Born in Devon, author Mick Escott pursued a car starting at the Victoria Theatre, Stoke-on-Trent. to freelance work in the West Midlands and his pursues a wide range of interests, one of which, football, led to his previous book, *Round the Turnstiles* (2008) about his 45-year tour to the grounds of all the 92 English Football League clubs (and more). He also contributes to the *Football and Real Ale Guide*. His interests include travel and buildings, which helped considerably in the 19-month long tour for this work. From Carlisle to Canterbury and Norwich to Newport this has been a rousing undertaking. He loves every one of the 49 cathedrals in this volume.

To Ruth

With best wishes

Mick

ROUND THE CLOISTERS

49 ANGLICAN CATHEDRALS IN ENGLAND & WALES & THE ISLE OF MAN

MICK ESCOTT

SilverWood

Published in paperback by SilverWood Books 2011
www.silverwoodbooks.co.uk

Text copyright © Mick Escott 2011

ISBN 978-1-906236-72-4

British Library Cataloguing in Publication Data
A CIP catalogue record for this book is available from the British Library

Set in Sabon by SilverWood Books
Printed in the UK on paper certified as being from responsible sources

Thanks to:

The individuals who gave their time and consideration on the tour itself:
Ven Dick Acworth, Robert Aldous, James Armstrong, Andrew Aspland, Very Revd James Atwell, Canon Wealands Bell, John Bethell, Neill Bonham, Canon Neville Boundy, Geraint Bowen, Karen Brayshaw, David Brown, Martin Brown, Richard Camp, Andrew Casewell, Revd John Coldwell, Pip Comper, Canon Sam Corley, Christopher Craddock, Jackie Davidson, Naomi Davidson, Canon Dorrien Davies, Leighton Davies, Nathan Dearne, Michael Deason-Barrow, Canon Trevor Dennis, Very Revd Adrian Dorber, Canon Clare Edwards, Rt Revd Wyn Evans, Very Revd Vivienne Faull, Rt Revd Richard Fenwick, Toria Forsyth-Moser, Canon Giles Fraser, Joan and Ian Freeman, Sarah Friswell, Rt Revd Jonathan Frost, Jim Godfrey, Canon Nigel Godfrey, Very Revd Rogers Govender, Very Revd Jonathan Greener, Very Revd John Guille, Malcolm Hanson, Margaret Hetherington, Canon Tim Higgins, Jon Howard, Very Revd David Hoyle, Marcus Huxley, Dave Johnson, Very Revd Keith Jukes, Fr Malcolm King, Ted Lachlan, Canon Philip Lambert, Canon James Lancelot, Rachel Lupton, Very Revd Geoffrey Marshall, Otto Martin, Canon Melvyn Matthews, Ronald Matthias, Thelma McIntosh, Steve Mellon, Rt Revd Jonathan Meyrick, Robin Moor, Canon Geoffrey Moore, Mervyn Murch, Richard Newell, Maureen Nicholas, Gerald Norris, Very Revd Catherine Ogle, Helen Parry, Rt Revd Robert Paterson, Rt Revd Michael Perham, Canon Alvyn Pettersen, Rt Revd Stephen Platten, Dave and Jo Plimmer, Gill Poole, Very Revd Chris Potter, Dr David Price, Jonathan Price, Jeremy Purseglove, Elizabeth Rae, Canon John Rogan, Chris Romain, Canon Bruce Ruddock, Leonie Seliger, David Snell, Kevin Spears, Celia Tate, Very Revd Charles Taylor, Canon Kate Taylor, Phil Thomas, Dr Tony Trowles, Terry Waite, Vince Waldron, Ian Walters, Chris Ward, John Webster, Bill Weeks, Rt Revd Martin Wharton, Most Revd and Rt Hon Rowan Williams, Revd Christopher Wood.

Sue Thomas and Sir David Davenport-Handley of Clipsham Stone Cutting Company, Rutland.

Mark Venning, Nancy Radford, Chris Batchelor and individual staff of Harrison & Harrison, organ builders, Durham. Alex Bunn for drawing the icons for each cathedral in this book. Simon Russell Beale for the foreword.

To the following, who have given vital information, advice and support: Constance Barrett, Pam Beddard, Dorothy Benison, Mike Butler, Margaret Cartledge, Lesel Dawson, Ian Duncan, Harry Fairhurst, Clemmie Farley-West, Pat Francis, Philip Gale, Maggie Goodall, Michael Hoadley, Andrew Lewis, Paul Lewis-Smith, Jason Parker, Stephen Perry, Ray Price, Warner Quick, Tom Rebbeck, Patrick Roberts, Paul Rogoff, Pamela Rudge, Revd Christopher Scott, Judith Walker, Mick Ward, Rob Wilson, Pat Wollaston.

Regarding the production process Helen Hart and her team at SilverWood Books, Richard Jones (Tangent Books), Karen Bysouth (proofreader), Roddy Peters (wizard on photos and icons).

Finally, to anyone I've unwittingly omitted, humble apologies. I am grateful, truly.

Palms progress to guide

49; one, Ripon, hosts

Wilfrid with prized lights.

ROUND THE CLOISTERS

Contents

Table of Photographs

262	30	Derby	Robert Bakewell's iron screen
	31	Newport	View from St Woolos's tower: Newport and the Usk estuary
	32	Llandaff	A rare cathedral gargoyle
	33	Oxford	Lierne vaulting in the chancel roof
295	34	Peel	Vice-Dean Nigel Godfrey has been gardening
	36	Peel	Wakey and Gill Poole at Tynwald garden party
	37	Brecon	The biggest cresset stone anywhere
	38	Gloucester	East window in celebration of the Battle of Crecy
346	39	St Davids	Bishop Wyn Evans in conversation over a cup of tea
	40	Wells	Oaken Jack strikes bells with his heels and right hand
	41	Wells	Roof corbel of a fox devouring a chicken
	42	St Paul's	Sir Chris's motto: Resurgam = I will arise
387	43	Bangor	Tile on choir floor: rabbit with bow and arrow
	44	St Asaph	The tower: two types of stone weathering away
	45	Coventry	1969, new cathedral: verger David Dorey and Graham
	46	Coventry	2010, old cathedral: Graham, Ragnhild and the author
420	47	Manchester	Misericord depicting dynamic dragon
	48	Manchester	Abstract stained glass window: red and yellow
	49	Norwich	Rare pelican lectern
	50	Peterborough	Leather goblet in the treasury
	51	Peterborough	Clipsham Quarry: stone destined for cathedrals
455	52	Birmingham	Charles Gore, 1st bishop, in front of his home patch
	53	Blackburn	*The Healing of the Nations* greets you at the east end
	54	York	Roman emperor Constantine in charge of the café
491	55	Ripon	13 bells and a wakeman for the Market Square curfew
	56	Carlisle	The best baldacchino has a strong presence
	57	Canterbury	The north aisle from above the Martyrdom
	58	Canterbury	Laptop gets the top cat award

524	59	Wakefield	The dean didn't like the kneelers
	60	Bradford	Bradford's pure ogees on the way up the steps
	61	Bradford	World War I memorial window
	62	Portsmouth	Organist David Price on his instrument
	63	Portsmouth	You can see the cathedral tower from the sea and marina
561	64	Newcastle	This dignitary seat is a feature of the nave
	65	Durham	You may take photographs of the cloisters
	66	Durham	Leslie Cooper, foreman pipe maker at Harrison & Harrison
	67	Winchester	A rare Tournai font: stories on each side

Foreword

This book is a good read, a fascinating journey undertaken in the spirit of fresh engagement with the cathedrals of England and Wales. The author does not adopt a traditional approach to the study of cathedrals, but allows us to look at these great buildings through his layman's eyes. It is about the enjoyment and the sensuous impact of these marvellous places. It is full of interest, acute observation and anecdote, but does not ignore the impact of current events and social change. As an example: at St Paul's Cathedral, where I spent a few years as a chorister, the author and his party waxed enthusiastic about Sir Christopher Wren's stunning application of physical laws to a seemingly impossible self-supporting staircase; at the same time, the coffee in the crypt was declared one of the best to be found in the country – there is an appendix giving a league table of cathedral cafés in the book. As ever, in our cathedrals, old and new worlds meet.

Simon Russell Beale

Introduction

WOKINGHAM – there's a name to conjure with. I've never been there but by weird, and wonderful, and wasteful, association, it's etched forever as the origin of *Round the Cloisters*. The seedling, which burgeoned into this excessive tome, hit my brain as Rand and I whistled, wet and windy, along the M3, past a road sign to Wokingham. As a cathedral-less place, it is all the more potent.

The short storyline goes as follows:

1   My companion, had recently attained retirement age and an improved body (triple heart bypass). He professed an architectural persuasion and wished to build a project, gradual and selective, of visiting the major cathedrals of England.

2   In bleak December 2009, we were on the way across southern England from Exeter (for football), via Salisbury (my Christmas treat to him, as a 'Sarum virgin'), to Rochester (near his abode), offering three cathedrals in as many days.

3   For me, it was blinding flash time. My previous book on football grounds was by then, unfortunately, consigned to history. I had been trying, in vain, to turn a lifetime of arts experiences into a workable formula for a writing project. The subject was too big. Why not cathedrals instead? At least it was a finite concept. There were only so many available.

Enter Celia Tate. That morning at Salisbury Cathedral she had been appointed as guide for us, rapt and curious, round many people's favourite place. These include my Foreword contributor, Simon Russell Beale. This small matter was serious. The seedling of thought grew during that sodden journey, by way of a country pub in Hampshire, intermittent roadworks and occasional exchanging of Rand's glasses, to my own desire to build up a tour, with the itinerary hung on cathedrals, and write about it along the way. The driver was enthused. The focus would be Anglican, and came to take in Wales as well as England; also the Isle of Man, which was to provide an ideal minibreak. The essential maps at the back of the resulting book would look better with the Gallic bulk included, and its territory was comparatively accessible, in fact, more so than Carlisle or Newcastle/ Durham. And a visit to the lovely St David's would fall into this package.

I had long harboured an interest in church buildings, cathedrals in particular. Rand was driven by Alec Clifton-Taylor's 1967 book *The Cathedrals of England,* something I had purchased when new, and which I had lent him. Coinciding with the project was a reading of J B Priestley's 1929 novel *Good Companions.* Its heroine, Miss Trant, is encouraged to embark upon a 'little tour… visiting all our English cathedrals'. She did embark upon the tour, which became the springboard for the plot, having achieved just one on the list: Ely.

Cathedrals are the most thrilling and satisfying buildings we have, also the best. They are always worth the time to enter, and, where requested, make a 'voluntary contribution', for the cathedrals' coffers, gift-aided of course, as no official financial support is forthcoming. Or, sometimes, pay because you have to. That very Ely was worth the price of a football ticket. Eighty years before, Miss Trant would have got in free. Once comfortably inside, enjoy and absorb. The buildings elate through their architecture, space and spirit. The differences between them are palpable, to be explored, while the similarities, the common basics of substance, are to be treasured. Every one is grand and worthy of scrutiny, while remaining essentially inscrutable. They can be grouped in a number of ways and separated by the many distinctions between them. They defy restrictive categories because in the end they are individual showpieces, for themselves, for their locations, for liturgical expression and cultural delight.

The plan opened with lists, something for which I have a predilection. Without a routine and methodical approach none of this could have been achieved. These were the general time frames:

1   The future: at any one time I was working out the order of play, arranging the next moves, from transport to accommodation to interviews. The present: enjoying the visits, sometimes returning, sometimes going to other church buildings as well.
2   The past: writing about the experience.

Sustained interest and balance were central considerations.

six Welsh cathedrals in pairs in quick succession and undertaking a diverse East Anglian tour comprising Chelmsford, St Edmundsbury, Ely and St Albans. What became surprising was how the predicted league rating didn't always materialize in the estimation of those present. Unfavourable reputations have built up. Peterborough had a low rating as a city compared with Norwich (they were seen on the same trip), but those present loved Peterborough just as much. That was unexpected, with the bonus of being shown round a quarry in Rutland the morning after the cathedral exposure. It was also refreshing, many a time, to find riveting features in parish church cathedrals, such as Sheffield (the Crypt Chapel of All Saints, where a Russian Orthodox service was in progress) and Derby (the baldacchino). I was to collect baldacchinos after that.

Now for the weather. I believe the climatic conditions proved to be irrelevant, at least in failing to damage our responses on bad days, though Salisbury, right at the beginning, was experienced in such torrents of rain that, even at the time, Rand and I were as one in mooting a second visit in springtime to enjoy it in good light; also to scale as much of its height as we were allowed. On the other hand Coventry was good to Ragnhild, Graham and me, and Oxford to Michael and myself, in awarding fine weather, as both were day trips comprising more than the respective cathedrals.

From the start every cathedral had to yield an icon to represent it in illustration at the top of the chapter. Most of these came easily, often in consultation with the companion at the time. In Blackburn there was much to do with football, which was then chosen. It was in the news at the time – the new owner of Blackburn Rovers FC had made a contribution to the cathedral. The 'heart' of York was easy, glaring at us from the west window before we entered, having examined abbeys and minsters in its diocese. York produced its see's lifeblood, all right!

Some things are more consistent. Cathedrals were the chosen subject partly because of their antiquity, in a world which reveres history and 'heritage'. Meanwhile, some are comparatively modern, though by now well-established. Some of the best building development has been seen at parish church cathedrals. The wide range has helped to sustain this enterprise. At the expense of brevity, this yarn has been spun. This book does not aim to compete with the wealth of erudite writing about cathedrals, and if you want a detailed guidebook, buy one at the cathedral shop. Finally, there will always be people who look at illustrated books of cathedrals and say: 'but they're all the same'.

1

Hereford

St Mary & St Ethelbert

Province: Canterbury
Founded: c.676 as secular cathedral
Present building: Early 12th century
Restored: 1788–87 by James Wyatt, who shortened the nave

Website: www.herefordcathedral.org
Tel: 01432 374200
Email: office@herefordcathedral.org
Address: The Cathedral Office, 5 College Cloisters, Cathedral Close, Hereford HR1 2NG

Three to See: Mappa Mundi and chained library; geometric arch in north transept; ball flowers on tower

'Golden fleece'

Sunday 22 November, 2009

We timed it for evensong, at the early time of 3.30 pm. It grew dark during the service: there was less than a month to go to the solstice, and it had been a dull day. That wasn't all: the river Wye, just outside, had burst its banks, prompting the signs warning off would-be walkers from the adjacent path. In the cathedral the choir was full in number and voice, filling the two front rows of the stalls, shapely and alluring in sight of the nave with its immense Norman pillars. This was only a sneak preview: we were to return in daylight the next morning, but the fulsomeness of the choir made me curious about how it was run. At a later date, Geraint Bowen, Organist and Director of Music, was to tell me. We sipped tea, which Geraint served from one of those teapots which incorporates an infuser full of leaves. I have one, too. The unction produced is very tasty. This was an exclusively male establishment, leading to the full complement in both rows of the choir, back (men) and front (boys). The cathedral school, dating from the 13th century, was an old foundation. So was the cathedral itself, having no monastic tradition. The diocese was founded in the late 7th century. The school took boys right up to the age of 18, thus incorporating that masculine phenomenon, the breaking of the voice. This had a more worldly-wise effect in the issue of funding. The cathedral provided two-thirds scholarships at primary age; and would continue to do so, during the secondary years. This was fundamental to keeping it all going. At the other end of the scale were the lay clerks. Four of the six (including one job share) had built up 'unprecedentedly long service', of over 25 years. The longest-serving came from Birmingham in 1974. They are 'phenomenonally loyal', said Geraint. The full choir was the standard here, the total back row comprised 12, with 18 boys. The youthful element was all recruited from the city, and diocese, the most distant commuting from Ludlow, Shropshire, near its northern extremity. Gap year choral scholars were now in evidence here, as there: normally three. Geraint felt Hereford had been lucky with clergy. He had already termed it a 'comfortable place to be'. Both the dean and precentor were music graduates. This helped, as did the housing of all key staff 'on site', giving rise to the aesthetically rewarding look of the surrounding cathedral close, replete with stylish properties. The organ had been attended to in the recent past, a lesser undertaking than the new one at St David's, Geraint's previous employer (he had a picture of that instrument on the wall; also in evidence were *Flora Britannica* and *Oxford Latin*. For the former, the cloister properties seemed to provide worthwhile gardens). Meanwhile the time of day precluded admiring the misericords under our seats. Darkness fell during the service, to the loss of the subtle hues through the stained glass.

Speaking of the diocese and its remoteness, here is a snippet about the Black Death:

Those clerks who complete Episcopal registers have the best measure of the scale of the mortality: they can see how many clergymen are dying. In the dioceses of York and Lincoln, forty per cent of all the beneficed clergy die in 1348–9. Some of them infected while administering to their dying parishioners. In the far south-west and Herefordshire, the figure is higher, almost fifty per-cent. The peasants fare little better: half the population of a manor dying is not unusual... to put these figures in proportion, remember that less than six per cent of the adult male population of the United Kingdom perish over the whole four years of the First World War, and the overall mortality figure is just 1.55 per cent.

The Time Traveller's Guide to Medieval England
by Ian Mortimer 2009

Monday 23 November

The project outside the building had been under way for two months. Most of the perimeter was marked by pedestrian diversions, which we had negotiated for evensong hours earlier. It was the subject of funds from Heritage Lottery Fund. Some interesting things were unearthed: deliberately in the case of an oak tree planted for the Prince of Wales' first marriage in 1981, and in the course of digging, 800 skeletons had come to light. The skeletons had served to slow down the process, as did the cold weather in the 2009/10 winter. 'It looked like a film set for the Battle of the Somme', said Geraint. A 2005 statue of Elgar was moved to a new, better position, the composer admiring the architecture in nonchalant fashion, leaning on his bike. One aim of this project was to enliven the area, to draw people into the close, and reduce the antisocial element. The building has suffered considerable erosion and undergone restoration and repair. One example of this was the stonemason encountered at Lichfield in May 2010, who had been provided with fairly local sandstone (from Staffordshire) for Hereford Cathedral work.

In the clear light of day the splendid tower rose above the messy work-in-progress. The tower dates from 1320 and is noted for the ubiquitous ball flowers, clustered handfuls of crumbling red stone, defined as 'decorative motifs consisting of three petals enclosing a ball'. Obvious, really! A pair of binoculars would have helped. At eye level the pleasing two-storey north porch presented itself. That is later, from the late Perpendicular period (c.1530), erected by Bishop Booth. Approaching it was tricky owing to the fencing all around. We negotiated the entrance, opening up to the 14th century side aisles, acting as a buffer to the 12th century pillar arcade. The priority for Wakey and me had become the new extension on the south side. We were aiming for something truly iconic.

Mappa Mundi! This could well be a piece of Latin vernacular, but we know better. It is a fabulous invention on vellum, by Richard of Haldingham, dating back to c.1280, which even includes names of key Roman settlements such as Lincoln (where Richard was Treasurer), Exeter (Excestris) and, of course, Hereford (prebendary) in completely the wrong literal position. On a conventional map from a British point of view, it's where South America should be. Exotic beasts are featured. One of them inspired the identification as a 'spread-eagled cat' from Wakey. It didn't take long to correct the error: it was the golden fleece. In fact East is at the top and the display reflects a medieval approach to the world and its inhabitants, with a very wide definition.

Of course we were very lucky to be able to see this fabulous object. The dean and chapter were somewhat impecunious in the 1980s, leading to the desperate decision to sell the map. In the event the British government, and John Paul Getty Jr to the tune of £1m, saved the day. The outcome was the new building, sympathetic to the character of the cathedral and its cloisters. The New Library houses not only the Mappa Mundi, but also the huge collection of books in the Chained Library Exhibition, in the final room. You just ogle at that, so many magnificent ancient tomes being housed there, arranged like rows of school benches. 'Nowadays', Dean Vivienne Faull of Leicester was to say: 'The importance of such a treasure to the nation would provoke preventative action'. When I saw it on my previous visit decades before, there had not been the organization, or even actual bricks and mortar, for its presentation. There certainly was now: round the corner from the cloistered café – the Lady's Arbour – (pretty good, including the cake) the Bishop's Cloister had been converted for modern use, giving an admirable exhibition of the story and setting. It led eventually, and initially out of sight, to the thing itself. What is perspicacious is the English translation in a separate frame not far away, to aid the visitor.

One feature highlighted by Nikolaus Pevsner was the north transept (c.1260) 'the highest level of architectural art' and the tomb situated there, of Bishop Aquablanca 'who died in 1268 and is buried in it'.

The cathedral's virtue was in its warmth. The dedication, to Ethelbert, King and Martyr, is honoured in a thirteen-panel structure (painted by Peter Murphy, designed by Cathedral Architect, Robert Kilgour and made by Stephen Florence) east of the High Altar. There was a pilgrimage tour leaflet, which told the story, summarized as follows: 'Hereford's Ethelbert (as opposed to King Ethelbert, the Canterbury one who became the first Anglo-Saxon monarch) was born in East Anglia in the late 8th century. He journeyed to Mercia to seek the hand of Aelfrytha, daughter of King Offa. For political reasons, Offa had the young king murdered – traditionally on 20 May, 794 – at Marden, five miles from Hereford.' The subject matter of the display was full of excitement. Here are some examples:

3   On the journey to Mercia the sun is darkened and there is an earthquake.
8   Ethelbert is beheaded.
9   Ethelbert's body is thrown into the river. A light shines, a spring rises.
10   Ethelbert's body is taken by ox-cart to Hereford. The head falls from the cart.
11   A blind man stumbles on the head and retrieves it. He receives sight.

It goes to show how strongly a modest piece of history can be embellished into shrine and pilgrimage status. Ethelbert actually had nothing to do with Hereford and would have spoken a different language as an East Angle. The poor boy was bumped off before he had a chance to prove any kind of mettle.

In the east end I shall highlight the treat in the corner. This was the show stopper, which would prove a hard act to follow in the contemporary glass found in many subsequent cathedral fixtures. *Welcome to Hereford Cathedral* stated: 'The recently restored chantry chapel of Bishop Edmund Audley (d.1524) contains new stained glass (2007), designed by Tom Denny and dedicated to the 17th century Herefordshire poet and cleric Thomas Traherne.' Stories were told and detail emerged from the four lights. The accompanying leaflet included: 'The windows seek to be a visual expression of the visionary beauty and the richness of Traherne's imagery… ' Wakey was bewitched. One example of images emerging from the panes was the cathedral itself, appropriately executed in shades of red.

Making money is permanently crucial for this cathedral. Events had included a Hereford Choral Society Concert the previous night, and the Messiah on 12 December, followed a week later by the Cathedral Advent Fair and Carols for Shoppers. The notice stated: 'We do not charge admission to this beautiful cathedral but costs continue to rise. It costs around £4,000 each day to keep open. For 700 years visitors and pilgrims have given donations at the shrine of St Thomas and your gift will help us a lot.' And perhaps St Ethelbert is providing a service with her shrine and story.

Hereford Cathedral is a seductive mass. Its rich russet look combines with its compactness, underlined by restorer James Wyatt's removal of four pillars at the west end in the late 18th century. Admittedly, this followed the collapse of the west tower in 1786. Alec Clifton-Taylor wrote in *The Cathedrals of England*:

> *Whereas in the 15th century towers were sometimes designed from the outset to be no more than towers, in the Decorated period they always culminated in spires, even though these might only be of wood. Hereford was no exception; the lead-covered timber spire survived there until 1790, and it was not until forty years later that the large corner-pinnacles were added. The tower is not very high, but is at once so massive and gorgeous that the loss of the spire does not seem to matter. The buttresses are like Siamese twins, and project diagonally from the corners. This arrangement, though somewhat complicated, is very successful, and the clustered pinnacles are delightful.*

Inside, dating from the 14th century are stalls and misericords worth examining. And upwards is an example of the green man phenomenon; the head of a lion, linking animal, vegetable and mineral.

The tower presence gave reassurance and pleasure from wherever it was in evidence, such as Edgar Street to the north, the ground of Hereford United FC. To me there was a comforting consistency of design between the four floodlight pylons of the stadium and the central tower of the cathedral. The pylons are squat and square, containing a mere nine bulbs each, almost lost towards the top. Perhaps the look of the cathedral inspired them. The pleasure was muted, as the home team won 1–0 in a cup replay, beating Tranmere Rovers, the team of my friend, The Toff. The tower, floodlit in a roseate hue, provided a little compensation. The Toff and I were to join forces later in the tour for Liverpool Cathedral and Westminster Abbey, that eminent 'royal peculiar'. For that I had to link it with St Paul's, the cathedral for London!

What we found worthwhile was to spend some leisure time in the city. It was the regional centre for an extensive area, and diocese (the population figure given was 250K for that, which included southern Shropshire). However, it was the 14th smallest city in the United Kingdom, with a population of 50,154 in 2001, and most visitors took it in as day trip material. We chose right to take it easy and spend a night, on this occasion at the old, atmospheric city centre hotel, the Green Dragon (which had seen better days), absorbed by the Best Western chain. It, too, offered St Mary and St Ethelbert as a view, but only partially, if you were allocated the right room. We struck lucky. Then we enjoyed a cluster of old streets and the timbered Town House. We were thwarted at the Cider Museum, officially open at 10 am, but not, it transpired, in winter (no information to that effect until we arrived at the front door). The City Museum and Art Gallery compensated; again opposite the cathedral it conveyed helpful local information, was selling redundant books cheap (a cookery one for 25p) and entertained us with a contemporary photography exhibition on the stairs. No toilet, though: 'You have to go up the street, sir'.

Saturday 26 March, 2011
Initially this is a progress report. The ambitious landscaping project had advanced over the 17 intervening months, as you would hope. The northeast side looked promisingly green behind the metal fencing. Wakey and I were also here to attend the choral society's engagement in the west end of the nave: Haydn's oratorio *The Creation*. Geraint was conductor and his wife, Lucy, the soprano soloist. Something else had become essential, through the gradual acquisition of related information over this time, immersed in project and architecture. Kilpeck Church, in the diocese and a handful of miles away, had to be seen.

First was the rehearsal. We sat for a soupcon. It was refreshing to observe that the event was being staged in the west end, like the Monteverdi at Lichfield. Geraint was to point out that Lichfield and Hereford had very different acoustics. This was the less challenging, though the next public performance was to be held in a more traditional layout under the crossing. The concern was the beautiful, and empty, space: at the east end of the nave you look up to the tower. An effect of red pervades at the top, but immediately above you is a 'crown of thorns-type structure' (I heard it called) of golden hue, a modern application of the Romanesque chevron. It bore a number of candles. At intervals it served as an excellent photographic foreground to a view of either transept. It conveyed a shining gold impression, at the point where the Scott screen had been situated until 1967. (It was made available for viewing at the Victoria and Albert Museum in 2001. I saw it in summer 2011. It is stunning). I had to agree that, given the modest dimensions of this building, the open plan worked well, from the west end right through to the altar. While we were there, we took in individual features. The north transept dates from the mid-13th century. It is a one-off: triangular geometric arches. They were crisp and satisfying. Like the crown, there was something new here, too. 'The recently refurbished shrine of St Thomas of Hereford has been a focus for pilgrims since the end of the 13th century. The stone and marble tomb is one of the best-preserved shrines in England,' instructed the caption. Hereford Cathedral was not well off. Shrines have traditionally provided a source of much-needed income.

We went through the south transept, where stood a fireplace. Durham has the only other Norman example, something for the following month's visit. The cloister beyond housed the shop, where I procured a rare shot glass for Wakey (£6.25, below the going rate). He might appreciate this as he revised his marks up to 17 out of 20 for the cathedral. That put Hereford in his top group, so productive was this second visit. Familiarity certainly enhances impressions, perhaps polarizes them, as rare bad feelings about churches and their bits can get even worse. All the cathedrals receiving subsequent attention had yielded more enjoyment. This could go on for ever!

Beyond lay the Cloister Café, set to assuage our current need of nourishment. We enjoyed a pot of tea, most tasty cakes and the bad news that the Mappa Mundi exhibition and Library were closed for several weeks. We both rated the coffee cake highly. It was good to return to the medieval ribbing, which acted as the surround. As for the exhibits, we had plenty on the agenda already. This was likely to turn into a place for periodical weekends.

After a break of a couple of hours, the concert was enjoyed from the start from the crossing (tickets courtesy of Geraint), with the subtly gleaming crown above the seating. After a rousing first part, the interval was marked by a lack of refreshments. No wine! Not even orange juice. I procured a glass of water from a verger, in case of a tickling throat. For the second part, the upper levels having plenty of space, we tried the (boys') front row of the choir, for a more elevated, if sideways, view. It was a rewarding first live exposure to this 1798 piece for both of us. The programme note pointed out: 'It is the work of Haydn at his greatest – a man in his mid-sixties, with a wealth of experience, known throughout all the musical world.' The previous week it had been Bach's *Mass in B Minor* (1749) for me, the two concerts entirely complementary, and stylistically representative of their two generations. When would this trajectory be extended further, for the next work? Berlioz's *Te Deum* (1849) would be just fine. I hadn't heard it for decades.

Naturally afterwards, denied alcohol for several hours, we applied previous experience to pay visits to two pubs. Most satisfying, as the beers, from various local sources were good.

Sunday 27 March
The weather was slightly disappointing again. The sun just couldn't break

through. That did not diminish the brilliant displays of daffodils and pale, fresh leaves ready to burst forth on many a tree. And the clocks: 'Spring forward.' We had doubled up the bodily challenges of losing an hour by starting early with a swim in the Hereford Leisure Pool. We emerged feeling worthy, and I said as much to the parson, the reader, who passed us with a quizzical look, where we were parked by St Mary and St David, Kilpeck, an easy eight mile drive from the city. She caught us in mid-munch of the sandwiches, which passed as breakfast. We received a warm welcome at Mattins. It was Sheila Hughes' last service there. The music was administered by the pressing thumb of the warden, James Bailey, except when Sheila delivered from a music machine concealed in the chancel. 'I've brought a choir with me,' she explained, for 'the difficult *Te Deum*.' She didn't expect those few gathered to attempt to sing it. It was a tricky setting.

We were to examine all the Norman-ness of this untouched building, which had survived the assaults of time (except erosion) since c.1140. A striking comparison could be made with the cathedral, of the same period. The church stands in rolling countryside, by a handful of ancient houses, also most desirable. The best thing was the detail: corbels illustrating delightful beasts, such as a pig upside-down and a 'horse of God' (as opposed to His lamb), wrestlers and a sheela-na-gig (woman with exposed vagina). The south doorway featured zigzags and was 'sumptuously decorated', assessed Nikolaus Pevsner, with a new motif, beakheads. Inside, an outstanding feature was an enormous font, quite out of proportion with the tight space. 'The best have a comic-strip character', wrote Pevsner.

Lunch followed in the very 'green' Kilpeck Inn (formerly Red Lion), featuring many devices, from solar heating to rain water recovery. It was a brief stroll away, looking very new and recommended to me by vicar Ashley Evans, when I telephoned him to check the church's opening times. He was elsewhere, taking 'six services today', James had said. Also open was our next destination, a further few miles to the east: St Catherine's, Hoarwithy. I shall quote Simon Jenkins' *England's Thousand Best Churches* to give a flavour of this extraordinary Italianate Romanesque construct.

> *On a summer day the loggia of Hoarwithy hangs over the valley of the Wye as an Umbrian church might over the Tiber. The building was commissioned by the vicar of neighbouring Hentland, William Poole, in the 1870s to replace a chapel... The architect was J P Seddon and the style was Italianate Romanesque. The southeast campanile rises over the trees, the long rise of steps from the road under the yew trees culminating in a cloister walk... The interior is of a piece with the outside,*

a work of scholarly sophistication... This is a complete work of revivalist art, rare for its date and an astonishing creation to find in a backwater of Herefordshire.

You have to see it, proud above its village, which happens to have a tempting pub, for which we had run out of time. We were to see a football game, re-arranged because the powers that organize these things decided that England's fixture with Wales on the Saturday afternoon would have a significant effect on the attendance. As it was, a paltry 2,234 souls witnessed Hereford's 1–0 dispatch of Crewe Alexandra. They seem to specialize in the most modest goal productions. This time it was pleasing: we were there for the Bulls. And some – us, at least – admired the floodlights and distant cathedral tower.

Finally, we reflect upon the cathedral. For Wakey: 'Just a small stained glass window made everything worthwhile.' He had made a return to Bishop Audley's chantry chapel. Familiarity certainly worked here. St Mary and St Ethelbert just got better and better. The next visit might just be for the *Three Choirs Festival*. It would be Hereford's turn in 2012, and Geraint was Artistic Director. It all had to be sorted out for announcements at Worcester in August 2011. He had looked ahead, too, to 2018. That could well be his swansong as AD, as he would be due to retire that year.

2

Salisbury

St Mary

Province: Canterbury
Founded: 705, secular at Old Sarum
Present building: 1220–58 as New Sarum
Restored: 1789–92 by James Wyatt; 1862–78 by Gilbert Scott

Website: www.salisburycathedral.org.uk
Tel: 01722 555120
Email: visitors@salcath.co.uk
Address: Visitor Services, 33 The Close, Salisbury, Wiltshire SP1 2EF

Three to See: The view of the tallest spire and the whole exterior in the largest cathedral close in the country;
Magna Carta in the chapter house;
1386 clock

Daffodil

Tuesday 29 December, 2009

I would like to thank Celia Tate for this. At first reluctant, she was the cathedral guide allocated to Rand and me. She told us she could only allow a few minutes to introduce the building to us, as she was wanted elsewhere. They were short staffed. The weather was dire, which may be connected to this lack. Some hadn't turned up for their shifts.

But we must start at the beginning: arrival the previous evening. We stayed at the city centre Red Lion Hotel, one of the old coaching houses adopted by Best Western Hotels. For our evening meal Rand and I chose a pleasing smoked haddock dish in one of a tempting network of spaces in the hotel, plus a tipple of Wiltshire beer. Having got our bearings, we strode forth into the elements, to drop into the New Inn. While Rand purchased pints, I ventured into the slippery and frozen garden out of spire-related curiosity. A man with a fag, suffering this exposure, confirmed that there was 'a great view of the cathedral, mate', round the corner. I called Rand, who was now extracting his own smoking materials. And so we got our first full glimpse of the illuminated spire, silhouetted against the night sky. We'd already enjoyed a preview approaching the city from westward Wilton, which had required craning of necks. I think the pint of Ringwood bitter tasted better after that, reclining on an age-old settle in the New Inn bar.

In the morning our cathedral visit was intended as the first scheduled stop on an engrossing and healthy city walking itinerary etched in ball-point pen on the maroon-on-white city map by Lynn the receptionist. The grand Cathedral Close is a fine weather place, most of all the spring for the meadows, which were most likely waterlogged on this occasion. So I nominate the daffodil as the embodiment of St Mary's Cathedral, Salisbury. It grows bright and tall amid the burgeoning greenery. In the vicinity I noted Mompesson House (National Trust) for another time, also Sarum College. Wrapped up warm, we enjoyed the magnificent approach to the close through a medieval gateway and escaped from the elements, after an enforced peregrination to the south west side. Rodney, the cashier, greeted us from a state-of-the art till, which required a 'suggested' donation, with the temptation of gift aid benefit. I was happy to complete the form and file away the receipt, for tax purposes.

And that was how we met our guide Celia, identified by her green sash. She launched into her anecdotal routine. 'The weather vane on the stone spire,' she related, 'used to whizz round in sympathy with the Beaufort Scale to tell the speed of the wind. If it was more than 80 mph they have to clear the cathedral.' This had ceased owing to a recent insertion in the machinery to comply with Health and Safety regulations. We were regaled on the changes over the ages with an entertaining turn of phrase, by turns eloquent and dismissive. We started with the prime statistic, always worth repeating: 'The spire is the tallest in the country at 123m or 404ft. Meanwhile the foundations are only five feet deep, the local land being considered 'particularly stable', unlike Winchester down the road. There was a model of the cathedral, on a scale affording much illustration, such as workers pushing wheelbarrows full of building materials. There was also the enjoyable diocesan map, which showed the southeastern boundary to follow the traditional division between Dorset and Hampshire. Salisbury is the cathedral church for Dorset as well as most of Wiltshire (Bristol claims Swindon and the north and yielded Dorset in 1836), but does not include the Bournemouth area, which for this purpose remains under Winchester's aegis (in the old Hampshire), from which, for local authority purposes, it was transferred to the county of Dorset in 1974.

We admired the massive clock complete with medieval workings dating from 1386, on display in the north nave aisle and without a face, as medieval clocks employed a bell to ring out the hours. By contrast we were then treated to the opposite end of history – the emphatic font installed in 2008 in honour of 750 years' history. Fonts are usually to be found as an immediate feature upon entering such a house of God. It was the winner of a competition. Here it was resplendent in the middle of the nave, and held your attention utterly. Flat water brimmed over in perpetual motion. Celia, not Clare or Cicely, as Rand referred to her later, conveyed understated disapproval. We both concurred: it dominated. The effect of modern introductions was sometimes that the look jarred. Salisbury is aesthetically pure – it does claim to be 'Britain's finest 13th Century Cathedral' (on the Cathedral tour leaflet we were given). That single-mindedness also applies to the 'Gothic' of the modern builds at Guildford and Liverpool.

We arrived at the east end, called the Trinity Chapel, and looked up at the strong blue Prisoners of Conscience Window, dating from 1980. I had liked the Tom Denny ones at Hereford. The revolving glass prism by Laurence Whistler (in the Morning Chapel) is an impressive modern piece. The sides are delicately engraved to invoke a magical illusion. You see the spire, west front and birds in the sky by turns. Celia Tate, upon whose every utterance we were now hanging, approved. She pointed to the strainer arches, inserted in anticipation of spire movement. They turned out to be of little use. Passing a cigarette paper through the gap would demonstrate this. Rand understood this better than me.

One of her observations was that 'people just don't do brass rubbings any more', not even that of Bishop Wyville (c.1375), now attached to a wall. We were introduced to the effective combination of contrasting stone employed. Beside the Chilmark oolitic limestone, the dark 'marble' from

Purbeck, within the diocese, provided a satisfying, though rather cooling effect. Rand, who at that stage had not been to York, was entranced by the grisaille glass, impressed by its contemporary look.

The hour struck, and we were urged to sit for the prayer session, including Rand, a tad embarrassed as he was 'not a believer'. We were to disagree about the screen, dismantled in James Wyatt's 1785 restoration. I thought it was a mistake, bearing in mind the benefit the screen gave to Rochester, for one. It often helped to have a division between nave and quire. You are provided with a magnificent sweep from west to east ends, to enjoy the gradient upwards beyond the lofty altar. At Salisbury the pointed English gothic arches stretch up to the tall roof and admit all that light. What a novelty it must have been when it was built, in fact overwhelming as it was painted in red, blue and gold, partly promotional for fund-raising purposes. In the nave the congregation would stand, a routine amended to kneeling after the Reformation. Next we ventured into the fabulous 'earliest surviving complete choir stalls in Britain' (c.1236); it was good to pause among them, of which there are 106.

The choir stalls were largely the habitat of nine-year-old Michael Deason-Barrow from 1963 to 1966. His is a happy story. He hailed from an unpromising background in Wootton Bassett, up country from Salisbury and more than a daily journey away. The town featured rather too frequently in the news over recent years for the returning victims of strife abroad. In his youth schools in the diocese habitually covered the choirs during cathedral school half-terms and holidays. He was star singer of the local Church of England school, and duly performed a solo in the cathedral. The organ failed, an act of God, but he knew to carry on regardless, to the end of the verse. Asked whether his parents were coming that night, he later observed a man engaging them in conversation. Soon after, he was diverted from the family holiday in Bournemouth (he was the third of six children) for a day trip to Salisbury with his father, who told him to 'sing to that man in there'. Back from the vacation, he was bemused to find his mother and grandmother battling over a fine uniform – for him, for school. He had been awarded a full scholarship to Salisbury Cathedral School. Only that way was it possible for him to take up a place. It proved a mixed blessing. It was hard to integrate with colleagues further up the social scale, used to the regimen of dormitory life. The cathedral choir was held up as a paragon. However, through the regular services and singing exposure, he was surprised how poor those apparently more advanced other boys were in quality. After ten days, he was instructed: 'Deason-Barrow, you're in the choir tonight.' 'I didn't have a clue,' he said.

Within a month he was awarded a solo. The service was evensong, the regular 5 o'clock slot. From that 'I effectively became a little professional musician,' amid homesickness. 'No room for wobblies.' At the next solo the press turned up. He became a child star, in the days before the success of Aled Jones and Charlotte Church. There were no agents or deals. He was singing Mendelssohn's *Hear my Prayer* in his North Wiltshire brogue. In speech he would utter 'gert' rather than 'large' or 'big'. Vowel training was an essential part of the schooling. His first term report commented on the need to 'rid him of the rusticity of his language'.

At home he'd slept on a bunk bed, in Salisbury in a dormitory with several others on a bed of iron with metal railings. In the eerie moonlight he was overlooked by 18th century bishops with fixed grimaces, so much as to snarl: 'You filthy boy'. On the other hand the view of the cathedral through the window would inspire him. And at times when mist enveloped the body of the church the spire would appear detached. Fog and dew would produce atmospheric effects. A similar experience was related by my friend, Paul Kaynes, who boarded at the choir school in the 1970s. It could be freezing cold but the view of the cathedral through the window compensated. He was not a chorister, but did turn pages in the organ loft.

Once, when a royal visit was imminent, Michael was suffering from tonsillitis. Penicillin for the posterior and heartfelt prayer aloft solved that one. He prospered. He has records – EPs and LPs – to show for it. 1966 was a bumper year, fronted with an angelic dark-eyed 12-year-old. An example was *Music in Salisbury Cathedral* for a performance of Charles Stanford's *Evening Service in G*. Delivering that on one occasion on a windy night in the pure gothic of Salisbury, the piercing top G from the star treble shattered a window. The glass fell in. He felt at one in that building: during a recording session he would be alone in the choir stalls, where the only light emanated from a couple of individual lights by the stalls, with overspill from the organ loft. The recording company technicians would occupy the vestry. Sound had to be pure, and the experience was intensely spiritual. It was at such a time that he felt the presence of those nocturnal occupants the bats, phutting and flying.

This experience was essentially limited to childhood. At 13, pupils moved onto the next phase: broken voices and more earnest schools. You can't rely on retention of voice quality. He did achieve a magnificent culmination in his career as a treble: Vivien Leigh's memorial service at Westminster Abbey. The actress had asked for him, requested that he sing an anthem. Sir John Gielgud gave the address.

We now return to the Celia Tate tour. Salisbury Cathedral was a mid-Plantagenet project, achieved within the reign of Henry III (1216–72), the fourth longest serving monarch in our history. He succeeded his father, King

John (1199–1216), who was fundamentally upstaged in political power by the execution of the Magna Carta in 1215. Signed in Runnymede, Surrey, somehow one of the four extant copies made its way here. We admired it as a piece of work in the chapter house. The initiative was led by Stephen Langton, Archbishop of Canterbury. It was made of vellum. Hair and flesh were removed from the animal skin. Once prepared, beautiful ornamental script – calligraphy – was applied in Latin. There were translations of a few passages on display. One was: 'Let there be one measure of wine throughout our whole realm, and one measure of ale, and one measure of corn.' There would be no imprisonment without fair trial, a principle which led to the legal practice of Habeas Corpus. This is defined as 'a writ requiring a person under arrest to be brought before a judge or into court'. Around the frieze of the chapter house were carved Old Testament images such as Noah's Ark. The room was really one for artefacts and exhibitions, admittedly most impressive, so you couldn't experience the building in full. One of these was a cute and perfectly formed chalice, unearthed during restoration. It was one used by George Herbert (1593–1633), poet and hymn writer (such as *Let all the World in Every Corner Sing*) at his parish in Bemerton, a village during his lifetime, now absorbed into the modern City of Salisbury. It is used on his calendar day, 27 February.

My friend Pom, mezzo soprano, who was to be my companion at Wells, related an experience she had when performing in Salisbury. 'I was not feeling 100% at the rehearsal' and afterwards decided to recline on a pew in the nave. An old lady from the choir took pity and offered her hospitality. Pom replied that she was already catered for – at the Bishop's Palace, as the incumbent's wife was in the choir. The would-be hostess said: 'But I live here in the Close.' Pom still demurred. The lady was persuasive and emphatic: 'You can't easily say "Fuck it!" in the Bishop's Palace.' That was in recent memory.

William Cobbett, of *Rural Rides* fame, had this to say of Salisbury during his trip there on horseback on 31/8/1826:

> *Yesterday morning I went into the cathedral at Salisbury about 7 o'clock. When I got into the nave of the church, as I was looking up and admiring the columns and the roof, I heard a sort of humming, in some place which appeared in the transept of the building... At last, I thought I could distinguish the sounds of the human voice. This encouraged me to proceed; and, still following the sound, I at last turned in at a doorway to my left, where I found a priest and his congregation assembled. It was a parson of some sort, with a white covering on him, and five*

women and four men: when I arrived, there were five couple of us. I joined the congregation, until they came to the litany; and then, being monstrously hungry, I did not think myself bound to stay any longer. I wonder what the founders would say, if they could rise from the grave, and see such a congregation as this in this most magnificent and beautiful cathedral. I wonder what they would say, if they knew to what purpose the endowments of this Cathedral are now applied; and above all things, I wonder what they would say, if they could see the half-starved labourers that now minister to the luxuries of those who wallow in the wealth of those endowments. There is one thing, at any rate, that might be abstained from, by those that revel in the riches of those endowments; namely, to abuse and blackguard those of our forefathers, from whom the endowments came, and who erected the edifice, and carried so far towards the skies that beautiful and matchless spire, of which the present possessors have the impudence to boast, while they represent as ignorant and benighted creatures, those who conceived the grand design, and who executed the scientific and costly work.

How Old Foundation cathedrals are funded almost two centuries later would make an interesting comparison.

After the tour was over, after profuse thanks to our guide, Rand and I failed to make it to the shop and café, between aisle and cloisters, because:

1   We were still replete with Red Lion breakfast. However, we were still knocking back our bowls of fruit when they attempted to serve the 'full English but, sorry, no black pudding, sir'. The bacon is recommended.

2   The Old Mill Hotel beckoned, situated at a later stage of the untried map tour. It is near where John Constable painted the evocative pictures of the cathedral, which hang in many a living room. 'You can park there', Lynn had said. That was good news, having run out of time in the car park abutting the hotel in the city centre.

The Old Mill turned out to be the kind of place you would avoid at peak times for congestion and noise levels, enough to scare off any wildlife hoping to make the weir and sedge outside their habitat. For us it was ideal. Still not ready for food, we enjoyed coffees: white for Rand, black for me, with biscuit samples.

On our way after this break, Rand anticipated another occasion hereabouts with relish. He would sketch and we would explore this venerable city at leisure to engage our senses, 'chuck a frisbee in the meadow and admire the daffodils, one and all', he enthused. That was the aim at the time. Bill Bryson should have the last word. He wrote: 'There is no doubt in my mind that Salisbury Cathedral is the single most beautiful structure in England and the close around it the most beautiful space' (*Notes from a Small Island*, 1995).

Friday 20 May, 2011
This was the long-awaited repeat visit in the summer half of the year. Graham, Kevin, Spencer and I enjoyed a coffee sojourn at the Old Mill. Where else but this emporium, considering its location? The cathedral's spire and west end looked stunning through the iron garden gate of a private house. With a foreground of tulips and carnations, then river, then meadow, this was true picture postcard stuff with babbling brook and dipping ducks by the hotel.

We were soon in the cathedral. In answer to my first question to one of a row of guides, Celia Tate wasn't there on Fridays. What a shame! A private wander ensued. A plaque on the south aisle wall attracted Spencer's attention. There was an inscription in Greek, which he translated loosely to mean 'The end is nigh'. 'It's the apocalypse, and we're here,' he said. I'm sure it was a coincidence that the end of the world had been predicted in a news bulletin for the next day at 6 pm, our time.

The first impression this time was of activity: the nave was cordoned off on the aisle side for a concert for Salisbury Festival, which had just opened. Also, the cloisters turned out to be partly given over to an exhibition. The brochure informed: 'You will be enveloped in the meditative sound' of John Tavener's *Towards Silence*. Most of the chairs in the body of the nave were facing a dais near the west end, with a bank of seats under the window. We were able to move around the masses of visitors, mostly in groups led by badge-wearing guides. The nave now seemed extremely tall and narrow to me, having seen all but one of the other cathedrals.

We found ourselves by the choir stalls. For more detailed examination than last time. The *Cathedral Tour – Salisbury and Magna Carta* leaflet bore an interesting entry below the floor plan: 'Monkey, Cricket and Cat.' It drew attention to three bits of fun to seek out. The rather large cricket was easy to identify, decorating an arm rest in the choir stalls, along with other delightful carvings. I wondered if Michael the chorister had noticed or enjoyed this detail of his workplace. I happened upon the equivalent leaflet from my earlier visit, which had listed a beaver, rather than cricket. Apparently the beaver was native to England in the 13th century. Next I continued up towards the high altar, and noticed, to my joy, ogee arches on both sides of the presbytery. Last time I was ignorant of their existence. Now I loved them. There was a plaque announcing: 'Queen Elizabeth II distributed the royal Maundy in this cathedral on 11 April 1974.' This was a matter of annual progression round the country by Her Majesty, so I was surprised not to have noted similar commemorations elsewhere. I rejoined my colleagues at the Morning Chapel, coming across a cluster of people peering at the Laurence Whistler prism. Kevin grumbled: 'The trouble with the prism is that people get all crowded around, and they don't see the glory above.' We looked up at three ascending levels of stunning architecture. 'That's the problem with showpieces,' I replied.

Attention was drawn to the 35-year link with the Episcopal Church of Sudan. This involved visits by bishops and 'considerable support, both financially and personally is given particularly in the areas of education and medical work'. There were displays to illustrate this. I shall mention another accolade, as all these contribute towards a feel for aspects of the life of cathedral and diocese. This one is about the building: 'The Commission of the European Community has... given generously to the repair of the spire 1989–90'. Then, on a board by the south aisle headed 'Salisbury Cathedral Community Forum' was a detailed tabulation of offertory collections, listing income and expenditure for 2009/10 (results). The 2010/11 budget was shown with actual figures for part of the year, based on anticipated receipts of £158K. Nearby, leaflet in hand in the south quire aisle above the vestry, I invoked a guide to show me the carved stone monkey, 'poised to hurl a nut at passing visitors'. It was obvious, once you were aware.

I went from there to the café as arranged at 1 pm to meet the boys. As they hadn't arrived I wandered through to the shop, at the other end of the space. I noticed a fridge magnet on the counter, depicting 'Wolfie, Salisbury Cathedral'. I established from Judy Bedford, the assistant, that he, the black cat in *Cathedral Cats* by Richard Surman, still roamed. I embarked on a one-man search party in the Stonemasons Yard, 'where he is probably about'. Judy added: 'He's often here in the winter', meaning in the shop and sometimes elsewhere in the cathedral. Celia Tate wasn't the only absentee. The yard abutted the cloisters (the biggest in the country), on the southwest side. I left the building and pursued a detour round part of the green perimeter to the next gate down, which was wide open. It was very extensive and would offer many a warming surface to a pampered cat for slumber. This was an inactive drive area, numerous ramshackle buildings and people's unidentified working spaces, cluttered with piles of disused stuff: machinery, stone, bits. Young glazier Tom, who was enjoying a tabloid newspaper and sandwiches on a bench, directed me: 'You need Steve, who looks after the cat' in the cabin 'two doors down on the right, round that heap'. This was Steve Mellon, misspelt as 'Mellor' in *Cathedral Cats*, he told me. He was in, just closing his lunchbox, and admitted to being a 'general dogsbody' by way of function. He was keen to talk about his charge, for it seemed that Wolfie, now 13 years old, had for 10 years relied on him for personal expenditure of around £40 per month. This mainly consisted of a range of two or three types of biscuits, also occasionally salmon as a treat. The pet was no longer part of the fabric of the cathedral, which meant no petty cash was now available to keep him. Currently he was turning his nose up at Whiskas, but would consider Go-Cat. He had just consumed a helping of this, and was probably resting somewhere on this sunny afternoon. Steve couldn't help me further: 'He's a funny cat', he said. Neither could Tom. There was nobody else in evidence so I walked around the yard, fruitlessly. I had observed the unusually elaborate provision for the works department (they are mostly confined to a space between buildings) and gained insight into the animal and his habits. It was unfortunate to have missed out on an encounter with Wolfie himself. The fridge magnet was £1.99, cheap enough. I also saw my first 2012 calendar, of Salisbury (£3.75), but wasn't quite ready yet.

I returned by way of the shop to the Restaurant to find my friends munching a snack. The café and shop area was formerly the Plumbery, which was unsurprisingly once the site for workmen and materials. Queueing up with my tray, a man in front urged to anyone near: 'Stand back!' This was for the frothing oak-aged beer by Innis and Gunn. To maintain consistency in this highly subjective tour-long survey I had to keep to tea, though that bottle did look appealing. Kevin and Spencer were enjoying paninis (£3.50) and tea (£1.40), which was thankfully poured loose in the individual pots. I elected for the lemon drizzle cake (£2.05) with tea. The prices were competitive. Next came a lull, sitting in the café, with the chapter house on one side and the south nave aisle on the other. A translucent roof led up from one to the other at an angle. I found it strangely constricted. The others liked it well enough, but I could remember much better layouts. You could at least say that it was an efficient, economical use of space. Ingestion? Tea excellent, cake poor, suffering from the customary deficiencies regarding flavour, succulence and freshness. Afterwards Kevin identified the stone cat in the leaflet. It lay opposite the Restaurant entrance ramp as 'part of the medieval graffiti still visible in the Cloisters'. In the high sun it was eminently photogenic, carved deep into the horizontal stone.

The tower tour time of 2.15 pm was upon us. It cost £8.50, £6 concessions. Local man David Brown was the guide, informative but prolix. Graham, who couldn't manage more than a dozen stairs, let alone 332, was forced to wait for a very long time near the car, fortunately parked in a disabled spot with a view of the building from the northwest. All such tours are invigorating: we saw plenty and gained detailed insight into the history and purpose of much of what we saw. Guide David brought the west window to life in his analysis. I took photos of a green serpent, which I probably wouldn't have noticed without instruction. Heating was explained. With the new installation it was much less of a drain on resources than hitherto. Above the triforium, nudging the west window, we looked down on the nave to witness a preview of a dancer synchronizing movements with a sleek blanket tossed into the air. Having mounted another level, the party of ten looked around the vast bulk above the nave. Repairs to the north and south side of the roof showed different methods of building with wood. How needs must vary with contrasting climatic exposure. Wind was blowing through the sculpted gaps on the west face, outside pins which had been pushed into the stone, presumably to scare birds.

Narrow spiral wooden staircases had been inserted for these public tours of which five were scheduled daily. We scaled the two of these, which I found unsatisfactory as a modern intrusion. It all came to an abrupt halt at the base of the spire, where the motley sequence of exposed ladders up to the summit looked appealing. 'No unauthorized person allowed beyond this point'. I wouldn't have looked down, honestly! 'There are bronze rings on the outside of the spire', said David. The top of the tower, where we were able to shuffle along the contained walkway, provided the expected open views. I tried to piece together my various previous destinations in Salisbury with modest success, I think: theatre, river, hotel. David, who had displayed comprehensive knowledge, pointed out landmarks. In the distance were the sculpted mounds of Old Sarum. He urged us to try out an unnamed church due north, which had the largest Last Judgement portrayal in the country. The tour had proved comparatively painless for all the steps trodden, as it was interrupted so much with pauses and information. It was one we were all glad to have done, just because of the iconic status of this building for its height and external brilliance. At the end David distributed blue badges saying: 'Salisbury Cathedral, I've reached the heights'. We had, almost.

Fig 1

[1] Hereford: Crown of thorns under the crossing.
[2] Salisbury: The picture postcard view across river and meadow.
[3] Salisbury: Memorial to Sir Thomas and Lady Gorges, 1530s.
[4] Rochester: 12th century arch on the west front.

Fig 2

Fig 3

Fig 4

Rochester

Christ & St Mary

Province: Canterbury
Founded: 604; Benedictine 1082 to 1541
Present building: 1178–1240
Restored: 1871–74 by George Gilbert Scott; tower rebuilt 1905

Website: www.rochestercathedral.org
Tel: 01634 843366
Email: administrator@rochestercathedral.org
Address: The Chapter Office, Garth House, The Precinct, Rochester, Kent
ME1 1SX

Three to See: Wheel of fortune;
south quire transept doorway;
Pilgrim Steps

Shell

Rand and I (I think both) were fired by the newly-concocted – the day before – project to face the gracious Rochester, not a city but part of the unitary authority of Medway. The day was foul and fetid, evocative of a threatening scene from the novels of local writer, Charles Dickens.

This time it was a case of treacherous pavements, and roads, too, on the way from car park to west door. There we left our umbrellas, indeed overlooking them on our departure. It was a good thing they were still there – a friend of Rand's once left a buggy in the cathedral entrance. It was no longer there when she went to retrieve it. Why didn't we wonder at our heads getting wet in the dank, sleety afternoon? Probably because we were still thrilled by cathedral-going with a purpose, and we'd enjoyed a pint of Nelson's in the Coopers Arms a bit deeper into the historical section, much-employed by Mr Dickens (1812–70). *Edwin Drood*, set largely in or around the cathedral precinct, was under the quill right up to his death. So many purveyors of nourishment used by him in his writing survive, from the time he lived at Gad's Hill Place, over the Medway, in his Swiss chalet-inspired residence. The Bull Hotel, in the High Street, became the Blue Bull in *Great Expectations*. In *Edwin Drood*:

> *A brilliant morning shines on the old city. Its antiquities and ruins are surprisingly beautiful, with the lusty ivy gleaming in the sun, and the rich trees waving in the balmy air. Changes of glorious light from moving boughs, songs of birds, scents from gardens, woods and fields – or, rather, from the one great garden of the whole cultivated island in its yielding time – penetrate into the Cathedral, subdue its earthy odour, and preach the Resurrection and the Life. The cold stone tombs of centuries ago grow warm, and flecks of brightness dart into the sternest marble corner of the building, fluttering there like wings.*

But the author would not have known the cathedral with its current tower. John Oliver, in *Dickens's Rochester* (1978), commented:

> *The earthy smell came from the 13th century crypt, which was unpaved and full of builders' debris from repairs that had been going on in other parts of the building. Since then the crypt (has been) paved and restored – the whole building is much warmer due to the use of oil-fired heating. The earthy smell has at last been subdued and replaced by a faint 20th century odour of diesel oil.*

In 2011, the BBC was to commit itself to fundamental invention. *The Guardian* had it thus:

> *The BBC is about to finally provide an answer and expose the murderer, in a new adaptation… Dickens died in 1870, exhausted by overwork and his gruelling public performances, before he could reveal all. He had finished two-thirds of the book, and caused Drood to vanish in mysterious circumstances, when the author had a stroke on 8 June and died the following day without regaining consciousness, leaving only a sketchy outline for the remainder of the novel.*

The author was quoted on the cathedral's audio guide. This was £3 and pretty good, my first ever such hiring in a place of worship. Well, Rand and I were surprised not to be demanded of an admission charge, but given the suggestion of a £3 'donation'. I didn't begrudge the cost.

An *Edwin Drood* reference was conveyed at the south quire transept. I love the spelling 'quire', and it has to count for Scrabble encounters, surely, not that actual usage has anything to the official dictionary for the game. The author's wish to be buried in beloved Rochester was upstaged by his status as a national icon. He was destined for entombment in Westminster Abbey. At least the Abbey can lay claim to a period of cathedral status, for all of ten years from in the 1540s. And our author made this observation: 'Dear me, it's like looking down the throat of all time.' This was the second oldest foundation after neighbouring Canterbury, as in the apse, evidenced by two parallel arcs etched deep in the floor by the west door. Speaking of our premier see, the division of territory seems to be straightforward. Rochester has west and north Kent, topped by Tunbridge Wells (eight parishes), Gillingham (seven – Chatham, the third Medway town, has six), and Beckenham (nine). This is according to the rather shabby diocesan map relegated to the crypt. This, with the model of the cathedral, is treated with more pride at Salisbury, in the nave. Rochester was described as 'Norman/Early English' and there are fine examples of the latter in the extensions in the eastern part.

At the upper end of the quire itself, a substantial part of a fresco of the Wheel of Fortune was discovered during rebuilding, mainly in startling, well-preserved red. Carl Orff's *Carmina Burana* was quoted in the audio commentary, and plain to see is Fortuna herself, with three levels of related experience round the perimeter. The apex of the wheel has a seated achiever, looking down on the lesser mortals. In *The Time Traveller's Guide to Medieval England*, Ian Mortimer states that in the 14th century:

The Wheel of Fortune – which lifts men up only to set them down in their pride – is a familiar image to all medieval people. And it is this understanding of vainglory which powers medieval satire.

In 1348, you can even see the king (Edward III, very keen on disguising games) himself take part in one of these mummings, dressed as a giant bird. Mumming does not always involve a play. Witness the procession which takes place before the ten-year-old Prince Richard (II) at Kennington in late January 1377. One hundred and thirty London citizens "disguised and well horsed in a mummer", ride out of the city via Newgate, with trumpets, sackbuts, cornet, shawms, and other instruments, and innumerable torches of wax.

I have enjoyed modern mummers' play productions, though they have proved elusive – not well-advertized in my experience.

In the body of the quire some original medieval work survives, such as the panel showing the red English leopard alternate with the blue French fleur-de-lys. The proximity of church and state couldn't be better shown. This was executed in the reign of Edward III, in the mid 14th century during the Hundred Years' War. The quire action area was furnished with service listings ready for each chorister for January, starting with the Circumcision/Naming of Christ. That seems logistically odd – surely the Holy Family was travelling towards Egypt on the eighth day, fleeing the wrath of Herod? Perhaps they dropped into a synagogue on the way for the operation. In the grand scheme of things, perhaps it's a trifle sophistic to enquire.

Copies of 1340s illustrations adorn the surrounding walls. They make fascinating anecdotes: images of fish and ears represent Bishop Fisher, who was duly executed by Henry VIII. Meanwhile we have the colours of Nicholas Ridley, destined to be burned at the stake by Bloody Mary in the 1550s, a somewhat contrasting regime.

We have to honour William of Perth, a Scottish baker, whose exploit, saving a woman from madness, earning sanctification, spawned the centuries-long knees-on-stone abrasion of the Pilgrim Steps in the north quire transept, in the Early English style of the 1180s.

Rochester Cathedral
It's Rochester Cathedral I meant,
That Perth bloke where pilgrims' knees bent;
Charles Dickens was here,

Norman pillars stay there,
This is the cathedral of Kent.

The conventional route led up to William's shrine, then to St Thomas at Canterbury, whence to Rome, then the Holy Land. You'd have to be sound of body and full of faith. 'Let peace fill our universe.' And ribald too, as Geoffrey Chaucer often was in his pilgrim-related yarn, which undoubtedly involved a stay at Rochester (the Crown Inn has been identified as the watering place, though without evidence), that is close to Watling Street. One tome carrying a related entry was Albert Hyamson's *Dictionary of English Phrases* (1922): 'Chaucer's jest: "An obscene or indelicate act or remark, in allusion to some narratives in Chaucer's *Canterbury Tales*"', (related by Jeffrey Kacirk in *Forgotten English*).

In truth the Norman nave is very fine. The monolith has survived fire, siege (by King John, we have to agree, a 'bad' king) and alteration. There are beautiful chevrons and other enduring abstract designs in pillars, as well as deeply-etched medieval graffiti. And the roof makes sense of the term 'nave': the upturned hulk of a warrior ship. We look up through various styles past triforium to later clerestory, admitting much-needed light. The view from the west and to the high altar through the rood screen is marvellous, showing clearly the upward drift from dying day and bad habits towards new life in the east. There, in the sanctuary was the Flame, small, but always lit. Rand wondered whether the candles were associated with war. This is the only cathedral not to have rows of arches either side of the sanctuary, giving a feeling of space.

The main man here was Gundulf, identified with the Benedictine foundation set up in the 11th century. Even this is advanced history for a cathedral originally founded in 604 by St Augustine – the original abbey cathedral was destroyed by the Danes.

There was a contrast in the timing of work here. The 1490 Lady Chapel was the newest part. Meanwhile we could admire tapestries by Bobbie Cox (1991), evoking a fusion of the abstract and the divine. A notice offered the skills of the cathedral organist: 'Roger Sayer is available to give organ lessons, as well as Aural, Theory and Sight Reading Training.' There was no music on offer during this visit, but his responsibilities included organ recitals and the instruments themselves.

I liked the taboo, in our times, doorway design at the south quire transept. Hamo de Hythe was responsible, he who secured his own depiction in a tiny figure, quite naked, at the top of the door, observing from above Synagoga, for Judaism, blindfolded, opposite Ecclesia, glamorous by comparison, who is clearly favoured. Emerging, this time, through the neighbouring door into a bleak and slippery Cloister Garth, we found solid evidence of Henry VIII's reforming zeal, an unroofed chapter house leading to the gloomy prospect of the Cathedral Tea Room, closed that day. The next time we did try it. To sum up the experience, the dominant aroma was not of coffee, something in keeping with the coffee itself. This had been a royal palace, briefly. How many did bluff King Hal own? And the old steps once leading to the refectory, now led to nostril-battering toilets. At least the architecture, featuring rounded bits of wall in a rich red hue, was more evocative than the Salisbury portacabin units that are the standard provision at original cathedrals where you can only guess at how calls of nature were formerly answered.

We moved on to the pursuit of a lunch break, rejecting the rolls in a café (85p, 98p if heated), also a number of other food places. The Two Brewers Inn looked tempting, offering splendid local Shepherd Neame beers, but apparently no food. Later we passed by again and noted a sign about the 'daily specials', facing the other way. We should have asked, only needed soup or equivalent with pub grub supper in prospect later on in Bromley. The Italian restaurant nearby was too expensive for our current reckoning. We didn't fancy bruschetta or garlic bread. Then we attempted the Coopers Arms, past the cathedral, successfully retrieving our umbrellas on the way. We'd realized this omission in Cancer Relief, where we saw some apparently for sale, but actually the property of shoppers currently scouring the shelves. The Coopers, quoth the smiling barman, was to serve 'no food until Saturday'. It was Thursday. So we settled for salted peanuts. At last we were driven back to the unpromising 'Goldings Bakery and Café', where Rand said he'd survived modest fare on previous occasions. I risked a residual sandwich and he tried a pasty, with a cup of tea each, the staple in such establishments. We then guessed the name of the austere assistant. I thought 'Irene', Rand, 'Margaret'. He was semi-triumphant as, though she was 'Anne with an "E"', her mother's name was Margaret. The conversation, at first tentative, turned fruitful, involving anecdotes, as she was a local girl (now aged 67) and there hung supporting props of exceedingly old photographs on the wall. These showed landmarks since vanished, much building and road change over the years. It was a hugely congested area, deep into the ground with changed use, with the Norman castle above the main road to Canterbury in one direction and London via the Medway, in the other. The cathedral is a veritable truffle in this scheme, something choice to be searched out, growing out of flinty ground among the complexity of local business over a millennium business. Remember Dickens' 'earthiness.' And in the café stood notices on every table: 'Due to changes to the health and safety regulations we are no longer permitted to heat or prepare any baby foods. Sorry for any inconvenience.' So no young families came in any more, for a couple of years by now, said Anne. A young mother couldn't be trusted to handle a hot vessel. This seemed a draconian knee-jerk reaction to some heinous incident in the past. But we were able to enjoy the visual treat of an unnamed assistant attempting to manipulate a Ewbank carpet sweeper.

Outside we were confronted again with the Dickens Café, which earlier had been full of that noisy part of the population discouraged from Goldings, and 'Pip's Corner' a greengrocer's shop, one of many references to today's themed celebrity, Mr Dickens.

We voyaged westwards in Rand's trusty VW, to Bromley, the parish church lying temptingly close to the car park, but by then unfortunately closed, so we were unable to compare and contrast with its senior church, which had proved so engaging. Also rewarding was one of the best pantomimes I could remember, *Sleeping Beauty* at the Churchill Theatre. Bob Aldous, a veteran actor and St Paul's Cathedral welcomer (his star turn as our guide in the Diocese of London was seasons away in September), played the King most regally, and I have to give comic Kev Orkian a plug. We were impressed – this certainly included Wakey of the belly laugh, who had joined us for a fine pre-theatre imbibement in the Partridge up the road in downtown Bromley. He was fortunate to join us at the bland, not very clean, Patisserie Valerie too late for a pot of tea. The tea was insipid. Where can we see Kev again? Never heard of him before – all of 5'4" tall, playing Chester the Jester, but perhaps for me rarely watching mainstream television was a drawback in such cases. Then he appeared in the weekly theatre magazine, *The Stage* (19/8/10), for the Edinburgh Festival Fringe 2010. He was to present his *Illegal Tour* at the Underbelly venue. 'It's basically me telling the story of the Armenian people. My tour combines mainly piano playing with acting and a little bit of dancing too,' he said. No mention of cathedrals, but it was too late for me to rearrange the diary to get to Edinburgh.

The best bit, conducted by Chester and two villagers (dancing boys), was a reinterpretation on the Twelve Days of Christmas recanted here:

1   A bra that was meant to hold three.
2   Two Bromley shirts (somewhat dull – white with black trim; what an improvement the all-red away colours would have been).
3   Three juggling balls.
4   Four pots and pans.
5   Five toilet rolls (which were repeatedly tossed into the audience,

with increasing vigour).

6   Six tatty frocks.
7   Seven smelly socks.
8   Eight rubber chickens.
9   Nine scrubbing brushes.
10 Ten pairs of pants.
11 Eleven cuddly toys.
12 Twelve gallons of water.

This was written by Kev, as well. It got the entire audience going, culminating in a drenching for the front rows. Upstairs we would whisper to him: 'Here's to the king'. Meanwhile the memory of the truffle that was Rochester Cathedral was set to endure.

Saturday 15 January, 2011
It was time to return to Rochester. This was a rather long weekend, combined with paying full attention to its big brother, the one that started it all.

The weekend was inclement overall, but nothing on the drenched exposure on the previous visit. The first, superlative change had been the opening of the new west door, largely glazed, introducing us and light into the nave. The structure itself was impressive. The six pairs of Romanesque pillars benefitted from this, to be enjoyed in all their varied massiveness. It seemed easier this time to admire the depth of the triforium. There were mini-arches inside the narrow pairs of pillars, revealing very early pointed arches. Then, proceeding to enjoy the choir decorations and especially the Wheel of Fortune, it came across to me in the vein of a reunion with an old friend. Retracing steps over this building delivered a sense of reassurance. You latch onto different things on a repeat visit.

In the crypt, tidied up somewhat, we spent some time before the *Textus Roffensis*, a local 12th century reliquary courtesy of a monk at the Priory of St Andrew, in two separate manuscripts, brought together in the 13th century. Among other excitement through its history, it had been stolen and fished out of the neighbouring River Medway. The contents comprised the written laws from the conversion of Ethelbert (c.560–616) through to Henry I, on the throne at the time of composition. Rand pointed out the unusual 'cushion' capitals. Two of them were placed by the Treasury. Cushion capitals, shaped like an upturned cushion were an economical way of making a capital, typically Romanesque, Rand read out to me later. I had been looking forward to the worn Pilgrim Steps, some so thin they were fractured, and all planked over. Nowhere else has there been such an intensity of knee traffic. The Lady Chapel, still seeming strange on the south side, on this occasion featured an exhibition of a Russian iconographer from 2004, the 1400th anniversary of the cathedral.

This time we followed the visit with a stroll up to the castle and over its grounds. An English Heritage adoption, the tower was open as well. Castle and cathedral made a fine double act. That corner of old Rochester showed its age – you were drawn into the literary world which was suggested by so many Dickens relics and souvenirs. After a showing of the brief film about him in the Guildhall Museum, we repaired to a pub on the other bank of the river, closer to Gad's Hill. It was the Kings Arms, Upnor, with a number of local brews on offer. It was an enjoyable conclusion to the morning's endeavours.

Sunday 16 January

It was again the turn of the see of Rochester – some of the hinterland of the Archdeaconry of Tonbridge. All Saints, Tudeley attracted tourists at all times. For practical purposes this was a hamlet, this Anglican establishment operating in a collective called 'Tudeley cum Capel with Five Oak Green'. This included a United Reformed church and, overall, made a viable unit.

Philip Gale, a member of the Private Archive Team at the National Archives, met us there. First, we immersed ourselves in the Marc Chagall windows, a dozen of them massed colour, often blue, with a lot of yellow, was relieved by the periodical image, as it all told the story of Sarah d'Avignor-Goldsmid, who died at 21 in a sailing accident. She was featured in a pane at the bottom of the original, east window. We noted Chagall's favourite motifs, asses and 'red tumbling angels' (said the leaflet *The Message of the Windows*). In a small, undistinguished church they served to overwhelm. Of the church, Philip told us: 'The lighting shifts. It dusks. There's something timeless about the windows: there's a sense of continuity.' A high percentage of Tudeley's income was contributed by tourists.

In an email Philip had written from his wide experience: 'I think what is impressive is the sheer variety of Anglican cathedrals from the towering form of Liverpool Cathedral to Southwark, tucked between Borough Market, the railway, London Bridge and the Thames.' A lot of what he said served to reinforce or add to our acquired knowledge. No bad thing. 'York Minster can raise funds more readily than Portsmouth.' That was propitious as 'Pompey' by then loomed only three visits away. I could only ask about their funding. This matter would be something to ask about concerning that 'parish church cathedral' diocese carved out of the ancient see of Winchester. Philip added, of many an old foundation: 'The further out lands have been lost,' such as York. Formerly you would find pockets of territory in the hands of a bishopric many counties distant from their base.

Endowments were a productive topic – in a practical way at Durham where 'the university was established as a way of using up its endowments.' This whole area of cathedrals and bishoprics required an intimate comprehension of concepts: endowments, canonries (Durham again: a special system there), archives. This last has undergone a transformation since Bletchley Park. 'Digital' had come to rule, and someone had to decide what was kept, sifted, and in what form. Philip waxed eloquent with the phrase 'system of benign neglect'. There had been a lot of that.

So on we drove to the pertinently named St Thomas a Becket, Capel. Directions presented no challenge for once, as it really was 'down the road and left at the sign'. It was a traditional parish church. Philip had said of it: 'You hear *The Lord is my Shepherd*, with sheep bleating outside. The Churches Conservation Trust works there – look at the graveyard.' Wakey, the conservation enthusiast, tarried awhile at the car park notice giving information about the woodland thereabouts. He had spotted a barn owl in the middle of the Medway conurbation the previous night. I was sitting in the obscured back seat and Rand was keeping his eyes on the road, so we missed it. We found ourselves up the path and below the tower 'built of local golden-brown Wealden stone'. The leaflet, for sale in a rack, was worth purchasing for detail about the coloured medieval wall paintings. Roy Tricker was the writer, spinning a good yarn: 'The masonry of the chancel and north nave walls is covered with protective render and one wonders what features of interest may be hidden beneath it.' The paintings, straddling a narrow Norman window, were discovered in 1868, 'uncovered by Professor E W Tristram in 1927, and were conserved by Mrs Eve Baker and Mr John Dives in 1970'. We should thank them all. The paintings extended over much of the north side of the nave, telling many a tale. 'Cain slaying his brother, Abel, and God reprimanding Cain for this dreadful act' touched me, as not only was it a lovely image, mainly in red on the (clammy) white but repeated the Genesis story told on the radio only a week before in a sequence of broadcasts commemorating the 400th anniversary of the King James Bible. We were to admire a copy of that very thing the next day in Canterbury Cathedral. Further, the Thomas a Becket connection was pointed out. The narrative continued: 'This Old Testament act of violence may well have also reminded Capel people and passing pilgrims to Canterbury of the murder of Thomas a Becket in 1170.' We were cast in the role of pilgrims in these Kent dioceses.

It was dark when we reached Rochester, after the service for the Blessing of the Plough. I wanted to be sure about Rochester's lack of cat, having met Laptop at Canterbury the previous day. Post call of nature, we entered the crypt by a conveniently open door, in the wake of a pair of uniformed sous-chefs, or some-such, who had just finished their fags; they stepped down into the kitchen space, which opened up to reveal a tea party in progress. I approached an imposing clerical man, with wife in tow. It was the Revd Dr Gordon Gatward, who had delivered the Plough sermon and was on the point of departure, back to Stoneleigh, Warwickshire, 'Diocese of Coventry,' he confirmed, and was ignorant about animals. Mindful of the accommodating bishop, with whom the appointment was nigh, we sadly left the array of tea and cakes unassailed and moved into the nave, as the quickest way out. We happened upon a team of vergers. To the one who conveyed an aura of authority, in the midst of furniture adjustments, I posed the essential question. 'Not anything you'd call a cat', he replied.

At length, we found the Rochester shell, plus a mitre, dark above the apex of a very smart iron gate a few houses beyond the Cooper's Arms. It was indeed Bishopscourt, and we were soon sitting with cups of tea in the elegant Georgian drawing room with curtains draped on a sofa on the other side of the room awaiting attention. 'Call me James,' he invited and a hearty hour of exchanges ensued. The Rt Revd James Langstaff was the first church official, not to mention bishop, to eschew his work gear for an open-necked shirt. He was engaging and forthcoming, admitting to a more evangelical persuasion (welcomed women bishops, but found the prospect of gays 'more difficult'). Mind you, it had been reported concerning Ebbsfleet, in this diocese that the flying/floating bishop looked after parishes who didn't want any truck with women clergy. Canon Clare Edwards of Canterbury was not surprised about this characteristic of the neighbouring territory. The two Kent dioceses were coming across as two sides of the same coin.

The time before James' arrival had been marked by the departure of Michael Nazir-Ali, and a gap of eighteen months, during which the workload had been covered somehow. The delay was partly explained by the General Election in May, as the recruitment of bishops was a matter for the (current) Prime Minister, delegated from the Crown. James had been heralded surrounding his inauguration on 11 December, in the press, and on the spot by the King's Lynn Festival Chorus, singing an Irish blessing: 'May the road rise to meet you. May the wind be ever at your back. May the sun shine warm on your face and the rain fall soft upon your fields, until we meet again. May God hold you in the palm of his hand.' Quite a mixture of contributions!

James could now forge ahead, partly with a different emphasis. Bishop Michael had found an echo in his fellow African, Archbishop Sentamu, in his international and interfaith interests. James would spend more time at home. He had left a very different post as Bishop of Lynn in the diocese of Norwich, living a rural life in Swaffham, Norfolk. His wife had retained her employment there, his children were pursuing careers of their own. So the image accrued of a solitary working week, in this showpiece of an official residence. Solitary, but unlikely to be lonely with so many friends in the business, and so much to do. Anyway, he said he was already becoming known to be at the end of his mobile phone (except for half an hour earlier, when I tried to call him). I commented about overdoing it: you can be too accessible. On the other hand, I reminded myself that we were enjoying an out of hours encounter, my memory fresh with the difficulty other similar situations had presented. I did meet Bishop Michael Perham of Gloucester – in the end. James had 'grown up with' Dean Vivienne Faull of Leicester, whom Rand and I met so profitably at her workplace. They once compared baked potato options in a queue. It was easy to imagine him going for it: there would be one forthcoming instance in the Gravesend deanery as part of a series of visits to each of them. There were 17 deaneries in total. He considered the diocese 'not coherent' but embraced an interesting mix, from the London boroughs to Medway to West Kent, where we had spent the earlier part of the day. Very nice too. And commutable from the capital. At 55, he was starting on the bottom rung as a first time diocesan bishop. It would take some years to rise to 21st position, and qualify for Lordship. I suggested that it probably would happen; he thought it would be right here, as he was unlikely to leave for another diocese. Though pleased to have been invited to become a bishop, he had been quite happy as a parish priest. Housing had been an interest up to now and this would continue. A central issue of Gravesend would be housing growth, and the ecumenical factor. There was the prospect of relationships with other churches in the region, and with the neighbours – Bishop Trevor of Dover (perhaps called 'Trover'?) would be a talk-mate, and perhaps a future diocesan bishop of Canterbury, and Southwark and Chichester shared borders with Rochester. The Kent Constabulary dealt with both Kent Anglican presences. On the other hand, bearing in mind the current, in fact endless, topic of diocesan reform, it was possible that Rochester would find itself the subject of a split between Canterbury and Southwark. As it was there were expressions of regional intercourse – periodical meetings of Diocesan groups, of the House of Bishops, for the Synod. Bishops were busy chaps.

For light relief I broached the issue of 'your favourite cathedral.' He touched upon his previous spot, Norwich, in terms of 'splendour', Ely for 'the vista right through – quite special', then Birmingham. This was where he had spent the body of his career, and to him the see of Rochester had much in common with it. As for the cathedral, yes, Birmingham got his vote. 'It's not a cathedrally cathedral, but I love the Burne-Jones windows, and association with events over 18 years. It's on a human scale, with clean lines.' He also enthused about St Martin in the Bull Ring, the parish church.

There was more, and on parting he showed us the display in the hall and up the stairs of the delicious watercolours of Donald Maxwell, whose subject matter included the house of God down the road, as well as Kent villages. 'It's the largest private collection', said James, counting 14. The artist had been a church warden, and now these gems were the property of the bishopric. Incidentally, the new incumbent was intending to appear on a daily basis for early services and attend rather more than I had heard bishops doing elsewhere. After all, they lacked any status in the cathedral itself. We wished the new bishop luck, and stepped cautiously onto the slippery garden path. My only regret was provoked later on visiting Wakefield, where I found a fine bridge chapel. These are rare. Rochester's was built in the 15th century, resting beside, not on, the River Medway. Close to the castle, it was reputedly isolated but in good repair.

4

Lichfield

St Mary and St Chad

Province: Canterbury
Founded: 700 as cathedral; history associated with Coventry and Chester
Present building: 1195; 1250–1310
Restored: 1855–61 & 1877–81 by George Gilbert Scott

Website: www.lichfield-cathedral.org
Tel: 01543 306100
Email: info@lichfield-cathedral.org
Address: The Chapter Office, 6 The Close, Lichfield, Staffordshire
WS13 7LD

Three to See: East window, whether to see the Herkenrode panes or, if
not installed, rarely seen clear glass;
pedilavium, with towel for visiting parties;
chapter house with cat carving

Dictionary

Saturday 2 January, 2010

Staying from time to time at the Lichfield house of my friend Tiptoes, I had been getting to know this lovely red edifice hand-in-glove with attendance at Aston Villa's home games, at their English Premier League shrine, Villa Park, (Trinity Road) Birmingham, 18 miles distant. Lichfield Cathedral's strongest image is of the stone spires, the only such British threesome (symbolizing the Trinity, of course). On most occasions it's on the A38 that you espy 'the Ladies in the Vale', as they are called, the vale being that of the River Trent on its journey to the North Sea. The central spire was destroyed in the Civil War and mercifully rebuilt and renovated in 1950.

This part of the city is restful and indulging, cohesive and elegant, giving a domestic ethos. Erasmus Darwin's house has pride of place, and is worth a visit for architecture, atmosphere, information and the herb garden. His pallid bust looks out of an upper storey window onto passers-by on Beacon Street, leading away from the city centre. Further up is Tiptoes' front door, and at the back those spires are in direct view. There is also a bird-bound pond in the vicinity. Also, there is rewarding building work style in the canons' houses in the cathedral close. Lichfield was the birthplace of Samuel Johnson (1709–84) and David Garrick (1717–79, premier actor of his day and pupil of Dr Johnson) and the centre of the see of Staffordshire. Prosperity has been mixed over the centuries, reflected in the history of the cathedral itself. Sam and Dave reached the summits of their worlds, after they had left their Midlands base. During my studies, most of all I enjoyed Johnson's *Life of Richard Savage,* to be revisited when time allows. Since words are important, and we have *A Dictionary of the English Language* (1755), a major contribution from Dr Johnson, a dictionary is chosen as the icon for Lichfield.

The patron saint of Lichfield is Chad, bishop from 669 to 672. The original building dated from 700. St Mary enjoys a joint dedication and both are commemorated in the Lady Chapel. Going back so far makes this one of the very first of the old foundation of cathedrals, though architecturally it dates only from the 13th century.

During the Wars of the Roses, when the see was termed 'Coventry and Lichfield', Bishop John Hales (or Halse) was in office as long as the House of Lancaster was in charge. During his tenure, 'when (he) called his 60 guests to table for the Feast of the Assumption on 15 August 1461, they were served with two salmon, two chub' (a dubious choice: Izaak Walton, of *Compleat Angler* fame, called the flesh "not firm but short and tasteless"), three pike, four perch, half a dozen dace and trout, and two dozen each of grayling and eels'. When Edward IV regained the crown for the House of York in 1471, Bishop Hales lost his office.

In Chad's time the diocese stretched from the Welsh border to the North Sea; and from Northumberland to the Thames. Despite having shrunk somewhat over the years as bits and pieces were chopped off to form new dioceses, Lichfield remains one of the largest in the Church of England, serving a population of just under two million people over 1,744 square miles. The diocese has 583 churches and 427 parishes in Staffordshire, the northern half of Shropshire, Wolverhampton, Walsall, half of Sandwell, and even three parishes straddling the Welsh border.

In 2010 the Diocese was headed up by the 98th Bishop of Lichfield (since 2003), the Rt Revd Jonathan Gledhill, and was served by 294 full time stipendiary (paid) clergy and an even larger number of non-stipendiary (volunteer) clergy and lay ministers. The Strategy stated: 'It is not about cold numbers but about health, life and relationships. We believe that healthy churches produce new disciples and fresh initiatives. We look for growth in disciples, welcome for children and young people and transformation of communities.'

It came to enjoy missionary partnerships with the Dioceses of Kuching, West Malaysia and Singapore in South East Asia; the Diocese of Qu'Appelle in Saskatchewan, Canada; the Diocese of Matlosane in South Africa; and the Evangelical Lutheran Church of Mecklenburg in northeast Germany. I have heard references in services to this admirable overseas work, and witnessed the welcome given to natives attending services, from more than one of the partnership countries. The whole initiative appears dynamic and healthy.

An irresistible attraction became the 10.30 am Eucharist service. One trademark here has been the quality of the sermons, featuring yet another invigorating delivery from a canon, perhaps Wealands Bell or Pete Wilcox or another, increasingly familiar, working in the fabric of this cathedral; or maybe a guest from somewhere else in the country, or perhaps a partner from a linked overseas diocese. Now for the opinion of Wakey, who has attended Lichfield Cathedral quite a few times: 'It's my favourite because it's so different – it's the stone, the three spires. You don't expect to see a red cathedral. The "3" – theory of balance of numbers – 3s, 5s, 7s, all instil something in the natural harmony; recognition that this instinctive kind of stuff works so well.' Add the comment of Priv, first and foremost a footy fan (Stockport County): 'There's a nice pitch and putt nearby.' But he liked cathedrals too, and a wide range of them, stretching from Chelmsford to Manchester. Also include Rick, who chose Lichfield for the golden balls on the spires. As a 10 year-old pupil at Yarlet Prep School, close to the Potteries, also in this diocese, he remembered them from visits to Lichfield to play St Chad's.

Wednesday 19 May

Much further down the trail line, having visited 22 cathedrals, this visit followed the delights of a jaunt around the East Midlands over the preceding days, from Southwell to Derby. The latter was spawned from the diocese of Lichfield in 1914. It involved a lot of driving. You end up looking like tarmac. The main bit of fun on the A38 was Eddie Stobart's lorry honouring Jemma Francesca on the driver's door. Eddie's girls' names, rarely realistic, could last for decades.

Wednesday arrived: at 9.30 am on a day yielding sharp shadows and shiny surfaces, Rand and I stood before the west front of St Chad's, which is no Lincoln Minster, but appealing in itself. This is where my friend Graham used to sit in the close: 'I enjoyed the collection of houses (home to so many on the diocesan payroll) rather than the shops you see around at other cathedrals.' On the west front were set in individual alcoves the kings of England, from William I to Richard II, in stately still pose above the viewer. Below was the wide green lawn more or less surrounding the cathedral. The man from Green Thumb was tending to the fertilizing. Yellow and red particles, like my blood pressure tablets, were spraying from his manual barrow. 'The Council does the cutting,' he said. This was under the squat central tower, propping up the biggest spire. Squat was sometimes best, I had decided, contributing to a sense of majesty from the unusual trefoil design in the clerestory level below. Further along, we found the building site that was the east end. Chunks of red stone lay there, ready for erection into some of the weathered masonry sections. Also lying there, by the apse, mellowed a handful of yellow-garbed workmen on a tea break (at 10 am). We bumped into an official, who I realized on the next visit was Dean Adrian Dorber. He was happy to inform us, ever-inquisitive, that the buttress project was scheduled for three years, at a cost of £3m. We asked about the east window, where the 'Netherlandish' (a broad definition applies) 16th century Herkenrode glass had been dismantled for a complete overhaul. Four years were allocated for that challenge. It tempted us inside, having done a full circuit of the delightful exterior, patchy in colour and state of repair, the patchwork look enhanced for me, as at Lincoln recently, by its erratic look.

The nave offered wicker chairs, fitting and comfortable, which empathized with the warm stone throughout, not so much red as dark, certainly after the limestone in the other buildings recently enjoyed. A feature here was the mechanical section of the floor, at the nave altar. In black and white, it was 18" above the floor, but at the press of a button could be flush with it. The altar was of oak and walnut, also modern (2003) and effective. Further up were 6-sided choir stalls placed there recently. This separated the nave, for general use, from the quire, which lay tantalizingly behind the Giles Gilbert Scott gate. That was good. And of course further on lay the presbytery and the high altar. So, when the place became fully operational again, there would be three altars, the newly conserved (not 'restored') Lady Chapel producing a tour de force below the brilliant east window.

Rand did not anticipate much satisfaction from Lichfield as, overall, Alec Clifton-Taylor had dwelt on bad restoration and decay in *The Cathedrals of England*. What we saw in this modest Staffordshire city was a cathedral busy on a sunny day, full of groups being shown around, the time limit at each station expressed by a strong but silent woman bell-ringer, clocking up many a mile. There was the north transept, where the font, curiously distant from any entrance, offered two handsome shells in which to dispense the water within. Also the stone pedilavium, another first, and as efficacious, for ceremonial foot washing, which we witnessed school children trying out (supervised). Jugs of water and towels were provided. Round the corner was the rich and active chapter house, where, for once it was possible to imagine real, live cathedral meetings taking place. The seats and backs were padded in a comforting ruby red (like altar wine, and raspberry parfait, or something out of a chocolate box). I reckoned it to be larger than Southwell, and modest compared with Lincoln. The point was that it might have been small enough to dispense with the elegant, ribbed central column (none at Southwell). There was lovely fan vaulting. But no, another device had been introduced to necessitate the upright support, as the library lay above. The building boasted two floors, so never monastic. The history was clear. Bishops were elected in this room. The canons, the residential clergy staff, had regular business to transact. Focusing on the individual eye-catchers/story tellers, the chapter house had plenty. Oliver Cromwell was as responsible here as elsewhere for defacements. Attend instead to the small model of the cathedral, next to its ground plan, easily admired in the sunlight, and thankfully not made of matchsticks. And next, almost to my relief, an icon at the Shrine of St Chad. You do need an icon in every cathedral, I'd now decided, and this was so apposite, marking the cathedral's saint solidly rooted in those dark days of the 7th century. He became bishop in 669 and died of the plague three years later. His was the most relevant dedication anywhere: the first cathedral bore his name – in 700. In the retro choir, west from there, was a quirky sequence of marble statues facing away. Apart, that is, from one each on the left and right extremity, who looked us in the eye: very odd. Through the gaps, between each of the figures, was visible the great west window.

Let's move on from this reverie to pass by the cathedra, piscina and consistory court. The last was sited in a curiously cramped manner to share a modest room with the treasury display and robe cupboard for celebrants and priests. So the big boys were able to admire the ancient (Hacket Silver, 1660) and modern (Lang Collection, 1991) exhibits as they awaited the call to hop and skip to their service workstation. I was to visualize all this at the next Eucharist attendance – would Archbishop Rowan be admiring the silverware during his wait? There was no riffraff box room for the service officials, nor any personal space.

Making contact with Head Verger Christopher Craddock, over 20 years in the job, we were waiting in the nave for him to join us. Rand and I enjoyed the exchanges between a very informal guide and some young lasses. 'Girls, are you ready?' he asked. 'We must be quick.' Rand's assessment was: 'Certainly a good teacher. They're rapt – the children.' 'Down to earth presentation' I posited. 'He doesn't patronize them' he added, having witnessed other such parties elsewhere. Then the bell would ring. It always did, without fail, soundly shaken by Silent Woman, who managed to convey a stentorian message.

Chris arrived. The acoustic was apparently used to best advantage with performers placed at the west end. Twice a year the modern choir pews were removed: at Christmas and during the Lichfield Festival. We moved to the organ, which I had been informed was a semitone sharp, in the high and tight loft. You see straight down, inducing vertigo in some. This was aesthetically satisfying to an observer, above the north choir. However the climb there was not for the squeamish. Rand was reluctant to join us two in scaling the height, but was ultimately glad to have been persuaded by Chris, with me coaxing: 'You'll regret not doing it.' On the way we had further exposure to the backstage rabbit warren, via vestries for boys and men (very untidy, complete with discarded white surplice lying on a table beside a packet of digestives), and an age-long list of organists. As at Southwell the wood-wormed board was tucked away from the public. It was for inmates only. Then, as we shuffled onto an exceedingly narrow platform, Chris brought us to the organ itself. Rand survived and I loved it – it was at the same level as St Chad's Head Chapel on the south side at an angle in sight of it, beyond the quire. To the east, work was in progress, hidden under a gargantuan plastic sheet, with ropes. I heard myself say: 'It's going to be magnificent when it's done,' but I articulated from imagination only – they should have covered the area with one of those artist's impressions of the finished product I've seen on major buildings in Madrid, and Manchester. There was either a failure of the committee or its funding. The legend stated: '… after the stonework repairs are complete… the window spaces will be filled with clear glass to help protect the painted glass in future and the Lady Chapel will return to use... a programme of conservation, not restoration, is planned'. Conservation – a precious 'c'. Of course it was the 'restoration' of zealous and egocentric 19th century architects that had served to diminish the former beauty of Lichfield Cathedral.

The organ, supremely historic, and finished in 1908 by William Hill & Son (of London), had been restored by Harrison & Harrison (of Durham) in 2000. We were treated to a display of the Cyclops camera, all-seeing and unbeknownst around the building. I mentioned Kim, the grey cathedral cat, by now 20 years old and retired. No rodents had survived here, as almost everywhere else. Health and Safety, restoration (or conservation) and the cleanliness of the modern world have all contributed. Chris had his own beast to offer: Comet, a black Labrador. The best, and solitary on the day, was on the chapter house wall: the stone cat, showing some evidence of pre-Reformation whitewash. With rodent in mouth, it made a fine corbel above a seat, as did the Coventry-inspired man's head facing askew in recrimination. We overheard the spiel of a tour guide: 'There's always art to do with the church. We see the role of the artist – for the glory of God.'

Next Chris told us who did what on a service day. The assistant organist played, the organist conducted. And there was a piano in the nave. There was spare accommodation there, unlike the chapter house, for one, which served plural functions, represented by various items occupying the space. It was noticeable that there were no periodical prayers delivered in the cathedral, which had been the practice in other cathedrals.

After a second perambulation round the close to the sunny south side, we met a stone mason: Phil Barnacle, working separately from the team of hard hats at the eastern extremity, and somewhat on show. Deliberately positioned? Phil told us how the stone was being chiselled down to replace worn out originals. That was local, while this was from Lockerbie, Scotland, the outcome of backstage discussions: down to money, it appeared. But consider the transport costs – big orders and somewhat heavy. Still the Ollington Quarry, near Rocester, Staffs did have an input, as it had when Phil worked on the just-as-jaded Hereford Cathedral. And at Coventry, too. Phil was the third, and last, generation in the trade in his family. On the other hand there were currently four apprentices, learning their method with a handful of chisels and a mallet, which reminded me of the display of tools at Liverpool Cathedral. There was pride in this. Those tools have made these wonders.

Thirsty now, we moved on to Chapters Restaurant & Coffee Shop, opposite the south side. We were able to sit with a view of a ruined wall. Chapters was geared to satisfy appetites from corporate or private arrangements to a simple cup of aromatic coffee, plus biscuit, which was essential in my view, but far from standard. A flyer invited us to 'Vote for your favourite business in Lichfield', for which four of the 11 questions applied to this emporium. Par for the course, and I was tempted to enter and submit 'Chapters'. It would have been unfair, though, as it was the only contender I'd patronized, except for the George and Dragon, Tiptoes' local, which I would recommend for Marston's Pedigree. That ale's excellence may be partly due to the short hike: it's brewed close-at-hand at Burton-on-Trent.

We ruminated over the building above us. It earned more points from Rand than anticipated, and quite a lot from me. I already felt good about it. As a second division traditional cathedral it ticked many boxes. It didn't aspire to outdo its greater rivals. But they are not in competition. It had plenty to do and was kind to us. There was no charge for admission, but encouragement to contribute on departure, in a small gift aid envelope.

The final journey followed. We overtook a 'Stobart' truck down the M5. This time Eddie had gone macho and dropped his first name. The name on the cabin was Jodie Hannah.

Monday 19 July
Lichfield Festival was not in the remit of Canon Precentor Wealands Bell. Wakey and I had enjoyed two concerts on Friday 17 May. The first was by Birmingham-based Ex Cathedra, performing Monteverdi pieces, from madrigal to missa, in a programme called In Search of 1610. That was good, in the setting of the nave, enhanced by the illumination, in blue, then purple, of the west wall, drawing attention to the line of discrete fan vaults below the window. Neither of us had noticed that before. But then we had normally faced the altar. We did that for the second event, the 10 pm candle-lit recital of Bach's Goldberg Variations in the Presbytery. This was performed by Catrin Finch, on the harp, which made a change from piano, which I've enjoyed a few times producing this work over the years. I have also played it on my music machine when needing to concentrate on writing about cathedrals. The candles were lit, so were considerable electric bulbs, rather diminishing the effect. Not very intimate, though the backdrop of the screen was transfixing. We emerged elevated and thirsty, destined for Tiptoes' customary hospitality, this time of cheese from food fairs in Shropshire, and well-drinkable red wine.

Onto the Monday I visited Canon Wealands who lived in The Close, just over the grass from the west front, a truly lovely setting for a senior chapter notable to live, complete with wife and young son (who had been enjoying Cheerios for breakfast, I learned). At 1.16 pm I rang the sonorously antique bell and a perky young woman answered it: 'He's in there'. 'There' was through the hall to an office on the left, full of books and business. The great man rose from his computer and diary-laden desk. 'Wealands,' he said. 'Mick,' I replied. There was no mention of my tardy arrival. I was concerned because it had been so difficult to tie a date around this visit to a diary entry. Theresa Willmore, his p.a., had said: 'Not before Monday,' and 'any time from 1pm.' Well, Wealands was laid back about it, and explained after her departure a few minutes later that his door-opening companion was Cathy Lamb, Director of Lichfield Cathedral School Girls' Choir, and part of a husband and wife team. The male part, Ben, was to join as Director of Music. This was the end of the working year, a time of change. Much-admired Organist Phil Scriven and two choral scholars were moving on. The meeting had been about fixing events in November. 'We have to plan ahead,' explained Wealands. I also noted the special guest sermonizer, a VIP (Very Important Preacher?), scheduled for Eucharist on Sunday 7 November. These snippets were in the back of the Festival Eucharist programme. This was actually the service booklet for the congregation the previous day, but it gave so much information that you would keep it for future reference. Wealands admitted to having written much of it. I have to quote from his passage about the VIP, headed 'Fiery Preacher', which came from the flyer on his wall board: 'The visiting preacher will be the Most Revd and Rt Hon Rowan Williams, Lord Archbishop of Canterbury (Lichfield is in his province), Primate of All England and Metropolitan, First Peer of the Realm, who is making a pastoral visitation of the diocese 5 – 8 November 2010. Pick up a leaflet (the one on the wall, but not yet in the cathedral), or go to the surely ill-advisedly named www.churchonfire.org.uk'.

In connection with the musical function of the cathedral, Wealands' domain, he referred to the difficulty of working in this building. The surfaces were far from flat, in the quire and elsewhere. The ceiling space was made of plaster. 'Flat' would be the acoustic ideal. Also, the organ was notoriously sharp. The result was that 'for tenors top B flat becomes natural. It's nice for bass and alto. I would say that; I'm a tenor and I was a treble.' Meanwhile brass bands play sharp, added the expert. The overall effect is that you're in danger of 'burst larynxes.' Of the organ he recounted the poser of ten years previously: 'Shall we buy another instrument or retune the current one? The decision was to buy new: Phoenix electronic organ for work with orchestras.'

His job was as 'Praecantor' – first singer – to lead, primarily attending to liturgy. In practical terms, responsibility, in a world of meetings, to defend his departmental funding (meaning the level of activity) in straitened circumstances. Singing officers cost £300K. It cost several hundred pounds per service. The paid staff included nine lay vicars (after their day's work at teaching, publishing, etc.), two directors of music (sharing) and a full-time organist. In total there were 12 adults on the payroll, and a page turner. They provided education for 18 male choristers. Scholarships were worth 50% of the fees, sited in the beautiful old Bishop's Palace on the north side of the cathedral. It was on public record that expenditure was being reduced. Some cathedrals lacked a paid choir. Cuts were expected. Next year there would be no choral scholars, following an excellent year. The two leavers went on to higher education at Durham and Cardiff.

Among further topics we touched on, Wealands admitted to a penchant for Guinness – he used to drink real ale, but his time overseas being forced to drink lager-type stuff had changed his palate. Concerning jobs, by no means did he covet the posts of bishop or dean. 'Who'd be a dean?' he posited. 'People imagine deans and bishops are smarmy Machiavellian characters. They are actually people with a profound belief. Their job involved immense workload in the life of a diocese with a very curious shape.' 'It's the shape of a head,' he added and pointed at the dimple in his chin to show where the cathedral lay geographically. This led to problems of association, as the current see was still substantial. Parts of Shropshire remained within. Oswestry felt disconnected, being so far away. 'When I was at St Albans Abbey, Bedfordshire didn't feel related to the cathedral,' (which is in Hertfordshire). He referred to moves within the Church of England. 'Some are coming back together.' An example was neighbours Newcastle and Durham. For administrative purposes there was a possible move to Tyneside. He knew that area well, having been born in Gateshead in 1963, and was at Jarrow as curate. 'We are attempting to keep ecclesiastical peace, dealing with damaged people. They would beg: "I'm hungry." You shouldn't give money,' (when your instinct is to be generous) but help with something practical, such as where to go, that is, which agencies. So he had direct experience of the social function required of a cathedral in an urban setting. Not so much here, anyway – Lichfield Cathedral rarely had anyone appear at the door in need.

We moved on to a specific of his role: the Precentors Annual Conference in September, applying specialities at each host venue, cathedrals, royal peculiars and some Greater Churches. To list recent and future ones:

2008 – Salisbury (the particular issue for discussion had surrounded 'Sarum')
2009 – Coventry (included was a visit to the Royal Shakespeare Company, for a meeting of minds with theatre directors)
2010 – up-and-coming at Windsor (a Royal Peculiar: on the

agenda was: 'how to answer needs of the Royal Family')
2011 – Sheffield (would feature the silver assay office)
2012 – Norwich

The delegates would share solutions – encouragement to people doing the same as you are.

We turned to the nitty gritty: the future of the church. The prospect was of less of everything we've been used to over the last 200 years. Some dioceses were becoming impractical. They might have to use other people's buildings – hold things in common. Stipendiary priests were a thing of the past. Have to work for a living – in the 1950s church people kidded themselves that all was well.

On a personal basis Lichfield for Wealands was 'a glorious coming together of all that has been. I miss teaching – the daily contact, though I am involved with the school quite a lot.' He was head of the choral foundation. The stated aim was to introduce girls (it's fully funded at Durham – meaning absolute parity of life). 'Poor Lichfield has no general endowments.' The Millennium music campaign aimed to reap good rewards – people died and left money. 'But not yet as they're living longer,' I posited. He concurred. 'These are undeniably challenging times,' he said, 'but it's good to be forced to look in mirror and (examine) what's going on.'

'We have to stop the place from falling down.' The immense physical challenges of the building's soft red sandstone were a few yards away for all to see. The purchase of the Herkenrode stained glass by an earlier regime had now come home to roost. The stonework was soft sandstone. The panes were in danger of falling out, so were removed in April (I was so glad to have seen them while they were still vertical. The climatic effect had been 'like steel brush on your teeth. Most churches are now dust on the wind,' he said sadly.

I had to move on. Wealands had been brilliant and only looked at the clock once. I had already noted Archbishop Rowan's autumn fixture for yet more exposure to St Chad's.

Sunday 8 November
Saturday the 7th saw Wakey and I sample a contrasting delight on a wide arc from Birmingham to Lichfield. We ventured into opposition territory, to the Roman Catholic St Giles, Cheadle, an unexpected glimpse into how church interior design had been in the past. It paraded painted pillars and blazing brasswork. It was a wildly colourful extravaganza cooked up by the excessively named Augustus Welby Northmore Pugin. In 1852 he expired woefully at the age of 40, incarcerated in Bedlam on account of

madness (or syphilis). Everyone should make the journey there to gorge themselves sumptuously. We left Cheadle and Welby's (my favourite of the architect's names) church full of the mind's eye of church and local fare, from Blacksticker Blue cheese to Russet apples purchased in the outdoor market. And there was an Eddie lorry on the A38: 'Dazey.' Wakey had to look twice to confirm. After all it was a rarity that the name comprised a single word.

The next morning found us once again in Lichfield Cathedral on the Third Sunday before Advent. Though arriving with half an hour to go, the nave was full. We ended up by the south aisle wall, with cushions, or kneelers, to sit on, and a clear view of the pulpit, for the star turn. It had been advertised, as per the dedicated website, as 'Church on Fire, Four days of events celebrating the pastoral visit of The Archbishop of Canterbury', presumably an output of Lambeth Palace Promotions. The 'i' of 'Fire' was a flame. All went well, including observance of a point made on page 10 of the service booklet: 'Please make your way to the communion stations efficiently.' We all did, because it was well handled by the considerable staff, most unlike the cock-up in recent memory at Manchester! The sermon was duly delivered and appreciated. 'He's got a lovely rich voice,' opined Wakey.

For Rowan the tour would not have all been 'duty': 'The Archbishop of Canterbury launched a new beer in Telford. It has been specially blended by Brough's Brewery, in Netherton, West Midlands, to commemorate his four-day visit to the Lichfield diocese. The ale is named Sticky Wicket, which has prompted a rash of puns around the word "ailing", and led some commentators to suggest that it represents the present state of the Anglican Communion.' Pat Ashworth, *Church Times* (12/11/10). That would have served to quench the fire a little.

To conclude the service, Dean Adrian extended 'a warm welcome to so many across the diocese'. He spoke of the availability of books by and about the Archbishop in the shop, opposite the front (we found an outlet inside the cathedral as well). Adrian referred to him as 'a distinguished author,' whose biography carried 'a very winning photo... He'd appreciate royalties and we'd appreciate the income.' I read that the Dean hailed from Manchester and was a lifelong Man U fan, something I discovered too late to introduce into our brief exchange afterwards. There would have been a possibility of negativity, given Wakey's attachment to the other Manchester team. Dean Adrian knew Rowan of old – the Archbishop had taught him at Westcott College, Cambridge in the 1970s. Not only that: in 1978 they joined forces with others to study Coptic Monasticism and Christian/Islamic relations in Egypt. And here they were together on Rowan's first visit to the Diocese of Lichfield. The extent of the see came home to me when I bumped into a tour-leader in the queue for the facilities in the café after the show; their coach-load had come from Shrewsbury. It's not surprising outlying parts felt detached. The lengthy evacuation of the building afforded us a chance to look around. Freshly equipped with insight into the nave altar, courtesy of English Heritage among others, we stood over it, with the pleasant backdrop of the wide open west doors, while the congregation seeped out, many by way of handshakes with the president and guest. The new dais was in pole position, erect. I mentioned it to Dean Adrian in favourable terms. 'It's not high enough,' he retorted, adding: 'that was the previous regime'. I reached Wealands, for once in my experience in a supporting role, in a small group in the north aisle. We shook hands. The gist was that it was over now, after all that preparation. I said: 'Remembrance Sunday next week.' 'Oh, yes, I'd forgotten that.' Outside the Archbishop was free for a moment – we shook hands and I introduced myself. 'Oh yes, you wrote to me,' he said. He was due to spend the next day in the Potteries, but not in any churches. He gave me a recommendation as to whom to contact for the visit to Canterbury two months hence.

As we left, yet again, Wakey concluded: 'Lichfield is just the right size. The information is well organized – telling you where to go.' Then, after a pause, 'It's impressive but you don't feel it's bragging – it's got a homely feel': an opinion, but a mature one, from comprehensive exposure to the Cathedral of St Mary and St Chad. By April 2011, the east window tracery had been rendered able to receive plain glass (the Herkenrode work continued to be a matter of fund-raising). The effect was unique in cathedral exposure: so much light! After all, everywhere else there is a showpiece window, often richly-coloured, or a wall. The Lady Chapel could now be admired in all its glory.

Fig 5

Fig 6

Fig 7

[5] Lichfield: Stonemason carving a red stone
   grotesque for the east end.
[6] Lichfield: Quire floor after cleaning.
[7] Bristol: Henry II: stained glass in cloister.
[8] Chester: The original refectory, now the
   cafe, containing a fine wall pulpit.

Fig 8

Bristol

Holy Trinity

Province: Canterbury
Founded: 1140 as Augustinian abbey
Restored: 1868–88 rebuilding by G E Street
Cathedral: 1542, absorbed into Gloucester diocese 1836; new diocese
of Bristol 1897

Website: www.bristol-cathedral.co.uk
Tel: 0117 926 4879
Email: reception@bristol-cathedral.co.uk
Address: College Green, Bristol BS1 5TJ

Three to See: Norman chapter house;
medieval candelabrum in Berkeley Chapel;
ogee arch in quire screen

Pincushion

Tuesday 10 February, 2010

Bristol has a plethora of ecclesiastical buildings. It can boast a veritable cornucopia of sense-gorging. Erstwhile second city, it grew fat on Merchant Venturers, wine, slaves and tobacco. It has glorious bits, is most uncohesive and difficult to know, and certainly to drive in. No grid system and much complexity (give me Birmingham or Leeds to comprehend and move around in).

There is a lot of history here and such a mishmash of styles and developments that many of the city's church buildings merit comment. We can start with its ancient foundations. The Augustinian abbey was founded outside the city walls before the Norman Conquest. In 1539 the abbey was surrendered to the king, and in 1542 the diocese of Bristol was founded, carved out of that of Worcester. This subsisted for 294 years. In 1836 it was all change: James Monk (1784–1856, a classical scholar) became bishop of the newly combined Diocese of Gloucester and Bristol. The building, still a cathedral, was to undergo profound improvements, such as a new nave and addition of the two west towers by G E Street between 1868 and 1888. (It's our loss that 'he who must be obeyed', Dean Elliot, disapproved of the vigorous misericords and ordered their removal.) The inconveniently detached part of the erstwhile diocese – Dorset – was simultaneously annexed to Salisbury, which itself ceded Berkshire to Oxford. That we are considering Bristol here at all owes to the campaign in the late 19th century, which resulted in the diocese being restored, with very different territory, in the present curious dog's bone shape. It now comprises the City and County of Bristol, north Wiltshire, embracing Swindon, as well as south Gloucestershire. This may be complicated, but is far more manageable than the earlier version.

The abbey, turned cathedral, is right in the middle of the modern city. On one occasion, just before Christmas a bomb scare at the Council House was timed just as Bristol Old Vic Theatre School was scheduled to get a truckload of paraphernalia for a performance of the touring production *The Nativity* into the cathedral. Park Street, the arterial road and only access was blocked off, owing to a traffic problem. Unceremoniously, Dean Dammers (in post 1973–87) declaimed to the staff, including the stage manager, the student in charge: 'Surely you can carry the scenery down?' No, they certainly couldn't. An impression was conveyed by the imperious staff of 'Whatever you want, you can't have it.' Things seem to have changed since then. June Burrough, was director of the Pierian Centre in Bristol (Pierian means 'of Knowledge or Inspiration'; the centre was, until its closure in December 2011, concerned with 'Time, Space and Clarity'). June was helped by the cathedral to facilitate the Legacy Commission-funded lunchtime event entitled 'Working Together for Positive Change' (22/3/10). Hearing speeches, poems and singing from the middle of the nave, the cathedral was supportive in hosting several hundred people involved in poverty and social exclusion. Many would not have entered the cathedral before, and it turned out to be a most suitable venue. This was a cathedral working with its flock. Tim Higgins, City Canon, was committed to it as part of the work of the diocese of a major city. For him this included responsibility for the city church of St Stephen's. On the way there in the 'Centre' (yes, it's as dull as the name) stands a stern statue of 'Burke', more fully Edmund Burke (1729–97), statesman and philosopher. He was elected M.P. for Bristol in 1774, when it was England's second city. He lost his seat in 1780 after opposing restriction on free trade with Ireland. Of course buoyant trade had been a significant influence on Bristol's commercial success. A generation later, the cathedral's urban setting produced some hearty action during the Bristol Riots of 1831. The mob burned books and were set upon razing the cathedral to the ground. It was saved by the sub-sacrist, who was awake and alert, and got the rescue initiative going. That mostly involved water.

Bristol is the only cathedral built as a 'hall church', meaning that the aisles are the same height as the nave. You don't regret the lack of upper levels. The substantial nave windows admit quite enough light and the design works. It conveys a harmonious, uniform appearance, a welcome change from the skyward height of some peer constructions. Perhaps this aids acoustic quality. You will observe this well from the choir stalls. While enjoying a rest there, it is worth looking up to observe England's oldest lierne vault 'reinforcing rib in the vaulting', as opposed to the usual continuous line. Furthermore, the arches at the foot are the country's highest at 50' from the floor. Afterwards, peer under the seats – there are some entertaining misericords. Examples of subject matter include marital discord with brooms, a mermaid and slug racing, with a whip. The kneelers are particularly good, as they depict the scene underneath: a sneak preview. The experience of organ music, from the back of the choir stalls, is admirable, and there is a bonus in the stylish ogee-arched screen, which acts as a divider from the nave.

Tuesday lunchtime concerts can be combined with lunch in the Coffee Shop, sited at the far end of the cloister. It abuts the row of cloisters and, outside, the quadrangle of Bristol Cathedral School. There are some flinty bits there and among many good stained glass images is a fetching window depicting King Henry II, during whose reign (1154–89), much church building was achieved. The catering facility has improved in recent memory, yielding bright walls hung with empathic photos. The soup was better, too, reaching the heights of a tasty tomato with rosemary. The more-helpful-than-average assistant came out with: 'Have whatever bread you like, my lover' (an example of Bristolian).

Make time after a snack to explore the garden. There were a few impressive exhibits in the garden. One was a metal sculpture *Refuge* by Naomi Blake, with the subtext 'to the victims of all racial persecution; *Survivor of Auschwitz*.' The smattering of flowers helped, too, at that time of year crocus and hellebore, with some roses eagerly awaiting the advance of the seasons. Something of a retreat as a small, valuable oasis it looks out onto a modern insurance building and the side of the Bristol Marriott Royal Hotel, formerly plain 'Royal'. Stars at the nearby Hippodrome Theatre have routinely occupied suites there, such as the octogenarian Mickey Rooney for Cinderella over the 2008–09 Christmas season. He didn't always remember his lines.

Back along the cloister, towards the south transept, you would find the stunning empty, that is uncluttered, Norman chapter house (1161), rectangular and decorated with delightful chevrons, a stock-in-trade Romanesque design feature. Nikolaus Pevsner admired the size and grandeur of the chapter house. He also wrote favourably of examples at Bristol of design in the first third of the 14th century.

We should now address the body of the cathedral. South of the quire lies the anteroom to the Berkeley Chapel. It involves the need to look up around and down to take in everything on offer, then use the steps down into the chapel itself. This is a recess for quiet prayer. Up to the left are some impressive tombs. This aisle is where day hair braiding was one of the attractions on the Working Together day. In the middle of the Berkeley Chapel space is the country's only medieval candelabrum. All of this area is worth close examination. Bear in mind 'snail' and 'flying ribs'.

There are two Lady Chapels. The Elder, on the north side, was completed in 1220 in pleasing, simpler early Gothic style. The designer was clearly a monkey freak. There is a proliferation of the beasts. He did accommodate an occasional alternative representative from the animal kingdom. Look for the lizard, for one. Between 1298 and 1330 the monastery's eastern arm was completed, including a new 'Eastern' Lady Chapel in the customary position.

Examining maps of Bristol over the ages is illuminating. The city still provides an array of churches; fortunately many survived the bombing raid of 1940. One that served as a potent reminder was Temple Church, in the heart of the old city, built at the height of Perpendicular prowess in the 15th century. The tower started to lean at once. Half a millennium later, we were lucky that the shell, including that strange tower, was still there. Its survival had been in question during the war, until it was impressed upon decision makers that its skewed look, in Pisa mode, dated back many centuries and was not the consequence of war damage. That's where the candelabrum in the cathedral came from.

I have observed the Bristol skyline many a time. Even in the 21st century, it is full of tempting church towers and spires. The biggest and best is that of St Mary Redcliffe, traditionally the city church, built by the water. That was a central motivating force in planning to attend Bristol Doors Open Day the following September.

Saturday 11 September – St Mary Redcliffe
This church must be accorded special treatment. I believe it to be the only church in the country which might be put forward as a rival to its city's cathedral. The preference was for abbey, not city church. The setting for this will become clear shortly. The point is that, along with Westminster Abbey as a non-cathedral, it deserves a visitor's attention, as follows:

> **Three to See**: the elaborate north porch;
> the organ, now overhauled for many a decade's pleasure for anyone listening;
> the statue of Queen Elizabeth I, under whose regime this, the main commercial church of Bristol, prospered

'Bristol Doors Open Day – now in its 17th year – is the day when many of Bristol's significant contemporary and historical buildings open their doors to the general public', stated the brochure carrying 58 such venues (by no means all ecclesiastical). It was a joint venture of GWF Business West and Bristol City Council (plus sponsors). It was to prove an excellent framework for visits to a number of centrally located churches, in the fraternity of the pincushion of Bristol. The pincushion was inevitably to be the icon of this city, with its multitude of churches. The most prominent focal points are the two, so different, top buildings: the manfully towered king, the Cathedral of the Holy Trinity, and St Mary Redcliffe, in queenly pointed garb, echoing women's dress from the period of its invention, the 15th century. I have to repeat Elizabeth's accolade from 1574: 'the fairest, goodliest and most famous church in England'. And at that time it lacked today's fine spire, added in the 1870s.

I met Kevin and Spencer outside the north porch, hexagonal and a fine expression of Decorated style. We chose it for the opening at 10 am, convenient and providing something good to admire while we waited. The porch had an association with Thomas Chatterton, the 18th century boy poet, whose house survived on an island site on the other side of the inner ring road just outside. Rucksacked punters joined the waiting throng. One source was Temple Meads Station, a few minutes' stroll away, impressive for its Victorian Gothic tower (people sometimes think the station to be the cathedral from a view of this). There were two reasons for starting at Redcliffe:

1   It was the furthest point on the itinerary, though the programme, displayed on my board for a few months, divided the map up into several areas bearing little relation to a long-term resident's picture of Bristol.
2   Anticipating the popularity of a day of visits offered so rarely, it seemed wise to focus first on something with a high profile, with queues at a minimum. So it proved. Somehow, casting our eyes round the organ area, now clear with the restored instrument in place, recently returned by Harrison & Harrison, organ builders, and a refreshing look at the captions referring to local magnate William Canynge (d.1474), who was responsible for this church. There was a four-poster monument to him and his wife. He was mayor five times and depicted in rich merchant's robes. Spencer, especially keen on local history, was riveted.

We were given yellow laminated plastic passes for 'Roof Tour', and without much wait were soon up some steps on the west gallery admiring the nave and east window. We later realized we had, inadvertently, jumped one queue or other. The organization had clearly made sense in theory (run by a bunch of volunteers retired from an incompatible discipline, I suspected).

We were satisfied by the lengthy (must have overrun) session in the bell-ringers room, donning ear muffs in the chamber itself, where our trusty guide, a proficient bell man delivered a fulsome speech about the bells, which dated back to 1622 and comprise the fifth biggest group in the country, after Liverpool, Exeter, St Paul's and York. It's impressive for a parish church to beat so many cathedrals. There was yet another addition due in the near future from the bellfounders Taylor's of Loughborough. Bell Man asked: 'Why are there holes in the chamber wall?' 'For scaffolding', replied Spencer, correctly, without demur. We did wonder how a late gothic structure like this tower could bear the weight of so many tons of the things. Hearing the demonstration through our hearing protectors was effective. We could tell the difference between the swinging smaller bells and the chimers. It was my turn to break the silence: 'How do you determine whether it's a ring or a chime?' It didn't seem a stupid question, but then I am totally untechnical. 'A ring is all the way over – 360 degrees. A chiming bell just swings,' said Bell Man, patiently. Somehow it did seem a bit obvious, once I knew. There was a total of 6,000 rings, and the ringers could go on for hours. This recalled what had been said about bells at Guildford and Peel, but they were eclipsed here, actually getting a close view of metal bells as they rang/chimed.

Our party of 12 rescaled the steps. 'Bottoms first down the ladder,' instructed Bell Man. He was good, and, though a bit short with his colleagues, who perhaps should have been more on the ball (or bell, when he was forced to shout three times 'Give me a tenner,' or was that 'tenor'?), then actually retrace hurried steps to get someone to produce a chime. It happened at last. Then came another. In BM's absence a caring father of two had suggested: 'Guys, I think we should wear the protectors: it'll ring before he gets back.' The bell house was very cosy. It was wise of them not to warn us about confined spaces. However, the provision of protectors had elicited a caveat about future tinnitus should you refuse them. Some of the score or more of multi-coloured head appliances 'came from my school yesterday', informed Bell Man. A teacher, then? A good one too, I suspected, but what subject? There was no chance to pursue anything further as the ringing room was small and very crowded. The two other officials, both apparently regular ringers, seemed overwhelmed by the sardined bodies, looking like several tours' worth. We had to evacuate the small area for the next batch.

Our band of three had been split up and now I made Kevin out as I mounted a flight of steps, apparently to the open west end gallery, where a timid little girl who hadn't wanted to make the trip was still sitting motionless on the stone bench. The view from there was splendid, though even with my binoculars I didn't make out any specific golden bosses in the roof. Of course I had in mind the one I'd read about (also at Wells Cathedral) whose subject was 'three men at stool'. It was probably sited discreetly in a remote corner.

Next we faced the almost vertical ascent on the southwest side. Several dozen narrow steps up we found ourselves on the roof. Chris, the guide stationed there, drew attention to the flat lead surface, surmounted by decorative pinnacles: very Perpendicular, unlike the ones I had seen recently at Exeter Cathedral, which served a practical purpose. We now enjoyed the panorama of bits of Bristol without any feeling of pressure. The Temple Church tower stood out idiosyncratically askew. I was imagining hundreds of frustrated bunches of people awaiting their tour time below. There emerged the following categories of the Bristol pincushion:

1   Those still operating as churches.
2   Buildings surviving so as to offer something to see above the rooftops.
3   The ones open to us on this tour – given both to God and Mammon.
4   Closed.

A woman, having been intimidated by the narrow, worn steps, she said, asked Chris if there were many casualties on such tours as these. 'No,' he replied, 'But, as an examiner at the university you get used to casualties: students fainting and needing ambulances.' And some of those were the ones with A*s, I'm sure.

We moved on to St Thomas (1793, with a yard shortly to be relaid with Churches Conservation assistance), then St Nicholas (1400). This was now deconsecrated. An immense William Hogarth triptych dwarfed the open plan office. The crypt presented a display of the story of St James Priory, the oldest foundation in Bristol, a Benedictine house from 1129, 'a daughter of Tewkesbury Abbey'. There is widespread cross-referencing between the multitude of churches in this city. In Henry VIII's post-Reformation period the monastic way of life was gradually suppressed and the number of monks at the priory dwindled. By 1535 it was occupied by just 5 brothers, the next year only two. The Abbot of Tewkesbury leased the building out, and within a few years parts of the church were in ruin. Like other buildings of its ilk it was sold to a domestic buyer. Henry Brayne bought it in 1544. Moving on a few centuries, during which many of our top notch church buildings fell into neglect, the modern world overtook it. In 1877 Bristol Tramways stables took over much of the site. Then, during the war: the west end was the only surviving substantial part. It was a shame not to be able to visit the priory on this occasion, having thoroughly enjoyed the present stately interior at Christmas concerts. Check out the singing group Exultate, and not just for carols. Conductor/creator David Ogden has for long been an inspiration on the choral scene in Bristol.

The rain had abated as we passed St Nicholas Market, the sight of which reminded me of the need to buy bananas and tea. That would have to wait. We arrived at the gates of All Saints. They were firmly locked. It had been taken over by the Parish Commissioners. At least we could admire the appealing cupola, its shape enhancing the skyline. Round the corner from that was the 1786 construct of Christ Church, now correctly 'Christ Church, with St Ewen, All Saints and St George' (the last is the Brandon Hill concert hall, worth patronizing). The musical director and organist Jonathan (JDR) Price looked decorative in motion around his domain.

Were those crisp trousers cream or off-white, JDR? *A Short Guide* stated: '… in the City of Bristol'. Names and locations apart, the guide told us: 'It was designed by Willam Paty and completed in 1790. The Paty family were architects and craftsmen involved in building and joinery as well as design. Christ Church is arguably their masterpiece.' For me the best of many features is outside 'the clock and quarter jacks which strike the chimes', over the entrance. It is enchanting to watch the moving display on the hour. Also worth attention were the bi-monthly Wednesday lunchtime recitals. This is a convincing 18th century church. It's so good that I shall simply give one sample of its features: the semi-circular altar table, along with iron rails and compelling screen, which started life as a reredos, and contains a dove: the Holy Spirit, echoing the dedication of the mother church.

Next on the list, after refreshment in the Bank Tavern, was John Wesley's Chapel, an impressive relic in the middle of the bland Broadmead Shopping Centre. Restored in recent memory, it represented an achievement as one of the most authentic complete historic buildings to visit in this city. Within, an interesting point was made about the pews, which dated from 1930 as 'authentic'. Not so, as John Wesley liked simple benches 'cheap to make and easy to move', also, essentially, egalitarian. He was disingenuous about wig-wearing. He didn't do that, as was the standard practice at the time. However, it was noted that he possessed fine Adonis-like auburn locks: 'hair which he took infinite pains to have in the most exact order, which with his benign and humble countenance gave him a pleasing aspect,' (*Field Preaching*, Bristol, 1739). Of the building, we were able to see it all, so it was a benefit to stand on the two pulpits facing the congregation, the lower one for readings, the higher, more awesome one, for preaching. On the top level were living quarters, and we were to read much about the man and his times (1703–1791), much of which was spent in Bristol, resident in this building. One feature to draw attention to was the octagonal lantern. Not only pleasing to the eye, it minimized the incidence of tax levied; it counted as a single window. The lingering mood of the building was one of welcome, its harmonious design pervasively green and brown. You could imagine many a conversion to Methodism here. On a more contentious note, the man's words about harmony and spiritual feeling, which underlay his approach to belief, could be just as easily applied to Buddhism (whispered Kevin), or indeed other forms of spirituality.

The chosen route took us back towards the city, to St John the Baptist, its tower rising above and traffic passing under its bowels through an old city gate. It used to, that is, before the road system was changed. On the ground below, by the redirected St John's Conduit, rested what looked like a pair of discarded knickers, of a dark hue, blue I think. Nearby were the doorway and steps down to the crypt. In what seemed like a grate area at the west end, were bits of stuff, including a damaged lectern saved from St Mary le Port, the relic round the corner which we had passed by on the way to St Nicholas. It went to show the close link between the churches hereabouts, as it stated that the lectern was originally in the cathedral before St Mary, which was destroyed in 1940. Above, in St John's church itself, the 1621 pews were accommodating and worth a rest amid the milling throng, as much here as everywhere else, and of all ages. Let's hope they all enjoyed the portable music machine by the altar, which intermittently yielded choral sounds. I cannot be more generous than that. The communion table there was from 1635, and the essence of the building was of that era.

The White Lion beckoned, on the Centre. This pub was splendid with local Wickwar beers and a seat outside. 'Le temps, it fait beau', said a neighbour, relaxing in the sun. I must mention this: the spiral staircase down to the gents, even tighter than the steps at St Mary Redcliffe, and designed, I surmise, to ensure that blokes in need of relief didn't fall down. Corpulent customers wouldn't even be able to make the journey. It faced the austere and classical Roman Catholic St Mary-on-the-Quay, a Victorian construction. It may have origins on the quay, but this was sadly redesigned in 1930. It became a frustrating space with sundry items lost within it, one of which was the statue of Neptune. The god formerly held sway at the Pier Head, which itself was built over the River Frome. Neptune was far more impressive in his old position. When a city has water, it should be shown off.

We were now to see the old and new St Stephen's, round the corner working very hard to serve contemporary needs. This means a good catering facility, toilets and, today, tambourines. We arrived there, not actually for tambourines, which I introduced for alliterative purposes, and were lying on a bench, but a cittern, its strings being stretched melodiously. We were handed leaflets at the temporary entrance. The place was undergoing renovation, not only the newly-commissioned reredos, but the west end. Fortunately the building boasted several external doors. The leaflets provided were most informative, addressing this day's happening and much in the future. Music was by West African Kora, and Jazz Piano. For me the best feature of the building is the tower, elegant and complex, modelled on Gloucester Cathedral. Apparently it was paid for by a Lord Mayor in the 15th century.

After a short time there, jostling with enthusiasts and musicians, we traversed the centre, with a wave at Neptune somewhere in the middle, to walk up to the College Green and the 13th century Lord Mayor's Chapel, opposite the cathedral itself and hemmed in between more recent developments. Formerly St Mark's Hospital it is still a gem. It inherited bits of William Beckford's ruined Fonthill Abbey. Greeting us were Marek (his mother chose the name) Barden, the verger, and the Revd Preb Harold Clarke, Chaplain to the Lord Mayor and a Methodist. The point was that, as the property of the Bristol City Council, this is the only church lacking a constitution or parish, therefore gift aid is also inapplicable. This made it equivalent to St Margaret's, the neighbour of Westminster Abbey.

The whole place succeeds in its clutter, as it's of high quality in an interestingly shaped and lit setting. To enter you descend a flight of steps, below a large, plain window. The natural light on an average day (grey, but still mild, on this occasion) was augmented by a strange collection of dangling light effects. 'The chandeliers have been restored and should have arrived for today', explained Harold. The bits were curiously anomalous, even as stand-ins. I turned to a stall at the foot of the steps and bought a calendar for £4.95. 'They only came today.' the lady with the tin told me: a more efficient supplier than the illumination people, I reckoned. She added: 'They've done very well. Nearly sold out.' I elected to invest in one because they were so attractive with a good choice of subject matter in the photographs. It was my first such purchase in all these visits. In due course it became my token church-related wall adornment in the New Year. It was good to be directed to the south aisle, which had been closed for repairs on my most recent visit. Work there had been completed, in time for this event, unlike the lighting order. I was shown an effigy, of Maurice de Gaunt, memorialized for many a century with his 'dagger or missericorde', explained as a 'mercy sword'. Well, there's another angle. A further detail was the black iron entrance to St Andrew's Chapel in the south aisle, 'Edney Gates'. Under the current leadership of this, the only such civic church in the country, there had developed an increasing programme of events. The building was now open to the public on a regular basis. It was outstanding as an intimate space, where the thrill of just being settled in a pew is accentuated when there's good music to hear. At certain points of the year, the 11 am Sunday service featured a substantial procession of uniformed dignitaries, on occasion outnumbering the lay congregation. I have attended a wedding at the LMC, and a funeral, and a procession, even a concert. It's a satisfying auditorium.

To depart briefly on a related tangent, that is 'performance', St Paul's Church, on the north side of the city, was open each year on Doors Open Day, but this time out of the way for us. Completed in 1794, its beguiling feature is its wedding cake spire, entrancing to note above the inner city horizon as you approach the city down the M32. A Grade I listed building, it was closed in 1988, but remains consecrated. It was embraced under the umbrella of the Churches Conservation Trust in 2000, after years of decay. The Heritage Lottery Fund was instrumental in funding the rescue. In 2005 it became the home of Circomedia, a circus training institution, also regularly playing host to such theatre productions as those of Bristol Old Vic Theatre School (often Shakespeare plays). There is plenty of space for ropes and trapezes above! Also, there are other good features: stained glass and handsome columns, as well as the ceiling, of its time. This can all be admired should the production design allow you to do so.

Back in the city centre the three of us were nearing the end, after, we counted, seven entrances and several near misses or 'should have-beens'. Leaving St Mark's, we paused for a glance at the cathedral and repaired to the Bristol Ram, up the hill, that is Park Street. We sat with our final pints, ruminating on a quiet Bristol Saturday replete with such variety of stone and style.

Sunday 5 December

Deep and crisp and even was the ground underfoot, after a cold snap, which had started in November, and taken a hold. No football games, but the gathering in the south of Bristol, in Whitchurch. This is the modern representative in Bristol's churches, but the 1970s St Augustine's Church had become unusable and was closed in 2000. Services took place in Bridge Farm Primary School opposite, where I received a fine welcome. The vicarage, next to the church, opposite, had also been abandoned as a ruin.

The Revd Canon Neville Boundy took me there, and then officiated at the communion service. A merry celebrant and sermonizer, a propos of something he told the congregation at one stage: 'You get seven years' bad luck if you set fire to a vicar.' An overhead projector was used for the hymns, reminding us that this was a school. This included a cup of tea and a bourbon biscuit. Notices were delivered about forthcoming Christingle and Carol services. One year I would be trying out the former, thus far outside my experience. The priest in charge, Revd Canon Nicholas Hay, in post since 2009, had been translated from a similar role at Bristol's Horfield Prison. He was absent at another church in the group that day.

From one extreme to the other, we drove to the cathedral for a monthly Friends lunch. It was a jolly occasion in the refectory. I was to meet the cathedral's Canon Emeritus John Rogan, who, along with many other retired priests in the Church of England, performed much-appreciated work there and elsewhere, including at Redcliffe. He would periodically be called up to the Lord Mayor's Chapel for official duties

I was on my own at the end, an opportunity to round off the pincushion. I kept it simple as I left, with a quick glance at two of my favourite things: the chapter house and the stained glass image of Henry II.

This piece has embraced a handful of the churches of Bristol. They are listed below by date of foundation.

Date of Foundation of Current Churches
    1126 – St James's Priory
    1140 – Bristol Cathedral, as St Augustine's Abbey
    c1150 – Temple Church
    1220 – Lord Mayor's Chapel
    1292 – St Mary Redcliffe
    pre 1374 – St John the Baptist (on the Wall)
    1400 – St Nicholas
    1470 – St Stephen's (fully rebuilt)
    1739 – John Wesley's Chapel
    1790 – Christ Church, City
    1793 – St Thomas the Martyr
    1794 – St Paul's (Circomedia)
    1840 – St Mary-on-the-Quay, RC Church
    1970 – St Augustine's, Whitchurch

6

Chester

Christ & St Mary

Province: York
Founded: 1093 as Benedictine abbey
Present building: Early 13th century with 15th century additions
Cathedral status: 1541
Restored: 1868–75 by George Gilbert Scott

Website: www.chestercathedral.com
Tel: 01244 324756
Email: office@chestercathedral.com
Address: Chester Cathedral Office, 12 Abbey Square, Chester CH1 2HU

Three to See: Consistory court;
choir stalls and misericords;
original refectory, now the café

Poppy

Monday 15 February, 2010

We approached the cathedral from the east (A51 from Staffordshire). Graham thought he had espied our grail approaching the ring road, but, no, it was a spire not a tower. Working towards somewhere to park is no fun in a city built in a different age, but here we did catch sight of the squat red tower, which served to lead us to its doors round an unwitting detour – a chance to see old buildings flash by. The tower is wondrous, with turrets added to the top corners – something to applaud Sir George Gilbert Scott for in his widespread restoration of cathedrals in the 19th century. In 1645 Charles I watched the Battle of Rowton Heath from the tower, which I read was held up by intersecting arches called the Crown of Stone, a feature unique to Chester Cathedral. Today the weather precluded any watching up the steps.

But first we had to refresh ourselves with a dose of the city's renowned Rows, 'a system of walkways that form continuous covered galleries running above shops at street level. They occur in all four main streets in the city centre, so there are shops at two levels. Although the Row buildings have been re-built and altered over many centuries, they represent a building form that originated in the late 13th and early 14th centuries. The upper level was approached straight from St Werburghs Street, from cathedral and car. We alighted upon Burlington's Coffee Shop. We could have sat outside and immersed ourselves in half-timbered urban buildings, i.e. chains and cafes, plus the odd pub, but thankfully not in sight here, as it might have tempted me in. We had business in hand.

Thence to the Forum Market, partly historic, which has to be mentioned for the cheese stall. My favourite at the time was Snowdonia Bomber, an exceedingly tart cheddar. Graham was satisfied with some royal blue material for his jewellery box (contents = valuable stock, to be sold at antiques fairs) and a ferrule for his walking stick. That's the kind of thing, which can be a bugger to find a shop for. The last had recently been lost in boggy ground in Exmoor while enjoying the snowdrops.

There had been a Bishop of Chester as long ago as 1075, when the seat of Lichfield was transferred there, the town church of St John the Baptist being nominated as cathedral. The remains of that were to be the subject after our tour of Christ and The Blessed Virgin Mary's this afternoon. This status didn't last as the immense diocese of Coventry and Lichfield was to employ the wealthy monastery at Coventry as the headquarters. It's likely, given the territory involved, not to mention travelling times on rutted roads, that Chester was kept as an essential facility, but the cathedral we know was not awarded that status until the Reformation, when Chester diocese was carved out of the revised Lichfield. 1541 saw its elevation to become a see, succeeding the status of the dissolved abbey. This was complicated. Here goes! The new diocese comprised two archdeaconries. The other was to the north – based on Richmond, the old town of that name being situated at the far northern edge of substantial chunks of both modern Yorkshire and Lancashire. Originally in the Province of Canterbury, it was given to York later that year. Some of the area lay way up the map, north of the city of York! Richmond itself was in the North Riding, then North Yorkshire. The next big shake-up occurred in the 19th century, starting in 1836, a year before Queen Victoria ascended the throne. The northern part went to the new Diocese of Ripon. Other marginal bits were stuck onto more obvious sees: Welsh acreage went to St Asaph, the Leigh part of Warrington (Lancashire) to the new Diocese of Manchester, the rest of the Deanery of Warrington to Liverpool, also newly created, and the deaneries of Kendal, Westmorland and Lonsdale (North West Lancashire), were ceded to Carlisle. Quite a transformation, but a shrewd one as population shifts over generations of Industrial Revolution were at last properly reflected in a practical revised map. That's the end of the regional geography lesson. By the way, you have a good view of Wales (Diocese of St Asaph) from the city wall, while providing a unique circuit of Chester.

The outcome of all this was that the boundary of the diocese followed the county of Cheshire, and still does, with the reservation that demographics were to develop further, culminating in the nationwide local government overhaul of 1974. The Greater Manchester Metropolitan Boroughs of Tameside, Stockport and Trafford remained under Chester's aegis, while the City of Salford was with Manchester, contiguous to, but administratively apart. The Wirral is also part of Chester's domain. The sum total makes it a sound mixture of urban (Chester's population is around 77K) and rural, its centre seeming a pleasant market town to visitors, and there are always plenty of those, mostly day-trippers shopping and admiring the beauty of the place. Chester has plenty of the trappings of a modern town, which include the blights of drugs and alcohol. Just so you know, the diocese has two suffragan bishops, of Birkenhead and Stockport, and is divided into two archdeaconries: Chester and Macclesfield.

On the way in on the northwest corner we first observed the noticeboard. On Wednesdays (being Lent) there were Bible Talks: 'Who Killed Jesus', and on Thursdays there were lunchtime organ recitals. Busy and varied – the Chester Music Society had presented 'An evening with Mozart' not long before. On our visit the communion service was to be held in St Werburgh's Chapel, where the table was plain and bare. We learned afterwards that the service, which we had joined, was conducted by Vice-Dean Trevor Dennis, in a green cassock. The chapel abutted the north side of the Lady Chapel. Vice-Dean Trevor would have benefited from the manucca honey I'd just purchased in the market, as he was somewhat croaky. Included in the prayers were the linked parishes: three of them in Russia. The Friends had embarked upon fundraising for them, at Kondopoga, near St Petersburg, leading to pilgrimages there. Trevor also announced the forthcoming memorial service for a Chester drugs victim. The family had come to the cathedral of their own volition, and a number of new visitors were expected for the event. This was a piece of work of the cathedral in the community. Just before this visit, in January, an event had been held here in the aftermath of the Haiti earthquake disaster.

Afterwards we engaged Trevor in an exchange. Fundamental was the day-to-day need for cash. The local council had helped with the current Anne Frank exhibition. An anecdote: the horse chestnut tree where she hid from the Nazis during the Second World War was blown down the following September in a storm. She could see it from her attic hideout, and had reported on its progress in her diary, such as: '13th May 1944: Our chestnut tree is in full blossom. It is covered with leaves and is even more beautiful than last year.' She died in Bergen-Belsen concentration camp in March 1945. Grafts from the dead tree were taken, one of which was put in the care of Batsford Arboretum in Gloucestershire. It was reported to be 24' tall and in full leaf (*Country Gardener*, October, 2010). Trevor noted that there was no theatre in Chester (the professional Gateway having closed – I remember seeing a frothy production there years ago) – and limited performance spaces, so the cathedral was often used. Politician Frank Field (Lab) had been vocal in the need for public funding of cathedrals. They serve the community. Funding is largely the preserve of the great and the good.

This is St Werburgh's place. She, the daughter of a Mercian king, died in 707, and became known for miracles of healing. Her remains were returned to Chester in 907. She is now honoured in the eponymous shrine and chapel. The shrine is a medieval construct, in the open upper level of which stands her small figure, a statue which was given by John L Borrow in 1993. Below this in construction is an ogee arch. The chapel in her name is regularly used for communion services. The name lives on in the area, for relics and street names, but not the cathedral itself, as the dedication for the elevated church went to Christ and the Blessed Virgin. It was therefore a bonus to find a Lady Chapel, as this is not required in a building ascribed to her. It has colourful stained glass – 'Lets in lots of light,' I commented. Graham rejoined: 'There are a couple of pieces missing, letting in even more light.' The ceiling bosses were described on a sign. There were three, from 1250–75, when the Lady Chapel was built. They feature: East – Holy Trinity; Centre – Our Lady with adjacent holy images; West – martyrdom of St Thomas Becket, which is held to be the earliest, the crime having been perpetrated five years previously. Apparently other images of him only occur at Exeter and Norwich. Something to look out for. The colouring was restored in 1960.

I found this a special cathedral for its civic identity. It's right in the middle of the city, built in frail new red sandstone, emanating from the ground. On the other hand it was apparently in a better state than those others of a red hue on this side of the country: Lichfield, Worcester and Hereford. There is plenty of rewarding architecture and archaeology here. The best thing is the choir stalls (c.1380), perhaps the finest in England, with, indeed, strongly depicted poppy heads capping the pews. To represent the cathedral we must have a poppy, a red thrill, fragile and engaging. The choir area is sumptuous, a word borrowed from a mat on the floor elsewhere in the building, and appropriate here. The covering structure is unique – a complex wooden network over each stall, interlinked, each forming a jagged spire reaching upwards. They lead the eye up to the clerestory windows and roof. Immersing yourself in these, you then have to attend first to the pews themselves and of course the poppies, lastly investigating the seats, lifting them for the misericords. They are marvellous and varied, frightening (ghastly beasts pouncing) and practical (how to till the soil); so many of them, too, 48, of which 43 share the building date of the choir as a whole. Here you can see them without encumbrance. As a punter, having paid your £5 admission fee (£4 concessions) you are free to roam, guided by the *Short tour* leaflet (£2). While the cathedral is comparatively small it has plenty to engage the inquisitive. The ground plan is almost square, reflecting the purpose of the abbey, and containment within the city wall. It is largely 13th and 14th century.

Returning to Chester Cathedral for an evening 'Easter Day Carols, Music and Readings' event in the choir (24/4/11), the choir proved a lush setting for what was effectively a recital. We sat amid numerous images adorning the stalls, whose physical presence was emphasized by the purposeful canopy terrace above. The Cathedral Nave Choir, all in red and white, comprised nine each of men and women, largely to entertain a good crowd to their rear, and on both sides, all in the unlit (unusual, that) choir stalls. They did have the benefit of understated crenelated black cylinders hanging from above, with effective bulbs concealed within. This was a design some of Chester's peers might consider emulating.

We heard *Easter*, ascribed to Michael Ramsey in the *He is Risen Indeed!* Service sheet. If that was correct (RamsEy, not RamsAy), this was Chevalier Ramsey (1686–1743) a Scottish Christian Universalist. That means he believed that everyone would in the end be saved. Moving to

France, he later converted to Catholicism. It was followed by an anthem, *Surrexit Christus* by Samuel Scheidt, which was a cue for me to relax and cast my eyes up to the triforium, subtly lit to emphasize its sculpted three-dimensional shape. This was a bit of a rarity: the shape and its telling illumination. Afterwards we creaked up some seats to admire the misericords. The end one revealed a bold notice on the underside, therefore to little effect once the damage was done: 'Please do not touch these seats.' It was hard to make out the subject in the subdued light, but I'm pretty sure something like a lion and a dragon featured, one eating the other. At the eastern end of the south choir stalls lay the mighty uplifting cathedra. It kept faith with the stalls in being fulsome and chunky. My friend Swallet, who lived in that strange part of Cheshire with Stoke-on-Trent postcodes, liked Chester Cathedral 'quite a lot. I used to go in for musical sessions at lunchtime – for Thursday shoppers.' A charge of £3 was introduced for an organ recital. 'You're kidding me,' was his response, but he continued in one place: the 'nice garden – flowers in summer, pool in the middle'. This didn't require any disbursement. The organ certainly sounded good during this event. It was made by Whiteleys in 1870, with 4,864 pipes.

Back 14 months, we wandered round the building, as full as any with entrancing features from every age – the place had a long history. In the north aisle was a rather modern clock, not at all out of place.

Below the clock was inscribed:

When as a child I laughed and wept, time crept;
When as a youth I waxed more bold, time strolled,
When I became a full-grown man, time ran
When older still I daily grew, time flew
Soon I shall find in passing on, time gone.
Christ will thou have saved me then? Amen.

Henry Twell

Speaking of 'time gone', the clock seemed to have disappeared on my 2011 visit. That was regrettable.

In the south transept we admired the display of the free Anne Frank exhibition, capacious enough for a regular programme of displays, this one being augmented by a film in the captivating 13th century chapter house (a good way to absorb its beauty over half an hour). I should note that the 2011 visit gave us a Kate Herbert exhibition, which was somewhat meagre in the huge transept space: *Great Lovers of the Bible*, depicting Adam and Eve, Abraham and Sarah, Samson and Delilah, David and Bathsheba, Joseph and Mary, Jesus and bride. All were modelled on the same basic template images: clever, but insubstantial. It did allow us to explore more of the transept, including the Children's Chapel, one of several along the east wall. Involving Chester Cathedral Education Department and Kettleshulme St James CE Primary School, it had produced some Noah's Ark inhabitants: Noah, a lion and an elephant. It evinced a smile, at least from me. The south transept 'is so vast that the old church of St Oswald may have still remained in use while the transept was building around it,' wrote Francis Bond in *The Cathedrals of England and Wales*. It was well filled by the voluminous Anne Frank display. It was extended in the 14th century and even assumed the role of parish church.

Stone seats were a perpetual facility for the weary around the vestibule on the way to the chapter house for the film: handy for those who had business with the monks and, after the Reformation, the cathedral, and now Anne Frank. The structure is a popular view of the cathedral, with the idiosyncratic tower turrets rising above it, as the hordes approach from the shops below St Werburgh Street. Nearby stood the scarlet twins: telephone kiosk and letterbox.

We wandered right down the nave. On the west end notice board there were more leaflets posted for 'Friends of cathedral music', and 'Mystery or Miracle' plays? The question was posed to refer to a performance of the Chester Cycle. The answer is that 'Miracle' plays have come to signify the involvement of saints, rather than the telling of Bible stories, which characterizes 'Mystery' plays. The Chester plays are thought likely to be made up of 24 pageants, a 16th century concoction of works from the Middle Ages, the time when the best known cycles, such as York and Towneley (Wakefield), were assembled. An example of the pieces is 'Noah and his ship', perhaps the most familiar as it is a good yarn full of character and drama, such as Noah's wife, drinking and gossiping until her sons had to manhandle her onto the ark. This was performed by 'waterleaders and drawers in the Dee' (before it became silted up). Another evocative one is 'The Harrowing of Hell', in sequence between the Crucifixion and Ascension, performed by cooks, tapsters, ostlers and innkeepers. I gleaned from notices that the next full production of Chester Mystery Plays was due in 2013. However, a notice announced at Easter 2011, '… a Mystery Plays in Miniature production of Creation will be performed as part of *Chestival* from 17–19 June at Chester's famous Roman amphitheatre. Free of charge – bring the family and a picnic to this event and get a taste for 2013'.

We arrived at the southwest corner: the 1636 Consistory Court, under the tower, is unique. Mind the entrance steps – they are very worn. It is the oldest example in the country of an ecclesiastical court room. It does look like a court, enveloped with seductive dark wood, which worked so well in the Stuart period. At the time of construction this was a productive use of a small space under the southwest tower, dedicated to the aegis of bishop and diocesan chancellor over matters ecclesiastical. Its function was as an Old Bailey of the world of the church. Be sentenced here: live by the church, and you could die by the church. The chancellor of the diocese would hand out fines for not attending services, for slander, gambling and drunkenness. One culprit, in May 1614, was the Vicar of Ribchester, Henry Norcross, too drunk to read divine services, marrying persons unlawfully and, most outrageous of all, pawning a communion cup. The court has not been in session since 1964. The cathedral can serve as a performance space more than most, perhaps a small-scale production for the Consistory Court? The cathedral, unfunded, was forced to be resourceful for such initiatives.

We were informed by a guide about the Chester Imp. It required identification, being high up, at a binocular-defying distance. Legend tells us that, centuries ago, during the construction of the nave, a priest was startled by the sight of a demonic face leering at him through one of the windows. This he took to be Satan himself, in person to investigate this latest fortress to apply his dark powers. Prompt action was taken and stonemasons were ordered to carve an equally ugly image and mount it where, should the Devil dare to look in again, he would be frightened away! The Imp was carved in chains in the north clerestory above the nave, where it is darker. That's where the Devil makes his entrance. Meanwhile, in the south aisle were three most effective windows, from 1992. Further up, towards the Consistory Court, was a richly coloured drape over the door, to go with an even bigger one, in slightly different hues, under the west window which was worth pausing to absorb, from anywhere up the nave, and into the eastern parts.

In the shop (on the way to the Refectory), imps were for sale but mostly Lincoln Imps. 'Imp' wasn't quite right, as it sounds like cheeky competition for a superior opponent. It's more of a ghoul. Graham, an antiques enthusiast and lover of quality – favourite pursuit buying things – noted the W H Goss souvenir crested ware. 'Highly collectable' he said. I found books by Trevor Dennis on the shelves. He turned out to be correctly the 'Vice-Dean and Canon' and was a storyteller. He had been tutor in Old Testament Studies, previously at Salisbury and Wells Theological College, where he went after the Chaplaincy of Eton College. He was next spotted at an Antiques Road Show from Chester Cathedral (18/4/10). In a brief interview with presenter Fiona Bruce, he admitted to keeping an eye on the proceedings throughout the day, rather a long one in view of all the support activity. 'It's just wonderful seeing the place full of people like this... All abuzz with it... We are for the people, for the community and they're here'. Back to Graham. This is how to sell a 'Cloisonné Cage for a Cricket' (don't ask for an explanation of that): Buy it at a car boot sale, or as part of an auction lot for £36; decide on a sale price (plucked out of the air) of, say, £84; attract the interest of a collector at your stall, and haggle to a mutually satisfactory deal at £65. The 2011 visit again involved pausing in the shop on the way to the coffee sojourn. The stock had become more locally relevant, in fact Lincoln Imps were absent. There were misericords and corbels. Angels and 'grotesques' (that is, imps) were for sale at £12.99, green men £1 more and a wyvern with a human head was £14.99. Lincoln was still represented, by several items, such as a knight with sword and shield. The shop was an attractive space in which to linger, outside which, further down the many tortuous passages, was that all-important staging post, the admission desk. Cough up and go in!

The February visit took us to the lunch break. The high quality of the monks' refectory was notable as an original purpose-built space that is a dining room, fit for the same modern purpose. In evidence were the arms of the barons of the court of Hugh Lupus. The fellow, who was Earl of Chester, was responsible for the building's new status, which subsisted until the Reformation. This initiative needed the help of St Anselm, well known in religious circles over the country.

On the wall hung the arms of the ancient earls of Chester, to the Blood Royal. Also on the wall above us, projected a curious pulpit, a relic from those ancient monkish practices, no doubt. Was it used often? Then we addressed the purpose: a snack. We were bearing in mind a repast to come that evening with our culinarily-adept hosts. It was easy to visualize monks, clerics, anybody doing something similar here down the ages. However, this was betrayed by the staff – a slovenly waitress and a gaggle giggling in the distance by the wall, all in white uniforms. The soup and sandwich February deal for £5 offered a single sandwich (crispy bacon and egg mayonnaise) and dull, lukewarm soup (pea and mint). There was no water left in the single jug and no glasses. There was plenty of space – the serving area could have catered for coach parties. Our mutual reaction was one of shock after the intelligent care and conversation found in the cathedral itself. Well, yes, I asked Graham how his coffee had been, in view of rich, late medieval panels and a barrel roof. 'The latte tasted of fish – it was rubbish.' he replied, adding 'the potential of the refectory is good, but the staff let it down.' I pressed him further on the wider subject of the cathedral. 'Chester is not the most interesting one I've been into.' I wonder if his impression would have ameliorated had he been with me for the 2011 visit. The 'provision' category was much improved, from smiling and helpful staff to a tempting range of food. I didn't yield to the temptation of the pear, almond and chocolate tart or even the raspberry and rhubarb option (both £2, which made it all the more appealing), as Wakey and I had dropped in on the way to the station on Easter Monday, following a lush breakfast at The Queen's Hotel, which had involved kedgeree. I normally choose that, when available. The coffee in the Refectory, cheap at £1.70, was delivered by a worrying self-service machine. I just pressed a button. But the liquid was fine, a cup of steaming black coffee, of satisfying aroma and taste. This was one of several cathedral catering facilities which had been transformed in a comparatively short time. That, eternally, speaks for restaurants, cafés and pubs. It's worth returning to revise a bad experience. Not so the obverse. How many times have I been disappointed in going back to where the memory has been good?

Having left the building from the café and shop through a cloister or two, all most pleasant, you reach Abbey Square, and an unseasonal but promising garden, part of which was now host to Barclays Bank and a car park. It was here that the Chester Mystery play cycle was performed when the cluster of buildings formed a Benedictine Abbey, itself inheriting the space from a 10th century minster.

It was imperative to try a local inn to recover from the café. The choice was the lovely 17th century Bear and Billet, serving well to harbour from the elements, complete with an open fire. I glugged away at Okells Ales, from the Isle of Man, with Graham's favourite, an extremely strong pint of lime and soda. It was essential to be potent, sometimes to the extent of being levied a charge for several shots of cordial. It was good, he said, to my relief, therefore not requiring a further bar visit for more green stuff.

So we faced the cold rain, which had started up again (a relentlessly bad winter, this) and followed directions past the amphitheatre (under restoration) to the former cathedral of St John the Baptist, surprisingly close, but outside the city walls. The view from it offers much inducement – gateway, old walls, the original city. How marvellous to find this tantalizing dark ruin. In fact it's been a parish church since 1581, its glory the Romanesque nave, particularly complementary to the more demure, later, cathedral. While the latter's lectern was in the shape of St John the Baptist's emblem, an eagle, the whole of this church is dedicated to him. A wander round the buildings was essential, for there are clumps of red stone at either end. Splendid deep red fragments and ruins outside enveloped the church, and inside there lay a shrouded skeleton. Archaic reference of re-sited tombstones 'Grace Jones is relict to the above John Jones'. The reason for such a church not to sustain cathedral status was linked to the diocesan map: the see was moved to Coventry. Many diocesan decisions later, the newest version of Coventry itself was later carved out of Worcester territory in 1918.

Finally, some words from Jonathan Swift in the 18th Century, after Chester was desecrated by the Puritans, and a century and a half before the Victorian restoration:

The church and clergy here, no doubt
Are very near akin,
Both weather-beaten are without,
And mould'ring are within.

7

Worcester

Christ & St Mary

Province: Canterbury
Founded: 679–80 secular; Benedictine monastic cathedral from 969
Present building: 1224 onwards
Restored: 1863 through to 1874 by George Gilbert Scott

Website: www.worcestercathedral.co.uk
Tel: 01905 732900
Email: info@worcestercathedral.org.uk
Address: The Chapter Office, 8 College Yard, Worcester WR1 2LA

Three to See: The view from across the River Severn, perhaps enjoying cricket or the races;
1130 chapter house, the oldest, in fine condition;
King John's tomb

Pear

Tuesday 16 February, 2010
Jeffrey Kacirk's *Forgotten English* daily tear-off calendar came up trumps for Worcester, as this was actually Shrove Tuesday. However there was no sign of pancakes, alas. I shall quote the entire entry, hung on the day's word 'cock-sqwoilin'. It was defined in John Akerman's *Glossary of Provincial Words and Phrases in Wiltshire*, 1842. A point has been stretched in the location, but Worcs and Wilts did have in common rurality, both occupying the western half of the country and boasting a medieval cathedral. 'The barbarous practice of throwing at cocks, formerly a custom at Shrovetide. This unmanly pastime is, I fear, not entirely abolished in some parts of England... ' There followed:

> *Fasteryn-Evyn: an older British term for Shrove Tuesday. A popular pastime in schools on Fasteryn-Evyn was cockfighting, some guidelines for which were mentioned in William McDowell's History of Dumfries (1867): "The under-teacher (shall) keep the door and exact not more than twelve pennies from each scholar for the benefit of bringing a cockerel to fight in the classroom. What money is given by the scholars, the under-teacher is to receive and apply to his own use for his pains and trouble." But according to John Brand's Observations on Popular Antiquities (1813), money was not the only reward for teachers. "The schoolmasters were said to preside at the battle and claimed the runaway cocks, called fugees, as their perquisites."*

The preliminary stop this Shrove Tuesday was at St John-in-Bedwardine, absorbed by the city of Worcester in 1837, on the west bank of the River Severn. Fortunately, it was set on rising ground, as the area is all too familiar with flooding. The Worcestershire County Cricket Ground has been under water regularly over the years. That evocative piece of green can be seen from St John's, the parish named after the church – round the corner and onto the road to Malvern. The choice was for my maternal grandfather, who was incumbent there from 1917 to 1927. When he left for Devon, this was inscribed in a little black book, which was among my mother's possessions:

> *To the Rev. F.E. Benison M.A.*
> *Rev. and dear Sir,*
> *We the parishioners of St John-in-Bedwardine, Worcester have heard with great pleasure of your preferment to the Curacy in*

charge of Littleham cum Exmouth after upwards of ten years
faithful service in our parish.

While we rejoice in your preferment we also part with you
with great regret. You have endeared yourself to us by your
unfailing courtesy and cheerful bearing, your work being
especially marked among the young folk of the parish.

We ask your acceptance of the accompanying purse of
money as a token of our esteem and goodwill.

We wish you 'God speed' and many years of useful activity
in your new sphere.
Yours very sincerely,
Charles T. Powell
Vicar

J W Noake
E R Bowen
Church wardens
December 1927

There followed a list from 'Mr Adcock' to 'Mr & Mrs Wassall',
numbering 215 and written in blue-black ink, with a suffix 'and many other
friends and well wishers.'

We enjoyed the church for a while, chatting with ladies arranging
flowers and cleaning. We were told that this was not just a Tuesday job.
There was a Norman arcade on the north side of the nave and some fine
medieval stained glass windows in the chancel, which defied my camera.
It was actually too bright through the yellow panes. There was unusual
framed glass on a tombstone. Also on the north side, a pillar had a squint
cut right through it, so the priest conducting a service in the chantry chapel
there (one of several in the church) could observe the progress at the main
altar to assist his own timing. Changes have been a feature of life here, as
everywhere. The most recent one was the removal of the balcony along the
north and south aisles. The church looked good from the outside, the 15th
century tower providing some character to the surrounding streets. The
church, which was advanced in a restoration appeal, lies at a busy junction.

Graham and I moved on the short distance via the bridge over the
Severn, affording the classic view of the cathedral proud above it. Having
sorted out parking thanks to 'Guide and Welcomer' Andrew Casewell, we
enjoyed his discourse on the merits of the cathedral. We were interrupted
immediately by a smartly-dressed man in distress. He was searching for a
funeral – of 'Tom Barker' I think. It was the same enquiry as at St John's

half an hour earlier, and met with the same response from the ladies there: bafflement, though the welcomers, discussing it between them, had some idea that there was such a happening at a Roman Catholic church nearby that day.

With the same dedication as Chester, Christ and the Blessed Virgin Mary, the cathedral had immediate glories in common with most of its peers in the league of cathedrals. The nave with its decorated roof, and, looking back, the overwhelming west window is a pretty good opening gambit. The presence of Edward Elgar (1857–1934), Master of the King's Musick for the last ten years of his life, was palpable: a plaque and window near the north door honoured his memory. Also his image appeared, along with the west façade of the cathedral, on the obverse of our £20 notes from 1999 to 2007. We were instructed to exchange these by the end of June 2010 for the new style, picturing Adam Smith. I preferred those redundant ones. I still found one or two in trouser pockets after that. The bank was accommodating.

It was at once time for 'Prayers for Healing' held in the extensive crypt, a Norman phenomenon, courtesy of Bishop Wulfstan which dated from 1084, a mere 18 years after the Conquest. Part of the crypt housed an informative exhibition. All was whitewashed, compelling to view and suiting its contemporary purposes well. I liked the fragment of jagged original wall below the entrance from which you should cast your eyes up and see a much later pillar resting there. And there was a fetching model of the old cathedral of Wulfstan (Bishop of Worcester 1062–95), off-white against the brightness of its setting.

Stepping upstairs, as a mortal you are dwarfed by the organ, which dominates the south transept. Making your way to the Prior's Parlour would be an admirable idea, but there are bells of various sizes in the cloister on the way. One is for the venerable Wulfstan, apparently cast c.1374 by William Burford. And not only these, which shine even on a dull day (like this one), but the chapter house. This is the oldest in the country and overwhelming. Having tried to say something therein, the sound bounced all over the place. How did meetings work with the long distance between each sitting space round the perimeter? The 1120 design was pure, an unadulterated circle, and four types of stone are used, including two shades of red. There was no clutter there apart from a covered piano. Graham considered: 'This would be a superb venue for an antiques fair, and they've got power points there.' And most discreet they were, too. The roof is of timber from the late 14th century. This is known from the cathedral's Cellarer's Rolls; also that the name of the carpenter was Hugh. His annual salary was 52s (plus 26s for food). This is a beautiful space.

So, on to the Prior's Parlour, a modest catering enterprise occupying a single cloister arch but achieving much. There was not only the stained glass beyond the cloister and more Norman pillars, sunk in the wall, but a convincing range of snacks. 'Bishop's Tea' (scone with butter, cream and a cup of tea or coffee) was £3. 'Dean's' involved a teacake, 'Canon's' two crumpets and 'Chorister's' a choice of homemade cakes. I think they'd got it right. Graham's coffee, however, had a slightly herby aroma, but he decided it was an improvement on 'fishy' at Chester. The toilets, too, were admirable. From the stone entrance a passage (peppermint green walls) led to the facilities, which were clean and up to date, even sporting one of those efficient Dyson Airblade hand dryers. It turned out to be a recent addition. Here there was no admission charge, with the Parlour convenient for the public to lunch in. It's very close to the lovely environs of the Close, the cathedral enclave behind the macho Edgar Tower, and walkable from the Worcester Porcelain Company down the hill. There wasn't time to see if there were replacements for gaps in my Evesham design collection.

The cathedral shop was down the way in a similarly congested, even economical, space to the cafe. There were artefacts coveted by Graham, small and expensive souvenirs I reckoned ('Celtic Lands' designed by Sea Gems and Fine Enamels by Ayshford, Staffs were on display). Royal Worcester should produce something for this local outlet, we thought, but nothing to tempt us to mark the occasion, except a few photos. The new welcomer – at the door that is – immediately asked to see my permit when she espied me aiming at a medieval glass panel in the north aisle (one of a somewhat small complement). Well, I'd already been told by Leighton Davies, a welcomer with some authority, to take as many pictures as I liked, including the misericords. It was he who took over when I asked the verger if I could have a more detailed look at them, in the choir stalls. He was changing the covers, as Ash Wednesday and Lent were imminent. 'Yes, of course,' uttered Leighton. What we did see was enchanting – three-dimensional carvings of stories, fables and advice. One set feature the Labours of the Months. At a higher level is the single piece stone pulpit, from 1642, during the Commonwealth: the Cavalier Worcester suffered for its resilient support of the monarchy.

This dialogue led to an exchange of phone numbers for my next visit, for which he would look up his book on the subject. It was he who recommended Ripple church and Malvern Priory. While the latter is well-known on a number of subjects including the matter in hand, St Mary, Ripple does not appear in many books covering churches, proving that personal suggestion and word of mouth is frequently worth following up.

We admired some glories of this place: 'Bad' King John's tomb, in startling polished Purbeck marble at the top of the quire by the altar steps, and, above it, in both senses, the chantry and tomb of Prince Arthur (1502), a scramble up shallow, worn steps. BKJ died at Newark, Notts (not far from what was to become Southwell Minster). He instructed that he should be buried in Worcester, something which serves to exonerate him from his wickedness just a little. And (Good) Prince Arthur, destined for the throne of England as Henry VII's successor, died on honeymoon not far away in Ludlow (diocese of Hereford). His interment in Worcester must have helped in saving the cathedral during the Dissolution. The best thing was the shaggy lion (I expect that was intended, as a royal beast), apparently licking the feet of the king's effigy. That was the monarch who yielded lands to France, autonomy to the barons (*Magna Carta*, 1215) and the crown jewels to the Wash. In St George's Chapel to the north of the altar was a memorial to Studdert Kennedy (Woodbine Willie), whose family was part of the congregation at St John-in-Bedwardine. One of the signatures in my grandfather's book was that of one of his family members. Behind the reredos was the Lady Chapel, with a mirror presented by the Head Postmaster, A A Dewar, in December 1974; a nice touch. Not far, is a simple two-piece cross, a gift from the bishop and people of Coventry to honour Worcester's 1300th anniversary in 1980. It is made of forged nails from the roof of the old cathedral, which had been bombed and destroyed in 1940. It is a fine symbol of reconciliation in a divided world. An item of sub-text is the removal of part of Coventry's territory to Worcester in 1918, at the end of the First World War.

Out we ventured into falling snow. I tried to do a circuit of the whole structure, which seemed massive in such conditions, but was foiled at the southwest corner. The tower was magnificent. We had admired it on the way from St John's, the detail and rich red carving, for new red sandstone is most conducive to a skilled sculptor. Then it starts crumbling. Now it presented a presence along with the very best. The west front and the view across the curving River Severn to the cricket ground and swans is iconic, as chocolate box as Salisbury across the meadows. I had a painting of it at home, which I admired daily, as did guests. It dated from the time of my grandfather's curateship and mother's childhood.

Of Worcester and its cathedral, William Cobbett had this to note during one of his *Rural Rides*:

Tuesday, 26th Sept 1826
Mr Price rode with us to this city, which is one of the cleanest, neatest, and handsomest towns I ever saw: indeed I do not recollect to have seen any one equal to it. The cathedral is

indeed, a poor thing, compared with any of the others, except that of Hereford, and I have seen them all but those of Carlisle, Durham, York, Lincoln, Chester, and Peterborough; but the town is, I think, the very best I saw; and the people are, upon the whole, the most suitably dressed and most decent looking people. The town is precisely in character with the beautiful and rich country, in the midst of which it lies.

In more recent times – 2010 – the *Independent on Sunday* reported:

Sport has... found an unlikely haven (or perhaps that should be heaven) in Worcester Cathedral. A unique exhibition, showcasing a century's worth of sporting heroes' stories and memorabilia, featuring the likes of W G Grace, David Beckham, Sebastian Coe and Stanley Matthews, and highlighting the changes in equipment and apparel, will be on display for a week starting today. The Dean, the Very Reverend Peter Atkinson, says that it is a fundraising event for the cathedral, but also an important celebration of sport. "At its best, sport is a force for good in the world and deserves to be celebrated as God-given." Amen to that.

Independent on Sunday 8/8/10

Unfortunately a subsequent bulletin reported a loss of £51K for the *British Sporting Heroes* exhibition. The Chapter asked the Cathedral Council for a review to unearth reasons for the failure. Only 2,000 had attended against the budgeted 10,000. Reasons? Pretty obvious, really: inadequate advertising and the target market, which 'did not match the Cathedral's normal visitors and would not have appealed to many of them', plus a lack of connection between the subject matter and the cathedral. However Worcester did have a good year overall financially – more donations and 'Rimes in Time', a poetry-reading marathon making over £20K.

The emblem of Worcester had to be the pear, given a black pear tree as the County's arms, and you have to sample local Vale of Evesham produce, including pears and Badsey asparagus, while in the area. Even Worcester Pearmain, the local apple, contains the word within it.

Wednesday 16 February, 2011
This is a preamble to Malvern and Worcester, a day out a few months before the February trip. Ripple church, dedicated to St Mary, diocese of Worcester, is right on the border with the county and diocese of Gloucester.

It was with some relief that the church was open: beseeching emails had come to nothing. The highly recommended, in fact amazing, misericords at Ripple were considerately displayed, in a vertical position and fortunately placed near plain glass windows on a light afternoon. I purchased a set of postcards, which carried photographs of the Labours of the twelve months with the sun (with a half smile) between March (sowing) and April (bird scaring), and the moon (with a man's face) dividing September (corn for malting) and October (acorns for pigs, no doubt being fattened for the November activity – pig killing). They are great fun as well as a reflection of 15th century life, the work of an artisan coming straight out of the working culture of the time. My immediate favourite was February: hedging and ditching, providing a sketchy modus operandi. Go out and do it yourself! A close second was May, when crops were blessed. I noted the story on display about a stagecoach. Ripple was on the route from Birmingham to Gloucester – a mail coach team conveyed two passengers from Worcester:

> ... it bolted at Ripple and the reins broke. The coachman and guard jumped clear and horses, in mid-career, with swaying coach. It passed from sight. One of the passengers, a young lady, in a panic and fear, flung herself from the coach and broke her neck. It was far more perilous than railway travel and local records recount a whole series of catastrophes at or near Ripple.

On that cold February day, I dropped into Malvern, a modest detour on the way up to Worcester. Great Malvern Priory had been widely recommended for a misericord sighting. I was to spend an hour there. It made a proud presence, nestling under the Malvern Hills, in respect of which we may quote Piers Plowman, a poem composed at the time when parts of the cathedral were being built during the Plantagenet regime:

The Vision of Piers Plowman
On a May morning in the Malvern Hills
I met with a marvel that seemed made by magic:
I was weary of wandering, and went to rest
Under a broad bank by the side of a brook.
William Langland (written between 1360 and 1387)

The tower of the priory was modelled on Gloucester Cathedral. Its square monumentality and varied stone slab tones impressed. Once inside, the nave was marvellously confident, with the plainest Norman design –

tactile round pillars – and medieval glass to compensate for the cathedral's lack of it. The priory complements Worcester. Take them as a double act.

It was 925 years old in 2010, a celebration which had passed me by. At least I'd managed a day of the *Three Choirs Festival* at Gloucester. Malvern Priory was a delightfully simple structure, stocky and ripe, placed amid ponderous cedar trees in the middle of a spa town, clearly a well-heeled one. It offered a series of set pieces, bold statements, which somehow reminded me of Coventry Cathedral in a totally contrasting way. I sat, entranced by the body of the nave from a very comfortable chair. Upwards, in the clerestory, there was fine, rare, ancient (15th century) stained glass, and more in the chancel, together with satisfyingly rich stonework; and yet more in St Anne's (southeast) Chapel. But that was having examined terrific misericords, easily admired on upturned choir stalls, complete with another Labours of the Months sequence. Simon Jenkins commented in *England's Thousand Best Churches*, about 'the medieval glazing. From a distance, the effect is kaleidoscopic, rather than narrative, a shimmering refraction of pure colour.' Finally, at the west end the window was a copy of the equivalent one at Exeter Cathedral.

The next breath-taker was the profusion of medieval tiles, decorating the choir screen on all sides. The numbers I picked up were: 1,200 tiles in 90 patterns, applied from 1456 to 1520; the most varied assembly and the only remaining mural tiles in England. Then there was a Henry VII relic: the north transept window. The central image, of the Coronation of the Virgin Mary, is not in the middle at all, owing to the stone in the way, but lies quaintly to the right (or east). The blue sky and bright stars shout at you. It managed somehow to escape the anti-Marian purge of the iconoclasts.

I purchased some economical, and tasteful, greetings cards for £1.30 each, at the shop which dominated the north aisle. There was a stock of leaflets on subjects as broad as 'Great Malvern Priory bell-ringers' and 'What's On for children and young people'. It seemed a busy place. Back round the building and up the hill, appeared tempting Vale of Evesham provender: the russet apples were so succulent! Next I happened upon Malvern's original purpose: the spa water, gushing from a Victorian spout. A woman stood filling a basketful of empty bottles. I had my more modest item to hand, and followed her example. It was cold and delicious. I imagined how good it would taste after a walk over the hills above, something on the long list. Having made the ascent, you could see for many miles in all directions on a clear day.

Worcester was calling. I ended up in the cathedral close. This further visit was earmarked for architecture. I had arranged a session with Chris Romain, the contracted cathedral architect. One is required for every cathedral. This was the first, and only, architect I met on this quest. I chose Worcester because of its particular susceptibility owing to the intrinsic character of its dominant red sandstone. Worcester certainly merited a second visit, to meet this expert. Chris had qualified in 1979, and had now spent 15 years as part of the fabric, inheriting the established 20 year restoration project, five years in. He had endorsed its substance, and costing, and, indeed it was to be completed on time and within budget. Chris's duties were to advise the chapter on the general condition and fabric of the building. There was a quinquennial inspection – very thorough – and his first one was particularly detailed. This situation was common to all cathedrals, one of the standard requirements embraced in the Cathedrals Measure of 1999. Architects were appointed as individuals, and operated through their firms. Chris was based in Wiltshire. This was his only cathedral, and he looked after three abbeys, shortly to be reduced to two (Sherborne and Milton), as well as 200 parish churches: 'from London in the east to Devon in the west, and from Swanage in the south to Worcester in the north', he said. Some architects had more than one cathedral in their remit. This was the opportunity to unearth his favourite cathedral. 'Oh, Worcester,' he replied, reinforcing the relish he oozed throughout our tour of his building. It was unique in the challenges and character it yielded, and was essentially friendly as a middle-ranking cathedral with a low profile (the city was not on the tourist map). There had been special events and parties, which had been arranged around the one or two days he spent there each week, for example a stonemason's birthday. He was touched by this, as he had been by his interview all those years ago. When asked what he would like to do with the building, he retorted: 'Do you mean after the new spire?' It was taken in good heart, with the response: 'How high would that be?' '405 feet'. Laughter all round, as that would just top the one at Salisbury, the tallest in the country.

We covered the whole place, serving to convince me of the interest of the building, which ranked low for many for its darkness, poor restoration and lack of good glass. Chris turned aspects of this into a virtue. The 'tufa' stone in the north aisle vaulting, from a quarry by the Teme in Shropshire, comprised considerable vegetation. Over time there arose a 'cheesy appearance'. Once this was explained, I agreed that it contributed something different. That aisle had been coloured until the 19th century overhaul, something we detected on close examination.

Chris drew attention to the strainer arches. More or less horizontal struts of stone were introduced to hold up the sagging tower. Think of the equivalent at Wells (the Scissor Arches), or those at Canterbury, which were erected to admire, as well as support, also flat ones at Salisbury, of which

I was unaware but now longed to return to see. 'These days those would never be allowed. It would be considered a major intervention. Things are subject to so much external regulation,' he told me. On the other hand the destruction of well-designed (if decayed) medieval features had proceeded without objection in the Victorian age. We looked at pillars. Some had been treated with linseed oil in an attempt at preservation. It now seemed preferable to leave it to its own processes. Purbeck stone was used as much at Worcester as at Salisbury (with similar problems – see its pillars) and elsewhere.

We aired the inevitable subject of funding. Architect Chris told the sad tale (which took me back to instances relating to the Arts Council and theatre company funds), where English Heritage had a pot of £3m pa to offer to cathedrals for building projects. 'All cathedrals could apply,' he recounted. 'Some had facetious plans, submitted because the money "was there". Also some found difficulty with the (required) matching funds overall. Less than £2m was spent by the end of March deadline, and the Treasury proceeded to reduce the pot,' arguing that it wasn't needed. These days, while English Heritage was waning as a source, the Wolfson Foundation and Pilgrims Trust had joined the fray, 'and funding was enhanced for next year'. There was the Scheduled Management (Assorted Landscape) Scheme. This enterprise possessed capital of £2m, administered by the Worcester Cathedral Restoration and Development Trust. When Chris came into post interest was being earned at 10.5%, affording some real work. The capital was still untouched, indeed sacrosanct, and, since the trust was wound up, was in the gift of the dean and chapter, interest recently being negligible. We both anticipated that to change in the future, now inflation was starting to rise. All in all, the chapter wasn't badly off, while the cathedral was hard up.

Another thrust was apprenticeship, which came out of my introduction to the stonemasons' yard, quietly situated on the southeast side. There was an abundance of slabs of many tones, ancient and modern. They would all be used, I was informed. I met Rowan Mackay, one of four masons doing 'banker' work, and 'fixing', not 'carving', as I called it. He was at work, on his day off, focused on a chunk of hard, pale French stone for a private commission. He had benefitted from the foundation degree, through Gloucester University, in which eight, fairly obvious, cathedrals were involved, financially and intrinsically for the perpetration of skills, and exchange of experience: an excellent scheme. This linked with what Chris had related a bit earlier: a common sense tale of building practices in the Middle Ages. The east end of Salisbury was commenced in 1220, Worcester four years later (Chilmark stone at the former, from local Cotswold Bredon

Hill here). 'The detailing is so similar. Did they build out of love? Did they heck! If they found out the rate was a farthing more at Worcester, they'd migrate there.'

I was lucky that my host could show me a display of the Guesten tracery in the south transept, comprising crisp crushed-raspberry pink segments laid out beautifully on the floor. I photographed them, some with the confidently-smiling Chris as backdrop. The Guesten was a medieval hospitality building adjacent to the masons' yard, and we were to meet Master Mason Darren Steele by the covered lightless building. We noted it to be keenly cold by then, with a lovely aspect of snowdrops, aconites and the medieval close all around. The Guesten repairs were at an advanced stage, from a starting point of stone crumbling to touch, and under the aegis of the Cathedral Fabric Commission and English Heritage. The exhibition was eloquent, to demonstrate 'a record of what the window was like. This is "restoration,"' urged the architect. 'The wall has gone to one side.' Decay was further exemplified in the mixture executed by the Victorians of sandstone and limestone. 'Limestone eats sandstone for breakfast,' he said, 'highly calcareous'. Incidentally, 39 different types of stone had been counted in the building. Its problem derived from the original choice of stone – red and soft from the Severn Valley, exacerbated in the Victorian restoration.

In answer to my wish, we now turned into the seductive chapter house. It was well-used, but no longer by the chapter itself. Chris told of one incident to demonstrate the acoustical properties. On an occasion when the perimeter places were all taken, one woman said to her neighbour of another opposite: 'I don't like her pink shoes.' The target spoke straight out: 'I heard that.' Like the Whispering Gallery at St Paul's. The wall was largely green – Highley stone, again, and once more each slab was different in hue, to satisfying, if accidental, effect, as was the yellow part, from the Cotswolds. False economy had been exercised in the choice of materials on the floor. 'If I had my way, drinks would not be allowed in here,' said the man. 'Soon after the floor was laid, one of the chapter was promoted to Peterborough, and red wine was split on the floor.' Quite a lot of it, and it kept happening. Looking down, it was indeed very patchy, in colour and quality. Up to then, no antiques fairs had taken place in this building.

Chris had to finish off in the nearby office, and drive home to Shaftesbury. But he took me up to the top of the tower, which meant a nodding acquaintance with a bell man in the practice chamber. Worcester has the fifth largest ring of bells in the country. Would-be campanologists have to train on dummy bells before they're let loose in the chamber proper, a level higher. After all those steps we stood on the roof, taking in a splendid panorama, including that territory owned by the host organization: Worcestershire County Cricket Ground; also, beyond, St John-in-Bedwardine. Even a leisurely absorption up there, complete with a photo session, didn't stop the guy from taking me to the Prior's Parlour for an exit tea and coffee. We parted company at almost 5 pm after a superlative three hours. Chris Romain had been an outstanding guide. And Worcester Cathedral was firmly established for me as a pear of a place, ripe, inconsistent and fascinating. Alas, Fatcat, a former resident feline, was now living with Canon Alvyn Pettersen in College Green, leaving a complete absence of cats in the cathedral.

Fig 9

Fig 10

Fig 11

Fig 12

[9] Worcester: Watercolour of view from the west, mid-1920s.
[10] Worcester: Chris Romain, cathedral architect: stonework for the Guesten.
[11] Guildford: west window: damaged pane not replaced.
[12] Guildford: Coffee cake in the excellent refectory: delicious.
[13] Chichester: View from the choir stalls: Norman magnificence.

Fig 13

111

8

Guildford

The Holy Spirit

Province: Canterbury
Founded: New diocese 1927, created out of Winchester
Building: 1936–61

Website: www.guildford-cathedral.org
Tel: 01483 547860
Email: visits@guildford-cathedral.org
Address: Guildford Cathedral, Stag Hill, Guildford Surrey GU2 7UP

Three to See: Angel weather vane/mobile phone mast;
font in south aisle, all a clean look;
stained glass, set off well in an uncluttered setting

Tupperware

Thursday 25 February, 2010

There was a curious preamble to Guildford: the Roman Catholic Cathedral Church of St Michael and St George, Aldershot, 'The Cathedral Church of the Bishop of the Forces', whose red spire is a landmark in the forces quarter, to the north of the town centre, picturesque football ground nestling on rising ground, and the most excellent pub crawl via the Three Lions (White, Red and Golden in descending order of quality and distance from the town).

The cathedral was under wraps, in the process of work at the west end, where some interest was on display: patron saint St George, triumphant over the dragon, most appropriate to inspire the battling congregation on entry. The active nature of the establishment was clear from forthcoming events: a military pilgrimage to Lourdes three months hence, in May, and sooner, 'The Chrism Mass' on Thursday 18 March. The current year was 'The Year of the Priests' and Bishop Richard was aiming for a 'renewal of priestly vows'. Next door to the cathedral is St Andrews, the Church of Scotland's presence in the neighbourhood.

There is a geographical anomaly hereabouts. Aldershot, Hampshire is in the RC diocese of Portsmouth, but the Anglican congregation looks to nearby Guildford, Surrey, sensible enough as this built-up area also comprises Farnham, Surrey and Farnborough, Hampshire. It is where three counties meet.

This conveniently takes us to Guildford, where I picked up Rand from his train. Oddly, the 'station' car park did not allow me access to the all-too-visible station, beyond a high metal fence and the railway lines, so through judicious use of mobile phones I timed it to open the doors to the intrepid traveller, who had journeyed from Kent to London to Surrey, though he had just unwittingly chosen a (very) slow service. We sped off to the abode of the Norrises for lunch. They were named Gerry-Bee and Mary-Wasp (her spouse's concoction), nominating Southwell and Exeter as their favourites. She was a Devon girl. On the way we espied, through the gloom, the Cathedral of the Holy Spirit soaring high on its mound, Stag Hill, above the university campus. Over lunch, Wasp recommended the Children's Remembrance Garden, which we duly witnessed as a rarity among our major churches. We arrived through appalling weather, up to now an alarming failure rate. It was nevertheless refreshing to park easily and discern that there was indeed an open aspect: 'discern', because you couldn't really see it properly. Set somewhere in the grey heavens, there was the red brick cathedral building, capped by an angel in gold, the weather vane, which the media-and-children-sensitive Rand, in a moment which smacked the gobs of Gerry-Bee and myself alike, deemed to be politically incorrect. I just thought it looked old-fashioned, an opinion I stayed with. This was in keeping with the whole place as a 20th century Gothic entity tied to a traditional, yet austere, view of the past, almost reminiscent of Giles Gilbert Scott's approach to restoration while Victoria was on the throne. The angel's location has also given it status as a mast for Orange mobile phones. Mine wasn't on at the time for me to check its efficacy. I was engrossed in matters in hand. The shade of red had a lot to do with the wife of the architect. It was Lady Maufe, a dyer by trade, who dictated the tone, a terracotta, almost earth red. Anthony Cyprian Bridge (the second dean, from 1968 to 1986) referred to it as 'puke pink'.

But I'm not really complaining – the west front had figures etched in the glass panels, another way you might see the view of distant hill and housing. The trouble is that one of the panels – featuring an angel's midriff – had been vandalized, and replaced by a plain pane. We all agreed this to be a mistake, Gerry-Bee, as a regular attender on the campanology front, considered it to be 'an irritating blank space', and Rand as a practising artist 'you could easily replace it with something convincing'. Anyway, the decision to leave it has prevailed, guided by the thinking that you can't replicate a piece of original art. 'Crap!' I thought. We moved on to the most impressive nave, singularly tall and narrow with empathic pillars. The style, and its execution, were an appealing interpretation of 'Gothic', in particular the columns which were shaped, sculpted, into seductive octagonal, vertical curves throughout. And below, every one of the 1,400 kneelers carried a different embroidered design.

In the south aisle, a short few steps from the entrance, was the covered font, the canopy reaching up to the roof just like the ubiquitous pillars, all in a pleasing creamy Somerset limestone. The emblem of a fish was displayed on the side, representing the early apostles. Gerry-Bee recalled a visit in the 1960s soon after it opened, when the lighting was effected by contemporary plastic lampshades, then chandeliers (remember that period for awfulness of look). His comment was: 'it filled me with a desire to make racist remarks'. The lighting was now innocuous, most discreet, leaving the main complaint to concern the sound. Acoustics were not the best, we imagined. Rand's suggestion was the introduction of 'mushrooms' like the Albert Hall.

We moved on to the crossing and organ aloft, looking good in its dedicated space, not cramped and disfiguring like those squeezed in unsuitable gaps in some medieval churches. In the south transept was reference to the (Anglican) Mothers' Union, with connections to the church in Nigeria, by whom a statue had been donated, on display here.

I always find diocese charts and maps fascinating and the one here was no exception, showing much of the county of Surrey embraced in the see. This was possible when Guildford and Portsmouth dioceses were carved out of the traditional, extensive territory of Winchester in 1927. From that time Holy Trinity, in Guildford High Street (with, reputedly, an attractive garden sloping up south of the church), was used as pro-cathedral, until the new building, designed from that time by Sir Edward Maufe, was opened at last in 1961 – the Second World War served to delay the building. Now 'Holy Trinity and St Mary's' it operates as a parish church. On the board each parish church was illustrated on a carefully-plotted plan, aided by the literal shape of the diocese, a landscape-shaped mass conforming to standard paper measurements. We wondered if it had been a student project. It was well-executed and we examined it for ideas for interesting churches to visit, eventually deciding that could wait, as there were already a number of exciting prospects imminent in the diocese of Chichester.

Stained glass is worth a mention, because it assumes a comparatively significant presence, the whole space being light, empty and uncluttered. In fact, with the image fresh in my mind from Wasp's lunch (rice and various flavoured toppings cooked cleverly in Tupperware vessels dating from the same aeon as the cathedral), it could be represented as just this, clear, slightly used Tupperware containers, sealed and promising good things within. The nave windows contain the action, the life of the church, clearly, with the gradual vertical encroachment of colour as official bodies suggestive of the welfare of the congregation, such as Surrey Police are displayed through coats of arms. More than this, in the south choir aisle is a unique, most dramatically tall window in vivid colour, which strangely seemed to work among its pallid surroundings, for Surrey County Council. Meanwhile we had reached the entrance to the bell tower. It's 160' high. Gerry-Bee embarked upon a lecture on bell-ringing: '12 here, from both of the main manufacturers, Mears and Stainbank and Whitechapel', which he had undertaken since the age of 13, half a century before. 'You remember your path. Rhythm comes into it,' he said, and regaled us with a lecture about blue lines, the Stedman Cinques based on 11 and the order: 1 to 5, then 5 becomes the fifth place and so on, the order changing. I can't quote him direct, being a total lay person in this, that is, ignorant. At that point I decided I must return on a practice evening to climb up, see the bells and receive practical explanations of what we were hearing; also see Gerry-bee at work.

Another anomaly was the Treasury and Exhibition room, the most extensive I'd seen, in an unambitious building. It displayed much impressive silverware, also a record of Christmas carols from 1976 by the Choir of Guildford Cathedral; there was mention, too, for a pilgrim's staff carrying the arms of the five dioceses of the Pilgrim's Way. It was illuminating that these were Winchester, Guildford, Southwark, Rochester and Canterbury.

We did manage to ascend the gallery and enjoy a direct view of the organ, and the aspect without, though it was still raining hard. After this came a round tour, embracing the chapter house, which seemed modest for the needs of a modern diocese, more like an inter-war morning room. I loved the contrast here to the pure and simple Early English design recently observed at Worcester. There were some fetching Art Deco touches here and there. And there was Eric Gill's work – St John the Baptist outside the south transept.

Rand was to observe, after complete absorption here: 'Everything's made of brick. I thought it was concrete.' He liked the honesty of the unadulterated red bricks on the exterior. The brick may serve to enhance acoustic quality. It was the preferred church performance space of guitarist Jon Cooper, a local lad (from the Horsham area) who had turned to West End musicals, such as *Hairspray*, to ply his craft. Saint Saëns' 3rd symphony, the organ one, was good for him at Guildford. 'It has the wow factor,' he said of the cathedral. 'It dominates the landscape.' It was his favourite. So does Worcester Cathedral from the west, as do the Angel of the North and wind turbines. It's all a matter of choice. However my cousin Tony Hill opined: 'Comparing Guildford to Wells (his local cathedral) is like Banksy to Michelangelo.'

Time was advancing and empirical testing of the facilities was become urgent in the dying light. The rain was relentless, putting paid to the day. The bookshop was closing as we passed, but over the dividing driveway, I had to pause by the shop, where, five minutes earlier, we could have purchased Clotted Cream Fudge, Lemon and Lime Curd, Summer Fruits with Pimm's preserve, a Wild Honey Set, or a blue and white clock, a tray or placemats, all promoting the cathedral of Surrey, by way of its logo. We did manage cups of tea and some coffee and walnut cake in the Refectory. The whole facility was in keeping with this purpose-built complex of the ecclesiastic. Should you make your way up from the town (no city this – no such award has been made), you'd be in for a pleasant, contemplative sojourn: lots of space, pale wood and an admirable array of food all day. It won the *Eat Out 'eat well'* bronze award from the county in 2009. It was to stand the course of this tour as one of the best cathedral cafés in the country. Guildford Cathedral sums up the best of the place – efficient and bright, the best kind of Tupperware creation, and apart from the population it serves, but, then, so is Durham.

9

Chichester

St Richard

Province: Canterbury
Founded: 681 at Selsey, moved to Chichester 1075
Present building: 12th century
Restored: 1861–66 steeple, after collapse and other work

Website: www.chichestercathedral.org.uk
Tel: 01243 782595
Email: info@chichestercathedral.org.uk
Address: The Cathedral Offices, The Royal Chantry, Cathedral Cloisters,
Chichester, West Sussex PO19 1PX

Three to See: Marc Chagall window;
Roman mosaics, also at other sites in the area;
detached bell tower, a building in danger

Mosaic

Friday 26 and Saturday 27 February, 2010

Following on from Guildford, Rand and I endured the weather-affected rush hour down the A281 to Horsham, in the Diocese of Chichester. The aim was to sample some other, varied ecclesiastical delights as well as the cathedral. This was a long weekend. All went well, including a reunion with Tony and Christine. I had known Tony for 53 years (oh my God!), longer than anyone. He provided some potential help with the churches of Norfolk. This was very much in advance, as that part of the world was scheduled for the autumn. These quests always produce the unexpected, and sometimes snippets of relevance. Tony's good health, or at least his resistance to cold germs, he attributed to his preventative action as soon as symptoms become manifest: take ½ a teaspoon of Manucca honey (from New Zealand and extremely expensive) three times per day; also Echinacea dissolved in water. A tincture. Not only that but Vick's First Defence in a bottle, 3 times per day, gargle almost neat TCP, and take a dose of Vitamin C – heavy duty, once per day. Unfortunately, the next time I incurred such a virus, I completely forgot this conversation.

Breakfast was sparse in the Premier Inn. My pomegranate and white tea was an insipid mistake ('an acquired taste,' surmised Rand), and my request, a large porridge, came with honey and strawberry jam. I swiftly replaced these with milk (the green topped type, alas) and Demerara sugar (not soft brown available – I'm fussy about porridge). St Mary's, Horsham is beautifully set in the Causeway, the old part of town. We met Verger Keith Farran in the church and immediately ventured forth to the churchyard to be shown the north-south skewed Muslim grave close to the path. The weather always improves on non-cathedral-visit days, and this being a mere church, Friday was almost springlike. Indeed there were daffodils here and there.

We admired the Norman nave and touches of interest around. Keith gave us a marvellous tour, starting with the controversial new build at the southwest corner to provide better facilities than many other churches. A complete extra south aisle had been built in the 19th century, to good effect. The 20th century addition to this seemed to us to be in sympathy, built of mellow stone in a neutral design. The new vestry upstairs was spacious, replacing the medieval two-storey extension on the opposite corner, hidden away between organ and altar, and sporting old, low beams, and below, the verger's office. On the equivalent of a dado rail had been inscribed the names of the three churchwardens (three is very generous, not often encountered) in 1649. In 1949, to honour the landmark, the current names were added further along. There was a chapel for private prayer by the main entrance facing the Causeway (north side), which was locked to prevent entry into the church. Not long before, this didn't prevent a felon snatching a banner and attempting entry into the nave via a broken window.

Henchwomen Margaret (originally from Tyneside) and Eileen (proud Cornishwoman, but both had lived in Sussex for years) were polishing the brass eagle lectern and many a pew throughout our ramble round the church. We talked about church vandalism. Margaret had been relieved of her purse by a young man in the church. Still, 'most of the crime is in Crawley'. We enjoyed a stroll round the bits left to nature at the back, then up the Causeway, a lovely concourse, with buildings from many generations. We were bound for the Black Jug to meet Wakey, joining us for the duration, and his friend Frankie Deegan, a Norwich Cathedral enthusiast, who was now based in Horsham.

Lunch was good. We were then bound for Shoreham-by-Sea for our stay. Towards the end of the journey, Lancing College Chapel, 'the cathedral of the Downs', looked irresistible from the Adur valley. So we scaled its hill. The very fact of its function as a college serves to deter many, and its relative inaccessibility enhances this. However, parking opposite the west door, almost on the advertised closing hour of 4 pm, we shared the space with three others, perhaps from the Mediterranean. It was strange to experience Lancing so soon after Guildford Cathedral, as both were comparatively recent concoctions. However, the college showed later thinking, from the choir canopies inherited from Eton College to the tryptych which commands the whole, light space from the east end.

Its role was as minster for the group of Woodard schools, founded by Nathaniel of that name in 1848. Indeed there was a substantial celebration in 2008, which involved a cantata composition and a live broadcast on Radio 3 featuring organ and singers. It is a listed building, of warm Sussex sandstone, and terms require it to be open every day. It turned out that this day it was still unlocked after hours for a strings rehearsal in the crypt. The strains of youthful fiddle playing wafted through the building as we admired its features.

It was dedicated to Saints Mary and Nicolas, after Norman namesakes in Shoreham, over the river Adur to the east. St Nicolas, Old Shoreham and Lancing Chapel are in clear view of each other. The magnificent and immense rose window, the largest in the country, had been in the planning stage during my time at the college in the early 1960s, and 32' in diameter, since completed to great effect. The detail is carefully contrived to illustrate each school in the Woodard Foundation (16 round the perimeter, with the host college in bull's eye position) and, of course, some, like St Michael's, Petworth that have gone. These are augmented in an inner ring by related dioceses – 16 of them. It is immensely detailed using over 30,000 pieces.

Wakey's opinion was, 'a bit overpowering,' and the whole building 'intimidating inside, harsh and austere – more suitable plonked by the banks of the Seine'. But he liked the Trevor Huddlestone window, being 'on a more human scale'. This was in complete contrast, a modern piece primarily in blue and yellow, commemorating the Lancing Old Boy who became a key 'anti-apartheid campaigner and champion of the poor and repressed'. He died in 1998 and the window was dedicated by Archbishop Tutu in 2007.

The building project which remained outstanding was a porch at the west end. However, it did seem reassuringly complete to me after a school career there attending a building always incomplete. It did employ full use. 'It's like a hall,' said Rand, and 'It's so high. It dominates the local area. It's a simplified version of a cathedral – it's like Notre Dame,' added Wakey.

It was an easier journey down to the dual carriageway A27, and very soon taking the route back to the banks of the Adur (pronounced 'Ada'. Both Rand and Wakey guessed at 'a'Dour', kind of French, which was understandable as we were within striking distance of the Newhaven to Dieppe ferry terminal here. The next stop was another canny detour, doubling back on ourselves for St Nicolas, Old Shoreham (note lack of 'h', a spelling subsequently adopted for the college on the Downs), actually abutting the main road, so we had a tempting preview of both the west end and the tower.

This was a Norman gem – all heavy circular doorways in Sussex flint. Wakey commented: 'It's squat outside and simple inside.' That meant he liked it, I think, but you can't account for a Yorkshireman. The church was small but most imperfectly formed as it now stood, and all the better for it. It was complete with an age-old yew tree outside the door. In fact we almost gave up on ingress, we had done a complete circuit of the church. It offered no obvious entrance. I had a go at the rusty handle of a shabby door on the south side, heralded by the windswept yew tree. It yielded, to my relief. The church was most rewarding within. The panorama from it featured Lancing Chapel strongly, no doubt even better in more dramatic, or subtle, light. This was an atmospheric place, by the muddy banks of a tidal river, with ringed plovers darting in the brackish sedge.

We were staying in the Crab Tree Inn by Shoreham railway station, an easy way to get to Brighton, 20 minutes away, and cheap, too. Finding an economical crashpad in the City of Brighton'n'Hove (title conveyed by HM the Queen in 2004) had proved too difficult. The pub was excellent, both for ale and the breakfast, including succulent black pudding. In the morning we ventured forth not many yards to St Mary de Haura (of the harbour, which indeed used to be nearby before silting up), in New Shoreham. We'd missed performances, scheduled for the preceding Saturday and the one after, the latter being 'A Concert of Song (retiring collection)'. It was no use to us, anyway, as we had other plans for the rest of the day. But we did witness a women's group rehearsing in the south aisle.

The west end had been truncated in the 15th century, as the harbour silted up, bringing hard times. Pictures on the subject were a gloomy record. 'You have to imagine it extending and being more impressive,' commented Wakey. 'If there were even more ruins you'd feel sadder.' It remained a busy and attractive church, dating from the same period as St Nicolas, and, these days, strongly linked with it. Old and New Shoreham were of a piece, and well worth looking around. Glories of St Mary de Haura included a bit of examination outside: the Mary Garden and another dedicated to the Hospitallers, which presented a selection of herbs, well overdue for some pruning. These were preceded in installation by the odd humps of flinty wall, which could be traced on the church diagram, as a considerable percentage of floor space had been razed to the ground centuries ago.

And onward we walked to the train and, once in the new city, took a stroll down Queen and West Street, Brighton to the seafront. It was a harsh exposure to the sea breeze on a day below freezing, as we clutched hot, steaming mugs, for warmth through gloves and to prevent their disposal by the wind. At least I didn't have a repeat of the fish and chips incident at Broadstairs the previous summer, when, the parasol having blown away, a forbiddingly massive seagull swooped down and snatched more than half my cod, in greasy paper in my hand at the time. This was deft indeed, as nothing else was upset, my cup of builders' tea untouched by the thief. This time we admired the Palace Pier (I can't bring myself to call it what the flashing lights proclaim 'Brighton Pier' – no *What the Butler Saw* there any more, for certain). It remains to record, and shed tears beyond those induced by the punishing wind, the residual hulk of the West Pier, now irretrievable as anything other than dramatic sculpture bashed eternally by the tide.

There's no more to say about the proceedings (bad football, and double burgers and Bovril). So we shall move back, in a westward direction, to more churches.

Sunday 28 February
St John the Baptist, Findon, with Saxon origins, was the first stop on the westbound drive to Chichester, but we timed it badly. Morning Communion was just starting, so a tour of the ancient church was denied. In any case, its main glory remains the view of it from below, especially to enjoy the spire.

We were now bound, in foul weather, for another spire, that of Chichester Cathedral. One of my favourite cathedral views is the approach westwards at the point, somewhere near Tangmere, when you can see light through the two window spaces on the spire: a fine chink indeed.

We reached the fair city itself, to park the vehicle in North Pallant, opposite the highly reputed eponymous gallery. This was worth noting as even on a Sunday, as on this occasion, parking presented a challenge in old cities full of quaint streets, prohibitions and parking restrictions. Later on, we drove into a space behind the pre-booked Vestry Hotel, which offered free parking from 6 pm through to 10 am, a lot better than the equivalent at Salisbury.

The tower is a good one, once you get to see it. There was a fire in 1187, the central tower collapsed in 1861, a replica being erected, completed in 1866. Fortunately the organ escaped damage, and, in any case, the Victorians were not able to afford to replace it, unlike many of the cathedral's peers. But still much survives of Bishop Luffa's late 11th century Norman construction. This was an example of William I's policy of moving cathedrals to centres of population, in this case from small, coastal Selsey.

By way of charming, deserted old streets, which would have been full off shoppers on any other day, the cathedral immediately presented us with the Cloisters café, and the adjacent shop. Venturing in, I spotted Harvey's beer, from Lewes, the base of one of Chichester's two suffragan bishops. There was also some tempting red wine (though a sip of the communion variety was forthcoming). The menu was what you'd expect in the county town of West Sussex, a magnet for the prosperous Sussex and Hampshire population. Here the Chichester Festival Theatre was a massive, and regular, draw, its box office selling productions all round the year.

We were soon in the cathedral, where the precentor took the service and the dean treated us to a mellifluous sermon. Wakey and I were in the quire, complete with a cobweb or two, afterwards noting the entertaining misericords above which we had been seated; for him a dragon, for me a gryphon. Rand had taken up position at the back of the nave, so was in a position to enjoy the vista of tall roof and screen. In fact, he saw the dean's performance. We did not from our eastern position, but I found much opportunity for my wandering eyes. To the left was the organ, well-fitted between two massive Romanesque pillars, above the wooden quire. They all seemed of a piece. Even more in this was the triforium, and to some extent the clerestory above, benefiting from light spilt over from the body of the building. It was deep and hemispherical, surmounted by the chevrons and other geometric shapes adorning its curves.

The Triforium
A cavern below the Clerestory,
The Triforium holds many a story
Of frolics round pillars,
Anecdotes that would thrill us,
That space must be Chichester's glory.

A momentous sight was the triple tapestry on the altar screen, devised by John Piper in 1966 (with assistance from the purposeful Friends of the cathedral). A sensation of red, most of all, as well as green, yellow and white, conveyed the central images of the Trinity, centred upon a staggered, interlocking green triangle. Speaking later to Finance Director Vince Waldron, he quipped that sunglasses were needed after the altar screen was cleaned! The whole display I found to fuse gradually with the abstract Norman shapes up and over. It was a staggering thought that fragments of Roman mosaics had been discovered behind the altar on the south side, and were now on formal display. This qualified a mosaic as the icon for Chichester. At my last visit this area had been under wraps, in mid-excavation. Now, for 20p pressed into a machine slot, you could feast upon these gems. It was a small but brilliant exhibit, and, another time, just down the road, Fishbourne Roman Palace and the villa at Bignor were available for more Roman exposure. Another memory I conjured up was of a Festival of Flowers some years past, held here in June. It was stunning and I was pleased to pick up a leaflet for the 2010 edition. How about comparing the dates with the summer Chichester Festival programme for double indulgence? Another reason for a visit would be the Southern Cathedrals Festival, to be held in Chichester, a month after the flower show. However, this was most unlikely to be realized in a year committed to countrywide cathedral trips. I noted that Winchester was scheduled to host the event 2011 and Salisbury in 2012.

Cathedral policy was not to charge for admission, but to make it up on other initiatives. The collection during the service largely comprised gift aid envelopes, duly filled and inscribed. There was also the Trust, which was by then engaged upon seeking funds for the repair of the unique St Richard's Bell Tower. James Christmas, a steward, told Rand bout it. During an unusually cold, frosty winter, the medieval tower had developed a serious crack, from top to bottom. The tower was built separately outside the cathedral, a few yards to the northwest. It's something extra to enjoy, but was showing its age badly. It had been filled in temporarily, but how many years would elapse until the funding for this critical need would be raised? How did the matter fit in with the following piece? '*The*

Independent reports that English Heritage says six cathedrals – Lincoln, York, Salisbury, Canterbury, Chichester and Winchester – need to carry out major renovations in the next 10 years. The twist in the tale is that there is no money coming from English Heritage to pay for the repairs now that the body's ring-fenced fund for cathedrals had been stopped. Lincoln Cathedral has launched a public campaign to raise £2.5m to fund badly needed restoration works.' (*Arts Industry,* 21/5/10).

Engaging in conversation with stewards was most profitable. This was easy given the post-communion welcome session. Rarely, both red and white wine were offered. I was quite happy to make the contribution suggested for the former, Wakey the latter and Rand warmed himself with a cup of coffee. Steve Holloway was my mine of information, providing me with the visitor's tour sheet. Funding, again, was an issue. He confirmed they maintained resistance to charging for admission, but earn from activities, like a retiring collection at lunchtime concerts, covenanted surpluses from the catering operation which served city visitors, this being both a wealthy place and attractive for daytrips. The Cloisters ranked among the best cathedral food emporia in the country. Then there were schemes such as the Friends and stewardship. We gained a helpful picture of aspects of the running of the vast and historic enterprise that is Chichester Cathedral. Along with Portsmouth, not far west from here, it is visible from the English Channel, and similarly has nautical connections.

The Vicar's Close, hidden behind the south side, away from the business of the city, gave notice of its Prebendary School. This fed into its hosts' work. The choir that day comprised six men and 16 boys, the latter crammed into a stall for 14, so the last two had to share with the older guys behind them. The six, termed 'Lay Vicars', enjoyed grace and favour houses, but not much remuneration, so needed other day jobs, such as at the Prebendary School, and in recruitment and teaching. They created a good sound. I recalled high quality back a number of years, in a different form: a solitary trumpet engaged our senses for *Hark the Herald Angels Sing* during Midnight Mass one Christmas Eve.

The three of us embarked upon exploration. The most vivid sensory delight for me was the God the Father image on the altar tapestry within the brilliant John Piper tapestry. We entered the south aisle to be greeted by a 20th century work, by another artist also well-known for his work at Coventry; Graham Sutherland. The painting was *Noli me Tangere.* Next, behind the high altar we found the site of the Shrine of St Richard of Chichester (Bishop, 1245–53), a man associated with a fig tree. Now what we saw was an Anglo-German tapestry, 'an authenticated relic, probably St Richard's arm, which had been preserved at the abbey of La Lucerne in

Normandy, was interred beneath the altar'.

Very bold on the north side of the Lady Chapel shrine, even in this day's dullness, was the 1978 window of Marc Chagall, providing colourful impact. Like the altar tapestry the more I looked into it the better it grew; and then the Treasury: it was good to find that the cathedral could boast this, given the loss of territory in the city centre. There was fine representation from parishes of the diocese. There was a list of organists from 1545, with a compact disc of the incumbent, Sarah Baldock (since 2008), on display.

After a moment absorbing the fine view from the west end, we left the cathedral, for the crumbling Bell Tower, 'campanile'. We could do no more than perambulate it and wish the crack-filling fund pursuit well. Once in the arterial street Eastgate it was time for reflection. Having enjoyed the distant foretaste of the cathedral, Wakey found it disappointing not to have further sight of it until right by it. 'It's a very strange cathedral, hemmed in. You're not allowed to have any breathing space. We turned a corner and there it was, tucked away. But I did like the cloisters. Coming into the cathedral that way was better than the main door. I fancied myself as a young acolyte with an itchy tonsure!' Rand kept his counsel, later revealing some disappointment: 'Not enough.' We did spend a rewarding hour that evening with Vince Waldron, and his wife Francesca. Some discussion related to his job for the chapter, secular after all, managing the finance. This was crucial in a demanding old building, given its remit in the modern world. We also talked about Gwen John, the artist, and her more famous brother Augustus. We all expressed an interest in her work, currently being exhibited in London. A final shared topic was the 20th century art in the cathedral. It seemed to work among the Roman mosaics and extremely well-established stone.

Monday 1 March
The weather cleared up for our final morning. It was a lovely sunny day – still very cold but the best conditions for church-hunting. We had driven back east a few miles to Arundel Roman Catholic Cathedral, dedicated to Our Lady & St Philip Howard. Rand and I met my aunt, AD, who was set to sing Mozart's *Requiem* with her choir in this space at the end of the month. She left posters to that effect on a table at the back.

The building was a reminder of Lancing Chapel, in high-naved medieval style. The pillars here involved 12 mini-columns superimposed, for enhanced effect. On our arrival, we saw Father Malcolm King, engaged in worship with nine communicants at the St Philip Neri Chapel. I enquired about the laminated tour guides on display. I wanted to take one away. 'I tell you what: I'll go and get the secretary to take a copy.' He returned with double-sided ones. What a technically-expert secretary! We were standing at the west door, in the evocatively named Narthex (under the gallery). This had been in the diocese of Southwark for its first 100 years, being awarded its own see in 1965. The name of the diocese is Arundel and Brighton. I felt the suffix to be unnecessary. Why not add 'Hove' as well. In 1971 the dedication was also changed, from one Philip for another, Neri (the 'Apostle of Rome', 1515–95) being dumped in favour of Howard, whose remains had been transferred from Arundel castle down the road. That made some sense, I admit.

Much cleaning of corners had been completed, noted AD. Father Malcolm confirmed that this as 1996. AD also reckoned the paraffin heaters and sea air contributed to the murkiness. The building certainly faced the elements, though it would always be upstaged by the stunning Arundel Castle, in a dramatic skyline, which confronts travellers from the east. The small town is full of impact, and the Fitzalan Howards. St Philip was one, as was the commissioner, acknowledged in a plaque from the benefactors' daughters as follows: 'To the memory of Henry 15th Duke of Norfolk 1847–1917, who founded this Cathedral in 1868, and of Gwendolyn Duchess 1877–1945. May they rest in peace.' This plaque was given by their daughters. The shrine lay in the north transept – wrought iron with a design appropriately 'based on a representation of chains, the crossed palms of martyrdom and the 'crosslets fitchee' taken from the Howard arms. It was impressive, as was St Philip's statue complete with dog (no cat here – no nooks and crannies, nor rodents). The hound was reported as having stayed with him faithfully during his imprisonment in 1585. Condemned to death, 'he languished in his cell until the rigours of prison life led to his death six years later'.

After further observation we enjoyed the sunny weather on the way down to the rival church: the part-Roman Catholic St Nicholas Parish Church. Firmly, it sports the 'h'. Dating back to Saxon times, the earliest of what survives is post Black Death (1349), officially dated 1380. There are murals extant on the north wall, depicting Seven Works of Mercy and the Seven Deadly Sins. More dramatic and bright were the encaustic tiles. 'Unmistakably Minton,' said Rand from his time in the Potteries. It had been introduced in the chancel along with Sir Gilbert Scott's restoration of 1874. The Roman Catholic half (actually more than 50% of the total length, though it doesn't look it) was only accessible from the castle, as it is very much a Howardian attachment. Through the opaque and very solid screen, we did observe the wooden fan vaulting all along the roof, for me a welcome first. Another new sight was the space built into the north-west corner of the Anglican church, complete with two male staff, coffee cups and accoutrements of an office. Quite useful, I thought. There was further fan vaulting in the Fitzalan, for which read Lady, Chapel.

We noted the stone pulpit, carved and venerable, and the font, of Sussex marble. Octagonal, it was most striking and thought to be the oldest relic in the building. Like the RC cathedral, St Nicholas was suitable for concerts given the layout and bare tiled floor, which was rescued from the carpet, which had covered it until the arrival of new vicar Revd Keith Richards in 1997. The church would now appear to present itself in the best possible light.

AD told us of the changes outside the building – she was to return with a friend to see the new structure in the garden, topped with a shiny gilt weather vane. We sauntered down the steep hill opposite the castle to a café for welcome refreshment. Then Rand and I departed, elated I'm sure, and drained after so many exposures to the heritage of this part of the South East.

Let's finish with a small bulletin from mid-October: the Rt Revd Kieran Conry, Bishop of Arundel and Brighton, condemned the ghoulish costumes chosen by children at Halloween. They should dress up as saints instead. He wanted 31 October to be reclaimed as a Christian celebration.

10

Southwark

St Saviour & St Mary Overie

Province: Canterbury
Founded: 1106 Augustinian priory of St Mary Overie
Present building: 13th century following fire
Building changes: Much restored; Lady Chapel demolished 1830 for London Bridge
Cathedral status: 1905, from Rochester diocese; originally part of Winchester

Website: www.southwark.anglican.org
Tel: 0207 407 5740
Email: cathedral@southwark.anglican.org
Address: Southwark Cathedral, London Bridge, London SE1 9DA

Three to See: 13th century retrochoir;
John Gower's tomb, with the poet's head resting on books;
excellent extension including fine café

Goose

Tuesday 9 March, 2010

The awesome presence of the bishops of Winchester still pervades at Southwark. It was only in 1905 that this territory, haphazardly grasping at south London, over north Surrey with bits of Kent and East Sussex, was consigned to the new see. I found my friend Nicky Sloane reading a biography of Beatrix Potter in the churchyard, in view of an unidentified shapeless heap, a sculpture in the direction of the omnipresent, in this bustling area of the Borough and London Bridge. The heap made a fine photograph, complete with a worker in warning yellow, eating his sandwiches on a bench behind. The sculpture was a pale stone item suggesting a rarely-found geometric phenomenon. The other thing to see outside was a more traditional memorial to George Gwilt, architect, who died on 27 June 1806.

I later unearthed information from the cathedral's website about the heap, which was put in place in 2006. It was a five tonne sculpture, commissioned from Peter Randall-Page, a memorial to the Mohegan tribal chieftain Mahomet Weyonomon, buried in the churchyard in 1736. 'It is in the form of a boulder made from pink granite, taken from the New England reserve of the Mohegan tribe.'

We paused to note what passed for a churchyard garden. London Bridge and its station network breathed down the cathedral's tower, or neck, having benefitted from a change of purpose of part of its former territory. Entering by the south door, it was suggested, gently, that we make a contribution of £4 (mandatory for groups). A photo permit would cost £2, obtainable from the shop, whither we were bound, along with the café, in anticipation of the main event, a recital in the nave.

Nicky bought Mothering cards, as that Sunday was imminent; I was tempted by the appealing range of Easter eggs, Kashmiri and by Gisela Graham. The shop had been a Millennium commission project and served its purpose well, in, perhaps, an octagonal shape. Modern Perpendicular. Round the corner was the Refectory, which immediately merited a place near the top of the cathedral list, most likely even after they were also sampled, way into the future. A barrelled ceiling set the tone for an elegant space, with quite a few covers on a variety of sizes of table. Nicky, in the acting profession herself, noticed the acoustics, suggesting the vaulting helped to reduce echo. The profusion of pictures of New Zealand (£195) on the walls may have made a difference, too, but now we're getting technical. The tea was £1.60, shortbread £1 (an afterthought) and sausages and mash £7. The hot food looked luscious. I would have tried the bean casserole if I didn't have a repast to look forward to that evening. Anyway, it was a busy, mellow, mottled space. I refer now to the whole extension abutting the north side of the cathedral.

Next was the recital: piano (Johannes Mnich) and mezzo-soprano (Mareike Braun), delivering nine widely-ranging pieces from Handel to Britten, whose 'Recitativ and Aria' was interrupted when Johannes failed to turn the page quickly enough. 'Wait,' said Mareike, *sotto voce* (we were close enough to hear the command), meaning the cue to restart: the word 'Wait' was on the sheet we'd been given; a good thing for the dozen of us scattered around the nave that it was the one item in English. The previous nave had been demolished in 1838, and the current one completed in 1897 in medieval style by Sir Arthur Blomfield. The entertainment suited it well, an excellent three quarters of an hour of Teutonic choices, during which it was possible to become immersed in the beauty of the setting – a sea of stone: a sultry statue of John Gower, who died in 1408, his head resting upon three of his books, in the north aisle; the varied column and frieze design towards the north transept, pillar within pillar, giving an intriguing lighting effect. Below, in a job lot with the modern chairs in a comfortable choice of wood, were uniform kneelers in a bright geometric design. It could have been Romanesque in another building. Above apparently extended an open-mouthed gargoyle. On close examination it turned out to be a boss with part broken off. Gargoyles are outside buildings, carrying water. The two bosses together did provide welcome relief at the entrance to the quire.

Later I saw another attractive cathedral event advertised: *The Southwark Mysteries* (22/4/10) billed as a 'new production of John Constable's work inspired by the history of Bankside and medieval mystery plays, £20, returns only Tube: London Bridge'.

This duo performance had a mellowing effect, we agreed, as we toured the cathedral, bumping into the volunteer day chaplain, Ken Woodhouse, first passing the tabby cat, reclining on a heating vent. He didn't know its name. 'Transept' I reckoned. 'He lives in the cellar – knows where the heat is' opined Ken. I later gleaned much more information on this from the magazine *Featuring Felines:*

> *Between Christmas and New Year of 2008 a tabby cat turned up unexpectedly at Southwark Cathedral, near London Bridge on the south bank of the river Thames, looking for some food and warmth. This seemed like a heaven-sent opportunity, because for some time there had been a growing problem with increasing numbers of church mice in and around the building, and members of the cathedral staff had been actively considering taking on a cat. Just at the right moment, as enquiries were going to be initiated — one appeared! As the doors were being opened one cold*

morning he appeared from beneath a bush near the main doors, and made it quite clear he would be pleased to "make friends". It was at first thought that he belonged to one of the nearby residents; but as time went on and he appeared each morning to greet the vergers, it seemed he had adopted the churchyard as his new home. As a result he is now fed regularly by the vergers and, although not baptised, has been given the splendid name of "Doorkins Magnificat" — because he hangs around the door in the mornings waiting for them to arrive and let him in. He has an uncanny sense of timing and is there without fail each morning, awaiting his breakfast ("Felix" brand is a favourite, as is "Sheba"!). If he is particularly hungry he will wait by the door again for something further to eat in the evening, when the cathedral is locked up, but not every day. Regular donations of food are made and so he always has plenty available, and parishioners and visitors frequently enquire after him. Doorkins seems at home now within the cathedral community, loves to lie on the grass in the churchyard when it's warm enough, and enjoys the attention of office workers who come to eat their lunch on the green space. At the moment he finds the hustle and bustle of visitors inside the cathedral a bit daunting, so "prefers to say his prayers in the morning, when there are fewer visitors around", says head verger Paul Timms. It turns out that Doorkins is not unknown in the slightly wider community, and spends some time at the nearby Borough Market, where he has been seen hunting mice. At night he currently sleeps — if he is not outside — at the foot of the stairs to the cathedral boiler-house, but it is hoped he can be encouraged to spend more time indoors as the colder winter nights approach. Failing that, a small hole will be cut in the boiler-house door and a cat-bed placed inside, so that he can be snug and warm in winter.

I am grateful to author Patrick Roberts for this. Hats off to Doorkins to his status as a rare cathedral cat in 2010, especially as a working animal. Watch out, you rodents!

Further on we found a sad cathedral model lacking a turret or two. The retrochoir was notable, however, and suitably described as 'superb in design and quality' and the erstwhile Consistory (ecclesiastical) Court – for the medieval bishops of Winchester, who came into their own here during Bloody Mary's purging of Protestants. In 1555, the Bishops of Gloucester and St Davids were consigned from the court to the stake. We bumped into

Ken again, this time with a cup of tea, for a vagrant, loping round the nether parts of the building. Ken adopted a paternal manner. We had observed signs alerting us to the alarmed antique chests, one of which was briefly occupied by the plastic cup. The man was diverted into a huddle by the chaplain. And one more thing we noted: a model of the area, covering the extensive territory of the see. There was a lot going on in this busy square of the map.

Next for us was the separated Harvard Chapel, where the famed college founder lay, baptised here in 1607, and in the north transept a memorial to Oscar Hammerstein 'playwright and lyricist'. Nicky had sung his works before now. It was surprising to read his lifespan: 1896–1960. He died so long ago! That production of *Oklahoma!* at Chichester Festival Theatre in 2009 was yet fresh in my mind: traditional composition, but still entertaining. On the subject of musicals, the most recent time I'd seen my companion on stage was very close to this, at the Menier Chocolate Factory, in Sondheim's *A Little Night Music*. A fine evening, preluded by a trip to a local eatery, Wagamama.

Something impressive from 1674 alerted us in the north transept: a red, black and gold sword rest, secured by a lion's head. So English! We now managed a direct chat with Ken. In answer to my question, he said that around March was the best time of year to visit: 'In the summer you're pressed by the crowd all the time,' he said, adding that such needs as we had observed being catered for was a substantial part of the work of the day chaplains. He was immediately diverted at the behest of a woman in distress, previously praying in the Harvard Chapel. In advance of this visit, I had failed to tie down anyone in authority at the cathedral to speak to, in particular the dean, normally the most appropriate interviewee for the purposes of this undertaking. Unfortunately it was never to be, as the incumbent, the Very Revd Colin Slee, OBE, died eight months later, from pancreatic cancer. Giles Fraser, Canon Chancellor of St Paul's Cathedral, writing in the *Church Times,* amplified the most eloquent obituary, elsewhere in the edition, in recounting a couple of stories about him which told a great deal about the much loved, and admired, man.

My favourite Colin Slee story involves his campaign against the swingers' sex club that opened just a few yards from Southwark Cathedral. In his office, Colin had rows of box files marked "Club Wicked". He was gathering the evidence that he needed to close the place down – which is what he eventually did… In the course of this campaign, he hired a couple of private investigators to go into the club one night and record what they saw. That particular evening had a costume theme. To those who frequented "Club

Wicked", that meant leather and rubber bondage gear. But the private investigators thought it meant fancy dress. They turned up as two of the three Musketeers. I would often tease him about this... At the lunchtime Eucharist on the day he died, a few hundred people turned up at the Cathedral to mourn his loss. Some went to the pub afterwards. "He made the church a colder place, he made the church a warmer place," one priest commented with a smile. Why colder? Because he was always trying to save money in the cash-strapped cathedral by turning off the heating. Why warmer? That is easy. His was a gospel of welcome and inclusion for all.

We meandered on. The plaque listing those running the show had priors in the transmogrification from Allgood (1106–30) to the first bishop, Edward Talbot (1905–11). Mervyn Stockwood (1959–80) was there, standing out like his reputation. I recalled his prominence in the news during his tenure. It is worth quoting parts of his obituary, from *The Independent* this time:

Stockwood was born in 1913, the younger son of a solicitor killed on the Somme when Mervyn was three. That same year, 1917, the family moved to Bristol, and it was there, at All Saints', Clifton, later destroyed in the Second World War, that Mervyn discovered the liturgical delights of Anglo-Catholicism, and where he was later to spend 19 years as curate... He served as a Labour councillor both in Bristol and Cambridge, and in Bristol he established the first health clinic in the country. Being unorthodox to his fingertips, he managed however to get expelled from the Labour Party no fewer than three times...

In many respects a prophet, he created in his diocese of Southwark visionary enterprises now regarded as commonplace, and during two decades he attracted to inner-city areas south of the Thames some of the most able clergy available. His name became synonymous with South Bank Religion (synonymous with radical theology and public controversy. Its most famous expression was the book Honest to God (1963) by John Robinson, whom he had appointed as his suffragan at Woolwich in 1959. Another controversial work was No New Morality (1964) by Douglas Rhymes, a gay priest on the staff of Southwark Cathedral, which questioned the traditional view that Christian morality was based upon absolute laws. Mervyn Stockwood was a celibate gay bishop. Within the Church of England he was liberal in his view of the morality of homosexual behaviour. He spoke in favour of homosexual law reform, included gay couples among the guests at his dinner and on at least one occasion blessed a gay relationship…

The diocese had no endowment, yet Stockwood raised the stipends of all his clergy, and Southwark was the first diocese in which parishes were encouraged to produce from among their congregation their own incumbent…

While he often looked with indulgence on some sexual lapse, what he could never tolerate was idleness. He once had occasion to discipline a lazy clergyman, who said to him, "You are only treating me like this because I am black." "Indeed I am," said Stockwood. "If you were white I should have deprived you of your living"…

His capacity for alcohol was prodigious, but it never impaired his mental facilities; the more wine he drank, the sharper his memory became.

Arthur Mervyn Stockwood, priest: born Bridgend, Glamorgan 27 May 1913; ordained deacon 1936, priest 1937; Assistant Curate, St Matthew, Moorfields 1936–41, Vicar 1941–55; Vicar, Great St Mary's, Cambridge 1955–59; Bishop of Southwark 1959–80; died Bath 13 January 1995.

Southwark has indeed been associated, or blessed, with some potent forces.

At the front (southwest) door reclined a substantial horizontal floor memorial to those who sank in the motor vessel, the Marchioness, which sank at Southwark Bridge on 20 August 1989. The 51 victims ranged in age from 19 to 46, most of them in their 20s. It was telling to recall that awful incident.

The *Spiritual Tour*, a leaflet we picked up, carried a poem by John Dryden (1631–1700):

The Angels
The trumpet
Shall be heard on high,
The dead shall live,
The living die,
And music shall untune the sky.

This is from his *Song for St Cecilia's Day* (Handel penned a work by that name, too, in 1739) and seems apposite enough for this place. Cecilia is the patron saint of musicians. There was certainly noise here – regular activity involving the world outside – and there were two choirs: the Main Cathedral Choir and the Merbecke Choir, no school as such, but a profusion of choral endeavour – six choir lay clerks and up to six choral scholars, plus a wide range of recruits from the area, with bodies such as the Vernon Ellis Foundation to support the activity.

This Southwark is a district abounding in life, as electric as ever. Going back in time, down the road was Clink Prison, one of seven thereabouts, giving rise to the vernacular expression. It was owned by the supreme bishops of Winchester – witness the striking residual arch in the eponymous House. The area was beyond the limits of the City of London, and through its immunity able to spawn theatre venture. Think of William Shakespeare and the Globe Playhouse. There is a Shakespeare statue in the cathedral, actually for his brother Edmund, buried there in 1607. There is also a 19th century stained glass window depicting every play. The church of St Mary Overie, as it was at that time, became a place of sanctuary, that is, an escape from authority. The Winchester Geese, the prostitutes in a ghetto of licentiousness, took full advantage, and so shall I in attaching such a goose as the emblem for the cathedral. There is more: 'Stewed prunes' were 'London brothels where customers "stewed" in hot water, creating prune like wrinkles in their fingertips,' (*Forgotten English* by Jeffrey Kacirk). After all, the market is nearby and any number of carnal and bodily needs are still satisfied in this crammed corner: Vinopolis, restaurants and pubs and everyone disgorged from London Bridge station. It is also notable for the motley crew emanating from the George Tavern to embark upon a pilgrimage, which, just for a start, led to the cathedrals at Rochester, then Canterbury. There is, in any case, a proliferation of cathedrals in the borough: St George's (RC) and St Mary's (Greek Orthodox).

And then there is literature: Geoffrey Chaucer entertained me in the Middle English class with *The Canterbury Tales* (and *Troilus and Criseyde*, another ripping yarn). It all started in the Tabard of medieval 'Southwerk' as the author spelt it, to culminate in 'Caunterbury'. He embarked upon the Tales in 1388. Along with the George (formerly with his Dragon) the Tabard was consumed in the serious Southwark fire in 1676, ten years after the Great Fire of London, over the Thames, which destroyed Old St Paul's. The difference is that while both taverns were rebuilt, only the George survives, as the sole coaching inn in the capital with a gallery. It became a National Trust property, and a hotspot for trippers and imbibers. The Tabard was lost to the world in the late 19th century. *The Canterbury Tales* live on replete with yarn-spinning and character-development. It was good to study, the Middle English of the poet being comparatively accessible.

After the recital, Nicky and I wandered round the building and westwards along the South Bank, as much as we could, given extensive road works, and reached that other cathedral of the area, the National Theatre. She was unlucky in her attempt to obtain tickets for Dion Boucicault's *London Assurance*, a terrific production (I saw it later on) with Simon Russell Beale (Sir Harcourt Courtly) and Fiona Shaw (as Lady Gay Spanker – what a name for a part, very 'Restoration' for a work gracing the stage in 1841). It was good to be able to persuade Simon to join the tour of St Paul's a few months later. The attraction we did achieve within the environs of the National ('Nash' to some) was the designs of Alison Chitty, which I was pleased to note included *Fanshen*, which she designed for the Victoria Theatre, Stoke-on-Trent in the 1970s.

Southwark looks to the river, the delightful but touristic waterside, but operates to the south. The reverse is true of St Paul's, which was to remain a carrot for many months. For the while the memory of the former sanctuary of Southwark was fine by me. In *The Time Traveller's Guide to Medieval England*, Ian Mortimer recommended 'Ten Places to See in London'. This was in the 14th century. Here is no 10: 'The Southwark Stews or bath houses are a tourist attraction of an altogether different sort (from London Bridge, St Paul's Cathedral, The Royal Palace in the Tower of London, or even Tyburn, where Roger Mortimer, Edward II's assassin, was executed in 1330, his naked body being left on the gallows for two days).' He relates the character of this part of the Diocese of Winchester in detail. I think it a good way to leave the subject of Southwark Cathedral:

> *Prostitutes are not tolerated in London except in one street, Cock Lane. Hence Londoners and visitors resort to the stews of Southwark, on the other side of the river. Here men may eat and drink, have a hot scented bath and spend time in female company. In 1374 there are eighteen establishments, all run by Flemish women. Contrary to what you might expect, there is little or no stigma attached to those who frequent the stews; there are few sexually contracted diseases and the marriage vows only require fidelity of the female partner; the man may do as he pleases. Some clergymen rail against such immorality, of course; but few directly allude to Southwark. Most of the bath houses are rented from the bishop of Winchester.*

Winchester itself was a world away, eventually to become the setting for the closure of this project, though at the time of this visit that was a long way ahead both in thinking and planning.

Fig 14

Fig 15

[14] Southwark: Peter Randall-Page sculpture and
Borough Market luncher.
[15] Sheffield: Stainless steel swords along east side of
St George's Chapel.
[16] Truro: The font made mainly of north African red
marble, with a brooding canopy.

Fig 16

11

Sheffield

St Peter & St Paul

Province: York
Founded: 15th century parish church
Building: 1880 rebuilding, 1919 enlargement
Cathedral status: 1914 – from York diocese

Website: www.sheffieldcathedral.org
Tel: 0114 275 3434
Email: enquiries@sheffield-cathedral.org.uk
Address: The Cathedral Church of St Peter and St Paul, Sheffield Cathedral, Church Street, Sheffield S1 1HA

Three to See: 15th century roof with angel bosses; St George's Chapel with figurehead and swords; modern lantern tower

Sword

Saturday 13 March, 2010

The first impression was of space, feeling like a city centre location with trams and buses immediately outside, and an open view of the amorphous shape of the cathedral from the south. On this visit, we mounted downtown Sheffield from the station with a number of obviously serious edifices on the way. You couldn't miss a recent addition, the Wheel of Sheffield, nowadays a common provision in many a major city, for the paying public to enjoy an aerial view, while in motion. They also serve as an extra landmark. It's an honest place with no frills, i.e. what you see is what you get. That includes the cathedral. The entrance door is of clear glass, affording a view of the multi-layered space inside to anyone wishing to peep in. The view through suggested the potential drama, should the decision be made to enter: chapels, a variety of styles and different angles. And the roof had grown into an eyeful of interest.

Outside, James Montgomery (1771–1854) provides the solitary piece of display – his statue greets you beyond the east end, whose window provides an interior monument to him. A Scotsman from Irvine, Ayrshire, he settled in Sheffield, becoming renowned for his hymn writing: 'One central creative thought, shaping for itself melodious utterance, and with every detail subordinate to its harmonious presentation.' He was also a prolific poet, including one volume, much of which denounced the practice of slavery. Once, in reply to the question as to which of his poems would live, he said: 'None, sir, nothing except perhaps a few of my hymns.' In his later years, he occupied himself with the promotion of philanthropic and religious movements, earning the almost universal esteem of the citizens of Sheffield. He was given a public funeral and remains a famous son of the city; hence the statue and panel of glass.

We turn from the cathedral's celebrity to celebrate the building itself. The eastern part is the oldest element. With its several chapels and elegant roof, topped off with shiny modern angels as bosses, it is a light, open space. You notice the stained glass, which is effective, in broad Perpendicular style. The choir stalls provided no kneelers, nor hooks, an honest reflection of what nearly every worshipper does – they sit. That's what all the ten communicants did at our 10.30 am Eucharist, using the book of Common Worship. It was a most efficient half hour's worth, during which I was able to admire the detail of the chapels and dramatic use of arches from St Catherine's Chapel through to the east end. I suffered an unfortunate 'first' – being ignored by the priest as I was forced to start a new row, there being no space after the nine others had placed themselves at the rail (kneeling essential for this). One of the nine communicated dismay on my behalf. She, it transpired, was Liz Arnesen, the wife of Paul, in orders, courtesy of a bishop's licence. The other official, with the wine, was a verger. This was a significant role for him in tending to the personal, and psychological, needs of parishioners.

Let's mention a key staff member: the Dean, the Very Revd Peter Bradley. In this role at Sheffield, he spent much of his time developing new relationships with business and community leaders, in pastoral care and evangelism. He was the senior priest at the Bishop's Church, this cathedral, leading the team of clergy and lay people who share in the mission of the Cathedral 'to know, love and serve our Lord Jesus Christ, and so become true witnesses to God's kingdom, and a place for all people'. There you have it. A chat ensued with Paul and Liz about practices in the cathedral. There was a Russian Orthodox service in the crypt following hard on from our communion. On Mondays there was a meditation session with Buddhists.

And now a piece about the Bishop, the Rt Revd Steven Croft: 'Singer Lily Allen was once described by David Cameron as unsuitable listening for his six-year-old daughter. Now, one of her songs has been suggested as ideal for churchgoers preparing for Easter. The Fear – or at least the radio-friendly version without the expletives – is recommended as a scene-setter before Bible study for groups on a new Lenten course entitled Exploring God's Mercy. The Bishop of Sheffield, who drew up the five-week course, said the 25-year-old's song captured a "certain spirit" of contemporary culture with its theme of materialism. He added: "There is the kind of mindset expressed to which I think the Christian gospel has a great deal to say."' (*Metro*, 25/1/11).

This was also a Grade I listed building, one of five in the city (the others include the impressive Town Hall and two parish churches). Liz had sung in various cathedrals. She nominated Peterborough as the best acoustically, along with Guildford, which I had already heard from guitarist Jon. From Liz we heard about the cathedral's lively music department, providing choir members – men, boys and girls.

The cathedral lacked a choir school and a café most of the time. The latter was open, in an extension on the north side, for breakfast for the homeless every morning and the public at weekday lunchtimes. At the time we were told of the aim to extend this, and also provide a shop. At the next visit the cathedral offered a shop but no catering. Something to be kept on the agenda, perhaps. It simply bore out the impression that this is a city cathedral, geared constructively to the needs of the people, not only established members of the church. Perhaps there is no space for further outreach – abroad for instance – when there is so much to do in South Yorkshire. The Friends here provided an interface – a good word from Liz – with the community. They served to fund essentials; next in line were flooring and heating. The project for a new organ, hopefully to be supplied by top Swiss organ builders, Kuhn, had in effect been suspended as a lower priority. There were concerts, events and the essential involvement of local business.

Now for the history: the diocese of Sheffield was carved out of that of York in 1914. Up to then it had come under the care of the archbishop. From 1901 to 1914 John Quirk had been the Bishop Suffragan of Sheffield. Since then there had been seven bishops. Provosts were appointed up to 2000, to be succeeded by deans, following the practice elsewhere. Going back in time, at Sheffield there are stones which date back to the 11th and 12th centuries. 'With their dog tooth pattern, (they) can be seen set in the east wall,' stated the guide. The 15th century parish church was duly elevated to cathedral status, the borough having been made a city in 1893. There has been considerable extension and change, in fact improvement, in the building since then, partly in tandem with the progress of the city and region.

Wakey liked the 'untraditional layout' of the cathedral. The style involved different levels and directions, with the Chapel of St George facing you on entry from the south, itself above the crypt. Beyond it, and below, on a half-landing, is the Chapel of the Holy Spirit, for me a modern Arthurian-style space including a seductive blue in the decoration, and pale wood. It faces north. There is more exciting stained glass there, by Christopher Webb (1940), 'a celebration of the Church on earth and in heaven'. On the way there past St George's Chapel, first you happen upon a figurehead on the brow of a ship. You quickly realize that this refers to HMS Sheffield, famed for Falklands War exploits. Forming a division from the passage/aisle on the east side of the chapel is a subtle display of swords and bayonets. It is this that suggests the sword as emblem for the cathedral. It's 'so Sheffield' in its reference to local industry and the many generations of citizens who have worked in steel; also symptomatic of the brave developments in building enhancement in pursuit of fitness for purpose. A further evocative image is on the other side – a stained glass polar bear in memory of victims of the Second World War.

Overhead, between St George's Chapel and the front door, was the comparatively recent addition – the Lantern Tower, high above, which I only caught sight of and examined as the last delight before leaving, as a sort of culmination of the multi-faceted features of this, almost, new build. The *Brief Guide* stated 'typifying the crown of thorns, coming down into the cathedral… the glass (1998) by Amber Hiscott is an abstract interpretation of how resurrection and the Holy Spirit (golds and reds) transforming human conflict and struggles (blues and violets) and leading to healing and growth (greens)'. I couldn't put it better myself! This was truly a civic amenity. But had we attended a service on Sunday morning, we might have witnessed, even joined, the breakfast initiative, which served for a while to bring communities together in Sheffield. No matter that we weren't able to try their tea and cake. There were pubs of high merit nearby. The Wig and Pen had served Wakey years before. Both of us rated the Kelham Island Tavern, CAMRA pub of the Year in 2009. Round the corner were the entertaining duo, the Crucible and Lyceum Theatres. World Snooker would be on offer in the former a month hence, and high quality acting throughout the year. Sheffield was, after all, one of our eight major cities, comprising the English Core Cities Group. No matter that its cathedral's origins are humble. It is unique and, above all, suitable.

So we ventured, on a fast train, into the diocese of Derby, a handful of miles away and ten minutes by train, to Chesterfield Parish Church (CPC), primarily for a football game. That twisted spire provides a shock on a first viewing, topping the hill upon which the town perches, and clearly visible from road and rail. It is referred to as the 'Parish Church', rather more than its dedication 'St Mary and All Saints'. Tours were scheduled for 11.30 am and 2.30 pm (£3.50 adults, £1.50 children) – we had just missed one. The facts:

The spire was added to the 14th century tower about the year 1362. The structure is an oak frame, clad with lead, and an interior view of the timber frame is one of the most remarkable sights in the whole church. Where the top of the stone tower and base of the wooden spire meet no fixing is apparent, so that the spire merely sits balanced unattached on the top of the tower. It rises to a height of 70m (228') above the ground and leans 2.89m (9' 6") to the south-west and it is important to distinguish two elements in the spire's "crookedness": the inclination and the twist. The inclination (lean) is due to a number of factors: the use of unseasoned (green) timber, the absence of skilled craftsmen (Black Death) and the neglect of cross-bracing. The spiral twist is considered to be by design. The use of "green timber" was a normal part of medieval carpentry, owing to the fact that it could be bent and shaped during construction. It was also less wearing on tools.

It is the highest lead spire in England.

Next door to the Rutland Arms (on the visit, good for both beer and food) you could actually go for what Sheffield Cathedral lacks: the 'café over the churchyard' as the shop-keeper at the back of the church informed us. The shop was splendid, selling everything for Mothering Sunday (the next day) except shot glasses, which Wakey always wanted, rather than a tea towel, of which there were plenty. The 'Saints Parish Centre', aka

'Saints Coffee Room', was very busy and full of tempting snacks. It was cheap, too. We were bound for something else in the town centre mishmash of the age-old Shambles: pints of local ale (Brampton and Peak breweries) in the Rose and Crown with friends Mickey G and Dick, who were joining us for Chesterfield vs. Port Vale, a bottom division Football League fixture.

Wandering round the church, its purposefulness was striking. Gift aid envelopes sat on each pew and there were families with prams viewing. Unlike Sheffield Cathedral, CPC was traditional and very dark – a Jacobean look pervaded from pulpit (c.1620 and possibly carved by the same team who did the work on the Long Gallery at nearby Haddon Hall) to choir stalls. Haddon Hall was well worth the visit a couple of years before. The font, which was obscure and easily passed by, was found in the south transept, which was fine as there was little room anywhere near the south west entrance, with screen, tables deep in leaflets and paperwork, and the shop occupying considerable space on the north side. Back to the east end, there were a number of impressive tombs, for the Foljambe family, the earliest dating from 1510.

The Friends organization was prominent, established in 1942, the membership fee currently £5. In 2000 it had paid for the re-gilding of one of the clock faces (with its case, like everything there, brooding and impressive) and two years later financed security door refurbishment.

In both places, indeed, we were blessed with a fine day, the first one of those in the eleven cathedral visits in this quest. It repeated the weather on offer when my old friend, the Mine, and I made an initial visit to Sheffield in April 1971, from the deepest south of England, similarly connecting cathedral with soccer. So, the sun always shines hereabouts, does it? It certainly helped, in both these contrasting churches. CPC would have been even darker otherwise. The cathedral's pale pillars were uplifting, connecting the various bits of St Peter and St Paul in a mass of interconnected fresh spaces. Would it have come across like that had it been raining as at Guildford, or snowing as at Worcester?

We were on to a winner, that day, in every respect: fine experiences in two church buildings, an excellent bap from Linda's Sandwich Shop on the corner of Saltergate, the moribund football ground, and a result we couldn't have anticipated: Chesterfield 0, Port Vale 5. I have harboured a quiet leaning towards the Vale, having lived in the Potteries. The football ground, 139 years old, believe it or not, hadn't weathered nearly as well as the much older church. After all, Saltergate was constructed of corrugated iron and cheap materials. Weather beaten and wonderful! And it sported an aspect of the brooding Peaks of Derbyshire.

Wakey had happened upon a flyer in the cathedral advertising a performance of Rossini's *Petite Messe Solennelle* by the Sterndale Singers, plus soloists, at the Roman Catholic Cathedral of St Marie. So it was that we enjoyed a nocturnal cathedral visit, of a contrasting persuasion. The building, serving the Diocese of Hallam (carved out of the see of Leeds in 1980), was consistent with others of the ilk. We were able to wander with glasses of red wine in the interval. Built between 1847 and 1850, it did hark back to Edward the Confessor in the south aisle windows, and the west window was by the inestimable Mr Pugin.

The day seemed complete with a pint of Thornbridge ale, a must at the station. This feast of exposure drew on many senses, and had proved quite exhausting. While on the subject of ale, please give some attention to the Blue Ball pub on the outskirts of Sheffield. The 150-year-old tradition of carols in the bar has long attracted both locals and visitors from all over the country. Most of these are not from the usual repertoire, but come from a 20-mile radius with some from all over the country. Sets of words tend to be a lot older than the tunes. People choose tunes they love, with words they like. They are more rumbustious than the 19th century model of carols (inception from the new Truro Cathedral in the 1870s), which prevails. The Victorians considered it decadent to be having fun and enjoying yourself.

Life
Ah, the beauty of life should not hide,
From those we love, cherish or even hate.
At times we must strain against the tide.
    Through Winter's long tears and Summer's short slide,
At Spring's bursting and Autumn's spate.
Ah, the beauty of life should not hide.
    Racing along life's rollicking ride,
Yielding passions and prowess, minor or great,
At times we must strain against the tide.
    We know our joys are bruised by Pride.
Let it not keep us captives of Fate.
Ah, the beauty of life should not hide.
    Wondrous heights toiled and goals we tried.
Constrained not by deeds or date.
At times we must strain against the tide.
    To nourish hopes that have not died,
Let all learn lessons not too late.
Ah, the beauty of life should not hide.
At times we must strain against the tide.

Mick Ward

12

Truro

St Mary

Province: Canterbury
Founded: 1876 diocese created from Exeter
Present building: 1880–1910, 1965 chapter hall

Website: www.trurocathedral.org.uk
Tel: 01872 276782
Email: colin@trurocathedral.org.uk
Address: 14 St Mary's Street, Truro TR1 2AF

Three to see: The tall, dark font;
St Mary's aisle, what remains of the original church;
Tinworth panel in terra cotta

Jerusalem artichoke

Palm Sunday 28 March, 2010

The ingredients were right: foul weather for a newish cathedral hemmed within its urban constrictions and the tail end of a liturgy to preclude our entrance on arrival. Thanks to Graham's disabled card we were able to park on the adjacent street and join a patient bunch of non-worshippers behind the glass west doors. It was a magical beginning, being drawn into the spirit of the cathedral at work on Palm Sunday through the vocal soarings up to the roof. The Director of Music (Christopher Gray) had, by all accounts, produced a splendid structure of choral activity. I can believe it from this evidence. There were scheduled Sung Eucharist services, 'sung by the Gentlemen of the Choir'. I'd like to witness one of those. (The website also provided a Virtual Tour, whisking the viewer all around the building). What we heard of the organ was impressive: a claim was made that the cathedral's Willis organ was one of the finest in the country. This is the opportunity to note that the format of nine lessons and nine carols was based on an Order drawn up by Edward White Benson, later Archbishop of Canterbury, but at that time Bishop of Truro, for use on Christmas Eve, 1880. That was early in the career of the diocese, created in 1876. The Cornwall Youth Choir, with roots in wassailing, used to start out from the cathedral, for carols in the street. Lesson readers started with choristers and ended with Bishop Benson himself. Even Baptists and Methodists joined the congregation to enjoy the Christmas carols, aided by Truro Cathedral Choir. From then on you could hear them more or less anywhere. Tradition says that the bishop organized the service at 10 pm to get men out of pubs in the last hours before Christmas Day, initially in a temporary wooden shed, which served as his cathedral. Through the new service he wanted to show the process towards redemption.

The comparison is made of Truro with Lincoln Cathedral. The architect John Loughborough Pearson, a leading light of the 19th century Gothic Revival, worked at Lincoln before being engaged at Truro. The building is Early English with some Gallic overtones – the spires and rose windows (Pearson had spent some time in Paris). Sarah Smith, a friend of mine who lived in Cornwall's county town for a number of years, had no compunction in choosing St Mary's as her favourite, one of the main influences being the way it dominated the city in an appealing way, as a contrast to Chichester, for example, which is lost in its city's buildings. Sarah also thought there to be a presence of ley lines in the area, but could find no evidence. Very much in evidence was the model of the cathedral that Christmas time, brightly illuminated at the city's Trafalgar roundabout. Newspapers carried photographs of this phenomenon, with the model in the foreground, and the real thing, also lit up, in the distance.

Now for a history lesson: going back to the 10ᵗʰ century, Cornwall had a joint diocese with Crediton. It lay at St Germans, near Saltash, near the Devon border. Crediton was succeeded by Exeter in 1050, which then spent 800 years in charge of Devon and Cornwall. During the 19ᵗʰ century, a period of great ecclesiastical change, new dioceses were created up and down the country, to reflect changed needs and much building restoration was undertaken. The choice of Truro as the centre of the diocese for Cornwall followed a considerable debate, rivalry coming from the old St Germans, St Columb (on the spine of Cornwall) and Bodmin, which boasted an ancient pedigree as a religious hub. Truro was given the nod by statute in 1876.

In this comparatively new build, we joined the coffee session in the north transept and were able to engage in dialogue with several people involved in the cathedral and diocese. One was the Canon Missioner, Philip Lambert, formerly of Curry Rivel in the diocese more familiar to me, based upon Wells. He had arranged the current icon exhibition. We were most impressed as we bumped into Eastern Orthodox art around the building. Another friend, Frumps, formerly an inhabitant of St Agnes, on the coast not far away, and a convert to the Russian discipline, would have loved it. Unfortunately she had moved to Westward Ho!, Devon, in the northern part of the see of Exeter. She had visited St Mary's on a number of occasions while a local. The exhibition served to enhance the busy feeling. Meanwhile, there was no gap available for colourful golden images in the north transept, it being cluttered with items from the old parish church and the odd modern addition. I was eagerly anticipating a cup of coffee, as that was what I had foregone for 40 days – in penance and to see if the loss of caffeine made me feel any better. The latter part had failed, and I was longing for a steaming brew of 'proper' coffee. Not on this occasion as, necessarily, all the provisions were instant – tea, orange juice and coffee. We spread the risk: Rand had coffee, Graham orange and tea for me, with a digestive biscuit. Lovely! It had been a while since breakfast. I observed the notice about the Truro Cathedral School and the memorials to John Robartes (d.1614), Mayor of Truro, whose family 'established the estate of Lanhydrock, near Bodmin'. That was interesting as, on a previous spring visit to Cornwall, I had enjoyed that pile, or rather its glorious garden, bursting with daffodils. I don't think that was the bit of which the Canon Missioner, contrasting it with Somerset, stated: 'it's a bit grittier here in Cornwall'.

The narrowing of the eastern areas excited Rand who was particularly interested in structure and form. Graham pointed out, from his vantage point at the west end, north corner, that the left hand stained glass window in the east end was out of sight because of this narrowing. This owed to available space. When planning a cathedral in a city centre every inch counts. There was none of the dimensional luxury available to those other new builds, Liverpool and Guildford. But here it created an interesting effect. Working round the top end, in the north choir aisle you came to the Tinworth Panel, in terracotta. Again, this was of interest to Rand having dabbled in just this while living in the Potteries. George Tinworth, the creator, worked at Doulton's, Stoke-on-Trent. The Cornish connection was strong, china clay being transported from the mines in the St Austell area. Now you go there to see the Eden Project, perhaps along with the Lost Gardens of Heligan. It was thought that the head of Pontius Pilate, on the far left of the piece, was modeled on the future Edward VII, who laid the foundation stone in 1880. It certainly looked like him, having seen a lot of the man as Prince of Wales and monarch in a lately broadcast BBC documentary.

In the quire I found it refreshing to note the plainness of the seating. There was none of the detailed misericord invention of older cathedrals, as at Exeter, to come in three days' time with a reputedly excellent selection. There were blank planks, and fine as such. And through we went to the best part, the residue of the 15th century Church of St Mary's the Virgin, still the parish church as well – with some old glass and a wagon-roof. The central tower (250') was a memorial to Queen Victoria. It was 300' long with a simply-treated interior, showing a fine mastery of proportion. It held the second organ. There was a service now being conducted by the archdeacon, soon after he had greeted us, post-liturgy. The worshippers comprised the small group we were later to observe discussing a forthcoming baptism at the rich red cathedral font, elevated within its own space near the south door. At the back of St Mary's, a fine medieval remnant, was another font, close to the rich red one in location but a world away in the setting. From here, as you mount the steps and pass the elaborate door to the street outside, can be admired the various vistas up, down and around the quire, aisles and east window. The solid red font was my favourite item, composed of North African marble font with a brooding canopy soaring to the roof.

Back at the west glass doors Rand commented: 'It can be quite interesting but you have to look for the interest,' noting the creamy vaulting in the nave and plain brick blocks. He liked bricks. Meanwhile, a visitor (young, female, possibly from the Mediterranean) asked Graham, who was sitting quietly in yellow pullover and vigorous tie, why the building narrowed further down. He gave a lucid explanation and her response indicated that she thought he was a guide. Well, his spiel was worthy of guidehood – we'd all been exchanging views on the matter for several minutes up to then. He was to turn guide for our small party at Coventry six months hence. For me, my friend Judy Torrens' comment about Truro should serve: 'It has a nice atmosphere. Lots going on there.' Judy's speciality was gardening – her display would rival Lanhydrock in the Spring.

The final thrill was the Norman arch into the shop, that same facility which housed the paper guide to the cathedral (only available when the shop was open, which was not to be until the afternoon, that day). Strange that, when there were leaflets for organ recitals, *Rick Stein at Truro Cathedral* (Monday 26th April – the menu to include 'fish and shellfish soup with rouille and parmesan – Yumm!), *Save Our Spire (sponsor our stones)*, all 250' of it, and of course *The Friends of Truro Cathedral* – what's on and an event booking form. Never mind, I did find a flyer headed *Welcome to Truro Cathedral*, which carried a map on the back. Anyway it was an easy place to assimilate. Graham liked the chapter house, a latterday addition at the northeast. It successfully doubled as the Restaurant and Coffee Shop (coffee £1.70 – reasonable enough). Built in an era when function presided over style, it still worked well enough here. So did the crypt. I sneaked a look at that. There were red and white recently doffed surplices hanging up. Quite appealing, really. During our wander I rescued a palm from a nave seat, child-sized, discarded by a member of the congregation.

We had missed the bells that day, but no matter as it was only later that they attained their full complement, as reported in *The Times* (28/10/10): 'Truro cathedral will become the only church in Cornwall to have a "ring of 12" bells when it gets four new bronze bells to mark its centenary. They were cast last week at John Taylor and Co in Loughborough, Leicestershire, the world's largest bell foundry. It is hoped that the first peels from the new bells will ring out before Easter.' Accompanying this, a large and colourful banner was made by students at the local Penair School featuring the new acquisitions. It was part of a centenary exhibition. I wished I'd seen it, and the bells. There was more of a story in that the total funding of £150K was raised largely from bell-ringers around the county.

Once outside in yet more rain – my umbrella was to expire the next day in the bluster – we peered at the central tower, under wraps and the subject of the fund-raising initiative. What had already been restored was the southern exterior – sharp stone edges greeted the passer-by from the railings on approaching, quite a contrast from the weathered edges further up. *The Observer's book* on cathedrals considered: 'From whatever point they are viewed, the grouping of the towers is striking. They rise dramatically from the huddle of buildings, which tightly enclose them. Built 1880–87 (western steeples completed 1910).'

After that we noticed some of the trappings of a city centre, even if Truro, with a population of around 17,000, was the 8th smallest city in the

UK. Shopping chains abounded, and the odd tea house, plus recommended pubs not far away – but it remained a miserable day and we were bound for St Ives, so off we sped. We might have chosen the summer months for this visit. One such (with the benefit of luck and judgment in achieving fine weather) saw 'a bring and share picnic in the grounds of Truro Cathedral' during Christian Aid week. (Along the same lines Exeter Cathedral hosted a cream tea, with a jazz band and speeches.)

The smaller spires sported fetching green sections. This contributed to the choice, over a boiled egg back at base a few days later, of the Jerusalem artichoke as the icon for Truro Cathedral. Rand said: 'Not sure – it shouldn't be wasted there – save it for a better cathedral.' You see, his priority was for the top ones, those majestic masses of which only Salisbury had been experienced thus far. As Sarum, it had, in 1220, been the most recent cathedral built on a new site, until Truro's inception. I thought the Jerusalem artichoke suited Truro very well: fitting that on Palm Sunday, with Holy Week upon us and the growing season just beginning, we attach an irregularly-shaped vegetable.

Mrs Beeton's assistance was invoked. My copy provided:

Boiled Jerusalem Artichokes
To each ½ gallon of water allow 1 heaped tablespoon of salt; artichokes.
Mode – Wash, peel, and shape the artichokes in a round or oval form, and put them in a saucepan with sufficient cold water to cover them, salted in the above proportion. Let them boil gently until tender; take them up, drain them, and serve them in a napkin, or plain, whichever mode is preferred; send to table with them a tureen of melted butter or cream sauce, a little of which may be poured over the artichokes when they are not served in a napkin.
Time – About 20 minutes after the water boils.
Average cost, 2d. per lb
Seasonable from September to June

She went on to list *'Uses of the Jerusalem Artichoke'* uttering the point that in some parts of north and west France *'the fibres of the stems may be separated by maceration, and manufactured into cordage or cloth'*. Why not in Cornwall, which is related to Brittany, and for the most part a poor area? Mrs Beeton died, aged 28, in 1861, sixteen years before Cornwall's diocese was created, reducing the see of Exeter to the county of Devon only but still big enough for any dean and chapter to run. Meanwhile so much has changed. Salt has been largely outlawed, and probably butter. But the artichoke should be nourished.

Monday 29 March

Having moved in the storm for a stay in St Ives, a visit to the parish church was on the cards, with pieces by Barbara Hepworth. Given the appalling climatic conditions, ambitious forays into the country provided little temptation. As a result, we stayed in the town more than intended and enjoyed the Hepworth house and garden along with several pubs in the vicinity.

Church Wardens Brenda and Bob were on duty. The former, who had known Hepworth as a local attender, considered the Madonna and Child piece in the Lady Chapel to be 'the best thing she ever did'. We didn't agree as, though it was a touching memorial to the artist's son who was an RAF casualty in 1953, there was so much more character and quality in the sculptures at the artist's house. From the garden there opened up a fabulous view of the church tower through skeletal trees (it was a delayed spring after the hardest winter for years). What was missing was enough of her work in the church to make a presence: just a pale, sinuous statue and two candlesticks, comparatively tall but not particularly interesting.

The other item worth enquiring of the vicar, then guides, was the dark wood medieval pew end in the choir stalls depicting the tools and image (with wife) of a blacksmith, named as Ralph Clies. No one could find it. 'Dunno,' said Bob, and Brenda showed us one at the back of the nave, clearly unrelated to the query. The image she alighted upon looked more like a warrior. There was an odd mixture of ancient and modern in the seating – a number of impressive pews and ends carrying images more familiar as misericords elsewhere. Intermingled were lighter modern ones. Vicar Revd A S Gough had arrived. He was engaged in discussion with a colleague about the following day's funeral, which was to require closure of the main road into the town. It confirmed our departure as early – by 9 am, after a hearty breakfast from our hostess Pom, she of the dulcet tones (Catch her delivering Rossini's *Petite Messe Solennelle*). I caught a conversational fag end. Said one parson to another: 'We normally have the condemnation, sorry commendation, under the tower.' The sadly-departed was an Afghanistan fatality from the relentless war.

The Anglo-Catholic tendency was seen in the perpetual lights and three rear altars. After all, St Ia, to whom the church is dedicated, was an Irish émigrée, one of a plethora who aimed for Cornwall. About them little is known. Looking up I reckoned the bright bosses in the Lady Chapel would have been more suitable depicted on kneelers.

We left the west door (there was another close by opening into the Lady Chapel), noting that we were to miss an illustrated talk and signing (£3.50) by Simon King on 'Wildlife' and 'Shetland Diaries'. Graham ventured out tentatively without his wheelchair, over the cobbles to the Parish Hall for an antiques event we had seen advertized. Rand and I did the church circuit, noting the strangeness of the path partly made of horizontal tombstones. The patch of grass round the building was just that – not one grave as adornment. The east end comprised four vaults with windows more impressive from outside than within. In the distant past they would have formed a landmark for vessels approaching by sea, which was right there, pounding on the pebbles below the wall. However, the RNLI (and public conveniences) building now had pride of place, a sad addition. Practical, we were sure, but not aesthetically pleasing.

The church, 15th century and making the mark for the settlement which became so prominent for fishing, then art and tourism, was a complement to the Victorian cathedral a handful of miles away. Next for something quite different – the millennium old foundation at Exeter.

13

Exeter

St Peter

Province: Canterbury
Founded: 1050, diocese moved from Crediton
Present Building: 1112–1200 – twin towers survive; c.1270–1350
Decorated rebuild

Website: www.exeter-cathedral.org.uk
Tel: 01392 255573
Email: reception@exeter-cathedral.org.uk
Address: Exeter Cathedral, 1 The Cloisters, Exeter EX1 1HS

Three to See: 1484 clock and door with cat hole at the bottom;
59' tall wooden cathedra;
minstrels' gallery projecting from nave

Cat

Wednesday 3 March, 2010

Yet another windswept day took us past the biblically-multiplying wind turbines on the backbone of Cornwall, some of which were irritatingly stationary. Rand told us he had heard that it would cost a fortune – millions – to repair them. It seemed a waste, overall, to suffer them as eyesores and lose the advantage of conserved resources when they cease to function: best to reinvent them as public art perhaps. More appealing was snow-capped Dartmoor – there had been a bulletin earlier about drifts in Northern Ireland. It was meant to be spring! Next was relentless rain taking us to the puddles and dead umbrellas of Exeter.

Graham, a native of Wellington, up the A38 and under the aegis of Wells, had the greatest familiarity with the ways of the city, garnered mainly through antiques auctions and whist drives. We located disabled spaces behind the building and sought the magic passport to a stay long enough to enjoy as many delights of St Peter's Cathedral as possible. This meant braving the elements, mainly a ferocious wind by then, a tour inside the west end via the cashier (£3 for seniors, actually voluntary, including entitlement to take photos). Rand might have suffered the same fate as Lot's wife for sneaking a glance at the country's longest continuous nave roof. We were accompanied by one of the mature and helpful (all female) guides to the office outside in what had, in pre-Puritan days, been the site of a cloister. Claire, the provider and groups organizer (busy with bookings now the season was beckoning), and a bit too tall for the low ceiling, went in search of a day pass, duly committed to us day trippers, thence to the windscreen. The three of us turned the corner to the warm and welcoming café, which turned out to be discreetly placed in what must have originally been another cloister within sight of the office we'd just been in (address: No. 1, The Cloisters), bedecked with stained glass at the opposite end, illustrating a selection of worthy forebears. There was also a Victorian bust of a benefactor. The coffee was adequate this time – one variation for each of us, but Graham, a connoisseur of cakes-on-tour as well as the niceties of whist technique, gave only moderate marks for the apricot cake, and, for that matter, to the lemon one. Where were the strong flavours?

The exposure to this ancient pile commenced. The nave seating was modern in an effective quiet blue-grey. Aloft on the roof were bosses 'bright with Dulux paint, and gold leaf' said Mary, the first guide who greeted us. She pointed out the figure of Thomas a Becket, head to head with the majestic Bishop Grandisson (in post from 1327 to 1369), who had seen the building project through. Apparently a recent predecessor, the studious Walter Stapeldon, left a pair of spectacles in his will. 'Wooden-rimmed spectacles were invented by Italians in the late 13th century,' recorded Ian

Mortimer in *The Time Traveller's Guide to Medieval England*. Stapeldon was murdered in 1326 for his affiliation with the doomed Edward II, but two more incumbents were to grace the cathedra before Grandisson's ascent in 1327. Stapeldon was the founder of Exeter College, Oxford and contributed very liberally to rebuilding the quire and reredos. His tomb is on the north side of the high altar there. I liked the story that Bishop Walter Bronescombe (appointed 1258 and known as 'Walter the Good'), on attending the launch party for Salisbury's bespoke new cathedral, initiated his own project, rebuilding more or less everything at Exeter except the immense Norman towers.

The Little Guide to Devon stated: 'The best thing is that so much was built at a time when Perpendicular style was in full swing. Nevertheless it is constructed throughout in the purest Decorated style, except the east window.' And that is a marvel, as well. From the west end, when looking up, the vista is of a single space. Beyond the chancel we could admire the fetching Last Supper adornment, constructed at local schools and mingling well with the other Eastertide exhibits. The 1665 (date inscribed thereupon) organ is sited above the pulpitum screen, I think to the benefit of the overall look. Rand didn't like it, preferring to see a continuous open space from east to west. The organ certainly makes an unanswerable statement. It's monolithic. This place is full of strong images.

Upfront and confident, yes, and in parallel there was a sensitivity of execution borne out by the atmosphere throughout the cathedral. There was fun to be had, and a challenge. Stone had been imported from 22 different sources, and most of the cost was transport, some from far afield. At least Purbeck was only a county away (in the diocese of Salisbury). There was so much to learn and be aware of here, especially compared with the much more recent foundation at Truro, so discourses with Dean Jonathan Meyrick, and two guides, just tapped the surface of whatever topic was being pursued at the time. One of the guides, Roger, wasn't quite official yet. He'd passed the tests and was due for launch into guidehood the following day. Rand and the dean discussed the Crown of Thorns currently being put in place overhead. Good Friday was two days away. 'It didn't work,' Rand opined afterwards. 'Not impressive enough.' My turn (Dean Jonathan was in a hurry to complete the C of T) involved an exchange about the nature of the diocese and how style filtered down the hierarchy. He was proud of the organization of the cathedral: 30 clergy, 50 stewards and 12 guides. Dean Jonathan, a Lancing College old boy, was to become a Right Reverend in 2011, when assuming the mantle as Bishop of Lynn, which for me illustrated the sense of mobility in the world of the church. After all I had met the former bishop of Lynn in his current guise at Rochester.

We admired the vast 59' high cathedra ('Bishop's throne' in the Cathedral Tour leaflet), the tallest in the country, with a backdrop of the south choir aisle windows. Made between 1312 and 1316, 'using local Devon oak, it was constructed without any metal nails or screws, being held together with pegs'. 'Humbling' is the word I've chosen to describe it, a huge statement towering above, with a figure (a bishop) demurely set within it. 'One of the greatest achievements in 14th century woodwork in Europe' was written. This was one of the features, along with other items such as the massive east window, misericords and the effigy of Walter the Good, which was removed during the Second World War, and stored in a remote place on, or under, Dartmoor: most wise in view of the bombing sustained in 1942. St James' Chapel is close to the throne. All of these artefacts were successfully reintroduced after the war.

Back to Roger, who seemed to have special responsibility for the mid-13th century misericords in the quire: 52 of them, completed in 1260. I managed to procure a viewing of a selection. They were not readily available to the public. The stalls were roped off. Under the Dean's seat (no.1) raged a ferocious dragon in combat with a lion, in the name of St Eustacius. Others I was shown depicted a green man, one of several such dotted around the cathedral in sundry places (one involved a red spewing head) and a female centaur. The most extraordinary misericord (no.44) had been granted its own place, behind glass in the north choir aisle. This was the Exeter elephant, flanked by a man on one side and a woman on the other, carved from the imagination of a medieval artisan – with cloven feet, after an equine model from the farmyard. Terrific stuff!

It was approaching the hour of noon, clock chime time, so we made for the north transept, under the towers. There were some effective Gothic additions, such as galleries above. The working medieval clock was one of four, all in South West England, along with Ottery St Mary (read on), Wells and Wimborne Minster. It had a fleur-de-lys hand, giving the time with the sun's position, the interpretation derived from the late 15th century view of the solar system, with Earth at the centre. The chimes duly announced that noon had arrived, heard but not seen. Below the clock was sited a most unassuming structure complete with two substantial holes, one near the bottom. Tallow used to be applied to ease the clock workings (and there was a rusty model of the previous clock on the floor whose parts we could examine). Rodents like a free meal. Cats were introduced, their brief to enjoy the rats. So Exeter has been for long a cat place, though in reality no longer, except for the odd pet, such as a vertical tailed beast belonging to one of the canons. I nominate the cat as the image of Exeter, which appears aloft as a corbel in St James' Chapel, on the other side of the building. This chapel was rebuilt through patient reassembly of the stone. It had to be a rebuilding initiative as it represents one Tom, the pet of the Head Verger, E R Hart, who was in post at the time the chapel was bombed. The cat is mirrored by its victim, a rat. Unfortunately the heroic feline lost an eye to his opponent for the spoils, an owl. This state of monocularity appears in the carving.

This is not to deny its prime enemy: the canine species. The best story, after all, is of the pre-Reformation Dog Whipper (perhaps a verger), who, with his family, was resident in the upper storey of the north porch, and of whom a primary duty was to precede processions in the nave (employed until 1856). He was paid an annual salary of £5 for the job of 'controlling dogs and kids. Cathedrals were not holy, sacred places,' said the Rev Canon Geoffrey Moore, who retired here from Lancashire in 1993. 'Business was done in the nave, and recreation. The Dog Whipper's accommodation was big enough for quite decent living quarters in medieval times.' No doubt this procedure also served to keep the congregation awake. Incidentally, from the 18th century, there used to be a day set aside up in York for dog flogging: 18 October. In the Minster one such beast had devoured the sacrament (some wafers). 'Beginning in the 16th century, many English churches employed churchwardens, or beadles, who not only supervised the sometimes unruly canines that traditionally accompanied their owners to church but were often charged with keeping parishioners awake during services,' (*Forgotten English* by Jeffrey Kacirk). The same author unearthed the word 'bytesheip', as a 'mocking expression for a bishop, intended as a play upon his official title, likening him to a shepherd who bit the animals he was charged with protecting'. Animal abuse would seem to be widespread. And, projecting from the north porch is a minstrels' gallery, built for Palm Sunday services and decorated with angels playing musical instruments. Palm Sunday was ever a big processional event.

After talking to Geoffrey I joined Rand in the north transept, early on in a group tour with Rachel Lupton, one of the qualified guides, at the last minute called to stand in for an absentee. On the north wall was a mural, below which, to finish the picture, hung a tapestry. The towers were Norman in themselves, but inside had benefited from 'a Gothic makeover', said Rachel. The high gallery was pleasing to the eye, and several of them around this building replete with spare walls. Rachel referred to the collapse of Winchester's central tower, in recent memory at the time of the Exeter project, which may have influenced design decisions, to my mind to its benefit, and ours. It didn't seem cluttered to me.

On the hour of 1 pm we were conjoined in prayer by Canon Geoffrey in the pulpit (an hourly engagement. He used St Richard of Chichester's prayer, reputedly his last living words. This jogged memories from my youth in the eponymous diocese. It was adapted for the song *Day by Day* in the musical *Godspell*. Speaking to him again, Geoffrey waxed lyrical about the library and its spectacular offerings. As there were Tower Tours on certain days, I entertained excited anticipation of another visit for these delights.

It was Geoffrey's lunchtime. 'I'm going off for a bowl of soup,' he said. Carrot and coriander, I believed. For me, the shop. It was in an appealingly converted space, connecting chancel to chapter house. There, having passed Shipping Forecast Areas and Food Glorious Food tea towels pinned to the access wall, in the shop I found a number of items connected with cats, including Babbacombe cat figures, busy cats' trays and a well-stocked book section, where I bought *Cathedral Cats*, now convinced of the strong association of the beasts with this cathedral.

I then moved to the south transept, close by, where the delightfully off-the-wall Rachel was regaling the rapt audience with her speech on the immense organ pipes attached to the west wall. 'They give a deep rumble,' she commented. 'In normal cathedrals the pipes are hidden away and lie horizontal.' In many medieval church buildings the later introduction of an organ has been an awkward insertion between pillars. Here it is a real statement and serves to amplify the overall look. She countered Rand's negativity with the organ, which brooded heavily over the stone pulpitum. 'It doesn't work artistically' said he. She retorted 'Where else would you put it?' No reply. This had also been a quickly-covered topic with the dean, who conceded it to be controversial, adding 'But I like it – it's the only one like it.'

A minor tour de force remained. Discreetly secreted within the west wall, right by the doors, was Bishop Grandisson's chantry chapel. After peering at this through the clear glass (it was locked), it was time to face the elements, and have a wander round the building. The north porch, formerly used as the main entrance, assumed more interest having heard the Dog Whipper story, and opposite beckoned antique hostelries. It's often said that the west front doesn't work, the window being out of proportion with its setting. True, the porch was added to the façade between 1369 and 1394 by Bishop Grandisson, and the overall effect becomes diminished. Meanwhile the west front offers the largest array of 14th century sculpture in England, said *The Observer's Book of Cathedrals*. In any case you can cast your eyes up, right and left to the bulk of the building and its perkily-pinnacled towers, and go in and gorge yourself.

Or do just that with a pint in the Well House Tavern, opposite. With the old Clarence Hotel, of which it was now part, it offered haute cuisine, courtesy of Michael Caines, the famed restaurateur. In the pub there were fine beers to be sampled. I remembered the time I did just that, sitting in the window with my pint of Yellowhammer, admiring the illuminated towers, looking wrinkled and massive, and somehow exuding a lightness of touch, from the comfort of the bar. They served Gargoyles Best Bitter there. What an enlightened choice of name for the brewery, started in 2005 by Roger Strudwick, in a former cowshed a few miles outside the city. A further cathedral connection is that 'Roger formerly produced cider under the name Green Man Cider,' (*CAMRA Exeter & East Devon Branch website*).

Next we drove to St Mary's, Ottery St Mary, ten miles away and modeled on St Peter's. It was a fine thing to park within inches and spend an involving hour in the church. There were several green men, 'a remnant of pagan symbolism, adopted by the Christian church – an unending circle of life and death,' informed the legend, for this parish church was well-signed, used to its appeal as a drop-in for church hunters, many of whom had read the high praise from Simon Jenkins (top notch 5*, one of 18 in the country), or had discovered its connection with the cathedral up the road. Rand gave it 7½ out of ten, noting the 'bosses – undoubtedly very high quality. That it echoes Exeter is incredible'. 'Very interesting' said Graham, who had rejoined the party. He was referring, I recall, to the mother church, as well. Down the road was Seasons café, which we adjudged to provide unusually high quality offerings, that is the tea (real tea leaves), latte and Graham's apple pie (and cream). My treacle sponge wasn't. Treacle appeared to be a vanishing species, golden syrup being termed 'treacle' on an alarmingly widespread basis.

> ***Ottery***
> *To find a good cake is a lottery*
> *Most tearooms care more about pottery*
> *The Seaton sponge sagged*
> *The Budleigh buns bounced*
> *The best was the apple at Ottery.*

During our wander round the town centre after tea, I took the opportunity of buying some Easter chickens in a charity shop with a card nearby assuring us 'knitted by local ladies' and containing a chocolate egg. They were really egg cosies. A nice idea, but I gave them away, complete with the red ribbons.

That was it, the diocese of Exeter being left behind for a detour towards Somerset over the Blackdown Hills. On the spine, say at the Wellington Monument, we enjoyed a stunning view of two dioceses.

Tuesday 13 July

This was the visit, prebooked, essentially for a Tower Tour (it's advisable to check availability). It was raining again, after not a drop over the spring and summer visits to 11 cathedrals. I had brought it with me, following the precedent of the previous visit. This was of concern in view of the roof tour an hour hence. They might not allow the party outside in case of injury on the damp lead.

There was time for more observation in the body of the building, but let's go straight to the tour: seven of us gathered under the west window to meet David Snell, our Guide, with the support of yellow-topped John Norman, the 'backstop' steward. David was erudite, to the point of having published a book on the subject, which we could buy in the shop. But first he had to check a detail with the overalled Gary, on the payroll as master mason, who passed by opportunely, bucket in hand. There was a whole team of workers employed by the cathedral, I was told.

David was steeped in the complex and advancing science which facilitated the building of this place, and since then, its survival. He had been a guide for 28 years. It was a case of stepping up, then along, and down a number of times over the extremities of this Gothic pile. We saw the work over many centuries, culminating in a modern walkway, which took us a great distance. First was a comparatively cramped vertical initiation up the southwest corner, to see drainage channels and the works of eons to keep the building up and, latterly (this year) safe for just such an event as this. Next, the longest haul was right along the roof, a continuous flat walk from west to east. There was plenty of space – no fear of an attack of claustrophobia. There was blue netting and red tape and pipe (fire protector system) here and there, as well as pipes and fresh timbered walkways. Drainage had been a challenge, and Exeter was unique in the method of addressing it, inwards.

At the crossing, we were shown the point where the chandeliers by the screen were suspended – they had been winched up for events in the recent Exeter Festival. We were taken further along, to be informed, to the alarm of a few (there was a family of Germans of various ages in our group), that the blank floor of the south transept was directly below. David referred to the 'rainlike noise', actually the sun and wind against the structure. Unfortunately it was real rain that we were hearing that day.

We moved to the south tower, down to the lead workshop, adorned with weighty pieces of the metal. I tried to lift one. They had been transported from St Botolph's, Lincs, by sea as far as the River Exe at Topsham. The rest of the journey had to be by land, the river passage having been blocked at Countess Wear. Up more steps and down again we were treated to the capacious bell chamber, so different from the last one I'd seen, at Peel. The massive tower housed this space, architecturally redesigned in the 14th century from the original Norman. It reeked of history, with the striped pulls hanging from the resting place of the ancient bells in the top of the tower, with individual platforms of a range of heights for each ringer. There were boards round the wall listing the achievements of teams over the years, and, covered in a blue cabinet, the published list of Victorian rules, as follows:

RULES, TO BE OBSERVED IN THE CATHEDRAL TOWER OF EXETER
I Whoever Curses or Swears, shall for each offence forfeit 6d.
II Whoever Fights or offers to Fight, shall forfeit 1s.
III Whoever Pulls a Bell off its Stay, shall forfeit 6d.
IV Whoever Rings with their Hat on their Head, shall forfeit 6d.
V Whoever comes to the Tower disguised in Liquor, shall forfeit 6d.
VI The Bell Toller to have the Ringing-Loft Swept every Ringing-Day, or forfeit 6d.
VIII Whoever Reads these Articles with their Hat on their Head, shall forfeit 6d.
SPENCER, PRINTERS, St SIDWELLS, EXETER

The inference to be drawn from those involving hats on heads was that it was a male-only activity. It was chaps who wore hats. This was in *Gargoyles and Gutters, a personal tour round the roof of Exeter Cathedral* by David Snell. I recommend it.

This comprised the second heaviest ring of bells in the world – 14 of them here, and one over in the north tower. They rejoiced in exotic names to accompany their absolute splendidness as creations: Pongermouth and Doom were two. David demonstrated his own mobile phone ring tone: yes, a peal of 12 bells. The musty sensation of a long history pervaded. It was quite a hike up to your workstation, compared with Peel, where it was a few yards through the main door, followed by a score of steps. This tower, at once seductive with its pinnacles from outside and satisfyingly square and solid outside and in, was the home to supremely magical sounds. It was possible to imagine a Pied Piper effect of peals of bells enticing a congregation. David told us: 'A full peal of 5040 changes takes over four hours – there are four full peal attempts a year.'

Also inside the towers were signs of the Romanesque stonework – solid bits of arch left exposed in corners as a reminder. That was as welcome a sight as any, like the solitary Norman gallery within the Decorated north transept, accompanying the double act of the current clock at work and the mechanics of the old one on the floor alongside. The clock was the determining factor for tour timing by our trusty guide. The rain had relented, so we were allowed on the roof after all, with grave notes of caution and Backstop John reminded of his duties, waiting for all to pass, and closing, firmly. The view was pretty good and better, obviously, on a clear day. The best reward was the building itself – the towers, their decoration and those purposeful, and pretty, pinnacles; and, like the interior of Lincoln towards the west end, the top of the roof of St Peter's was irregular. The upright pinnacles on the roof were not decorative but functional, keeping buttresses in place. I must emphasize the contour of the roof: it was extraordinary how far out of kilter the axes had strayed: not the four lines of the compass but diverging by significant degrees. As David said: 'See how the movement of the timbers has dragged the crossing out of shape.' The line of each section was askew. At Lincoln the building was at fault; at Exeter it was a kind of wear and tear. Somehow they fused into an effective cruciform design. The building has stood up for 700 years, so it must work. By now it was almost 4 pm – back we went down a single flight to the clock workings, to witness the cog advance at the hour, and the dull thud of heavy metal. The cord connecting machinery to display was one long thread. That concluded the tour, or rather the 175 steps down did (plus two at the bottom), to admire the beautiful clock as we emerged into the cavernous cathedral interior. The cord was just visible, now we knew what to look for against the limestone wall.

What remained for me was the Library, which closed at 5 pm, allowing a reasonable introduction. This involved navigation – David showed me the way – outside to the southeast corner. Pressed buttons and a greeting later, I was upstairs, being welcomed again, by Richard Newell. Welcomes abounded here, a most friendly place. They've got the training right on the customer service front. This Richard, keen to attend to my needs, first pointed out the display of a medical book from 1300 (the time of Bishop Grandisson). A conference of dermatologists had visited recently to look at it. The page on show featured pustules among other unappetizing skin afflictions.

He then showed me the two showpieces. One was the Exeter Book (*Codex Exoniensis*, a 10th century anthology of Anglo-Saxon poetry and one of four source books of English poetry, with Beowulf, at the English Library in the Bodleian, Oxford and one in Italy), donated by Leofric, the first Bishop of Exeter. The other was the Exon Domesday book (1086), bigger and tattier than its neighbour, by which it nestled. It predated the

DB proper, and covered land use for the broad southwest in minute detail. Winchester was then capital of England and home of the central Treasury. It received the Domesday Book, later transported to London, and eventually back to Exeter. This was the best extant version, 'Books have always been in the cathedral,' said Richard. 'A bit of the Lady Chapel was once set aside.' The books were successfully hidden away during the Civil War. A plan was currently afoot to relocate the Library – one example of its shortcomings was the lack of disabled access. I beat a retreat by way of a massive wooden door, which opened near the quire.

My next visit to St Peter's was again on a wet day (24/8/10). It was a tragic occasion, a Service of Thanksgiving for Adam Stansfield, a leading Exeter City FC player, hot-scoring centre forward, who died of bowel cancer a month before his 31st birthday. How good that the cathedral embraced the event, welcoming many who would never otherwise think of entering St Peter's.

Fig 17

Fig 18

Fig 19

[17] Exeter: The cat door for rodent pursuit up the greased clock pole.
[18] Exeter: You have to undertake the recommended roof tour to see how skewed it is.
[19] Liverpool: Modern cope chest with Toff and guide Robin Moor.
[20] Chelmsford: Crouched statue of St Peter in fishing boots, facing out to Bradwell.

Fig 20

14

Liverpool

Christ

Province: York
Founded: 1880 created from Chester
Building: 1904–1978

Website: www.liverpoolcathedral.org.uk
Tel: 0151 7096271
Email: info@liverpoolcathedral.org.uk
Address: Liverpool Cathedral, St James Mount, Liverpool L1 7AZ

Three to See: The well (western part of nave) for a view of the whole
building, and, perhaps a game of football;
stained glass window featuring women;
tool display;
lets add the embroidery gallery, also a rare display

Eagle

Friday 16 April, 2010
Frankie said: 'the entrance to the Anglican cathedral would make a fine 5-a-side football pitch'. This was the same Millwall-supporting man, with whom I had lunched in Horsham, Chichester diocese. On his annual pilgrimages to the Norwich Beer Festival visits to the cathedral for tea and cakes were factored in between sessions. He meant the sunken nave, the well, and following my visit I had to agree. In this vast open place it was the last bit to be completed and is separate and unemphatic, quite the opposite of a nave, in any other church. Frankie was also inquisitive about peregrine falcons taking up residence on the very obvious, red roof, extending to several hectares. And it's the one topic I failed to pursue during my two sessions, later discovering that the Royal Liver Building, as an example, sported falcons' nests. The Liver Birds (part eagle, part cormorant) hardly served as scarecrows. Speaking of which, it became obvious that the icon of Liverpool's Anglican Cathedral had to be the eagle, the symbol of the city, and half of the eagle and child duet, the emblem of the Stanleys, whose benefactor member, Lord Derby (1841–1908) inspired one of the best things in the cathedral, his bronze memorial in the southwest transept.

Also associated with Liverpool is St Nicholas of Bari (270–343), as a patron saint. In *Forgotten English* (1997) Jeffrey Kacirk writes of the Old English expression 'barn-bishop, for a traditional holiday dignitary – associated with St Nicholas of Bari – who was called the "boy-Bishop" because of his very early exhibitions of benevolence, said to have begun "in infancy." From time immemorial, "bot-bishops," as barn-bishops were later called, were chosen from the choirs of various churches on Saint Nicholas' Day as a reenactment of the story of Jesus teaching the doctors in the temple.'

Returning to eagles, a streamlined one serves as a sinuous rest for his feet, face to face with the child. There is many a pub in South Lancashire called 'Eagle and Child'. There is, too, a fine model of the original two-tower design (press the button for a few seconds of illumination). The whole concept is that of a single architect, but there were implemented a number of variations, not always reductions, during the interminable building process.

The Toff had driven us carefully up among the all-day Friday motorway traffic. The trip was painless enough, having adjusted to this prolixity and settled down to interminable conversation about football, our teams, the state of the nation, the General Election being nigh, and the first three-leader television debate freshly experienced. We did abandon Strensham Services as our coffee stop, as a coach party or two appeared to have arrived minutes before so the Costa queue was a mile long. Frankley

Services, the next one up the M5, was better. Though causing the customary dent in the wallet, the latte, americano and egg sandwich (sans mayonnaise, praise the Lord) proved to be the right kind of ballast as we were to reach Liverpool well after 2 pm, too late for the snack in the café to be termed a lunchbreak.

It was quickly established that: a) A tour was essential as the welcome desk was the first thing in evidence after entering via the northwest aisle, a pillar or two and the sunken football space, and b) The cathedral was proud to make admission and the wisdom of a guide chargeless, though there is written encouragement to contribute £3 each – gift aid please. However we had committed ourselves to the car park, to which Toff, with considerable local knowledge, had taken us without demur and it was to be £3.50 (£5 standard) for a Great Value Attractions Ticket. With this we underwent the Tower Experience (The Vestey Tower – 'Go To The Top' – and Elizabeth Hoare Embroidery Gallery, and on my return the next morning the Great Space Film and Audio Tour). The attitude was undeniably welcoming. It would be churlish to begrudge the charges. In the case of the Tower, for example, the lifts cost something to maintain, and so did the fabric of the whole gargantuan place. It's been completed in our lifetimes (1978) and I remember an earlier visit to the area when it was forbiddingly unfinished. The whole is even bigger than the parts in my opinion.

We were hugely lucky to have Robin Moor as our interpreter (or guide). Despite the job title he didn't speak languages other than our mother tongue, but hoped to convey information to the widely varying range of visitors. He did speak in dulcet tones – as a cultured Wirralian, who had moved to Wales. Rather like the Toff, whose origins in Merseyside made him a supplementary tour guide. Before our departure, the next day Toff's daughter Vicki had a tale to tell. She recounted the story of when she, who hadn't then reached double figures, and her mother attended the cathedral during a visit of HM The Queen. 'Arriving, there were lots of cars and people. I wanted to get to the front and weedled my way there and found a nice spot, next to a black girl. The Queen spoke to her. Then I saw my mother up on some steps, surrounded by police. I had no idea, but there had been a full search, as she thought she'd lost me.'

Toff did say, during the return journey: 'I was most surprised at how good it was – a wonderful place.' That came from an atheist and cultural enthusiast. He then expressed interest in future involvement in this project. I was keen, as he contributed a fair share of questions and observations. Westminster Abbey was set up as a sequel, for me an inevitable coupling with St Paul's.

Robin embarked upon a detailed and unprompted sequence through the building. Giles Gilbert Scott (1880–1960) designed the whole thing, taken on in his early 20s. That's some trust to invest in one so young! What appears to have been partly a mentor role, though officially to oversee the project was given to George Bodley. He was also involved in the choice of designer. His approach turned out to be at odds with Scott, starting with the very first section, the Lady Chapel. It transpired to be a good thing that the much older Bodley died in 1907, thus leaving the young master, still only 27, to it. The first thing to strike me was the idea of four transepts; two, west and two, east. It is symptomatic that the prosaic basic 'Gothic' approach has taken on a latter-day interpretation, as we also have Truro and Guildford which both work perfectly well in their own right. Not one is dull and all merit hours of study and enjoyment. However, the idea of traditional Gothic may well be distancing for would-be virgin visitors. It looks too 'churchy'. I'm sure the Metropolitan Cathedral of Christ the King at the other end of Hope Street is more immediately appealing – a picture of it even featured in an Antiques Road Show programme (from Chester Cathedral on 18/4/10). We are used to progressive looks in our buildings. The point for the Anglican cathedral is that once inside you are transformed. Scott's transept approach is the epitome of this.

The diocese of Liverpool was created out of Chester territory in 1880. City status was conferred in tandem, late for what had already become England's second city and has come across as a proud majestic centre even during times of trouble and decline. The former produced a heyday with David Sheppard (1929–2005; Bishop of Liverpool, 1975–99), along with Derek Worlock (1920–96; Archbishop of Liverpool, 1976–96), both evangelical in persuasion and productive partners serving the city at the time of the Toxteth riots and following the tragedies affecting the football fraternity in a local context – Heysel (1985) and Hillsborough, Sheffield (1989). 1994 saw their joint award of Freedom of the City of Liverpool – ultimately they both succumbed to forms of cancer. Hope Street assumed official recognition as the link between the Anglican and RC disciplines in 2008, when the Sheppard-Worlock Statue in the form of two bronze doors, by sculptor Stephen Broadbent, was unveiled to honour them both, midway between their buildings. The money came from public donations. That says it all, for two inspired and dedicated men, set on inner city improvement and reform. This is a true conurbation cathedral, its brief South West Lancashire, which embraces the conurbation of Merseyside, from Southport in the north, round Ormskirk to Wigan (the metropolitan borough is in Greater Manchester) and down to Warrington. That is an oddity as it was transferred through local government reorganization to Cheshire in 1974, and remains there.

The new construct replaced the largest city parish church in the city on the site. St Stephen's, also in the vicinity but later demolished, served as pro-cathedral from 1910 until the Lady Chapel assumed the mantle in 1924. The foundation stone was laid in 1904, by Edward VII, who as Prince of Wales had done the same thing in 1886 at Truro, the previous new build, itself the first since St Paul's, two centuries previously. 19 July sees an annual celebration of this. On the nearest Sunday, the youngest choirboy/girl brushes oil onto the surface lines of the foundation stone, so as to keep it fresh.

We spent time here, at the crossing, termed Central Space. Vernacular works better in a modern, purpose-built setting, and 'crossing' would not convey the complexity and scale of what you see in this part of the building. Looking up we heard the story of the elevation of Great George, the biggest bell, the roof soaring 330' above ground level. That point is only halfway to the top, above the bell chamber we were to gawp at from the steps up the tower. It would have been good to see and hear them in action: a trifle ear-blasting? The vastness bore out Robin's comment that the single quarry used, at nearby Woolton, was exhausted.

The Central Space leads to the eastern transept on the cathedral plan (the term applies not just to the north and south sides but the body of it, too). This is where to find the permanent seating and recline in awe. Further east, before the choir, was an altar space flanked by diagonally placed chairs, of a more elegant design. I tried both types for different views and was rewarded, the building's character coming to life through its many angles and diversions, horizontal and vertical. Our choice of day helped – sunny springtime, so not too cold. Outside, people in shirtsleeves were enjoying the daffodils and blackthorn. In admitting it was cold inside in winter Robin did allude to the underfloor heating, which retained its warmth, pointing out that it costs more than £4K to run the cathedral day by day, from staff to electricity. The Toff opined: 'The sandstone has a warm feeling to it. Though huge and empty, it doesn't feel cold to me.' And light: to my opinion that there were few stained glass windows, Robin replied, 'There are 50, mostly way above our heads.'

You do have to look up a lot to take it all in. That included the northwest transept where the café had been installed in 2008, discreetly above the shop. Complaints about this facility – within the working building – have emanated from local traditionalists and overseas tourists alike. While the chinking of teacups and culinary aromas would prove a distraction during services, it's fine as it is, a modest, 40-seater money-spinning (think of the £4,000 per day) enterprise, designed as a subtle clear curve made of glass and light wood pleasing to the eye from afar and upfront.

At 4 pm, in time to catch the tower before it ceased business for the day, we enjoyed tea and cakes under the northwest transept stained glass window. My treacle and ginger sponge may even have involved a treacle tin. Toff's iced honey and lemon cake was on the sweet side, but not dried out as so often. I ventured into the longer-standing refectory, which can afford to create steamy fare as it is sealed off with the option of sitting outside with an aerial view of Georgian buildings afar and tombstones and greenery below. The promotional material stated: 'We have four styles of catering at the Cathedral to suit your every need and occasion – 2 public eating places: The Mezzanine Café Bar and the Refectory and 2 ways to accommodate private and occasion dining: The Western Rooms function suite and large civic receptions and dining in the Main Cathedral.'

The Café Bar was further described as 'contemporary "light bite",' and it offered 'free wireless broadband internet access', all truly C21 state-of-the-art.

Another artistic addition was introduced in 1996 by Dean the Very Revd Derrick Walters. There were five contemporary paintings dotted around, the strongest of which were in the choir – not the only rendering of the parable of the Good Samaritan. Another, in the chapter house, involved the artist's favourite quirk, a Bedlington terrier. I didn't think it worked.

The cathedral's economics have come good with its massive and many spaces. Conferences and corporate dinners are held in the extensive basement. 'Crypt' would not be the right word. This is undoubtedly a modern business place. While the city's St George's Hall was being refurbished the cathedral stood in to please all involved, and earn a tidy sum. The top hotel, the Adelphi, couldn't cope. Similarly with the Philharmonic Hall, a near neighbour. When receiving a complaint about use of facilities the appropriate response was 'You're entitled to your opinion, but we're going ahead.' Provision rather than prohibition.

We came to the cope chest, unworkable in its massiveness, and most handsome, adorned with a double cross echoing the ground plan for the transepts. This double cross would have been second choice after the eagle as iconic image. The caption mentioned:

> … there are examples of cope chests in just under a third of the Anglican cathedrals in England. The oldest ones are in Wells and Salisbury dating back to the 13th century. There has been a resurgence of interest in these historic pieces of church furniture with seven of the thirteen being constructed during C20.

Down the southern corridor, we came to the Lady Chapel by way of an intriguing illuminated passage, behind a gate. This would be the triforium for the chapel, but uniquely we could look down it from this gallery above to chapel from which there is a glorious overview. It was easy to imagine this as a separate parish church, similar to Truro (the bit remaining of the original St Mary's church). The lie of the land is responsible for the odd levels. A separate entrance is used for christenings, weddings and funerals, for which it is an ideal space. There is a direct view of Scott's chandeliers, actually designed by him and like most things, executed by top class craftsmen, whose tools were on display in the southeast transept, presenting a varied array. A feature of the chapel is the stained glass depiction in a yellow hue of celebrated women. We picked out Josephine Butler (1828–1906), who attended in particular to the plight of prostitutes in the city.

Round to the east end we passed Elisabeth Frink's 'practice sculpture, for the west door', (said Robin) and came to another inspired idea. There was an arch on either side of the altar screen for the Lay Clerks (12 men), and any of 24 boys or the same number of girls to ascend to the choir. The youthful members were drawn from local applicants, there being no choir school, and would be found, between practice and performance, outside the east end playing football. Alas, the Easter holiday break was not over so we heard no live music. A rehearsal would have been welcome to assess the acoustics. Robin felt the long vista through the opening to be inspiring. We both readily agreed. It provided yet another chance to absorb various elements of the structure. Giles Gilbert Scott had certainly inherited his forebears' affinity with the spirit of church architecture. It was convenient that the initiative was embarked upon early in the last century, inheriting the extensive output of the Scott family, the Tractarian movement and the whole network of Victorian architects. We hoped that it would coax choristers to enhanced vocal delivery.

The chapter house was next, opposite the Lady Chapel. Robin observed that in practice the Dean and Chapter would sit in far more comfortable surroundings. The bishop was ascribed the status of 'Visitor'. Absolutely! I noted the Suffragan Bishop of Warrington on the list. I muttered my line about Warrington now being in Cheshire to which Toff noted Robin's silent reaction and whispered 'You're in the wrong company here.' Well, footballers playing for high profile clubs habituate Cheshire, and the Wirral. The two 1996 paintings were noted, and a Bedlington Terrier, apparently a trade mark. Bedlington is in Northumberland, so that's another misplacement! I think the idea of introducing a more up to date interpretation of 'modern' could work, but not all the paintings are of the highest quality. There was the inherent flaw that they would fall out of date. In the end the chapter house is primarily symbolic and cannot compete with much of the rest.

We had reached the high altar and stunning stone screen, the reredos, behind it. The gold paint on it melded well with the dusky red. The Last Supper had, rarely, been devised without Judas, who had departed on an errand, so there were actually 11 at the table. The cathedra was in clear view, again not terribly practical for the bishop, situated so far from the body of the church, and lacking a canopy to assist acoustic projection. On most occasions he delivered his orations further down. We were at the choir and, satisfyingly snug between pillars on both sides was the organ, console to the north, with some of the pipes above. Otherwise it was a case of 'hunt the pipes': the organ was the biggest in Britain with over 10 thousand of them. The smaller ones were upright. Robin pointed out a few in the Corona gallery.

This time it was the organist who needed assistance in communication, being disconnected from his/her cues, a number of square feet removed along and up (expressed as metres here as usage is contemporary throughout). In Liverpool a closed-circuit television in the organ loft would be entirely in keeping, in fact something to do with spare space. Mirrors were a thing of the past, so I imagined a room downstairs full of redundant ones. A painting in the choir section depicted the subject of the Prodigal Son. The winding road may have been of a 'yellow brick' order. The piece opposite was another approach to the Good Samaritan, but we both reckoned it to be weak and compromised the integrity of the design of the space.

By contrast we were now led to the northeast transept for the mobile organ console, used for recitals, that is to be visible to an audience. We witnessed an exchange between Robin and a female organ enthusiast. It would take a series of evening classes, with an instrument to hand, just to make sense of a cathedral organ. I misted over when she mentioned 'swells'. The War Memorial Chapel filled the transept itself. Over 40,000 men are listed in the 700-odd page tome, whose pages are turned periodically. George V signed the front page in 1924. There were also galleries above, reminding me of the Gothic ('makeover') galleries in the equivalent position at Exeter in a real Norman tower.

This was when time ran out, and we made haste to purchase the tickets and tea. Robin demurred about both, unwillingly, as the Metrorail beckoned. It had been a superlative tour, and I had decided to return the next morning to fill in the gaps.

The tower involved speedy lifts and 108 stairs. The view of the region was breathtaking, of course. We couldn't quite make out Tranmere Rovers' ground over the Mersey (as a preview for the next day's action), but the local boy, Toff, showed me St Luke's, an elegant ruin between the turrets and city centre. In the Embroidery Gallery, I noticed Ninian Comper, Toff's great grandfather, assertively placed in an illustrated family tree of architects, with portraits. This also included all the Scotts and William Morris. We had, perforce, to look out for his work at Westminster Abbey a few months later. The embroidery was bright and shiny, a treasure in itself. The room offered a raised area to admire the interior. We were on Level 3, above the nave. The west window was a lot bluer close to than it had appeared from further off, but that was partly to do with the time of day, now 5 pm.

Off we went to car park and Hope Street, after a spot of misunderstanding about the method of escape. It all came good when a discreet ticket machine came into view. Toff was eager to show me one or two streets, tributaries of this short artery. 'It's improved so much,' he said, recalling how run down, even dangerous, the area had been. It now sported a number of hostelries recommended for high quality, civilized drinking, even on the street, as it were a promenade. We reached the Metropolitan Cathedral of Christ the King during a communion service, at a distance, so sat quietly, inhaling the essence of a totally different environment. Brilliant red, and some green, light streamed in through the slabs of stained glass and spilled onto seats and floor. 'Paddy's Wigwam' was an apt nickname, and circular, compact and fit for purpose it seemed. 'The Mersey Funnel' shows some wit, as well. The choir was on holiday here too, so the intended choral evensong experience was off. We noted the points of contact. The architect had been Anglican, and organ pipes looked like a display of crafts on the wall beyond the central altar.

The crypt, by Anglican Edwin Lutyens, which Toff wanted to show me, was closed by this time, but we were able to peer at photos of it in action – an elaborate display in the entrance area. The Crown of Thorns was ingenious, covering the space above the altar, concealing functional matters such as microphones and electrical cables. This was the seat of an archbishopric – there were hangings listing the bishoprics of Salford, Hallam, Middlesbrough and the others of the north. By contrast were the permanent pews and curved kneeling bar, an encouragement to pray. The Anglican cathedral offered a few red kneelers here and there. Finally the building had notoriously suffered from funding challenges during execution and the consequent need for repairs. Up the road it took many decades to build what convinced as a solid structure: there were none of these lead and brick problems at the Cathedral Church of Christ in Liverpool, but if anything went, the cost was likely to be massive.

We decided upon refreshment. I was keen on the Philharmonic (pub), part of whose entry in the *Football and Real Ale Guide* reads: 'Described by Egon Ronay as the most ornate pub in Britain I would prefer the qualities of gob smacking, jaw dropping stateliness. The Grand Lounge must be unique in its scale'. Like the Anglican cathedral? I had been there before, and new experiences were the order of the day. We crossed the road and Toff pushed open the doors of the Philharmonic Hall, for the ascent into an Art Deco delight. Built in 1849 – we saw the pictures – it was burned down and rebuilt to open in 1939, in the style of its time. The result was convincing, complete with Lloyd Loom chairs. They were 'on their last legs', said Peter the barman, who kindly unlocked the 1650 seater auditorium for a look. An Abba tribute band, Bjorn Again, was to play that night. It was all right as we had to leave Liverpool soon, but not before a pint, for me of Liverpool Organic Brewery Bitter, 'a delicately hopped ale'. Peter was good value to complete the day's experiences. He called Toff a 'plastic Scouser'. Even the object smiled in admission. The conversation moved on to catering, microwave treatment being termed 'chicken ding ding' by Peter, just the kind of thing which would be an aberration in the cathedral café. It would ring all over the building – I could hear the sound ringing all round the bare stone.

Saturday 17 April
This time it was Noel Andrews, full of respect for Robin, and apologizing for his paucity of knowledge. On the way I took the route via the shell of St Luke's, noting the empty vodka and Peroni beer bottles at the top of the steps, and a recumbent figure in the glorious sunlit gardens. All-pervading on the streets were the purple refuse bins. Liverpool Cathedral announced 'Welcome' on the west door and this time I admired the Frink figures of rival, nay brother, Bishops Sheppard and Worlock. This was followed by a private examination of the nave, and up the stairs to the tower entrance, guarded by a Giles Gilbert Scott creation – a red telephone box, his smallest creation inside his largest. It was surprising and impressive in that position.

Noel had a background in the Philharmonic Choir and apologized, 'I don't know if I'll be much help to you, but I'll try.' He was very good, taking me to the baptistery and Italian marble font. He pointed out the fish, swimming in synchronized mode round the base, and the apostles etched out on the thing itself. The seductive stone was enough to encourage a person to re-undergo the sacrament of baptism. The first victim had been the architect's granddaughter, Louise Gilbert Scott, in 1951 and she was still alive to tell the tale. I was told about the nature of cathedral visitors, such as how Scandinavians combined cathedrals with football games. I know the feeling and it's good!

We descended to the extensive basement to witness preparations for one of the many events for which the cathedral is geared up. Here it must be an essential and wide-ranging source of income, both in the nature of business needs, such as conferences over several days, and sheer entertainment. Mike McCartney, whom I remember performing Lily the Pink in his Scaffold era (McGear was his cognomen in those days), was a forthcoming gig, 'In Conversation' (Tickets £15.00 from the website). There was an abundance of activity beyond the regular services, other examples being 'Learning in the Cathedral' and 'Living History – Victorian Days', to celebrate 100 years since the consecration of the Lady Chapel, focusing on the Nobel Women of whom Josephine Butler was one.

Back up the stairs, I trudged one higher, to the bridge, this time with Liverpudlian Alan Dodd. Noel had requested him to take over, not wishing to scale the height. Once up there, I fulfilled the universal desire in a cathedral, to hear music. It was in the form of an audiotape, heard through earphones, along with a direct view of the whole building. I concentrated on the choir to the east, as the tape comprised the moments when the choristers joined the body of the church and delivered a few bars in harmony. St Augustine was quoted: 'He who sings prays twice.' The man had a point.

I heard anew, and now record, John Betjeman's opinion that this was 'one of the great buildings of the world.' I was now in a position for my own opinion and concurred, inhaling last breaths of red sandstone atmosphere among unbelievably tall arches. 'Don't look up at my arches, look at my spaces', Giles the architect once said. Alan waxed mundane, though it was in answer to my question about acoustics. An aggressively efficient hand-dryer had been installed in the new ladies toilet by the shop. On occasions when the door was not yet closed (it does happen) the sounds permeated through the building. The one for males only had paper towels, which this proved to be preferable.

The final enjoyment, after a period of essential reflection deep in the expanse dedicated to 'Christ', was a perambulation round the leafy perimeter, way down below the building. This became a prelude to fine ale in one of the better, and more historic, of Liverpool's public houses: the Thomas Rigby, named after one of so many industrialists and, in effect, benefactors of Merseyside. I chose Okell's ale from the Isle of Man. The diocese of Sodor and Man was not yet scheduled in this quest. It was something to relish if accompanied by a quaff of beer like this. The final fixture was the football game, by way of the Mersey Tunnel to Birkenhead. Tranmere Rovers beat Exeter City, to my chagrin, but the prevailing memory was of the fine 20th century cathedral.

15

Chelmsford

St Mary, St Peter & St Cedd

Province: Canterbury
Founded: 15th century parish church
Present building: 1926–29 east end
Cathedral status: 1914 – created from St Albans diocese

Website: www.chelmsfordcathedral.org.uk
Tel: 01245 294489
Email: office@chelmsfordcathedral.org.uk
Address: The Cathedral Office, New Street, Chelmsford CM1 1TY

Three to See: 1480 south porch;
statue of St Peter outside on southeast flint wall;
map of diocese, which embraces Essex and east London

Mallard

Monday 26 April, 2010

The first treat on meeting Rand at Gillingham Station was dubious: a pint at a pub he'd noticed on the way down, the Fleur de Lys. He had noted the sign saying 'Traditional Ales', outside, but the sign was very old and chipped. We settled for keg cider – Blackthorn – and settled down to plans for the East Anglian cathedral tour. The place was busy, with balloons afloat and in the process of inflation. It turned out to be the 21st anniversary of the landlords' tenure: Clive and Terry, together with Fran the bar-propper, this side for now, who'd been around since 1975. Twenty one years was also the time since Steve Davis's last World Snooker Championship triumph, prominent on the red button at this time, as he doubled up as quarter finalist and commentator: double and quits.

Rand had a spicy chicken casserole a-bubbling in his kitchen, along with fresh veg, as yet not from his allotment, at the time a mere glimmer. We talked about that – his back had to improve first. The next morning we left behind the scheduled 9.30 departure. Blame an excess of toast. No matter, as Chelmsford was an easy ride and we found a street with a space almost in sight of the destination. £1 for two hours. We admired town centre buildings of variety, character and a number of generations of origin, on the way up to a picture postcard view of the surrounding churchyard, a vivid green in the sunlight, complemented by seasonal flowers in bank and bed. It was good to arrive at such a setting, enhanced by a fetching range of memorials and tombs. If you were to look up at the southeast corner of a remarkably flint-bound building, you should espy a modern statue of St Peter 'complete with fishing boots, net, some of his catch and, of course, his key. He faced towards Bradwell-on-Sea (on the Essex coast), where St Peter's Chapel is to be found' (*A Pocket Guide to the Cathedral*). This was the nearest thing to a gargoyle for a while. We circled round the green sward, admiring what did look like a parish church, in size and presence, albeit an appealing one. Nearby Rand identified a trig point caved out of the wall. The west door carried a Latin motto: 'Ad dominum oculos levavi'. Lift your eyes to the Lord? This we did, admiring the tower and roof and noting on the board nearby, that there was a funeral scheduled for noon. It was elevenses time, but our viewing opportunity was limited. It was time to venture in.

First was the south porch, easiest approached from the cutting edge of the town centre. This is indeed no city – Chelmsford City FC has got it wrong as the place has 'borough' status, this being one of the latter-day new dioceses, initiated in 1914. These did not automatically make the place a city. It's a complicated affair, but the list of cities is growing. Her Majesty the Queen would be conferring city status on some lucky place in 2012 to mark her 60th year on the throne. The porch dates from 1460: the original parish church.

One indication of the confidence bought by elevation to cathedralhood was in the 1953 additions, reflecting Anglo-American friendship. It was good to see the arms of George Washington. Chelmsford has embraced real life in its burgeoning presence and open-heartedness. While there was no café, there was a welcome extended to all. Hospitality was dealt with in the kitchen or by caterers. No problem there. The brief was wide, as this was the second largest diocese, by population, after London. It was transferred from the same St Paul's, London to Rochester in 1845 and later to St Albans, when that see was invented in 1877. Chelmsford diocese ranges from the whole of Essex, itself by no means England's smallest county, to Leyton and Dagenham, now in East London: inner city to remote rural. That direction, eastwards, reflects the long-term population drift.

Regarding origins, the guide book states: 'The first authenticated incumbent, Richard de Gorges, was presented in 1242, the living remaining in a gift of the bishops of London until the 16th century.' This church was rebuilt in the 15th and early 16th centuries. The 20th century upgrade served as a catalyst for change. John Betjeman wrote:

Chelmsford... Remaining a late medieval parish church in spite of the changes effected in 1926 by lengthening the chancel... Attractive "Gothick" plastered ceiling. Archway between chancel and north chapel most unusual in form being semi-circular divided into two pointed arches. Very fine south porch and west tower showing East Anglian knapped flint work within traceried panels. Charming mid-C18 spire to tower.

The context was a book about churches, not cathedrals. He should serve as a tour guide: thanks John. We did pay attention, sir.

Meanwhile Rand commented that the cathedral was 'pretty nondescript. The blood's not going round me'. That was partially down to his back pain. He enjoyed one of the understated brown chairs in the nave. He, and I, would have enjoyed sitting there for the Chelmsford Sinfonietta Festival 2010 concert (£25 – must be good for that, and a necessary fund-raising event).

In the southwest chapel to St Peter, the cast bronze statue featuring a seated woman with dead child on her knees – 'the Bombed Child'. 'Already I'm impressed,' said Rand. 'They can't be political, can they?' The answer was there before him and the cathedral displayed its commitment to addressing social needs in many ways. Above, in the corner was an altar upon which was what looked like a discreet display of vessels of dry sherry, no doubt locked away behind the glass front. My henchman was new to the broader setting of religious life, such as bishops imparting their wisdom on current issues. You could listen to the Radio 4 *Today* programme for edifying examples in *Thought for the Day*. Bishops are flock custodians, after all.

Some displays were detailed, such as The Tree of Life. Mark Cazalet had produced a bespoke work, a painting attached to the space formerly occupied by the north transept window. It's large – 20 feet high in 35 wooden panels. 'Difficult to find the detail – it's turgid,' decided Rand, 'and too much gold, making it gaudy. They should commission a modern artist, instead of a naïve, poorly executed work.' He spoke as a contemporary artist himself – bloody good, too, but not for sale, alas. I needed binoculars, now a regular aid to cathedral touring, to identify the key subjects in the painting: for example a woodpecker and Judas in number 12 shirt with accompanying thermos flask and snap (sandwiches), though I preferred my initial assumption that it was a depiction of a green man. You can never have enough of those around. It's the same as gargoyles.

Invoking the help of welcomer Ronald Mathias, he proved helpful but not particularly knowledgeable. The verger or dean would have been good on information, he said, but the one was unwilling owing to the imminent funeral, the other unavailable (we just missed him). Still, we amassed many leaflets and had much to observe in a modestly-proportioned building. It reminded me of Sheffield – light, in fact sunny, in both cases, and well-augmented since attaining a higher level in the ecclesiastical hierarchy.

Ronald came from Leyton, 'metropolitan Essex', reaching the county town of Chelmsford via Eton Manor Cricket Club and that of the county of Essex. 'It's a multi-racial club,' he said, with whom the cathedral has good relations.' Also there were boys' clubs. Frankie Vaughan had been one of their sponsors.

Another thrust of the cathedral's activity was charitable work for the homeless. Once a year the dean spent a night in a cardboard box. To me that and the bishop's question in Parliament below suggested a productive and dynamic attitude to the cathedral and see. Being a town centre church had its drawbacks, however, which were borne out by the notices to beware of theft; also, perhaps, Ronald's discovery, while we were discussing the expanse of the bishopric, that the diocese map had vanished from the notice board. Attention was drawn to local information – lots going on. The map would have been more interesting to us objective observers.

I had found this on my computer:

The Diocese of Chelmsford is Europe's premier region for regeneration. The Thames Gateway, the M11 corridor and Stansted airport, Harwich seaport and the main site for the

London 2012 Olympics are all located within the Diocese.

As well as being a place of worship, the Cathedral is a popular venue for concerts, lectures, civic events, school prize-giving and university graduation ceremonies.

The Rt Revd John Gladwin, Bishop of Chelmsford, asked a supplementary question to the Minister during Lord Astor's Question, "To ask Her Majesty's Government what is the future role of Her Majesty's armed forces in Afghanistan' on 13 July 2009:

"My Lords, we on these Benches too send our condolences and our prayers to those who have lost their lives. Perhaps we in the House might also remember those in the Chaplaincy Service, for whose services there will be considerable demand as a result. Is not one of the difficulties that we face in a situation such as this that the presence of large numbers of particularly American and other western troops in Afghanistan can add strength to the radical Islamist argument that this is about western imperial ambitions? Will the Minister accept that, unless we are absolutely clear about the purposes of this operation and the boundaries of what we are seeking to achieve in a very different and distant culture, hopes for success will be undermined?"

Rand and I went our own way, reaching the pulpit, in a contemporary metal sweep, which worked here. It led quickly to the series of icons round the chancel. They suggested the Orthodox discipline, and by extension the inclusivity of the Anglican brief, a question not finding a convincing answer in this building. The ones in the quire illustrated Mary, John, Jesus and St Cedd. The last was an immigrant to the East Saxons in the 7th century. He was also the inspiration for the Mildmay Altar Frontal to the left of the chancel, quite a celebrity hereabouts. One of the cathedral leaflets claims '(it) is very serene and still and invites the onlooker to pause and contemplate'. Fair enough, and complementary to the more vigorous recent introductions elsewhere.

While we were at the east end, Ronald came over to proffer a few handouts, somehow leading to the subject of the choir. There is one, of considerable repute, the cathedral school proudly furnishing it with talent. Rand asked about regional focus, to which Ronald cited 'CM' postcodes, referring to Chelmsford as a series of villages. Visitors, from Italy and France as much as locally, would come for silent prayer. This was the church of the family, the regularity of the services, beginning with

8 am communion, supporting that.

We arrived at the shop, occupying the northwest corner, and as well-filled as I remembered from the last visit in 2008 as part of a weekend for football at Dagenham & Redbridge FC in the metropolitan part of the diocese. My companion, Priv, had espied and acquired a copy of Peter Lupson's book *Thank God for Football,* something I'd read about for my own football book *Round the Turnstiles.* Wakey, who was also there (on the way to the Chelmsford Winter Beer Festival) recalled: 'Though the cathedral wasn't big in size, it felt spacious. It was a sunny day and we'd not been drinking (yet). Maybe it was because a service had just finished and the building was being used… A feature was the stained glass – quadrants centred round a tree of life in vivid colours. Local Essex stuff – wheatfields, agriculture. I had to look at it closely to see the owl and other things and different birds in the trees'.

Apparently ordering stock was in the remit of the Canon Pastor (Ronald asserted), worth noting for the future. One book in the economically displayed but amply stocked shelves was 'Cathedral Appeal Cookery Book' (£5), collected by Pat Dean and including, I noted with delight in view of the fixture two days hence, 'Ready in no Time Pizza: St Albans Pizza'. This was the offering of Janet Pettifer, who had embarked upon married life in the Hertfordshire city. Not a mere town, you note. History was on its side. Unfortunately there were no whisky shot glasses (I wanted one for Wakey, a whisky souvenir enthusiast), which we concluded reflected an official pro-temperance attitude. Later the same day, St Edmundsbury shop was selling a choice of goblets and wine glasses, but no shot glasses either. Did this betoken a widespread 'no spirits policy'?

By now the noonday hour approached and the non-believer, but socially sensitive, Rand was keen not to interfere with the funeral. I did spend a minute in St Cedd's, Chapel at the west end, to observe something else. During 2010 the cathedral received icons from anonymous Orthodox iconographers. They get around, but I was undecided how successfully. I've since come to the conclusion that anything goes in a cathedral gradually establishing a history and physicality. Icons turned out to be universal. It was good to find a constant in these diverse buildings.

The variety of display in the cathedral lent to its identity, For instance I loved the barrel roof, freshly painted in pink and blue, reminiscent of a subtle version of Aston Villa's characteristic strip, called 'claret and blue'. There were golden bosses in the centre of each section, pointed at by a dozen arms from the perimeter. It was most distinctive.

We left amid increasing numbers of black-garbed congregation, by the south porch, now a noble frame for funeral attenders. I paused long enough for a young woman to ask me if I needed help. I asked the identity of the unfortunate one. She replied that it was her grandfather, Basil Rolfe, who had been long associated with the cathedral. He had died in Scotland. *Morning has Broken* started up to open the proceedings. I well remembered Cat Stevens' big hit, and it was chosen for the wedding of the brother of a friend of mine for his wedding in the 1970s. There's a point to make about the circle of life, and remote connections. It opened:

> *Morning has broken, like the first morning*
> *Blackbird has spoken, like the first bird*

and evoked the spring season we witnessed satisfyingly around the cathedral, and, indeed everywhere on this three-day quest.

We departed to search for the chapter house 'over there'. Ronald had waved vaguely to the northwest. We found that, but not the cathedral office where he had said we would find the dean's email address for further enquiries. 'He'll tell you all you need to know at once', he claimed. The chapter house was an effective, fairly recent addition. On the top floor it was good to see a meeting in full flow, perhaps of the chapter, through the glass panel in the door. Clerics in purple abounded under the pleasingly irregular shape of the room, which was evocative of a traditional chapter house we reckoned. On the stairs were coloured engravings of the town centre from previous centuries, with the narrow green spire of the cathedral, then parish church, penetrating clouds above the mayhem of secular life on the streets below.

Back by the sward, the funeral procession approached, followed by an elderly woman on stick and dressed in pale clothes. It was coffee time. We ventured over the green to meet a solitary duck. There was no water in sight, and we did not know how far away the River Chelmer lay. This prompted the mallard as the unofficial icon for this place: an urban/rural creature, both wild and familiar, of all time and for now, like the life and work of the hub of the diocese 'serving the Church of England in Essex and East London'.

We eyed the Saracen's Head just over the road, in the true town centre. In the foreground we noted the burly pall-bearers and accompanying hearse with not a single cigarette between them (a disciplinary offence I'm sure). A local landmark stood there: the memorial statue, to Right Honourable Sir Nicolas Conyngham Tindal, 1776–1846. It looked over to Tindal Street. It's worth a verbatim quote of the inscription, such was the man's valour and the eloquence of description:

> *... to preserve for all time the image of a judge, whose administration of English law, directed by supreme wisdom,*

animated by purest love of justice, endeared by unwearied kindness and graced by the most lucid style, will be held by his county in undying remembrance.

Some accolade! We went on to a contented coffee break in the Saracen's before the journey north into Suffolk. The only problem was my single espresso. It proved a tad powerful. I told Rand: 'I'm going to have to give this up.'

The visit to Chelmsford Cathedral had taken almost exactly the two available hours. With 11,270 sq ft it rates as the second smallest English cathedral, one up from Derby. I'd sum it up as 'modest but purposeful'.

16

St Edmundsbury

St James

Province: Canterbury
Founded: 1503 as parish church (1065 abbey demolished at Reformation)
Restored: 1862 nave roof, 1865 chancel, 20th century further extensions, 2005 Gothic tower added
Cathedral status: 1914 – from Ely and Norwich dioceses

Website: www.stedscathedral.co.uk
Tel: 01284 748726
Email: visitor.officer@stedscathedral.co.uk
Address: The Visitor Office, St Edmundsbury Cathedral, Abbey House, Angel Hill, Bury St Edmunds IP33 1LS

Three to See: The Millennium lantern tower, a diocesan landmark; treasury, the subject of considerable attention;
Susanna window

Lion

Monday 26 April, 2010

'Not another roundabout,' muttered Rand, 'look at the price of petrol there,' as we passed a gas station on the A131 charging the seriously excessive rate of £124.9 per litre (average price at the time £121.9). A jousting competition was advertised at Hedingham Castle. I remember being amused on my previous visit to the area at the adjacent road signs to the village, Castle Hedingham, and Hedingham Castle, for touristic purposes. It was curious seeing the two versions one above the other. Next was Holy Trinity, Halstead. I realized the quest had got to me – I was putting churches before towns, and while Holy Trinity was early on in the Halstead experience, the town did seem to offer something to investigate in the future. In the country again, we were reminded that the General Election was nigh. A double placard reared itself among the greenery – blue with the loud phrase 'Vote for Change', and, below, even bigger 'Conservative'.

'How far to Sudbury?' asked the driver. 'Two or three miles; the way you drive it seems like quite a few.' And we found ourselves in this town, on the best route from Chelmsford to Bury St Edmunds, resolutely resisting the temptations of the birthplace of Thomas Gainsborough, and I'm sure, the charms of Sudbury. Bits of it we did observe: the impressive and stately houses in various colours. Also a curiosity: a solitary statue of a seated figure outside the church perimeter wall facing the road. What was the story? Further on was parked an Eddie Stobart lorry, with the name 'Lucie Sandra' on the front. That indicated an ideas decline in Eddie's name vault.

Rand was reflecting upon the Chelmsford experience: 'Funerals upset me therefore I don't want to go to any more,' referring to his own family. 'You don't have to, it's your life,' said I. 'They don't suit everybody.'

We continued meandering on the northbound road. The occasional blackthorn eased by on either side, a piggery or two came into sight, taking up whole fields, and lunch beckoned, having established that the Theatre Royal, Bury St Edmunds would not provide much of a show, on the food or any front, before it opened its doors for the evening show. The prospect of Lavenham emerged as a modest detour, its reputation for scenic town and church preceding it.

The first sight was of the late Perpendicular church, surrounded by well-sculpted spherical bushes, in a fascinating geometric layout. Dedicated to St Peter and St Paul, it boasted a substantial porch, much cleaner than the rest of the building, conjuring up in my memory Leeds Town Hall, in the 1970s, after it was de-grimed, surrounded by its neighbours still blacker than grey. The best thing here was the gargoyles (on the porch and all down the roof) which I had found to be a rarity among the 15 cathedrals and supporting other church buildings so far. I was using 'Round the Gargoyles' as a working title for this book at the time. Its inappropriateness became apparent fairly soon – cathedrals aren't really in the gargoyle market compared with parish churches such as Lavenham, and you don't go round them so much as strain your neck gawping up.

Built between 1486 and 1525, which puts it very late as a medieval-influence build, it had surprisingly simple, modest benches as pews, which belied the luxury of the rest of the church. There was an abundance of wealth there. The kneelers showed merit, and imagination, with a wide variety of images. I took pictures of the obvious sheep motif, and a harvesting scene. These had been the outcome of the Millennium Kneeler Project.

At the back, by the second hand bookstall, was a notice saying: 'Help yourself to a recycled carrier bag (for books from the stall).' Outside again, we faced a choice of three paths at equidistant angles from the south side, for town, houses and country respectively. On we sped, aiming for the famed Swan, ancient coaching inn. But I was mistaken: the Angel was the one in the *Good Beer Guide*, I discovered too late. The chosen tavern seemed expensive from the board outside and reeked of something untoward from the kitchen within, so we wandered up the street and spotted the Greyhound, This served us well. It was a shame about the Angel, but Rand kept quiet. Local Greene King IPA was chosen, as a light brew, to wash down fish pie (salmon, fulsome and tasty), in the garden. There, two eponymous dogs came into view, accompanied by a character who may have been to do with the management, judging by his imperious manner and badinage with a decorative female in tow. A brief perambulation of the town followed for us, taking in enough of the medieval houses to mark it as a place to which to return at leisure; and perhaps to Halstead church.

Now for Bury St Edmunds. The diocese of St Edmundsbury and Ipswich was invented in 1914. I would prefer St E on its own, as that is the location of the cathedral. For over 1,000 years the site of Suffolk's more recent cathedral has been one of worship and pilgrimage. The death of Edmund, King of the East Angles, at the hands of the Vikings in 869, led to the building of an abbey to house his remains. St James' Church, its forebear, was built within the precincts of the abbey.

The stunning new tower is the tour de force in this charming (West) Suffolk town. It was completed in 2007, immediately to gain status as a key landmark from the A14. It commands the ancient territory of the former Benedictine abbey of St Edmundsbury. I had been forewarned about the brilliant addition to the complement of England's cathedral structures. I cite a bulletin:

Also, photographs of the painted fan vaulting were to be seen in various magazines through the year. It was bold and impressive.

We found a car parking space for 3 hours outside the Angel Hotel for £2.70, (4* and expensive, but the Gents was good, the need a direct result of a whole pint at lunchtime). Rand declined, despite his much-proclaimed bladder deficiency. I reckoned that shyness of using hotel facilities was something to do with it. We entered the cathedral by way of the new cloister, completed as recently as 2009. It seemed very fresh. We delayed the essential visit to the catering facility until we'd earned it. A 'first' ensued. We entered by the northeast door, straight into the recently-completed St Edmund Chapel with something much older: a 16th century German picture of Jesus with the martyred Edmund. The temporary treasury was nearby, housing some bright goblets. The Lady Chapel was unavailable. Its altar was visible; otherwise it was all work-in-progress and obscured. The benefit of visiting at that stage was the viscous atmosphere and fresh textures of novel cylindrical and square pillars. 'It still has dust on it – it's so new you can smell the stone dust,' said Rand of the first one. The stone was comparatively local, given the total lack in Suffolk. No longer was limestone quarried from the now defunct Barnack, Peterborough up the road, but Clipsham, Rutland. Barnack has become a valuable resource in a quite different way, in the guise of Barnack Hills and Holes National Nature Reserve.

We were indulging in the utter novelty of the space. The high altar, with quire in the centre, abounded with strong square red and gold tiles. The altar was furnished with similar hues. Workmen were busy on the organ space, while the instrument underwent construction in Durham at the time, courtesy of Harrison & Harrison. Mark Venning, the firm's chairman, remembered this:

The contract for St Edmundsbury Cathedral was a slow-moving

*one, with my first visit in 1994 and completion only last year.
The old organ did not have a proper case and, with its internal
pipes and mechanism exposed, it looked rather like a disused
chemical factory. At an early stage I attended a memorable
meeting with the cathedral architect, Stephen Dykes Bower, who
had always envisaged a beautiful organ as part of his design for
the enlargement of the cathedral. He was 91 years old and very
frail, but he expressed firm views about what should be done.
Seventeen years on it was moving to see his wishes successfully
realised: the two new organ cases, beautifully decorated, have
caused a sensation.*

Mark Venning 2/6/11

The forthcoming evening prayer session would clearly be just that, with no music on offer. Further on in our self-determined meander, Rand drew me to the lower end of the quire, or crossing, for an upward view of the tower. Excellent, but more of that after tea.

We must move to the underlying design, of Stephen Dykes Bower. The high altar sanctuary had been constructed in 1959–60, and the architect was deeply involved in the immense project of augmenting the recently-devised cathedral as a funder, too. We noted the cathedra by F E Howard of Oxford, and his font cover, not exciting but fit for purpose, we thought.

Rather than delve in the original, western, half, and bearing in mind the time constraints of the Refectory Restaurant, we retreated to the cloister, its newness adorned with plaques and tomb slabs from a previous generation, with the substantial annexe on its south side, which had been built up as a complete two-floor building. Having alerted the reluctant, and stroppy, cateress, we went for cups of tea (95p) rather than a pot for one (£1.30), for two (£2.60), or three (£3.90). Not much of a deal there, and her attitude would hardly encourage a return to make more contribution to the cathedral's coffers. The cakes were above average: iced lemon and coffee and walnut, by now so routine that we might order in advance. However the iced cake did prompt for Rand a reminder of Nellie the cook's sugar-rich cakes at the Victoria Theatre, Stoke-on-Trent in the mid-1970s. I think we originally met during a break over one, or two, of those in what passed for a café in those days. Rand was Assistant Designer there and needed regular escape from the 'endless demands', as well as a roll-up.

The time was nigh for the conventional approach to our destination, up the cloister again, in a fresh Gothic style consistent with the straightforward look inside. We couldn't resist the main road, cheek-by-jowl with the wall. It disallowed any space at the west front, but a pleasing urban view up to the Angel with hotel, car park and Abbey Gate, and southwards to St Mary's Church and towards the Greene King Brewery. A veritable feast lay before us with the notable exception of the 1819 Theatre Royal which was out of sight. The shop abutted the entrance in the northwest corner, and stocked the cathedral cats book, leading to my first question to the guide once inside the cathedral. There were no cats here but she immediately diverted attention to "the new tower", advising that the best view was from the crossing. Meanwhile, as we were in the appropriate area, we heard about the Norman tower at the west end. This area was now significantly below street level, indicating road metalling (Rand's word. It failed the word scan), that is the trunk road, which had been built up over the centuries.

Fresh from the abundance of icons suggesting Eastern Orthodox influence at Chelmsford, we were reassured to see a few here, too, starting on a pillar. The guide (part-time from elsewhere in Eastern Europe) was unable to help with our enquiries: what/why/whence? She had no idea, and directed us to the verger who was attending to another query beyond the nave, a long way off. This was Amy Bull, four years into the job, wearing an unfamiliar working habit in black, which involved cleavage revelation. We established that the icons were recent, perhaps aiming to spread the C of E word in a wider context. There was more about the tower. We had enjoyed it first as a landmark, a fresh, newly constructed Gothic structure, reminiscent of Guildford in pure execution. Up at the divide between old St James' and new build, the workmen had finished for the day, leaving a silent display of the 43 Anglican coats of arms on a mounted display. The home diocese was represented round the perimeter at the foot of the tower. I noted a few, such as the boat and keys of Portsmouth, the azure fleur-de-lys of Wakefield, the mitre of Manchester and the bull of Oxford while we waited, first for the shop manager, then the PR Manager, Sarah Friswell. She turned out to be the best source of information.

The scene was set with a basic fact: scaffolding had been in place since 2000. Much of the initiative had been linked to the investing euphoria of the new millennium; money thus made available augmented by private support from the Vestey family, whose plaque we noted in the north aisle under organ-wraps. Such was the complexity and permanence of the project that we were told of the tearful leaving party for bricks and mortar men Dave and Bill, who had been on the job for nine years – pretty long contracts. I've also heard reference to whole legal careers based upon North Sea Oil.

To me, Sarah's assessment of the development of cathedral artefacts suggested a well-meaning interest in expressing the traditional, adapting to the current. The presence of icons supported that. Meanwhile, a project she would like to see in the future would be to extend the cloister on another side. The current single one was fine, 'but once you've started… ' She didn't finish the sentence. Upon request, she led us to the crypt, clean and fresh in its central space, seeming just right for the new treasury, when built. We were aware of the goblets at present on display at the east end, but now we learned of the Bury Bible, at Corpus Christi, Cambridge, and the Bury Herbal, in Oxford, at the Bodleian Library. This, itself, was only completed in 2009. Reports of the new Bod have varied. Daytrips from Bristol have been sold out, whereas someone I bumped into, who was involved in the project, criticized it as 'far too much staircase'. There was a copy of the Bury Cross, in walrus ivory, whose original was housed in the Metropolitan Museum, New York.

The Treasury, if it was to be so called, would be a fine addition to this invigorating new building. For that is what it seemed. Having recently been immersed in the inestimable glory of Liverpool Anglican Cathedral, here was its peer in East Anglia. Once again the plethora of the officially top C of E buildings had produced something remarkable, fulfilling and individual. I felt confident after a wildly varied range of cathedrals that the game would run right to the end. Of these this was only the third in sunlight, which certainly showed it off well, more than most owing to its newness.

Sitting in the squeaky-clean choir stalls, I reconfirmed the theory transformed into practice. We were here at a critical time. With work incomplete, though much had just been done, it echoed the recent completion of the other modern builds, and equally the idea of a medieval cathedral. It simply revealed the world at large, where wheelbarrows and loose planks still abounded. We were so privileged to be at St Edmundsbury when the tower presented a pale, powerful quality, bright Lincs-stone-white, and the weather vane cocks shone resplendently against the clear blue sky. The air was heavy, icons flashy, floors made of regally sobre red and gold-yellow, to produce the majestic growl-free lion of the coat of arms. This is not an aggressive part of the world, but lordly and quietly assertive. The lion was then chosen as my image of the cathedral of Suffolk, golden and proud in the sunlight: a lion rampant, standing erect with forepaws raised.

Moved by the immersion, a remedial stroll was essential for Rand and me round the public park, which once upon a time had been an extensive monastic institution. Local resident Terry Waite, whom I met at St Asaph that September, thought it appalling that this magnificent historic site should meet its end as such a ruin. He put strong voice to the thoughts of so many. Meanwhile, hellebores and daffodils were yielding to the next stage of the spring floral display, but the cosmetically maintained ruins of the flint-built abbey remained, to our delight. Venturing towards St Mary's, at the southern end of the ground plan, we passed by the main event again with a satisfied glow, and indulged in the houses built out of ancient flint walls. The Norman gatehouse provided reassurance in its certain, sequestered and sunken pen. There's nothing like a Romanesque church building for solid confidence. It reminded me of a Bach composition, almost any, for structure, certainty and, above all, inspiration.

Enough, as St Mary's Church was closed. It was now after 5 pm. I had to note what to return to see in the church: 'a marvellous hammer-beam,' (John Betjeman) and 'impressive interior' (Treasures of Britain). This was yet another reason to return to Suffolk. We sought out the Regency Theatre Royal for another architectural piece of newness – refurbishment completed only lately. That evening Pam Ayres was to provide the entertainment and we had the brief opportunity (despite warnings of sound checks for this one-night stand) of enjoying another sharply-designed, lucid interior. Not much comfort was evident (wooden seats) but plenty of style. I'd like to spend an evening in one of the circle level boxes for six. My previous visit had been to see Timberlake Wertenbaker's *Our Country's Good* in 1998. The Theatre Royal remains one of the country's most glorious old theatres. It opened in 1819 and is a National Trust property, one of the few open during the winter months. It has to, as it presents shows all year round.

Departure was urgent. Failing to pinpoint a pub in Bury St Edmunds itself, we made for the Bear at Beyton, off the Ipswich road, for a pint of local ale, Cannon Brewery's Gunner's Daughter. A man at the bar recommended the Dog and Partridge, which brewed its own ales. Unfortunately I had espied it as we drove down the one-way street by the brewery, but our concern for parking obviated a visit. East Anglia is evidently good for premier buildings and ale. It remained to try to visit the quarry, which spawned the building in this leonine construct. Clipsham was a new target. Regarding domestic feline, as opposed to leonine, matters, Sarah Friswell was to tell me a year later that from a total of two residents cats a few years earlier, there were now none. However cats and other pets abounded at the houses of canons. The update included the news that two sides of cloisters were now open. This was a place of expansion.

Fig 21

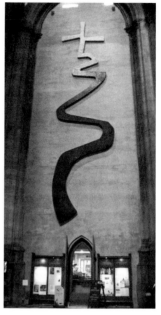

Fig 22

[21] St Edmundsbury: Suffolk's landmark: the splendid
     2005 tower.
[22] Ely: *The Way of Life* by Jonathan Clarke, in cast
     aluminium.
[23] St Albans: St Matthew = Lord Grimthorpe, restorer.
[24] St Albans: Medieval paintings in Norman nave.

Fig 23

Fig 24

17

Ely

Holy Trinity

Province: Canterbury
Founded: 673 as monastery, becoming cathedral in 1109
Present building: 1081 through medieval period
Restored: 1847–78 by Giles Gilbert Scott

Website: www. cathedral.ely.anglican.org
Tel: 01353 667735
Email: visits@cathedral.ely.anglican.org
Address: Ely Cathedral Chapter House, The College, Ely, Cambridgeshire
CM7 4DL

Three to See: The Octagon by way of a Tower Tour;
Stained Glass Museum, obtaining a 'Whole Experience Tour' for this, the
tower and more, expensive but worth it;
eel sculpture 'The Way of Life' at the west end, north wall

Eel

Monday 27 April, 2010

The party was three-strong: Mary, a friend of Rand's and our hostess for a couple of nights, joined us regulars. Her disabled parking permit proved to be a considerable boon on the day. It was a 40-something minute drive from her house, awash with blossoms and pond life, and well-situated near the previous item on the list, St Edmundsbury. Past Wicken Fen, the famous landmark hit us across flat terrain. Wicken Fen itself, evocatively introduced by its mentor Jeremy Purseglove, was to send Rand and me a-quivering after the visit to Peterborough Cathedral in the autumn.

That eyeful of Ely accorded with the reports, verbal, oral, everything. 'The Ship of the Fens?' Well, yes: 'enticing' might serve, and we'd be there soon! And we were, and allowed to park free for the whole day. Admittedly anyone can do that for three hours, with a longshot view of a cannon, and beyond that, the oddly unbalanced west end of the cathedral dedicated to the Holy Trinity. The cannon was Russian, captured during the Crimean War in 1860, at which time our medieval cathedrals were over half a millennium old and undergoing widespread restoration.

There was a clear plan. Ely had been a daunting prospect. On investigation a challenging set of options was available for guided tours. We went for the mega-one 'The Whole Experience' (£11 concessions, but this was to be a long performance). Once inside I reserved places on the next cathedral tour, at noon, to be followed by the Octagon Tower Tour at 1 pm and the Stained Glass Museum thereafter. There was also tea or coffee in the Refectory, as 'This is the whole experience', affirmed the uniformed cashier. We could have chosen the West Tower as an alternative to the Octagon, but the cashier advised the latter when I asked. Photography was included, too. Just as well, as I was to take 142 that day. Oh, the benefit of digi-tecnnology!

As it was, just after 11 am, we elected for a wander round the perimeter in the welcome sunshine. This afforded sight of some gargoyles, whose function appeared to have been replaced by black lead down pipes. Three of these proudly announced '1994' at the top and a fourth '1995'. The gargoyles were ageless and mostly in an advanced state of weathering. The bits we were unable to enter comprised an expanse of former monastic dwellings. We were later given an aerial view of these. The city of Ely was a pleasant domestic, seemingly affluent place. It's always good at this time of year to witness the encroachment of shorts and repose on grassy slopes in the knowledge that the summer months were imminent. We admired the 12th century west front in all its Norman magnificence, bemoaning a little the decision, so long ago, not to replace the northwest tower. We re-entered the portal for our free cup of – what? I wanted espresso but was denied –

'You can have regular tea or coffee'. Mean spirited, don't you think? Mary had espresso anyway – she wasn't doing 'The Whole Experience,' so had to pay, or rather Rand did, the £1.80. 'Regular' would have been £1.50. My filter coffee was insipid, and I almost made the decision to abandon it in future for raspberry'n'cranberry or fennel tea. The café was cramped, with a stained glass roof, of an early velux variety. I don't mean coloured, just murky. It provided an obscured view of the north wall above. The adjoining shop looked considerably more spacious and well-appointed. We had already decided to try everything while we had the opportunity. The Almonry Restaurant was earmarked for later refreshments. It was secreted in the corner of the lawns on the north side of the cathedral, with a door onto the High Street. It also boasted a bloom-filled garden.

The tour started, conducted by the splendidly dry Ted Lachlan, a guide for 'a mere ten years'. We were immediately interrupted by a prayer call by the canon for the day, involving a reference to the University of the Third Age, and the Lord's Prayer. This, as at other cathedrals, was conducted at most hours. I'm sure this was a good thing, as while Ely is an expensive tourist stop, both town and cathedral, visitors, of universal range, should be made aware of its *raison d'être*.

Ted referred to its status as one of eight monastic (Benedictine) foundations, now with dioceses. Here is some history:

- 673 – with Etheldreda, a local Saxon queen, later Northumbrian, then back to Ely as abbess
- 869 – destroyed by Danes
- 970 – new Benedictine monastery
- 1081 – third monastic church (the present building), intended as abbey
- 1109 – Bishopric (900 year anniversary celebrated throughout 2009. We should have come then)

It was under the jurisdiction of Lincoln whose aegis covered territory east of the line from the Humber to the Thames. The revised secular county of Cambridgeshire had absorbed the Isle of Ely (1965) and 'gobbled up Huntingdonshire (1974), so Ely has 308 parishes', said Ted, also the Soke of Peterborough, at the northwest end of this general area. However the Anglican diocese of Peterborough now looked after the Soke together with Northamptonshire and Rutland (part of Leicestershire). Finally there's a bit of west Norfolk (the Downham Market area) in the see of Ely. Confused? Try negotiating the Fens without detailed local knowledge.

The west door was in Transitional style, moving on from

Romanesque. Ted was telling us about the part behind us, as 22 of us sat in the commanding Norman nave. 'The unique silhouette is of the west tower. The top stage has turrets on each of the four corners.' It is a familiar image, ranking as one of the best of English buildings, along with famous paintings, which many know but few actually see in the canvas. He drew attention to the Millennium exhibit, *The Way of Life* in cast aluminium by Jonathan Clarke, cleverly shaped to embrace the numbers 1, 2 and 3 downwards like a sinuous eel; rough at the top and sharply shining. The cathedral leaflet said of its theme 'travelling from darkness to light and leading us to the cross of Christ'. A prayer is attached to the piece:

> *Lord God,*
> *Through life's difficult path,*
> *Be with us on our journeyAnd lead us from darkness*
> *To the light of Christ.*
> *Amen.*

The eel is the symbol here, hence 'Ely' (the district of eels) and its isle, formerly rising above the water proliferating with the creatures. However, we chose this as the icon over a ship, as a more potent image of the cathedral's character, in its terrain. One of my favourite culinary experiences has been smoked eel with new potatoes and Chablis. Such was provided in a lovely restaurant in the Somerset Levels, an area akin to the Fens. Jeremy Purseglove covered them both in *Taming the Flood* (1988):

> *Alfred the Great led the resistance against the Danes from Athelney in the Somerset Levels; and... William of Normandy conquered England in 1066; he did not succeed in subduing Ely and the surrounding fens until 1071, when Hereward the Wake submitted.*

Imagine the hero marauding in dank reed beds, peering through bulrushes, at the time when the cathedral was under construction. He was inspiring in so many directions, the legend of his resistance (he died in 1072) lending later to Robin Hood stories further up the country. The connection extended to Mike Riley's novel *The Legend of Hereward the Wake*, also involving drug-taking, psychopathy and arson. His very name means 'army guard' and Wake means 'watcher'. It was even rumoured that Hereward was the son of King Leofric of Mercia and Lady Godiva (the eventual inspiration for the eponymous 1966 hit by Peter and Gordon, one of my favourites at the time). I was glad to note the emporium, a bar in the town, named after the hero. There were other tempting taverns nearby which we didn't try, either, such as the King's Arms, Minster Arms and the Royal Standard.

There was also a local reference to the zealot to whom anyone interested in cathedrals should not refer: 'Cromwell's', after Oliver the Protector, born nearby: 'Mr Cromwell of Ely'. In power after the execution of Charles I in 1649, Oliver Cromwell, 'erstwhile champion of the commoners, was named as one of the commissioners under a new Act for the Draining of the Great Level'. Dutchman Cornelius Vermuyden, also instrumental in the Somerset Levels project, was to follow this through. 'The two massive channels run straight towards the Wash, enclosing a flood-land which fills up in winter, as Vermyuden intended. They are his greatest monument. In 1653, after the remaining works had been completed by Dutch prisoners of war under Vermuyden's direction, a service of thanksgiving was held in Ely Cathedral,' (*Taming the Flood*).

On the tour we turned to the geometrically devised nave, of the 11th and 12th centuries. Looking up, it looked standard, until you considered the detail: 'arcade, gallery (triforium), clerestory, in a ratio 6, 5, 4'. That was of arches, and in the nave, the Romanesque columns, solid with rubblecore, faced with limestone. The quarry employed was at Barnack, near Peterborough and the journey was tricky, by the river Nene, the Wash and the Great Ouse, arriving south of the site for carving. The structure was magnificent.

The whole place must have been very colourful up to 1539, when Henry VIII closed the monasteries. Traces of red and blue paint are still visible. The transept arches have faint blue and white stripes. But the monarch required all imagery to be removed once he had assumed the mantle of religious control in England. This was supervised by the incumbent bishop (thank God). Had an outsider been appointed it might have ended up a roofless ruin like some of the abbeys of Yorkshire. There was too much Maryanism, especially the ubiquitous Lady Chapels, which drew attention to some churches. 1770 saw the removal of the stone pulpitum, a divider between the monks in the quire and general public in the nave. Since then the vista from the east end has been of 537' to the west, a longer distance than all except Canterbury and Winchester.

Ely, alone among England's cathedrals, has a central feature over the crossing that somewhat resembles the polygonal vaulted lantern towers of Spain. The tower collapsed in 1322. It fell eastwards, impacting on the chancel. The rebuilding, by Alan of Walsingham, was on a new ground plan. At ground level there is an optical illusion. It is an irregular octagon – the '8' was significant: the eighth day, linked with eternity and immortality. Ted directed the audience, sitting in chairs on the edge of the crossing, to look up, right up. Depictions were in Byzantine form. At the top the Christ figure appeared in the centre, ruling overall. Next down was a ring of standing angels on panels. This was refaced in 1541 and the glass was Victorian, with 12 stone apostles (3 x 4 formation): heaven to earth and darkness to light in the lantern tower. The whole appeared strongly iconic, that is Byzantine, and suddenly made sense of all the apparently Eastern Orthodox imagery we'd been seeing in East Anglian cathedrals, and not been convinced. There was an historical context in the history of the church, a Byzantine reference, successful in this magnificent wooden octagon lantern, hovering in the central tower, itself resplendent with more of the same. Pevsner summarized:

> *The Octagon is a delight from beginning to end for anyone who feels for space as strongly as for construction* (Rand was the construction enthusiast and loved the Octagon). *For the basic impression created by the Octagon as one approaches it along the nave is one of spaciousness. We found we were taking a deep breath after the oppressive narrowness of the Norman work. Then follows, as one tried to account for that sudden widening of one's lungs, the next moment's feeling, a feeling of surprise.*
>
> The Buildings of England: Cambridgeshire by Nikolaus Pevsner

And that was having been entranced with the nave.

Guide Ted continued: 'The crossing is 74' wide and the Lantern Tower weighs 200 tons. You'll appreciate there was no mean problem to be solved. Not a stone mason but a carpenter': Edward III's 'king's master' William Hurley (working 1319–54) started here in 1334. He used 280 interlocking beams. I caught Rand's eye, sated with this and thrilled with the prospect of the forthcoming climb up to angel level and beyond. Mary looked demurely satisfied.

At the pulpit we moved to Victorian restorer George Gilbert Scott, cathedral architect in 1847, until his death in 1879. Three quarters of the building had become unused because of its dangerous state. Above the pulpit was hung another Millennium artefact, 'a wooden figure of Christ (which looked burnished close up) with his right hand raised in blessing and the left pointing to whoever was preaching in the pulpit'. Ted said no more. No more was needed.

The nave altar demonstrated flexibility of use. 'One extreme is the annual teenagers' Rave in the Nave,' reported Ted with an air of drollness.

It was clear to see – a substantial space easily adapted from altar to seating. The seating was certainly varied, suggesting a sequence of different deals over the years. And there'd been plenty of those.

The 1090 east transept was in austere Norman style, the roof unique to Ely: an East Anglian hammerbeam. There were horizontal angels looking vertically down. Angels did abound in the building, but I wasn't concerned about Rand's defensiveness about them as he was transfixed in awe at the all-consuming beauty of every new sight. There was a private prayer chapel dedicated to St Dunstan (10th century), and St Eswold (bishop of Winchester in 970. Winchester was a key to so much), Christ and St Mary Magdalene. The northeast transept contained two chapels, one military, featuring St Edmund, 870, whom we'd already met at his place in Suffolk.

We were taken down the Processional Way. Next to it were toilets, discreetly located. Rand didn't notice them, but I, lagging behind at the back of the posse, took advantage of the facility. There were paper towels there – great! The Way, paved in York stone, connected the Lady Chapel to the main building, uniquely separate from the body of the cathedral at the northeast point. Originating in the 14th century, it was rebuilt for 2000, not in the favourite Barnack limestone but Fritsham. There had developed a strong Maryan cult, expressed in her vibrant figure in dashing blue, with hands raised (by David Wynne) above the altar in this, 'the largest and most beautiful Lady Chapel in the land,' commented Ted. The inscription: 'Behold the handmaid of the Lord' made sense of the pose, considered our guide. I suppose so, but it seemed a bit ungainly.

'It is unusually on the north side – the east end was already extended in the 6-bay presbytery. It would have been very awkward to extend it further.' It was a 1321 foundation – 100' x 46', the final straw – the central tower crashed. John of Wisbech did both projects in tandem in Decorated style, with a mass of decoration contained within the stonework. At the time it was the widest vaulted ceiling, involving lierne vaulting, crossed. It allowed so many more bosses.

The Reformation brought destruction of the figures. 'The Virgin was over-venerated,' said Ted, hence the focus on places like this. We were glad to peer at the same section in a window on the south side. Assembled there was evocative medieval stained glass: streets ahead of the Victorian. The prospect of the Stained Glass exhibition loomed, where we would find out more about this. It had been assembled and placed there in 1992. Underfloor heating had been introduced before the laying of dark Purbeck marble. We were interrupted by the hourly prayer session, a moment for reflection in this chapel, which assumed an identity of its own. This was the area where O, my future colleague for Welsh cathedrals, objected to an exhibition of photos, which screened the beauty of the building.

In the quire came the tale about misericords. Old and infirm monks had the opportunity to take the weight off their feet when engaged upon three hours of prayer. How soft are we that ten minutes upright in a cathedral makes us want to try the seats, with or without the concealed decoration of a form of folk art? I sneaked a look at one or two, difficult to perceive easily owing to their situation, depicting scenes of everyday life. George Gilbert Scott (19th century) was instrumental in the lower/minor stalls and canopy panels. The rear stalls are more historic – 1300s. There was no cathedra here, but two stalls at the nave end of the choir stalls, for the abbot/prior and bishop/dean. The earlier users in the stalls would have been attending King's School, Ely, latterly King's New College. The organ was next, following the model of Strasbourg. I loved that city for its fusion of German and French culture, and a rather good bar offering jazz with fine beer, culture leaning more towards the Teutonic. In answer to the question to the audience: 'How many organ pipes are there?' And, following a predictably crass guess '250,' Ted amazed us with '5,606, in the Gallery, and everywhere.'

My friend Pom told a tale about a concert in Ely Cathedral. A baritone friend of hers was engaged to sing in two movements at an event to be recorded for Radio 3. It was high profile, being recorded live and edited down for broadcast. He duly went to Ely, booked into the hotel and did the rehearsal. He returned to the hotel to rest and change. On approaching the cathedral for the performance he heard the music, but at a much more advanced stage than anticipated: towards to end of the second movement. He had been told it was to start at 7.30 pm, in ignorance that it was actually 7 pm. He hoped they would go back to re-record, but no. That was it. He didn't sing, nor receive the fee. The recording was transmitted without the solo bits.

The presbytery was added in 1234–52. There was pale Purbeck marble, which originally sparkled. The Norman had been apsidal. The Early English design of the east end was square. William Wailes was responsible for the stained glass, equivalent to French cathedrals, showing Christ's life story. St Etheldreda, from near Stowmarket, Suffolk, founded it in 675. Four years later she died of a cancerous growth in her neck. All signs of this vanished, spawning her shrine as a centre for pilgrimage. There was a modern sculpture in place – candles were lit there. The reredos was by GG Scott. Eucharist was celebrated at this altar every Sunday. 'The last thing it is, is a museum,' Ted had nearly finished. 'It's a place of prayer.'

That was it. The tour finished near the high altar. We were late for the Octagon Tour – Ted had overrun by a quarter of an hour, much to our benefit. We eased back to the desk and arranged the next one, almost an hour hence, giving us time for the Stained Glass Museum. Mary had retired outside. Rand and I ascended stairs in the south aisle to the south gallery/ triforium and the museum. It was a good choice for this. There is hardly any good glass in the building, and the outfit is well-attuned to packages and tourists; to me, one of the negatives. Not the charge itself as much as the arrogance of the way it's done. 'We are the best, so YOU must pay.' An example occurred on entering the museum with the big, bold ticket I'd been given on production of my credit card. The girl in the reception box, formerly back of the gallery, as Ted would have put it, offered me a Gallery Guide for £3 and an Audio one for £1. The exhibition was fascinating in the way modern displays usually are. You come away thrilled by what you've been shown, and, perhaps, slightly the wiser, both as to what has been achieved and shown and how to do it. The trouble is that there's so much here, the Exhibit that is Ely, and this exhibition is itself engrossing. Perhaps all you can really expect is to emerge with good memories. Perhaps buy the gallery guide, after all, to dip into on the coffee table.

Notable individual stained glass items and illuminated stained glass panels, included:

- A boar medallion, black on yellow, the badge of the de Veres, 1340–560 (East Anglia)
- Portrait of George III, 1793, by James Pearson (1740–1818), the same image as is familiar in oils, and evocative in this medium
- A peasant figure, from the Lady Chapel, Ely

What goes round comes round, it seems. After exposure to many Victorian exhibits, I confirmed my prejudice, that at worst Victorian Stained Glass is equivalent to late Perpendicular architecture – over-ripe and unpalatable, like a banana closer to brown than yellow, or green. Also the display had involved a walk the length the triforium from west end to crossing and back.

Back at the bottom and past the font (at last something below par) I happened upon the Prayer Net. It's what it says: a fishing net stuck to the wall. The answer to the question: 'Why not take a piece of wool and tie it into the net?' was to do just that, accompanied by a quotable prayer, of St Brendan, written below:

Shall I abandon, O King of Mysteries, the soft comforts of home? Shall I put myself wholly at the mercy of God? Shall I

leave the prints of my knees on the sandy beach?
O King of Heavens, shall I go, of my own choice, upon the sea,
O Christ, will you help me on the wild waves?

It was 2.15 pm. Octagon time at the gathering point of the display boards opposite the entrance desk. But first we bumped into Ted Lachlan, while awaiting our new guide. No, he wasn't conducting this one – the steps were too much for him. 'I'm not sure about them myself,' said Rand. We had noticed a man chatting with the welcome/cash till staff in between sips from a sturdy white mug, not anything you could buy in the shop. There was plenty of west end for lurking potential. You can spread activities too far! The mug man crossed the nave to join two other punters (who turned out to be from Retford, Notts, on holiday in a tent) further up. Then he summoned us. He told us: 'I'm John Webster.' Duly emptying the mug with a final swig, he led our thankfully small group to the crossing itself for an introduction, then to the entrance to the tower in the north transept. The ceiling was painted to look like Heaven, 142' high inside. The opening part of the tour was to marvel at the construction, and of course to admire the endless views for various levels. 'The horizon is 12 miles away' he said, therefore still in Cambridgeshire. The tower is of 200 tons of lead, to which add the same weight of wood, cut in the green and mellowing, maturing forever in place. It was transported by water from Bedfordshire, 40 miles distant. After all, this part of the world is stark when it comes to building materials. But it is perfect as a setting for a majestic building.

Feeling the strain, Rand accepted the offer to leave his shoulder bag at the first level, one of four, at least 41 steps up, but not quite up to triforium height, I reckoned. My count was different up and down, but John was adamant that the grand total was 167. The bag was placed alongside a suitcase or two (one in an extravagant sky blue) and personal effects. 'The choir,' said John, by way of explanation. We didn't stop to look down for too long as much better was in prospect: initially the next stage, the walkway between the south side of the Lady Chapel and the north of the quire. This was the immediate view, spying on people on the grass below. Nothing untoward was going on. Also we could admire the Almonry garden and its blooms. This was just the right time of year, though the day was turning a little misty.

Up and up, John waxed lyrical about detail of the building process. I shall restrict comment to the stunning experience we were undergoing. Imagine immense organ pipes grumbling low. There they were, or some of the 5,300. Then the 17th century tower timbers, wooden buttresses resting on stone walls and still standing. Remember the collapsed tower, and similar disasters at many other cathedrals. The architects, designers and craftsmen must have developed a supreme confidence in an age when ecclesiastical building was a familiar source of work for many and for several generations. You'd done St Albans and/or Peterborough, so how about Ely next? It was still wondrous to consider 63' of oak hanging in space. There was a notice not to deface the beams, and plenty of signatures from over the years. John opened panels in the side of the top of the lantern, where the angels had been painted in the Victorian restoration. I wondered how long it would take for a pin to drop from there.

At last we reached the very summit, the lead roof where we could perambulate round the louvered wooden tower. John pointed out the monastic buildings way down on the south side: the red brick Bishop Alcock's Palace, built in the late 15th century; the Bishop's House, built into the former great hall of the monastery; Ely Porta, the broad gatehouse, from 1397.

Photos were taken with the west tower in clear view, as was the gap that had been the northwest tower, completed in 1397, collapsing in 1430. It was quite a blank space, resulting in an incline of the west tower to the left, with consequent removal of bells. Its story followed: the Norman spire, in oak, was removed in the 14th century for the stone replacement, which successfully completes the look today. Gothic on Romanesque: we agreed to better effect than a spire.

Making the descent it was time for casual chat. The couple from Retford (diocese of Southwell) rated Lincoln the highest, not even mentioning their local cathedral. In fact they said they were from Doncaster at first, thinking nobody had heard of Retford – we narrowed it down gradually to get to the actual town. John was from Leicester: 'No cathedral there,' he asserted. 'Oh yes there is,' I countered. It spoke of the understandable condescension at Ely that a modest conversion (the Diocese of Leicester was established in 1884) wasn't in the same league, in fact didn't exist. I pondered on the merits of Chelmsford and St Edmundsbury, of Sheffield, explored and enjoyed, and quietly welcomed the prospect of the next tour of four cathedrals. Derby and Leicester, centres of the last generation of new dioceses, would be among them. So would Southwell, Notts, humble perhaps, but old and atmospheric, and Lincoln. Say no more about that. Requested for a suggestion for post-tour tea, John recommended the Peacock.

It wasn't over yet. Rand was on the point of speeding through the shop, to tend to Mary, who had opted out of the more strenuous endeavour. I asked him where his shoulder bag was: not on his shoulder, but in the wooden space where he'd left it 41 steps up. 'Oh No!' he exclaimed.

We interrupted John's next tour, in its early stages. Rand was looking despondent and feeble (what he'd already done was a triumph: recent triple heart bypass operation. Tennis next, I was hoping). I volunteered to retrieve the item for him, so my total steps in the Octagon Tower rose from 167 to 249, not to mention the scaling of the triforium for the glazing display.

Heroism and stamina apart, the cathedral was satisfyingly despatched from the pending box. Rejoining the resting Mary in Rand's jalopy, after various attempts we reached the Peacock, scenically sited by the river. Having got there, even securing a parking place, a discreet notice informed that it was closed on Tuesdays. We hastened back to the Almonry, where the tea was achieved. Rand, no doubt a bit displaced, was trying to impress with his avoidance of sugar. I had witnessed his resolute devourings of candied confections elsewhere. He now chose buttered toast. The waitress, evidently of a sympathetic persuasion, noted his expression and tendered some jam. Rand yielded meekly, selecting the raspberry option, with no encouragement from Mary or me. We had both ordered apple pie, and we all pigged out with a direct view of the Lady Chapel and east end of one of the best.

Later on, hardly sobered by the journey home, Rand was to eulogize: 'O Ely how beautiful you are with your spires and towers. Oh, rhubarb, rhubarb.'

18

St Albans

St Alban

Province: Canterbury
Founded: 793 Benedictine monastery; from 1539 parish church
Present building: late 11th century, using earlier materials; a bit of each generation
Restored: 1871–80, including work by Lord Grimthorpe
Cathedral status: 1878 – from Rochester diocese

Website: www.stalbanscathedral.org
Tel: 01727 860780
Email: mail@stalbanscathedral.org
Address: The Cathedral and Abbey Church of Saint Alban, Sumpter Yard, St Albans. Herts AL1 1BY

Three to See: Tower, featuring Roman brick, to be seen with neighbouring Verulamium site;
watching loft;
medieval murals in the nave

Rose

Wednesday 28 April, 2010

The route from the heart of Suffolk – diocese of St Edmundsbury (and Ipswich) – took us through Constable Country. Rand, an aficionado, drove to East Bergholt, John Constable's birthplace in 1776. Back we went to the A12 to reach Dedham, over the Essex border, for St Mary's Church and the Essex Rose café. The church impressed Rand, being newly decorated, and sporting a fine organ and floor tiles. In the café I foolishly chose coffee and soon rued the decision. The coffee was not strong enough! In Chelmsford it had been a knockout concoction. Soon enough we were told 'for Old London Road, follow Bentley'. Droll, I thought. The contributions from Eddie Stobart were 'Josephine Mae' and 'Vivienne Esther', representing a slight improvement in invention. There was more fun with Rand's ongoing concern over petrol provision. An infusion of fuel was duly obtained (121.9p – palatable). Then we resigned ourselves to the M11 and M25. Actually the (slower) alternatives were mostly trunk roads, so perhaps not the country route we had in mind at the outset.

St Albans was our destination for the ruins of Verulamium as well as the cathedral. They are next to each other. It now required pressure in the throttle, not Rand's preference, and recent indulgence in dioceses had depleted the tank. We arrived at the cathedral, fortunately finding a rare space (£2.70, maximum 2 hours) just outside. The exterior was bulky and varied, beckoning ingress as soon as possible.

We entered by the west door, to be greeted by a 'welcomer' in blue. 'Welcome to the Abbey,' she said with a smile. This appellation is confirmed, with knobs on, on the website, where it is not only 'Abbey' but 'Saint', not 'St'. The first view was stunning. The nave stretched almost out of sight, and involved mounting a few steps for an eyeful of vastness.

However, initially we decided against this and made for the Café in the Abbey by way of the flat south aisle. It occupied the ground floor of the 1980s chapter house building. We both ordered spinach soup, leaving anything sweet for a later break. We sat outside on plastic garden furniture, in an empathic green. It was easy to embark upon acclimatization to the stunning prospect of this ancient, and more modern, building. We enjoyed an uninterrupted view of the square red tower, made of Roman brick and dating from the 11th century, unique in England, being situated on the crossing. The materials had been pillaged from the Verulamium site. From there the endless length of the exterior convinced as awesome. It was monolithic and proud.

On the route back to the west end I couldn't resist the board near the rood screen upon which was presented the history of management in the building: from abbey to parish church to cathedral. It all started in 793 with the wonderfully named Willegod, abbot, through to the final incumbent of that title, Richard Boreham or Stevenage, who surrendered the monastery for dissolution in 1539. It was granted to Sir Richard Lee and gradually savaged. The abbey was retained by the Crown until bought by the town for its parish church on obtaining its charter in 1553, when Edward VI succeeded his father Henry VIII to the throne. From then on the incumbents became rectors and deans, right through to 2004. Meanwhile elevation to cathedral status was made in 1877, since when there have been nine bishops, including Robert Runcie (1970–80) who clearly did well in charge of a busy, progressive suburban diocese. Home Counties North had enjoyed an influx of population from London. We were told St Albans was 25 miles from the capital (though my *AA Members' Handbook 1984/85* stated 23). It's on the direct route, appropriately the Roman road, Watling Street. Runcie was promoted to the archbishopric of Canterbury (incumbent 1980–91), showing that our primates may be selected from any diocese. He is buried at the cathedral. A notable occurrence in his career was his recognition of Argentinian war dead at the special service marking the conclusion of the Falklands War in 1992. This incurred the wrath of Prime Minister Thatcher.

The abbey's allegiance was moved several times, to Lincoln in 1542, and London in 1550, back to Lincoln and to Rochester in 1845, finally achieving its own see through the Bishopric of St Albans Act in 1875. It's a good thing that the issue of time did not muddy this issue further. It was an abbot of St Albans, Richard of Wallingford, who experimented with mechanical clocks. Edward III was credited with the introduction of mechanical clocks to his palaces in the 1350s and 1360s.

We had picked up a *Children's Guide* from the welcomer, who suggested looking out for a real live guide. We commenced the long haul. Soon enough, on the north aisle wall, we admired the collage, 'which tells the story of how the Abbey was built and discover what materials the Normans used'. It seemed most suitable for children, and us. Rand commented on some of the content. The medieval-effect script indicated the role played by 'the people'. He observed: 'For peasants this must have been the icing on the cake, and joy, like we watch television. It's like magic, a magical effect, that feeling… a miracle, outside their lives.' This was the ill-educated, post Conquest era of Normans, then Plantagenets.

A 'Guide' (said the badge) was spotted. It was Joan Freeman, who was then to regale us on a most entertaining tour, pointing out that this was the second longest Gothic English cathedral (after Winchester, six feet longer). She spoke of the collapse, during a mass in 1323, of two of the massive columns on the south side of the nave, and part of the roof as well. The contrast in style between Romanesque further up in the east nave and Gothic (south and west) is remarkable. I found this effective. The massiveness of it all is overwhelming, and I began to enjoy the juxtaposition of whitewashed and painted Norman with the maturely carved stone of the medieval part.

Joan sat us down in the nave, which was slightly worrying as we'd already established that we had limited time. I don't remember the nature of the seats, which is a good sign. We came to the rood screen, interrupting the sweep of the nave, but to no ill effect as the building's scale could accommodate it. Underneath, beyond raked sets being introduced for an event, Joan alluded to 'the cellar, for naughty monks'. If they were really bad they'd be sent to the daughter house, Tynemouth Priory in the far north, which was much worse: cold and grim, with wailing seabirds. The current guide book promoted it by quoting a letter from an inmate:

> *Our house is confined to the top of a high rock and is surrounded by the sea on every side but one... Day and night the waves break and roar and undermine the cliff. Thick sea frets roll in wrapping everything in gloom. Dim eyes, hoarse voices, sore throats are the consequence. Spring and summer never come here. The north wind is always blowing and brings with it cold and snow; or storms in which the wind tosses the salt sea in masses over our buildings... Shipwrecks are frequent... No ringdove or nightingale is here, only grey birds which nest in the rocks and greedily prey on the drowned, whose screaming cry is a token of a coming storm... See to it, dear brother, that you do not come to this comfortless place.*

The screen, two feet across, was the only one in use in the country. Above it the 1420 organ had been pushed in, one half on either side, opposite each other.

She took us outside the west door to recount the story of the zealous restoration of Edmund Beckett, Lord Grimthorpe QC, from 1870. 'He did grim things,' said Joan, 'He was an absolute rotter.' Nikolaus Pevsner called him 'a pompous, righteous bully,' known for his 'arrogance and bile' (*Oxford Dictionary of National Biography*). His portrait was there for all to see in the porch. The heads of the four apostles were sculpted, with Mark as a lion, Luke as a bull and John an eagle, as tradition dictates. Matthew was not an angel, but a man, a winged poser depicted as Lord Grimthorpe. This contemporary rhyme serves well:

Said the builder who built the great west door:
"What shall I put in the spandrels four?"
Then answered the architect, thus quoth he:
"Put St Mark, St Luke, St John and ME!"

There was a saving grace: he invented the depressible door knob in the 1870s, for he was technically, rather than artistically, expert. He didn't appreciate colour. The west window contained plain glass until 1921 when the present stained product was inserted. St Alban's martyrdom, of the 3rd century, was shown. The abbey's site was elevated and water supply was from a well 'in the bishop's sitting room,' according to Joan.

The construction was of flint and clay. The diocese derived from the foundation of Offa II, King of Mercia, in 793, with the Benedictine abbey. Sacked by Danes c.890, it was rebuilt after the Norman Conquest, in 1077. Rand's supposition was confirmed: the pillars were based upon rubble, or clunch, finished in plaster and surfaced with smarter flint and tile 'so hard it can't be carved'. This was from the ruins below. Verulamium had expired around the 5th century. More modern, carvable stone had to be imported from another part of the diocese: the Tottenhoe limestone quarry. Where there are frescos, for example in the Norman section of the nave, they were painted on, dried and soaked. A true fresco is painted onto the plaster while wet, in small sections. We saw not only depictions of St Christopher, with child in arms, and Thomas Becket but on an arch above handfuls of small red flowers. The faces had been scratched out before the great whitewashing of the Reformation was embarked upon. We learned that Alban the Martyr's motif was a rose, so that was to be my icon for St Albans Cathedral. He was the first English Christian martyr, executed by decapitation.

Joan didn't think the flowers painted in the nave above our heads were roses, and I admit them to be modest in size and looked more like periwinkles, or something from the hedgerows of rural Herts/Beds, which surrounded in the real world. Even more in the Norman part: altars were placed on the front of each flat pillar, for there are bulky circular and smooth flat parts side by side. On the south side was good late Decorated gothic work, by Henry Wy, with the figures of Edward II (1307–27) and his queen Isabella painted on. Behind, in three south aisle window alcoves, stood a series of electric blue figures, now almost a decade old, made to commemorate St Albans Day (22 June).

We reached the quire and were told of the groups of girls and boys, who formed the choirs, along with a men's choir, whose members are remunerated. There was also a congregation choir. Above the space was a colourful roof, flat and wooden as throughout the building, but of superior quality depicting castles of Edward I. This was redesigned by Pete Herbert in the 1960s.

By this time, overwhelmed by the scale of the building, I felt a reminder of Spanish cathedrals. The same conditions prevailed today: clear with sun for light and warmth. We'd come here at the right time. Mind you, the majority of cathedral visits during this project had been on bad days, and still rewarding. Just wrap up warm, as my mother used to tell me. The real question was one of light in the building. This had not proved problematic.

Another consequence of collapse and stone weight was noted. During the restoration of the 1870s, it was reckoned that the nave was askew, an estimated 27" out. The technically supreme Grimthorpe used hydraulic means to level it off. 'It's a pity they took the faces back to the stone each time', said Rand. Joan added: 'Also *that* Grimthorpe elbowed into the job ahead of Gilbert Scott.' The latter, and his works, has stood the test of time much better, his inventions turning out to have been rather more sympathetic to the buildings. 'St Albans hasn't seen much kindness,' said Rand. Unfortunately he was right – there was a lot to enjoy but much has reduced the character and quality of the former abbey.

The back half of the cathedral came across as being as large as any complete building, it was so extensive. In the south transept was a series of stalls, a shop, where second hand books were for sale. It was easy to pause there and thumb through a *Pears Cyclopedia* (old section) and a book on gargoyles in the new part. Unfortunately there were no gargoyles attached to this building. There was also an internal shop space close enough in the chapter house building. Above the transept were steps leading up into it, built with replica Roman red bricks. This was from Bedfordshire, a noted centre for brick production. The building was opened in 1982, and seemed fit for long term purpose, unless the shopping outlet had been introduced as overspill. Partly, I suspected, the building is so huge that it's handy to be able to apply some of the blank space to profitable use, and again it was along the south aisle, uphill beyond the presbytery, that a ramp had been placed, and, near it, a wheelchair.

We reached the monumental limestone screen at the top of the quire. The figures standing in its cavities were 6' tall. They didn't look it. While you're casting your eyes up, look along the ceiling, which is 13th century wooden gothic and as astonishing as many of the best cathedral roofs. There were 19th century Minton tiles on the floors. I'm sure one of the best improvements on what they replaced. Some were in a patchy green, much of it worn away so as to appear dark. Or was this to do with a chemical reaction, as Rand thought? Further up in the north aisle, along the wall, was the pilgrim seat, a discreet low stone ledge, where the weary could rest, 'where the weak go to the wall,' quoted Joan from an unidentified source. One of the glories was nigh: a loft, the strange, bulky oak Watching Chamber from 1400. It was built for observation purposes for the medieval monks as guardians. It's the only survival of many built in the Middle Ages. It was adorned with a range of beasts. The upper chamber, reached by way of heavily timbered stairs, looked into the shrine of St Alban, where, in another luxurious space, stood the fenced off shrine. Behind it, abutting the screen, was an eastern icon on the wall. Icons had by now taken on a role of expectation for Rand and me, starting out quizzical as to why an Anglican cathedral chose to display them. 'Trying to encourage universality?' was what Rand suggested.

It looked out towards the final zone: the Lady Chapel, added to the east side in the 14th century. Sealed off, in 1553 had become a school for the post-Dissolution boys. At the same time the Great Gatehouse, outside to the west, which we were to admire on our return for tea, cake and girls' singing, was turned into a town jail, and the abbey itself ended up for sale to the town for £400. In the Lady Chapel was the second, smaller, organ, on the north side. We were now in a hurry to get back to the car. Our time was up and the voluble Joan had overrun, while simultaneously worried about traffic wardens. She had been effusive, and entertaining, abetted by our endless inquisitiveness. She had to mention one last item: Humphrey of Gloucester, Henry V's youngest brother, whose tomb was discovered in 1703 and restored by Hertfordshire Freemasons for the Millennium. There was spirit as well as bones in evidence. Poet Quinn, a visitor along with his friend the Lichfield actor David Garrick, wrote:

A plague on Egypt's art I say
Embalm the dead! On senseless clay
Rich wines and spirits waste!
Like sturgeon or like brawn shall I
Bound in precious pickle be
Which I can never taste.
Let me embalm this flesh of mine
With turtle fat and Bordeaux wine
And spoil th'Egyptian trade.
Then good Duke Humphrey, happier I
Embalmed alive, old Quinn shall die
A mummy ready made.

Humphrey was deeply involved with learning and the arts. Unfortunately his second wife, Eleanor of Cobham, was convicted of sorcery and heresy (work done to aid the advancement of her husband). The eventual outcome was his death, in 1447 at our earlier stop, St Edmundsbury, conveyed to rest in peace next to St Alban. I read about that bit. As we made for the door Joan had urged: 'Read about Humphrey. The story's fun.'

This episode with Joan had run its course, but there was more to come: at Gloucester Cathedral during the 2010 *Three Choirs Festival*. Rand, Wakey and I bumped into her and Ian, her brother, a stone specialist. Following an interlude in the café, they were to furnish me with copious reproductions of fascinating and helpful abbey matter. I want to thank them by quoting Matthew Paris (c.1200–59), most likely local to St Albans and a sharp observer. He referred to his monarch, Henry III: 'as a perfidious, avaricious and weak-minded tyrant whose soul would have been seriously endangered had it not been for the liberality and constancy of his alms-giving'. This was one of our longest-serving monarchs, 56 years on the throne, during whose reign so much cathedral building was done. This piece is from *Matthew Paris* by Dr Richard Vaughan, fellow of Corpus Christi College, Cambridge, at St Albans Abbey (29/10/59), to commemorate the 700th anniversary of his death. Two reasons are cited concerning his importance, a world away in the 21st century: 'He must be numbered among those few writers of any age who successfully enshrine the vices and the virtues, the foibles and fancies, the prejudices and the outlook, of the ordinary man in the street.' That is, he was an effective journalist, writing way ahead of his time. The art is to judge some semblance of a true story from such work as his magnum opus, Chronica Majora, covering events over Europe as well as England. He says: 'The papal court stinks to high heaven', and of Richard Marsh, Bishop of Durham an 'inexorable exactor of money, drunk with the poison of Satan'. Matthew's huge output is worth dipping into for the invective alone!

Returning to a mellow day in the English spring, Rand manoeuvred the car down leafy residential roads awash with tempting pubs, mostly named after flora and fauna – there was at least one lion. Spring was in the air and the gardens. Cherry blossom was most in evidence, a white variety above us in the Verulamium car park (£1 for 3 hours). I obtained a photocopied map from the Museum desk and got directions for the Hypocaust. We were facing an extensive undulating park, where you could imagine a city had once stood. The sign said 'Mosaic' when we arrived at the white building, on the side of a hill. It was quite different from the experience on my previous attempt at entry in 1971.

The Hypocaust
Several signposts severally say
The hypocaust is that way
We wander round in some earnest search

Past white geese, weeping willow, coots,
Fragmented city walls and cricket match
And find at length
The Museum
Old St Albans,
Verulamium;
Myriad mosaics and plaster walls
In vivid rust and verdant green.

Then departing for elusive heatworks –
Hypocaust -
Another sign we see -
Hypocaust Bungalow -
This is the key to our deception
We have reconnoitred
Roman ruins
Almost assailing the walls, ramparts now reduced to ruin
Like ancient invading marauders
For the hypocaust.

In the grandeur,
Verulamium's once,
We envisaged a pillared dome
Or Doric gazebo
Majestic shelter encompassed by a landscaped arbour
At least a stately permanent home
For the hypocaust,
In a civilized municipium –
Third century Rome on English soil.

But now we find
Ten minutes too late
The bungalow
Windows open, low hedge surrounding
Doors locked and tickets away,
Seeming no more than a building of utility.
Herein the hypocaust
Is instated.

But observe a little
The sunlit field,

Open green heart of
Verulamium;
Cathedral afar
Parts of stone antique wall
And plumaged pond.
Everywhere is green
And in the midst
A bungalow.

The building, new to me, containing the Hypocaust was open and free of charge. I read 'beneath the main mosaic is an underfloor heating system or hypocaust, from the Greek "hypo = below/caust = heat."' We were admiring an almost complete mosaic floor mainly featuring squares of tiles in the usual colours (red, yellow, black and white), depicting abstract and floral shapes. It had opened in 2005, when it won a Commendation from the St Albans Civic Society. After this we went in search of Roman defences (the oppidum), eventually finding a good stretch behind a mound, trees and a metal fence. This was Prae Wood. It was worth the effort, the structure comprising 'mortared flint layered with red brick'. 5 m high and 3 m wide at the bottom. It was laid out in AD50, one of the finest towns in Britain, and destroyed ten years later by the Iceni warriors under Boudicca (she did the same at two other places, the wanton Amazon), and further by a devastating fire 100 years later. Rebuilt soon after its destruction, it had many excellent buildings, including a theatre and forum, and its full municipal status signified its importance. Now we connect with the abbey, proud on the hill to the east, as Alban was martyred here in the 3rd century.

We'd achieved a quota of exercise and, at 4 pm it was time for tea. The park facility would have been good at another time, but there were no tables in the glorious sunshine, a long queue in front and noisy children and dogs. No thanks. We returned to the car for the next challenge: to find a parking space back at the cathedral. Having achieved this with difficulty, in St Albans School car park, we were again in the abbey for an all-important pre-evensong refreshment. We had noted that the café closed at 4.30 pm, it was urgent to get there for tea and cakes. This we did, the food section offering slices of far-too-creamy lemon and a banana-ish products. Jane, the same cashier as for the soup, was most obliging: 'I do hope we'll see you again', having whispered a reduced charge to Rand. She undercharged a bit too much at first. It eventually settled as a total of £6.25, perchance because she'd taken a shine to my companion.

There was time for a more relaxed stroll round the east end, then into the quire for the musical service. The 20-strong girls' choir delivered a challenging version of the *Magnificat* (St Paul's Service by Wilby), and a mellow anthem, Mendelssohn's *Laudate Pueri*, which brought a tear to Rand's eye. However, the two readings caused consternation on his part. The first (Deuteronomy 10: 12 to end) included the words 'circumcise' and 'foreskin' and the second (Ephesians 5: 1–14) 'fornication' and 'whoremongers'. 'Were they suitable for those young girls?' he posited afterwards. I doubted if those sopranos and contraltos had even been listening. There were six people in the congregation and three priests, one conducting the service, two delivering respective readings, as well as the choir conductor. The aspect from the south stalls was majestic and peaceful: Norman arches, massive masonry and the dark, flat roof; in the opposite direction the screen with the organ shining large. It was dawning on me that this was a suitable culmination of the recent intense immersion in cathedrals: four in three days. The core of the cathedral was cordoned off, so we returned to the car on the south side, noting the pale arch-shaped patches on the wall. 'Former cloisters', said I, later realizing that three c's were missing there: cloisters, crypt and cat. It was overdue to notch up another feline. These cathedrals seem to have become rodent-free places. The image of the Romanesque prevailed, as it did with Wakey, who had visited the abbey in the past: 'I remember the zigzags so well,' he said, but didn't like it much as a whole.

The coda was the St Albans road system – hellish like many old towns. We made it to the Goat Inn, Sopwell Lane, the old coaching route from London and appropriate, as Sopwell was the site of a nunnery ('Priory') founded in 1140. Our final indulgence was two brews, each from local sources, and platters of pub grub. Jeffrey Kacirk's 2010 dictionary *Forgotten English* had a relevant word for this day: 'Sile. It relates to liquids, especially milk. John Ray's 1674 *North Country Words* (hardly relevant here, however) defined it: "To soil milk, to cleanse it." Francis Grose's *Provincial Glossary* (1787) gave: "To pour. He siled a gallon of ale down his throat."' That's more like it – at least we were in the right setting for such an accomplishment. We were well-sated, and 18 cathedrals to date represented progress into the second third of the complete list.

The final space has to go to one St Albans emigrée of my acquaintance. 92-year-old Eileen Shillcock said feelingly of this building: 'It's an abbey. It's only called a cathedral for tourists.'

19

Southwell

St Mary

Province: York
Founded: 8th century monastery; from 11th century collegiate church
Present building: 1108 with continuous additions
Cathedral status: 1884 – from Lichfield and Lincoln dioceses

Website: www.southwellminster.org
Tel: 01636 812649
Email: office@southwellminster.org
Address: The Minster Centre, Church Street, Southwell, Nottinghamshire
NG25 0HD

Three to See: 1300 chapter house, adorned with foliage;
sedilia in chancel, rarely with five seats;
the pale west window by Patrick Reyntiens

Bramley apple

Saturday 15 May, 2010

This was to become a nature day. We started with a piggery seen from the A614. 'Pigs,' said Rand 'have a life of gorging themselves, not worrying about body mass index, foraging around all day, indulging.' Wakey added: 'Wallowing in mud.' 'And at the end the pig is slaughtered,' concluded Rand.

Arriving in this small market town of Southwell, it was immediately apparent that the roads just weren't suited to modern needs. They were only wide enough for 1.5 cars, and fewer buses. We underwent an unaccustomed number of pauses to let cars through, finally finding fortune in parking outside Burgage Manor, home of Lord Byron from 1802 to 1808. From a distance it looked suitable for fine living, but Byron was to describe the town as the resort for 'old parsons and old maids', and move out again. Wakey's decision to park there (free all day) proved wise, or fortuitous, and we enjoyed a sedate stroll towards the town centre. Southwell is not a city. This amounted to a preamble, commencing just on noon, ideal to culminate in a Minster Café coffee stop. On the way we noted some individual shops – upmarket we surmised. Perhaps this serves as a dormitory town for Nottingham, 12 miles away down country roads. In the open air market Wakey almost invested in come calico in order to black out his bedroom window. It was an interesting discussion, engaging the stall-holder in advice. The lack of proper measurements brought the initiative to a close. I was imagining leaving a bulky parcel at the desk in the minster for later collection, then forgetting it as we had done in the case of the umbrella at Rochester.

Noting the Saracen's Head, famed for its association with Charles I, we crossed into Church Street, for Rand to replenish his wallet at HSBC. Next door was the 'Minster Centre, Southwell Minster', which informed: 'If you wish to enquire about Baptisms or Weddings at the Minster, the Canon Pastor is usually available to meet you on the first Monday of each month, 6.30–7.30 in the Minster Centre. Well, that's nice, and next door was the Minster Café, first in evidence through a placard announcing 'Douwe Egbert's'. Great, thought I. Free Trade, too, though that's not always a guarantee of satisfaction. I'd almost given up on quality in a cup of coffee during cathedral visits in the light of recent ghastly experiences in East Anglia. The shop was first. At last, here I found a shot glass, and the intended recipient was in the party. Wakey was to receive this clear glass memento, engraved with the image and name of the building we were soon to enjoy. £6 was a lot, but it was a boxed item and rather too smart for regular infusions of whisky. Wakey found a most suitable spot – the furthermost table outside by a tree and in view of the north side of the

Minster, where we could admire the singular Romanesque features. Round windows at clerestory level, a substantial north porch with windows above, a space for use and accommodation in the past. It was sunny, but cool, and most welcome to sit and observe in the open air. Distressingly the provisions were so poor much of it was left to birds and waitresses. The coffee was weak and the gluten-free cake tasteless. There were no spaces inside and the building fell well short of others we'd experienced – such as Guildford or Chichester for modern café builds. 'Number 2, or even 1,' said Rand of the coffee. 'You need number 4, or 5. They've not made it right.' Cathedrals need money, but not at the expense of quality, or maybe it was just poor training of the (very young) staff, as the lass who served us was probably a schoolgirl on her Saturday job. At least we could enjoy the diversion of a puppy, identified by Wakey as a Border Collie, subject to much attention and patting on the path leading to the west front. And there was a squirrel gambolling in a fir tree.

The north porch was the entrance, with 'Craft Fair' the attraction, in the nave. We were requested to make a '£1 donation'. This we declined: we were here to meet steward, Thelma McIntosh. The nave was crammed full of stalls and shoppers, though not as many as the November fair, the dean told us later. The fare at the fair looked worth examining, through nave and transepts. The south one was also given over to an internal café, which we would try at the end of our tour. I acquired the £2 *Cathedral Companion*, a 16-page volume with a glossy cover. The front cover depicted the minster from above. There was also a £5 book. 'More of a Souvenir,' I had been told in a telephone conversation the day before by David Turner, the guide organizer. This had followed an initial call to the minster to discover what was happening that day, the date and time already being fixed in our diaries. I was informed about the craft fair, 'so there is no chance of a personal tour, and there is no audio, as the old one has been withdrawn and its replacement not yet launched. You're coming at just the wrong time,' David had laughed. But he was perspicacious in mooting that a spot visit was what we were doing (to some extent), and there would be stewards on duty, whom he would prepare for the invasion. I liked the idea of a craft fair and doing our own tour, in the interests of variety of approach in a few days dedicated to a bunch of cathedrals. The event presented Southwell Minster at work, making a welcome contribution to the coffers. So would Willard White, bass, who was to appear for a performance of the music of Paul Robeson (£25, £15). Wakey showed interest, briefly, until he saw the cost, and pondered on the journey there, and back.

So, without any impediment from the business at ground level, we pursued the guide from A to L. The nave was a hugely satisfying Norman extravaganza, the small scale and light windows helping the experience. So many 11th and 12th century churches are dark and ponderous. Not this. The pallid hues of the Great West Window worked well. 'It was designed and painted by Patrick Reyntiens, who described it as 'a great gathering of angels, enjoying being with God, just all joy and worship.' It was installed in 1996 and complemented the millennium-old nave magnificently. Its name 'Angel Window' elicited 'Oh dear' from Rand, sensitive to the reaction of others to his antipathy to angels. At the other end was another modern addition, equally effective: the Figure of Christ (Christus Rex), dating from 1987 and by Peter Ball. 'It is made of elm and oak, covered with copper and gold leaf'. It provided an optical illusion. From the west end it looked flat, but actually projects at an angle from bottom to top. The outstretched arms, seen from the crossing beyond it, suggested a crossbow, also evocative of the ethos of American Indians. Wakey was reminded of an albatross, but he had recently returned from the supreme credit of seeing more than one of the creatures in New Zealand's South Island. Meanwhile, another late alteration produced good effect: the barrel-vaulted nave roof, from 1880. This solved the problem created by a lightning disaster in 1711, resulting in destruction of much of the minster (as it was then in function as well as name) including the flat roof. Many cathedrals have suffered acts of God. The circular shape echoed the predominant roundness of pillars, windows and arches. We approved of the lightness of the window, Rand pointing out the lack of dangling lights. He drew attention to the organ – the quire one – resting on the pulpitum in the distance, and objected to the effective interruption of the eastward view. 'Where else would you put it?' I asked. Wakey, keen to divert the topic, posited, irrelevantly as well as irreverently, 'That's the question asked by many a man – where to put it?' 'Get rid of it,' muttered Rand.

On the way down the nave, among the stalls of provender, I did sample Smokehouse Chutney on the stall of Mr Pitchfork's Pickles. There weren't many tasters on offer – quilts and wooden products were more in evidence. And alongside the nave, beyond the aisle, was a long stone ledge, inbuilt for 'the aged and infirm' to use, giving rise to the expression 'the weakest shall go to the wall'. Indeed there was otherwise nowhere to sit. We were shown the discreet wooden chairs, behind the scenes, which normally filled the nave. We had also seen the name-boards, which brought home the 1884 status promotion to cathedral, the diocese being carved out of the territory of York. Southwell was formerly a pro-cathedral for York. It's the only Midland see answering to York – all the others look to Canterbury.

The crossing beckoned, and the ever-stunning impact of the tower from below, with the floor of the bell-ringing chamber in sight. More from the *Companion*: 'Southwell is unique in that the bells are rung in an anti-clockwise direction. A carillon fitted in the Tower plays one of three different tunes on the bells twice each day, at noon and four o'clock in the afternoon.' We were between these, so missed out, but we did witness a campanologist scampering along the triforium after the bell-ringing session. It was good to witness this, drowning out the hubbub of the market place.

Avoiding both pulpitum and quire for now, we explored the north transept, which again offered extremes of display to great effect. The Millennium Pilgrim stood on a thin column, a sinuous and compelling design by Rory Young. Opposite was 'an ancient lintel or tympanum, thought to be part of the Saxon Minster, which stood on this site before the Conquest'. The subject matter, involving David/lion and St Michael/dragon, was lost to me in the awe of absorption in the whole piece. At the other end of the transept's west wall was the, now, famous Bramley Apple Window 'celebrating 200 years of the first propagation of this variety in Southwell in 1809'. Two hours later, we passed the very house of its invention, that of Matthew Bramley in Easthorpe in 1837. We have to give credit to Miss Mary Ann Brailsford, who planted the original pips. I came to nominate this culinary mainstay as the image of Southwell, also as it is of the country. No cathedral is more imbued with rurality. You have to negotiate an underpopulated green route to get there. And nearby was a sign hidden away behind clutter today, announcing: 'Welcome to Southwell Minster. It costs some £3,000 a day to keep this church open.'

The pulpitum, the screen, had to be next. Work began on it around 1340. It was a splendid mature Perpendicular thing, three-dimensional with a crucial contemporary function. Steps within it led up to the quire organ. Beyond were the choir stalls, where the first facet to seek out had to be the misericords. Six of them lurked under the seats of the senior clergy. In the clear light it was good to be able to make them out. Not so in many cathedrals.

The whole quire was a substantial Early English (c.1240) replacement of the Norman original. It took me back to Exeter, where the entire building replaced the Norman original in (current) Decorated style. The wood carvings on the quire side of the pulpitum included one image which occurred to Wakey as reminiscent of Lofthouse's Fisherman's Friend – the gnarled old seafarer. Could it have been the inspiration? The lectern involved a story worth repeating. This is the version of *Harris's Guide to Churches and Cathedrals*:

> The fine medieval brass eagle lectern dates from c.1500...
> This, a cross and a pair of candlesticks were found in the lake

at Newstead Abbey c.1750, purchased from the Fifth Lord Byron in 1775 by Sir Richard Kaye, prebendary of Southwell and later Dean of Lincoln, and presented to the cathedral in 1805. The cross and candlesticks are the only original ancient set remaining in England.

Moving up to the high altar, to the left was a modest cathedra, with a bit of fun – a mouse carved in the wood. Is it the only one such? Opposite were five sedilia. The dean was to tell us that it's most unusual to have so many. The creamy and smooth local stone enhanced their appeal. We made for the chapels at the east end – the Chapel of Christ the Light of the World, offered candles and informed on the Southwell/Natal link, with a cross seemingly made of South African materials as an emblem. Prayers and thanksgiving were requested in the area, along with paper for them. Someone had written (verbatim): 'Please pray for all the animals who are trated cruley – especially ferrets. They are not the creature they are made out to be.' And in the north quire aisle was an assembly of medieval glass, an effective abstract display, from which Wakey picked out an heraldic boar. Close at hand was a wheelchair, awaiting a call to duty.

We were making our way round to the ultimate glory, the chapter house. The Airmen's Chapel had as altarpiece a tryptych by Hamish Moyle, inspired by Edith Sitwell's poem *Still Falls the Rain, The Raids, 1940, Night and Dawn*, dealing with the sacrifice of war. It could be pondered over on a wooden replica. The first verse went:

Dark as the world of man, black as our loss -
Blind as the nineteen hundred and forty nails
Upon the cross.

A passage led to the chapter house, as independent and discrete as that at Ely. It was small but finely devised and the passage kept us for a few minutes, itself a small glory. In fact a cloister formerly abutted this walkway, and the east side was adorned with more work form Patrick Reyntiens, referring back to the Great West Window. We moved to the chapter house entrance. Again I quote the *Companion*:

… probably the work of the master mason… regarded as one of the finest examples of the art of stone carving of this period. Unfortunately the two small dragons on either side have been decapitated, but otherwise the archway has survived almost intact. The botanical species represented here are, from left

to right, vine along the moulding, then hawthorn, maple with ranunculus flowers...

'A truly wonderful creation!' it claims, and so it is. Craftsmanship at its peak like the best Perpendicular architecture before it became over-ripe. The grotesques around the cathedral impressed, but this foliage, repeated in bosses and around the chapter house itself, was overwhelming. Kenneth Clark in *Civilisation*, broadcast in 1969, summarized it:

As early as the mid-13th century Gothic sculptors had begun to take pleasure in leaves and flowers, and one finds astonishing accuracy and intensity of observation on the capitals outside the chapter-house at Southwell.

From Mike Harding's *A Little Book of The Green Man*, I like the entry for *Jack & the May King*:

Perhaps the clearest representation of a Jack-in-the-Green figure that we have, the head opposite, carrying his bower of leaves, like the Jack who could be seen in the May Day Revels until Victorian times, is one gem amongst many others in the chapterhouse of Southwell Minster.
One of the world's great works of art, the chapterhouse is more like an arboretum cut from stone than a room... many of the major plants and trees of Britain are cut out of the stone: hawthorn, hemp, nettle, ivy, bryony, hop, maple, vine, oak, buttercup, rose and mulberry... The Green Man... has earned the title of the May King, because the hawthorn bears the may blossom, the symbol of the coming of summer.

We had chosen halfway through May for this visit.
The structure was begun in 1292, while Edward I was hammering the Scots and erecting fortresses, and is unique with a stone vault without a central supporting pier. The building itself, is surely workable for meetings of the dean and chapter: intimate and delightful. Strangely the seat to the left of the 'Decanus' bore no identifying brass plate. In the open central space was a modern exhibit of the Stations of the Cross, in, perhaps, a steel alloy. The tourist was invited to touch and feel. And yet again it worked as a display, though I have to say I would have preferred an open space, this edifice is the most singular thing at Southwell.
A history lesson lay by the entrance – many want to know what a

minster is. The board instructed us that with origins in the Anglo-Saxon era, it is a collegiate church (any large or important one). Southwell lay in the Archdiocese of York as did Beverley and Ripon. Of these only Beverley has failed to achieve cathedral status, which reveals something about the region, blessed with exceptional geography.

We now took the air, leaving by the south transept and perambulating the east end, returning to bell-ringing and to meet Thelma McIntosh, our helping steward, in post since 1980. A widow, her husband, David (1938–98), had been organist, honoured as such by way of a plaque on the nave organ, which she showed us among a shopping unit or two, still busy selling. Being employed as HMI for schools (musical discipline) he was barred from assuming an official role as organist at the minster, but was able to perform during the summer recess, amounting to around twelve times a year. Thelma's family was closely involved here. One son was an organ scholar. Regarding the other, she told us: 'Choirboys used to dare each other to go across the walkway under the Great West Window from the triforium. My son did that.' This venture would have involved challenges concerning both height and width. From our vantage point in the nave, it looked too narrow, but we were informed that there was an adequate walkway. Indeed we could discern radiators. In a previous generation there had been seating at the bottom of the window. The triforium, was, alas, not available to us to mount. It looked to be a deep space, quite able to accommodate a canon or two in his duties. Above was the clerestory with its porthole windows. In the chancel this narrowed to a single, light level.

Thelma edified us with comments about the life of the minster – how the 3-Choir system worked. This involved the transformation of the school from Boys' Grammar to Comprehensive, still incorporating the cathedral choir connection. There was a men's choir (lay clerks on a stipend), boys (termly), augmented recently by girls, who received special voice training to comply with regulations. The third strand was the voluntary choir – the Minster Chorale. The Rector Chori was the responsible officer. What an apposite title! The system had grown into a comprehensive means of training and performance.

She took us eastwards to seek out wood carvings, when, from the pulpit, a voice boomed out the facilities available to those attending the day's event. It was the Very Revd John Guille, Dean, to whom she hurried to introduce us. We duly sat with him in the south quire aisle at a table laid for tea and cakes. He had joined the cathedral staff less than three years before from Winchester, and was shortly to be joined by the new bishop, similarly translated. Meanwhile the previous assistant organist, Simon Bell, had removed the other way, to Winchester. John was fresh with statistics required from on high: the last year had produced 90K thousand visitors, 17K at services, 12K at events, with a budget of £1m. St Mary's was not in a populous location. Few tourists made it to rural Notts.

The thread we pursued was to do with the commercial side of this charitable entity. There was a waiting list for the immensely popular annual fixture: the November Craft Fair. 'There was not one complaint about the £1 admission charge.' There had also been a food fair, with a local Bramley reference. This featured Apple products, such as Calvados. 4,000 people were involved. The cathedral was off the beaten track, but the failing Euro had helped recently. Income of £400K had dipped during the year to £250K, but rallied to over £300K more recently. To us, Southwell Minster Ltd seemed very viable.

After an illuminating and generous exchange he took us up to the high altar, to the sedilia face-to-face, noting the benefit of so many seats (in the Permian limestone from Mansfield, 15 miles away) in that each official at a communion service had a sedilium: the celebrant, deacon, sub-deacon and two acolytes. 'They were made to look like that – tactile,' he said.

I asked if we could ascend the organ loft and he obliged. My companions demurred owing to their mutual problem with heights. They could not resist, however, and the four of us tramped up the steps to face the instrument. All of us gaped at the vista, to east and west, of the mayhem of the fair, and, most cogently at this elevation, the triforium. We were looking over the crossing. It was amazing. I thought: 'Give me Romanesque.' Wakey and Rand were mute, with glee I'm sure. Gobsmacked. Wakey said, months later: 'Every time I think about it, it seems so perfect. It all comes together magnificently.' He had liked the noisy presence of the market. I manoeuvred beyond the organ to the side adjoining the quire. It offered another vista, bringing home the Early English design and the single space above the choir stalls. This organ was the instrument my friend JDR, from Christ Church, Bristol, had played a matter of weeks before. I was to return two copies of *A Guide to Sung Eucharist, Mattins & Evensong on Sundays for Choirs*, one for Alto Dec and one for Auxiliary Alto Dec, with the notice inscribed 'Please do not take away'. JDR had asked for them to be conveyed to Paul Hale as the interested party. He was Rector Chori, also organ advisor to other cathedrals and an Oxford college. This cathedral had two organs. What was new was the 1990s screen. Both of them can be played from the one in the nave.

I gave the books to Dean John. He placed them on the organ seat. I like to imagine that the Rector Chori (I have to repeat such an evocative title instead of his name) retrieved them in person.

On the way down was the long list of organists pinned to the wall, which we had overlooked on the ascent – a shame the congregation had no sight of this, as if it were private knowledge. John had to move on – he had given considerable time in a forthcoming way.

We strode the short distance to the south transept café. Tea and something edible were to be purchased. But I espied Thelma and further chat ensued. I extended this while the tea cooled down, discovering such anecdotal detail as:

1   The phenomenon of the Three Choirs Festival. Not Worcs/ Glos/Herefs but Southwell/Lincoln/Peterborough – something to Google soon.

2   The previous bishop, George Cassidy, since retired, had been instrumental in converting the Diocese of Southwell into 'Southwell and Nottingham', to get the main city into the name to be more relevant – recognizing the balance of the work of the diocese. I see that as patronizing – this is the diocese of Nottinghamshire. Surely anyone interested has the wit to find its cathedral. St Mary's, Lace Market, Nottingham had been turned down in favour of this place as the new cathedral church in 1884.

3   There was considerable continuing contact with European countries. The Rector Chori (oh yes!) was involved with France and Italy, not to mention a Southwell/Sweden initiative.

I let Thelma escape. We'd spent so much time in productive discussion, focused entirely on this building and its work. She was from Glasgow with an appropriate accent, but there no time to cover religion in Scotland.

The cherry cake was much better than the earlier gluten-free effort, but it was time to explore different avenues. Malcolm, on the door, obliged. 'For beer,' he said 'Go to the Bramley Apple, the Old Coach House and the Hearty Goodfellow in that order, the best at the end,' also advising Sandy Lane, by the Goodfellow for easy return to the car. We did all this, and it worked, only marred a little by periodical score flashes from the FA Cup Final from Wembley (Chelsea, champions of the Premiership versus Portsmouth, bottom). In the Bramley Apple (almost neighbours with the eponymous apple-invention house) the half-time score was reported: 0–0. We were supping local ales outside, in full view of the discomfort suffered by bus and car drivers alike in braving this narrow road to Southwell Racecourse and the Workhouse, a National Trust property, for which the quote is provided from Mr and Mrs A Rutherford, Harrogate: 'We had a real insight into the lives of the Victorian poor. The real shock though, was seeing the bedsit (post World War II).'

No television, so no score was available at the next one, the Old Coach House, in prime position to serve the junction of key local roads. It did provide interesting Spicy peanuts, strangely the mildest of the three options (we sampled them all). Finally the Hearty Goodfellow gave us the result. Chelsea had '30 chances to Portsmouth's four,' asserted the barman. They won 1–0. It was a saga of missed penalties and angst. I was so glad Exeter City had thrilled us all into saving their third division bacon a week before. That all the footy for now.

To honour Southwell Minster, the Bramley apple and its product calvados, here is a relevant recipe:

Calvados Gravy
Ingredients:
1 tbs sugar
½ cup apple cider
¼ cup calvados
1¼ cups low sodium chicken broth
1 tsp lemon juice
1–2 tsp salt (optional)
¼ tsp ground nutmeg
2 tbs water
1½ tbs corn-starch

Method (20 minutes):
Place the sugar in a medium-size heavy saucepan. Place over medium heat, and cook until sugar is golden (do not stir).
Carefully add cider, stirring constantly (mixture will bubble vigorously).
Stir in brandy; cook 1 minute.
Add broth, lemon juice, nutmeg and salt.
Combine water and corn-starch, stirring with a wire whisk; add to the gravy. Bring to boil and cook for 1 minute, stirring constantly.

Mikekey, 2007

That should be tried. At the time our sensibilities were suffused with the structure back up the road, assisted a little by hop products. Southwell had proved to be a comprehensively good experience.

Fig 25

Fig 26

Fig 27

Fig 28

Fig 29

[25] Southwell: Not money changers but a craft fair.
[26] Lincoln: Part of the glorious west front.
[27] Lincoln: The workforce battling with scaffolding.
[28] Leicester: Tombs and the author in the churchyard.
[29] Leicester: A bright welcome board at St Martin's.

227

20

Lincoln

St Mary

Province: York
Founded: 1072, moved from Dorchester, Oxfordshire
Present Building: 11th century west front, mainly Early English

Website: www.lincolncathedral.com
Tel: 01522 521600
Email: visitors@lincolncathedral.com
Address: Minster Yard, Lincoln LN2 1PX

Three to See: Before you go in look at the Romanesque columns on the west front;
the imp and while you're looking enjoy its setting, the Angel Choir;
Wren library, built over the east cloister

Imp

Monday 17 May. 2010

We were on the train, a branch line: two stops in an hour and no other stations to serve that we noticed. Cooling towers were rife in a 'desperate part of the country', as Rand put it. In days of yore he used to travel towards civilization from the 'it's so bracing' Skegness, facing the North Sea, not far away. 'I'd hurry along here – I don't like it.' There was acid yellow rape everywhere, to the extent that the drab urban introduction to Lincoln was welcome. Mind you, we'd already luxuriated in the previews of the three towers on the highest point of a hilly city for several miles before arriving.

Rand's back was playing up, so the immediate taxi was inevitable. It got us there quickly. We were before the vast west front in no time. The rampant Romanesque display in the lower levels invited us to caress and analyze the columns exhibiting exotic influences: Arabia and India perhaps, with a touch of Assyrian, evocative of exhibits at the British Museum. Rand said afterwards: 'It was the colour that caught me first.' And, on a day bright but showery too, the tones of Lincolnshire oolitic limestone did excite.

We ventured in. Expecting more of a fleecing, we were happy to pay the £4.75 (£6 for standard people), the charge the subject of an apology: 'over £50 thousand per week to run the cathedral'. An audio guide was £1, but, once inside, the tours were free. Unfortunately, undertaking the cathedral tour would preclude the roof one, as they started at 1 pm and 2 pm respectively; the result was overlap. This was confirmed by the cashier. A bit crass? There were also tower tours, but only on Saturdays. We were two days too late. The place already seemed old-fashioned, with much fuss from ancient cashiers, baffling us and themselves with the gift aid forms and further complications involving the entitlement to repeat visits, and special arrangements for groups. One of these had congregated in a long line, complete with a bevy of schoolmistresses. There was an eastern icon on the wall behind: something to divert you while you waited.

Rand and I made for the catering facility; somewhat gradually as every glance about us was a temptation to divert us. It was called the Cloister Café. There were only 25-odd covers in the café itself. We were to discover more outside on the lawn with views of houses to the northeast. There were tables and chairs in the cloister on the other side, where you could enjoy the sight of men at work on a lead roof project, members of the ample works department of the cathedral (on the payroll). Orange overalls pervaded on scaffolding. The café was pokey, given the dimensions of the cathedral, where some of the chapels had a surfeit of display compared with action. Big, in cathedrals, isn't always best. We had a pot of tea for one (him: £1. Coffee would have been £1.40, so the price was right), sparkling water (me) and baked potatoes (£3.95). Mine was soggy, but I did opt for cheese and beans for the filling. The enterprise was in decline from the evidence, which doesn't mean a thing as several cathedrals' facilities have been transformed to provide enjoyable experiences on subsequent visits. Meanwhile the wall boasted a commanding painting of the cathedral. 'Post-modern', opined Rand. We emerged from this, refreshed enough to do our own wander round the perimeter. This initiative was curtailed at one point by a metal barrier, backed up by a notice requiring hard hats to be worn, then by a sudden flurry of rain.

Next was the tour, conducted by Pat Palmer. We started at the west end, as is traditional. It wasn't the most inspiring, or complete, delivery. Perhaps there should be various options, as there is a vast amount of easily conveyed information. We weren't shown the chapter house or the cloisters, for instance. The building, Early English on Norman, was stunning. Wherever you look sits another delight for your entertainment. Pat pointed out the glorious green man, belching forth through the dense foliage of the screen/pulpitum (a double act like Southwell), and, later, dragons on the opposite, south side, one live, one skinned. Plus some traces of the original colour. As she mentioned the number 33, as the estimated sum of green men in the building, after that we examined every display, wooden and stone, for green men. We saw none, resorting to advice from a steward near the west end, on our way out. She said, quickly: 'Oh, that's easy, we have a location chart for green men.' There they were, nine of them, in puce marker pen. One was high in the crossing. We were hard-pressed to detect it even with binoculars – I don't know how we could unearth the unlisted 24 if some of the listed ones were elusive. They should have been easy to single out. This place was so immense and rich that the following (suggested by *The Charge of the Light Brigade* by local poet-knight, Alfred, Lord Tennyson) is aimed to spin the yarn:

A Tale of Lincoln Cathedral

1 Early
William came conquering
The first Norman king
God's houses to bring
For one, to fair Lincoln.
Remigius, war hero
Was Dorchester's bishop.
"God to town" manifesto
Saw the see go to Lincoln

Way up on high ground

Landmark far around
Looking down on the wold
An easy choice: Lincoln
From old Wessex country
Dorchester see –
Biggest one in the land –
Now moved to Lincoln

In 1072,
The castle there, bright and new,
What did Remigius do?
Ordered a stone or two
Cathedral for Lincoln
Then after the pile was done,
Matilda and Stephen fought
Battling in field, on fen,
Was it to do with them
That fire consumed Lincoln?

Alex, on Bishop's throne,
Replaced blackened stone
Added style of his own,
A new Norman Lincoln
Henry of Huntingdon and
"Magnificent" Alex won
Plaudits for what was done
The new Norman Lincoln
A bit smug you might surmise,
But flash on to '85
An earthquake hit countrywide
And worst hit was Lincoln

2 Middle
The bishop turned in his tomb –
The pale limestone came in bulk
All left of Alex's hulk,
Was the west front of Lincoln.
Hugh of Avalon, inspired,
Bringing Gothic up here
From the dense Romanesque
(Round mass, arabesque)

The new Early English
Made Salisbury, Wells, Lincoln

The sanctified Hugh
Got it going anew
In 1192
The new build at Lincoln
But eight years on he was dead
It was too much for him they said
(did trips in King John's stead).
It all took a hundred years
The new Gothic Lincoln

In 1200 a piece,
The dark Tournai font,
Arrived as he died
In the west end of Lincoln
Just one marble block –
Lions and winged beasts flock
For the new-born of Lincoln

Saintly the masons were
Heavy the barrows there
With fresh quarried stone
Shaping for Lincoln
Sharp arches soared in flight
Craftsmen strove day and night
Skills stretched well out of sight
For glorious Lincoln

Plantagenets on the throne
Three Edwards (oh how dull)
Saw first the chapter house
59' wide, and tall
For administering Lincoln
They all heard a frightful crash –
The central tower was dashed,
Too bold, it ended trash
In building site Lincoln

A new tower was built

Decorated style,
And angels to the fore
At the east of the choir
The Angel Choir, Lincoln
The Virgin Mary saw her
Her winged host installed
All over fair Lincoln

Decorations divine,
For generations in line,
The Dean's Eyes, so fine
The stained glass at Lincoln
And St Hugh has his shrine
The Imp pert and prime
On guard for all time
The ghoul of Lincoln

3 Late
Tudor times weren't so good
The spire fell where it stood
(spired tower a bad idea)
Flat tops for Lincoln
Puritan spoil severe
And more poor repair
Too good for its own
Good, that's sad Lincoln

Then a fine new enclave
The library of Wren,
(That's Chris of St Paul's)
Baroque came to Lincoln
In Charlie 2's reign
Over the cloisters
The old Gothic Lincoln

The west spires came down
Our poet came to town
Alfred. Victorian,
His tones so stentorian
His statue at Lincoln
Poet Laureate of renown

His Light Brigade charged
All over fair Lincolnshire

The modern drifts in
With Duncan Grant's mural
Bloomsbury 50s in
Middle aged Lincoln
St Hugh's shrine got spikes
Not everyone likes
For this is the rural
County of Lincoln

But now look around,
The perimeter's fenced
Scaffolds abound
The tour guide's intense
At tourist spot Lincoln
The green men are listed
Misericords dusted
It's not to be missed
This mecca called Lincoln.

Sir Christopher Wren's library, which we caught towards the end of its brief opening time, served as restful relief. The style was conducive to a chamber music recital, and indeed they are presented at St Mary's on a regular basis. But I had for decades harboured the memory of a concert in the nave. The good bit was a performance of Faure's *Requiem*, marred by a stilettoed woman who chose a quiet movement to stomp precisely from front to back and out. The conductor motioned the musicians to stop. Once the offender had safely departed they started up again from the top of the interrupted section. It just wasn't the same after that.

I'm sure fine concerts have been scheduled on a regular basis for a very long time. What has changed is how the place is run. In 1990, Lincoln had become notorious for bad relationships. 'The Dean and his Chapter said "And also with you", they didn't mean it.' Further up the Anglican hierarchy was sometimes a 'job-for-life' feeling. I recalled something of this and resorted to the *Independent* for this report:

The Dean of Lincoln, the Very Revd Brandon Jackson, has finally replied to the public appeal to him to resign made three weeks ago by the Archbishop of Canterbury, Dr George Carey.

In a statement issued to his local paper, Dr Jackson said he was prepared to resign, but only if the Sub-Dean and treasurer of the cathedral, Canon Rex Davis, also resigned. Canon Davis has said he will not.

Dr Jackson has spent most of his seven years in office trying to engineer the resignation of the other four canons he found in office when he joined the cathedral; Canon Davis, his chief opponent, is the only one still in office. Dr Jackson also demanded, as the price of his own resignation, that the financial arrangements made for both men be made public.

The Dean's latest statement, in which he claims the pressure on him to stay "is very considerable and growing by the day", is the latest development in a story that has veered between tragedy and farce since Dr Jackson's arrival.

He has survived a trial for adultery with a former cathedral verger; ... the Fraud Squad (was) invited by Dean Jackson (to) examine the accounts of a fund-raising trip to Australia for which Canon Davis was responsible; and the two men have rejected attempts at reconciliation from the Bishop of Lincoln, the Archbishop and a team of professional counsellors.

After his acquittal on charges of adultery last year, Dr Jackson accused the Bishop, the Rt Revd Bob Hardy, of being part of a conspiracy against him and demanded that he resign. Both Bishop Hardy and Dr Carey, wearying of conciliation, have urged both men to resign. At a press conference last month, Dr Carey described their feud as "a cancer" and "a scandal dishonouring the church". But he admitted he had no power to compel either man to resign unless they were found guilty of a criminal offence.

In his statement, Dr Jackson claimed yesterday that he was "co-operating with the spirit of the Archbishop's request, but must now leave it to others to resolve the other half of the equation needed to achieve the outcome requested".

Dr Jackson is 61. He need not resign until he reaches the age of 70.

Independent 19/7/96

This scenario provoked the establishment of the Lady Howe Commission, whose findings informed the content of the 1999 Cathedrals Measure. It had a profound effect on how all Anglican cathedrals and dioceses were henceforth to be run.

On display in the Library were two attractive volumes: *The History of St Paul's Cathedral* by William Dugdale (1658), a lasting memorial to Old St Paul's, perhaps helpful as a visit to the current one was scheduled in this tour within the following six months. Also on that subject was *Devotions upon Emergent Occasions* (1626) by Dean of St Paul's John Donne (1572–1631). The caption read:

> *Although Donne is best known today as a poet, it was as a preacher that he was celebrated during his lifetime... (he) used rich figurative language far removed from the plain prose favoured by the Puritans.*

We must therefore dip into his sermons. We had seen plenty of evidence of the direct actions of the Puritans, at Lincoln on the orders of the earl of Manchester: faceless corbels for example. Here was the linguistic equivalent. And we were able to enjoy the organ and girls' choir – practice by turns. This was fun, the kind of thing it almost seemed that the biggest cathedrals with pedigree and history behind them could afford and have inherited. On a visit to London's Victoria and Albert Museum in 2010 there was a fine exhibition, apparently to do with gargoyles: Gothic architecture and 19th century photography. Included was 'Lincoln stairway in SW turret 1898' by Fred Evans (1853–1943). Unfortunately, 'gargoyles' in the title will get the public in, like me, but not deliver. I didn't see one, like the lack of gargoyles on cathedrals. They are very rare, but are generically associated with church buildings.

Here's a piece of trivia, which happens to have a subject from this diocese, from this day's tear-off page from Jeffrey Kacirk's Forgotten English 365-day calendar of vanishing vocabulary and folklore for 2010:

Iatrochemicus
A chemical physician, or one who uses chemical medicines (John Redman Coxe's Philadelphia Medical Dictionary (1817).
Or
Iatrochemistry, the chemical theory of medicine adopted by Paracelsus (Sir James Murray's Oxford English Dictionary (1909).

Perpetual Pill-Popper
On this day in 1917, Mr Samuel Jessup, an opulent grazier of pill-taking memory... died at Heckington (Lincolnshire) aged sixty-five. From 1791 to 1816, the deceased took 226,934 pills

supplied by a responsible apothecary in Bottesford, which is at the rate of 10,806 pills a year, or twenty nine pills each day. But as the patient began with a more moderate appetite and increased it as he proceeded, in the last five years preceding 1816 he took pills at the rate of seventy-eight a day, and in the year 1814 he swallowed not less than 51,590 (and) 40,000 bottles of mixtures, juleps, and electuaries.
William Hone's Every-day Book, or Everlasting Calendar of Popular Amusements (1827).
Just before his death, the well-off Mr Jessup inconceivably appeared as a defendant in a lawsuit charging that he failed to pay his apothecary, a Mr Wright. The above-mentioned medicines were catalogued over the years by Wright, filling "fifty-five clearly written columns" of his notebook.

It was 4 pm and Great Tom, the mighty 5-ton-plus bell, clanged – it was time to try the café's pot of tea. We sipped it sitting in the sunny cloister, for which the Library served as a canopy. A sprightly blackbird joined us, but refused Rand's blandishment, in the form of the remainder of his rather dry cake. A column carried graffiti: 'Skelton 1686'. The aspect was of the north aisle mostly obscured by scaffolding, which earlier we had witnessed rather laid back action from three yellow-jacketed, red-helmeted workmen, with their props, sundry tools and a slab or two of oolitic. There was sadness about the state of the stone, extensive patches of weathered and crumbling edifice. I was not surprised to have read this piece:

The Independent reports that English Heritage says six cathedrals – Lincoln, York, Salisbury, Canterbury, Chichester and Winchester – need to carry out major renovations in the next 10 years. The twist in the tale is that there is no money coming from English Heritage to pay for the repairs now that the body's ringfenced fund for cathedrals had been stopped. Lincoln Cathedral has launched a public campaign to raise £2.5m to fund badly needed restoration works.

Arts Industry 21/5/10

We happened upon a notice saying: 'Adopt a stone from £25', backed up by a purposeful triple-folded promotional item at the entrance.

It was the vulnerability of this building that appealed to me. It is a hulk and an icon. Alec Clifton-Taylor wrote: 'Probably, all things considered, the finest of the English cathedrals.' My favourite defect was the nave mismatch. Building started at the east. When the project had advanced several hundred feet, the roofline had veered to the south. The west end, which, after all the nave was seeking to join, was out of kilter. Also fun was the presence of a stray pigeon. There were droppings on the floor under the crossing, suggesting that such an incursion was a frequent occurrence.

Rand and I also liked what might have been described as a mistake, the Duncan Grant mural in the southeast Russell Chantry. Applied in 1958, they illustrated, provocatively, sheep and fishermen, executed with a preponderance of gender display. Moving a little northwards, neither of us was sure about the 1986 superimposition of a sinuous steel snake around and above the Shrine of St Hugh's Head, under the east window and below the guardian Imp (20p was the charge to illuminate the 'darling thing', expostulated an American woman, with camera at the ready). The work was isolated in a cathedral little given to modern additions. Attention was drawn in our tour to the irregular ribs here in St Hugh's Choir, and in the bottom transepts. Again, being quirky, this was welcome, while Pevsner was referred to as describing it as 'overwhelmingly lopsided'. These arches over the quire are known as the Crazy Vault. Under 62 choir stalls, way below, lay the second best set of misericords after Chester (claimed Clifton-Taylor). I had seen those and the ones at Worcester and Exeter. All of them were fabulous. Here, tour guide Pat said: 'They're not on view.' I did manage to sneak a peak later on.

The list was endless. Any list would be in this building, which became a model, in the ground-breaking nave and elsewhere, for subsequent projects all over the country. On the other hand the sites of former brasses in the floor come across as scars, and here and there's so much space that it looks lost, and on occasion cluttered with paraphernalia.

Wandering slowly back down the south side, the Apprentices' Wall appeared, showing practice carving. Arriving at the Tournai Font, it was locked, where Lichfield's had been open and replenished with real tap water for school parties to enjoy. The single mass revealed exotic images, should you care to examine the dark, obscure surface. We were informed its use to be about 12 times per year. Then we saw the Paupers' Window, where alms were distributed. Rand commented: 'I find this delicious – this arch behind the font. Exuberant. What effort!'

We were now dealing with the delights of the cathedral in easing out mode. Finally departing from the cloister by way of the café, now empty (at 4.30 pm) we walked to the statue of the erstwhile Poet Laureate round the chapter house, which looked pale by comparison with the cathedral itself. It's a decagon. Ten sides! This was the largest in the country, and looked it, reminding me of the detached Ely Lady Chapel and Chichester's Bell Tower.

The surfaces were patchy, and unfortunately eroded. At the Judgement Porch (c.1260), the figures were beautiful but in a bad state, and the porch cramped between later additions. It whistled past as we approached the west front by taxi, jutting out from the south side.

Replete with limestone, we sought out refreshment of the hop-based kind, choosing the Victoria and its garden, which meant passing by the West Gate and Castle. Well-designed buildings proliferate in Lincoln. But the cathedral was quite enough for a day's preoccupation. Inevitably it should be identified by the Imp. Not only is it the single most familiar image, adaptable to reproduction as souvenirs but Lincoln City FC are the Red Imps, after all. This is of course along with the cathedral's profile, photographed and painted from the High Street or much of the county. All cathedrals are some kind of landmark. Down the road lies the substantial St Botolph's, Boston. Its west tower called 'The Stump', topped with a Perpendicular octagon, constitutes a most impressive landmark in endless flat country. Wakey suffered a vertigo attack as we did the circuit round the exposed walkway at the apex. Once I had engineered him back down the irregular, very spiral stairs, he had to rest awhile in the womblike nave. You have to choose your own parameters for best silhouette. Lincoln does pretty well in the landmark and icon stakes – not bad on bits of oddness, too, which all contribute to its singular character.

21

Leicester

St Martin

Province: Canterbury
Founded: 13th century parish church
Present building: 19th century tower and spire added
Cathedral status: 1927 from Peterborough

Website: www.cathedral.leicester.anglican.org
Tel: 0116 261 5200
Email: leicestercathedral@leccofe.org
Address: The Cathedral Centre, 21 St Martin's, Leicester LE1 5DE

Three to see: Archdeacon's Court;
carvings of ailments in Great South Aisle;
outside, afterwards look at the tombstones on the south side, arranged as
a display

Cloak

Tuesday 18 May, 2010

After a two hour drive on a Tuesday morning, we were early enough to find a valuable space in Leicester's open air Lanes car park, very close to the cathedral. The machine involved a battle. We had trouble entering the required registration number as the machine rejected the (correct) number four times. It was to our relief and that of a well-turned out business woman, that it produced the goods, a ticket for four hours. Business Woman was as perplexed as us, and she was a regular user. Rand's V registration VW could therefore be blamed, as BW had a sporty number with a modern-style number plate. While waiting for the conclusion of this business, I espied a Wetherspoon's establishment beyond, which would now be suitable for refreshments in the time left before our appointment with the Dean of Leicester. Rand, rarely troubled by the subconscious, revealed what he could remember of his dream the previous night. It involved Duncan Grant naughtiness (he averred vaguely) involving sheep, harking back to the provocative Lincoln murals. He himself was in the picture, though he couldn't remember what actions took place. They were of a lurid nature, by definition. And here we were, in the East Midlands, about to experience something at the polar opposite of the day before.

On the website of a cathedral with a vision statement: 'Reaching out to all, we witness to Christ holding all things in unity' is 'A Welcome from The Dean'. That's exactly what Rand and I received from The Very Revd Vivienne Faull, at the time one of only two female deans in Anglican England. The other was at Salisbury. We eventually found the correct building, and passed the 'big, red door' and entry phone, we were met by Julia Unna, the PA to the Dean. Rand's full name was taken as an additional guest, and we were provided with a welcome mug of tea. The dean had half an hour, she said, which had been arranged, most fortunately, through a person-to-person phone call. Thinking I was through to the PA, I said I wanted to arrange to see the dean, to which she replied: 'You're speaking to the Dean. What can I do for you?'

The conversation, which ensued after tea delivery and establishing that it really would be half an hour, was wide-ranging and cogent to ecclesiastical matters and business. Dean Vivienne, formerly Vice-Provost at Coventry, and Bishop Tim Stevens had both been in post for enough time to forge a productive partnership, him since 1999, her from 2002. She was Chair of the Association of English Cathedrals. At home a thrusting negotiating process prevailed to combine the bodies covering the work of deans, precentors, organists and architects to become unified in a single organization and one building. This bore out the nature of the dean's role as Chief Executive. This was in a diocese with its top building completely hampered by its physical position. Only Oxford, among cathedrals, had less space around, she said. This was an urban church, and the centre of most of the population of the diocese, the traditional county of Leicestershire. The parish church was promoted to cathedral status in 1927, ceded by the unwieldy diocese of Lincoln.

Leicester was set to become the first 'plural' city, with no white majority. Hindus and Muslims make up the bulk of the figures. The car park Business Woman may have been one. There were direct issues of deprivation: asylum seekers proliferate and destitution is all too much in evidence. There were more than a hundred sleeping on the streets every night. Global citizens had to sort out issues; dioceses such as Leicester were players in the world of economics and human problems. Meanwhile, following the recent General Election, Vivienne was confident in the approach of Leicester South MP, Sir Peter Soulsby (Labour), who had taken the seat from the Liberal Democrats in 2005. 'His policies tie in with the cathedral's', she said. This is a paradigm for church and state working together, as well as unity within the diocese, and an extreme model of the city presence, as I had witnessed at Southwark and Sheffield. Social needs were high on the list of activities. Rand had said on the way down: 'I'm sort of expecting it to be a big crèche.' Maybe later in the day it would resemble St Mary Magdalene, the parish church of Taunton, Somerset, which we had visited recently: busy, with a café at the rear of the nave and buggies rampant. Except that at St Martin there was no catering actually in the cathedral. On the subject of public figures – MPs and mayors – I'd like to add a subsequent snippet from the *Metro* (1/7/10):

> *Pants be to God*
> *It could be a case of the Lord moving in mysterious ways when a mayor who banned prayers from council meetings found his trousers slipping to the floor in a room packed with children. The trouser trouble struck as Colin Hall, the lord mayor of Leicester, stood up to make a speech in a library in the city. He has now apologised following the gaffe which drew gasps and giggles from the youngsters. "Whilst giving a vote of thanks, I suffered a problem with my trousers," said the 46-year-old. "I had chosen not to wear a belt and the trousers came loose and fell." On his Twitter site, Mr Hall appeared to blame the problem on his new diet.*

I asked about bishops and the House of Lords, as Bishop Tim was reported as a member thereof when making a statement on Radio

4 about marriage, civil partnerships and covenants (Sunday 28/2/10). This was a relaxed diocese, as was Southwark, another with urban and 'people' emphasis. There were the five premier bishoprics, and 21 others, determined by length of service, pure and simple. When you retired, the elevation evaporates. Of course bishops of the Johnny-come-lately Leicester, along with all but the Big 5, had to rely upon length of service and retirement of others to gain membership. Vivienne showed how the system worked by way of an anecdote about a former Bishop of Carlisle, who was desperate to make an appearance in the upper house, and was approaching retirement. Yes, he made it, just, in the end. The current one, the Right Revd James Newcome, rose to the challenging duty of making public statements following the mass murders by Derrick Bird in his diocese the next month.

Time, and the tea, were ebbing. For us it could have been prolonged considerably, given the flow of conversation and issues. Vivienne echoed the cathedral pecking order in the way I'd worked it out: there were about four levels, and Leicester was in the bottom division, but not quite as badly off, financially, as Bradford, in wooden spoon position. Events such as *Macbeth in the Cathedral* (£12/£8), was to be presented on 22 May between performances at Manchester and Norwich Cathedrals, should make a good contribution. When I asked about viability, she revealed the obvious, that some of them might become (re?)absorbed into others. Cathedrals with a track record were more able to take risks. Salisbury had benefited from a series of leaders pursuing a radical direction. 'That explains the font,' I speculated flippantly after we left. Rand expressed it thus: 'With Celia Tate, I'm very surprised.' As the entertaining, but reactionary, guide at Salisbury it had been she had contributed to inspiring this long journey.

Attendances here were in an upward trend, but high numbers couldn't really be expected. Meanwhile there had been a substantial success with the Good Friday 'Christ in the Centre' event. 300K people were involved, and, alas, it was reported nowhere. Finances were critical, informing the intricate management by the various bodies and individuals, stakeholders as in any business. They were responsible businesses, but lines must sometimes be drawn, as in the attempted sale on the open market by Hereford Cathedral of its treasure the Mappa Mundi. Cathedral treasuries were important. The dioceses were in the role of custodian, and a bit of opulence and quiet pageantry didn't come amiss. Antiques Road Shows had been conducted in many a cathedral. For the practical 21st century, the ongoing project was the investment in St Martin's House, Leicester's cathedral centre for mission and outreach. It would serve city and county, diocese and cathedral.

Formerly Leicester Grammar School, it was completed by the end of 2010, showing off its best old features.

We now had to see St Martin's as it had developed in the 83 years since its elevation in status. First was the grassed and paved area on the south side. The right hand part of this contained a cooling water feature and tomb stones arranged in a semi-circle behind a bench, upon which I sat to pose for a snap. The uprights resembled dominoes in sequence before a clown toppled the lot.

The 1897 south porch was admirable with carvings of Leicester's great and good over the generations. We now ventured inside to enjoy this former parish church. To celebrate the elevation of status the large wooden chancel screen was presented, designed by Sir Charles Nicholson, who was also responsible for other work of refurnishing the 13th and 14th centuries interior.

The building's capacity is 920 with no real possibility of expansion, but the interior was attractively medieval, of the 13th century, rising above a dull, regular layout. As ever there were fascinating features. My favourite was in the Great South Aisle where the coloured corbels depicted various human ailments, such as toothache. In the corner was a Consistory ('Archdeacon's') Court, put to use on occasion and benefiting from ample space. To start with we used 'A Pilgrim's Walk' until it turned out not to present detailed information. It probably sufficed for people new to the world of Anglicanism and churches. *Explore Leicester Cathedral* was more of a workable guide. There was a message from Vivienne. '... Look... Reflect... Pray... celebrate... and enjoy your visit,' were her words, as she smiled from the page. We did. It asked for a donation of 50p to cover costs.

Leicester is reported as the fourth smallest English cathedral. Birmingham (3rd from bottom) and Chelmsford (bottom but one) were eclipsed by our next focus, Derby. And Newport, Wales, loomed on the horizon. Tiny: half the square footage of even this compact building. However the Guildhall was next door, housing the catering facility. St Martin, to whom this cathedral was dedicated, had a predictable presence. A Roman soldier who became a Christian in AD334, he appeared, carved, on horseback on the cathedra, and sharing his traditional cloak with a beggar in stained glass near the elegant curved gallery under the west window. The legend went that in the beggar's face he saw that of Jesus. Cloaks and mantles, metaphorically, abound here, as an image of turbulent city life, borne out by its chosen martyr. Therefore a cloak is nominated as the image of Leicester. St Martin was a good choice for the dedication, in a foundation originally Norman.

The Dean and a Cloak
This parish church see, strong and tall,
Gives communion, concert, cakes, all.
St Martin, in cloak,
Helps many a failed bloke:
It's all down to Dean Vivienne Faull.

We found ourselves in St Dunstan's Chapel where there were two icons in evidence. We were getting used to one, but two? They were: one Greek, of Mary and Jesus, and one Russian, more detailed and interesting to look at, of the 'Hospitality of Abraham'. Dunstan was the patron saint of goldsmiths. I thought hosiery was Leicester's thing,

Leaving intrinsically valuable items for last, there were admirable paintings in the north choir aisle: *The Scourging of Christ,* painted by Luis de Morales (c.1520–86) was donated to the cathedral in 1966; *The Resurrection of Christ,* painted by a follower of Palma Giovane (c.1548–1628) was given to it in 1790. There's a Van Eyck copy – an altarpiece, *The Adoration of the Lamb.* Rand commented: 'A lovely piece – it's surprising no one has stolen it.' The cathedral is a custodian, indeed. Something seemed to have been added in most generations. The organ (by Harrisons of Durham, like Lichfield's) 'contains pipework from a Snetzler organ of 1774'. The font was made in 1849 and the spire added in 1860. The first two were good to look at. The steeple, by Brandon, has been considered over-high (*Observer's Book*) but I felt its presence in the city centre justified that. On the way out, the southeast chapel of St George 'contains the memorials to the Tigers' or 'The Royal Leicestershire Regiment' from which the rugby football team took their name and colours (green, red and white). After this the Tigers became champions, again, beating Saracens in the final. Along with Bristol, Leicester RFC was the last to dispense with letters, rather than numbers, on players' shirts: another old tradition banished by modern commercialism!

We were now replete with the cathedral, leaving to wander around the area, noting St Martin's Hall, conveniently opposite the west end. We then embarked upon a wander in an easterly direction through older bits of city centre to the newest presence of all: the Curve Theatre. It had replaced the Haymarket, whose hallowed space was now occupied by a shopping centre. I recalled a coach trip to the Haymarket to see *Mack and Mabel* in the 1980s. A leading regional theatre, it had been famous for musical productions, which regularly transferred to the West End. Also in the mental picture were the management meetings of the Midlands repertory theatres, in the days when 'repertory' was standard in the world of subsidized centres of arts excellence. In this contemporary building we did a circumnavigation of the ground floor, which meant going round both main house and studio, adjacent in a single space. We managed to see both, one by a sneaky snoop through a random door, and the other through the assistance of a purple-clad bar boy who let us in: 'Hurry, as work is going on.' *The Lieutenant of Inishmore* was in the offing, and tours of *The Rat Pack* and other popular fodder.

It was coffee time. Rand duly sank a white one. I chose Blueberry tea, with some anodyne addition. It sufficed, and was in keeping with the elegant, curved, environs. We repaired through the market and pedestrianized street to where we had begun. Lacking a *Good Beer Guide* and the time to perform instant research, we hit upon the High Cross Inn. I chose Nethergate Red Poll bitter, to wash down sausages and mash and Rand opted for Black Sheep to accompany something Italianesque on the plate. We sniggered at the trials undergone by a substantial queue in our car park, which was in direct view. I took a photograph. As there were spaces for about a score of cars, the line of five represented a considerable percentage. We agreed we would try a multi-storey car park next time. We left, easily, for the ring road onto the A6 and over to Derby.

22

Derby

All Saints

Province: Canterbury
Founded: 15th century collegiate church
Present building: 1500 tower; rebuilt 1723–25 by James Gibbs; more work from 1960s
Cathedral status: 1927 – from Southwell

Website: www.derbycathedral.org
Tel: 01332 341201
Email: office@derbycathedral.org
Address: Derby Cathedral Centre, 18–19 Iron Gate, Derby DE1 3GP

Three to See: Robert Bakewell's wrought iron screen;
Bess of Hardwick's memorial;
1963 stained glass windows, which work well in the east end

Peregrine falcon

Tuesday 18 May, 2010

This former collegiate church has been a cathedral since 1927, when the Derbyshire territory was transferred to the new diocese from Lichfield. Its modern day idiosyncrasy is to host peregrine falcons.

The 1530 west tower was what governed the choice of car park, aided by road signs to the Cathedral Quarter. It was easy to find, facing what must have formerly been a busy thoroughfare. Not so these days, and the café 'Derby Cathedral Centre' closed its doors at the unprecedentedly early time of 3.30 pm. In practical terms the shop was being shut up as we arrived, soon after 3 pm. This flew in the face of the protestation that it was a welcoming award-winning enterprise. Tea would have been good.

We were met by 'John, Education', actually John Armitage. There's a good name redolent of the industry of the area. We launched into the obvious: 'Where are the peregrine falcons – can we see them?' the outcome of which was to leave the binocular scanning of the roof until after we'd finished in the cathedral. I had actually remembered to bring the bins. We then agreed to try out the *Walk Round Plan* and ask him any questions afterwards. It was subtitled 'A special place of prayer, open to the world, at the heart of the city'. Somehow every cathedral's mission is slightly different. Derby is the smallest cathedral in England at 10,950 sq ft, so it really is compact. I prefer that to other adjectives, as the size suited the contents. It was a rewarding building to examine.

All Saints Cathedral is on the site where 'there has been a Christian church for over 1,000 years', on the edge of what is now a city centre (status conveyed by HM The Queen to mark her Jubilee in 1977). The position bears this out, at the top of an attractive green space rising from the River Derwent. People of a studying age were draped over municipal seats and reclining on the grass. The only break was provided by the statue of Bonnie Prince Charlie. His presence needs an explanation. Here is what *Peak District Online* states:

> *December 4ᵗʰ 1745. On that day a six and a half thousand strong force of Jacobites led by the "Young Pretender'", Charles Edward Stuart, known to history as "Bonnie Prince Charlie" marched from Ashbourne into Derby on their way south to claim the English throne. Two days later, on December 6ᵗʰ, the Bonnie Prince and his band of followers had turned tail and were retracing their steps northward, pursued at a distance by English troops.*
>
> *Four months later the Jacobite Rebellion, as it came to be known, was over. The Bonnie Prince's highland army made it*

back to Scotland, only to be completely routed by the Duke of Cumberland's troops in the savage battle of Culloden Moor on April 16th 1746.

Two and a half centuries later in December 1995, a fabulous bronze statue of Bonnie Prince Charlie on horseback by sculptor Anthony Stones was unveiled on Cathedral Green in Derby to mark the 250th Anniversary of the Prince's advance to the city – and each December, the Charles Edward Stuart Society hold a colourful pageant and re-enact a battle in the city centre which culminates in the laying of a wreath at the foot of the statue.

An interesting piece of history, I thought. Inside the building, which is a 1720s concoction by James Gibbs, we were aided by another bright day, helping to clarify some of the items there. Photos were free of charge: a notice greeted us on entering: '(To) Amateur photographers. We hope you will take lots, show them to all your families and friends and encourage them to visit us and see our lovely cathedral for themselves.' That was such a good message compared with some elsewhere, notably in the big, proud cathedrals.

Rand and I sat first in the comfortably-pewed nave. We found the whole place had a formal character, as a model of 18th century achievement. Its look was rare and cohesive. The limited dimensions served to allow us to embrace everything easily. There were no additions or extra bits, though there was space outside, especially to the south, to extend the building. It was all the better to have resisted. It might have the effect of dilution. We decided to follow the number order on the plan, broadly anti-clockwise. Nº 1 had been achieved by the sojourn in the pews. Nº 2 was St Katharine's Chapel. This was downstairs so I partly withdraw my comment about the whole interior being in sight. The chapel, hiding discreetly in crypt mode, was stunningly modern like a rather select basement restaurant. It had whitewashed walls with bare stone and a cleanly carved dark marble table. This would serve as an altar though the room lacked a cross. We wondered about its history: I applied an asterisk to my notes, signifying 'Ask John'. Only a very few bodies could squeeze in there at once, but it permeated calm and peace. I felt better already.

Above, 'The Cavendish Area' awaited us. This provided an abundance of friendly relics and connections, as well as one disappointment. I shall get that out of the way first. First in the firing line was a tomb chest. That was fine. From, dangerously, reading round the subject, we were expecting a cadaver in the space below. ('A shroud covers the head but the face is visible. These are the only wooden effigies in Derbyshire', *Harris's Guide to Churches & Cathedrals* by Brian L Harris). What met us was a blank space. The item was absent on the leaflet. Rand was particularly upset, following his enjoyment of the cadaver at Lincoln. Preserved life and death, provide a special kind of art. But we were able to gorge ourselves on the display board and memorials of successive generations. In pride of place was the splendid 16th century monument, which was Bess of Hardwick's memorial. That is, Elizabeth, Countess of Shrewsbury (1518–1608). Her pile, Hardwick Hall, lay a few miles up the road; we had visited, and thoroughly enjoyed it in recent memory (it did provide refreshments). In the vault below lay her descendant, Henry Cavendish (1731–1810), who discovered hydrogen. This was a family of achievement and celebrity: hot property and cool gas.

On an informative board display, was related the engaging life story of Georgiana, Duchess of Devonshire (1757–1806), and that of her successor in marriage Elizabeth Foster (1759–1824). The artist was Thomas Gainsborough, to great effect. The man concerned was the 5th Duke (1748–1811), one of the *roués* of the Classical period. There were plenty of Cavendish links in many of the stately homes in Derbyshire it seems. The refreshingly down to earth local painter Joseph Wright (always called 'of Derby') was also represented here, prompting our next foray, of which more in a minute.

By way of diversion the font was found in this southeast section, unusually at the furthest distance from the entrance at the west. Above it our attention was drawn to the two 1963 stained glass windows, solitary in the building, by Ceri Richards (1903–71), which suited the place admirably. In gold and blue they appropriately depict the themes of All Souls and All Saints, showing the ancient struggle between darkness and light. And on the north side was a consistory court. That was two in one day, with Leicester earlier. The Derby one was predictably more structured and official in appearance. Dark wood always helps.

I've left the best until last: the intricate wrought iron screen by local expert Robert Bakewell. It was executed between 1725 and 1750; the arms displayed being those of George II. We had devoured the glory of another of his works at the gates of Wentworth Woodhouse, near Rotherham, days before. Even Alec Clifton-Taylor mentioned the screen, despite the *ingénue* status of Derby as a cathedral. AC-T favoured 'old'. It was an exceptionally rich piece, worthy of close attention, involving anti-dog devices, inset rectangles, motifs with linear patterns, and finials, known as the 'Bakewell border' (*Robert Bakewell, Artist Blacksmith* by S Dunkerton).

Eastwards lay the altar. It was surmounted brilliantly by my first 'baldacchino'. This was absent from my Concise Oxford Dictionary, and from the Apple one. 'Canopy' is the mundane vernacular translation. Dating from 1972, it was the work of Sebastian Comper, the son of 20th century cathedral and abbey architect Sir Ninian, the great grandfather of my friend the Toff, with whom I shared the joys of Liverpool Cathedral. We hadn't yet arranged the visit to Westminster Abbey, where Comper's skills were reputed to have produced excellent results. The east end had also been extended with plain glass windows, and all the better for that. It complemented the 18th century screen well, making a unified look. There was someone practising on the organ, which soothed our senses, as it was moderately proficient. Raising your eyes to the ceiling the main paint tone might have been chosen for a colour blindness test. It was a pinky buff. Was it a prescribed Georgian recipe, or even suggested by the National Trust paint chart?

We were back in John's company. He was ignorant about the ceiling colour, but thought he knew someone who did know. Unfortunately no more was said. I do have photos of it in case of future visits to NT properties or those where Heritage authorities have required restorers to use authentic Georgian colours. John did then give valuable advice about Joseph Wright of Derby. I love that name – why is he the only painter with works in museums to be appellated, if I can call it that, after his hometown? His namesake, the wordsmith, may have been a Yorkshireman. The entry for this very day in Jeffrey Kacirk's *Forgotten English* daily calendar was 'nazz'd', meaning 'confused through liquor, slightly drunk (C Clough-Robinson's *Dialect of Mid-Yorkshire* (1876). 'Nazzy' meant 'stupefied through drink' and Joseph Wright's offering was 'Nazzle, to be in a dreamy, stupid, abstracted state; Yorkshire', in his *English Dialect Dictionary*, 1896–1905. We didn't reach 'nazzledom' until well into the evening, staying with my friend Tiptoes in Lichfield, with the cathedral nearby, of course.

The Derby Museum and Art Gallery now beckoned. John said it was five minutes away. There was sufficient time so off we trotted. Everyone in our ambit was proving so helpful. The reception man, labelled 'David', told us where Mr Derby's pictures were displayed: 'the biggest collection anywhere'. He also told us how to get there and a lot more besides. With diminishing time we reached Mr Derby's room. He had a first floor gallery to himself, and fully deserved it. The ones we both liked best were his chiaroscuro industrial subjects, especially the one involving an astrolabe, of which there was a replica you could illuminate at the touch of a button. It was fun seeing Saturn's moons flying round the planet. Joseph Wright of Derby? Yes, very good.

We spent some minutes on some Crown Derby porcelain. It was displayed through the centuries. I was in search of an image with which to associate the cathedral. Nothing from the china occurred as helpful. I was considering the acanthus leaf, in abundance on the cathedral screen. But that was mundane, thought Rand.

A wander through more streets further enhanced our opinions – nothing tied in with my previous experiences there, most recently by train to see Derby County FC play at the new stadium, Pride Park, which we'd passed during Rand's circuitous approach to the journey from Leicester. That sporting day had been good, opening with most palatable ale in a pub near the ground. Fish and chips came from next door, the publican encouraging its consumption in his bar. This time, we kept the route brief in the city centre and missed the notorious Hippodrome, a listed, but unviable building, vandalized in 2009 and unfit for future use. I also recalled an evening in the 1970s in the then new Derby Playhouse, *Tommy* the production.

We also missed the Cathedral Quarter Hotel, covered in the *Saturday Guardian* (9/10/10; Sally Shalam waxed promotional): 'Derby's Cathedral Quarter is a clever bit of branding for an extremely historic handful of streets, a mixture of Victorian arcade, Georgian and Renaissance buildings, independent shops and – in what were once council offices and a magistrates' chamber – a boutique hotel.' She particularly liked the six pillows, 'on a king-sized bed, with padded headboard in a kind of bronze PVC (which looks better than it sounds)… Morning, lying against the pillows. I watch the sun rise over the cathedral tower, shower with Aveda, and drink tea with James Naughtie (so to speak). Quiet for a city centre.' I liked the woman's style. Next time I'm in Derby the CQH would be a must, at least to feast my eyes on the 'grandiose marble and alabaster lobby', if not to plump a plethora of pillows.

What was outstanding in the cathedral was music. We were returning to All Saints for 5.15 pm Evensong. On the long stretch back we happened upon the best view of the cathedral, the one familiar from an illustration somewhere. We reached the Chapter Café, 'opposite the west door'. It doubled as the cathedral shop. I stood by the plate glass window absorbing the display. There, in pride of place were soft toys: peregrine falcons.

Inside again, the choir stalls were accumulating attenders. There didn't appear to be two spaces together, apart from the front row from which we were shooed away by a woman saying they were 'for the choristers'. Fine, and in the other (back) row, someone moved up to yield a splendid position. We could see it all: choir, in red and white (17 boys), master and four priests (black and white), and another official who remained mute near the bishop's throne, that was supposedly 18th century Turkish. The kneelers were huge. Rand's was embroidered 'D Fenn' and mine 'Canon'. Eventually the congregation swelled to 15, and the opportunity for absorption in the screen to the left, the altar and that marvellous baldacchino to the right. Georgian-ness all around was imbibed among the strains of the canon in charge and the conducted young voices, delivering familiar material.

Afterwards it was the turn of the falcons, bearing in mind the date with the carillon, 7 pm we were told. It was just after 6. We did hear its tones, and bell-ringing, in the form of rather hesitant practice. The website referred to them as the oldest ring of 10 bells in the world, most of them dating back to 1678. Down to the river, past Bonnie Prince Charlie, binoculars were extracted. There was no siting of birds except the ones we hoped were on their menu, failed racing pigeons. With no peregrines we might instead have spotted a Rolls Royce artefact in the sky, from Derby's major employer over several generations. Perhaps the latest showpiece would appear: a Trent 700 jet engine, fuel-efficient and environmentally friendly. Key boxes were thus ticked. Harking back in time, we recalled a Spitfire, not a peregrine but the Merlin, securing funding in 1933, in the early period of this building's enhanced status. That's not to mention the ultimately iconic luxury vehicle bearing the company's name.

I had listed *Good Beer Guide* pubs to try. Near the Silk Mill, one of the recommendations from David in the museum, was the 'Old Silk Mill'. It offered nine real ales but no garden, and opposite was another 'Old', actually the Olde Dolphin, also on the list, with an outside yard (serviceable enough), part of which gave us a view of cathedral tower and roof. I had chosen Solar Power bitter from the Isle of Purbeck brewery, evocative in view of the proliferation of Purbeck marble in our major churches. Rand had Black Sheep, as at Leicester. And that was it, including a false alarm when a bird was spotted on the roof. Briefly we harboured hope, resigning ourselves eventually to its true identity as a fledgling pigeon. We wouldn't make ornithologists. But the image of Derby as the peregrine place was assured. That seemed to be happening to Chichester Cathedral, according to a bulletin on BBC2's Countryfile on 22/5/11. A family of beautifully marked peregrines was filmed on the roof.

Good churches in the diocese, such as those at Tideswell, Castleton, Youlgreave and Hathersage, would have to wait for a purely touristic venture into rural Derbyshire. I had been to Chesterfield Parish Church along with Sheffield Cathedral, not so much a cheat as an opportunity taken. This is a rich part of the country to spend leisure time.

23

Newport

St Woolos

Province: Wales
Founded: c.800 origins
Present building: medieval parish church, with Norman parts;
1960 east end by Alban Caroe
Restored: 1854, 1913
Cathedral status: 1922, created from Llandaff

Website: www.newportcathedral.com
Tel: 01633 212077
Email: administrator@newportcathedral.com
Address: Newport Cathedral, Stow Hill, Newport NP20 4EA

Three to See: Norman arch on the way, enjoying the Galilee Chapel
as a vestibule;
tapering nave pillars, reputedly made of stone from the Roman foundation
at Caerleon;
ascend the tower for a view of the Usk estuary and, on a clear day, Exmoor

Lych gate

Friday 4 June, 2010
This is the smallest cathedral in England and Wales at 7,850 sq ft, seating 600. O navigated me to Stow, the English-sounding district just south of the centre of Newport. In fact the name means 'enclosure' in Saxon. It seemed a world away from this city – status conferred by HM The Queen in 2002. It was a pleasure to arrive with the Friday morning rush hour traffic – half-term may have explained the ease of the journey. Two hours of parking awaited us on Stow Hill above which St Woolos rose above on an island, or mound. At once it is essential to explain 'Woolos'. The 'Churches in and around Newport' leaflet told the story:

> *According to legend (in the 6th century), the soldier-prince Gwynllyw was converted to Christianity when he was told in a dream to search for a white ox with a black spot on his forehead and, when he found it, to build a church as an act of penitence.*

Somehow 'Gwynllyw' also got converted to 'Woolos'. That building was made of mud and wattle. 'The essentials of the modern church date back to the Norman period.' Indeed, on entry, having passed through a long anteroom, which contains the font, you are confronted with a typical Romanesque doorway, squat and impressive with dense curved stone and chevrons.

The first welcome was from the Very Revd Richard Fenwick, Dean of Newport, with whom I had hastily arranged a chat and cup of tea the previous day through Brian Cox, the Cathedral Administrator. Very accommodating; the role of a dean is always pressurized, and he gave us a generous amount of time. First of all he waved in recognition, as we emerged from the fine Norman arch, ushering us to the southeast corner – St Luke's Chapel, aka 'Of the Presentation' – for the Eucharist service, for which all the other participants were assembled. It was conducted by him with the assistance of three canons: Keith Dennison, residential, the Director of Education for the diocese, with a specialism in 17th century spirituality, said the Dean (I had asked him what to call him. He replied 'How about 'Dean'?'). He was also a Welsh speaker (and, it transpired, a champion of the language), as I witnessed when the host was being delivered. Three of the six communicants were addressed in Welsh of whom he was one. Some of the service, basically Anglican, for it is 'The church "in" Wales', had been imbued with local practice. Having said that, services around England always seem idiosyncratic in some way. The chapel featured some worthy items: first the obligatory (by now) icons, not just the eponymous one of St

Luke the Evangelist but two, the other to St George (of England – well, I remember 'England and Monmouthshire'); next the seating, shaped in four desks for two, two facing the altar, the others alongside it at right angles. It worked well in a small space; also the extensive use of contemporary light oak, allowing open spaces between the furniture.

Canon Keith kindly opened both of the green books for me at the correct page more than once. There was none of the usual fumbling in an unfamiliar tome, which had happened everywhere else. The altar chalice was handed over individually for sipping. That was a nice trusting method. Afterwards the junior canons, Robbie and Geoffrey, were keen to engage in conversation.

Then it was over to Dean Richard. Having observed the informality of address, I repeated the earlier question. 'Call me Richard,' he replied this time. He took us backstage for a tour of one space after another, the total square footage feeling more voluminous than you might imagine. This included the Dean's Loo, of which I availed myself while the kettle boiled. We pursued threads of discussion in the kitchen, where Canon Robbie brought a case of wine, which I indicated might be preferable to Tetley's tea. He replied: 'Gentlemen, you shall go straight to Hell if you touch those bottles.' O was offered a blue mug for his coffee, Richard adding 'because you're wearing blue.' O replied, having noted the alternatives: 'I'd rather have the St Albans one.' He hailed from that diocese, actually Letchworth, Herts. We settled into a diversion about St Albans and its identity as abbey or cathedral. Like others in pursuit of this topic, he much preferred 'abbey'. Then we discussed the use of Roman materials in cathedral buildings. I had discerned red bricks in the central tower, introduced from the city of Verulamium. Were some of the tapering Norman pillars we examined really from Caerleon, the Roman foundation on the edge of Newport? We were mellowing and the conversation shifted as we settled in seats surrounded by the gloriously bright vestments draped over tables. St Albans had also cropped up in my brief exchange with Canon Geoffrey after the service. Explaining my quest, I told him: 'The next trip after today is Oxford.' The train of discussion got to Reading, a Suffragan Diocese of Oxford. 'Small cathedral, big diocese.' He mentioned Jeffrey John, the Dean of St Albans since 2004. It was he (born in South Wales), whose appointment as Bishop of Reading caused a rumpus as he was openly gay. In the end the appointment was withdrawn by way of persuasion of Dr John from the very top, by AB of C Rowan Williams. The Church of England was not ready for such an advance. Meanwhile in the USA, hardly noted for liberal values, the Episcopal Church had approved the appointment of homosexual Gene Robinson as Bishop of New Hampshire.

Richard was articulate about the role of the church – the expression of people in the pews – and the wide variety of style within the Anglican church. The choral work of Newport became clear. It was not a wealthy diocese, in fact hard-up. There was a productive network of choral contributors in the area, developing into a tradition. This owed to the cathedral, not the diocese. It was local. Boys would ask Richard: 'What do you think Mr Dean?' Mr Dean referred to the 'two fabulous choirs'. In the Song Room we admired the new Waldstein piano, the selection of sheet music including Buxtehude, the New English Hymnal and the Oxford Book of Tudor Anthems. In the robing room, full of cupboards, the notice was pertinent: 'Please do not use the robes in this cupboard'. Following the increase in status and greater responsibility, a building programme had been launched. A new east end was built in 1949.

The Diocese of Monmouth was carved out of Llandaff in 1922. It was a clearly defined, cohesive unit. One archdeaconry become two (Monmouth and Newport) in 1929, when St Woolos was promoted to pro-cathedral. Various ecclesiastical buildings on the fringes of the new see were considered for elevation to cathedral status (Abergavenny, Chepstow, Usk, and even the exposed Tintern, with a new roof – the railway ran past it). St Woolos was chosen. After all it was in the main centre of population: Newport is the third largest place in Wales, with a substantial working class and attendant social needs.

The political setting for this was the culmination of a thirty year long campaign to disestablish the Anglican church 'in Wales'. David Lloyd George, evangelical Welsh wizard and powerful enough to push it through, with, disendowment in tandem. Back in 1893, Dean Vaughan of Llandaff wrote: 'Bits of Wales (were) still established and bits of England disestablished and poor Monmouthshire shoveled into disestablishment for the crime of belonging (though an English county) to the diocese of Llandaff.' The thrust of Lloyd George was 'an act of vengeance' said the dean. This meant the deprivation of sources of income. Church lands were appropriated. The first bishop of the Disestablished Church in Wales was Charles Green, consecrated at Llandaff Cathedral in 1921. Rowan Williams was to follow 50 years later.

One ultimate outcome of ensuing budget changes was shown in the need to present Jeff Hooper: 'The thinking man's Frank Sinatra,' opined our host. Scheduled for the next evening it was billed as a Fund Raiser Event, with special guest Alicia Hooper, 'an evening of swing and ballads' (£10 per ticket). The main thrust of fund-raising was through the leaflet *Emergency at Newport Cathedral*, complete with Gift Aid Declaration, the Royal Patron being HRH the Duke of Gloucester. Good for him! His local diocese, over the border, had plenty of everything compared with Monmouth, the Three Choirs Festival for one, which dated back to the 18th century and was to be hosted by Gloucester two months after this visit. On 4 June in the *Forgotten English* calendar a Gloucestershire custom was noted: the Cotswold Games, as a feature of Whitsun merrymaking, in Chipping Campden. 'They were instituted by an attorney of Bourton-on-the-Heath, in Warwickshire, named Robert Dover and like the Olympic games of the ancients consisted of most kinds of manly sports such as wrestling, leaping, pitching the bar, handling the pike, dancing, and hunting.' Rev T F Thiselton-Dyer's *Folklore of Shakespeare*, 1884. Something along those lines might appeal to Dean Richard for his congregation in the hamlet of Stow, bringing new use and initiates to St Woolos, and, of course, the Six Bells.

The recent bid for Heritage Lottery funding for essential work on the roof had failed. The hoops changed, the see couldn't keep up with the process. Appositely, it was a case of 'not singing off the same hymn sheet' while in the same arena as tourism – castles, great houses. By extension, cathedrals were in the melting pot. The bottom having fallen out of those coffers, the 'Dear Dean, Sorry but no' letter had been received. Working with local industry was key, producing joined-up thinking in the drive to raise funds. Everyone was in an industrial world. The effective chief executive was 'our Dean'. You get on with the city fathers effectively: cathedral, university, city.

The diocesan payroll reflected a shoestring operation and senior clergy needed other jobs to make up their income. On the other hand the work of the diocese reached far and wide, way beyond the geographical confines of the territory of Monmouth. There was a twinning arrangement with St Helena, five days and countless difficult journeys away in the South Atlantic. Richard had spent his sabbatical there while Sub-Dean at Guildford. The St Helena Diocesan Festival was to be held locally the next day, involving lunch and a visit to local spot, Tredegar House. The news broke early in 2011 that Dean Richard had been appointed Bishop of St Helena that May. Good luck to him so far away! His replacement was to be the Vicar of Abergavenny, Jeremy Winston: it has some merit to keep it local.

Speaking of refreshments, by the cathedral, through the strapping, well-sited lychgate, the local 'Stow Village' pub, right in the hub of things, was now called the Six Bells, a Punch Tavern with good beer, and was attended by churchgoers. Not so when it was called the Physiog and Firkin, part of David Bruce's pub empire, which encouraged wider patronage of real ale, but scared off the churchgoing community at St Woolos. It was the saint's day of James Hannington (1847–84) and other martyrs of Uganda, he added. A potted history revealed him as a zealous missionary bishop of Eastern Africa, who was apprehended, tortured and killed on the way to Uganda, up to then enthusiastically welcoming Christianity. Another, more recent, martyr was Janani Luwum, Anglican Archbishop, who died at the hands of Idi Amin's henchmen in 1977, aged 55. 'He's a hero of mine,' said Richard, who became involved in this during his Minor Canonship at St Paul's.

We heard about the organ, acquired from the town hall, refurbished in 1966 and remodelled in 1997 (elevated to four manuals) by Nicholson's of Malvern. It cost £200,000. In the Crindau Chapel (north aisle) stood an elegant organ case. Looking up to the east end, the round design on the window and border was not happy, rather faint-hearted compared with the potent round Norman arch. John Piper could have tried harder than the uninspiring painting in an impression of pastel shades, surrounded by a colour, which has been variously described, though not quite as 'puke puce' about which Richard recounted a story concerning architect's wife Lady Maufe at Guildford (you'll have to look up the entry), or possibly 'tasteful and domestic.' O muttered this, and the round stained glass crucifix above was insignificant. He was very disappointed after exposure to the same artist's work at Coventry and elsewhere, 'like something in a Thirties estate church'. What let it all down was that circular shape, too far away from the Romanesque presence in the building. It needed to continue the Gothic feel. We wanted a pointed arch. 'It symbolizes "Creation"', said Richard, I think wryly. Another detail: we had chatted with Jeannie the volunteer flower-arranger. So much work was charitable, and the blue kneelers were curiously awry throughout, as if they'd all just been left after a recent service. It looked odd. 'It's just a pity that people in the town don't know about it. It's more of a family cathedral,' said a lady from Rochdale who was glad to have moved to Newport. The overall character of St Woolos was 'local'. So the pied ox of the saint can also be seen as a bull, muddy, labouring, practical. Not the champion beast of Birmingham's Bull Ring, but a Welsh one, that is pied. That is important.

Into the heart of the building, a board told us:

> *Prof Freeman, the distinguished Victorian antiquarian, said of this nave: "No better or more typical Norman interior could be described." No two of the capitals are identical… The Norman arch is one of the glories of the cathedral… The Galilee Chapel is on the site of Gwynllyw's original church. Some of the stonework is pre-Conquest.*

The Galilee Chapel, like a vacuum chamber between west door and the rather small arch into the body of the cathedral, was slabbed with erstwhile tomb stones, quite effectively. This is Anglo-Norman Wales, and the cathedral amenable to a wide public, as witnessed by the photographic display showing it at work. Bell practice and the Sunday school were shown. Mundane, but the essence here is its status as a community facility, alongside a strong sense of liturgy. On one night the following November when I approached Dean Richard to join me at Newport's Riverfront Theatre for a production about the Chartists, very strong hereabouts in the 1830s, he declined, not for lack of will but because his diary that evening revealed two engagements: a Buildings and Works Committee meeting, and, yes, a celebration of the Chartists in the cathedral.

Time was marching on for us, and there was the tower to climb. On the way we were shown the shop, effectively contained within the restored south porch. It was built through Phase 1 of the Appeal, and had previously been 'an absolute mess'. Richard found an Illustrated Guide Book, which I bought, to amplify the detail of this enigmatic building. Keys in hand, the man had removed his cassock. It was inevitably dusty up there, and hot. He was destined for official duties after this. We both felt hot and dusty, replacing shorts – habitual for the summer – to don trousers, deemed appropriate for ecclesiastical exposure. One hundred and fifty four steps was my (fallible) count, via the office, and where we bumped into Canon Geoffrey hovering over the desk on the descent. The final two light bulbs up the narrowing stairs were off, so it was a case of fumbling up the final steps. Then the view! 'You can see Dunkery Beacon (highest point on Exmoor) on a clear day,' said Mr Dean. We did see plenty, including the Transporter bridge, under which I was due to sail in Paddle Steamer Waverley four days later. (That was not to be as the weather turned foul). Moving round, there must have been some bulls. The black and white Friesian breed would have been appropriate, given the Gwynllyw/Woolos legend. Inland, I saw the village square of Stow below, beyond the lychgate – seats, pub, post office, greenery, trees, cars parked – and realized we were half an hour overdue for removal. Richard gasped, putting into words his opinion that wardens were at work down there.

Retreating to the ground again, it was time to part company. Heartfelt thanks were conveyed to our host, whom we last saw hurrying to his vehicle, adjusting his hastily donned cassock. We did the circuit round the cathedral, all on a slope, the grass partly shorn, but not on the south side up which you could not comfortably walk. O relaxed on an 18th century tombstone with a roll-up. We were below the east end, whose exterior was as out of keeping as it seemed inside. Still, this had been a rewarding visit to a welcoming place. O turned again to navigator mode for the transfer to Llandaff. Looking back at the lychgate it became clear that this was the image of St Woolos, though I had been tempted by the pied bull. The new choice was what welcomed you to this little gem, and which stood in the assertive manner of a landmark in the centre of the small community of Stow, up the hill from Newport city centre.

[30] Derby: Robert Bakewell's
    iron screen.
[31] Newport: View from
    St Woolos's tower: Newport
    and the Usk estuary.
[32] Llandaff: A rare cathedral
    gargoyle.
[33] Oxford: Lierne vaulting in
    the chancel roof.

Fig 30

Fig 31

Fig 32

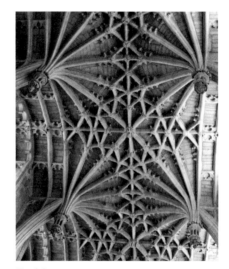

Fig 33

24

Llandaff

Ss Peter & Paul with Ss Dyfrig, Teilo & Euddogwy

Province: Wales
Founded: 560 by St Teilo
Present building: from 1130
Restored: Rebuilt 19th century, having fallen into ruin

Website: www.llandaffcathedral.org.uk
Tel: 029 2056 4554
Email: office@llandaffcathedral.org.uk
Address: The Cathedral Office, Prebendal House, Llandaff, Cardiff CF5 2LA

Three to See: Parabolic arch in nave;
George Pace's Welch Regiment Chapel;
St Teilo's Well on the southeast side, thus benefiting from a stroll round the building

Marigold

Friday 4 June, 2010

As this was such a singular place, I can't beat comments made by E A Fishbourne in *Cathedrals, Abbeys, and Churches of England and Wales* (1891):

> *From its completion in medieval times till late in this century, its only history has been one of "Decline and Fall". So that though Llandaff claims to be one of the most ancient sees, if not the most ancient, yet practically its bishopric, its cathedral, and its cathedral body are all alike new. No bishop had resided there for about three hundred years. For something like six centuries there had been no dean. The chapter was merely a nominal one... Of the cathedral itself half of it had become a roofless ruin, and the other half was hideously disfigured into the similitude of some pseudo-classical temple.*

When O and I arrived from Newport it was lunchtime and had become hot, local bicyclists and workers enjoying 21st century lunch boxes and carry-cups. He had been keen to join me for the day's forays, with his memory turned to anticipation of the view of the west end from rough ground high above, of buttercups and long grass. 'There is something exceedingly picturesque in the situation of the cathedral as it is usually appreciated through the little village-city. It stands on low ground near the river Taff (hence its name Llan-daff – the church by the Taff), but on the south and west the ground rises abruptly from the very doors of the cathedral.' What was on show in 1891 was just as good now – local architect John Prichard's west tower (mid-19th century), capped by an ornamental spire. It complemented the medieval tower at the southwest corner, contributing to the mottled look in the stone. Cotswold stone had been inserted here, to augment a myriad of more local quarry products.

The first sight had been from the lychgate, the most appealing feature in view being the Norman door on the south side. Compared with the one just enjoyed at Newport, this one occurred to us as discreet. Further along was a semi-circular mown area, dedicated, it turned out, to the memory of the bombing attack of 1941 – only Coventry Cathedral suffered more devastation. Along from that was the standard chapter house, shapely and traditional. It looked enticing from the outside.

We were to meet John Bethell, the experienced archivist, in post for seven years so far, whose ear we bent for a long period. O was further satisfied by his decision: 'Let's go somewhere quieter,' to take us through the door in the north aisle to York architect George Pace's 1960 Welch

Regiment Chapel, having completed his major work, which rendered the building ready for business in 1958. This chapel was the particular design structure he had come for and had prepared me for, succinctly: 'I won't tell you anything about it. I'll just say it's magnificent.' Absolutely right! It was white and shapely, suggesting gothic arches, aided by clear glass in the windows. 'Parabolic,' said John, who referred to the 'philosophical approach to medieval architecture. He continued the tradition. George Pace's work is so fresh.' No wonder John chose this space for our session. The processional way led beyond more empathic doors, medieval in inspiration, to the business zone of the diocese, that is meeting and store rooms, so tightly squeezed into the territory that we were unable to circumnavigate the building at the northwest point. In the corridor were two discreet cadavers, or so it looked in a poorly lit alcove. This was a whole new block, disguised from the general viewing area of the main church. The change of use of the chapter house on the other side was understandable. There was immense subtlety in Pace's designs. This echoed the new build at Guildford, where a traditional Gothic style had been employed by Edward Maufe. Pace had taken a fresh look at a time-honoured style. The windows involved sculpting to best effect: their design was subtle and, with artifice through clever lines, deceptively simple. We had the benefit of a long stay in the chapel, allowing us to absorb the intricacies of the chapel. O said after a while: 'The ceiling floats – where does it begin?' There had been a down side to this project, necessitating the use of asphalt, not lead, in the windows: a false economy, leading to a need for repair earlier than it might have been. I had reservations about the variously displayed panes of stained glass over on the west side. John replied cryptically: 'They were bought in – North European.' It was then that he suggested that, as George Pace fans, we visit St Michael's Theological College, up the road.

We talked around the politics of the Welsh church – more reflections upon Lloyd George along lines similar to those recently conveyed by Richard Fenwick at Newport. We moved onto another topic: the loss of pews. John was strong on this. Often nowadays the argument prevailed that an open look was more likely to encourage new congregations. A number of churches had become redundant. In fact the Newport ministry comprised eight churches under one management, all taking shares in the action. Pews were, in effect, in decline, as the church sought to widen the use of its buildings. They had become a familiar sight in reclamation centres. The nave here provided abundant chairs. The Welch Chapel did have pews, which could hardly have been described as alienating, low and tactile. Comfort was a telling argument, many pews being simply uncomfortable. A further traditional joy greeted us on the way back to the nave: the Norman doorway, which had been exposed to the elements prior to the building of the block. Adjacent was more admirable mid-20th century work: GP's gate. Presumably the fact that the architect's names are both monosyllabic accounts for the habit of referring to him by both names, where normally you would simply use the surname. Mind you, one has to be careful to be clear when dealing with dynasties such as the Scotts and, to some extent Compers and the one I was soon to encounter at Brecon, the Caroes.

It was now well after 2 pm and we were wilting, so we braved the access road up to the village. There were three options: lychgate and steps, a steep slope, and a westbound path not promising anything in the way of refreshment. We chose the slope, having sampled the steps on our descent. Soon enough we were in Jaspers, a café for the times, devouring a ham sandwich and baked potato (and tea and sparkling water – I needed a clearer brain. The bubbles always seem to work). Most restful. My beans and cheese would have melted even better in the heat outside. And back again by the east end route, which took us past St Teilo's original well. We explored the perimeter of the cathedral. I liked the inscription on one tombstone: 'John Richard Worthington Poole-Hughes 1916–88, Bishop of Llandaff 1975–88 and of South West Tanganyika 1962–74' and, later, inside again after a satisfying stroll, 'In Memory of Morgan Morgan, Verger 5/6/1860. This Tablet is placed by the Dean & Chapter... ' that was near the chest, by GP of course, for vestments, or anything, as it was voluminous, and probably capacious, too, a beautiful 20th century object in light oak, merging into a medieval wall, offering a ledge below, originally for weary clergy. In the choir, a shift across the building from there, was another aesthetic thrill: many shades of wood combining in the different surfaces of throne, stalls, canopy and organ.

The Diocese of Llandaff hadn't been lucky with its main building. Abandoned for half a millennium, bombed, then, as recently as 2007, struck by lightning. John confirmed that the requisite conductors had been in place, but a demon bolt still managed to knock out the organ (already in a state of decline). Telephones and a computer inlet were blown off the wall. The organ appeal in 2010, with HRH The Prince of Wales as patron, temptingly announced: 'As part of the appeal it is possible to sponsor specific parts of the organ, as follows: Pipes: 32 feet at £2,500.' The list was almost endless, culminating in 'Tuba Stop: £15,000 complete.' In an 'arts' capital funding list at the end of 2010, one item was 'Llandaff Cathedral had a new organ'. While we were there we heard some strains issuing from the instrument, courtesy of Huw Tregelles Williams, in full view above the choir as he rehearsed for the concert the next day. This was the start of the nine day *Llandaff Festival*. His repertoire would include works by

Bach, Franck, Karl Jenkins and Mathias. It was a pity we couldn't return to enjoy it. We would also miss the *Golden Heritage Festival of Flowers* (5–7 August), but hopefully this omission would be made good in other forthcoming cathedrals. O took great objection to the projection of the new organ, from each side of the chancel. It did appear a trifle indiscreet, undermining the fluency of the sweep through nave to Lady Chapel. He took it out on the unwitting duty guide on our egress. She took it in her stride. Nothing new, perhaps.

The amendments to the cathedral have not been subtle, but broad brush statements. Take the great concrete parabolic nave arch, topped with golden angels from the old choir stalls, of which three more surveyed us from on high as roof bosses. We agreed the arch served the same function as the scissor arches at Wells, somehow enhancing the look. It was breathtaking. Facing the congregation on the west side was the Jacob Epstein figure of Christ 'Majestas' in aluminium, of modest size compared by the structure behind it, according to John 'stark and severe'. Of course here there were two bishop's thrones, Bishop Dominic doubling as Archbishop of Wales. Meanwhile there had been an influx of clergy from England of late, the local supplies not being adequate. How did they cope with the Welsh language? Nationally it was strong in various parts in the north and west, augmented perhaps by the established promotional campaign. It was down to perception – alongside a growth in Welsh schools, fewer spoke the language. Priests had to learn some, of course, pertinently in Llandaff and Monmouth.

Even the cathedral's dedication is big: where Newport has dear old Woolos, Llandaff has Teilo, of local significance. It also boasts Ss Peter and Paul, Dyfrig (Dubricius in English), the earliest saint and Euddogwy, Teilo's nephew, Oudoceus in English. Teilo didn't need to be anglicized, and his shrine had been the main attraction over centuries. We should nominate him for sole dedication. Greedy having so many, I'd say! The foundation goes back to the 6th century, like St Woolos, but this has always been a premiership model, the top cathedral. The '*Dean & Chapter welcome you...* ' leaflet said of St Teilo:

> *Until the time of King Henry VIII, pilgrims came to visit the shrine of St Teilo (whose volume still stands on the south side of the sanctuary), and their gifts supported the church. When pilgrimages were forbidden it was no longer possible to maintain the building adequately and over the next 200 years it fell into a state of ruin. In 1734 restoration work began in the popular style of the day, but the "Italian temple", which John*

Wood (the Bath architect) began to build inside the near-ruins was never quite completed and the original walls and pillars were left standing. A hundred years later, new life and growing prosperity in the Diocese made possible a fresh restoration, undertaken by J P Seddon and John Prichard. To them we owe much of the present structure including the south-west tower and spire which replaced a tower which had collapsed in 1722.

This is quoted as symptomatic of what happened to so many cathedrals: centuries of inattention.

The ceding of land and population to the new diocese of Monmouth occurred when the previous move had been forgotten, before the huge commitment to rescue and modernization of the building:

About 1836 it was seriously proposed to unite Llandaff to Bristol, which would have given the coup de grace to the unfortunate see; but from this it was saved, and under its last two bishops, Copleston and Ollivant, the new era began. In 1840 and 1843 two important Acts were passed, which resuscitated the dean's office.

In fact Bristol was absorbed by Gloucester in 1836. More energetic deans followed at Llandaff.

They gave their whole energies to the noble work of raising their ruined minster from the ground. It has well been said: "There may be other churches which in some points come nearer to ideal perfection, but then there is none which has in the same way risen to a new life out of a state of such hopeless ruin."

There came across real pride and importance in what was not a big building, as Anglican cathedrals went. The design conveyed more than was actually offered. When in the dead end that is the Lady Chapel, the vista back to the west was of a different space, which you could not reach without rejoining the south aisle. Looking from the west you saw how short it was. GP seemed to want an observer's impression to bethink the cathedral was larger than it really is. The Lady Chapel had much to enjoy: extensive, again, the altar screen boasted much varied, strong colour, including the reredos, with gold-leaf bronze wreaths, panels by Frank Roper, abutting a statue of the Madonna and Child, white because the anonymous donor stipulated it was never to be coloured. That yielded some relief given the abundant colour all around it. A dozen panels illustrated wild flowers in Welsh and English on red and green background, each 'in honour of Our Lady'. Gold Mair = Mary's Gold = Marigold, which is duly chosen here as the emblem for the cathedral, recalling the country-like setting of the building. It proved a difficult proposition for Alex to draw one for this entry, until I unearthed a photo of a hybrid marigold variety, which lent some structure. Mark, a singer/musician of my acquaintance, not only alluded to the 'country environment in a city', but considered it to provide the best cathedral acoustic. Last to see, and close to least, was the dull, ill-lit triptych depicting the Seed of David by Dante Gabriel Rossetti, currently in the St Illtyd Chapel. The artist had been difficult to deal with, said John, demanding payment up front. This was at the foot of the northwest Jasper Tower, reputedly a Tudor construction, by Jasper Tudor, uncle of Henry VIII. The triptych was originally placed behind the high altar, and moved during the restoration, resulting in the current extravagant and effective display.

We left the cathedral behind to scale the hillock above. I found I was light-handed and realized I'd left my notebook on a pew in the Welch Regiment Chapel, while taking photographs of the cleverly-designed windows. I was hoping to produce at least one sharp snap of something interesting in each cathedral, rather than predictable towers and triforia. I left O relaxing with Golden Virginia on a bench at the car park end of the greenery – the mown part. I made a short detour to inspect the chapter house, which I had registered as an omission up to then. It was only predictable in external appearance. Inside, use had been awarded to officials as a vestry.

On my final mounting of the mound I heard shuffling noises in the undergrowth. Looking up I got an eyeful of the naked back, and nether parts, of a young man. He was clearly enjoying himself, and, hearing my steps, broke rhythm to lift his head upwards. He would have been visible from the west and south sides of the cathedral, and from the tower, though we hadn't been given the option of experiencing that. I rejoined O, who confirmed: 'Oh yes, two boys went past here.' We wandered through the centre of Llandaff village, past the Butchers Arms, the Maltsters, and a pub in the name of some black beast I forget, to St Michael's College, which we'd been assured by a guide, greeting visitors in the west end, was a couple of minutes away. Spotting it over the main Cardiff road, we gained admission to reception, the outcome being the accommodating assistance of Denise ('Dens'), from East London, a student there.

She procured a key and led us into the chapel, the George Pace chapel. Hurrah! Another 1950s creation, it turned out to be another joy. Over 50 clear windows made up the far side – the building was skewed to the south, we reckoned, not facing east. There was an excellent sculpture/hanging piece above the altar. The corners were faced with images of the four gospel writers with their emblems. There was a distinct lack of marigolds. Christ was seated in the middle, humorously referred to by a woman who entered after us as 'Nankipoo'. All was distorted metal, chrome and gold with bits of colour, to great effect. We also tramped upstairs to the organ and library, and back again to the vestry below. The furniture comprised old chests of drawers and cabinets, I suggested ecclesiastical use might be a good way to dispose of similar items I had at home when the great downsizing operation drew nigh in the future. 'Oh yes,' Dens concurred. 'Lots of churches need somewhere to put their stuff, and may have the room space.' Good point. I now wanted to see more of GP's work. His insightful interpretation of the brief of cathedral design was quite at odds with some of the 19th century restorers who savaged the cathedrals in their charge, such as Lord Grimthorpe at St Albans. Dens told us she was bound in due course for a parish in West Wales (Diocese of St Davids).

Finally, we sought our reward. The rush hour was looming. We decided upon the garden of the Butchers Arms for pints of locally brewed Hancock's nectar. Cathedrals and beer are both concerned with history, and we were imbibing both in the present tense. To borrow again from the 1891 text: 'There may be other churches which in some points come nearer to ideal perfection, but there is none which has in the same way risen to life out of such hopeless ruin.' We could renew that observation, imbued with the genius of George Pace, dealing again with a ruin.

25

Oxford

Christ

Province: Canterbury
Founded: 735 as nunnery; 1122 Augustinian priory
Present building: 1158–85, but nave reduced in 1525 by Cardinal Wolsey
Restored: 1870–76 by George Gilbert Scott
Cathedral status: 1542. It is a dual foundation with the college, for which it is the chapel

Website: www.chch.ox.ac.uk/cathedral
Tel: 01865 276155
Email: cathedral@chch.ox.ac.uk
Address: Christ Church Cathedral, St Aldates, Oxford OX1 1DP

Three to See: Lierne vaulting in chancel;
stained glass – see 1631 Jonah window for one;
St Frideswide's shrine

Mortar board

Tuesday 22 June, 2010

The modest River Windrush led cousin Michael and me across western Oxfordshire to Christ Church, the hub for a diocese of three counties. Bucks and Berks were thrown in to augment the hub of dreaming spires. We were treated to vistas of the river valley and the odd spire, as well, quite at odds with the city of Oxford, in-your-face on alighting from the Park-and-Ride bus. We wandered in fine June sun down Cornmarket Street, which transmogrified seamlessly into St Aldates. In 1941, Michael, as a Christ Church scholar, had embarked upon a degree in Classics, on a scholarship. Fired up with enthusiasm following the pivotal Battle of Britain, he embarked upon training during that first year. 'I joined the Air Force in 1942.' Older and wiser in 1946, he was lucky enough to re-enlist, at the university, thanks to A S Russell 'as senior tutor, one of the few dons left'. Grants were available to people from the services at the time, so the scholarship became less urgent.

In June 2010, as we approached the entrance, before turning collegewards, a cup of tea was needed, my first of the day, and a chance to read my notes in advance of this visit to the half-way cathedral – number 25 out of the 49. Attracted by its appearance, and wishing to note what the average student-oriented café had to offer in those days, I dropped into G & Ds, open '8 am till Midnight everyday'. 'Regular' tea was £1.25, the cheapest thing on the menu, which announced a 'decaf surcharge' of 15p and cream for 25p. Also highlighted was 'Oxford's own ice cream – hand made in our shop on Little Clarendon Street, Jericho.' I remembered Jericho, having enjoying evenings there in 2000. It was substantially a student enclave complete with an independent cinema. That was at the time I was almost a local resident, living in a caravan and commuting through delightful countryside to a gruelling and unrewarding job. The compensation was nearby, the delightful town of Woodstock.

Rescuing my cousin from the seat where he'd been enjoying the sun – no elevenses needed by him – we passed gracefully under Tom Tower. A doorkeeper barred our way, but on hearing the magic phrase 'I'm a Houseman', we were admitted without payment. Across the extensive and empty (more or less) quad, were two discreet Norman doors. They were open. This was the not-so-grand entrance to the cathedral, in this guise lending more credence to its status as college chapel than its alter ego. Once inside we were greeted by a man and a woman with badges announcing 'Cathedral Welcomer/Mothers' Union/Oxford Diocese'. Nearby lay a memorial to John Locke '1632–1704/Westminster scholar/philosopher then and forever'. The quote was: 'I know there is truth opposite to falsehood that it may be found if people will and is worth the feeling.' Michael had also been a Westminster scholar, almost 300 years after the philosopher.

Welcomer Alan, having greeted us unctuously, pointed out someone with a steward sash, who turned out to be Maureen Nicholas. 'She's the best,' he whispered confidentially. She was knowledgeable and lucid. We started in the 14th century Latin Chapel. The Burne-Jones window, an early work from before the time of William Morris and recently restored, did seem a tad brash, colours bright so as to illuminate the best thing there: the shrine to Frideswide. I have to tell the story of this lady, from the best version I've come across. The top part told of the saint's conveyance to Heaven in a fetching ship of souls, with her earthly story below, as told in Leland's *Collectanea* and retold by R St John Tyrwhitt in *Cathedrals, Abbeys and Churches* (1891).

> *About AD 727 an alderman of "subregulus" of the name of Didan is discovered ruling the populous city of (Mercian) Oxford, in all honour. He and his wife Saffrida have a daughter named Frideswide. She embraces the monastic life with twelve other maidens; her father, at her mother's death, builds a conventional church in honour of St Mary and All Saints, and thereof makes her prioress. Their munificent kings of Mercia also built inns, or halls, in the vicinity… St Frideswide's death took place 735–740, or even later. Her priory became a house of secular canons; and her remains were laid beneath the already-existing tower.*

Maureen extolled the saint, emphasizing the apocryphal tendency of a yarn spun since 700 AD. The supporting columns were of Purbeck marble. What else? It gets around, but the limestone in the building was from the quarry at Taynton, Oxon, near Burford, where there is an impressive church. On our route there, it lay close to the Windrush, a tributary of the Thames, like its neighbour, equally appealingly named River Evenlode. Back a millennium, the *Domesday Book* assessed the eel fishery at Taynton 'to be worth sixty-two shillings and sixpence a year'. This is in the following context:

> *Eels have been harvested in the Thames for aeons, probably since our heavy-browed Neanderthal ancestors first shambled down to its banks a hundred thousand years ago. The first documented reference to the fishery is in the Chronicle of Abingdon Abbey, dating from the middle of the 11th century AD, recording the payment of a hundred eels a year by the*

people of Oxford in return for leave to dig a navigation channel
on church land. The Domesday Book listed a total of twenty-
two fisheries on the Thames, which – calculated for taxation
purposes – produced 14,500 eels a year. The eels were speared,
netted, bobbed for, caught in baited traps, and intercepted in
the V-shaped weirs known as kiddles. According to Domesday,
Walter of St Valery paid the State five shillings a year for the
right to net the Thames at Hampton.

The Book of Eels by Tom Fort

Back at the shrine in Christ Church, which doesn't quite go as far back as William the Conqueror, one dark-stoned pillar had survived and, passing the acid test, in recent history had triggered insertions to make up the six to prop up the shrine. Maureen averred, with a smile: 'At 6" you can tell, at 6' you can't.' And carved delicately upon it was sycamore, from the first representation in the 13th century, proving it thrived in England even then. I'd heard the suspicion that, like rhododendrons and grey squirrels, the sycamore was a mistaken introduction from overseas. The negativity was still worth a mention as one has imposed itself beyond reach over my garden wall, the bastard! On a neighbouring section was a primitive facial image gesticulating (tongue out). It was, Maureen confirmed (or, more accurately, surmised), a green woman, one of several in the building. I adopted the image as the token for Oxford there and then, with the guide's approval – she was keen on the idea of the female version. Above the shrine, on the Lady Chapel side, brooded the watching chamber, affording a view of the riches of St Frideswide's shrine.

Reassurance is a prominent factor in Christ Church Cathedral. See the brasses in the Latin Chapel floor. Four of them lay there proudly, inescapably on the route for the footwear of all who venture there. How good this was after Lincoln where acres of space lie: the scars of brasses long since removed. 'Nothing was ever thrown away at a college, especially a male college,' said Maureen, showing a number if items, which would have merited more examination. There is plenty of detailed interest at Christ Church, needless to say, not just the cathedral. The *Pitkin Guide* to the cathedral covers Peckwater Quad, the Library and the Picture Gallery, before signing off with 'The Cathedral Today'. This is the first sentence: 'Oxford is the largest diocese in England yet its mother church is one of the smallest'.

We then doubled back to the crossing replete with Transitional work. This was early 12th century, with Henry I on the throne. Builders were perfecting the round Norman arch, while stretching their skills to introduce the Rome-influenced pointed style. The arches abutting triforium, ambulatory, and roof made a cohesive whole, which took your eyes all around, up, across, down. This was entrancing and kept Michael going all the time I was preoccupied with guide, verger and shop manager. It was entirely comfortable and comprehensible, built as a small Augustinian priory, not aiming to answer comparisons with other, bigger ones, which have not all made it to cathedral status in the various upgrading initiatives over the centuries. Its turn came in 1546, as 'a unique dual foundation of both college and cathedral' for the newly founded diocese of Oxford (*Pitkin Guide*).

We paid attention to the stained glass. The *Pitkin Guide* again: 'Christ Church is very fortunate in its possession of a particularly varied and interesting collection of stained glass.' It was rather better in range and appeal, than the display in many a higher-ranking cathedral. I had thoroughly enjoyed the lierne vaulting in the body of the cathedral. Much as I love the 'fan', especially at Gloucester and Wells, the lierne was a brilliant success here. I thought it cooperated with the stained glass here and there to assertive and comforting effect. Alec Clifton-Taylor defined it thus: 'short subsidiary vaulting ribs serving a purely decorative purpose: characteristic of the later Decorated and Perpendicular periods'. The bosses, espied aloft in the Quire through the binoculars I'd remembered to bring, were another thrill – presenting two versions of Frideswide. And by the end I found the cathedral entirely delightful.

Over on the south side was the endearing portrait of St Thomas Becket in the window. Portrayed in pious pose between monks, representing the church and knights for the state, the image was a victim of Henry VIII's reforming zeal two hundred years later. He proclaimed that '… his images and pictures through all the realm shall be put down, and avoided out of all churches' (1538). So the monarch's representatives decapitated him, and so it remained until modern times when a new head was applied. I agreed with Maureen that this was a mistake. I would have preferred it without, so that the whole panel was of a piece. Back diagonally to the north aisle, in the nave, was the window of the 1630s. I was told that the man was stained glass but the much more extensive surrounds, including the city of Nineveh, were painted on. It showed and lent to the fascination. Still on stained glass (Maureen being able to dart around the building as it was so small), the Dutch glass had 'been ground, mixed with colours, chemicals and various things and THEN fixed,' said Maureen. 'The Victorians took this all down, and it was found in big boxes of broken glass. They didn't throw anything away.' Speaking of bits, she added that the spire, c.1210, among the oldest in the country, was capped by slightly lighter stone. Only in this 21st century had it been added, to bring change to bear on the public image of the cathedral. Tom Tower was the iconic image of the university and city. We broke to admire the organ playing. Cousin Michael was in view, apparently lost in a 'transitional' reverie, while the swells darted round pillars and tombs. Maureen told how Gillian Weir, the organist of note, had played here, and filled the cathedral to bursting. It's not surprising the place was known for its music, the tradition dating back to Tudor times. The year 1525, during a period of change, had seen the establishment of the cathedral school and college.

At this point we were interrupted by an American woman, accompanied by another, hijab-clad. It was the Alice Door they were after. Maureen procured a substantial key to the door leading onto the glorious mid-summer Dean's Garden. I took the opportunity to see it with them, complete with the 'Gate' within the wall opposite. The Cheshire Cat's chestnut tree stood proud above the wall. I wondered how many times the guides had shown the curious, and curiouser, garden and gate. Maureen said she had been in Oxford for 30 years. The lawn was perfectly primed for a picnic. This begged the question: 'Who runs cathedral and college?' The reply was that the Sub-Dean ran the cathedral with other canons who are also professors. The Dean was preoccupied with university duties. Christ Church was forever at the top of lists of Oxford colleges, starting with its buildings, all too clear to see. The resident Cathedral was certainly strange on many counts. It was rather special: I immediately warmed to it as an enclave within something magnificent and public, and as the minutes ticked by, for its singularity. There is a lot packed into a small space (16,143 sq ft) as cathedrals, especially medieval ones, go. It has no space for development, being completely surrounded. The only lesser ones in square feet are the former churches at Leicester and Derby and over the border in Newport. Oxford lost a significant percentage of its hectarage courtesy of Henry VIII's Chancellor, Cardinal Wolsey. The west end was demolished, reducing the nave by half (four bays). Mr Tyrwhitt wrote of 'the lamentable shortening', to enable Wolsey to build his 'Cardinal College', as it was called, peremptorily. The odious (many concur) man lost favour in 1529. The rest is history, and Oxford Cathedral is testament to those times.

I put the question about attendance figures, as there were mixed messages surrounding the £6.50/£4 admission charge, the God/Mammon association and Oxford's position as prime tourist destination alongside its convenience on the map. You can't get more 'South Central' than this, applying a term used by the statistical and the tourist trades. Blenheim Palace, the Thames and plenty of good living are available in the area. Maureen, who had been wonderful, but may have felt the need to become more generally available as we were now in the peak viewing period, said:

'I'm a mathematician – never could remember numbers,' and handed me over to the conveniently placed Jim Godfrey, Verger since 1987, i.e. man and boy. It was, almost, his first job after graduation. He took me backstage through, I estimate, seven rooms to the Priory Room Office, with a southern garden aspect. Jim brought my attention to a list, giving paying attendance figures to the cathedral, neatly displayed on the notice board:

	Total visitors	Highest month	Lowest month
2001	144,122	21,218 (Jul)	4,826 (Dec)
2002	170,204	28,347 (Aug)	5,301 (Jan)
2003	212,836	35,149 (Jul)	6,554 (Jan)
2004	252,296	44,621 (Jul)	8,567 (Jan)
2005	240,085	46,813 (Jul)	8,963 (Jan)
2006	253,325	48,408 (Jul)	9,526 (Dec)
2007	252,703	46,633 (Jul)	9,701 (Jan)
2008	278,990	53,746 (Jul)	11,258 (Jan)
2009	265,771	48,025 (Jul)	9,933 (Dec)

So, there has been a substantial trajectory with July taking the honours and bleak January dramatically poorer in attendance. The greater popularity of 2008 could not be explained by Jim, as obviously more popular than the rest. The early years owed something to the *Harry Potter* films, whose key dining scenes were filmed in the Hall, but mitigated by '9/11', 2001, after which the American market dried up. Weddings affected the summer months, and income. Jim held the view: 'We can't charge too much, and they are popular in the summer.' This was a fabulous setting for a wedding. The gardens and medieval buildings were eminently photogenic. The hard, and welcome, news was that the upkeep and payroll (bishop, dean and chapter, treasurer, vergers, lay clerks, cleaners) were in the remit of the college. A massive benefit indeed! On the other hand it inevitably rendered the cathedral exclusive. An absent function was pastoral care, strongly in evidence at Southwark and Sheffield, where the needy could walk in and seek succour from a chaplain, or even sanctuary if desperate. The setting of Oxford Cathedral, off Cornmarket Street (the 'Corn' as Michael called it, rendering it even more 'gown' as against 'town') precluded the general public entirely.

Jim took me to the shop, occupying the chapter house, contemporary with those enjoyed at Salisbury, Chester and Lincoln. At least it was good to see it in use – others are sometimes desolate or cluttered. While there was, predictably, no catering facility, this was an elegant edifice, later than most of the good stuff – Early English from 1225–30, full of light. The eye was led to the stained glass, as you stepped down into the room from the cloister. In the roof was another boss depicting local lass Frideswide along with colourful medallions of saints and angels. But within were a wide stock of products, and the staff: manager Sally Druce and two volunteers. Sally was working on her budget when I was introduced to her. Two tills were in use, reflecting the expected custom. The profit the previous year reached over £100K and was duly handed to the cathedral. I applied the acid test: 'Do you have a shot glass?' She left her station to fetch one. Wrapped enticingly, it was only the second one I'd encountered in all the visits up to now (the other was at Southwell), suggesting a high quality of product selection. I bought one, and a postcard of the fan vaulting, a late and gorgeous creation of 1638, above the stairs up to the Hall, completed earlier, in 1529. The Hall, the refectory for undergraduates and *Harry Potter* actors alike, was dotted with portraits, the subjects including John Locke, philosopher, and W E Gladstone, Mr Disraeli's sparring partner; also John Wesley, the founder of Methodism, responsible for the lovely chapel in Bristol. Another consideration was that access there was only to those who were already in the complex, most of whom had already paid the entrance fee.

Egress led me round the neighbouring cloister. The toilets were sited at the far end. Round another corner was the nook presenting the cathedral video, which I had enjoyed while at the *Oxford Literary Festival* in March 2007. On that occasion, comprising a two night stopover, the Bodleian library had afforded the double benefit of:

1   An Auden Panel, chaired by the then Poet Laureate, Andrew Motion, who was surprisingly inarticulate, as well as inaudible. Technical problems did not help.
2   The building itself and 'Christ Church Festival Room 1'. There was more stunning medieval stonework wherever the audience was led. The next morning produced an entertaining delivery by Richard Aldous on his new book, the subject Benjamin Disraeli.

Following this diversion, Michael and I reunited, to mount the steps to the Hall, heads uplifted to absorb the fan vaulting in the ceiling. Much is omitted here, including points of interest which Maureen Nicholas did show me.

Oxford is rather good at erudition. I unearthed the annual *Oxford*

Symposium on Food and Cookery – Middle White Pork from the Wye was on the menu. From the 14th century I happened upon *Cormarye*, an 'easy' and 'travel safe' recipe:

> *This is an exceptionally simple and very tasty recipe. The combination of coriander and caraway, a bit unusual for medieval English recipes, gives the meat and the sauce a strong, complementary flavor:*
>
> **Cormarye**
> *Ingredients:*
> *2 lbs. pork loin*
> *1½ tsp. coriander*
> *1½ tsp. caraway*
> *½ tsp. pepper*
> *½ tsp. salt*
> *2 cloves garlic, minced*
> *2 cups red wine*
> *1 cup broth*
>
> *Method:*
> *Mix spices and garlic with wine and pour over pork in a roasting pan.*
> *Cover and bake at 350°F until cooked through, basting regularly.*
> *Strain the drippings from the roasting pan into a saucepan, along with the broth.*
> *Bring to a boil and simmer for about 15 minutes.*
> *Serve sauce with pork.*

It's not in *Mrs Beeton*, where it would have been listed between 'Corks, with wooden tops' and 'Corrosive sublimate'. That reminds me of an American friend who, to dismiss tedious simperings from his partner, would say: 'If you want sympathy, look in the dictionary between shit and syphilis.'

We were set for a ramble towards refreshment, both liquid and solid, the latter perhaps not stretching to medieval pig dishes. There were plenty of outlets in the city centre outside. I photographed my companion, pointing out his erstwhile lodgings in the next quadrangle, on the way to the comparatively tiny Corpus Christi (Maureen had pointed out the contrast), past Oriel, featuring the eponymous window, over the main thoroughfare, High Street. My cousin nodded back to Turl Street adding '"The Turl" starts out at the Broad, advances to the High and ends up at the Mitre,' while waving in the direction of Brasenore, Lincoln, Jesus and Exeter Colleges, as we passed the graduate college, All Souls, up past the marvellous early Christopher Wren building, the Radcliffe Camera, the two parts of Hertford College connected by the Bridge of Sighs. Next was the Bodleian, refreshing my memory, to note that King's Arms where I recalled a pint on a different occasion years before after a recital, at this glorious time of year. We were now increasingly beset by undergraduates in formal garb, '"Sub fusc" – dark clothes for exams in the University schools, where you sit for them,' explained the Houseman. Bicycles proliferated. So did small eager, seemingly carefree groups. Many were certainly not bothered where they were going – road or pavement. Michael took a discreet turn down an alleyway. It was pertinent to read in the *Evening Standard* (19/11/10):

> *Oxford students boast that they are the "worst behaved in Britain", bragging that they drink to excess and have sexual encounters "whenever they have a chance". One in three said they get so drunk they end up vomiting or urinating in the street "at least once a week". Students from eight universities were asked in an MTV poll which they thought were most badly behaved. Oxford came top, with 87 per cent believing they deserved the title.*

We arrived at a pub garden replete with lunchtime trade – perhaps the students in the survey were safely elsewhere until the evening. It was past 2 pm, when more conservative hostelries would batten down their hatches against the hungry, asserting as it were an inalienable right. Bar staff wore t-shirts with logo 'Turf Tavern Oxford' in the guise of academe. There were apparently no tourists here, Michael observed. We had enjoyed Everard's Beacon and the apposite 'Back of the Net' from Greene King. The World Cup was in full flow and England's now-or-never final group stage game versus Slovenia was 25 hours away (they won 1–0 to fight another day, against Germany in the last 16. Say no more). The ham sandwich contained 'the best ham for a long time', according to my mentor. My jacket potato with cheese and beans would stave off hunger for a session hence. There was no-one in examination gear but almost entirely of that age group. A few blackboards were on permanent display. It's worth repeating some of the content:

1   Bill Clinton, during the Sixties, did not inhale while smoking illegal substances.

2   Bob Hawke (later PM of Australia) in 1963 drank a round of ale in 11 seconds. That's some going.

3   1575. Forbidden: Cock fighting, bear baiting, cards and vice amongst other things. In the reign of the restored Charles II, in 1660, only deceit at cards was prohibited.

This pub was out of the way for tourists, by and large. We supped under a vast green, square parasol. My cousin settled into an observation: 'Cambridge is a smaller city. Colleges are clustered together, all on one street, down to the Backs. Oxford is much more interesting with buildings muddled up together.' My preference is for Oxford, as well, so that pleased me. After all, it has a cathedral. For me, ever amenable to influences, and observant of how close a link there would always be between cathedral and college, the icon for Oxford had to become a mortar board.

Michael related the story of his return to the university in 1946, as a relatively mature student:

> *I came back as a Flight Lieutenant in the Air Force and was luckily accepted for medical study. Having done physics, chemistry and biology, I progressed to anatomy. I was dissecting a leg. My fellow dissector was a fresh-faced young man straight from school. Roger Bannister was his name. We used to run together to the Anatomy Department along the South Parks Road. We were late, you see.*

It seems he kept up with the future running hero. It was time to leave. Our alternative way out took us down St Helen's Passage, so it was written quietly on the wall. It also said, below, 'Turf Tavern – an education in intoxication.'

On the return leg to the Park-and-Ride stop, I noticed a serious mismatch of goods for sale in Broad Street shop windows. The frivolous by design (balloons and faux-champagne artefacts) nestled among what was being treated frivolously: college rugby shirts – no doubt an end of semester/end of line disposal. We waited for the 300 bus, by the Randolph Hotel, where I recalled Elizabeth Taylor and Richard Burton making headlines while in residence in 1965 for the production of Marlowe's *Doctor Faustus*. I bought the Mario Nascimbene sound track and played it a lot. Thankfully it offered a lot more Burton than Taylor, and some haunting music. The Oxford Playhouse studio theatre still carried their names.

The trip had come to an end. Lupins, larkspurs and lambs' ears had adorned the gardens, pied examinees the streets and Transitional Taynton carving the cathedral. We returned to base, hot from a steamy car. At last I was able to meet the Windrush in person at the end of Michael and Ragnhild's garden. It was to be her, my cousin-in-law's, turn next: Coventry in September.

26

Peel

St German

Province: York
Founded: St German's built on St Patrick's Isle 1227, became a ruin
Present building: 1884
Cathedral status: 1980

Website: www.iomguide.com/stpatrickisle.php
Tel: 01437 720202
Email: secretary@sodorandman.im; mission@sodorandman.im
Address: Thie yn Aspick (Bishop's House), 4 The Falls, Tromode Road, Douglas, Isle of Man IM4 4PZ

Three to See: Cathedral: Treasury;
Bell chamber – the only one accessible to the disabled as it's only a few steps up;
St Ninian's Parish Church, Douglas, the mezzanine space and its stained glass

Kipper

Friday 2 July, 2010

This is the story of a long weekend marked by in depth involvement in the working of the Isle of Man. Wakey and I were immersed in the Diocese of Sodor and Man from our arrival, followed up by the public face of Tynwald, the Manx parliament, to express it in a mundane manner.

The prelude was a correspondence with the cathedral office over several weeks. Initially I had difficulty in identifying the cathedral building, a rather crucial matter, and getting the hang of the diocese and its personnel to arrive at a plan. I acquired the ministrations of Gill Poole, Bishop's Chaplain and Mission Adviser, the right hand woman of the Right Revd Robert Paterson. The project augmented over the weeks into something to marvel at.

Bishop Robert had provided entertainment on website delivery of his sermons since taking on this job two years earlier. In a recent Whitsuntide Convocation (27 May 2010) he was quoted thus: 'Have you noticed how many people love cauliflowers? Ever since it was announced that the sale of caulis has been dropping steadily, all the nations of these islands have been pledging their allegiance to cauliflower cheese – and I include myself!' Robert was open and talkative. We were all garrulous – the conversation could have lasted much longer, but Gill interrupted around 6 pm to drop a strong hint that we had to move on to the cathedral. She put it in terms of the lift to Peel, in her car, being imminent. The conversation curtailment was down to the procrastination of the ferry service. Robert had revealed that a benefit he enjoyed was entitlement to the superior lounge, which reduced the onerousness of frequent travel to England. We had witnessed the crowds swelling and swilling (motor cyclists and weekend travellers on a popular Friday crossing).

Over the tea in the bishop's office we covered a multitude of subjects, tangents and diversions to the extent that Wakey and I later agreed we had gained considerable insight into the life and works of the bishop and his domain. This was his first diocese, following wide experience, in 2004 being made a Canon of the Province of Wales, followed by Chaplain and Researcher to the Archbishop of York in 2006. He came to this, his first, diocese as a respected churchman well able to fulfil the demands of the bureaucratic side of the job as well as the hands-on bit.

Here is a potted summary of curious and germane points arising about Sodor and Man, the latter adjective in place as St German's, Peel was chosen to become the cathedral by public vote in 1980. The diocese of Sodor originated in 1154, 'Sodor' perhaps referring to 'southern' islands off the west coast of Scotland, as compared with the northern ones of the Hebrides, all of which were controlled by Norway until 1266. They were part of the diocese of the Norwegian coastal town, Trondheim, whose cathedral was enlarged to accommodate growing bands of medieval pilgrims. Cathedral status had come its way in 1152, when it became the seat of the archbishopric. Its authority stretched as far as Orkney and, rather incredibly, the Isle of Man.

- Sodor and Man as a name originates from 17th century. The diocese came to comprise the Isle of Man itself all on its own. However it needs on occasion to become attached to a neighbouring mainland one, say Carlisle or Blackburn, for the process of issues, which cannot be pursued locally. The Isle of Man is a Crown Dependency. Sometimes this separateness yields benefits: senior citizens who have been resident for more than 10 years receive an extra 50% on their pensions, from the Isle of Man government.

- St Patrick's, on St Patrick's Isle off Peel, IoM, was founded in the 9th century. The cathedral for the see was originally at Peel, within the castle walls on the adjacent rock, St Patrick's Isle. It became ruined in the 18th century, and pro-cathedral status was given to the Bishop's Palace at Bishopscourt in the northwest of the island.

- The 12th century tower house was abandoned in 1979. The new bishop's wife refused to live there, giving rise to the need for a new cathedral.

- The Bishop is ex-officio dean, while at the time of this visit St German's was run by the Revd Canon Vice-Dean Nigel Godfrey.

- The Bishop does not sit in the House of Lords but is a member of Tynwald, requiring attendance for a three-day session each month. It is mandatory to vote, but Robert is not always able to speak or, in his conscience, commit himself by voting. He admitted to taking discretionary toilet breaks!

- Child protection has been a burning issue, along with Criminal Records Bureau checks. It is these issues that have to be addressed on the mainland, not being within the realm of local institutions. Policy-making can be a problem. The previous bishop, Graham Knowles, embarked upon modernization, but was translated to the post of Dean of St Paul's too soon for much fulfilment, something Bishop Robert, in post for three years, was pursuing. Attendances were improving, but as is universal, after early years in which the church may feature strongly, young people are a difficult group to attract.

- A more productive element is in place for the Celtic churches. In 2009 bishops of various denominations (including Roman Catholic, Methodist and Elim Pentecostal) conducted their annual meeting in the see for the first time. There was agreement that 'the bishop is our bishop', which was welcome to Bishop Robert, especially from the RC quarter.
- Alongside changes afoot in Anglican diocese organization, Sodor and Man, which is in the province of York, like other bishoprics enmeshed in this process, might see its bishop become a suffragan.
- There were overseas links: Uganda and Germany; and working relationships in Ireland.

Having driven a willing and curious duo over the island, Gill reached the streets of Peel and drew up outside an appealing red church: there was space in front to park and admire the tower. Once inside, flowers were much in evidence, with a cohort of smiling volunteers applying their various skills in advancing the display, for the imminent Tynwald/Manx Week. She introduced us to Helen Parry, whose local connection was lifelong – she was 63 at the time, and baptised and married in St German's. She was Mothers' Union Diocesan President. This meant responsibility far and wide, most recently having visited Blackburn. She was concerned with Baptism and the Prison, for example. She was also 'hospitality' and one of six wardens ('too many,' she said). Some of the pews had been removed since the Millennium, many in the transepts. Vice-dean, or 'sub', Nigel had been reported as saying that creating space for other church users during quiet periods allowed the cathedral to 'work for its living' and 'adapt to meet the needs of the current generation'. Some pews had been subject to amendment to double ended ones, so they could more easily be moved around. We noted the columns adorned with grapes and acorns. 'It reminds me of Southwell,' said Wakey. Next was the 'Menorah' ('lampstand' in Hebrew), 'Commissioned for the *Anne Frank (+ You) Exhibition* earlier in the year, and made in Israel from rocket shells used in the Israeli-Palestinian Conflict' said the flyer. It was a finely-wrought piece, a lampstand, certainly, with three curved branches on each side on the central upright rod, the whole thing carrying seven candles. Nearby was the Hope Tree, for the Anne Frank events, which had attracted 10 thousand people to an opening event and two concerts. We were shown the wine glasses, containing the ersatz cochineal.

The organ was due for replacement (Mander and Wood had issued a report 'completely inadequate', we heard). It was effectively concealed behind choir stalls. 'Rand would love that,' asserted Wakey. The instrument was digital as a temporary measure.

The ponderous gilt eagle lectern had fallen down during a reading, Helen informed us. At the bottom was a fetching ivy-clad book. We all liked that, but the eagle did look precarious. Glancing to the side we saw windows dedicated to bishops. Helen said the bishop only appeared to preach for diocesan events – the wont of bishops, indeed. At last Nigel made his appearance, somewhat breathlessly, and briefly. We established that there would be a chance for a proper chat another day, in fact at the garden party two days hence. He was in working-vicar mode, carrying a trowel and so hot that his dog collar was undone, with neck, and bits of damp chest exposed: dishevelled with a shovel, so to speak. A photograph was duly taken. His pet project was the subject of the exhibition we were to immerse ourselves in the West End: *'Bird's eye view of proposed cathedral garden, Peel. August 2007.'* It was ambitious and admirable, and Nigel was to elaborate on Sunday on the green sward.

We were told that over the road was Corrin Hall, which served as parish hall and café. The north transept fulfilled the purpose of refreshment at the time of this visit. This would come to life after a service or recital. There was no charge for recitals, perhaps missing a trick as the place was impecunious. Looking up there were John Nicholson creations: east window murals and paintings.

The church was named after German, the first bishop of one of the oldest dioceses in these islands. There had been a steeple, since taken down. The tower boasted eight bells. We were invited to clamber up there, a fascinating experience. In fact we were mistaken for new recruits, but not for long. A sign said:

Green – ok to ring
Red – do not ring

The troupe was the Sodor and Man Bellringers. We were to imbibe something of the essence of campanology, to be tried at some stage at Guildford, as an outstanding invitation. This one was cosy, or tiny. Seven pm was practice time, and at our departure the chamber was full.

The stopping point was the Treasury, in excellent evidence, illuminated at the back of the cathedral abutting the firmly closed west door. It housed a number of brightly shining exhibits, of the kind all cathedrals should own and display. Rather special was the communion plate from the old cathedral. There was the Lord's Prayer in Manx and a bishop's crozier posing as a shepherd's crook. There was a corner nearby for quiet contemplation. 'I would have done it quite differently,' said Helen, who had opinions on everything, and I can't say I disagreed with any of them, save perhaps the pews. But then they can be obstructive. It's a matter of appropriateness and style. As a last gasp I cast my eyes aloft to the dark pine roof – sure to create a feeling of comfort on all those dark, wet days in Peel.

Most generously she continued in hostess/guide mode to take us for a drive round Peel, past the kipper smoking factory and round appealing streets to the castle and the former, ruined, cathedral. It was raining, which served to change our minds about the next stop: beer and a bite. Wakey had identified promising hostelries, but we also had to consider the bus journey back to Douglas on the number 5. 'Will you know where the bus stop is?' asked Helen. I did have the timetable to hand, which showed a service at 19:51. It was now 19:43, so an expedient decision was made to go for it. It was still light, being only a couple of weeks after the longest day. The prospect of nourishment in Douglas became more likely, plus the appeal of observing the countryside during the half hour journey. Done deal. Helen drove back into the cathedral grounds – the bus shelter was right there. I noticed a gargoyle in silhouette on the tower. A snap was essential. I hurried that, as a maroon and white bus (just like Edinburgh) came to a halt at the stop. I cantered to the stop, where Wakey, following our driver's shrewd suggestion, had already ascertained that this was the one to the capital, and not to Ramsey in the opposite direction.

Back at base, we eventually found an apparently rare catering establishment, a Slug & Lettuce. Despite being knee-deep in raucous wenches and, later on, a stag group we'd witnessed earlier in the day on the boat, we devoured chicken dishes ('Tikka' for Wakey, 'Italian' for me, which I hoped would be better than the Cock au Vin in Liverpool 24 hours earlier).

Reflection on our Sodor and Man exposure was better afforded in the more empathic surroundings of the Albert Inn, our next stop, and we shared a demure sense of calm as the day's assorted events sank in. It had been magnificent – a sequence of enlightenments as initiation to Man. The only regretted absence at the cathedral had been a cat; there was not even a Manx one available. Douglas's party atmosphere was perhaps augmented by the World Cup, manifested on the streets and in the public houses. Evidence of vuvuzelas wouldn't have come as a surprise as Uruguay and Ghana fought to the death. The Urus went through on penalties (4–2) to the semi-finals against the Netherlands. A week later I saw the final, typing this lot, in living room comfort. I wasn't too bothered about who won – Spain and the Netherlands would both have been new inscriptions on the World Cup, which was good news, and Spain got the best press and popular vote when they won by just 1–0.

Saturday 3 July

This is told economically as it was the free day. Gill had provided just the right itinerary, for which read 'gameplan'.

A leisurely breakfast involved lush kippers. Meeting, Helen had referred to the Manager of the Empress, Brian Keenan, as a friend. 'She knows everyone on the island' was Nigel's opinion on the Sunday. 'If they don't have kippers', she said, 'Complain to Brian.' The advice was not required as this local fare was delivered efficiently and they were good. But we did enjoy a brief exchange with Brian, involving a compliment for his tight ship.

We activated 3-day travel tickets and opened the account with a bus to the Electric Tram terminus. We had the benefit of open vehicles on this fine day and were introduced to some of the best bits of the island. Having done the flat part as far as Laxey, the next section, on the tram, involved a steep gradient, to Snaefell, the summit of Man with rarefied atmosphere and panoramic views. A man with a need expressed quasi-alarm at our attire of shorts and t-shirts. That garb was habitual for Wakey, who fancied himself as a hardy Northerner, but I saw it as the only opportunity to wear this gear, the other days all requiring degrees of smartness.

Back in Laxey it was time for lunch. We sought advice from a local man as to the shortest route to Old Laxey, near the seafront and with ale supplied from adjoining premises. The Manx delicacy 'queenies' (scallops from the Irish Sea) were on the menu, but a woman at the bar, apparently the manager, said they were off. 'We've got chicken tikka,' she said, strongly, adding 'Home made.' Chicken in any form was becoming too much of a habit. Baked potatoes it would be. They were all right. The setting was better, by a babbling brook with seagulls swooping on ducklings.

After that came the exercise, up to the Laxey Water Wheel, the Isabella, the distant view of which, had provoked the Snaefell-bound tram to pause for a photo-stop earlier. We arrived at the Mine Inn and chose a local brew to quaff under a parasol, having just witnessed Serena Williams thrashing Zvonareva in the Wimbledon final. We realized I'd been using the wrong pink section on the timetable when a tram bound for Douglas drew in. Not right, I thought. Actually too right, and we bolted the best part of the pints and ran the few yards, just to make the half hour return journey back. We made it two Queen's Hotels in a few hours at the top end of Douglas: the score was Germany 1 Argentina 0 when we dispatched our next pints, with a further fetching aspect of the sea with oncoming horse trams and buses in the foreground. They turned there as well, as it was the end of the line. It may not have been far back to the hotel but the gentle rhythm and gleaming haunches of the chestnut nag was a fine indulgence, courtesy of the travel card.

When we reached the hotel's substantial television set, Germany had annihilated Argentina 4–0. I regretted that Maradona's lot failed to score just once. Wakey and I unwound in the bowels of the hotel: sauna, whirlpool and pool (not quite big enough to earn the prefix 'swimming'). Then, completely complementary to the 19th century churches here, we indulged in a Frank Matcham delight, the Opera House and Gaiety Theatre, which had been converted into a larger entity, the 'Villa Marina and Gaiety Theatre'. Securing two of the very few remaining tickets for *Joseph and the Amazing Technicolor Dreamcoat,* a frothy evening of family fun was just right. *Any Dream will do,* reprised ad nauseam, rang long and hard in Wakey's brain – he sang the refrain just a bit after that. The production seemed brighter (harsher) and more technical (gizmo rampant) than my memory of the previous time I'd seen it, over a decade before. In the interval we sank small bottles of red wine on the balcony with a transfixing aspect: the rippling petrol Irish Sea. I recall a ferry came into view.

Sunday 4 July

Rain! Oh no!! And a most foreboding sky accompanied pre-breakfast tea and mid-breakfast prunes.

The Tynwald Garden Party was only hours away, with the worrying prospect the following day of a rough crossing, or suspended service. We heard that the morning service was cancelled – ferry, not Eucharist – and, later, that vomitousness was much in evidence on the one that did make it over the turbulence.

The idle aim of a gentle stroll up the hill to St Ninian's turned quickly into an urgent taxi, rather like after our arrival in Douglas. We ran out of time, blaming an unwitting tourist mode. Everything was taking longer than expected, in this case breakfast. We borrowed an umbrella in ill-advised England colours, red and white stripes, or Exeter City, of course. Thereafter the challenge would be to remember to remove the borrowed brolly from Gill's car, as she had offered lifts. Anyway, we took a cab to St Ninian's, a confident and dashing church. Bishop Robert did us proud. We met him in the car park, while we were undergoing a circuit of the church in the rain. I needed some air, being deprived of it in hotel and taxi up to then. St Ninian's was quite a landmark, being perched on a hill, but visibility was minimal.

Inside we met the Rev John Coldwell, vicar, who made a clear welcome immediately apparent. He broached us in friendly direct mode (a Yorkshireman, like Wakey, but from 'West', not 'South', and supporting Leeds United along with the Terriers of Huddersfield Town). At the top of the service he made this public, asking anyone who wished, to talk to us over coffee after the service. Our attention was drawn to the 'mezzanine' structure, as it was termed by Chris Clucas, a warden from Man and the world. His was a local surname; he told us 'w' in English became 'qu' in Manx, so I'm not quite sure how 'Clucas' worked out. The mezzanine was built into the west end, where the entrance was sited. This had created an alternative to the straightforward walk through into the nave: the option of mounting wooden steps, up to this new space. Designed by people full of insight and skill, including David Roberts, architect, who was in the congregation, it was unique in my experience. Set into this Victorian Gothic church and built into seductive red brick, it empathized well. The space served as the parish centre, hosting weddings: we heard two lots of second banns during the service. In the room thus created, the main features were to bring the pillar capitals within it down to floor level, propping up the structure, it seemed. The west end stained glass windows were brought face to face, becoming strangely smaller in experience than imagined. The Island's TT Races provided subject matter: 'To the glory of God and in loving memory of his wife, Alice... dedications can be to all competitors in the TT Races.' These windows were presented by John N Anelay of Blackburn (a vice-president of the Auto Cycle Union) in June 1983. And, above, accompanying a colourful image of a motorbike in full throttle, 'Let us run the race looking into Jesus.' What a nice touch – Alice as the Lord's spouse!

We went into the service, imbued with common purpose and community. The space, the church, supported this as an empathic setting, the red bricks and gothic design comprising a unified whole. I wondered at the process of choosing St German's at Peel as cathedral, in competition with St Ninian's, and maybe other meritorious candidates. It would have been good to see more diocesan churches. Bishop Robert entertained with a challenge, in fact parable. Should you aim to turn a Weetabix into gold you must not utter 'Abracadabra'. But once that is in your brain, you cannot relieve yourself of it. Maybe alchemy was always thus. The bulk of his address was in admiration at the inclusiveness of Christianity, told through Paul's Galatian epistle, in contrast with St Peter, who had been more exclusively Jew-focused in spreading the word.

The service, coffee and chats done, Gill arrived from the Peel Cathedral Eucharist, to become our post-coffee chaperone. Vicar John invited the three of us to join his family, along with the Bishop and his wife, for 'a simple lunch, just pizzas'. This all came to pass and was good. The conversation was wide-ranging and invigorating. We got to favourite cathedrals. When pressed, I posited Southwell as possibly my choice of the 26 so far. 'Have you not thought about Durham?' asked Pauline, the Bishop's wife, seeming bemused that I'd mentioned one so modest. The favourites in the straw poll – I ask anyone who wants to engage on the matter – have nearly all been subjective, relating to experience. Thus Gill nominated Coventry, where her father had been Canon Precentor. For Robert it was St Paul's, where he had worked. Lunch at the vicarage was a veritable feast, featuring tasty slices of chicken (the residual pieces of which the dog snaffled off the table on our way out) and key lime pie, surprisingly tart, therefore welcome, and 'from Marks and Spencer's'. Hostess Maria volunteered the information.

Off we went to the garden party, by the country route round from the centrally-situated vicarage to the south of Douglas. The driver expressed slight concerned that Nigel, ticket holder as vice-dean, needed to be engaged as one of us visitors was to be his guest. Wakey had lent me his subdued purple tie (for work in the Health Service), which went better with my shirt and blazer. Mine, featuring yellow and blue daisies, hadn't worked, but Wakey looked the part in his worksuit. The effect was finished by the tie. I couldn't recall the thought process which had resulted in the mismatch. It may have been due to an undercurrent of resistance to wearing ties. Rarely was formality required in the pursuit of cathedrals. We arrived, parking in a mown field. Gill's persuasion at the gate won the day. The officialdom appeared to be all in the invitation, which threatened non-admission for those without tickets. We found ourselves among similarly clad hordes on the extensive lawns below the former Nunnery, another magnificent Victorian Gothic pile.

There was ample intercourse with guests before and after the formalities associated with this key social fixture. It was held on the afternoon before the opening of Tynwald, the Manx parliament. Some of those we met were vicars from churches around the island, the ones we weren't going to see. Gill introduced us patiently each time: of me that I was from Bristol and writing about cathedrals, and of Wakey that he came from 'South Yorkshire', or 'Doncaster'. At last I noticed her wilting a little, and interjected: 'And he's a Roman Catholic.' The conversation ceased. But these were nice people on a relaxed occasion, and his new status, from which there was no return, assumed the character of curiosity. We strolled into the extensive marquee, of society wedding proportions. It was surprisingly free-moving. We got to the cucumber and egg and cress sandwiches, and fairy cakes, directly, picking up cups of tea without obstruction. The next best thing was to hitch up, finally, with Nigel, who revealed himself as a fine wit and observer. He took the three of us to a redundant chapel on the fringe of the territory. He hoped it would be open, but it was merely redundant. Nigel was entitled to the 1920s vicarage (ultimately bishop's house) as his abode in Peel, but it would require £3 or 4 million to be rendered habitable; he lived in a flat. His main focus for fund-raising was the 'garden rooms' project, which we'd seen on boards in the west end of St German's. He warmed to the subject, which was presented in 14 stages. He described them as 'telling the story of Christianity in the overall context of Manx history from the 5th century to the present day', with interactive activities and 'the opportunity to walk a labyrinth'. It was displayed on; also inculcating the need to return and enjoy it when completed, should you live that long. Meanwhile 'the cathedral itself,' he said, 'would absorb £10 million and you wouldn't notice it.' Nigel had arrived in 2007. His previous position had been as Principal of Southwark ordained Local Ministry Training Course, and chaplain of Southwark Cathedral. 'It was a baptism of fire working there', he said.

Our leisurely approach took us up to and round the Nunnery building for a while. Back at the car, the reclining umbrella looking inappropriate in its ready-for-action posture now that the bad day had turned so good. We were next able to stroll by the beach and up an elegantly fenced path on the nearby coast. The abundance of seaweed was a trifle off-putting. I'm always keen on paddling possibilities. We were taken back to Douglas. Gill turned down our blandishments aiming at a rewarding drink. She was now committed to ticket duties for the Tynwald grandstand the next morning. But we did greet the fairies at their eponymous bridge, as she instructed us.

This is to Gill:

A fine woman driver from Peel
Had a style which approached the surreal;
She thrilled us with speed
But never had need
For emergency stops with a squeal.

A quietish evening was to follow. The World Cup was in abeyance in anticipation of the semi-finals. Ecclesiastical life as such in the Isle of Man had eclipsed the buildings, though St German's and St Ninian's were now both close to my heart. Wakey concurred.

Monday 5 July
The public holiday bus provision was normally that for Sundays, i.e. much-reduced, but this was the top public event in the island's calendar, so the No 5, and others, became a frequent service during the fair. Alighting at the early village stop soon after 10 am, we were well in time for the procedure and all the fun of the daylong fair. We could take it all in at our leisure.

I shall quote the Official Programme's opening comments:

The observer at St John's on 5th July, the Manx national Day, watches a ceremony which has continued unchanged, except in detail, for more than 1,000 years. The annual outdoor sittings of Tynwald, the Manx Parliament, date back to the Viking settlements which began in the 8th century of the first millennium AD. No other parliament in the world has such a long unbroken record.

The Isle of Man is not part of the United Kingdom, but a Crown dependency. Her Majesty, The Queen is acknowledged as Lord of Mann. King George VI was the first British Sovereign ever to preside at St John's, in July 1945, and Her Majesty, The Queen presided in 1979 when the Millennium of Tynwald was celebrated...

Public announcements abounded, and we got close to Lady Haddacks (with Vice Admiral Sir Paul, her husband a few paces ahead). We had already been their guests at the Nunnery. I caught her Ladyship on camera in mid-exchange, close to where we were standing. She was clad in a fine black and white number. There had been a brass band there; here massed military bodies performed by invition from the state. Tynwald Hill was a terraced mound bedecked with seats and topped by a conical tarpaulin, resplendent in the sun and rippling in a tussle with its taut tethers. We caught final glimpses of some of our weekend hosts as they took their seats on various levels of the hill. Wakey had acquired souvenirs from the fair section, such as a pair of Celtic cross cufflinks, and baps for lunch on the ferry. I secretly acquired an Isle of Man calendar for 2011.

That was the final act. The process of the return journey was due for inception. And, blessed by clement weather, we were back in Liverpool in good time. It had been a very good time.

Fig 34

Fig 35

Fig 36

[34] Peel: Vice-Dean Nigel Godfrey has been gardening.
[35] Peel: On the altar in wood, a rendering of peace.
[36] Peel: Wakey and Gill Poole at Tynwald garden party.
[37] Brecon: The biggest cresset stone anywhere.
[38] Gloucester: east window in celebration of the Battle of Crecy.

Fig 37

Fig 38

295

27

Brecon

St John the Evangelist

Province: Wales
Founded: 1093 as Benedictine priory, parochial since Reformation
Present building: 1215
Restored: From 1860 by Gilbert Scott; from 1923 by W D Caroe
Cathedral status: 1923 – from St Davids diocese

Website: www.breconcathedral.org.uk
Tel: 01874 623857
Email: admin@breconcathedral.org.uk
Address: The Cathedral Office, The Cathedral Close, Brecon LD3 9DP

Three to See: Wooden effigy of Mrs Thomas Ganes with comely shoes; cresset stone full of candles for monks;
lancet windows aloft

Shoes

Friday 30 July, 2010

This venture into Wales coincided with sort-of local boy Tom Jones topping the charts with his controversial piece *Praise and Blame*, which David Sharpe, the vice president of Island, his new label, referred to as 'some sick joke'. They wanted 'upbeat numbers, reminiscent of the classic *It's Not Unusual*, not songs with a religious content' (*The Big Issue* N° 908). The record even featured on *Thought for the Day* the next day. Rhidian Brook took the angle of retirement. To quote from the opening of his piece:

> *It's not unusual to be productive at 70. But it is unusual to be a 70-year-old with a N° 1 record. And if Tom Jones's new album… holds its midweek position on Sunday he'll be the oldest male artist ever to hold the top spot. It'll be an impeccably timed achievement in a week that's seen the Government announce the scrapping of the compulsory retirement age of 65. Men and women can continue to make hit records well into their 8ᵗʰ decade with impunity.*

Unfortunately it only made no 2. The tenuous link with this narrative was to take the opportunity to mention that 70 remained the retirement age for bishops.

I had been granted an audience by Geoffrey Marshall, Dean of Brecon following his Shelter Cymru commitment in Cardiff earlier in the afternoon. He would make time before and after 5.45 pm evensong. Initially there was a bit of confusion for me in that his email was signed 'Geoffrey Msrahil'.

The Tour

Graham and I arrived in Brecon. We wandered down from the car park to the busy bit approaching 12.30 pm, with the immediate need to have lunch as my tour was at 2 pm. We decided upon Ye Olde Cognac for a Yorkshire pudding with sausages, mash, peas and gravy (and pints of VERY STRONG lime and soda and Hancock's bitter respectively). The meal served its purpose, though taking an age to arrive. Too late I noticed the entry on the laminated menu to the effect that meals were cooked fresh, so 'customers should be patient at busy times'. It was indicative of this town centre pub that our co-patrons were at least our age, and tended to eat early, as codgers seem to prefer. The couple who moved in next to us, arrived after us, and were irritatingly served with theirs far quicker – note this for next time. In due course, leaving Graham for a wander round the shops, I took the car to the cathedral, situated on the northern edge of this small but Friday-busy town. I arrived in the nave at precisely 2 pm.

The tour had started, so I shuffled into a back seat, where pleasant red chairs had replaced the Victorian pews. I extracted my bound notebook and one of an assortment of ball point pens. The one I happened upon was from the previous week's hotel in Oslo, one of the local Thon group, which I recommend. See also the cathedral (RC), which had undergone a recent restoration: it was very colourful, of Baroque design. And the Thon pens were worth removing, being of the chunky type. Richard Camp was the guide, immediately demonstrating a sharp turn of phrase and plenty of opinions. His badge said 'Welcomer'. There were over 30 of these, whose brief was 'not to be a guide, but to find answers'. He had enough answers for ample satisfaction, to the point of handing me a 14 page draft of typing at the end. He had been briefed through my earlier phone call. It was headed: 'Brecon Cathedral: some key points for Welcomers'. That was helpful in filling in some gaps where my brain and pen had lost the pace to keep up with his delivery. Dean Geoffrey said later that he had a copy for proof reading (it did need another look). What was missing from the cathedral website was just this: information about the cathedral. As Graham observed: 'There really isn't very much there,' having mentioned a few special items for which read on. Thank you Richard for many of the facts and phrases which follow.

The central points include:

- The building, dedicated to St John the Evangelist, was founded as a Benedictine priory in 1093. It was always small, with no more than eight monks.
- This is English-speaking central Wales. A mere 10 miles to the west the Welsh language is spoken.
- Though originally Norman, the earliest architecture is Early English, with some good Decorated gothic and no Perpendicular.
- It suffered from the ravages of the Tudor and Puritan periods…
  … and from neglect thereafter…
  … and from inappropriate restoration by Gilbert Scott from 1860.
- In 1923 the Diocese of Swansea and Brecon was introduced, the priory being designated as its cathedral. This led to the employment of W D Caroe and subsequently his descendents to improve on Scott's efforts, and make some of them good.

In medieval times the priory was always open, a hub of secular activity, acting as a market place. More recently a village hall had opened in the town centre, open daily. This was perhaps a shame as the cathedral has remained a minority interest for churchgoers. The current regime was aiming to improve on that. There was now more going on in the building, from visiting choirs at evensong (today from Croydon Parish Church) to Brecon Jazz Festival and Fringe events, also serving to replenish the coffers a little. Perhaps £2K would be earned from Festival concerts, of which it was hosting 9 out of 47.

In the building the first gem was the font, a Norman delight, showing obvious damage. There were deep incisions. An extensive green man spread out to the fore, his locks intertwined with various beasts – scorpion, eagle and fish, all executed vigorously round the heavy piece: grotesques and all the better for it. Part of the font was obscured by flowers, lily-based and strongly scented, in place for a forthcoming wedding. Richard wrote: 'Ours is the largest Norman font in Wales dating from c.1150; it is of limestone, not the sandstone of the rest of the cathedral, and may have come from elsewhere... ' He pointed out an impressive candelabrum above, which was from Bristol Cathedral, in the Berkeley Chapel (where the present one was also good). This one dates from the 18th century and was made in Bristol.

Nearby, at the back, was 'the largest cresset stone in Britain', something of a curiosity but formerly serving a crucial purpose. With 30 candle-shaped cavities it lit the way for monks embarking upon attendance in the priory at 2 am. That was having negotiated the steep, narrow stairs in the south west corner of the nave, from their humble accommodation in the network of spaces overhead. There was a rather substandard colour photograph adjacent, illustrating 30 candles in glow mode. I suppose at least it gave some hint of its quality for those poor monks. It produced considerable light.

Perhaps the best part was next, certainly Graham's favourite – the St Keyne's (as in Keynsham, Somerset – this saintly woman lived in a hermit's cell there) Chapel with its fine Tudor entrance screen. The Victorian and Edwardian stained glass was shown: 'The most interesting ones are alongside and above St Keyne's Chapel, depicting Celtic holy men and women who brought Christianity to the region. Long before St Augustine landed.' This was the sole surviving guild chapel, its cognomen being 'Corvizer's Chapel'. Corvizer means 'shoemaker'. And there were shoes in evidence on the 1555 effigy just outside. Most rarely and effectively the figure of the wife of Thomas Games (probably, and surviving from a three-tier tomb of the family). There were flowers 'to keep away the common herd,' said Richard. At the top end was a good example of that quirky device, a squint, or hagioscope, to enable a priest in the chapel to observe progress at the main altar to aid his own timing.

Here's an aside about the Gameses. Brecon men were identified by

Master Shakespeare in *Henry V*, on the eve of the Battle of Agincourt – 5 October 1415, St Crispin's Day, the patron saint, of course, of shoemakers. 'Davy Gam Esquire was one of the few casualties. (Historically he was leader of the King's bodyguard).'

The effigy was wooden, therefore extremely rare, with flat feet in relief at the bottom, facing the chapel. That's enough to gain the nomination for the image of the cathedral. It's a shoe, as the working history in its prime featured shoemakers, for the guild, taken further in its (tatty) banner within. The alternative choice would be a 'ballflower', dating from 1320–30, 'a three-petalled flower enclosing a ball', and of which there are many here, adorning the elegant ogee arch in St Keyne's Chapel and elsewhere. The story went that ballflowers died out in the second half of the 14th century, following the Great Plague, aka Black Death. Richard also noted: 'The tower of Hereford Cathedral is bespattered with them.' Very true. Another thing here was the Tudor screen, which 'includes square bosses that came from the oak roof of the chancel. The Tudor rose is prominent; the screen was part of the chancel screen.'

This prompts the rant against Gilbert Scott, engaged as restorer. The precursor was the period, particularly the 18th century when, along with so many church buildings, Brecon was abandoned. The roof was stripped of lead,

> *... so that a woman, and later a boy (in 1750) hunting bats, fell through the rotten timbers... Owls, bats and jackdaws nested in roofs and had ready access into the church. Stones from the monastery building became a handy quarry for later houses. The church walls on the south were invisible under the ivy; windows had been boarded up. A convenient sandstone statue... was in general use for sharpening knives. Purbeck marble columns were found to be useful in timber-rolling. By the mid-19th century, the relative comfort of the dissenting chapels lured the congregation away from the extreme dampness and cold of the church; conditions there, according to the curate, "endangered the health of the venturesome few" remaining adherents to the established church.*

Enter the man Scott. The trouble was that, in completing his project in 1862, he betrayed his undertaking to conserve, to return the building to how it looked in 14th century. He was unaware of Welsh traditions in working with wood. Carved screens had been a feature. When built the edifice had been unusually high, following the imagination of Henry III in the mid-13th century. With Paris's Ste Chapelle as the model, it was designed 'higher than it needed to be'. Richard then waxed lyrical about the Caroes (W D Caroe was 'my hero'). He voted for St Davids Cathedral, a mark of credit as this guide was so persuasive. I was already anticipating the forthcoming visit to Pembrokeshire with relish. Meanwhile he drew attention to a Raphael oil copy, *Madonna of the Goldfinch*. I hadn't clocked before that the bird's redness represented Christ's rood. I've always liked Raphael, whose sheer expertise expanded the potentially mawkish subject matter into great painting. This was not the only one in the cathedral. Our attention was drawn, again, to the laminated sheets, in English and Cymraeg, for use at several points. This made good the lack of a helpful leaflet. One such sheet explained the lack of a rood screen, lost in restoration. At least now we had a direct view of the best bit, for me, the east window with its five symmetrically arranged panes, leading down north and south to the lancet windows, 'very tall with elegant pillars', where you would usually find triforium/arcades and clerestory. Sometimes it helped to design a church on a smaller scale. I recalled the chapter house at Southwell. Meanwhile the dreaded Scott had inserted commonplace stained glass windows elsewhere, with a negative on both quality and light. He installed 'his own conjectural vault; the medieval vault was given up for financial reasons. He said he would leave medieval work untouched. In fact he covered it up'. One positive thing he did do was to recommend cathedral status, as the issue was under discussion in his time. However, it did take another 50 years to come to fruition. Another pro-Caroe point was the organ case. WD designed it, placing it most aesthetically within an arch in the chancel, pinnacles at either side reaching up to the apex.

In the Havard Chapel, the misguided Scott 'covered up beautiful windows and filled them up with stones and plaster'. The Havards were even now a strong family locally, for example winning trophies at the local show. Then, over on the south side, the group found the St Lawrence Chapel, initially examining a hefty 17th century chest, 'The Llewellyn Cupboard', one of a cluster of items in relief in a single sweep of the eye. Its four top panels, 'earlier Flemish of about 1500', depicted most evocatively scenes from the early life of Jesus: the Circumcision (apparently a theatrical performance to judge by the number of rapt onlookers), Flight to Egypt (with an entertaining show of bushels of corns which miraculously flourished to protect the Holy Family), the Magi conveying their gifts, and one more for which Richard requested nominations of the group. The most vociferous of them thought it to be Christ entering the Temple. 'That would fit,' said our guide. The chest was from Neath Abbey, which earned a quiet cheer from the company, who were on a daytrip from a day centre at Neath.

The tomb of the first bishop lay to its right, then, on the wall was hung a sculpted picture of the Last Supper from Oberammergau: 'Modern, but with lovely detail' said Richard, and it did harmonize with the other items, which begged to be touched to compare textures. This was good for the blind, I thought, as visually challenged group members tried it out. Once within the chapel, the omnipresent oak had not faded. This was because Richard's hero had used the technique of immersion in lime, to be left for several months. We all looked up, at Richard's behest, to observe weird angles in the ceiling. The vaulting, brickwork and all lines were delightfully awry. Not as basic at the nave ceiling at Lincoln or the roof at Exeter, where spines were skewed a bit worryingly, but erratic in line and link, reflecting all those generations.

Finally came more bulk, in the form of the lavishly funded alabaster memorial to 'Sir David Williams miles' ('miles' is Latin for soldier, I hazily recalled). This lay as the main point of interest in that area of afterthought, the south aisle. Actually the man had paid for display in the chancel (he died in 1613), but in 1862 the 'The Great Scraper' (the great Scott) transferred the thing to the Harvard Chapel. Finally (for now) in 1923, WD put it here. Poor Sir David. And, as Richard said, 'the untouched effigy of his wife is clearly out of reach'.

Once bereft of guide and group I wandered around the cathedral snapping away. There were plenty of subjects. I had learned how to charge up the new camera, but only having been forced to read the Nikon instructions thoughtfully enclosed among the packaging. So the inconvenience of a failed machine had proved temporary. Good. I didn't want another digi-dumping.

In the north aisle was an exhibition of paintings by Mark Cox, priced at £135 and £145. That may have been good value, also serving as potential souvenirs of this trek as St Davids and other cathedrals were depicted. So were the local beacons and Venice. The notice announced '30% of sale proceeds go to Brecon Cathedral.' I didn't notice any red stickers to indicate clinched deals. Perhaps they were discreet hereabouts. But I did happen upon a pillar nearby. It was very scratched and a notice informed: 'When a stonemason finished his apprenticeship, he adopted a trademark which he carved on each stone that he dressed. All these marks have been found in the Cathedral… The pillar was covered in them 'perhaps as an advertisement for the tradesmen who had worked on the building', apparently similar to the tower at Hereford Cathedral. Disfigurement turned art? The pillar was as pitted as the old oak beams in the Octagon Tower at Ely – that had been scarred by the initials and dates of tourists over an abundance of centuries. This places these lived-in structures in a context of living history.

The Dean

I returned to the town centre to pick up Graham at a quaint emporium, where he had finished his latte and looked pleased about a couple of bric-a-brac shop purchases. The self-imposed shuttle saw me park the car, this time in the cathedral grounds. We then enjoyed a tea break in Pilgrims Tearoom, formerly the granary. The Welsh cakes were adequate, the service inadequate (from a grumpy girl – this happened so often) and the view meritorious. The aspect was of the cathedral buildings, formerly of the monastery, lost at the Dissolution and eventually restored to the new diocese for excellent work, again by W D Caroe. A demure mushroom-coloured statue of St Francis beamed from the flourishing herb garden in the foreground – we had opted to sit outside, as the rain had stopped and the seats were dry. There were captions close to each appropriate bush, such as feverfew for migraine and rue ('garden' it said) for 'antiplague'.

4.30 pm struck as we entered the cathedral for my appointment with Dean Geoffrey. When he arrived, the choir rehearsal was in full flow. Graham elected to roam around, using the laminated information sheets while the dean and I walked the few paces to his residence for our discourse. Evensong would be at 5.45 pm.

In the Deanery it was a mug of tea and a cosy chat in his dining room. On the mantelpiece were cards quoting: 'Oi', 'Thank you' and 'Musical Eisteddfod'. Geoffrey was eloquent about being a dean, first and foremost to assert: 'To me the building is less important than the people.' He certainly came across as a people person, for a start in being so willing to accommodate my wishes, making time before and after the evensong service at which he was the scheduled reader. This was his first incursion into a deanery. The interesting thing was the entirely contrasting roles his life in the church had produced for him: going back in time Rector at Wrexham, Sub-Dean at Derby and an earlier post at St Albans. While at work in Wrexham the choice of a new city for Wales had arisen. He put the outcome pithily. In 2002, Newport was the right decision being the larger town 'It's better to be the largest TOWN' than the smallest city. St Davids is tiny. The situation at Wrexham was the opposite of Brecon. It was the biggest centre of population of the see of St Asaph. The challenge in his current diocese was to get Swansea involved in something run from far away, ideologically, though Brecon was situated in the geographical centre of the diocese.

Geoffrey was wearing subdued shades: downbeat purple shirt, dark jacket and charcoal trousers, unlike most of the clerics with whom I'd engaged in discussion and tea, who kept to on-stage gear. He did, of course, don the official floor-length mulberry cassock for the service. There was a yowling from the tabby cat who had brushed past as we entered. This was Linford, named after a certain gold medallist sprinter. That was easy to guess, as there are not many of that name. I don't think this one could run very fast, though he was a sort-of cathedral cat, appearing from time to time in the nave, which was only a stroll from his home. There was another feline, Smokey, owned by the erstwhile dean, John Davies, now Bishop of Swansea and Brecon, and now living a few hundred yards away, as opposed to inches. Smokey's attendance had been more regular, but there was something of a need for rodent control in the choir room.

That was an interesting phenomenon: did the spectre of his predecessor haunt him? 'No,' he said. 'We are very different people; he is younger than me, and I am not musical. There isn't competition. Also it was an archdeacon who recommended me.' There were two archdeacons in, of Gower and Brecon. There were no suffragans in Wales. The position in Wrexham had been advertised. Both he and the Bishop spent a considerable percentage of their time in Swansea. Also he made a point of attending every induction of a new vicar. That's 12 so far in two years of incumbency. They had a constant need to make sure the cathedral was part of the diocese.

He had produced a sheet headed: 'What is a Cathedral Church for?' Here are three of the eight bullet points:

- It is the seat of the Bishop and a centre of worship and mission; other churches have a seat for the Bishop and they too try to be centres of worship and mission (from the cathedra, standing proud in the chancel for dozens of parishes in a diverse diocese).
- It must extend hospitality to pilgrims and visitors of every kind (I realized my visit fell into this category and was a fine example of his approach to work).
- As the mother church of the diocese I trust that it will share with the parishes in every aspect of the Church's vocation, which is why I'm particularly pleased to have been asked by Bishop John to have some responsibility for the care of our Readers. (In fact Geoffrey has made this a key part of his work.)

Even so, I suggested it might be a poisoned chalice to follow a man promoted to the top spiritual job. Geoffrey was positive: 'The Bishop loves the cathedral – he is musical (a recurrent theme), and the building is now in better shape with endowments and legacies. When musicians visit, I make sure I give a welcome: a couple of sentences. I milk that.' There were so many preoccupations – the liturgical, centrally, burials and functions, and flower-arranging. Meanwhile Mark Duthie, the Director of Music, was spearheading a tour of the choir (all volunteers) to Powys's twin town in Germany.

The challenge of Wales's second city reared again: 'Getting Swansea (itself only being awarded city status in 1970) on board is not that easy.' They were working towards a big event involving the great and the good in 2011, to encourage the relationship. It was a poor industrial city, its main church St Mary's, with the work associated with its location, and a full-time lay reader, ministering to down-and-outs and alcoholics. This was a far cry from rural Brecon. He added: 'When I was first appointed I spent half a day with the Vicar of St Mary's.' That had been very wise politically, and the two had become friends. We touched on the opposite pole of cathedral practice: the old-established Lincoln Minster, which in the 1990s had become notorious for bad relationships. 'The Dean and his Chapter said "And also with you", they didn't mean it.'

Moving on, I heard about the benefits of the cluster of buildings now run by the diocese, very good for a comparatively modest entity. The Diocesan Centre was a good facility, as was the two-bedroom canon's flat. The whole cathedral enclave could come into its own at the present time, hosting and entertaining a visiting choir for a week – Organist Mark, or the Succentor, received many an entreaty for such a visiting group. They would hike over the Beacons first thing, returning for practice and evensong in the afternoon, and enjoy a slap-up Sunday lunch before they return to Croydon (also dedicated to St John the Baptist) in the Diocese of Southwark. The Festival Fringe would benefit, too, taking over the green spaces.

It was time for the official to don his apparel, and as we rose I noticed a Rolf Harris print on the wall behind me (Nᵒ 248 of 695 of Durham Cathedral from an unusual angle), which prompted my standard question about his favourite cathedral. He elected for this very Brecon, following consideration of many others on various, all individual, counts, such as Southwell, St Davids, York, in fact probably most of them. I was introduced to Hazel, his wife, who ran the shop, which I had visited briefly and pleasantly. She concurred that she enjoyed living there, though it was rather enclosed when the big gates were locked every evening (we had transferred Graham's vehicle to the official car park, nearby, to avoid the need to request the drawbridge to be opened). She didn't want to nominate any cathedral, as she preferred quieter, more humble churches. Fair enough.

Exchanging buildings, I caught the procession in time and joined Graham rather far to the front of the nave. The 16-strong team took up the entire choir stalls, backed up with their instrumentalist, whom Mark told us was the organist, yes, the main man, at Southwark Cathedral. After the service he chose a Mendelssohn sonata as voluntary and I feasted on my chosen sight – the east window. I hadn't witnessed his skills on the Southwark visit as it was a recital for two that Nicky and I heard, no organ involved. The dean read well. You do find interesting facts at such times as this: from 2 Samuel 5 it emerged that David reigned for 33 years. There was a bloodthirsty theme on this occasion. Apparently Matthew's gospel had made up one reading ever since April. 'This is the end,' said Geoffrey, adding helpful comments to the scriptures, a rare practice. When it came to the hymn we found we lacked hymn books. We hummed along to Nᵒ 198.

Afterwards we spent more time with Geoffrey in the nave and covered the subject of funding. His main focus was the £1m appeal for the Choir Trust. He said there was still nearly £400K to find to secure the future of the choral tradition in Brecon. This was now significantly aided by 50% support from the magnanimous Hufton Trust, through which matching funding of a more attainable £200K had to be found. 'Good luck', I said.

On a daily basis the cathedral did struggle to break even. This had only been achieved twice in the last ten years, so it would be tricky to afford emergency costs 'like if the organ blew up'. Even so, as elsewhere, concerts and events were presented with more than one purpose. One such was to entertain, as exemplified so well by the annual Brecon Jazz Festival. I had attended a few over the years, as punter and volunteer. The latter, in 2005, was not so good, being tied to one marquee, though we were there for the Georgie Fame Big Band.

> ### Brecon Cathedral
> *Those rocks of red, those fine lights serve to beckon*
> *But first some tea, lukewarm, and Welsh cake, foul,*
> *You're drawn inside and find it's time to reckon*
>
> *Explore those grounds, owned by the see of Brecon;*
> *For years monks worked with hand, voice, habit, cowl –*
> *Those rocks of red, those fine lights serve to beckon.*
>
> *So, push doors north or south to enter Brecon,*
> *Enjoy that Norman font, whose grotesques howl,*
> *You're drawn inside and find it's time to reckon.*
>
> *The lancets high, east window, pride of Brecon*
> *Reach to the roof, once habitat of owl,*
> *Those rocks of red, those fine lights serve to beckon.*

It's evensong with reader, Dean of Brecon,
The strains of praise by choir from Crickhowell,
You're drawn inside and find it's time to reckon.

That rich endowment, ex-priory called Brecon,
See limestone carvings – ballflowers, feet and fowl,
Those rocks of red, those fine lights serve to beckon,
You're drawn inside and find it's time to reckon.

28

Gloucester

Holy Trinity

Province: Canterbury
Founded: 681, as St Peter's Monastery
Present building started: 1089
Cathedral status: 1541

Website: www.gloucestercathedral.org.uk
Telephone: 01452 528095, 01452 508210
Email: christine@gloucestercathedral.org.uk
Address: 12 College Green, Gloucester GL1 2LX

Three to See: 14th century east window;
cloister fan vaulting;
exhibition (there's usually one) or, if not, the tomb/shrine of Edward II is a permanently brilliant exhibit.

Sheep

Tuesday 10 August, 2010

Tewkesbury would do just fine as cathedral material. The trouble is its proximity to the fair Gloucester, one of our premier edifices and full of crowd-pleasing attractions. Failing that, it's only a cough and a spit down the map from Worcester, of similar heritage to Glos. The evocatively named Touching Souls Tea Room at Tewkesbury hosted our first sojourn, complete with an illustrative eponymous sculpture at the entrance. Rand commented: 'I'd like to draw that for the book.' My reply: 'It won't be included – Tewkesbury is an abbey, not a cathedral.' We enjoyed coffee in this facility, choosing a table which would normally give a view of the north side of the abbey. That was under repair. However, the planks and boards were hardly conducive as an outlook. The cafetières (£1.50 for one, £2.50 for two – there were three of us) flowed with above average coffee, but only just that. After a score of samples in tearooms I had yet to be transported with delight at the mid-morning fix. The cakes were promising but, again, really betrayed the promise: the lemon drizzle (£1.50) was sweet and tangy on top, but the lemon hadn't seeped adequately down into the sponge. When I pointed this out Pauline, the cake organizer, and on duty that day, said: 'Yes, I'll tell her (unidentified) to make holes in the cake for it to drizzle through.' Her own effort, the coffee sponge (£1.50) was the best. Lucky Wakey – but we did all sample each one. This time mine was the oaty cake (£1), for all intents and purposes a flapjack, certainly more so than my culinary effort, which I renamed 'flopjocks'. I admit I did use treacle, not golden syrup. Why is 'treacle tart' made of syrup? Treacle is such an underused commodity. It doesn't grow on trees, despite the rumours.

Tewkesbury and Gloucester

Three guys supped at Tewkesbury and Gloucester
Cake, coffee, chords, wine, paternoster
They went to great lengths
For Free Trade, of all strengths,
Decided the best was at Costa.

In the Touching Souls toilets a notice faced standing males: 'If you would like to help keep these toilets clean and tidy, please leave a donation in the chest inside the Abbey. Thank you.' All right, but I wanted to gift aid it. We made our way to the abbey entrance under evergreens dripping with rain. It was an umbrella day up to then and were we equipped accordingly? No. Outside, on the road, you face various pubs, hotels and teashops. After all this is a pretty tourist town. I remembered the excellent fish pie in the Bell after an evening concert. That was during the floods in 2007. Tewkesbury was eternally subject to flooding as the Severn and Avon converge there. I took newspaper cuttings showing the spate at the time: only the abbey rose above the river/lake, with an identical photograph below from 1947. The overflow (unfortunate name) car park where we had been forced to leave the vehicle was had a sign saying 'flood area'.

We entered the abbey, where the leaflet rack was fresh out of guides in English, much to the consternation of the welcomer, Brian, so I used *Bienvenue à l'Abbaye de Tewkesbury*. It was very gratifying that my O-Level French was at last drafted in to serve a purpose. We were immediately confronted with a stack of fund-raising material referring to the appalling recent flood disaster in Pakistan. That had particular resonance here.

We did a circuit in anticipation of the lunchtime organ recital, after which Gloucester Cathedral would beckon. The Norman nave was spectacular. Round in the ambulatory we happened upon an embroidery endeavour in full flight, involving shifts of several local ladies. One said hers would take three months to complete. Were they destined for kneelers in the nave? We asked another official if we could sit in the choir stalls for the recital. 'Best seats in the house,' said he. Brighton's Nick Houghton was listed as soloist, on the main one of three organs. We admired the effigy of Sir Edward Despenser, 'porte-étendard du Prince Noir, à genoux au-dessus de la Chapelle de la Trinité'. It was more intriguing in French.

The programme comprised seven pieces covering three centuries, from J S Bach to Paul Hindemith. We immersed ourselves in the 45 minutes of glorious music. From our seats at the back we imbibed the apsidal east end; and the triforium and clerestory, which appeared to merge. Clever, that. Above the stalls was a profusion of wood with Norman shapes. Wakey pointed out the corbels (bright gold) and bosses (red) above, as well as angels to exercise the binoculars. There were also fine abstract floral designs on the kneeling benches: roses on the kneelers themselves and on hymnbook stands. Then you looked up to the bosses (roses) and along to the east window (roses there too). This was the dominion of the Red Rose. From the Black Prince and his son, Richard II (represented by his emblem, the Red Hart on bosses around the tomb), to Edward, Prince of Wales, heir to Henry VI of Lancaster, killed at the Battle of Tewkesbury, 1471, when the Yorkist claim was consolidated with the victorious Edward IV returning to the throne for the rest of his life (died of excess in 1483). From Wakey: 'I do like the abstract decorations,' which were nine hundred years old, and looked modern. A benefit of the building's age and changes undergone was its very variety of look: a faded Norman doorframe where a cathedra might have been placed, with different status, by the south stalls.

Most of all this applied outside in the patched up walls, harking back to the building's role as the domain of monks. Perambulating the exterior, the far east end showed a scar on wall and ground, though it had looked complete within. The south side had all too plainly lost substantial space. Had this been a cathedral with requisite public function and resources, the mess there would surely have been dealt with. This didn't matter as we watched the gardener pruning and enjoyed a display of August colour in the border abutting a wall, which would in the 13th century have been inside the building. Wakey, ever mindful of his allotment, said: 'I'd like some of those (fulsome fuchsia bushes).' In the end we have to be grateful that the citizens of Tewkesbury showed the resource both in energy and finance to raise £453 to buy the abbey at the 16th century Dissolution.

The first bad people experience this time was due to happen as we had become smug and content during the Tewkesbury prelude. We reached Gloucester city centre. We, actually I, as driver, were in search of somewhere to park for the rest of the day. I inadvertently interpreted the road signs as meaning 'Left 5 mph' or 'Right 20 mph', both in the direction of a gruesome multi-storey car park. I tried the 5 mph one, and at once found it to be straight into the bus station, so beat a hasty u-turn. Not speedy enough, as we were all shocked by a thumping on the roof. It was a bus driver. Winding down the window I was bombarded with hostile attitude from the man: no expletives but hot aggression. The outcome was not advice as to the correct route, but dismissal accompanied by the abrupt uplift of a finger. Woman problems, we surmised. We were left to work out a direction whither to wend. The multi-storey car park noticeably revealed many gaps between cars, we were that close. But it had now been consigned to potential nightmare status. Rand suggested: 'Why don't we try the other way into it?' Wakey retorted: 'No we won't. We're going to another car park.' Definitely. Assisted more by hazy memory than road signs, we found an open-air facility and parked. This time the problem was one of interpretation – of the board of instructions. There were others with a similar challenge, an elderly couple dressed for festival exposure, I reckoned. The situation was hardly helped by an inanely smiling yellow-clad official. I was able to avoid feelings of paranoia that it was just me who had problems with parking there. 'Don't worry, mate,' he retorted at our concern about validity. We didn't and all was fine on our return that night.

It was in the medieval streets in the vicinity that Beatrix Potter's tale *The Tailor of Gloucester* was set. Hitting the bookshelves in 1903, the story was told of a poor tailor who fell ill while making a waistcoat for the mayor, so not making the deadline of his Christmas morning wedding. He was rescued by mice who completed the job, almost. One buttonhole was unfinished. The villain of the story, Simpkin the cat (alas not a cathedral cat; there was none at Gloucester), had imprisoned the mice under teacups, which the tailor turned over while he was out, enabling them to escape. Returning from his errand to purchase cherry-coloured twist for the garment, Simpkin hid it on discovering the absence of his next meal. The finale comprised the explanation that the incomplete button was due to 'no more twist'. The inspiration for this came from an actual incident, where the tailor (John Pritchard, 1877–1934) was bailed out by his assistants. The story passed into local folklore. The tailor pushed the part apparently played by fairies, who, essentially, left a note stating 'no more twist'.

By now it was past 2 pm. To the cathedral we marched, for the utterings of Rand, who had been reading up the relevant pages of Alec Clifton-Taylor's *The Cathedrals of England*, to equip himself for a guided tour. This was for Wakey, whose first visit this was. We were to attend concerts at 4.30 and 7.45 pm. In pursuit of my companions following ticket procurement in a room dedicated to festival activity, I bumped into the charming form of someone I recognized. It was Joan Freeman, who had been such an entertaining guide at 'St Edmundsbury, back in April,' I said in my haste. 'St Albans!' she corrected me, introducing me to her brother Ian, a stone expert. It is strange that the mind/tongue comes out with inaccuracies like that, when you know what you mean to say. We hadn't seen enough of her place of work ('The Abbey') that day. The two of them were at the festival among a coach party. The only time we could find to converse was at that moment, and so we did, in the crowded Coffee Shop while Rand took soup, Wakey a bagel, with a fat sandwich for me; and tea for everyone. Following a discourse, mainly amplifying Rand's and my knowledge of St Albans, Joan was good enough to write to me a few days later with extensive information: 'It was nice meeting you and your colleagues during our Gloucester jaunt. It was rather more fun than some of the music.' As for the catering facility: out of the way and uninspiring; in fact 'adequate'.

Rand's tour began. Wakey was 'knocked out' by the cloisters with their stunning fan vaulting. In the green interior he espied sheep, a diverting exhibit for all the family. The exhibition was called *Sheepscape*. Children with painted faces were climbing on them, extending the gamut of a *Three Choirs Festival*. Initiated in 1724, this was the 283rd such fiesta – pretty mind-boggling. Hereford had played host in 2009 and Worcester was to come next. The sheep were life size in fibre glass and physically uniform, but each individually treated, that is daubed with paint, from substantially black to multi-coloured. One depicted 'Bling King', another 'Do Androids Dream of Electric Sheep', and 'Very Educated. You could sheepstakes with those Shoes'. So the sheep was to emblemify Gloucester. The ones we saw might be temporary, but Gloucestershire is wool country. Wool = wealth. We owe so much to it. Returning to the honoured event, William Cobbett gave the 103rd festival serious consideration, as follows:

12th Sept 1826 Stroud (Gloucestershire)
Huntley, between Gloucester and Ross
… but, when I came to Gloucester, I found, that I should run *a risk of having no bed if I did not bow down very low and* *pay very high; for, what should there be here, but one of those* *scandalous and beastly fruits of the system, called a 'MUSIC-*
MEETING'! (The Three Choirs Festival. William did like to disparage!) *Those who founded the CATHEDRALS never* *dreamed, I dare say, that they would have been put to such uses* *as this! They are, upon these occasions, made use of as Opera-* *Houses; and, I am told, that the money, which is collected,* *goes, in some shape or another, to the Clergy of the Church, or* *their widows, or children, or something. These assemblages of* *player-folks, half-rogues and half-fools, began with the small* *paper-money; and with it they will go. They are among the* *profligate pranks which idleness plays when fed by the sweat* *of a starving people. From this scene of prostitution and of* *pocket-picking I moved off with all convenient speed, but not* *before the ostler made me pay 9d for merely letting my horse* *stand for about ten minutes, and not before he had begun to* *abuse me for declining, though in a very polite manner, to* *make him a present in addition to the 9d. How he could I do* *not know; for, I soon set the noise of the shoes of my horse* *to answer him. I got to this village, about eight miles from* *Gloucester, by five o'clock…*

It's a case of 'Those were the days'.

We turned off the cloister into the chapter house, adapted into an elegant shop, then, as it were coerced by a magnetic pull, back into the cloisters. Wakey happened upon a table displaying leaflets concerning 'music for dementia' and 'mindsong'. Embracing this area into the work of the church was most encouraging. In the body of the cathedral we tried not to collide with urgent choristers in red surplices bound for a rehearsal in the nave, as well as with double bass cases in primary colours. The brash pink worked best, I thought: more of a statement. The *Welcome* leaflet was only helpful regarding the general shape of the building, so at least we knew we were to traverse the quire to arrive at Robert of Normandy's effigy below the east window. He was the eldest son of William I, and died in 1134 in Cardiff castle. It showed the figure off demonstrably. The duke's display comprised the following features from the Norman era:

- Surcoat (long and red)
- Hauberk (over the head)
- Ornamental coronet (with strawberry leaves and fleur-de-lys)
- Red cushion (under the head)
- Handle of sword (grasped by right hand).
- Iron spurs (on feet)

I can only add that it was splendid. Rand commented, on seeing the reclining Robert after much else: 'It's a treat, this place – Perpendicular arches covering the Norman... fine lierne vaulting.' It was a case of feasting your eyes wherever your feet led. Next was the north ambulatory for Edward II's tomb. A consequence of serious propaganda, the glory that has become Gloucester cathedral was, to a significant degree, brought about by the much-revered monarch Edward III (1327–77). His futile, destructive father was transformed into a demi-god, assisted by the nature and location of his demise (assassinated in Grand Guignol manner at Berkeley Castle), with his tomb elevated into a shrine. It is a pretty good piece. 'The beautifully pinnacled canopy and superb effigy of the king attracted many pilgrims in the Middle Ages and their gifts made possible the rebuilding, remodelling and enlarging of the Norman cathedral we see today,' *(Harris's Guide to Churches & Cathedrals.)* 'A lot more use dead than alive' I thought. And then there are Gloucester's land and endowments.

Here's an irresistible non sequitur: Remember the rhyme?

Doctor Foster went to Gloucester
In a shower of rain.
He stepped in a puddle right up to his middle
And never went there again.

The origin of this is reputed to involve Edward II's dad, the first of that name. He visited Gloucester only to tumble from his horse into a substantial puddle. Muddy of course! But how did 'Edward I' transmogrify into 'Dr Foster'? While we're on kings, please note that the 9-year-old Henry III (1216–72) was crowned in Gloucester, possibly at the Fountain Inn on the south side of Westgate Street, between the cathedral and our car park. It claims to be the oldest inn in the city.

For me the cathedral's crowning glory is the great east window, conveying a dual essence of red and blue. It's the second biggest in the country after the 20th century Coventry build and the largest using tracery. The Lady Chapel beyond and below is good enough (1457–83, mature Perpendicular) with roof bosses comprising exotic flora and fauna. That east window entranced us in both forthcoming concerts, as we ended up in the quire, first one side then the other. That gave us several hours with direct views of the showpiece. Edward III is to be thanked again for the tour de force, a phrase in a tongue running through this narrative. It commemorated the part played by locals in the triumphant Battle of Crecy (1346, in the Hundred Years War). A curiosity was the widening of the walls at the very end, to make the window wider than the quire. I wonder why – at Truro the equivalent narrowing is explained by urban constrictions. Gloucester had loads of space in its close. And while we were awaiting the afternoon concert, not one or two but six musicians alternately carrying stringed instruments, and trombones, passed by us to their positions. It was the only opportunity we had of seeing them, as the wooden choir stalls, complete with enticing misericords and the proud cathedra, was entirely enclosed. We lifted up our own seats after each concert to admire:

- Pilgrim riding goat
- Man sleeping with dog
- Horseman hunting duck
- Football – noted as an early expression of the game

Or so we deduced, as the light down among the choir stalls wasn't the best.

The concert was titled *Venetian Splendour,* with early 17th century choral works by Giovanni Battista Grillo, Giovanni Gabrieli and Claudio Monteverdi. The performers comprised The Three Cathedral Choirs, His Majesty's Sagbutts and Cornetts and two organists. All proficient, but not well-attended. My head-on view was of a curious beast topping the end of the stall in front. Wakey contrived to leave his bottle of water (a horrid recycled purple plastic fruit drink vessel). It was still there when we returned for the evening event. I wasn't surprised no-one had wanted to purloin it.

We were able to pass through the nave, whose pillars are 30' 7" high, while Tewkesbury's are 30' 8", the highest in England: a bit of a close call! It's their bulk that is so impressive. The vast space abounded with punters, floral displays and, under the west window, a substantial grandstand, like the one I had recently encountered at a cricket match.

Time was fairly tight as we rejoined Westgate Street, in the hope of finding a hostelry for ingestion. The Dick Whittington looked welcoming and people were tucking into plates of tempting food. (The Dick Whittington of legend was a local landowner.) The barman was reminiscent of the bus driver a few hours earlier. Pints were obtained, but no help regarding food orders. The baked potatoes might have been quick and easy, but we lost the chance as the man went on to serve someone else. Showing off to his regulars lined up at the bar, I thought. Rand had unfortunately already paid for the round. It was to be a quick quaff, fortunately in the yard, where we moved the wooden table into sunlight, with vistas of the west end of the cathedral in one direction and the truncated St Nicholas Church, complete with a comparatively simple tower, opposite. We proceeded to another bad ingestion experience up the road at Hedley's. The salient point was that Wakey ended up with no food, and all of us with little time.

We arrived at the south transept entrance. A cleric with whom we'd had contact in connection with the afternoon concert said: 'You know where to go by now. You're rather late.' I didn't answer that but sought confirmation that the choir stalls were now the best option. 'Yes, and the best sound,' he replied reassuringly. Though the ST would have provided a new experience, and offered a partial view towards its opposite number, I, like the others, was pleased to return to that fabulous setting. Now experienced in seat choice at Gloucester, we wanted the back row which was padded. However, there weren't three together. Even so, this did complete our 'three choirs' in terms of our seats at the concerts we'd attended that day. Rand and Wakey took the programme, which I'd perused before handing it over (and Wakey the chocolate). At least I knew the first half order of play – Holst's *St Paul's Suite* and Vaughan Williams' *Fantasia on a Theme by Thomas Tallis*. I mellowed into the obscured environs, a few spaces down from our afternoon situation. Up and over I espied Rand and Wakey, and a woman in front, all in strange postures, perhaps looking for a lost brooch. A mature female near me, very county, and local, was engaged in discourse with an American man. I know he was from the US because he alluded to that – several times in as many minutes. She said: 'This is very special, in fact unique. The *Fantasia* is exactly 100 years old. It was first performed here.' The voluptuously-bewhiskered gentleman on the other side said: 'You won't mind if I snore?' 'I probably won't tell it from the bass notes,' I replied. The evening light made an empathic backdrop in the east window.

At half time, I made my third enquiry about the location of the drinks dispensary (having broached two different ushers on the way in). The cohorts of smiling volunteers hadn't been briefed with that information and looked vacant. Once again, we happened upon a man with a sash who received my entreaty: 'Do you know if there are refreshments?' (i.e. red wine). 'I expect there's something somewhere,' said he. A brainwave hit me: the cloisters nearest the nave, closest to A to C sections (top price £38, ours were £9). We trudged our merry way past lurid lime green and puce stringed instrument cases and the fibre glass sheep. Performers clustered in black. My eyes happened upon uplifted hands holding plastic glasses of what was likely to be House of Prayer wine. Two red wines and an orange juice were obtained (Rand was already succumbing to the role of homeward driver). They were priced at a high £3, to suit a major festival with a direct view of the action. We mulled over the glorious tower above, and the concert. Wakey was sated with wine, and chocolate, and took a swig from his purple bottle, by way of mellowment. Rand made reference to the crouching episode *a propos* the misericords. 'The lady in front told us about the football images underneath us.' 'Oh that's what all the stooping was about,' said I. He did a seat swap with me.

Regarding volunteers, of course cathedrals benefit immensely from individuals' willingly donated time. Familiar among them were the flower arrangers, largely females of retirement age, whose contact is discrete, focused upon display only. However in 2010 the cathedral sought to apply Criminal Records Bureau regulations to their floral cohort, as the ladies shared a lavatory with choirboys – there was 'a risk of paedophile infiltration'. Annabel Hayter was chairman of Gloucester Cathedral Flower Guild. She refused the check, and ended up resigning with five others, asserting that it was unnecessary as they had no contact with children, which underlay the purpose of the procedure. One is tempted to remark: 'Bollocks!' at such a crass misinterpretation. Mrs Hayter's compensation was subsequent offers of similar work from parish churches. 'No mention of CRB checks,' *The Sunday Telegraph* (12/12/10).

Elgar's *Violin Concerto* had been the driving force in selecting the date for this day out. This was a magnificent performance, with Philippe Graffin, soloist, and Sir Roger Norrington conducting the Philharmonia Orchestra, though we saw absolutely no performers through the rigid screen. The next week I saw an effusive review of the festival in the *Daily Telegraph* (in my optician's waiting room) glowing about its emphasis on English composers. Four stars.

Afterwards we examined the misericords under our seats. One or two really did evoke sport, one a football encounter. Rand trolled over from his assumed domain, armed with my jacket and a small black umbrella. The latter was a mystery. Whiskers and wife had denied ownership, and I had lacked an umbrella small enough for my shoulder bag ever since the previous one perished on the seafront at Douglas, IoM. Girly the replacement might be but it became a practical souvenir of this event.

It was time for final inhalations of this hallowed setting, down the nave and up the path. I was to ask my friend Dave about his experiences living for a year in the close. Other bits of reminiscence have emerged, such as Bristol Old Vic Theatre School's touring production of *All's Well that Ends Well* being performed there: 'A good experience,' said John Hartoch the director. The date had been arranged through the auspices of a serious supporter of the School, the then High Sheriff of Glos. Another friend, who for some years held a teaching post at the cathedral, and was resident there, referred to his joy of seeing it in all the different morning lights. That's the benefit of familiarity – we had sampled a little of this with the east window going through a sunny afternoon to night time.

Monday 8 November

I reached the cathedral, detecting a hallowed parking space outside it, and within the close, which is an elaborate affair. I was surprised to find the Bishop's Office to lie in a modest building facing the south side of the cathedral. This was for my 4 o'clock appointment to see the Rt Revd Michael Perham. I had sufficient time to relish more of the cathedral and was fortunate to happen upon the tail end of *Crucible*, a sculpture exhibition of 76 items, both strong (massive exhibits inside and out) and sexy (many graphic nudes). Artists displayed included Eduardo Paolozzi, represented by the vast *Vulcan,* greeting you at the main entrance, Antony Gormley and Damien Hirst.

This brings me to Dave and Jo Plimmer, friends who lived in the close in the late 1990s. It was a time when the Gloucester's docks were undergoing expansion and arts offices were funded to include an artist in residence at the cathedral. Jo secured a three floor Georgian flat as part of her terms. It was good to witness current artistic endeavour in both these 2010 visits, especially as, by general consent, the city of Gloucester was a sad place, in Jo's words: 'The wider hinterland was quite bleak.' Dave found it 'melancholic', and the landscape 'Brueghelesque, with no spirit'. Other residents in the close were awarded flats following waiting list experience, as Rand and I had found at Norwich. This led to a deeply conservative range of occupants (complaints were made to Jo and Dave about displays of washing). There was a strange coincidence of lifestyles in the strong community link afforded by the residency, and the daily sight of the evensong congregation, which would include scurrying regulars, and a slow-paced African man. Then the open space would offer a haven for waifs, strays, beggars, drunks, druggies. Clergy would see them on their way. This was quite unlike what Jo discovered in the Barton Street area – a big Asian community, but self-sufficient, where projects found some success.

The initiative has found fruition in still retaining an artist, and working hard to provide for the downside of modern society. But Gloucester always loses out to Cheltenham, eight miles away. That's the choice of location for Gloucester RFC players to buy houses.

Inside the west end once more I was struck by a large and intriguing piece, in an elusive spiky but silvery metal seductively revealing body contours. It was *Calvary*, by David Mach, showing the Crucifixion. The shop beckoned. It stocked a rare thing: a shot glass for £5.99, alternatively 'whisky' glasses for £9 and £10.50, stated the labels. Something rather appealing was Cotswold Lavender: foaming bath soak for £2.99.

I moved to the nave and found myself quietly absorbing the architecture, alongside a verger with a walky-talky and technicians dismantling exhibits and wrestling with containers, together with a mixture of sculptures still in place, including an anomalous orange effort in the south aisle. I asked a passing guide/welcomer about the Anglo-Saxon candlestick about which I had read first in Kenneth Clark's *Civilisation* (1969): '(the candlestick) made for the Cathedral of Gloucester, is only about eighteen inches high, but so highly wrought that one can imagine it eighteen feet. It is an extreme example of Cluniac elaboration.'. The welcomer enlightened me: not only had it been transferred to the Victoria and Albert Museum decades before, but the Treasury was now closed for the winter. Exhibits come and go. So do Three Choirs Festivals.

My meeting with Bishop Michael was the outcome of an ongoing correspondence between me and his personal assistant, Diane Best. Thank you, Di: nice cup of tea, too. Michael was famously knowledgeable about the running of the Anglican Church and cathedrals themselves. The House of Bishops comprises all 44 diocesan bishops (in 43 buildings in this book plus Gibraltar, but not Wales) and a few others. It forms one of the three Houses of the General Synod, concerned with 'the Governance of the Church of England and the Anglican Communion'. Michael had a long list of activity to his credit, for example a speech in 2010 on 'affordable housing', also 'post-conflict stabilisation', in the House of Lords. He has been in post at Gloucester since 1994 and acceded to lordship in 2010. He was previously Dean of Derby. While there he 'was a member of the Church of England Liturgical Commission from 1986 to 2001, also playing a major part in the production of the Church of England's Common Worship,' (*Bishop Michael's Homepage)*: a busy man and, it seems, most productive. I was grateful that he made time for our chat.

Bishop Michael set the scene of how the Anglican cathedrals are run, recently streamlined for more consistency. So the various groups, with traditions and methods originating from their contrasting backgrounds, broadly Old Foundation, New Foundation and Parish Church Cathedrals.

The Cathedrals Measure came into effect in 1999, following the Archbishops' Commission on Cathedrals (the Howe Commission), set up in 1992 at the request of the cathedrals themselves, and published in "Heritage and Renewal" in 1994.

That was Lady Howe, wife of Prime Minister Thatcher's erstwhile right hand man Sir Geoffrey. What it meant was that cathedrals were to have a constant structure: deans (no provosts any more) and chapters; also scales of pay. This was effected promptly. The Church of England reported that in February 2000, the provosts of Blackburn (Province of York) and Chelmsford (Province of Canterbury), both Parish Church Cathedrals, became deans. This worked at the top end of the hierarchy as well as the more modest, and recent, entities. Lincoln (Old Foundation) had become infamous for bad practice and ill will in the previous generation. Its running would now become more accountable, and fit for purpose.

We touched on another movement under current discussion: the viability of certain dioceses. 'Dioceses' was a word whose every syllable Michael articulated, somewhat awkwardly. It sounded like a lisp, though I admit to being lazy in pronouncing the plural as the singular. I admired his persistence, though even he, an articulate and attractive speaker, stumbled over it on one occasion. Yorkshire was a bit of a mess at present, indeed, but this issue was to be addressed a few months hence through preliminary recommendations by the Dioceses Commission. I would be visiting the sees concerned over the winter. Before I left I tackled the question of favourites. He demurred at first, yielding to duty *a propos* his work place. In the end he opted for Norwich, providing a persuasive array of its virtues. Rand and I had indeed enjoyed it, only nine days earlier, but neither of us ranked it in the top group. That was the benefit of such a survey, subjective as it inevitably was. It's (almost) all personal, why anyone chooses a particular heap of stone.

Gloucester Cathedral would continue to figure near the top of my list. I departed after a final stroll round those cloisters. Later I would catch up with BBC bulletin about gargoyles. It was something that had already been reported before this visit. In October five new gargoyles were installed as 'part of the South Aisle Restoration project, which is due to be completed in the spring of 2012'. Those put in place on this occasion were 'a mad king, the Gloucestershire peasant, Sir ram, the lady goat and sea-monster', (quoted verbatim). There has simply been a dearth of gargoyles on this trail. This was certainly something to note for later, and lent further force to this place as an exhibition specialist.

29

St Davids

St David

Province: Wales
Founded: by 589, by St David
Present building: 1180–82
Restored: 1862–70, George Gilbert Scott

Website: www.stdavidscathedral.org.uk
Tel: 01437 720202
Email: info@stdavidscathedral.org.uk
Address: The Deanery Office, St Davids Cathedral, The Close, St Davids, Pembrokeshire SA62 6RH

Three to See: The sloping nave floor, preferably with beetle in motion;
the (secret) garden;
the discreet Holy Trinity Chapel

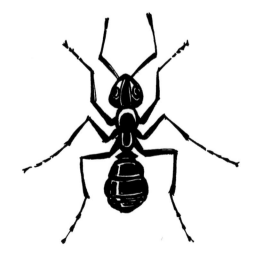

Beetle

Wednesday 11 August, 2010

It took a few hours to reach this gem, with a lunch and interview stop in Carmarthen. It was described as: 'An animated old-world Welsh town with bent-backed houses and narrow winding streets crammed onto a bluff above the river Towy', in *Nicholson's guide to Great Britain*, undated but published in the 1970s. The lunch break was at a *Good Beer Guide* recommendation, the Queens Hotel, in the town centre. This animated settlement was the location of the offices of the Bishop of St Davids, the Rt Revd Wyn Evans. Rand and I were to see him at 2 pm.

Round tortuous streets the pub came into view, but without anything except congestion to offer, certainly no parking. I had vainly hoped that as a hotel it would boast a car park. It was Rand's department to search for somewhere to leave the vehicle, while Rutz, Hel and I settled into a bottle of Pinot Grigio and menu perusal. The offer was two dishes for a tenner, doing the job of reward for hours of effort: sitting like stuffed dummies while Rand entertained us with his driving style. We did note the Victorian extravaganza Castell Coch as somewhere to visit. This stop would provide ballast for the final leg, which would culminate in a late afternoon cathedral visit. Sitting quietly in the garden at the rear in dappled shade, we chose a selection of succulent pies. The pub was just right. That was helped by the landlord's attitude to passing trade. He was friendly and helpful. Though I would have preferred some Double Dragon to white wine – remember the pub was chosen from a beer guide – Rand and I both had to take account of bladder-affected restrictions. It was also easier for all of us to share a bottle.

The Bishop's House was simple to find, in Abergwili, effectively an eastern suburb of the county town, right next door to the County Museum. Through the black iron gates, open and giving way to an enticing display of high summer blooms in the garden borders, we alighted upon a selection of 1970s buildings, intended both for living and working, very similar to the bishop's official residence in the Isle of Man, similarly on the edge the main centre of population. This was the outcome of a sequence of email exchanges with the bishop's personal assistant, Anne Rees. She now brought cups of tea while we waited for the bishop to finish his previous meeting.

Soon enough we were sitting opposite Bishop Wyn. 'Oh yes, call me Wyn.' He confirmed the impression of immediacy I'd obtained from various website publications, including sermons and bulletins surrounding his work, clearly energetic and progressive. It was obvious that the discussion should pursue his career with this diocese. First it transpired that the bishop did actually live in St Davids and his wife worked there as a potter.

The basics spoke for themselves: Wyn had spent 14 years as Dean of St Davids, and was chosen as Bishop in 2008. He professed reluctance when hearing of his nomination. He was a project man, a mover and shaker, and the list of issues and improvements, sounded to be endless in his gift as dean. 'Death watch beetle' was his most frequently uttered phrase. A beetle had to become the emblem of St Davids. We were to imagine them sliding down the slope of the cathedral nave, perhaps echoing the fate of the lemming. It was near the sea, too. Anyway, the process of appointment was written in tradition, involving an electoral college of 47 people, who represented various interests. A maximum of three days was allowed for a decision to be made. He said it actually took two. Then he became bishop. The parallel issue of the choice of Archbishop of Wales was currently under discussion, the post held by the Bishop of Llandaff, situated in the nation's capital. The previous five had been from the other dioceses, the most recent being Monmouth: a certain Rowan Williams. Only at Brecon, had there never been a double act. The question had been posited: should it rest in Cardiff, given its importance as the public face of Christianity?

The bishop's relationship with the dean was 'visceral.' As dean Wyn's archaeological background had proved invaluable, Rand and I thought as much as a spur to motivation as practical in matters of the building. It was 'a quirky, difficult building,' said Wyn, 'not centrally planned – burnt down 7, 8 or 9 times.' It was built on a bog with the northwest nave lodged on a riverbed. He added that the wood in the nave roof was not Irish as the guide books assert, but British. English? Well, yes. His task throughout had been eased by familiarity with the people there. We could well imagine that, as he had an affable, bright manner, which suggested purpose and intelligence. He said he 'built on what had been done'. Everything was about 'building', which was apt as Wyn came across as a fundamentally constructive person. From the start in 1993, fundraising was key, through his position in the archaeological world he could keep pressure on the long process of preservation. He mentioned the 'west end to south end' where stone had been flaking badly. The west front (not the best feature) had to be refaced. The partnership with Caroe & Sons, architects, so productive at Brecon, had done well here too, as had Jerry Sampson, an architect noted for his work on the west fronts at Wells and Salisbury.

The cathedral had originated c.1180, and there was fine Romanesque work to be seen. It was built of purple Cambrian sandstone, dynamited out of cliffs nearby. It was a hard stone, later developing cracks. The quarries were a site of interest, owned by the National Trust and located in a National Park. St Davids boasted iconic status, which helped in obtaining approval for 600 tons to be extracted.

One of Wyn's initiatives had been to make sure the Bishop's Palace at St Davids stayed in existence, as a ruin. Roofing it had been a discussion point for a while, to house Graham Sutherland's permanent collection. I was looking forward to seeing the artist's large scale work at Coventry Cathedral. The first impression was likely to be one of bewilderment at such an idea as the palace is immense. Hel said: 'Surely this must have housed monks, it's so big.' The Victorian restoration work was now 140 years old. Whatever its quality (not much by all accounts) it was time for a new initiative. This was one of a number of major projects for Wyn; another was to get the organ right: the case was too small and deathwatch beetle in alarming evidence (for me 'deathwatch' is a great name for a destructive insect). This would involve an appeal subcommittee.

He also established a cloister project, which in turn would facilitate a greater range of activity. The appeal process was immense, involving professional advice, the tendering of firms, and the rest, leading ultimately to the transformation of the cathedral for a sum which reached £5.5m. Even the detached gatehouse, the first port of call from the village/city above, cost a tidy £ ¼m.

Wyn would note the audible gasps of surprise to be heard there at visitors' first sight of the cathedral enchanting all who happened upon it from above, as good an impact as any in this book. Again there were the inevitable pieces of ignorance, which might have jeopardized project completion: concerning the siting of 'loos', reported Wyn. Achieving approval for a common sense plan became an eleventh hour decision. In the end he got what he wanted. Partners included the Heritage Lottery Fund, 'Europe', the Arts Council (for the vaulted area for performance), and of course the ubiquitous Friends – Single £10, Corporate Membership £25, Life Membership £250. The outcome was a terrific structure, hardly conveyed by the term 'cloister', which Wyn called 'an area of refreshment' (refectory). That was only part of it.

The bishop's diary was the next subject. He opened up his current one, which was ample, and apparently drenched with black ink. Unlike his former appointments as dean, in this job the entries were spiritually-inspired, based upon such fixtures as 'inter-church' meetings: one such was recently held in Shrewsbury, over the border in England, for the facilities to discuss 'covenanted churches'. There were ordinations, and, in the many parishes, confirmations; also inductions and licensing. And then there was the quarterly tryst of a bench of bishops. He was president of the Cathedral Festival, a ten-day event every spring (Whitsun), which must be a joy to attend. The most evocative image of the place involved the foreground being plastered with daffodils or buttercups. It features on many an Easter card.

Having spoken to Dean Geoffrey at Brecon it was interesting to observe the other side of the coin. Wyn had been instrumental in choosing his successor as Dean of St Davids after 14 years in the job himself. It had presented no problem, he said, as there was a fundamentally communal atmosphere of cooperation.

We next heard about the choir, with a unique core of girls. This had been provoked by a flu epidemic among the boys. It was stunning to consider that Alexander Mason, Director of Music, had achieved so much and, above all, attracted so many singers, in this remote and under-populated place. It was the smallest city in the country – 1,900 souls according to Wyn, city status having been confirmed by HM the Queen in 1995.

Our time had proceeded apace – over an hour and a quarter – and I, not our host, made to move to leave. Our companions would be waiting, awash no doubt with acquisitions from the charity shops of Carmarthen, for that was where Hel wanted to go. Rand did ask when the best time of year was to pay a visit to St Davids. Wyn's answer was immediate: September to November. 'When retired people, like us, tend to come,' I posited. 'Well, yes,' he replied, again. My friends Nick Thomas and Barbara McNamara went to west Wales for a holiday soon after. Nick described the souvenir of the occasion, a colour photograph: 'The Bishop of St Davids holding a little open-air get-together on top of the old lime kiln by the sea at Cwmtydu. Also checked out lovely Brecon Cathedral.' This was all good news. Wyn was essentially a very busy bishop.

Rutz and Hel both appeared, empty-handed. That was a shame, really, as it would have been good to admire, or scoff at, their choice of new garb for the entertainment that evening. We reached the cathedral car park after, not the 'one hour and five minutes,' which Wyn had asserted to be the journey time, but several more this time. There were extensive roadworks on the A48, the only realistic route via Haverfordwest. We resorted to 'I-spy', which fizzled out after Rutz's offering of 'T' for 'Tree'. We arrived in enough time for a wander, round the fabulous Bishop's Palace, which was absolutely huge and craggily ruined. I could understand the need for a significant quota even to make it safe. There were so many jutting arches and apparently loose bits of stone, right by a stream. Hel had concluded mobile phone dealings with the appointed guest house, Glendower, which was perfectly placed on the first street above the cathedral in the city/village, adjacent to a car park which offered two hours' parking between 8 am and 6 pm, hence suitable for breakfast and a cathedral re-visit in the morning. We would therefore aim to leave St Davids at 10 am. Before that was a wealth of fun in prospect.

We first admired the exterior, of the striking purple stone. The tower was good from the direction of the Bishop's Palace, which we took initially, and later from above. We enjoyed the building we'd gathered much about.

Inside, the font was good, discreetly placed in the space opening up before you on entering the building. You were not immediately faced with rows of chairs. Looking down you notice that curious slope in the nave, especially as there was considerable open space. Upwards more admirable material was in evidence, such as the roof of 'Irish' oak. It dates from the late 15th century and has an unusual appearance, with two rows of bosses, the whole length of the nave designed with fine arches. It looked good, as did the tower: 116' tall. The view of it at the crossing was worth a bit of neck strain.

The building suffered serious neglect in the past. Bishop Wyn was one of a sequence of improving forces. Onwards, to examine the rich dark choir stalls, where the misericords were fun to lift to reveal. There was also one showing boat construction. I haven't seen one anywhere else depicting what some people do on a boat: a man vomiting over the side of one: this is a cathedral close to the sea. And then, further up in the sanctuary, there were mid-15th century sedilia, rarely made of wood. Nearby was the shrine of St David (1275). Looking up again was something else not often seen: Early English lancet windows. There was plenty to see, in three sessions: the main one now, around the recital and a last look before departure. Being at different times of day, I found this a catalyst for conveying a rewarding range of character. St Davids had that quality in abundance. The roof and walls have fine carvings. As the guide book had it: 'The fine stone screens at each side of the chapel show signs of the weathering they suffered during their exposure to the elements at a time when the chapel aisles were unroofed.' To me that says something about the sadness of the neglect in earlier centuries in many cathedrals. How lucky we are to be able to visit these buildings now in comparatively good repair. Cathedrals also offer, confidently, work closer to our time; here our party approved of the 1979 screen, erected as entrance to the Lady Chapel.

A verger now asked us to leave, as she was to close the doors to mark the end of the day's business. The concert was nigh. The next task was to check in at Glendower GH. This served our purpose well, though both Rand and I were to take baths, being too lofty for the shower attachment in our attic room. Hel, as organizer and lady, had chosen room five on the first floor. I then lost the toss for the double bed, winning what turned out to be a good night's sleep on a hard single bed under the window, with a direct western view of ecclesiastical buildings and, in the distance, the Atlantic. Rand's special request was to see the sea while we were still there. We started by taking a snapshot on arrival and another before departure. Different light, you understand.

We were next well-nourished by another pub dishful, on a garden table in the cooling evening. It was still warm enough to sit outside. It could be classed as a 'fine' day. We chose the fresh and dry Pinot Grigio again: Hel's influence. The good thing about this routine was in avoiding excess: one and a bit glasses each, but just enough quantity for a course of pub grub, if you paced yourself. The accompanying salad, self-served from the buffet, was the best bit, together with the prospect of the sounds to issue from the organ, restored as one of the achievements of Wyn's deanship.

The organ project was by Harrison & Harrison. Mark Venning, their managing director at the time, remembered this:

> *Organ contracts can take many years to come to fruition. My first visit to St Davids Cathedral was in 1975; we completed the organ, with its lovely new case, in 2000. This was another Willis organ, which had sadly been altered and was in a poor state. A number of important pipes had been removed from the organ, and one of my first tasks was to find them. It was rather like a treasure hunt – they turned out to have been stored in untidy heaps in an outhouse of the Deanery, and we were able to rescue them and include them in the new organ. An organ case had been built around all four sides of the organ; it was beautifully made but was too small for the poor old organ to fit comfortably inside. I remember seeing that case set up on the floor of our workshop to form a gloriously carved wooden encampment. Our designer paced to and fro inside it, like a soldier inside a large toy fort, trying to work out how much he could use for the completed organ. The new case has two Welsh dragons facing each other on the front. A few months after completion I received a complaint: the architect had noticed that one of the dragons was lacking a tail. My explanation (that female dragons don't have tails) was politely rejected, and the tail was duly provided.*

Walking in a crocodile down the incline, we arrived at what was now the box office (a desk near the south door). Once the rather sparse audience was assembled Dorrien Davies, the delightful Canon Residential, did the introduction. Dorrien had been a schoolmate of my friend Kevin, who described him as 'magnetic' at a young age, exuding a sense of spirituality, a powerful faith, which carried him through tough school years. The artist was the accomplished musician Michael Slaney, who had been a remarkable achiever during his 80 years. His performance that evening was magical. He emphasized that the organ, though new in 2000, actually conveyed the character of its older origins. It was a Willis instrument from 1883. It comprised 3500 pipes hidden around the building, by no means the only shiny, sparkling exhibit above the rood screen and the others we could see. He asserted: 'It's perfectly fair to say that it's still a Willis organ.' Rand and I exchanged a thought, sotto voce, that the triforium, which transmogrified into the clerestory windows above, must account for quite a few pipes. We did slightly disagree as the sound seemed somewhat bright rather than mellow. But I'd need a professional organist to confirm or otherwise. A big screen had been erected before us in the nave to see the action transmitted from the organ aloft. This succeeded. We were able to follow hand and pedal movements, some of which displayed the virtuoso, such as the canon (*Fantasia on Hanover* by Edwin Lemare), requiring extreme dexterity with the digits. Also, we had the option of making out the forms of performer and page-turner in the loft, above the massive screen. He kept us informed with erudite information which served the chosen pieces well. Hel and Rutz liked the Debussy *Arabesque* best; Bach's *Sonata No 5* for me, and Rand remained silent, perhaps transfixed, for it was a lovely session. Rutz liked it all. From Dorrien's introduction to the words of the valiant performer – over 80 years old and 'sharing, not wanting to be clever'. Both ladies liked catching sight of the actions of his feet 'amazing on the screen,' which was a rare opportunity.

A point was made which interested Rand and myself – that several of the seven pieces harked from the golden age of organ composition – 1900–20. Rich sounds indeed. On the way out Dorrien thought his workplace to be 'One of Wales' gems – we have to keep it in good nick.' There was a post-concert recovery in the Farmer's Arms, sampling Felinfoel Double Dragon for the first time in decades; large Pinot Grigios for Rutz, who said she was 'knocked out by the wood in the choir stalls,' as we ruminated over the cathedral. In the pub, where we happened upon the dying minutes of England's 2–1 defeat of Hungary at Wembley (I hovered briefly in the seething crowd under the television in the next bar), there was an abundance of noisy, mobile youth, who may have been on, or in, the ocean wave during the day. They hailed from somewhere Mediterranean we reckoned. I hoped they had ventured into that other gem of a building.

Thursday 12 August
I took the opportunity to investigate the cathedral buildings further after breakfast. The repast had been a streamlined affair. The star turn came from Rutz, who asked for 'Muesli' off the laminated menu. When it arrived she sent it back. Well, the deal was cheap at £33 each inclusive.

Sinking to cathedral level down the path from the Bell Tower, I attempted a complete circuit, but was thwarted on the northeast side. Still,

I did enjoy the high summer display in the garden. Being out of sight, it was very secret and conveyed a calming effect in providing benches, hydrangeas and crocosmias to support the view of stone above.

Once inside, the morning light didn't serve the place too well, though I was able to dip into the bits for which we had run out of time a few hours earlier. The marble artefacts in the Chapel of Edward the Confessor in the south chapel aisle appeared disappointingly flat, after the subtle tones produced there the previous evening. I did happen upon the obligatory icon, Cretan (17th century). And found its position of the crossing, over the choir, a pleasant change. This echoed Gloucester. It was strange to find such an approach in two consecutive cathedrals. There were bright silver-coloured angels blaring on the rood screen on the choir side, below the Willis organ. In the quire itself, lurked a number of delights – the misericords merited investigation, with a green man in evidence – there's one in the Lady Chapel, too. Delving into Bishop Gower's screen (his remains lurk there), there was a nest of recesses, whose contents included a chair and a number of hymn books ready for distribution. The cathedra was imposing, as it led the eye to the altar, where a lady volunteer was painstakingly arranging flowers. No, they weren't from people's gardens but 'Johnson's', said the arranger. They were attractively displayed there in the presbytery, in the nave to greet worshippers, and in the Lady Chapel, where a more modest organ was housed, 'S E Gilks, organ builders' of Peterborough.

Moving behind the high altar lay the unusual rectangular space of the Holy Trinity Chapel, darkly isolated as a discreet stop-gap before you ventured into the east end, but offering carvings and a casket. Perhaps this contained ancient bones. It was securely stored in an arched alcove behind an iron grid. At Durham and Winchester this area is termed 'feretory'; here it was an unassuming presence, on the ground floor only. You could easily miss it. Weathering was a significant feature of this chapel. The guide related: 'The fine stone screens at each side of the chapel show signs of the weathering they suffered during their exposure to the elements at a time when the chapel aisles were unroofed.' That would apply universally to decayed stonework, which remains worthy of examination even so. I had bought the guide book (£3.99) in the shop, thankfully open before the published time of 10 am. There were no shot glasses in the well-stocked outlet, which happily occupied practical open space in the northwest corner of the nave.

Wandering through the cleverly-designed cloister complex I heard the strains of choir practice. There were steps down to a crypt-level room. Surplices and cassocks were to be seen hanging in anticipation. Those participating in the session, or lesson given the stentorian male voice in charge, were out of sight. This, for me, reinforced the favourable impression of what had been achieved by the cloister project. An appealing extension in its own right, it was fully up and running as a centre of activity, with the refectory and art display aloft (open into the evening, in fact 7 pm, indeed was a boon), chairs and tables below with a view through the door and up the hill, or of the green sward within the cloisters, solidly succeeded by the ponderous buttresses built on the north aisle. Overall it would be a shame to lose them, which has been mooted, as they contribute to the varieties of different style in that area. Finally, having read about them before breakfast, I took a final stroll through the cathedral, noting ancient stone with carved crosses, which are a feature here, which we hadn't noticed thus far. Once you see one you start tuning into them, rather like green men. It is quite a collection, apposite in this part of the world.

Time was up and, having scaled the bank, I bumped into my companions on the wall by the gatehouse, enjoying a final inhalation of the delights before them. The car awaited us close by, and Rand now sought to try out the local beach. Whitesand Bay was formerly the point of embarkation for pilgrims, down a predictably narrow, windy road. We drove to the end, where the only option was a £3 charge to park. That would have been fine, if you wished to indulge in the pleasures on offer, but we decided upon a quick view only. The coffee stop could wait until a bit further on. With a few miles done on the homeward journey, Sands Café appeared, at Newgale, an easy stop right by the water. We stopped there partly because of the incredibly slow vehicle in front of us. It boasted an extensive beach, which we struggled up to, briefly. It was windy, I recall. The coffee was good as were the memories of St Davids. We variously reminisced with satisfaction on the visit. Hel and Rutz itemized the purple stone, the outrageously massive Bishop's Palace, the beetles and sloping floor, the wood employed in the choir stalls and the fetching pew ends. All this had been enjoyed in that anomalous cathedral somehow competing in the realm of our best church buildings in such a tiny place. Why was that site chosen, hidden away on hostile terrain below its settlement, when it could have been built on a rock for all to see? There are plenty of those around. On the outward journey we had admired the mountains to the north, Mynydd Preseli. Rand and I decided to return some autumn, as Wyn had suggested, for another visit.

St Davids was once the scene of an instance of divine intervention: my friend Iris Murch disregarded the signs prohibiting photography and snapped away at the delights on view. Later she reviewed her efforts. The film was blank.

330

30

Wells

St Andrew

Province: Canterbury
Founded: 909; 1090 see moved to Bath, in 1170 back to Wells
Present building: 1186–1239

Website: www.wellscathedral.org.net
Tel: 01749 674483
Email: visits@wellscathedral.uk.net
Address: Chain Gate, Cathedral Green, Wells, Somerset BA5 2UE

Three to See: Steps to chapter house (right) and to chain gate (left);
chantry of Bishop Sugar;
corbel of fox devouring chicken on the roof, which will require taking a
High Parts Tour

Mille feuille

Sunday 29 August, 2010

Professor Freeman had this to say in 1899: 'The traveller who comes down the hill from Shepton Mallet looks down on a group of buildings without rival either in our own land or beyond the seas,' (*The Cathedrals of England* by Francis Bond). A visitor should factor in time to embrace what lies outside Wells Cathedral: St Andrew's Well, where it all started, the Bishop's Palace and its garden and orchard, the Vicar's Close and the west front in the dying sun.

'Actually, yes, please,' I emitted, perhaps a little feverishly. This was in answer to my friend Pom's offer of a day out in Wells. She, a mezzo soprano, had been engaged to sing for the Wells U3A (University of the Third Age) Music Weekend final event. We arrived at 11.25 am, in time for the driver's rehearsal for pieces by Brahms and Wagner, in the Music School opposite the cathedral's north porch. I strolled round to the brilliant west front and through the creaky door. I bumped into a man and a woman, the former of whom carried a walking stick and narrowly averted an upending. He asked: 'Are you coming for the fair or Mattins?' 'Mattins' I replied, being ignorant of any fair. 'Oh, good' he smiled. A strange exchange, I surmised. Lo and behold, on reaching the north transept there was a conglomeration of silver-haired people with a few trestle tables just visible round the perimeter. A quick thought was how meritorious this was. Then I ruminated upon the curiosity of this happening on a Sunday in mid-morning. More I was not to evince, but entered the quire from the nave to be greeted by a man with a badge. I chose solitude in the second row, facing the east window. I was soon joined by a canon, the prime chanter. The stalls were dotted with patrons of all descriptions. To judge from the sound emitted and approaches to stance (the service sheet, as ever, instructed 'sit, stand, kneel' by turns) not a high percentage of attenders was aware, or responsive to how things were done – most likely tourists, and why not as this was a thoroughly rewarding slot in the cathedral's timetable to precede or follow a tour of the building. What surrounded us was a sublime piece of work, representing a gradual but insistent Early English project. Unlike so many beautiful choir stalls I'd snuggled into, the whole of the eastern part of Wells was of a creamy limestone piece, inspired in its complexity and fusion of style with purpose. The absence of wood in the stalls and cathedra was refreshing. Concerning this, on display in the Outer Hall at Dunster Castle, in West Somerset, is 'a bishop's throne canopy from Wells Cathedral. Originally a sounding board from above the pulpit, designed to help project the speaker's voice,' the National Trust had inscribed.

On this occasion the performance and volume produced by the

Tunstall Choir, which originated in Durham, took the audience to a level somewhere through the blind triforium up to the expansive plain glass clerestory and further still to the abstract tracery in the ceiling (delicate red and blue fronds). The architecture shows invention. After the blessing I approached a convenient virger (local spelling) to view the misericords, upon one of which I had been sitting. 'You'll have to get a special pass. If they were available to everybody they wouldn't last ten minutes.' He added: 'There are some good ones on display in the retroquire.'

Walking the cloisters amid public and Tunstalls singers, at the Gents a man kindly held the door open, evidently by now exasperated by the effect of his generosity. 'Anyone else?' he asked. 'Two and six please.' I had to give credit to the design, clean with a model of fast hand dryer the like of which was outside my experience. And in the recess abutting the entrance to the Friends and toilets extension there were crumbling bits of masonry on display. Ancient and modern – very good! I passed through the efficient shop, a big improvement on the old one, which, with the café, had previously occupied the west cloister. There were the books I'd been reading, along with the customary range of goods, including snowflake fountains and tacky items labelled 'Angela, Anthea, etc.' I spotted a greetings card illustrating Louis, the marmalade cathedral cat. The story was told: 'Cats have a long and honourable association with cathedrals. They are valued for their hunting skills. Louis adopted Wells Cathedral as its (surely should be 'his') home and is much spoilt by the staff all round the building. Louis spends much time in the shop and has many friends amongst the staff and visitors.' I asked the assistant where Louis might be. 'Oh, he's been fed,' she said, 'He'll be around the cathedral somewhere. He's usually near the bishop's chair.'

I mounted the stairs in the corridor to Chapter Two, the well-named catering initiative, new since my last visit where immediately in evidence was a light airy space, with a direct view of the moat and Bishop's Palace. The daily specials included Golden Vegetable Soup (£3.95 – what is 'golden'?) and Jacket Potatoes – filling of the day Egg and Mayonnaise with Coleslaw and Green Salad (rather expensive at £6.25). What I could have chosen was a Mendip Moments Ice Cream, such as Raspberry and Elderflower, Vanilla Bean and Latte Crumble or even Fairtrade Coffee in the interests of consistent empirical testing at each venue. I bit the bullet and ordered a black Americano. Coffee was the true test. Tea, the 'breakfast' version, was more standard in character. Also, I knew there would be tea and cake after the concert, which was beginning to loom. I was bound to appease belly needs on a cake. Lemon drizzle was on the list (all were £3.95, again somewhat overpriced), but I couldn't resist the fruit cake. With coffee at £1.80 I was undercharged, working it out seated in a prime position with aspect of the swans milling in the water beyond. The café wall was effectively festooned with well-judged photographs of the cathedral. A customer or two might even be tempted inside it by the fetching image of a corbel: a human head, though they could have done with captions. The only other punters were a family who appeared to have tried all of the seven ice cream flavours while I was there, a feminine (actually male) couple, well-got-up in chancel pink and nave mushroom, and two mature women in full ladies-who-finished-their-meals-an-hour-ago mode, but who were still lunching (that is gossiping). The cake, brimmed with ostentatious fruits, in hues from yellow ochre to burnt umber (as evocative on the palette as 'Ponder anew' in mid-hymn, earlier). A mouthful put Chapter Two at least near the top of the cake charts. But the coffee: insipid. I had recourse to the water bottle in my bag, and outside there were fountains in evidence here and there, most helpful for the thirsty. One more thing was well-expressed: hot chocolate made with real chocolate – the best in Wells! No temptation for me, though I did note bottles of Gem Bitter and an assortment of colours of wine for another time.

The image of Wells was suggested by Pros, an actor friend whose visits to the cathedral had been gluttonous. One definition of this abstruse item is: *Mille Feuille* (literally, a thousand leaves), a traditional French recipe for a classic layered pastry that separates into individual layers when baked.

Mille Feuille
Ingredients:
1 square puff pastry
5 egg yolks
90g sugar
375ml whole milk (I liked that – none of your green, red or purple tops)
40g flour
1 vanilla pod, split in half and scraped
Pinch of salt

Method:
In a medium bowl, stir together 80 ml milk with the flour and salt and whisk until smooth.
Add the yolks and 3 tbs sugar and whisk vigorously until the mixture is smooth and pale lemon in colour.

In a heavy bottomed saucepan, heat remaining milk with the remaining sugar and the vanilla scrapings over medium heat.
Heat until the milk just comes to a boil.
While stirring the yolk mixture, slowly pour ¼ of the hot milk mixture onto it. This will temper the egg yolks so they don't start to scramble.
Immediately pour yolk mixture into the hot milk in the saucepan.
Whisk over medium heat until mixture comes to a boil and thickens.
Remove from the heat immediately.
Cover with clingfilm to prevent a skin from forming and allow to cool completely.

You are now ready to assemble the Mille Feuille.
Cut ¹/₃ off the puff pastry square that you've made (freeze the remainder to keep until later).
Roll the puff pastry into a thin rectangle some 30cm x 40cm.
Line a baking tray with parchment paper and sprinkle with water.
Lay the dough on top and poke all over with a fork to prevent over-rising.
Chill for 15 minutes then bake in an oven pre-heated to 200°C until golden brown and very crisp.
Transfer to a wire rack and allow to chill completely.
Trim the edges of the pastry so that they're straight and even in shape, then divide the rectangle into three even strips, each about 10 cm wide.
Evenly divide the cooled pastry cream between two strips of the puff pastry. Spread evenly then lay one strip, covered with cream, on top of the first, lining-up evenly.
Top with the final strip of puff pastry. Dust with icing sugar and chill for 1 hour before serving.
To serve, cut with a serrated knife using a sawing motion and garnish each half segment with half a strawberry (one finger will yield 8 Mille Feuilles).

Celtnet Recipes.

It sounds fantastic, with strawberries, it instructed (or raspberries, my preference), from the growers nearby on the Mendip slopes. Roll on the day when Chapter Two was to offer this Wellsian delicacy on a day I'm visiting.

The restaurant is near the public entrance, at the corner of the territory closest to the Penniless Porch, leading to Market Square and parking. This has enhanced the west front as a feature, to admire as such. I walked up the west cloister to the nave, to wonder at the singularity, the deceptive simplicity of the Early English design. I love the Scissor (Strainer) Arches, on three sides at the crossing, the screen taking up the eastern side. Wells offers double fulfilment: as a single unit on a human scale filled with interest and character, and for the detail which keeps a visitor intrigued at every turn. The columns are largely uniform, and delightful as such. They also reward upward investigation as many carry thrilling images, of human, animal and myth. Examples are a merman, with a fish, a man-headed bird carrying a staff. The trouble with corbels and bosses is that it's not easy to discern the detail. Often you wonder: 'What am I looking at?' Even with binoculars.

At the transept end of the nave there are chantry chapels on each side. The south one is dedicated to St Hugh Sugar, from 1489, complete with a delicate fan vault, and attached pulpit (stone of course) from c.1540. There was a covered seat in the corner of the chapel, upon which was recumbent a ginger feline: Louis, who had extracted giggles from a young couple before me, as I approached. I wondered just how efficient he was at his job of rodent control. Even cats have to pay their way. I was thinking of all that shop fodder. His bulk suggested a well-nourished pet, rather than a rampant rodent remover.

I was bound to cast my eyes heavenwards again in the nearby south transept, for more capital depiction: a man with toothache and fruit stealers, one of whom is caught (it said). They did look good. Perhaps the detail would become clearer in subjecting the photos to technological treatment on my computer Meanwhile I had embarked upon a southside ramble involving a number of tombs:

- St Calixtus' Chapel, to note delicate carving on the side of the tombs, especially the treatment of quire clothing.
- Incised slab in the shape of a coffin – commemorating Bishop Bitton II (1267–74), it is one of the oldest of its type.
- The chapel and effigies of Thomas Bekinton, Chancellor of England, local bishop (1443–64), himself above in original colours, cadaver below with discreet cloth covering.

In the retroquire I did indeed happen upon three misericords clearly displayed. Marvellous stuff: I still wanted to see the others secreted under seats: in their proper setting illustrating intriguing subjects. I was becoming addicted these wonders of Plantagenet art.

The Lady Chapel followed, the stonework showing off the light to best advantage. It had recently acquired a boat, to honour the patron saint, Andrew, as fisherman. Opposite, facing east, were 14 Stations of the Cross icons, modest in dimension. I had observed a large icon at the foot of the southern Scissor Arch. Of St Andrew, it was painted by Aleksandre Gormatiouk of the Grabar Institute, Moscow. The accompanying notice explained the significance of icons to the church better than anywhere else I had seen. A further contemporary work was effectively displayed in the Chapel of the Blessed Sacrament. There stood part of an olive tree and its product, a flask of olive oil. Together with a reassuring vase of flowers at the opposite side of the altar it looked just right. Somehow Wells has succeeded with the fusion of unified Gothic and dots of modern addition.

There was a memorial to John Milton, Chancellor of Wells (1337). I had already seen that of Walter Raleigh, (dean 1642–46), 'nephew of the famous Sir Walter, murdered in the Deanery as a Royalist by his gaoler David Barrett, a shoemaker, and buried under the dean's stall by Mr Standish, a Priest Vicar, who was accordingly put in prison where he died'. Pondering on the more famous namesakes, one point was that Wells lacked originals, as a backwater, without much in the way of saints, pilgrims or profile. Glastonbury is only six miles away. That was all the better for the sake of its purity and sense of positiveness, and all the more surprising that in 1953, the Coronation 'custom' saw the bishop honoured in being placed next to HM The Queen. Also to its credit, it gave Canterbury an Archbishop in a recent generation – its former Bishop Rt Revd George Carey (1988–91).

Next for more practico/artistic architecture and sublime detail in framework: through to the undercroft, also worth a look, as was the 'stoup, inside which is a delightful carving of a dog gnawing a bone'. Gnaw on, hound! The items on display again provided variety of interest in a context much better used than previously. The undercroft fitted into the armpit of the graceful flight of stairs and chapter house to which they led. This is perfect, emblematized by the corbel of a peasant spreading the risk of propping up the vault, and by extension, the chapter house itself (1306), while slaying a dragon. This should all be seen while stationary on the steps, well-worn and the scene of many a tumble by misfooting patrons. Wildest dreams might conjure up this area. Each bay carried its representation, such as 'Wyviliscombe' or 'Comoc 1', up to 'Comoc XIV'. In the modern era the dean and chapter meet in a separate room, but clarity of speech should be sustained in this space. The upward flight takes you, should the way be open, to the Chain Gate (1459) and over the road to the Vicars' Hall (1348, year of the Black Death, which says something) and Close (1360).

Back in the body of the cathedral, the next pause was in the north transept. And there was the 1390 clock, the oldest complete mechanical one in England. It proceeded to strike: I had timed this for 1300 hours on the twenty four hour clock resplendent with sun, moon and much more, and witnessed the marvel of the clock in multi-dimensional action. The best visual aspect was the colourful jaunting jousters in circulation.

A wander round the cloisters was the next matter. There were worthwhile bosses in the roof, but I failed to find one of 'three men at stool'. I was pleased to identify a good one, however: 'A man playing the bagpipes'. There remained time for the garden area on the southeast side of the cathedral. There was an element of oasis about it with late summer blooms, flat tombstones, and a gargoyle set low in the wall. Elsewhere, as was common, the building had attached lead troughs projecting from the corners, with only functionality to recommend them. It was good to see this rather useless thing. It pointed at the centre of the bottom wall, where I now turned. It stated 'St Andrew's Wells,' to be seen through the glass panel nearby, through to the palace water section beyond. Finally, I returned to the fading floral display, noting that a few roses were still about to bloom. Summer wasn't over yet.

This is the opportunity to plug the Bishop's Palace. After an earlier visit, I came to regard it as worth the admission fee (many are alienated by this, as they were when a charge was made to view the cathedral). It is something to share. The prelude is the moat. Among the cedars, a mature mute swan played to its audience in arriving at the rope in the wall, and ringing the bell, a tradition dating back to the 19th century, and handed (or beaked) down through the generations. See the palace and its immediate garden, complete with tall walls and a statue of a wild boar. Continue the itinerary leading through to the eponymous wells, amid stream, vegetation and organic growth. Trees range from mature apple varieties, succulent in the autumn, to species previously not experienced. The wooded Tor Hill looms above, and in front is the ultimate picture postcard view of the cathedral, towards the east end over water.

Hastening to the concert venue, the Cathedral School music room, it turned out that I was really gate-crashing a recital of works by Schumann, Brahms and Wagner. Pom performed, always a joy. Joy is her middle name, so an easy word choice. My neighbour at this concert was a knowing lady. Our opening gambit was to concur about the tightness of the space and unyielding nature of the chairs. On hearing that I had been at Mattins while the 100-strong throng was learning about Brahms' relationships she commented 'Well at least there was no sermon.' I had to ask her favourite cathedral. She said without hesitation: 'Durham – it's fairly rooted – not going to blow away.' 'That's rather definite,' I followed. 'And I do like Wells. But I'm not sure about having Wagner on the programme with Brahms – they hated each other.' Afterwards we took tea and biscuits, followed for Pom and me by more bonhomie and ingestion at our hosts' house (David Naysmith had organized and conducted as well). Its outlook gave views of Glastonbury Tor and the tower of the fine Perpendicular parish church of Wells, St Cuthbert.

Monday 30 November
The South West of England was in the throes of early season snow. That was droll, having the previous day been informed by the BBC that 2010 was to be either the hottest or second hottest year on record. This spell of big freeze would surely result in an overall plummet in temperature to deny such an accolade.

I therefore allowed more time than was the habit to get to Wells, and made it, almost on time. I followed a tentative, crisp and fairly even trajectory, to the entrance to the cathedral, to meet Melvyn Matthews, erstwhile Canon Chancellor. My idea had been to grab a quick eyeful of the west front, but he was waiting, deeply concealed under a woolly hat, at the entrance to the modern bits. He immediately said that we'd managed to choose the day of the cathedral's saint, St Andrew, so the building was closed to viewing. We decided, easily, on coffee and cakes, in Chapter Two. While procuring refreshments, Melvyn asked me to select a table – there was plenty of space – so I elected upon a view of the Bishop's Palace. When we left I realized that his aspect, opposite me, had been of the west front, a good two-way design by the regime. Also, under the Creativity and Care scheme with English Heritage, the cathedral had also acquired 'New entry cloister, Education and Music Resource Centre, chapter house, undercroft, works yard.' Wells Cathedral was going places. The coffee was tastier this time, the brownie too (no lemon drizzle), so all-in-all the facility was doing well.

The Measure of 2000, while exercising an effective agenda to standardize practice, had not been beneficial for all cathedrals. Old Foundation cathedrals (Wells was one) did as little as possible to change their practices. Need had resulted in an increase in staff numbers over the years. The new level, 'cathedral council' had only one power: to see accounts and sign them off. The best practical scenario was one of good management, where the dean exercised consultative leadership. That all rang true, the cathedrals were modern businesses, whether at Canterbury or Chelmsford.

Converting the negative truism of a cathedral as 'a palace of the establishment', therefore discouraging to the public, Wells, though 'never a monastery, in spite of its cloisters' is the very model of the Benedictine essence of welcome. It is paramount for visitors, pilgrims and investigative tourists (me). Yes, that was the role of the guestmaster, with unfettered, unquestioning grace. 'There is not a scrap of "judgement" on the west front, anywhere,' Melvyn continued. It is all to do with life. The cathedral lacks shrines and dead bishops, and attempts to introduce them have failed. Rather, the imagery, such as on the pillar capitals, spoke of life – such as 'The Tree of Life. See the green men.' I mentioned the grotesques. 'But they're fun,' said Melvyn. It so happened that the building more or less coincided with the life of St Francis (1181–1226), he told me. He also said that the Gothic style, of the pointed arch, originated here, life straining up to the heavens.

My parking ticket was about to expire, and my host had domestic duties to perform. I would make fresh contact in the new year. I returned to the shop to pay for my High Parts Tour (£5.50 in a gift aid envelope) and noted the orange marmalade for sale, honouring that popular animal, Louis. There were samples on the counter.

Guide Neill Bonham arrived at 10.50, so we were able to start early. The High Parts Tour was just tremendous, one-to-one with someone who knew his stuff. It didn't surprise me that his favourite cathedral was Lincoln, a purist's choice. A fresh influence was conveyed: in 1300 the liturgy was changed, resulting in more processions, more complications and to more places – to all altars. The east end was rebuilt, parts showing Decorated and Perpendicular. It had already claimed the first pointed Gothic arches, and a revolutionary approach to columns and capitals. 'Even St Denis had round columns,' said Neill. We saw, in detail, the ingenuity of the Scissor Arches and supporting buttresses, some set in the surrounding stone. I needed to be shown this, along with the added vertical flutes on nave pillars, one style superimposed on another, and all seductive to observe and touch. Another historical snippet was revealed: King John's contretemps with the Pope (excommunicated between 1209 and 1213), resulted in the suspension of building. The detailed history was riveting, underlying what we now saw from the 13th and 14th centuries. We strode upwards. I shall just mention the Chilcote marble elements in pillars at the west end: purple and effective, they seemed quirky. I had to run my hand over the smooth surface.

From outside the building to the interior, the whole tour saw two hours come and go. Bullet points are best for some specialities into which to dip:

- Masons' marks in the pillars – more than 500 of them.
- Up the west front, the singing holes, allowing a voice to imbue the close with delicious sounds, reminiscent of the Sirens. A Palm Sunday procession was recommended.
- The sculpted inner towers – craftsmen applied their skill in places never to be on general display.
- The elaborately chiselled and painted clock, from triforium level, then behind it to note some of its winding gear. This was the second 19th century replacement. The 1392 item was to be seen in the South Kensington Science Museum. It has to be told that the manual clock chimer, Paul Fisher, had retired the previous August, necessitating electrification of the gear. Five generations of Fishers had wound the clock, starting 'after Leo returned from fighting in World War I'. Paul's title was 'Keeper of the Clock.' The brief involved 'an hour three times a week turning the three 250 kg weights 800 times'. (Wells Cathedral website).
- The triforium, my second after Westminster Abbey, was amenable by comparison, housing such items as the platens for painting the ceiling in its distinctively sinuous flower trail design.
- The north porch, workplace of the Master Mason. John Locke had been the artisan responsible for so much innovation in the building. The tracing floor, covered with refreshing plaster after project completion, was one of two such in the country. The space presented a remarkably smooth face, with a display of the method on an easel, looking like a series of concentric circles.
- Still on triforium level, candles on every surface in two rows, for the forthcoming carol concerts. Apparently one bank would be lit for each event – a huge amount for some minion to wade through. But only expect to witness it at this time of year.
- The traces of heat in the south transept, from a lightning strike in 1438. Part of the wall was pink, not a colour found in Mendip stone.
- Leap across to the north transept for some fan vaulting.

That's nine items – a tenth would be the fabulous view from the roof, including a sense of loss for the Reformation removal of the extensive chancery chapel beside the south transept, all too clear from above. On an ornamental pinnacle on the east side was the fresh figure of a fox with a mouthful of fowl as trophy. Seldom was a corbel so close that you could feel it.

We descended apace because: 'We've overrun – my wife will be waiting.' And so she was, by the doorway into the north transept. While Neill signed off in the virgers' office, she and I enjoyed a brief exchange about the mass of uniformed schoolchildren seated in the nave. 'They're going to Belgium, weather permitting,' she informed me. I had noted the importance of St Andrew here. Five services were scheduled for his day. The High Tour had been accommodated between 10 am Sung Eucharist and 12.25 pm Holy Communion. Ruth Clacee-Rowe, Visits Co-ordinator, did a good job in negotiating it. The final event, later on, was to be the Primary Schools Concert. That was one more than on Advent 2, the next Sunday.

The events so far were enough, but not all, as I confirmed my immediate visit to the Ven Dick Acworth, (Archdeacon Emeritus of Wells) at his house in a village nearby. The intention had been for him to join the High Parts Tour. He was unable to climb stairs having recently fallen on ice. There would have been 250 of them. For me, via a mutual friend, his claim to fame was the 26 day nationwide quest to visit all the 42 English cathedrals on his senior bus pass, a piece of economy extended by staying with a contact for every sojourn. Scores of years in the church had produced a host of, er, hosts. He did allocate one day of rest – day 16 between Sheffield and Southwell. I could understand that. The serendipitous Nottinghamshire country town was one you'd expect to present a challenge, and lovely to recline in awhile, if that is what he did. God must have been on his side, over 121 bus rides, over 2,371 miles! It was very clever, and rewarding, not least for the Wells Cathedral Girl Chorister Trust, who emerged better off to the tune of £14K from Dick's fund raising initiative. He left a handful of leaflets in each building:

1   A Bus Pass Pilgrimage to all Anglican Cathedrals in England: the fund raising document.

2   A bookmark on the subject of his present endeavours, with the invocation: Fact: Someone you know or love has experienced a mental illness and talking to you would help.

3   Cathedrals Pilgrimage: a collection of prayers, one of which, laid out like a goblet was the Chalice prayer. It was so impressive I shall reproduce it here:

A Chalice Prayer

Loving God, Father of all, you call us to
proclaim the good news of your Kingdom
in this beautiful but broken world.
in the power of your Spirit and by
the grace of this sacrament send
with joy and humility, with
steadfastness and truth.
Help us to use the gifts
and opportunities
you give
us,
and
so
make us
channels of
your peace that
all the world may come
to know and love you in your Son,
our Saviour Jesus Christ. Amen

Dick was good at compiling numbers. Here are some from the physical demands section: '37 towers climbed, 6810 steps ascended. At 8" a step I climbed 4540', so you could say I climbed Ben Bevis (4409')' Now, that's something to do in your retirement!'

On the subject of harmony within the corridors of Wells, Dick did report an instance during one of Canon Melvyn's month's residences, when he carried the can for staffing services. The new bishop, who was not president of a particular Eucharist service, insisted upon pulling rank over the dean and appearing at the end of the procession. In the Church of England the appointee to presidency holds sway. Melvyn insisted, thereby upstaging the bishop. Then Dick told me a snippet about a one-time Bishop of Lincoln. He had expressed the antithesis of the building's incredible status as a landmark in commenting on his diocese as 'Miles and miles of bugger all.' Dick's favourite was Ely, some way down the road from Lincoln, with the sheer wonder at the achievement of converting massive oak trees into the structure of the octagon so far off the ground. And it's still there.

I paid a further visit to Wells later on in the winter, for matters arising with Melvyn, in the rain this time. On the agenda were the following, for economy of space a further 'Three to See':

1   The mid-14th century Vicars' Close, evocatively chimneyed,
     and occupied by Vicars Choral among other cathedral
     personnel, the Cathedral School and, up the gradient at the far
     end, was available for lucrative lets to Americans. They would
     always have 'wonderful experiences' staying in such a setting.
     So would we all.
2   The Vicars' Hall, dining room (1342) – Melvyn employed an
     impossibly bulky key for access. Then we were able to peer
     up to the stairs on this north side. The story went that the
     bridge over the close was built in response to bad habits of the
     residents, who would engage with women of the town.
3   We met Kevin Spears, Librarian, who introduced his charge.
     The facility was in as good condition as that at Canterbury,
     the subject of a visit only a fortnight before. The role here was
     quite different, as there simply wasn't the profile for it to attract
     regular and erudite patronage. It was a resource centre for the
     cathedral and its guides. Mervyn had been intimately involved
     in its improvement up to 2000, when he retired, employing
     the cathedral carpenter to upgrade it to its present state. He
     had hoped that it would develop an appeal for the clergy of
     the diocese for theological purposes. The Library was blessed
     with some superb volumes, abiding, some chained, in elegant
     and ancient presses. Given recent developments, Kevin, who
     had been in post for three years, treated it as a resource centre
     for the cathedral and its guides. I shall cite a single example
     of the extravagant volumes we were able to see: 'De humani
     corporis fabrica (Basle, 1555) by Andreas Vesalius, or van
     Wesel of Brussels... the "Fabrica" is one of the great books
     of the 16th century. The dramatic illustrations, created by a
     student of Titian, brought new standard to anatomy... The
     work heralded the advent of biology as a subject'.

Mervyn had to leave. I was in the need of refreshment, and took the
opportunity to digest what I had been shown. Chapter Two was better than
ever. The Americano was steaming and full-flavoured, the Somerset apple
cake succulent to the point that I was tempted to wonder in which orchard
the apples had been plucked. And from which tree?
     The last words come from *Wells Cathedral 'The Minster beside
the great spring called Wiela',* by Robert Dunning, Richard Lewis and

Melvyn Matthews, (2005). Melvyn wrote: '… the crowd of statues on the West Front at Wells represents what one New Testament writer calls "a great cloud of witnesses", those who have gone on in front of the pilgrim and have reached the goal and are now standing in welcome as the visitor completes the last stages of their journey'. The west front is a fine place to start a visit, and close it.

Fig 39

Fig 40

[39] St Davids: Bishop Wyn Evans in
conversation over a cup of tea.
[40] Wells: Oaken Jack strikes bells with his
heels and right hand.
[41] Wells: Roof corbel of a fox devouring a
chicken.
[42] St Paul's: Sir Chris's motto: Resurgam =
I will arise.

Fig 41

Fig 42

31

St Paul's

St Paul

Province: Canterbury
Founded: 604
Present building: 1675–1710

Website: www.stpauls.co.uk
Tel: 0207 246 8350 (reception); 0207 246 8357 (admissions)
Email: reception@stpaulscathedral.org.uk;
admissions@stpaulscathedral.org.uk
Address: The Chapter House, St Paul's Churchyard, London EC4M 8AD

Three to See: The Dean's Staircase;
Jean Tijou iron work;
charred remains of effigies from the old cathedral

Red cross

Monday 13 September, 2010
Round on the north side of our destination Temple Bar had been translated from its traditional location at the boundary between the City and Westminster on Fleet Street, to form the gracious introduction to the almost demure Paternoster Square.

At 9.30 am precisely Robert Aldous was ready for the tour, having attached his badge of office. His on-call day job there was as a casual steward, which had been on and off for eighteen years. We mounted the steps and first bumped into Simon Russell Beale, paragon of the spoken and sung arts and former chorister here, and, level with the pillar base, Rand, ready for sprinklings into his sketch book. The start of our man Bob's spiel was promising, leading us back down the steps to an elaborate marble display – an 1886 copy of the 1712 statue of Queen Anne, illustrating the four kingdoms of her time: with England as Britannia, France wearing a helmet (QA wasn't in reality Queen of France. It is just that we didn't renounce our claim to the French throne until King William IV's time just before Victoria), Ireland clutching a harp. America was the best, illustrated by an Afro-Caribbean subject with a 'native' American ('Indian' to the Cowboys and Mr Longfellow) headdress. We were told that Queen Anne was often lampooned for her affection for spirits:

> *Brandy Nan, Brandy Nan, You're left in the lurch,*
> *Your faith to the gin shop, your back to the church.*

This statue was not included in the official tours, Bob told us, who was doing this as a special favour: we were his 'family' for the duration. And here was the 'red cross' (borrowed from Peter Ackroyd in *Illustrated London*, the cathedral of the second least-populated city in the country (2001 Census):

1   St Davids, of which we've heard enough for its size, 1,797
2   City of London, 7,185
3   Wells, 10,406
4   Bangor, next on the cathedrals list, 13,725

Once through the portals, our eyes were guided to the west door. By way of persuasive anecdote, Bob told us that recently a dead pigeon had been found on the stone gallery below with its innards eaten out, overwhelmed by maggots. Bob would be one of 18 stewards when scheduled for duty, nowadays, no more than three days a week as relief for those on holiday or off sick. 'So people can predict when they're going to be ill, or at the dentist,'

I wondered as he approached 76 years of age. He conveyed the impression that the cathedral was well off for such volunteer staff and so big and busy that a large complement was essential. 'It's a big job to coordinate it.' He showed me the roster page, a solid application of black on a white A4 sheet, to reveal who would be on when I returned for the service at 5 pm the next day. 'She's Scottish' he said of one. 'You'll have to listen carefully.' When the time came, I did. No problem.

Still pausing at the west door, Simon noticed features he said he'd never seen before. He had been a chorister between the ages of nine and thirteen, initially as a treble. In 1974, at 13, he left for the next stage of schooling at Clifton College, complete with its Ely-esque chapel tower, which Rand and I had admired from a tennis court below only weeks before. A frosty 'proper' guide, and guardian of her prerogative, enjoined in an exchange with Bob. He explained hurriedly, to which she replied: 'Oh, I see,' sternly, I thought. Bob was doing us a favour and made no claims to detailed knowledge. In fact he couldn't give answers on dates and numbers. Guides had to pass exams, while stewards were there to 'welcome'. He was emphasizing the benefits of the new century restoration, which took four years and had a stunning effect. 'The stonework prior to cleaning restoration', reported the nearby caption. The extensive detail, in this case projecting into the nave from the wall, was now to be observed. A plaque gave us the facts and a patch of uncleaned wall showed the murk in all its squalor, again hinting briefly at that wicked world, of which Peter Ackroyd wrote so evocatively: fire, disease, crime; streams of red and a moving feast on this site with five differently designed cathedral floor plans. 'Red is London's colour… London Bridge itself was "bespattered with the blood of little children"… the symbolism of the red cross and the words "Lord have mercy on us" has not been wasted on mythographers of the city' (during the great Plague of 1664, two years before the Fire.) A red cross is the quintessence of St Paul's Cathedral, City of London.

'Really you should come on a sunny day,' was the platitude from our guide. Rand had said of his back yard example: 'We must go to Canterbury on a fine day for the stained glass.' The aim this time was to deal with London, north of the Thames, in these two days. Simon woke me up in commenting: 'It's an odd cathedral, I think.' Somehow that lent reassurance. They're all odd, being singular, and already quirkiness was giving life to something tightly planned. Bach would have composed a cantata.

There was an Antony Gormley exhibit on display, above the southwest staircase, itself a marvel of geometrics/physics, one of Sir Christopher Wren's little aptitudes. What a bold decision, a self-supporting staircase, a 'mathematical folly' said Simon. It stood up all by itself, reminding me of M C Escher's monochromatic nonsenses of endless skybound blocks. A complex, formless piece, comprising a cloud-shaped (cumulus I guess) mass of aluminium-coloured metal thread, hung above the bottom on the flight of stairs, known as the Dean's Staircase, and worked superbly. I had already enjoyed Gormley artefacts in London, from the static figures on roof tops on the South Bank to the *White Room* in the Hayward Gallery. I wished there had been time to see more of this one, especially as the exhibition – *Flame II* – was temporary. I was disallowed from taking pictures as the policy here, exercised by both the current and previous deans, was to bar any photography. Shame! And misguided as far as I am concerned. Bob's official line was twofold: regarding danger, as cameras might drop from a great height and: 'Photography is not allowed because it detracts from the cathedral's function as a living church.' In all the cathedrals thus far I had not found a ban, only a charge, and that rarely. They had a point given this place's function as a tourist venue, on the Capital run. It was far and away the most popular cathedral in the country. In fact millions paid the large admission charge of £12.50. They came from a wide range of origins. The audio machines also did a lucrative trade in a number of languages.

As a chorister Simon had undergone the tough discipline of practice every day at 8 am. Some alternating was done. There had once been a bomb scare. 'We will go on', determined the dean. Simon also conjured up the image of the crib at Christmas. Actress Sarah Miles (daughter of Sir Bernard, of nearby Mermaid Theatre fame), constructed a crib from an immensity of seeds, both in variety and number. I asked him if this filled the space. 'Oh, yes, it made a presence' he said. Back to the nicely clean and clear west doors, Bob demonstrated that, massive though they were, they were easy to pull open. At St Dunstan's Chapel, next to the northwest tower, Simon told us how the choir used to practise there early in the mornings.

Up the nave we came across tall red panels. 'Part of an exhibition from Germany', commented Bob. I'd noticed a German phrase book in his flat (where I was staying), and he admitted to using his meagre schoolboy French and German on occasion when on duty. Then we spotted the man Wren himself, fully costumed and bewigged, regaling a class of children under the dome. 'But it's not him!' asserted Bob. 'He was short and stocky.' An imposter! We had arrived at the quire. Simon and I agreed, after an exchange, upon Decani allocated the left choir stalls, Cantoris the right, imagining that the former had to do with the Dean, who might suit the left. In any case, he thought that was where he was wont to sit. He recalled Barry Rose (but not with total affection), the Master of the Choir who had auditioned him.

In the north transept, a cavernous space with a single name,

'Middlesex Chapel', hung one of three copies of Holman Hunt's *The Light of the World*. It was refreshing to observe flags and light there, with a prevailing impression of the black and white tiled floor. Further on Rand and I, at least, enjoyed the sinuous form of a Henry Moore. Every such palace should have one, like the icons, of which I'd so far counted two, larger than average.

A better press than Barry Rose was reserved for Grinling Gibbons, one of Sir Chris's special contributors, and there were few enough of those. He struck lucky with the ones he secured. GG was responsible for the choir stalls, whose perimeter we now circled. First was the door. 'Organista' was inscribed for all the world suggesting a confessional, dark and forbidding, but actually led up to the organ loft, where our guest was detailed on occasion to turn pages. That was a penalty. He would avoid incurring such a fate. Access to the organ was now from Cantoris. He moved on to his memory of the cast of *Hair* attending the cathedral. What price dope or incense in his first term in 1969. On the other side was now a 'Viewing Point'. We'd never heard the like. It was the main entrance in Simon's day. Now it was where you were instructed to admire, gape in awe. Perhaps the ban on snaps fostered concentration. At this point in our proceedings an hour had been reached on the clock. This meant a brief prayer session, perhaps delivered by a pastoral priest. I told Bob we'd witnessed the same at Southwell, Exeter etc. He seemed pleasantly surprised.

Next we hit upon a joy: a baldacchino consecrated as recently as 1958. The present high altar underneath replaced the one destroyed in the War, along with the reredos. I put a name to the baldacchino without demur. I was glad to see one after Derby. Its introduction was a latter day reward for Sir Chris, who had designed it centuries before its construction. It was part of post war rebuilding, and a fine addition it is, completing the massiveness of quire and ambulatory. 'A bomb fell there,' recalled Simon. 'Oh yes. It didn't explode but caused a lot of damage,' said our host, whose brother-in-law had done the French polishing of the baldacchino's sugar twist columns. It did look good this morning. He said he liked to spin this yarn to Americans, who loved the long version of the story. There was a twinkle in his eye. In the American Chapel behind (also known as 'Jesus'), stained glass windows and surrounding carvings depict symbols connected with the USA. There hung a mural to 'America', on whose border were a few of its citizens in evidence. Bob showed us an easily-missed image of a rocket ascending, to indicate space travel. Quite cute, really, and so discreet. I'm glad he bothered. There were symbols of all the US states. 'Yes, 50' he confirmed. A bigger number followed – the 28,000 names of US servicemen who had perished, inscribed in a hefty book. This was the actual American

Roll of Honour. A page was turned every day. 'Very middle of the road', whispered Simon, and when a hint of incense was observed, 'We didn't do smells and bells.' There were stations for those so inclined to buy and light a candle. 'That's a new development.' 'It's universal', I replied, almost slipping down a shallow dark step. These developments amounted to a trend closing up the extremes of doctrine, with perhaps growing information and acceptance; also tourism, that other ubiquitous influence.

Rand was disappointed to note the date '1890' on the top decorated part of the iron gates. Bob reassured him that the gates were actually the original Jean Tijou works, but we felt it was confusing as it looked as if the whole lot was Victorian. He agreed. In the south choir aisle he had opened a huge tome, concealed under a cut of old pink velvet. This book was a copy of the American roll of honour, which relatives can examine and search for names. The introduction was beautifully phrased in Dwight Eisenhower's hand – two of them: A to J and K to Zee for 1941–45.

Simon then recalled the strict dress code: Eton collars set the stamp. When I asked he denied that corporal punishment was used, saying it wasn't needed. It sounded a bit like the discipline of drama school, something both he and Bob had been through. We arrived at the charred effigy of one of the 17th century's naughtiest boys, John Donne, who, from an upbringing of Catholicism underwent conversion eventually to become Dean of St Paul's. A processional staff was hanging there, which prompted Simon to inform us: 'The Head Boy used to carry it as high as possible.' 'You mean you did.' 'Yes' he giggled. 'To impress?' 'Of course.' And next, opposite, under the choir stalls, was the Bishop's Closet. 'Virgers' said Bob, 'are the stage managers of the cathedral.' That was their domain.

It was time for a Queen Mother story. She used to attend the annual service of the Friends of St Paul's. After the service she would retire to the Dean's Vestry while staging was set up for a recital by the choristers in her honour. During this spell a butler would prepare a gin and tonic for her. One year he couldn't come, so another butler, from the chapter house, had to do it. He was most agitated as to how to fix her tipple. Not being versed in our national aperitif, and fearing Her Majesty would be demanding as to measures, he asked if it was all right. 'Oh yes, but next time make it a double.' We watched as an official applied a heavy key to a south side door. 'Have a peak' said Bob. This was the Dean's Vestry itself. I made out some robes and not much else.

A ponderous marble memorial came into view. Prominent was a nude, perhaps angelic, male child. Bob told us how he caught an enthusiast kissing his bottom. And another: Sir Harry Smith Parkes, who had penetrating eyes, which on close inspection turned out to be hollow. Also in evidence were a bible, spectacles and slippers. The bust of the Queen Mother, marking her centenary, was unveiled by the Princess Royal but of course the subject was unable to see it distinctly. The good news was that she was able to be there at all. In most cases the famous were honoured by way of plaques: Sir Alexander Fleming was one (1881–1955: was it as recent as 1928 that he discovered penicillin?). One of the most striking exhibits, for that is what much of this had become for the relentless procession of visitors, was a mosaic, the product of Holloway prisoners.

We reached the crypt where Simon and Rand considered the Falklands display a lovely piece of work. Indeed it was refreshing to see something comparatively modern (April to June 1982) and vigorous. A strong dark casket had pride of place, erected on a plinth above us, perfectly sited under the centre of the dome. It was the place intended by Henry VIII for Cardinal Wolsey, who proceeded to fall out of favour. The honour had eventually been conferred on Admiral Lord Nelson, two and a half centuries later. This was commodious enough for a thousand talking points. High on the list were my favourites, which had spooked Simon throughout his career in the building: the charred and maimed remains of effigies from the old cathedral, truncated bodies rescued from the ashes of 1666. An American had asked: 'Were they thalidomide cases?' And to think that it was in the building then occupying this space that there was a fair in the middle at one stage, where horses were bought and sold, servants hired and lawyers met their clients, tombs being used as shop counters. In fact, it may have been that the standard trading measurement 'a foot' was taken from the carved boot of Algar, 1st Prebendary of Islington. Later, Oliver Cromwell had employed the crypt as a cavalry barracks. By the middle of the 17th century it was a near ruin. The spire of Old St Paul's had been taller than the dome which replaced it. OSP was overdue for a makeover by the time of the reintroduction of the Stuart line to the throne. Going back in time, in the 14th century, it would have been N° 2 in the 'Ten Places to See in London' according to Ian Mortimer (*The Time Traveller's Guide):* This church, started in the twelfth century and recently extended (finished in 1314), is one of the most impressive in the country. At 585' long, it is the third-longest church in the whole of Christendom. Its 489' spire is the second-tallest in England, dwarfing that of Salisbury (404') and only second to that of Lincoln Cathedral (535'). But forget statistics. It is the beauty of the church, especially its rose window at the east end, and its chapter house – for which it deserves to be on any list of London sights. The top recommendation was London Bridge.

On the north side of the crypt at the Treasury, Bob told us: 'The former treasury used to contain a range of silverware, ornate vestments and such like, but it did not belong to the cathedral, whose own treasures had been stolen at one time in its history.' It had experienced a profound change of use. What greeted us was innovatory and, at the time, I'm sure unique: a virtual reality display all round the walls, spilling over onto floor, columns and ceiling. After a while Simon was drifting off, and Bob called him back in an authoritative tone. 'You must stay for this – there's not much more.' So assertive! But what we were waiting for never materialized: a visual display of the upper galleries, where we would tread but Simon would miss: the climb up all those steps to the roof, with its spectacular panorama. That was a pity as it rendered the film rather superficial and gimmicky. There wasn't enough in it to inform or attract you about the building. This seemed to be a plaything of those detailed to organize it. Could do better! Bob was slightly abashed after his emphasis on its worth. We all left the paying guests part of the basement. Simon departed at this point 'to go to the supermarket', not to rest before the show as was mooted by Rand. His call was actually many hours later.

The crypt was a resting place for literati, artists and the military. We passed memorials to Sir Joshua Reynolds, J M W Turner, RA, the Duke of Wellington and my choice, Lichfield man Samuel Johnson among others. We three survivors repaired through the barrier to Café@StPaul's for recovery in the public section of the basement, beset by elegant pillars. My coffee was excellent but, as I expected, it was a franchise, a fully-developed business, as was the Restaurant (further on and up market, but offering what may well have been a tasty Express Lunch for £15). Everything was 'Premier League' here in its delivery. The trappings of St Paul's Cathedral were magnificent and sensitive to the market in which it found itself, vast and eminently accessible. I resisted the 'Barmbrack, Coffe walnut (sic), and Toffie Shortbread (sic, too)' but in search of a photograph for the book, being banned from snapping up to now, took one of another fetching item, where there could be no reprimand. I asked the fey assistant what it was. 'Furry cakes' said he. 'Did you make them yourself?' I immediately realized my crassness – he had said 'fairy' not 'furry' and no way would they have been made on the premises. The same products had been delivered to a multitude of enterprises in the City. Bob's coffee (up to the brim) was spilt by the cashier, and Rand was baffled by all the jugs and baskets for condiments and add-ons in search of milk. I expect it was skimmed, therefore insipid, and was most content with my (black) Americano. Bob then spilt more of the coffee himself. We chose the same table where Bob had introduced me to the top man, the Dean's Virger, on first arriving in the cathedral that morning. The chap was enjoying a quiet time with three of his underlings in anticipation of the rush. He had given a pithy description of the next day's 5 pm service, Eucharist, not Evensong, to celebrate the annual candle presentation. This was so off the wall that the information confirmed my need to attend it. While on catering, I have to mention the partnership Bompas and Parr (they have first names, too, even though they're old Etonians: Sam and Harry). They were jellymongers, according to Gerard Gilbert in *The Independent* (21/7/10). Their relevance is in some of the designs adopted in their creations: St Paul's Cathedral and the (wobbly) Millennium Bridge. That was down to Parr's architecture training. A slice, or spoonful, of the dome would have been more appealing than a furry cake. You do not have to wonder as to choice of flavour. The recipes in the article (by Nigella Lawson) were 'Gin and Tonic' and 'Easy Lemon'.

Leaving the seating area we bumped into a gaggle of guides. The frosty woman was one, who looked askance when I opined that Bob was giving us an excellent tour. 'Don't say that,' said he, aside. 'To them I'm not a guide,' so I added, for general hearing 'It's very personal.' A quick perusal of the shop was called for. Rand bought two post cards here: he rated St Paul's highly. One depicted the large model of the cathedral, something we weren't able to see. I found shot glasses, called 'tot' glasses, maybe to justify the exorbitant price: £16.99 (plain ones were £9.99). The one at Southwell had been £5.99, but that's in the sticks. Five Christmas cards cost £3.50. Well, the average punter would be a big-budget traveller or a Paternoster Square commuter, I surmise. The shop's staff haven't always subscribed to the assumed ethic of honesty: in 2010 Southwark Crown court heard the case of Alison Robinson, former manager. She was jailed for eight months 'after conning her employers out of £58,000. (She) ordered thousands of pounds' worth of 'worldwide' stamps on the shop's account before selling them on eBay... The 44-year-old moved to Brixham in Devon with her husband after falsifying internal records to cover up the swindle. But a private investigator tracked her down to her new home when an audit at the shop revealed huge unexplained losses. She admitted obtaining property by deception between February 2006 and May 2007 and sold her house to pay the money back to the cathedral... She later said she carried out the fraud as a 'means of escape' from acting as a carer to her parents. But Judge Martin Beddoc pointed out she continued the scam after they died, leaving her an inheritance of £150,000. He said: "This was a deliberate course of dishonesty, quite carefully planned." But the sentence was reduced because she had repaid the money.' *Metro, London.*

Emerging, I glanced back down the length of the space, abounding with every category of visitor. The crypt itself was further on, replete with tills and gift aid envelopes. The basement had been transformed into a very effective sequence of spaces.

Next we reached that high spot: the Whispering Gallery. Rand and I had mounted all 257 steps, while Bob used the lift (he claimed that he had to see someone, but I reckon he wimped out). We tried out the trick, to test the physical property of the wall to convey sound at a curved distance. We were 50 yards apart. It worked. Bob joined us. More numbers: 119 steps to the Stone Gallery and 152 to the Golden one of that name. We saw the Eiffel Tower to the south. Actually it was the Crystal Palace – I am relaying the comment of one American, or many. The view was the best, most pertinent at the time being the Stratford E Olympic dome, conveniently set between tower blocks. Should I ever venture here again, time only could tell what it would all look like, or be doing. Would it stay as a landmark building for other sports use? Round to the north Rand was asking about Newgate, The Old Bailey, Wren churches. And my emphasis was to do with this very afternoon: Temple Church, elusively deep in Inns of Court territory near the western boundary of the City. It was too low to be visible, though we made out the elegance of St Bride's in the foreground, whose tiered spire had inspired the design of wedding cakes.

On the descent Bob applied his privilege – the lift from Whispering Gallery to crypt. The steps hadn't been as challenging as those to the roof of St Mary Redcliffe, Bristol a few days earlier, as Sir Chris had designed one set up and another down. Once down and out on the south side of the cathedral, the man's epigram stood there for all to see, once our friendly steward located it, rather high up: 'Resurgam' – I will arise. And that was to represent the 'red cross' cathedral in photographic form. The man was as good as his word. This was his crowning glory. I liked the aphorism I read somewhere: 'Inside St Paul's is all church, outside it is all dome.' The final sight outside was Bainbridge Copnall's black statue of Thomas Becket, acquired in 1973, the year of the artist's demise, just over eight hundred years after the murder – the piece is strong in depicting the subject's agonizing last moments.

Bob steered us to the Old Deanery, the fine residence of the Bishop of London. Next, the Cockpit was Bob's chosen hostelry for a pint and sandwich, for a respite after his valiant tour. The pub was a good choice, but lacking what we had experienced at every turn in the cathedral: his colleagues. Instead it was busy with local people and visitors – our neighbours were from Germany. The barman unearthed a piece of publicity, which told us: 'The present was constructed in the early 1840s. After cockfighting was prohibited in 1849, the name was changed (from The Three Castles) to commemorate the last venue in London to hold, legal, cockfighting.' It got a vote of confidence from us all.

Rand and I were to pursue an afternoon of church and Inns of Court garden exposure. St Bride's was first, but not to be followed by Temple Church, which was closed that day for beautification. At length it was back to Bob and me to see Simon in excellent form in *Deathtrap* at the Noel Coward Theatre, a revival of Ira Levin's 1978 thriller. 'A play to kill for' announced the flyer. Rand's departure after a rewarding meal (cottage pie) at Bob's club was marked later by an urgent call: 'I've left my coat there.' Clearly the day had affected his focus. No matter, it was still there, when I returned the next lunchtime on the way to Westminster.

Tuesday 14 September – Westminster Abbey
This building is essential to include alongside St Paul's. London. It is writ large in public consciousness. Also, not that it matters, it was a cathedral between 1540 and 1550. 'Survival due to unique status as royal coronation and burial church' (*Observer's Book of Cathedrals*).

> **Three to See:** Ninian Comper's stained glass windows in the triforium, but gaining access might be tricky;
> Royal Ballet memorial;
> Henry VII's Chapel.

This was the complementary arrangement:

1   I couldn't go to St Paul's without acknowledging the Royal Peculiar of Westminster Abbey, so close to it in history and the heart.
2   The Toff did the organizing for Westminster Abbey, initiated by a letter to the Dean, The Very Revd Dr John Hall. It came to fruition as part of this two-day exposure to London things north of the Thames. This was so good, to have something taken out of my hands. The Pope was coming, to this building, not the cathedral.

Toff and I met at Westminster tube station for a quick snack at St Stephens Tavern next door, and a snizz of Pinot Grigio: 'We don't want to smell of alcohol.'

Right on the dot of 2 pm we met Dr Tony Trowles at the Great West Door. He turned out to have a most detailed knowledge of the abbey. Hot on his heels was the briefest of introductions to the Dean. Blink and you'd have missed him. Busy, I'm sure. I would have loved to discover what it meant to be dean of this abbey, this 'Peculiar' entity. As it was Tony took us round, thus obviating the need to pay £15, the highest admission charge on the tour. The 1 million visitors a year account for 85% of the total receipts.

I was burdened by rucksack as well as shoulder bag, having vacated Bob's abode, and got a really good transport deal for the day: £3.50 for several journeys and means of transport. 'Not really', said Tony when I asked if I could leave it somewhere. 'It's safer with you.' That didn't recommend security at the abbey. It was also most irksome. Perhaps there were extenuating circumstances as the place was beside itself with the forthcoming papal visit. Such top level occasions are no rarity – every royal coronation since William I in 1066 has taken place here. The pontiff was to visit Archbishop Rowan in Lambert Palace, say prayers with him at the Shrine of St Edward the Confessor, having shaken hands with the Canon Steward, Jane Hedges. That got the most media footage. And that was after meeting a mass of schoolchildren in Twickenham. He was to speak in Westminster Hall as well (the setting for the trial of Thomas More when he refused Henry VIII's moves to divorce Catherine of Aragon).

The thrust for the Toff, who was still revelling in the memory of our trip to Liverpool in April, was his great grandfather. Sir Ninian Comper (1864–1960) had designed a significant number of stained glass windows, most obviously in a long, full-length sequence in the north aisle. There, Sir Ninian worked with J Armitage Robinson (1858–1933), who wrote about the abbey in the Middle Ages. We saw Henry III, with a model of the abbey, and Henry V (a cat was lurking below his figure), coupled with William of Colchester (a pelican stood among many images). Seeing the cat I asked Tony if one was in residence. 'There was one – Biggles – but he attacked visitors. He had a tendency to wander up to visitors, innocently. They'd try to stroke him and he'd pounce. He went to the country.' 'Like valuables from the abbey during the War' I suggested. 'Sort of.' We found more windows in the north transept. The place was notable for its officials in red and then green. Red was for marshals, green for welcomers, I think. There was a bank of the green ones, several of each gender, along a trestle table under the windows, uneasily perched between endless memorials from an age when commemoration seemed to have been all (the tedious part of the 19th century). But we did find some good stuff. In the poets' section in the south transept was a recent one, which Tony showed us, funded and placed by the Royal Ballet in October 2009, the words in a quasi-artistic font to Ninette Valois, Frederick Ashton, Constant Lambert and Margot Fonteyn. Then Eddie the marshal came to our assistance as we reached another barrier: 'Can I help you?' Without demur he added 'This is east and that is west.' Actually some humour was welcome after all the earnest marble. Tony had proffered the information: there were 3,000 burials and 600 monuments. Over lunch I had heard from The Toff about the writings of Anthony Trollope (1815–1882) and the place of religion there. Here was his resting place. 'Creator of Barsetshire' it said. I still didn't have an answer as to which work to try out to help the narrative in this tome. Toff conveyed the impression that an awful amount of reading would be required. And a window in Poets' Corner had blown out in the War. Augustan poet Alexander Pope (1678–1744) was featured. It took my binoculars to read the caption: 'And heaven is won by violence of song.'

We arrived back at the southwest corner where through the door we were bound to mount 73 steps – my burden made it seem worse than St Paul's – to my first ever triforium, to see the best Ninian Comper work, two stained glass windows. Happily one showed Queen Eleanor, consort of Edward I. To her right was Lady Margaret Beaufort, mother of Henry VII. They were both good eggs, I'd discovered in recent reading. Toff wondered about the choice of position, out of the way of any audience. Beside this, Tony's news was excellent that plans were afoot to raise funds to turn the whole extensive u-shape of this space into a public area. The mooted cost was £12m – a brief of the Development Director. The conversion would be contingent upon a lift being inserted somewhere, possibly subtly outside by a projecting pillar. These windows would become a strong feature. This reminded me of an item in *The Independent on Sunday* (20/6/10), with the headline: 'English Heritage shows how to get a head at the abbey.' During the restoration of the 13th century Chapter House, 'A new collection of heads and gargoyles ("Great," say I, as there aren't enough gargoyles around), was commissioned to replace the weathered Victorian ones, and a select few bureaucrats involved in the project have enjoyed the privilege of having their contribution to the project carved in stone.' This was necessitated by 'years of traffic pollution, smoke from Battersea power station and weather erosion.' The revelation incited rage from various quarters, such as 'Will Hurst, news editor of the architects' weekly *Building Design*, (who) said: "It is hard to understand how English Heritage apparently saw fit to award itself such an honour. In contrast to the original gargoyles, this exercise seems humourless, unimaginative and indulgent."'

I was engaging Tony in conversation about Royal Peculiars. 'It's what we can't do that's important – it gives us independence not to have a diocese. We can do things other than mainstream.' It was a neutral space, for dean and queen, our monarch being a visitor to the abbey. Slightly apart in this vast barnlike space, Toff was in close discourse with carpenter Ray, one of many artisans on the Abbey's payroll, who was attending to duties in the mustier corners there, a location surely rife with possibilities for a resident feline. There was two of each, also plumbers, electricians and stone masons, as well as a handyman. There were probably others as well. And the choir was mentioned: 30 boys – no space for girls. Ray and his peers were managed by the Clerk of the Works, next up to the Receiver General. As ever, these titles come out as evocative, some from time immemorial. On the way to the steps, we happened upon poet John Gay's memorial. I found out that this had been moved out of the way of newly discovered, i.e. thought to be more important, wall paintings in the 1930s. Alexander Pope (1688–1744), though misshapen, was a pall-bearer at his funeral aged 47 in 1632. He wrote this:

> Of manners gentle, of affections mild;
> In wit a man; simplicity a child;
> With native humour temp'ring virtuous rage,
> Form'd to delight at once and lash the Age:
> Above temptation, in a low estate,
> And uncorrupted, e'en among the Great;
> A safe companion, and an easy friend,
> Unblam'd thro' life, lamented in the end.
> These are thy honours! Not that here thy bust
> Is mix'd with heroes, or with kings thy dust;
> But that the worthy and the good shall say,
> Striking their pensive bosoms -Here lies GAY.

A. Pope

The report went that the funeral was lavish. And the triforium was marvellous, with views right down the nave to the west window with not an ugly memorial in sight. Cousin Michael, the Christ Church Houseman who accompanied me to Oxford, was wont to sing from there while a pupil at Westminster School. The abbey was its chapel (three services on Sundays).

To invite the public would be another money spinner, which of course underlies the £12m project. Once back on tourist level Tony made his excuses. We received parting gifts: a postcard each of *Detail from a banner*, designed by J Ninian Comper, presented to Westminster Abbey by the Girls' Friendly Society, 1922. The illustration was of Virgin and Child with a lily and two roses, one each of York and Lancaster persuasion. We thanked him and made our own way up to Henry VII's Chapel, renowned for its fan vaulting, and the Lady Chapel for a final perambulation. At the top the way was barred by a conglomeration of Asians with black weapons. We retreated, deciding it was time for some tea. That was in the cloister. So were some mugs, on sale at £6.50 (carrying Westminster Abbey's image), and £4.50 for the earthenware version. The tea was delivered in a plastic cup, which we sipped on the cold and damp ledge in the West Cloister, with a view of the Houses of Parliament. I recalled staying with my friend Graham as guests of David Dorey, former Dean's Verger (in post from 1982 until his retirement in 2003). He oversaw such poignant events as the funeral of the Queen Mother. He lived in the neighbouring Little Cloister, so peaceful only yards from the busy thoroughfare, with peregrine falcons visible on the roof and a view of a fine tranquil garden. It even provided a car space for Graham, his friend from Coventry Cathedral days. The Queen once, on the occasion of the Fortieth Anniversary of her reign, asked David about his previous job. When she learned that it had been at the very modern cathedral of Coventry she said: 'Oh, different as chalk from cheese!'

I Just Love People, a celebration of the life of David Dorey by Revd John Richards. The author wrote alternative words to a favourite hymn, the content saying something about David's quality:

> *Chorus:*
> *All things bright and beautiful;*
> *All creatures great and small*
> *All things bright and beautiful*
> *King David wears them all!*
>
> *He wears his glowing colours,*
> *His scarlet shouts and sings;*
> *The envy of all creatures –*
> *Especially those with wings,* Chorus
>
> *Our God created colours,*
> *Some quiet and some loud*
> *But David likes the latter*
> *Of which he is so proud!* Chorus…

Red is the colour of Westminster Abbey, as is the cross of St Paul's. We both needed relief as we left. Eddie (favourite cathedral Durham, whence he came), who had been chatting with us about his 18-strong crew, conducted us back through the triforium door to 'The Queen's closet'.

Once on the streets, it was raining again as I leapt on a suitable bus. I found myself in the nave of St Paul's. The stewards were directing those bound for the service to the dome section, armed with 20-page 'Sung Eucharist – Holy Cross Day' service booklets. Seats were laid out in two halves, reflecting Decani and Cantoris for Simon's benefit had he not been preparing for his *Deathtrap* duties at that time. Another significant figure in evidence was no doubt doing just that. The Revd Canon Dr Giles Fraser, 46, formerly vicar of Putney, was to deliver the sermon. I had heard him on *Thought for the Day* on Radio 4's *Today* programme, and had formed the impression of a forthright, clear-thinking progressive cleric. Mention was made in the order of service of the emblems of the church. It read 'The cross on which Jesus Christ was crucified has become the universal symbol for Christianity, replacing the fish symbol of the early church, though the latter has been revived in recent times… ' (from *Exciting Times*). In the same forthright way that he habitually dealt with the few minutes' worth of subject for the day on the radio at 7.48 am he spoke out to the scattered listeners, who numbered enough to make a quorum of opinion. The seats were placed under that startling dome. The entire event was almost submerged in incense. The cross had an offensive connotation to early Christians, involving a rebranding after Constantine, the Roman emperor responsible for mobilizing the church (see his statue at York Minster). Preacher Giles was compelling in a curiously polyglot gathering. Then something extraordinary happened. A woman of uncertain description, but I recall probably youngish, easternish and in downplayed tourist garb, marched precisely up the centre to the geometrical decoration under the Dome and in front of the altar, behind which were seated the president and two officers (one of them our Giles). The woman knelt down, extended her arms skywards, immediately leapt up, stood, gathering herself for a second, and shouted: 'Go to fucking hell!' You couldn't be sure whether cross or fish, or even fowl, came into it. There was no disruption, the next point of singularity coming a couple of minutes later when the Prayers of Intercession from the President kicked off with 'Richard our bishop, Rowan our archbishop and Pope Benedict'. And again soon enough came the central feature of this special communion service. 'The Master and Wardens of the Wax Chandlers' Company make their annual presentation of candles to the Cathedral'. The Master Wax Chandler had risen from his seat at the front of Cantoris to explain to the President and all present that this was a simple traditional ceremony, appropriate at this time, 70 years on from the destruction of 1940. 'Please accept this gift of candles, for use in the divine worship of this Cathedral Church. May they be a light upon the path of all whose pilgrimage brings them to this place.'

For me that concluded this visit to the Diocese of London. It wasn't simple as that, given the Pope's imminent invasion, and reportage thereof. As he arrived we heard comment first from his attendant, Cardinal Casper, who slagged Britain off as seeming a 'Third World country', in the German press, before setting foot at Heathrow. He might have been right if provoked by that rather unpleasant airport, but his comments were interpreted in the context of the big issue of secularism. It seems he went straight back home, under instruction. Then, who else but Canon Giles was interviewed on *Today* (16/9/10) by Justin Webb, the subject the Pope's visit given this very new and aggressive secularism. A vigorous analysis ensued, Giles finally saying that at Putney he had a very strong relationship with his opposite number: parish priest to parish priest. There was plenty more broadcast and written on the subject of the Pope's visit and Cardinal Newman, but St Paul's and the Abbey had been absorbed. Next I was bound for North Wales, perhaps for some light relief.

Finally a non-sequitur: did you know that one of the chambers at Gough's Cave at Cheddar Gorge was named after 'the beautiful soaring chambers' of St Paul's Cathedral?

32

Bangor

St Deiniol

Province: Wales
Founded: 546
Present building started: main work 1496–1532, rebuilt from 1445 having been sacked by Owain Glendower in 1404
Restored: 1870–80, George Gilbert Scott

Website: www.churchinwales.org.uk
Tel: 01248 353983, 01248 362840
Email: martinbrown@churchinwales.org.uk
Address: Cathedral Close, Bangor, Gwynedd County LL57 1LH

Three to See: Thompson's Mouse Marks, carved in wood around the building;
rood screen;
floor tiles around the chancel

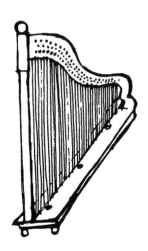

Harp

Sunday 19 September 2010

But first, the Saturday journey. The first of many stark and satisfying contrasts with the recent visit to the capital was transport. This trek to and around North Wales had to be by car. There was to be no repeat of the luxury of easy transfer in London from Cathedral to Royal Peculiar and all that lay between. This was a land of ancient traditions and an Anglicanism imposed in areas speaking their traditional vernacular.

It was a long journey and difficult to find the two things essential to break it: coffee and an abbey. My Bartholomew Historic Series orange (nasty shade thereof) *Cathedrals & Abbeys Map of the British Isles* did, in the end come up trumps, along with the trusty *Treasures of Britain*, perhaps a case of 'the old ones are the best'. I chose an unorthodox route which led to Ruabon, an attractive name I reckoned, and perhaps, in this age of the retired tourist, offering a coffee shop. The elegant Wynnstay Arms was most definitely closed, and nothing else reduced the unpromising look of a sad place. Perhaps this was linked to the local river Dee and former industry alongside it. I repaired to Llangollen, along a road reminiscent of the Pennine spine route (A646) between Todmorden and Halifax, which a few months before proved to be littered with dead road house pubs. It was the same here: much had been lost. Perhaps it was all now left to the big resort, famed for those leisure industry transport staples, canal boats and steam railway.

I found the Royal Hotel, on the bridge over the river, and enjoyed a change of seat types (comfortable armchair) and an Americano. The Bartholomew map had crosses for a number of ecclesiastical sites. This was the comment, a caption under a pencil drawing of the ruins of Valle Crucis Abbey nearby: 'Madog ap Gruffydd, Prince of Powis, established this abbey in 1201. Part of the church still stands, with a good range of monastic buildings.' There was no guarantee of anything – extent, quality or access – but as Valle Crucis was also in *T of B* and seemed to be located just on the north side of the coffee stop, I decided to go for it. There was soon a sign on the road, leading to a riverside caravan park. This enterprise had sensibly followed the example of the abbey, also on the banks. The leaflet stated: 'A visit to this fascinating site evokes the lives of the Cistercian monks.' They 'loved all things austere. Solitude ruled absolute. Finding this remote yet magical location must have at least raised a smile amongst the serious-mined brethren.' Indeed, and so long after the original building in 1201, much of it remains to enchant in a glorious setting. This is a beautiful part of the world.

But I was bound for Flint, to pick up companion Wakey. It started raining just as I (eventually) conquered the road system and found the little slip road, which led to the station. The weather did not improve, even until the next day. We found ourselves in Rhyl, that well-known seaside resort with golden sands and a notable social problem. As it was nearly 1 pm by now, we consulted the *Good Beer Guide* for somewhere to stop for lunch; also to escape from the deluge. Our choice was easy. The Swan was close. Over the pint, we devoured a lush omelette (I enjoyed that) and meat pie (and Wakey his). Both meals came with chips, which were very good: hot, crispy and fulsome. We set about preparing reading round the subject for the morrow: Bangor Cathedral.

Now for Sunday. Through the morning rain, we found an indoor car park. This was not an easy place for motor management, typical of an old market town adjusting to modern times. The message was: don't bring a car. We had done and opted for £1 worth of parking, for three hours. We did a perambulation of the cathedral, 'chunky' as Wakey said, and somehow the trappings of the ecclesiastical seemed to form an open enclave within the town. That was a clever contrivance in such a small space, and is down to the 'fence'. The word actually means fence, the enclosure on the site. We were to spend time examining a proud exhibit in the north aisle, explaining the origins of this. It provided a visual display, which included a (proverbial) fence, actually a massive basket, containing a collection of early medieval carpenter's tools, similar to the ones that would have been used to construct the first church. The centrepiece was a man-sized black-bearded puppet, which had been occupied by some lucky person in the procession through the city earlier in the year. We reckoned a poor chap required to get into that might have perspired somewhat.

But first came the service. We entered by the west door, in pleasing modern glass for greater light, to find the Welsh Language service drawing to a close. The 11 am Eucharist had the Revd Canon Dr Sue Jones as President. It was a rare thing to hear the chants sung by a woman. The greatest other presence was also female: The Revd Lynne Perry. She delivered the sermon and made reference to her youth in Somerset. She had seen Heinz perform in the Gaumont, Taunton. I'd seen pop group Sparks there in 1975, so that was worth an exchange afterwards, during which she nominated Bangor as her favourite cathedral. 'Small and personal', she said. In the sermon she also brought up Barbara Windsor's character in *Eastenders*, as an example of someone who tried to hold the reigns of power. She had left the drama a week before. It was news at the time, which is why I mention it! The Dean, Alun Hawkins, had been the prayer deliverer, mentioning Cardinal Newman, who that very day was to be taken on the first stage to sanctification by the Pope, in the final leg of his visit in the Birmingham area.

Cathedrals, Abbeys, and Churches of England and Wales set the scene well, albeit from the distance of 1891. R H Hill wrote:

> *Those who regard the historic monuments of Welsh antiquity from a general standpoint must be content to find fewer evidences of power, wealth, and lavish taste in the principality than on the other side of the English border. A more ancient yet scantier civilisation, the natural poverty of moor and mountain, the long struggle for independence, the isolation of a distinct race and language, have tended to produce this result, which is nevertheless in some degree atoned for to the sight-seer by the beautiful setting of the jewels which remain in Wales, and to the church (in North Wales, at least) by its continued possession of nearly all those rectorial rights which elsewhere became first the appanage of religious houses, and next the prey of the spoiler. In the first rank of these monuments stands Bangor Cathedral, the seat of one of the most ancient among existing British sees, dating as it does from the time when Christianity seems first to have gained a permanent footing in Venedotia or North Wales, and to have rooted itself in certain definite localities. St Daniel, or Deiniol, made the first settlement here about 550.*

The illustration accompanying this shows 'interior, looking west' which lacks the feature I concluded during the service to be an excellent unifier. This was the rood screen at the top of the nave, by Oldrid Scott (1841–1913), son of George Gilbert. Its curved central section echoed the residual round Romanesque columns beside it, and suited in size and shape, to bring the line of vision up the dark-pewed and bright-tiled floor through the chancel to the east end. The east window worked, too, even on such a dull morning.

The cathedral all seemed of a piece through its variations. This must partly be ascribed to the architect, of whom this was one of his 'choicest restorations'. Those tiles were succeeded among the choir stalls by copies of the medieval ones, now kept under the carpet in the shop. Double negative whammy for us: shop shut and tiles not to be uncovered anyway. It didn't matter as what we saw proved a delight with a wide range of colours and motifs: a sequence of ancient symbols.

There were aspects of the service to report: a choir of only ten men and boys, not a bit like the professionalism of St Paul's, and imperfectly executed. This didn't matter as the whole spirit of the service was welcoming and local, as a parish church rather than cathedral. A woman opposite made the effort to welcome Wakey personally after the service. There was no coffee session, partly because of the small congregation (40 against 90 the previous week, we were told) and the date: it was Fresher-time at the university on the hill above. Its towered landmark was often mistaken for the cathedral, but several generations younger and we heard of the occasion when the weather vane, at present a fine shiny cockerel, was stolen by students. The culprit was duly apprehended. The organ playing was accomplished. It transpired that Martin Brown, whom we had arranged to see, was the performer. I asked what the voluntary piece at the end was: *Triumphal March* by the Belgian Jacques-Nicolas (Jaak-Nicolaas) Lemmens (1823–81) and a prelude indeed to our tour in Martin's expert hands. So we had unearthed a rare Belgian who had made a cultural contribution. When we left the building it was to the strains of the instrument in practice mode for Graham Eccles, the new Director of Music, for a forthcoming service in Birkenhead.

Looking round the north aisle displays I found exactly what I had hoped for. There was an article pinned up about Aled Jones, former boy chorister at Bangor and now ubiquitous singer and broadcaster: very popular on *Songs of Praise*. I had known him during his training as an actor at Bristol Old Vic Theatre School (1992–94), one memorable contribution to public enjoyment being his Knave of Hearts in the Christmas production *Alice through the Looking Glass*. Since then I had seen him at the Grand Theatre, Blackpool for *Joseph and the Amazing Technicolor Dreamcoat*. Bob (my St Paul's friend and a member of the Frank Matcham Society) cited the Grand as his second favourite Matcham theatre, after the Coliseum, London. Aled put in a fine performance as Joseph, and I had made attempts in advance of this visit to quiz him about his life in the choir at Bangor. There was no reply, so I shall now quote from the journal *Church Music Quarterly* (26/6/10):

> ... *I've been involved with church music since the age of nine when I first joined Bangor Cathedral Choir as a probationer... when I was in BCC, you didn't dare tell your friends that you were in a church choir... I felt quite guilty when I received my award in Durham, because I felt I should give half of it to Andrew Goodwin, my choirmaster in Bangor all those years ago.*
>
> Stuart Robinson

He was referring to the recent (May 2010) honorary award from the Royal School of Church Music, during its annual Celebration Day, held at Durham Cathedral.' You can't deny his success. Think of *The Snowman*, which, as a popular children's play, was still presented each year by a partnership involving Birmingham Repertory Theatre. As so often with actors who move on, it is perhaps a pity that Aled didn't still do straight acting, but I'm sure the diversity of drama training helped him. It gives talented, diligent students a transferable skill.

Wakey, after some time to observe reckoned on 'a space within a space without – how that applies – spiritual as well as physical'. This was the benefit of a small cathedral, fit for purpose, echoed here for me recently from Wells, and, to jump ahead, later that day at St Asaph.

Something comparatively ancient occurred in a different vein. 'Gradual' hymn N° 466 'Teach me my God and King' by George Herbert (1593–1633) from *The Temple*, written as poetry in the year of his death, had a quality way ahead of the 19th century blatherings of so many hymns in the book used there: '*Hymns Old & New*, Anglican Edition 1996'. Read this, for use of language:

1 Teach me, my God and King,
In all things thee to see,
And what I do in anything
To do it as for thee.

2 Not rudely, as a beast,
To runne into an action;
But still to make thee prepossest,
And give his perfection.

3 A man that looks on glasse,
On it may stay his eye
Or if it pleaseth, through it passe,
And then the heav'n espie.

4 All may of thee partake;
Nothing can be so mean,
Which with his tincture (for thy sake)
Will not grow bright and clean.

5 A servant with this clause
Makes drudgerie divine:
Who sweeps a room, as for thy laws,
Makes that and th'action fine.

6 This is the famous stone

That turneth all to gold:
For that which God doth touch and own
Cannot for lesse be told.

These were what we sang – six verses – called *The Elixir* by the poet. Meanwhile hymns don't usually have names. Another exception is *St Patrick's Breastplate* 'I bind unto myself today... ', another telling and uplifting piece, translated from a Gaelic poem. It features the 'lorica', a mystical garment intended to protect the wearer from danger and illness and guarantee entry into Heaven. The standard practice with hymn indexes is to use the first line as the reference. Indeed, why not keep it simple, unless it's a special case, and I think both these qualify for that. The version of *Teach me, my God and King* found on a compendium of 'favourite hymns' lost the 'famous stone', 'drudgerie divine' and 'tincture' to render the whole somewhat anodyne, in a mere four verses. The tune alone merited the whole six. Herbert was a devout Anglican. So had been the RC convert John Donne, with whom he was friendly. This is where the 'tincture' came in. To move further up the tangent, here is Samuel Johnson's definition of the word, from his *Dictionary of the English Language*, which first reached bookshelves in 1755: 'To imbue or impregnate with some colour or taste, e.g. *A little paint will tincture and spoil twenty gay colours (Watts)*', wrote Dr Sam, in whose day the letters 'I' and 'J' were treated as one, in an alphabet of 25 letters, so the entries are in order of the second letter of each word. It may have been revolutionary for him to suggest this in the introduction to the letter: 'I is considered both as a vowel and as a consonant, though, since the vowel and consonant differ in their form as well as sound, they may be more properly accounted two letters.' In my local reference library – there were two mighty tomes of the Dictionary, so I wanted to look up more than just 'tincture'. I hoped to arrive at J for 'jewel' for its various definitions 250 years ago. It was coming up at Ripon Cathedral – it took a while to find amid all the 'I' words. For a while I thought he had omitted a block of his subject matter.

In *The Works of George Herbert* (1994), Dr Tim Cook wrote: 'The idea that even the simplest and humblest actions, such as sweeping a room, can be given religious significance if approached in the right frame of mind is the subject of *The Elixir*, a poem that makes use of the alchemical imagery associated with Donne.'

Pressing this even further, Henry Vaughan (1622–95) was influenced by George Herbert. I decided to follow the model of *The Retreat* to undertake a representation of this cathedral:

Bangor Cathedral

Bangor the name means 'fence,' you know -
Cathedral, close and down below
The garden – this all should be bound,
Imagine a fence which circles round
This chunky building, Deiniol's –
It's full of architectural rules,
The 19th century Norman – nice! -
Sits well quite near some modern mice,
And on the floor strut rabbits too;
Medieval tiles make quite a zoo.
We see so many styles survive –
Deiniol was here in 525.
The tower came a thousand years
Later – Perpendicular,
Producing the arcade, there now.
But pigeons, bats and people! How
They made the thurible a need –
The censer spiced and sweet, like mead,
Would kill the odours oh so dire,
Pervading all from nave to choir,
Where arms of Gwynedd's tribes now stand -
That's Venedotia's hinterland.

But turn to century 21:
Observe how practice now is done.
We scanned the north aisle noticeboard:
The Mothers' Union's links abroad;
A bright-garbed snap starred Sentamu
From ancient Wales to NZ new.
The Pope was here the other day -
In England, not so far away.
We shake hands, think World – prayers are said
For unity, then wine and bread.
The church provides both fun and praise
Get used to it, that's how it stays.

It was worth noting the bright kneelers, every one different, and, looking down the south aisle there was a shelf above a radiator with mantelpiece-like framed pictures displayed upon it. There was a more modest equivalent diversion than the swearing woman at Eucharist at St Paul's.

The sidesman (well, an official-acting man, who helped me to a gift aid envelope) sitting in the back row behind us, found it necessary to go to the north door to curtail the chatter of people gathered in the porch, no doubt sheltering from the rain. In the course of our pre-service circumnavigation round the cathedral, on the other, northeast, side we had noticed the traces of a former space. Every building has lost some bits. This was the former Lady Chapel. And, back inside again, powerful on the pillars above us, were papier mache constructs illustrating the gospel writer: the Bull (John), rather disconcerting overhead, with formidable flared nostrils. I thought the best to be the yellow-billed crow of Luke. It made a change from the traditional image.

The dean was in evidence afterwards and introduced me to organist Martin, who rejoiced in the title 'Chapter Clerk and Administrator'. He was from Tamworth, Staffs, and his favourite cathedral was his local one, Lichfield. That made two, with Wakey, who had made that choice. I love these bizarre job titles: different everywhere. We observed that his brief involved playing the organ and developing an impressive knowledge of the history and display of the cathedral. We learned a lot. The map of the dioceses of Wales showed a fairly convenient split in the north: Bangor had the west, St Asaph, the east. However, four thousand of Llandudno's population was in Bangor, the rest of it not. There had been an anomaly in the definition of each – bits of misplaced territory, rather liked the 'detached' part of Flintshire I recalled from school, long before all the complication streamlining Wales into Clwyd, Powys etc., more recently redefined into unitary and secondary authorities. Wrexham is on its own, but definitely looked after by St Asaph in see terms. Wrexham was the main centre of population. I'd heard all about that from Dean Geoffrey at Brecon, who had moved from one to the other. So Ruthin, in the middle of the St Asaph diocese geographically, was belatedly moved into its jurisdiction. The population of the diocese was 250K, of which 13K lived in Bangor. It is a city, ranking the fourth least populous in the country. It was difficult to get Welsh priests, and there were a number from outlying sources, such as Utrecht, Netherlands and Reading. The dean was a Welsh learner, and a considerable chunk of the map, to the west, used the Welsh language, but no-one in Llandudno. There were further consequences of staffing shortages. In Anglesey one vicar looked after nine parishes. Loss of population was also a factor, of course. There was considerable contact with the other five dioceses: there was to be a governing body meeting soon in Lampeter, way down south.

Next I can report something entertaining, as we were gradually wandering round the building. Martin showed us several of the 'Thompson's

Mouse Marks' dating from, the rodents mostly carved on wooden chairs, doorways, or anywhere. There was one on the font. 'Very valuable' he said. That's Robert Thompson of Kilburn, North Yorkshire (1876–1955). Adding a mouse to a piece of carving started by chance in 1919, apparently related to a comment about 'being as poor as a church mouse', while Thompson was producing a cornice. Linked to the Arts and Crafts movement inspired 1920s revival of craftsmanship, the practice of these charming additions increased, with the signature 'Mouseman'. It spawned spin-offs like 'Squirrelman', 'Gnomeman' and 'Eagleman'.

Martin took us right up to the reredos to admire the thurible (metal censer, but I prefer this evocative word), now used regularly, showing a sign of the times. There was a piece by John Wall in *Church Times* (18/3/11) which showed how telling a contribution thuribles can make:

> *I went to Canon Beaumont Lauder Brandie's retirement do at St Martin's, Brighton, a couple of weeks ago – and a splendid do it was, too. Many know Canon Beau from his Walsingham activities (they have named an arch after him there)... so the place was packed.*
>
> *Seven bishops (I think) sat in state, about 100 robed clergy were in the sanctuary, and as many again swelled the congregation of some 800. There was much incense (cartwheels with the thuribles were de rigueur), much unobtrusive shimmying by the teams of servers and taperers, and much singing from the massed children's choir.*
>
> *I especially enjoyed the post-do beer, which had been specially brewed for the occasion by a local (ecclesiastical) micro-brewery and named "The Last Canon."*
>
> *John Wall is Team Rector of the Moulsecomb Team ministry in Brighton.*

We examined its gritty contents. 'It also conceals smells', said Martin. Good point. Apart from people, the place was on occasion host to bats and pigeons – it was said that incense was used to discourage pigeons and disinfect against woodworm. 'There's a hole in the roof,' 'But no cat?' I posited. 'No, but my dog is sometimes here,' and was to be seen awaiting admission at the door. Martin lived next door in the deanery, which was divided into two. Attending to the structure of his workplace it was evident what wear and tear it suffered. There were cracks, still moving as time went on. The cathedral was a long and squat building, sited for convenience by a (navigable) river, but fortunately out of sight, reinforcing the argument that it had benefited from its obscurity. It had been roofless between 1404 and 1515. 16th century bishops Dean and Skeffington had initiated the new building. It was obvious in the south aisle how contrived some of the angles were to make it work, and the north was different in design from the south. It all worked and the contrasts served to stimulate interest, as did the fact that the west tower was not central, as the new 1532 addition had to serve as a foundation for the whole building. It is with some relief and admiration that you greet such tidings. Thank God for the experienced architects and engineers of the late Middle Ages! Fewer from that period have collapsed.

Looking more closely into the rood screen there appeared concise fan vaulting along the top, and, at last, an angel or two. Further up, on the cathedra was the ermine and spurs, the coat of arms of the diocese – white on black – and coats of arms of the tribes (said Martin, 'families' per the welcome leaflet) of Gwynedd, illustrating the tops of the choir stalls, looking down on the marvellous tiled floor. We should thank the great Scott for facilitating this. Reintroduced to the Norman pillars abutting the rood screen, it was a really good fit for a much later addition, and the columns had been a 19th century rebuild, stuffed full of rubble.

We were in the north transept, a clever rethink of use: modern bespoke oak, made by a talented local joiner, as a canopy over the passage to the vestry, meanwhile housing organ pipes. The building housed 4,200 of them. It was the largest organ in Wales, a £1m project. What we had heard had been impressive. Apparently American practitioner Carlo Curley, a voluminous man himself, as well as flamboyant, had produced considerable volume on the instrument. The customary mental note was made to attend, sometime, a concert featuring the organ at full throttle, perhaps while two high quality organists remained on the payroll. Martin also mentioned a caretaker. Welsh cathedrals can't afford more than the essential staff. The joiner had been with them on a contract for that project. It had been staff who made up the party, in suits, at Westminster Abbey the previous Friday, for Evening Prayer, the occasion when the Pope and Archbishop Rowan had united at Edward the Confessor's shrine. Every Anglican diocese had been invited, the Bangor party comprising the Bishop, his wife, Dean, Chapter Clerk, Archdeacon Designate, Senior Canon Diocesan Secretary. They were seated in the north transept, the corner for Prime Ministers, notable for the presence of Messrs Gladstone and Disraeli, together.

We were nearing the end. Time for refreshments, and, in our case, to retrieve the car, which had run its three hours. 'They're tight here, we were told, as we came to the displays in the north aisle. Martin pointed out the telling contrasts in a photograph from New Plymouth, New Zealand, at the Taranaki Cathedral Church of St Mary. Archbishop Sentamu of York, was there, in the newest Anglican cathedral, representing the oldest cathedral, that very place where we now stood. Sentamu, with teeth shining complete with the gap, was clad in modern dress, the Plymouthians in traditional robes. It made an amusing scene. I wonder if they approved of his choice of garb. It's a long distance to get a change in clothing. I enjoyed this, in the anticipation of meeting the man, to discuss his role. What <u>does</u> he do? As it happens I had approached him with a view to squeezing half an hour into his diary, sometime, anywhere. I received this email:

> *Thank you for your message through my website on 31 August and for your request to meet during your tour of Anglican cathedrals. Unfortunately I have already had to close my 2010 diary, and 2011 is almost as busy, and so I am unable to accept. I am sorry to have to decline but I am sure you understand the pressures on my time. I do hope the tour and your planned book go well.*
> *With every blessing*
> *Sentamu Ebor*

Nicely put. The Toff, during our discourse at Westminster five days earlier, had said that when he was writing for the *Diocesan News* Sentamu had been good to interview, so I immediately regretted missing the chance. There was plenty to unearth of his quotes, however, and his memory was fairly recent in Birmingham, which by then was not far off in the schedule. On top of that, it was pleasing to find him posing fairly regularly in media coverage on peripatetic visits. They seemed almost ubiquitous.

We hadn't quite finished, noting the medieval scaffolding marks in the pillars. For that to become a point of interest indicated how involved you got while enjoying a cathedral. The green men, in wood and stone here and there, were good, too, with the advantage in a small building of being able to get close. And of course I was encouraged to take photos. Forty eight survived the downloading and review process. At Westminster Abbey, where snaps were banned, I'd sneaked four in the cloisters.

Out we ventured into the rain. I had dumped an errant umbrella in a bin in Conwy before our watering hole visit earlier, so it was good to be parked so close. As a parting point, Martin drew attention to the erect extensions to the walls. Useless buttresses. At least the ones in St Davids, equally functionless, had been set at an angle, as was 'traditional'. They had looked like the real thing. Still, perhaps there were occasions when you could lean against these, like when chatting during a service, on a clement day. As it was, in the appalling conditions of the day, it was possible to imagine potential problems associated with the site, close as it was to water. There was also an issue of defence over the years. Thos McKenny Hughes summed up the geography of the Welsh cathedrals: 'You see nothing of St Davids till you are quite upon it; hills command Llandaff and Bangor all around. No one would occupy them for defence, except so far as the mere walls would protect those who took refuge within them.'

There was no fence in evidence outside, just yet, and not even one suggestion of a harp. Upon reflection I decided a harp would best represent this cathedral, for its music and its Welshness. Martin repaired to his residence next door. It was about twenty paces further to my car, and thence to St Asaph.

33

St Asaph

St Asaph

Province: Wales
Founded: 560 as monastery; became diocese c1073
Present building: Rebuilt from 1482 having been burnt by the English in 13th century and quire destroyed by Owain Glendower in 1402

Website: www.churchinwales.org.uk/asaph/cathedral/
Tel: 01745 582245
Address: Cathedral Office, High Street, St Asaph LL17 0RD

Three to See: Central tower in two contrasting swathes of coloured stone;
oak altar table with glass top;
unadorned nave pillars

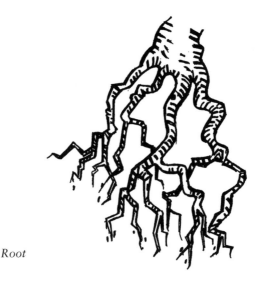

Root

Sunday 21 September, 2010

The good thing was that the rain abated as I reached the village that is St Asaph. Leaving the car for a respite in the cathedral car park (free on Sundays) I noticed the Dean's House adjacent and a 'For Sale' sign, which, on close inspection, related to the stables next door. That was a relief: selling off church assets? Entering by the west door I was confronted by a grandstand, which I swiftly realized would be our location at 7.30 pm for the North Wales International Music Festival concert, the event upon which this endeavour was hung. It was fortunate that The Very Revd Christopher Potter was willing to see me, the appointment fixed at 4 pm. The place was as busy as you'd expect for something which would involve 18 singers with Musical Director and Conductor Harry Christophers, baton in hand, and 400 lovers of Early Music. A quick perusal of the interior gave me a warm feeling, and I had arrived at the appointed hour. I chose a mature lady, who looked more likely than most to be linked with vestry not visitors. 'Oh, he's just left', she said. 'I'll show you his house.' She took me backstage, for that was its role for the event, and unlocked a door beside the modern extension at the southeast.

Over the lush green sward I walked, past the 'For Sale' sign and to the front door bell, duly pressed. The dean arrived quickly. I recognized from his photo on the website. 'Oh, yes, Mick?' from him. 'Where shall we go?' He decided upon the vestry, whither we went, through the door I'd just passed through the other way. It was to become the green room in due course, but the performing posse was in the process of arriving and he felt he could banish anyone else venturing in, for the time being. 'What do I call you,' I asked first, 'Chris, or a nickname?' I was hoping for the latter as I had a Chris already. In fact several. 'Oh Chris, please.'

He was comparatively new to the church, and his life story was fascinating, perhaps a model for future late arrivals to faith, given the contemporary paucity of recruits into ordination. After Leeds University (English Literature and Art History) and Bradford Art College, as a history teacher, he wanted to do something more practical. He invaded rural Wales for involvement in car components, and became immersed in hippy culture: a drop out situation; the beautiful Llangollen area proved a most empathic setting. Making furniture became a career. Features of life included swimming in the Dee and goats in the yard. Meanwhile we move on to the early 1980s, when Chris was in partnership, fitting kitchens with a friend, mostly a very successful business with countrywide orders. Chris was always handy, enjoying practical work, as currently at his cathedral in addressing problems with boilers (the new one, quite an investment, was serving to reduce fuel costs). I read an article later about thefts of heating oil from seven churches in Flintshire. More than 1,000 litres were stolen in three incidents, according to the Revd John Jones, of Treuddyn and Nercwys. It was to be hoped that the felons didn't extend their ambition to the mother church at St Asaph, where there might be rich pickings.

With a happy marriage, four offspring and a fulfilled life, a gradual conversion manifested itself, a calling. The catalyst for this was a series of hazardous incidents such as with a Scots pine, Chris barely escaping a direct hit; and lightning struck, again with no casualty. Business was volatile over the critical period up to 1983. Jenny, his wife, was to comment: 'It's been a funny old year', which rang a bell with him. A mirror fell to the floor, its string broken, the mirror not. The outcome was his decision on a change of life. The practical move was to train for the church, a complete transformation for the whole family, embraced by all. One thing that changed was their living conditions: a considerable forfeit. Chris's faith had augmented through the process affecting them all. No doubt an innate spirituality came to pervade his whole life: that's how it came across to me. At 16 years old he had undergone a psychological aptitude test (personal profile) which had concluded his best fit to be the church. He had ignored it for many years, then started going to church. It came upon a midnight clear. I asked him if he had any regrets: he replied easily that on inheriting £1,100, a princely sum at the time, he failed to invest it in a property in Yorkshire. Prices were low and the Hebden Bridge area later took off in the market. He bought a car instead. Cars are not forever. Certainly that one wasn't!

The western Welsh dioceses had become something of a dean scene. I had already spent productive time with Richard in Newport and Geoffrey in Brecon. Chris was the same, conveying the commitment and devotion required. The workload was immense. Deans have to make ends meet – apply husbandry, initiate and create. They all met twice a year. It's a productive fraternity. The dean and chapter didn't make money. Added to this was the minuscule population of St Asaph itself, a mere 3,800. The parish church lay 150 yards down the road from the cathedral, as well. There was a reliance upon volunteers. Infrastructure which needs maintaining includes similar staff to Bangor, like the administrator and caretaker. Praise the Lord for the stipend and two part time chaplains. There is inevitably sharing with the parish.

The building had to remain open 365 days a year (not so several churches I've tried to enter, including three in London six days before). This was where the boiler argument came in. 'Good administration includes containing fuel costs.' He wanted to change the lighting system. There was much to do. Dean Chris was 61, having been in the job for nine years so far. Retirement at 65 was anticipated. He would have no deanery after that but his modest abode in the country. The Old Deanery was now a retirement home. In mentioning legacies to the cathedral, I had suggested that some of the inmates might be prospective legatees. He didn't think so.

When it came to his introduction to the concert two hours later, he didn't miss a trick with the audience (they'd paid good money for the ticket, so were a target audience for future contributions). He mentioned the recent withdrawal of Arts Council funding, a serious set back. Sponsors would be welcome, such as Salisbury (Chartered Accountants) for this performance. You could invest £1 in a board of names, a modest fund raising item. I chose 'Roussel', and Wakey 'McCabe'. Neither of us has been notified following the subsequent draw, but the cathedral has earned something. We were ignorant as to the identity of our choices. Looking them up (in a hurry) there was an Albert Roussel, French composer in the impressionist style, going on neoclassicism and Anthony, a jewellery designer. McCabe? Alistair embarked upon pilgrimage tours and Helen made cardigans. None the wiser, really. Though the idea of creativity is appealing, using lumps of metal and loom, the gravitas of classical music and biblical trips rang more true. Or were they the names of stewards' dogs, or the stewards themselves? It's probably best not to know.

We left the vestry for the south transept and a feast of the more modern attractions. The Treasury was an illuminated arched cabinet of shelves, with a changing display relating to the work of the diocese. The cathedral is home to the William Morgan Bible, a practical link with Welsh culture and literature. The best thing was the *Naked Christ* by Michele Coxon, provoking a 'difficult and uncomfortable interpretation of the crucifixion' as the leaflet stated, having quoted gory passages from Isaiah. It continued: 'The easiest response, of course, is to walk away in revulsion. Crucifixion was designed to be excruciatingly painful and humiliating. Victims were nailed up naked as objects of deterrence and disgust. Our natural response is to look away, which is why, historically, there have been so few realistic depictions of Jesus on the cross.' It is made of natural products, mainly wood, from the core of the natural world. I found it awesome. Below it, Chris introduced me to a more recent piece, an altar table, of pale oak, purpose-built with seductively shaped glass on top. He was pleased with it, it appealed to me, as an artefact, let alone kneeling before it. Wakey later concurred as we rested our wine glasses upon it, almost guiltily. The Sixteen had embarked upon rehearsal, so we brought discussion to a close. Chris said: 'See you later,' and I found I had enough time for a wander round the parts of the cathedral behind the stage, erected at the crossing. The mufti-clad performers and conductor were facing west. This was to be the 12th concert of the 15 on the tour. Of these, eight were in cathedrals covered in this tome.

Ticket procurement for the event had developed into an unusually trying process, involving several phone calls to Katy Morgan, Festival Coordinator (very nice) and postal loss. The other piece of the jigsaw, accommodation, was easier. I had refused to believe the claim that Premier Inn rooms could ever really cost £29, as in the widely displayed 'From £29' banner. I was patronizing a lot of these, the average rate running at about £59. But the one at Rhuddlan, a couple of miles from St Asaph, turned out to be, yes, £29. I was so impressed that I yielded to their request of 30p for Water Aid.

With two hours to go, while enjoying an independent observation of the sanctuary, I mulled over this, in smug vein as I could identify the seats from afar. The chosen ones were in an excellent position, with an overall view. This included the Reredos, 19th century and of somewhat distant Derbyshire alabaster. Everything was individual and rewarding, from cathedra to dean's stall. The former was a memorial to Bishop Beveridge (1704–98), it said. He deserved an accolade for his longevity, at least, if it provoked production of this piece. The choir stalls, from 1482, were tempting enough for a dose of evensong. 'Notice the face of a man on one of them (south side) – possibly the Master Carver,' said the leaflet. The man looked a comely fellow, or was it a case of self-enhancement?

It was a bit of a trek to the Translator's Chapel, or north transept, round, past the organ, which would have meant disruption of the rehearsal, now in full throat and captivating. I settled for more time in the south transept, built in 1336. Wakey was to pick out the Madonna in the niche – 16th century Spanish – as the kind of quirky thing you find in such old buildings. It looked good at eye level, set in a pillar. It was prevailingly blue, of a paler hue than the colour chosen by Dean Chris. To my question about choices of colour, he said anyone apart from bishops (purple) could select their own colour of garb. His was the brightest so far, impressive against the white dog collar and darkness of jacket and trousers, He acceded to a photo. I have to say that his blue eyes were exceedingly complementary.

There was an oddity in the southwest corner. There were panels painted yet another shade of blue (a shade in between those mentioned so for, let's say ultramarine) along the wall panel. The last one was open, revealing hot drink equipment on a shelf, rather out of place beside a confident modern mural along from the chalices and platters on display in the treasury. I wandered quietly down the south aisle, as the posse disbanded. I wondered what refreshments they would receive before the show, making a mental note to ask my mezzo friend Pom about the routine surrounding such a concert. She was to open in a new opera that very week. There was an occasional effigy and memorial, including a hare and hound motif, leading to the font at the west end. This had been a victim of the Civil War. Oliver Cromwell, not content with using St Paul's Cathedral for stabling his cavalry, had been here too, or his soldiers had, using the font as a watering trough. Perhaps the twists of the Protector's mind related to his origins, in Ely. Psychologists: there's a case study in waiting!

We now fast forward to the return of the Wakey, refreshed after a slumber in the £29 resting place. It was just right, and we'd paid for a slap-up breakfast, for an extra £5.95. That's how they quietly acquire more coffers. The Plough, conveniently between resting place and venue, was our choice for ingestion. That comprised roast beef dinners, but the pudding offer didn't apply to beef, and the ham was finished. The pub was St Asaph's representative in the *Good Beer Guide*. It had a horse-racing theme, and Chelsea were winning on the wide screens. We avoided that, preferring peace and quiet. Real ale, there was not. It had been a busy Sunday. Bad management, I'd say, to run out of staple fare. Wakey opted for Guinness, which I had no hesitation in avoiding, so soon after enjoying the real thing during my stay in Ireland. I opted for the house red wine, (merlot), which was to serve as a precursor to interval offerings.

Having parked, care of a school up the road from the cathedral, we joined the queue, giving me a chance to show off my knowledge of building materials, newly-acquired from the cathedral leaflet. The cathedral tower was a fetching bi-colour.

> *There are two totally different types of stone used. The finely grained limestone came from quarries at nearby Cefn and the sandstone was quarried at Flint or Talacre. This is an unusual combination as the two stones react together chemically and are gradually eating each other away!*

It makes for a unique look, and, despite the inherent problem, was most appealing. The resulting snap ended up as my screensaver for a while. In we went and obtained the tickets, noting the 1738 iron chest opposite, now redesigned to accept donations. Wakey inserted postcard money there. Was it in a gift aid envelope? I made the essential investment in the festival programme, a wise decision even though we were only there for one concert on a long list. I learned all about the organization and the evening's event. One fact, which could have been useful in my exchanges during the tour of St Paul's was 'In 2008 The Sixteen featured in the highly successful BBC Four television series, *Sacred Music*, presented by actor Simon Russell Beale... ' but I had missed so many excellent programmes over the years, through a failure to examine broadcasting schedules. The series would be repeated, surely. My oft-quoted truism might even apply: 'In my retirement.' I came to hope. Armed with the passports to pleasure, I took Wakey round the bits I had seen earlier, and more, some fresh to me, in the interval. In the south transept, hiding the kettle cupboard, were trestle tables covered with glasses and wine. A bucolic bloke, who admitted to being agnostic, proffered a slug each of: 'They're Chilean – Cabernet Sauvignon or Merlot. Your choice, sir.' A choice, at a concert, in a church? This was a novelty in my recollection, to be followed hotly by one each then and another ordered for the interval: M then CS, I think I recall. He gestured to the distant, west, end of the auditorium, which the nave had plainly become, where a substantial chap in a white shirt was waving pen and paper around. He was taking interval orders. Another first. They were friendly here, and a glass cost a mere £2 – the one in the Plough had cost £4.95. The outcome was for me to write down our order on a page torn from my pocket notebook, noting the order. 'Then you can reuse your glasses,' said the Agnostic. How, I wasn't sure, visualizing the usual massive queue, bearing in mind that we were to be sitting in a most inaccessible location. Of course, in negotiating our way up to our seats, White Shirt had arrived at that very point at the same time. 'No problem,' he uttered, somewhat flustered from all his endeavours (clearly, he would be unable to cover the whole place before 7.30). Down we sat, with just one more seat unoccupied beyond my companion. Then I noticed Dean Chris below, chatting to a familiar, most fulsome, figure. I recognized him as Terry Waite, whom Chris was directing towards the standing Wakey. The seat was his, and an exchange was to ensue. I had noticed that an earlier event that day had been 'Festival Lunch – Siaradwr gwadd. Guest speaker / Terry Waite CBE'. I was to ask him: 'What subject did you choose at lunchtime?' 'Oh, music and language and what not,' came the reply. We giggled. It was the turn of the awestruck couple on the other side to engage him. The lights still hadn't dimmed when that exchange abated, so we spoke again. 'I said that on my release my wife told me: "I prayed for you for five years." I said that was good. "But you came back," she said. That moved them.' Eager to capitalize on the situation, I asked him which was his favourite cathedral. He paused and said 'Durham, I think, (how common, thought I), and I like Peterborough.' Terry cropped up on *Today* on 15 November 2010, following the release by Somali pirates of the retired seafaring captives Paul and Rachel Chandler. Asked how he would advise them to approach this period, he listed the order of processes:

1   Make a press statement.
2   Avoid further exposure but take time out.
3   Use a trained listener.
4   Make adjustments gradually.

The couple had said on release that the greatest emotions came with the loss of their boat; then the threat of separation, with ensuing beatings when they refused. They had been in captivity for 388 days – ransom of around £300K had been dropped a month before, but more was demanded. The further sum of £630K, which was raised privately and delivered, secured their freedom. Terry considered there would be an issue of trying to give the money back. It had been assembled from a number of sources. Meanwhile the Somali government should (obviously) address this issue, the country being well placed for piracy by busy shipping lanes. At least the northwest part of Somalia was fairly stable. That gave a modicum of reassurance.

I have more about Terry Waite. My friend Mickser, with whom I was to enjoy Peterborough Cathedral, told me this: the Romany Society was founded to extol the Revd George Bramwell Evans (1884–1943), who became a Methodist minister. His mother was a true gypsy, and he became known as 'Romany of the BBC', appearing on Children's Hour in the 1930s and 40s. The narrative followed adventures in his vardo (caravan) with friends and animals, such as Comma the horse. After a gap of many years, the society was re-established in 1996 with Terry Waite as Patron. In 2010 Hon Sec of the Romany Society was welcoming both information and new members. He, John Thorpe, wrote in a letter to *The Stage* (9/12/10):

> *Although he died 67 years ago, the work he did formed the bedrock of what we have now come to regard as quite normal – that is, the body of spectacular and authoritative wildlife programmes for which British television and radio are famous throughout the world.*

The lights went down for the concert, which opened with four sopranos just below us. I like that traditional device, to move around the whole space, though, once on the platform, the changes were just repositionings among them. There were eighteen of The Sixteen, and eighteen listed in the programme, so no-one was off that day. It comprised Tudor works by Byrd, Tallis and John Sheppard. Tallis's Canon is one of my favourite hymn tunes, and *A Theme of Thomas Tallis* had been marvellous at *The Three Choirs Festival* at Gloucester. These selections were magnificent, and I resolved to approach Musical Director and Conductor Harry Christophers after the tour (final performance on the 22nd) for his opinion regarding acoustics. This I did. We would well believe that St Asaph ranked near the top. How was it for performers delivering to perfection such disciplined work? Eventually I was to speak to one Zoe, on the telephone. She spoke for the boss, Harry Christophers. Basically acoustics were not a primary consideration in booking concerts. No building was the same, suiting different variations of music and group. You just have to adjust. There was a single rehearsal on the afternoon of a performance; then the event itself. I subsequently heard something else about The Sixteen from a friend running a venue – they were expensive, ill-afforded by many managements. Since then I have always kept a lookout for them when perusing classical music brochures.

From Row R, right at the top, we derived full benefit of the view of the cathedral. The image of 'root' was so right to identify St Asaph, the whole place an ancient organic entity full of basic materials. The short nave pillars unified the scene, reaching up unfettered by capitals or artifice. Being so few (five) helped. They did not dominate but served to introduce the viewer to the broadening transepts and heightening roof. The chancel area beyond was a darker development of the foreground.

Afterwards we bought The Sixteen's CD (£12 for one, then it became an immediate need to acquire one for each of us for £20). During the 20 minute break we somehow managed to arrive speedily at the front of the line and duly obtained the Merlot – delicious – from a bargirl who had overheard the chat with the Agnostic. 'Yours is the Cabernet Sauvignon, isn't it – give me your glasses.' Good girl. We reclined on the future altar table and Wakey went round all the joys I'd witnessed earlier. He was in full accord, especially liking the Madonna and Child in the pillar, not surprising for one of a Roman Catholic persuasion. I now revised my assessment of ultramarine with the paler type of blue worn by his football team, Manchester City. But I'm sure the reason for his choice was altruistically based. More perambulation followed, covering the chancel, then a return to our places, where the chat with Terry resumed. He revealed that he had received honorary doctorates from Canterbury and Durham. 'Then Durham is disqualified as your favourite. Peterborough it shall be – breaking its duck,' I said, I hope not too assertively. We talked about our journeys home. 'Are you returning tonight?' he asked. 'Oh no, in the morning.' 'I like night driving,' he added. 'Where are you driving to?' we wanted to know. 'London,' said he, having revealed that he had also a place in Bury St Edmunds. As well as Rand and me, Terry liked the new tower in St Edmundsbury cathedral, though the loss of all the monastic buildings there was pitiful. He was staying at St Asaph, with the dean. On discovering Bristol to be my base (we didn't get around to covering Wakey's) he told a tale about a children's charity there, giving holidays to the deprived. A couple of stories ensued: of one girl who turned up with only a pair of knickers to change, and a boy who didn't bring his payment, but later discovered it was wrapped round his soap in the soap dish.

After the concert what remained to examine, while the cathedral emptied, was the north transept, known as the Translator's Chapel. It wasn't remarkable for its contents, but its sense of tranquillity, in effect removed from the main body of the cathedral. The name derives from its commemoration of 'the men responsible for the translation of the Scriptures into Welsh in the 16th and 17th centuries'. Chris had told me that he had learnt the liturgy in Welsh as he couldn't do the job without it, but that was the extent of his knowledge of the language. 'Don't ask me anything in Welsh,' he smiled.

The next morning provided a follow-up to that. My friend Suts was local to this area. She went to school in Mold, and we met her near that market town for chat, walk and tomato soup straight from the garden – she was house and cat sitting for friends currently in Greece. She grew up in the 1970s, when learning the Welsh language was actively discouraged. She went on to do a degree in French, and having an aptitude for languages, has since learned some of her country's tongue. How things have changed. As a professional movement specialist, continuously acquiring many skills as performance artist, she has also done shows in church buildings. Another facet of Mold occurred, at Theatr Clwyd, the professional theatre venue on the outskirts. In the early noughties, Rutz (she was in the St Davids party), Graham and I saw a production of Noel Coward's *Private Lives* there. Before 'curtain up' a girl bustled, pressed against a wall, wriggling to escape her male companion. The action became alarmingly aggressive. It was the invention of the director. What ensued was a somewhat outré, sexy interpretation. A noticeable number of the white-haired audience left at the interval, not to mention in mid-speech. The derisive line from protagonist Amanda: 'Very flat, Norfolk' became Rutz's favourite, oft repeated.

After Suts's culinary creation I made my way home via Wrexham for Wakey's train – it was bizarre there. Was it Central or General Station? He understood Central to be the one, so I dropped him there. He later reported that he then had to change at General. Having driven right through the town we agreed upon the intricate church tower as suggesting a proper look at the whole church on another occasion. Next was the trek down the map, to notch up over 500 miles on this tour. I would be spreading the word about these modest gems of North Wales. Suts had never set foot in St Asaph, the local cathedral of her youth. There was an Eddie Stobart gem, too, on the M5: Tryphaena Berenice, and Eddie's place was to be the subject of a television series starting that week. That had to be seen, but first was to be number 34: Coventry, just two days hence, certainly another massive contrast from the charms of Bangor and St Asaph.

Fig 43

Fig 44

Fig 45

[43] Bangor: Tile on choir floor in chancel: rabbit with bow and arrow.
[44] St Asaph: The tower: two types of stone weathering away.
[45] Coventry: 1969, new cathedral: Verger David Dorey and Graham.
[46] Coventry: 2010, old cathedral: Graham, Ragnhild and the author.

Fig 46

34

Coventry

St Michael

Province: Canterbury
Founded: 1095–1129 as priory
Parish church: 1373–1450 until gutted by fire bombs 1940. There is still much to see.
Cathedral status: 1918 – from Worcester diocese. From 1539 to 1837 Coventry shared a diocese with Lichfield
Present building: 1956–62

Website: www.coventrycathedral.org.uk
Tel: 0247 6521200
Email: information@coventrycathedral.org.uk
Address: 1 Hill Top, Coventry CV1 5AB

Three to See: The nave windows, which are orientated northwards, so view from the altar;
the six altar candlesticks, which are the biggest thrown pots in the world;
the Chapel of Unity, particularly for the mosaic floor

Phoenix

Graham was the star of this visit, having been a cathedral guide not so long before, in fact in 1969. With cousin Ragnhild, he and I first of all benefited through the ease of parking his mobility car in the cathedral close all day, in a city overrun with traffic. Who knows what angst was thus averted. As it was we walked straight into a paradisical setting. Leaves were starting to turn and the bulk of Holy Trinity church was next to the vehicle, assertive and reassuring, though we failed to try it out, as we ran out of time. The main event was to prove all-consuming. Opposite was the prospect of old interfaced with new: the dark red sandstone of the well-maintained ruin of the old east-west church, the surviving tower at the southwest corner housing Tourist Information on the ground floor. There I established the parking situation, and location of the catering facility. Benedicts Café would involve walking round to the north, the 'east end' of the new cathedral.

But first we would acclimatize in the scarred shell, where we paused for a while. It had plenty of detail of its own, expressed in its own leaflet in two shades of blue, not the easiest to read. The medieval glass of the Sanctuary had been removed in anticipation of war, as at Exeter, Lincoln and elsewhere. This was just as well as it was now on display in the Visitors' Centre (newish, introduced since 1969, considered Graham). Squirrels were carved in the stonework, perhaps referring to leafy Warwickshire, the county of William Shakespeare, the Forest of Arden and the Diocese of Coventry. There were guild chapels along the sides, taking me back to study of the medieval Mystery plays, of which the Coventry cycle is as well known as any (along with Chester and Wakefield). Theatre Director John Doyle was one producer of performances of the Coventry Mysteries. My friend Jacquie Crago, who was associated with this, felt 'a sense of reverence and history in amongst destruction – there's something very moving about it'. She nominated Coventry as her favourite, citing the juxtaposition of ancient with modern as an influence. In 1969 the Charred Cross had been present in the ruins, which Graham told us was made up of two roof beams which had fallen in the shape of a cross. The original had been moved to safe harbour in the building, and we saw a replica, along with an altar, built from the rubble, with the words 'Father Forgive' carved in 1948. The original church, the new one being the third on the site, originated in the 12th century, dedicated to St Mary but becoming a victim of Henry VIII's reformation policy.

It was approaching 1 pm and we were in need of sustenance. Benedicts Café was down a number of steps, prompting Graham to enter 'Disabled access needs improvement' on the customer questionnaire, which the assistant thrust at us once our order was accomplished. Ragnhild and I chose the day's

Pensioner's Lunch for £4: cheese and broccoli bake with salad and garlic bread, fine but I wouldn't have guessed at the presence of garlic from the taste. It may have been an example of caterers being feeble about customers' tastebuds. The thinking would go: 'They probably can't cope with too much garlic, so let's just put in a pinch.' I was glad that we united in sparkling water and I avoided black coffee (£1.95), as this was not the kind of facility to stir more than a thimbleful into the machine. Raspberry and coconut slice and cappuccino cake might have been rewarding. Graham's carrot and corriander (sic) soup was good, he said. Next, the toilets were sampled and awarded a generous 'ok' (the third of four options) on the form. The hand dryer may well have dated back to the sixties like everything else that day. There was a picture of Ullswater on the wall. Why not something a bit local, to encourage those seeking relief to try out the cathedral? Patronage there could well comprise a wide range of users. And, despite a strident notice 'Wash your hands frequently… ' the door handle was not clean! Back in the café, the final aggravation was the floor. 'How noisy it is' said Ragnhild, in stentorian tones, as a (hefty) man drew his wooden chair up to the table. It was a hard floor. Graham, recovering from being asked to repeat, again, what he was saying, which had been drowned out, commented: 'It's a mistake not to put something on the bottom of the chair legs.' His pearl of wisdom concerned his old friend, the Head Verger at Coventry through whom he had done guide duties, learning the spiel informally, unlike the guides I had encountered in other cathedrals, who were now formally tested on their knowledge. The friend was David Dorey, who moved on to Westminster Abbey as Dean's Verger. David's familiar comment was: 'I just love people.' That's how it seemed when I saw him in action at the Abbey. But Coventry seems to have been his high point, latterly Provost's Verger from 1976 to 1982. He also said: 'I was attracted to the Cathedral because it is such a progressive place. It's not just a building. In its activities it is forward thinking and prepared for change. I think the Cathedral's work towards peace and reconciliation gives people hope for the future.' That states the mission at Coventry. No wonder he did so well at that time and subsequently.

Graham also knew the Dean's Virger (note spelling) at St Paul's. That was Tom Cameron, who retired from the church in May 2010. Graham said: 'It was in Tom's time that entrance fees were introduced at St Paul's.' And by this time it had risen to £12.50. We chatted about cathedrals. I wondered if Ragnhild would change her mind about her favourite. Durham was currently nominated. This would be her 14th in all, more than many. A list was compiled over lunch.

We entered the exhibition without paying, unwittingly, as we passed through a door from the café, apparently an unorthodox route. There were boards giving helpful information. A clear statement hung on the wall: 'Destruction experienced by Coventry during the Second World War changed everything. This cathedral's mission became the ministry of reconciliation. Our story became our icon of hope in the world.' The history thereabouts was well-presented. In 1102 Robert de Lynesey, Bishop of Chester, became the first bishop of Coventry and Lichfield, with two cathedrals in the diocese. In 1539 St Mary's, Coventry was the only cathedral to be demolished, there being Lichfield Cathedral available, and two large parish churches nearby in the city of Coventry. It was vulnerable to Henry VIII's sweeping programme of closures and the pragmatism of the city. Its community was dispersed, riches forfeited and stone from its buildings plundered and reused throughout the city. Coventry was taken over by the Diocese of Lichfield, and, later, Worcester until 1918 when the burgeoning Midlands population led to the creation of the Diocese of Coventry in its own right.

There was no doubt about the image of Coventry Cathedral: a phoenix rising from the ashes. The phoenix process is worth reporting, in the words of Alec Clifton-Taylor in *The Cathedrals of England* (1969):

> ... here at last is an Anglican cathedral designed in a contemporary idiom. It is certainly one of the best known English buildings of the 20th century (indeed it was voted Britain's most popular 20th century building in 1999). Its predecessor was one of the parish-church cathedrals: a very large Perpendicular church which was not accorded cathedral status until 1918. In November 1940 German bombs reduced this building to a blackened shell, apart from the noble tower and spire, one of the finest in England. At first the intention was to build anew in traditional English Gothic. Only after long controversy was the design thrown open, in 1951, to competition. The winner was Basil Spence, and his cathedral, with all the furnishings contributed by other artists, arose in no more than six years: 1956 to 1962.

There had been 200 applicants and the cost totalled c.£6.5M, using 30K tons of red sandstone, from Hollington, Staffordshire. Not so local was the Westmorland slate, used to good, contrasting effect. The Unity Chapel worked so well with this; AC-T again:

> Originally it was intended to use pink stone for internal facing too, but later it was felt that a grey-white roughcast, besides

being much cheaper, would set off to better advantage the stained-glass windows.

The decision to rebuild was made on the day after the destruction, which was the tragic outcome of a raid lasting eleven hours, killing around 600 people and injuring more than a thousand. When it came to the fundamentals of the rebuilding exercise, it could so easily have followed the model of Guildford. Whoever was the prime mover with the ambition to move forward in style deserves quite a lot of credit.

We timed entry into the chapter house, a circular construction, for the beginning of the 20 minute introductory film. That was a theatrical device. We were approaching the actual thing by gradual stages; a tempting build up, especially for Ragnhild, who had never set foot in the cathedral before. The film opened with the title 'Coventry TLC, not PLC'. Fair enough. 'Our task is great, but God is greater'. Handed the same subject, how does every cathedral manage to invent a different slogan? Marketing is as much in the brief as all the other ecumenical functions. Cathedrals and deans and chapters operate in the modern world of business. Much of the commentary was spoken by Dean John Irvine. While planning this trip I tried to engage the Head Verger, Janice Clarke, being a friend of the helpful chaplain to the Bishop of Sodor and Man, Gill Poole of Peel. Gill's father, Joseph, had been the original Canon Precentor of the new cathedral. She emphasized the date – 1962 – so an important factor by now was the looming 50th anniversary. This visit clashed with the Head Vergers Conference at Coventry's old friend, Lichfield. So I contacted the Dean's PA, to no avail, actually no reply, which prompted the idea of an in-house performance by Graham. It worked perfectly, allowing us the freedom to pace ourselves in such a way that synchronicity prevailed, culminating in evensong at 5.15 pm. Ragnhild's opinion was 'You had a lucky escape – he's not very interesting', of the dean. He did point out that Benjamin Britten's 1962 *War Requiem* enjoyed its first performance in the new cathedral, also the welcome extended to 'People who would never dream of stepping inside a church' to attend events 'from concerts to conferences, from banquets to balls'. After the credits we returned to the corridor to 'Emma Fox – Welcome Desk', at the, er, Welcome Desk, to confirm, in our exchange, that we had indeed been in the chapter house, used for film shows when the dean and chapter were not about. We bought tickets to the cathedral and, for Ragnhild and me, the tower climb, while Graham would recover with a cold drink in the Herbert Gallery, which we had noticed opposite the old cathedral. Benedicts, which I kept wanting to call 'Becketts' as there are others of those around, closed at 3 pm (rather early, we thought), but the

Herbert was open until 5 pm, so the welcomer informed us. The purchase involved the first automated gift aid system experienced. All I had to do was sign the printout having yielded all the relevant details. I wondered if the information was safe. Of course it was: Coventry Cathedral was just being progressive.

We walked round to the southwest door for the first full glorious impact of the whole interior in mid-afternoon sun. Up on the wall, stood Jacob Epstein's statue of St Michael and the Devil, black and potent. Once in the building, Graham coaxed us first into the Westmorland stone-built Chapel of Unity, erected for all Christian faiths in a circular form. On the way in was a colourful, illustrated map of the diocese, very upbeat, executed in 1993 by Coventry College of Art and Design. The well-named chapel was designed in the shape of a crusader tent (Graham's term), the floor composed of marble from all over the world. It was lovely. He pointed out: 'In the middle is the creation of everything: peace,' then the concentric rings of design, in particular teaching through the parables, such as loaves and fishes; also the signs of Alpha and Omega, with the four evangelists tellingly represented in their traditional images. The five continents were there, too, the whole effect fusing in harmonic sequence. It worked as a positive statement, with chairs set in a circle, and no altar as such. There was a chalice depicted. Ragnhild suggested it might be ice cream. It could have been, more probably the fountain of life, and the whole space might contain identifiable images and references, but it was down to the individual, or perhaps group, to find their own application.

A verger, 'Pat' we were told, spoke prayers for all to hear on the hour, also conveying the message of reconciliation, very much the buzz word here. Now we were some way down the building Graham drew attention to the nave windows, ten of them facing northwards. 'Colourings represent the stages in life: infancy, juvenile, maturity, autumn, death.' 'I'm in autumn,' said Ragnhild.

In the back of the nave we descended the steps, Graham with difficulty, on Ragnhild's arm. She said: 'We think there should be more facilities for the disabled', echoing Graham's earlier comment. There were not enough ramps, strange in this day and age and with so much space available. A class of children was sitting in a larger circle than the Unity Chapel could provide. Kitted out in plum coloured blazers they were being regaled by an ebullient master in full throttle. There was none of the bell ringing as at Lichfield, to move the groups on. The routine was on a bigger scale with more space in fewer areas, and we only noticed the solitary party. We came to the Baptistery Window, by John Piper. 'It's completely abstract. If you look in the centre, it's clear glass. Think of the world and Christianity as the light of the world. Roughly, all the yellow could represent the world. The bottom could represent land and sea – green and blue in colour. The top could be the heavenly sky. And there's a little cross or star at the top.' Yes, and it was worth spending time becoming absorbed in it. In effect, look and you shall see. It is the biggest window in the world, the Gloucester east window, seen not long before, next down in size and spectacular in a quite contrasting way. At the bottom was the font, 'a piece of boulder from Bethlehem. If your imagination lets you want to think so, you could have sat on that on the way to Jerusalem'. It was gouged out in the shape of a scallop for the purpose. Graham's speech could have been directed at the children, who had now moved on. Ebullient Master was quiet for a moment. It was entrancing, and of course the window would always defeat the camera. As ever in life, and certainly for this whole amazing edifice, you have to see it for yourself.

The pillars were an engineering triumph. AC-T wrote: 'The high piers, which taper down, are very slender, and could be more so, as is demonstrated at their base.' That was well put. Graham urged us to read the plaques, sets on each wall down the nave. Potency had been handed down from the graffiti of early Christians in the catacombs of Rome. As it was roped off, we could not yet enter the chancel: one of the forthcoming benefits of attending evensong. We did have a view of the Crown of Thorns above the choir stalls, the persuasive ethos continuing around the bishop's throne. This led us to the high altar, designed by Geoffrey Clarke. This evoked an abstract interpretation of the Charred Cross in the Ruins,' informed the *Welcome* leaflet. After the war crosses of nails were presented to the cities of Kiel, Dresden and Berlin. Three medieval nails found among the rubble were bound into the shape of a cross, which was to become a permanent symbol of peace and reconciliation.

We admired the oak nave chairs, very discreet and adaptable – 'Dove tail'. As an observation Ragnhild commented, for all of us: 'I'm amazed at the craftsmanship, of each item and in respect of the high quality specialities throughout.' You could see the different stages – much better than at most cathedrals. It was certainly straightforward and purposeful, uncluttered by generations of development and change: a handful of items compared with a gothic cathedral, but all imposing. She emphasized this after we'd done the rest of the tour: Millennium Chapel of the Stalingrad Madonna (new for 2000 AD, so Graham didn't know it) known for Jane McDonald's artistry, the huge Cross on the left above the stairs, then the Graham Sutherland tapestry. 'It's the size of a Wimbledon tennis court', said Alan Titchmarsh, on the television programme *Yesterday 12*. 'Christ in Glory,' it was called and endued majesty in its massiveness. The figure of man provided a telling image, naked and exposed between the feet of his maker.

Organ practice had commenced. The instrument and its practitioner were refreshingly in full view. This was soothing as we looked back from the tapestry, admiring the seductive curves of the seats at that end. It transpired that the same shiny dark wood and sinuous lines had been used in the choir. Our stalls were very comfortable. My favourite thing was here: the tall, bulbous candlesticks beside the altar, under which we stood on the way to the Chapel of Gethsemane, another utterly different design, the Angel Michael by Steven Sykes. Finally the Chapel of Christ the Servant, in a wing to the side, housing an exhibition of prints. We had passed another exhibition, the Tapestries of Bobbie Cox, which I recalled from Rochester the previous December. There are packages which do nationwide tours – the Anne Frank one was doing the rounds, too, noted in at least three cathedrals up to now.

Nikolaus Pevsner approved of the cathedral and Chapel of Gethsemane and expressed general similar sentiments as AC-T, writing in 1964: '... thousands still go on the pilgrimage and queue outside to be let in...they come to admire a work of architecture and works of art. And they are the same who wrote hardly more than twelve years before: "this unusually ugly factory... resembling a cockroach... the gasholder on one side and the glorified dustbin on the other... "' There was to be plenty to celebrate in 2012.

We read the inscription on the floor by the full-wall west window. By Ralph Bayer, it was incised in grey stone: 'To the glory of God + this cathedral burnt November 14 1940 is now rebuilt + 1962.' My friend O, who had accompanied me to Newport and Llandaff, had complained that this floor had been covered by an exhibition at his visit. It was designed to be a perfect piece and 'notices destroy', he said. I was glad to get it in full, below vast panes of glass in John Hutton's west screen 'The images of saints and angels affirm the continuity of Christianity down the ages. It is the link between the old and the new cathedrals, and represents resurrection.' 'It's like Wells Cathedral,' said Ragnhild simply. I saw what she meant – such detail, all etched in plain glass, so many figures. The whole made for something much bigger than the parts. On the notice board next to it was a photo of a youthful football team, with the caption 'Coventry Cathedral United FC'.

For the cathedral, as well as Graham's delivery from the past, I possessed *The Pictorial Guide to Coventry Cathedral,* inside whose cover my mother had pencilled her and my initials and 'Aug 1969' (a year which was cropping up rather a lot) to mark the visit. Therefore Graham may, perchance, have been our guide on that initial visit. That was when I had bought postcards of two of the creatures drawn from the Revelation: the bull and the eagle, always echoing what we had seen in the Unity Chapel and recently at Bangor: such an evocative subject, open to fresh treatment.

Also in my old paper bag, unearthed in a postcard and souvenir clearout, were postcards of items to be examined again now. Some things had been moved or amended in the 41 years since then, but essentially the cathedral turned out to be an easily comprehended delight, replete with large scale inventions, assertive, confident and meaningful.

Once outside the building Ragnhild and I were bound for the tower, and Graham for refreshments. The *Guide*'s version was:

The Tower and Spire
The tower was built between 1373 and 1395 and it spire, the third highest in England, was added in 1473. Along with much of the rest of St Michael's, the building of the tower and spire was made possible because of the generosity of the Botoner family, who are remembered by statues on the tower. Sir Christopher Wren declared it to be a masterpiece of Gothic building. It escaped destruction in 1940. Twelve bells were rehung for the Cathedral's Silver Jubilee in 1987 and rang for the first time in 100 years when Coventry City won the FA Cup Final.

We scaled the narrow staircase to reach, first, the bell chamber, replete with the rehanging in a brick-built Gothic space. After a rest we completed the elevation, which Ragnhild later revealed she had treated as a test following foot trouble – too much walking on asphalt of late. This proved successful and a worthwhile ascent for us both. We made out a number of landmarks from the perimeter, most interestingly the medieval remnants directly below us. To the north, out of the city by the M6, was the Ricoh Arena, where Coventry City now played. We couldn't identify Graham below anywhere – anyway he was meant to be imbibing a fizzy drink inside the gallery opposite. It was time to join him as we needed cups of tea. The descent was nearing completion, with me ahead, when the ominous sound of voices wafted up. A somewhat bulky man of around 30 came into view. We really couldn't pass each other in that environment of shallow, narrow steps. He gallantly retraced steps, forcing his slightly less weighty companion to retreat first. We emerged painlessly to the ground floor Tourist Information/shop facility, then crossed the old cathedral to reach the gallery, which was firmly closed. Where was our companion? We immediately sought to locate him and procure the refreshment which we had been anticipating with increasing relish since leaving the cathedral. Nothing else of a suitable nature was open, but on reconnoitring the area, I spotted our chap with bottle in hand stepping gingerly by on the far side of the tower. After a purchase of a can of Lilt, he had been ejected – it had closed earlier than the Welcome Woman had told us. Within minutes Graham was sitting comfortably on a wooden seat in the ruin. I had noticed the Golden Cross pub, also close to the tower, so we padded there to find it was a typical city centre watering hole for the young, formerly a coaching inn, perhaps. Not nice, but the barmaid was helpful. She'd never been asked for 'tea' before but had luckily brought in some teabags, which we could have. Once transformed into a drink – milk (semi-skimmed, I noticed), not sugar – she conferred with a spangled and ringed youth, punter-friend rather than co-bar-person, I reckoned, about what to charge. I said: 'How about £1?' 'That sounds right', she said. And so it was. We sat in the front bar enjoying the light through the stained glass, some of which was obscured by sheets announcing cocktails and forthcoming gigs. We regrouped with Graham, and sat awhile absorbing the mellow sun on the red ruins, cultivated into a pleasant environment, enclosed and apart from the hubbub of the city just beyond. A couple from overseas – we didn't agree about where – obliged in taking our group picture on the bench. It ended up in this tome.

It had reached 5 pm. We strolled to the cathedral. There were no restrictions this time; we simply walked up to the choir stalls and chose positions far up on the left, with the best view of the organ and its player. Those seats were wonderful to spend the duration of a service in, amply designed, not to say massive, shaped for both bum and back. Choral evensong featured the boys (being a Wednesday) with pieces by Bairstow and Bach. We could enjoy the architectural riches at close hand, sitting in those stalls with the nearby bishop's throne (more appropriate here than 'cathedra') surmounted by thorns; and those monumental candlesticks were in clear view. It occurred to me that I was harbouring a wish for more exposure to cathedrals' activities, this time for the performance of Benjamin Britten's *War Requiem,* due on 13 November. There were also Monday lunchtime concerts. I had picked up a flyer for the Saturday '2012 Golden Jubilee Men's Breakfast, an opportunity for men to enjoy each other's company – full English Breakfast (£5) and a short talk'. This was another major city church catering for the needs of the population. Subjects included 'Football & Stuff, Second Chance, Coping with Pressure and Trust'. It was required to book in advance, perhaps not entirely user-friendly, requiring effort, but it wasn't absolutely clear who this was aimed at, and in what way it was linked with the jubilee.

From where we were seated the nave windows came into their own, the angle allowing the strength of the stained glass to work its wonder in the late afternoon sun, reaching its peak at the high altar. Their theme was 'The Destiny of Man and the Revelation of God.' Shortly after this trip, I caught a BBC2 programme, *Climbing Great Buildings*. One episode was Jonathan Foyle's visit to Coventry Cathedral. We were able to see much of that now before us, close up. The 74' high tapestry was shown so we could see it close up. It weighed ¾ ton and incorporated 1,000 different shades of wool. The baptistery window up top showed the detailed subtlety of the glasswork and from above, the camera found the clear scallop shape sculpted in the font. Right in front of us as he and Lucy Creamer (a real climber, and they had both visited the cathedral, separately, in their youth) were hoisted high, was the etched 'west' (actually north) window, which employed the very latest techniques in realizing figure detail. Creamer said she hadn't taken much notice at the time of her earlier visit (not having then learned to 'Look Up'); Foyle was to say, of St Paul's Cathedral, mind you, that it was the 'scariest thing' he'd done. The presenters openly entered through that west door, showing that it could be done. So it should, all the time, to maximize visitors' experience of the building.

In an earlier programme, albeit in the same burgeoning territory of what might be referred to as history made relevant at home, was Michael Portillo's *Bradshaw's Railway Journeys*: 'Nothing dates faster than yesterday's view of the future.' Mr Bradshaw recorded Coventry's spires and noted the city's medieval importance. A relevant painting had come down to me, as my grandparents lived here. From 1915, it featured the three spires of Coventry, when they all topped parish churches, before St Michael's was upgraded to cathedral status. In the 14th century this was the fourth most wealthy city in England.

This had been a most rewarding day. We returned quietly satisfied to Ragnhild's home in the heart of the see of Gloucester. Graham regaled us with a seasonal rhyme from Somerset, which he claimed his mother told him: 'Apples be ripe, Nuts be brown, Petticoats up, trousers down.' I think it was the result of too many whist drives. I was next bound for a further culture, if not time, zone in North Wales, back from set pieces of brilliant recent invention to the organic confusion of age-old cathedral buildings.

35

Manchester

St Mary, St Denys and St George

Province: York
Founded: 1421, when made collegiate, having been a parish church
Restored: 1862–68 and through 19th century
Cathedral status: 1847 – created from Chester diocese

Website: www.manchestercathedral.org
Tel: 0161 8332220
Email: office@manchestercathedral.org.uk
Address: Exchange Station Approach, Victoria Street, Manchester
M3 1SX

Three to See: Early 16th century misericords in celebrated choir stalls;
colourful 20th century windows at east and west ends;
15th century angels playing musical instruments

Angel

Saturday 25 September, 2010

It was a frantic weekend in Manchester. The Labour Party Conference was in full flow, the Manchester Peace Festival was culminating its week on the Saturday. The Christian Socialist Movement was to attend the service we chose on the Sunday.

Wakey and I bumped into the Peace Festival at St Ann's Church, which had seen Tony Benn, 'veteran war campaigner' speak at the Concert for Peace on the first day. Owing to an appointment with a football fixture in Stockport, we were unable, most unfortunately, to stay for the lunchtime recital, but we did enjoy the practice session by the musicians as we went round the church. That was armed with cups of tea and a digestive biscuit, most welcome after train journeys from different parts of the country.

Wishing to sample a building other than the cathedral in Manchester diocese, St Ann's was an easy choice, being Simon Jenkins' suggestion in *England's Thousand Best Churches*. It was also geographically convenient, sited in the city centre, in fact close to the cathedral, though our visits to each were on successive days. He wrote:

> ... Here is a quarter of Manchester that has not been humiliated by the 20th century. The church was founded in 1709 by a local aristocrat, Lady Ann Bland, in honour of her own name and that of the then Queen. Her house, Hulme Hall, lay across Deansgate and the church stood on what were the outskirts of the town, facing a large cornfield. Those were the days.

The first piece of impact was two slabs outside the east end, headed: 'Please keep off the tombs'. They carried the same message, with information about a few key individuals. One was William, Lady Ann's son, 'who died in MDCCXXIII (1723)'; also the de Quinceys, whose most famous member, Thomas, wrote *The Confessions of an English Opium Eater*, published in 1821. We noted the best, north, side before entering, which happily faces an open pedestrian street, interrupted only by the statue of Richard Cobden (1804–65, famed for his contribution to the repeal of the Corn Laws), '... two storeys of handsome round-arched windows of equal height are separated by coupled pilasters. The north doorway has coupled columns and a pediment'. The exterior was omitted from the welcome leaflet. There was much to admire before entering, and I regretted that I had never before noticed it, on a number of passings-by over the decades. Its soft-coloured stone appealed in the sun that day.

Inside it was satisfyingly classical, especially given the prospect of the forthcoming cathedral, which represented rather different periods of endeavour. The solid dark pews were good to sit in with the cup and saucer, for contemplation of the unified interior, and, for that matter, a rest after the journey, having also checked into the hotel. We noted the numbers and names on them, recalling its age and its social rigidity. There were even receptacles of the time for umbrellas and sticks. The pulpit had been moved from the dominant position in the centre, in front of the altar, to the top of the nave, to better effect, following the building of a chancel, which was elevated, and topped by the gallery with its organ on the north side. There was a plaque I liked – in honour of James Prince Lee (1804–69), the first Bishop of Manchester, showing how recent was the conception of the diocese. One hundred and ten new churches were built in his time.

It was a matter of absorption, then a wander to the parts not in view: the Lady Chapel, occupied by ladies behind trestle tables dispensing refreshments. A screen masked the painting covered in the leaflet, *The Descent from the Cross*,

> *... in the manner of Annibale Carraci (sic) born 1561. The picture was brought from Italy by a church warden of St Peter's and used to hang in that church until it was demolished in 1907. In very different style altogether is the art deco window. It is in memory of Hilda Collens (correct spelling) who founded the Northern School of Music in 1920. This school is now part of the Royal Northern College of Music whose students perform regularly in St Ann's.*

The window was subtle, with curved and angular motifs etched into the glass. It was colourless and in no dispute with its single-minded surroundings. We both liked it. Shame we couldn't see the Carracci. There was plenty of evidence of the festival, in the form of people involved in various ways, and the opportunity to contribute to the cause of the Pakistani Flood Appeal. Alternatively, there was the ongoing 300 appeal, in anticipation of the church attaining that age in 2012. That's the same year that Coventry Cathedral would reach 50.

This church imbued a state of calm, helpful in view of the indulgent day ahead. Put simply, it comprised football, a pub crawl (real ale only) and good conversation. The score was Stockport 2 Aldershot 2, the home side recovering from a worrying deficit to earn a draw in style. They could well have won. The sorry footnote is that seven months later Stockport County were relegated from the Football League.

Sunday 26 September

The morrow saw us trundling suitcases up Cross Street to Manchester Cathedral, again in cool but sunny conditions. In we went, at around 10.15, to make a careful choice of two neighbouring seats in the busy nave, overwhelmed by full-throated and energetically conducted 'music... sung by the Sing Out Gospel Choir'. That was just about bearable, and had to cease at 10.30 for the action, but front row members of the congregation were singing along to unfortunate effect. The good thing was that the masses were drawn from a wide constituency, including, it transpired, clerics, from all over, well-used to singing (in tune) and conference attenders, who at least liked the sounds of their own voices. I noticed a few familiar faces, such as Ben Bradshaw, MP for Exeter. I regretted not finding him afterwards for an exchange about Exeter City FC, who the day before had beaten Rochdale, a side fairly local to this venue. We may be straying off the subject, but my favourite actress Debbie Reynolds featured in the news this week. Her ex-husband, crooner Eddie Fisher, died. On the death of Elizabeth Taylor's husband, Mike Todd, in an air crash, he lent support to the widow, who was Reynolds' best friend. Of the outcome the latter was to comment: 'You could say that he consoled her to the point of matrimony'. Taylor's ceremonial headdress from the film *Cleopatra* sold for $100K in June 2011 at a gargantuan auction of Reynolds' collection of theatrical costumes and props. The highest price bid was for Marilyn Monroe's crepe dress in *The Seven Year Itch*. It went for $4.6M.

Manchester's dean, the Very Reverend Rogers Govender, born in Durban, South Africa, was President for the service, and opened in welcoming mode, including 'the members of the Labour Party, who may join, and Peter Smith, the Roman Catholic Archbishop of Southwark,' engaged to preach the sermon; also 'the Gospel Choir, very different from usual. Refreshing'. Then he mentioned the cathedral's forthcoming new facility, the Cathedral Café (in the Welcome leaflet the entry was 'Visitor Centre – 20 seconds', to open that Tuesday at 10 am). The initiative had come out of a 'Reflection Day away,' and had taken ten days to produce. I wished we could have stayed to test it, as catering facilities on the trek had been thin on the ground recently, and not very good overall. At least something new held promise. I won't go on about the potential of the coffee.

The singing during the service was delivered by the Lay Clerks, eight of them, directed by Christopher Stokes, Organist and Master of the Choristers and connected to Chetham's School of Music next door. The service booklet was unusually bulky at 24 pages, but had a lot of information to convey, such as an introduction to The Christian Socialist Movement, and a page of information including the Hearing-loop and the availability of Gluten-free wafers for the communion. The first reader was Lord Paul Boateng, his voice as distinctive as remembered from his days in the Cabinet. When it came to the sermon, the Archbishop of Southwark opened with: 'Would you like to take a pew,' which set the tone and earned a round of chuckles. The whole morning's proceedings built up to an act of harmony, promoted by having the pink-clad archbishop at home with an Anglican congregation led by its green and gold, and black, dean. It is worth mentioning some of the content of the sermon – concerning the beggar Lazarus and the Rich Man who would not share even a crumb from his table. The preacher went into the 'unbelievable arrogance' of the Rich Man in Hades, when he assumed Lazarus should cool his burning body by getting him liquid for his tongue. When it came to the Prayers of Intercession, the subjects of poverty and tax were addressed. Tax justice had become a campaigning issue. Postcards had been left on the seats to sign and leave, amounting to a petition to strengthen the system. The President saw fit to point out that we were on page 17, for newcomers, maybe. During the communion ten goblets were used, sitting proudly on the altar until transferred to the hands of a number of servers, some of whom were at a serving point further back. The process was, frankly, an organizational mess, emphasizing the rare level of communicants on this occasion. The 6" altar platform didn't help, confusing as to where to stand or kneel. All those baptised were invited to partake. I didn't recall that being uttered before, as the practice was for the more advanced confirmees to take the sacrament. It was, however, another indication of the extension of the hand of goodwill.

Events like this are always an opportunity to embrace the surroundings. We were, in effect, a captive audience, augmented by the quiet incursion of delegates. Looking up at the repeated pattern of angels in the nave bosses, their instruments painted gold, it emerged that this was the icon for Manchester. It had to be an angel, affirmed afterwards in finding more in other areas. These were 15th century and the contemporary instruments, fairly obviously if you could make out the likes of sackbuts and rebbecks so far aloft.

The service over, we were treated to more than just the tea and coffee. Ed Miliband, narrowly elected as new leader of the Labour party the previous day, was there to give us an affecting speech, thankfully short, as the sermon had been. The tea (and the toilets) was inaccessible, being out laid out close to the speech area at the top, where senior clergy and politicians were standing.

While high level conversations pervaded over plastic cups and bourbon biscuits, Wakey and I embarked upon our tour of the building, armed with photocopies I had made of books at home, plus the Welcome leaflets highlighting 'Five things not to miss' and the more detailed 'A brief history and guide to architecture'. These were all we needed: a human guide was not essential. It was pleasant to observe, yet again for a 'third division' cathedral, that there was a cornucopia of goodies to admire, not just angels, though the first thing we now happened upon was the Angel Stone, 'the oldest object in the building'. The caption informed that it had been found in the masonry of the medieval porch of the cathedral when it was demolished in the 19th century. Saxon or early Norman, it may have been a former part of the tympanum (decorative panel of stone over a doorway) of the original south doorway of the church more than 1,000 years ago. An irregular fragment of stone, it justified its place beside the pulpitum.

The obvious glory of this building is the quire. As Alec Clifton-Taylor referred to the 'magnificent set of choir stalls' and that's all, in relegating the cathedral to the lowest division of quality, not part of England's 'vintage' set of 26. Ernest F Letts wrote in 1891, as Minor Canon and Precentor:

> *Entering the choir by the richly-decorated organ-screen, we find the interior small and narrow, but filled with exceedingly beautiful stalls, fifteen on each side. They are surmounted by the most elaborate canopies it is possible to imagine. There are niches for over a hundred saints, and the crockets and finials, cuspings and pinnacles, are bewildering in their variety and multitude. Nor less interesting are the quaint groups of the subcellae or misereres. Tavern incidents, hunting scenes, fabulous monsters, combats, legends, all find a place, carved with the most elegant minuteness, and fortunately little damaged by the hand of time.*

So well put, that could describe a number of other sets of choirstalls/misericords. At Manchester it is critical, as AC-T was right that they are the best thing there. It's best not to mention the cathedra, but I shall, for contrast. It is disappointing, and Letts, with his vested interest as a company man, agreed. His phrase was 'sad contrast'.

It's advisable to go modern after that, to the east end, where notice boards told of the work of the diocese elsewhere.

1   In Namibia, St George the Martyr, Windhoek, was the smallest cathedral in Africa. Links there 'stem from the time when Bishop Stanley Booth-Clibborn of Manchester spent with his wife in Africa'.

2   Tampere, Finland, of Lutheran persuasion: 'faces many of the

same post-industrial challenges we experience in North West England'.

3   St John the Divine, New York: 'both cities have suffered from terrorist attacks and face challenges of working with a wide variety of people in an urban setting'.

These were good points and initiatives.

We moved round and into the Regiment Chapel and Fire Window. That window had been in the line of vision from our seats in the nave, and was seriously provocative, i.e. stunning. Bright red and substantial, it lifted the whole area and elevated the theme of war in the chapel to a contemporary dynamic. The windows are really something. The 'brief history' states:

> *All the stained glass windows in the cathedral were destroyed in an air raid in December 1940 (the Fire Window was restored following the effect of an IRA bomb which exploded near the cathedral in 1996). At the west end, are five modern stained glass windows by Anthony Hollaway, who was influenced by the expressionist theories of Vasily Kandinsky.*

They are all impressive, and refreshing after the endless Victorian glass elsewhere. Manchester suffered serious damage during the Second World War.

Moving west from the chapel we were struck by the unique facet of the cathedral as a five-aisled building, making it the widest nave in England. The reason was the multiplicity of chantry chapels, complete with altars, established by notable (and wealthy) local families between 1310 and 1523. The intent behind it was fair enough: 'to offer regular prayers both for the souls of the departed and the welfare of the living'. There were eight of them, perhaps saying something about the prosperity of the area. It couldn't last and several generations later, reformers considered prayers for the dead to be superstitious. In 1546 the chantries were abolished, eventually followed by the partitioning walls. This immense width is quirky and allows greater accommodation in the modern world of popular events, also spinning money for the coffers. The downside is that it must be lost space a lot of the time, and expensive to heat, I imagine. Moving across the aisles one by one did allow for appreciation of the west windows, depicting The Creation (1991), St George (1973), St Mary (1980), St Denys (1976), The Apocalypse (1996). All marvellous, they put me agreeably in anticipation of the works of Edward Burne-Jones in Birmingham. The visit there was getting closer.

We were by the altar dais earlier attended by hesitant communicants. Looking upwards again was the pulpitum, the richly-decorated double timber screen, from 1509, modified in the 19th century. Reassuringly bulky, I thought, affording room inside for storage. You have to be practical. It also led up to the organ console. But you can't tarry with the pride and joy so close, that is the choir stalls and misericords. We've dealt with those, so move further south to the chapter house, again applying an individual approach. It is octagonal, completed by 1510, simple and effective.

By this time the hubbub had dwindled, and Wakey, returning from reconnaissance while I scribbled notes, imparted the bulletin that Dean Rogers had finished his sequence of chats. He had in fact vanished when I arrived in the south aisle, his station ever since the departure of the new Leader of the Opposition. An aside here: new chief Ed was going to have to accept the Shadow Cabinet members voted in by the party. Was that workable, especially in this case when it was the union vote that got him elected, and he was seen as veering to the long-lost Left? He would be working with men and women out of sympathy with his philosophy. It was all to come out in the wash.

Anyway, I made it through to the newer business section to the southeast of the cathedral, to gain admittance to the Dean's Office by, I think, a verger. I didn't ask owing to a perceived concern about time. Wakey remained in the nave to absorb and meditate, and look after our suitcases. The background to this was the phone calls with the Dean's PA, Alison Rowland. Most productive, the date for the visit had been governed by the holiday, to be springboarded from Birmingham Airport a couple of days later. We were very luck to hit upon this pioneering, high-profile time. Alison had confirmed that Dean Rogers would be happy to see me, but unlike most Sundays, when he was free after the service (in an old building), he would be rather tied up on this occasion. Hence the chance to do the tour round the cathedral with Wakey, and now to find the dean free for a chat. I had explained my agenda, in his case to find out how it was for him working in a totally urban diocese in the north of England, given his background in Durban. The map of the see, one of the clearest on the website, comprised the conurbation of Greater Manchester, with archdeaconries in Bolton, Rochdale, Salford and Manchester, but with Wigan ceded to Liverpool.

The Dean, 'Call me Rogers,' had been working in the Church of England for ten years, and was familiar with the urban element from his work at home. There were huge challenges, of homelessness, as one example. The centre downstairs offered covers for 120–150 per week, able to provide food and access to information, training and education. People released from prison would be an element of those in need, along with the mentally disturbed. There was a charity set up, independent of the dean and chapter. The cathedral could offer space and utilities. I suggested there had to be a budget for this. Yes, and funds were available from certain sources. Outside the building, there was plenty of evidence of needle pushing, the phenomenon of skateboarding and bottle breaking in the precinct. This was in the centre of one of England's biggest cities. Every morning the verger would gather glass within cathedral territory, which actually did not extend very far outside. Then there were the drinkers, the vomit, downers aplenty. All of this was part of the work, which got discussed with peer dioceses, such as Manchester's neighbours, Chester, Liverpool and Blackburn. Open all day, the troubled were able to approach volunteer chaplains, often retired clergy, with a lifetime of experience. One of them travelled from Lancaster (Diocese of Blackburn) to help out. That's a distance of 56 miles.

Benefits of the cathedral, by now with an extensive and varied experience, exercising its upgraded status, were many. The rare connection to Chetham's was one. The brief history referred to it: '… much of which is an extensive intact medieval complex very much like an Oxbridge college.' I wished we'd found time to cover the '250 m' to explore it. There was clearly a healthy outcome in the college producing boys and girls choirs (together with the lay clerks). On another tack, the cathedral had good civic connections. Its work contributed, after all, to local life, in some ways fused with it. Events were held in the nave – Rogers showed me a photo on his phone: an exotically lit (predominantly electric blue) happening the previous Friday night. The Coop had hosted 500 for a fundraising event. The dean had said grace for the UNICEF dinner. Harvey Nichols (their shop was in view outside) was to hold a fashion show. This opened up the cathedral for what it used to be. This comment echoed the Antiques Road Show at Chester and the Craft Market at Southwell. Pop shows were welcome, too, though the *Guardian* only awarded The Magnetic Field two stars when they performed there earlier in the year. Altogether it was an urban and community presence, an organization of the present and future – in the public domain. Word of mouth and the website played a vital role.

Dean Rogers had to leave to tend to a sick child, and Wakey and I left the building to take in the tower and peer at the gargoyles on the south side of the roof. A rarity they were, and surprisingly unweathered. Had they not been so high up, they could have solved the challenge of a photograph for Manchester. I hoped one of the angel pictures would serve, which would have been appropriate. It was already lunchtime. We therefore repaired to a pub, the Waldorf, convenient for the onward train journey, for a couple of pints and Aston Villa. This was eventually achieved, after some negotiation with the barman, whose interpretation of the pub's Sky deal proved questionable. Wakey made the shock choice of Walker's Turkey and stuffing flavoured crisps. 'I thought I'd give them a go,' he said, 'seeing as Christmas cards are already in the shops.' I wondered which would be the first cathedral to find a Christmas tree installed.

36

Norwich

Holy Trinity

Province: Canterbury
Founded: 630 at Thetford, Benedictine; 1094 moved to Norwich
Present building: 1096–1145

Website: www.cathedral.org
Tel: 01603 218300
Email: reception@cathedral.org.uk
Address: The Close, Norwich NR1 4DH

Three to See: Cloisters showing style changes;
chocolate font;
rare pelican lectern

Chocolate

Thursday 28 October, 2010
North Norfolk churches had reached the shell-like orifices of Rand and me as an essential precursor to the glory of Norwich Cathedral.

We opened the gambit in King's Lynn. 'Lynn' sports its own Suffragan Bishop, along with Thetford in the Diocese of Norwich. The see more or less comprises the county of Norfolk, with some notable funny bits: Lowestoft, Suffolk, is embraced, but the western area of Downham Market southwards is not – it's Ely's. St Margaret's Church is the image of Lynn, 'Bishop's Lynn' until the monarch elevated it during the Reformation. In the interminable flatness of the Fens, it stands proud above the wide River Great Ouse, the eastern boundary of the Wash. Indeed it has been awash may a time, some of such acts of God being noted by the west door. 1978 was particularly high – 4'. Imagine that! Above, safe from flooding the somewhat rum mismatch of the two west towers drew a snigger, the southern one so much bigger, and it displayed a 1650 moon clock in a fetching combination of blue and gold. Speaking of floods, apparently the clock 'shows phases of the moon and, by means of a green dragon's tongue, the time of the next high tide… using the 24-hour system. The letters in "LYNN HIGH TIDE" are each two hours apart,' (*Harris's Guide to Churches and Cathedrals*). I shall point out one more phenomenon, also from Harris: 'the two largest brasses in Britain. The earlier is of Adam de Walsoken, 1349. The other commemorates Robert Braunche (1364), who gave a peacock feast for King Edward III in 1349 and this is shown in the bottom frieze… Both average 9 feet in length.' They dominated the south aisle, and rubbings thereof decorated the wall, so they were quite a presence. The trouble was that, like bosses, it is not easy to discern what you are peering at, as they are flat and without contrast. I identified one of them as a post mill, in the resident caption as the first portrayal of such a thing. Following a wander round the town and along the waterfront, we finished the tourist session with the rewarding 'Seahenge' exhibition (Bronze Age timber circle) in Lynn Museum. These few days were to prove an extensive exposure to this area. The sense of pilgrimage started in this town, a Hanseatic port whose provender included religious sites and untamed fen. The evening was spent on (local?) fish and chips and a good film in the 1928 Majestic Cinema, refreshing for its fadedness. *RED* was the film. It stood for 'Retired, extremely dangerous.' Well, we were retired, technically… It proved just the ticket with the prospect of so many churches to come in Norfolk, leading up to that promising spired treat: Norwich Cathedral.

Friday 29 October
Replete with guest house breakfast at the Beeches, we realized a visit to St Nicholas Chapel was essential, to facilitate a more complete view of this

terminus of a town. It had been the end of the line, certainly, for me at that enchanting teashop in the station. This was exciting – we had to obtain a key to the chapel from the Tudor Rose Hotel, which was duly handed over by the management. I had to sign a book, but was not required to inscribe any details. Very trusting. What we hadn't established was which door the key would unlock. On a clockwise perambulation, we observed tombstones repositioned under the wall to look as if they were sheltering from the elements. This church is redundant, there being no congregation now, but it was available for weddings. We passed one door after another, each with orifices for nothing like the shape of the key in my hand (rather *Alice in Wonderland*). They all looked redundant, and rusty. Falling apart, more like. We reached the south side, arriving at a small door with a key hole obviously the right one as we approached. The metal round it shone through the windy gloom.

St Nicholas was an eerie, bleak building, enhanced by the awareness that we were entirely alone there, with increasingly skeletal trees visible through the plain glass windows. Mostly skyward Perpendicular, the nave and roof (termed East Anglian 'Angel') soared, and impressed. There was the relic of a consistory court in the northwest corner, and a bucket behind the organ; also some memorials and a poppy bench end among a number of highlights. This was a chapel of ease for St Margaret's, and, close to the north part of Lynn and the elegant and huge Tuesday Market. Back we repaired to the Tudor Rose with the key. On this occasion the market place was substantially given over to parking, the handful of stalls occupying a small corner. One of them, a greengrocer's, was selling 'Romanesque cauliflowers', at which we gawped, as they were most stylish and structured. St Margaret's was close to the smaller Saturday Market, serving the south part of the town. And on we went, dropping in at Hunstanton for a coffee with some kind of view of the Wash.

We arrived soon at the Burnhams, those locally concentrated, but tiny, mostly, centres of trade and pilgrimage on the North Norfolk coast. This meant six churches, starting with the Saxon Burnham Deepdale, right on the road, and offering us red herrings and an agreeably wide range of buildings. Bored we were not, even learning all about Horace (as he preferred to be called), Lord Nelson at Thorpe where his dad was the Rector. The interest of these was related through choice of photographic material. I've just looked at the Burnhams again:

- Deepdale: the font carried fetching illustrations of the activities of peasants through the months. Rand's favourite was November – 'a pig being brought in to be killed'; mine, August – 'a man binds corn into a sheaf'. We had to be told, on the supporting display board, as it wasn't always clear. Other good ones were 'drinking from a horn' (January) and 'at table for the feast' (December). Life wasn't always hard. Another essential note is about the medieval stained glass, one window centred around the Crucifixion surrounded by golden celestial rays.

- Overy Town, where windmills were the local landmarks. We had been directed there from Overy Staithe, which sadly lacks a church. But these places are very close together. St Clement boasted fine lancet windows, again a treat for Rand who by this time was developing a lancet passion. Also the chancel was unusual, enclosed within the nave.

- Thorpe, abounding with Nelson references, and refreshingly straightforward. We didn't follow through the prospect of lunch at the Nelson Arms (formerly Plough), as it was issuing an acrid aroma, to do with work under way. And the available seating areas were full. This was Half Term Week.

- Market, the centre thereabouts, and something of a second home haven (my friend Tony used to travel up from Horsham, West Sussex, for breaks there). Two churches, for Burnham Ulpha and Westgate. The former modest and workaday, its glory being the Jockey Inn opposite where we spent a brief sojourn over some Woodforde's Wherry. Westgate was on the way out of town, with a curiously patchwork tower.

- Norton, once unearthed, turned out to be closer to Market than the village of Norton: a true landmark on a rare hill – a cylindrical tower and an amazing pulpit, in the shape of a wineglass, restored to its original richly-coloured magnificence.

It was time for our appointment, with the Revd Christopher Wood, Rector, whose abode lay behind Brancaster church, which we had passed earlier on the way to Deepdale. He had been in post since June 2009, the brief being 'Rector of Hunstanton with Ringstead Parva, Holme-next-the-Sea and Thornham, Brancaster with Burnham Deepdale and Titchwell with Choseley (Norwich), formerly Assistant Curate of St Margaret with St Nicholas, King's Lynn. This is summarized by the epithet 'Rector of the Seven Seaside Parishes.' There you are! To its chagrin Holme-next-the-Sea had suffered the loss of Seahenge, as it came to be called, to Lynn Museum. And he was great-nephew of his namesake, the St Ives artist, which pleased Rand, an enthusiast of that discipline. Over tea in his living room, we enjoyed works by Gwen John and John Piper, and Theo the splendidly massive tabby cat, who was banished following a show of aggression aimed at the sofa.

Christopher was substantial himself, bluff and urbane. He set the local ecclesiastical scene for our amused edification. Pilgrimage was a central ingredient in North Norfolk, with Walsingham close by and emblematized by the Milky Way – Our Lady's Milk. Abbeys and churches abounded for travellers reaching the coast. Water is linked with milk. Other idiosyncrasies pervade, such as the presence of saffron, normally associated with more exotic locations. The Carmelite priory itself had links with the Holy Land, a hike from there, but it seems to have become a sometime itinerary by sea. The way the Church of England worked there meant considerable independence. It was extensive and the Bishop of Lynn served his own tranche at an impractical distance from the centre of the see at Norwich. The lack of motorways in the county affected communication. Chris was a man of many parts, riding his scooter back from Thornham just before we arrived and mixing socially in an area where the church might be more linked to the way of life than elsewhere. We could imagine him enjoying hospitality betimes, alongside judging village allotment produce. What if you hate courgettes? He touched on local white witchcraft in connection with the war effort, but we won't go into detail here. To mention this related a little to his origins. He came from Ramsbottom, or 'Tup's Arse'. Near there lies the Trough of Bowland, a centre renowned for the Pendle Witches.

When asked about his cathedral preference, the Rector reeled off a few favourites: York, Lichfield, Wells, St Davids. When pressed he said, in authoritative tone: 'Durham,' explaining that, as well as being magnificent and massive, it offered some quiet spaces. Having also admitted, quietly, that his favourite church under his wing was the local Deepdale, he revealed that his pastime was beekeeping, mentioning the intoxicating smell of the hive. It was addictive, he admitted, alongside involvement with the Beekeepers Association. He referred to Buckfast Abbey in Devon – Brother Adam was the man there. Our host was quite happy with his life in this remote enclave. We could see why. On our way out, prompted by Rand, Chris donned his crash helmet and posed for photos on his scooter. It carried L-plates, and the church tower formed a telling backdrop.

Rand sped down the map that evening, the only item of note being 'Ellie Joanne' on an Eddie Stobart lorry. Having settled in at the Nelson Premier Inn, we took the train from Norwich to Wymondham, to be met by friend and host for the evening, Linds. He made a brief detour to provide a glance at Wymondham Abbey by floodlight. We admired it through the iron railings. It would have been good to examine the abbey in daylight. It was a 'Greater Church' as well, of which more anon. I read a Wymondham Abbey anecdote about Alexander of Langley, once upon a time the Prior, who sadly became insane. Publicly censured by the Abbot, he was flogged 'to a copious effusion of blood', and kept chained in solitary confinement at Binham Priory until his death. He was buried in his chains. We were ready for the main act.

Saturday 30 October

A bracing river walk round old Norwich is recommended. That is what we applied ourselves to after a hearty breakfast in the Nelson Premier Inn, which stood beside the River Wensum and in sight of the station, and, one heard, had once been the city's best. It did just what we wanted, at £39 for the room. Not quite the bargain the Premier Inn near St Asaph had represented at £29, but most suitable. It even allowed us to leave the car there for the whole day's cathedral search and city wander. Rand was a Norwich novice, and confessed to being well-impressed with the day's experience.

It was bright, and stayed that way. This was one of the best times to visit, given the richness of hue in foliage wherever we went, eventually round the cathedral. The arrival point which had been suggested to me, the north porch, was curiously secreted behind the Cathedral School. It was disappointing not to be able to circumnavigate the building. We did what we could, noting Edith Cavell's mundane grave, and antiquity at every turn. She was a Norfolk vicar's daughter, who trained as a nurse and was instrumental in the escape of a number of prisoners. Her last words were: 'Standing as I do, in view of God and Eternity, I realise that patriotism is not enough; I must have no hatred or bitterness towards anyone.' She was shot on 12/10/1915. Our interest in her had been stirred by Christopher Wood the previous afternoon. I observed that both Chris and our guide to be, Ian, pronounced her name with the accent on the 'a', as in 'cavil', perhaps a little unfortunately. Or was that correct?

The first (free) tour of the day was at 11 am. This involved 15 of us and the excellent guide, Ian Walters, who was a tad daunted by the presence of the two of us, a bit obvious with notebook and sketch book, cameras, binoculars and printouts of information from a tome or two. 'Don't worry', I reassured him (I hope), 'We'll be attentive.' We were and the ¾ hour tour ran over the hour. Ian's stated reason was that it was a large group. He was full of fascinating detail, so I reckon we got the long straw: an informed and intelligent leader whose knowledge would always run over. There was a slight concern on our part, as afterwards we had to try the Café – empirical testing, and judgement of quality, as always. Then we had noticed that our other venue of the day, the 'Greater Church' in the city centre, St Peter Mancroft, purported to present a (free) lunchtime concert. Actually, to get ahead of myself, on scouring the leaflet during a lull, this was the only week with no concert, so we were let off the hook. Half term has that effect.

Ian had already imparted these relevant points:

- There was no cat, though the dean had dogs.
- It was wretched (Rand's favourite word) to be informed that Norwich had lost its chapter house. We had guessed wrong as to the former site. It was actually in the corner between the four-sided cloisters and the south transept. These are the only two-storey monastic cloisters. Peterborough, the next day, had suffered the same loss.
- He was fairly ignorant on cathedral property, except that the close visible from the city end was leased out to carefully chosen people, normally those involved with operations in some way. Income was always welcome. Cathedrals are hard up.
- The bells were a real disappointment: there were five, of which two were cracked. What remained was struck, not swung. These days 'Dial-a-Tune' was used, from the Lay Vergers office.
- His favourite cathedral was Lincoln.
- He emphasized that the Hostry, new in 2009, and the slightly older Refectory should be sampled.

On opening the tour, he emphasized that this was a house of prayer, so in the side chapels we would not disturb anyone there. That was obvious, but in all these tours had not been previously uttered. It was a good thing to mention, I thought. Equally, there was a visiting organist at practice. This was to be borne in mind. The cathedral had Romanesque origins (1068). Ian preferred the term to 'Norman'. We were happy with that, too. There was also considerable late Gothic work, including the spire, which works as a tempting piece of work, a landmark, second to Salisbury in height. The cathedral is awash with bosses, for which binoculars helped. Occasional mobile mirrors were available, to minimize neck strain. There was considerable colour, every boss depicting an event from the Bible, in sequence. The Crucifixion stood proud, and the Ascension. Christopher Wood had told us about the hole in the roof. His story was about feathery Norfolk angels, of local mystery play origin. There were fowl in the fields as a source. The hole in the roof opened. Down the chain came a man to feather those below. Ian's was the official version, presenting basic fact of the matter: to bring something down, such as a light or relic, or for swinging a censer. The feast of Pentecost would require the arrival of the Holy Spirit. There had been a major collapse in 1463, resulting in much of the building, such as lierne vaulting of great style.

Down the nave, between pillars, we admired what was to be my favourite artefact – the font, in shiny hemispherical brass. Like Rolos, it was the product of chocolate people Nestle's, or 'Caley's' – marching chocolate. The top was detachable, and the base would be pushed into the nave for use. 'Norfolk folk do different, 'commented Ian

Once in the choir stalls, I had read that the misericords were disappointing, but Ian showed a few brilliant images. There was one showing corporal punishment – schoolmaster and errant boy. There were two recent ones, showing aspects of contemporary life. One, under the seat of the vice-dean, one Jeremy Haselock, with whom I had unfortunately not managed to make contact, featured Norwich City FC, the Canaries, at a time of lesser achievement. They were now of higher status. 'But not performing,' opined the man next to me. In fact they were to achieve two promotions in two years. And their celebrity joint majority shareholder, Delia Smith, omelette-woman, was not in evidence. I had seen replicas in the shop, while we were waiting. Also, there was a jolly wyvern for £20, or squirrel, merman, dolphin, owl or bear. 22 ¾ carat gold was involved in items for £120, or smaller ones at £50.

The eye was caught beyond the choir stalls by the brass pelican lectern, at that moment sharply defined in bright sunshine. It dates from c.1450 and shows the bird feeding its young. Meanwhile the boss saga rolled on. Wherever you looked they lurked aloft – 900 altogether, more than any other cathedral. The fine lierne vaulting links with an intensive approach to boss insertion. Largely responsible was Bishop Lyhart, also remembered in stone. The high altar provided a diversion. 'This is the only cathedral north of the Alps,' recounted Ian, 'with the cathedra behind the high altar.' There it rested, remote and squat, compared with most bishops' thrones. There was also a more traditional bishop's seat – Victorian and drab. They would have been better advised to dump them both to be replaced by one impressive one. Our attention was drawn to the apparent fire damage to the stone. It was pinker in places. The Civil War had seen some sacking, as well as the fire of 1272. That came about as a result of taxes levied by monks on fairs. A riot ensued, and conflagration.

We were wondering about a crypt. The absence of one owed to the River Wensum, all too close on its way to the North Sea. In the northeast corner was the Reliquary Arch, bearing what was now the Treasury, where all manner of beautiful artefacts were residing in cabinets. 'Silver and gold was melted down during the Reformation.' There's a story. Further, in the Lady Chapel, now St Saviour's for the military, we learned something. Banners lined the walls, some threadbare. This was because they are not maintained. In several chapels attractive wall paintings on panels elevated the atmosphere. Some had graced the Victoria & Albert museum's exhibition in 2000. They were from different ages. St Luke's Chapel, so appealing from the exterior, with its Romanesque curve, was disappointing within. It served as parish church of St Mary in the Marsh. The bosses got a bit out of hand in the chapel – I counted nearly 50, though the five-panelled altarpiece was worth a close look.

We had done the circuit round to the south transept. One of the group asked about the netting in the crossing. In every other cathedral with a central tower, a glory was to crane your neck to examine the structure. This may explain the unusual positioning of pews in a circle below. Like the bell situation I was disappointed that to prevent damage, and of course for Health and Safety purposes, the entire square was covered in a crude manner. It also obviated access to the levels above: no roof visits here. Above that was the 313' spire. The height caused concern about stability.

But we were now at the recent pride and joy: The Hostry, funded by the Heritage Lottery Fund, the Friends and other foundations. The first thing to confront you as you enter by the orthodox route (unlike us – we happened upon it on departure, so bypassing 'recommended donation £5, £4 concessions') was this notice: 'Access via the Hostry Visitor and Education Centre'. This had been the brainchild of former dean, Stephen Platten, and cost £12.5m. Happily I was to meet him in his next guise as Bishop of Wakefield.

Ian told us about the opening on 4/5/10, when Ian shook hands with the Queen. Serious security was imposed throughout the service, attended by 'guys who looked like prop forwards – burly blokes', he said. The message was: 'All who arrive as guests are to be welcomed like Christ.' He was very enthusiastic about the new addition. Even the Christmas cards showed a new design this year. We were finishing in the cloisters, complete with blind arches behind which were crammed the trappings of a modern cathedral – coloured leads and ropes. Rand, very handy and as keen on repairs as reredoses, seemed to salivate at this point. But this was soon after a flurry of green man bosses in the east cloister, and at the end of a mouth-watering tour, so these factors may have contributed. It was good to apply our architecture knowledge and observe the tracery of the windows on each side to be in a slightly different style, reflecting the rapid fashions of the time over 130 years. These were the largest monastic cloisters. The largest overall, were at Salisbury. There was a rolling programme of stone masonry. 'Some need "tlc,"' he said, 'repair work.' He drew attention to the new builds adjacent to the cloisters, beyond walls of flint. The actual finish to the tour – a meritoriously long one – was back in the nave, near the chocolate font, and the shop.

Refreshment in the Refectory was overdue, and we enjoyed it. Reminiscent of Chapter Two Café at Wells, also a recent addition, this one paraded an ambitious mix of ancient and modern. The contemporary parts seemed effective and likely to harmonize over time. I just had a slight reservation that it felt detached from the cathedral, through the solid division in the south cloister wall. The aspect was a bit fragmented, of more building, bushes and cathedral properties. Perhaps I was spoilt by Wells, from which there was an open view of moat etc. The coffee was adequate, the pear cake fine, for lack of lemon drizzle, with a further negative that we were forced to share a refectory-type table with a couple on a Saturday jaunt there, not entirely at one with each other. There were not enough smaller tables. Rand was able to read a newspaper while I was queuing up, which was not a burdensome process given the hour (lunchtime, by now). It was only later that I was reminded of the cathedral's passive role in *The Go-Between* by L P Hartley, for 13 year-old Leo, boiling in a tweed jacket. Set in the hot summer of 1900, it must have been a cool oasis for the lad to be dumped there, allowing the protagonists Marian and Ted to give vent to their passion. That was set before the age of cathedral tea rooms, one imagines.

Onward to the impressive market and St Peter Mancroft, outside which we were faced with the statue of Thomas Browne (1605–82), 'contemplating with urn'. He once said: 'Oblivion is a kind of annihilation,' and was a writer who chose themes ranging from religion to the esoteric, in extravagant language. *Forgotten English* told more on a tear-off calendar item for 19/10/10:

> *English antiquarian. His first book Religio Medici (1643) received a mixed reaction from critics. According to Samuel Johnson's biographical sketch of him afterward (no 's' as the dictionary was an American publication), the undaunted Browne "experienced the delights of praise and molestations of censure, probably found his dread of the publick eye diminished, and therefore (it) was not long before he trusted his name to the criticks a second time, for in 1646 he printed Enquiries into Vulgar and Common Errors. As the title clearly indicated, this work contained a series of valid exposes of everyday "endeavours of Satan," or devilish misconceptions, ranging from the value of medicinally ingested gold to why beavers supposedly gnawed off their testicles and scent glands to escape detection from hunters. The God-fearing philosopher*

also posed some thought-provoking biological and theological
questions regarding such stories as that of Noah's Ark, about
which he asked what the carnivorous animals ate during the
long voyage and why all plant life was not destroyed in the
mighty forty-day inundation.

I should add that the day's word was 'Noaharchaic', meaning 'extremely old-fashioned and out of date,' which author Jeffrey Kacirk credited to Maurice Warren's *Dictionary of American Slang* (1934).

The antiquarian's effigy had been moved close to Norwich's Perpendicular treat. St Peter Mancroft had been closed on my previous visit, and it was a shame that there was no music, as the organ was stunning to look at. Its performance and the building's acoustic earned praise from Roger Youngman, the day's welcomer, who greeted us. This building dated from 1430–50 and was one of the Greater Churches, of which I was now keeping a parallel list, and a thrilling complement to the cathedral. Simon Jenkins gave it **** in *England's Thousand Best Churches*. The tower was unusual. Its Victorian 'fleche' pricked into the sky above. We ventured inside to find it full of rich detail. It was light and spacious, helped by a lack of stained glass, a preference I was developing in a general way after so much Victorian excess up and down the country. Roger told us of the ring of twelve bells, a bit of an improvement on Holy Trinity Cathedral! I noted a particular item on display: a humungous pewter jug. The campanologists concerned have been wont to use the jug, to assuage the thirst from so much exercise: it holds 33 pints. We were in search of just the two, which we accomplished in the Bell, celebrating which bell we failed to discover.

Fig 47

Fig 48

Fig 49

Fig 50

[47] Manchester: Misericord depicting
    dynamic dragon.
[48] Manchester: Abstract stained glass
    window: red and yellow.
[49] Norwich: Rare pelican lectern.
[50] Peterborough: Leather goblet in the
    treasury.
[51] Peterborough: Clipsham Quarry: stone
    destined for cathedrals.

Fig 51

37

Peterborough

St Peter, St Paul & St Andrew

Province: Canterbury
Founded: 970 as Benedictine abbey
Present building: 1116–80 after fire
Restored: 1882 tower rebuilt
Cathedral status: 1541

Website: www.peterborough-cathedral.org.uk
Tel: 01733 343342
Email: info@peterborough-cathedral.org.uk
Address: Cathedral Office, Minster Precincts, Peterborough PE1 1XS

Three to See: Painted nave ceiling;
fan vaulting;
baldacchino

Pomegranate

Sunday 31 October, 2010

We had been warned: Peterborough is ugly, in action and appearance; too easy to reach from London and the working north. The East Coast main line was reputed to be efficient, so industrialists might be persuaded by the city's accessibility and reliability, with all the trappings of fast-moving existence in the modern world. The Revd Christopher Wood, of North Norfolk, had grimaced dramatically when the name 'Peterborough' was brought up. He told how once he attended choral evensong in snowy conditions before Christmas. A snowball was thrown through a window – quite disconcerting, but unsurprising to him given the character of some of the people in the shopping precinct just beyond the cathedral's enclave.

Catherine of Aragon was buried here in 1536, and Mary Queen of Scots paused in her coffin on the way from Fotheringhay Castle to London. Fotheringhay was the scene of her final incarceration, leading to her beheading (after two strokes) in 1587. I dare say her spot here gets comparatively more attention than the Westminster memorial, where it is one among many.

It is argued that Henry VIII was swayed by his first queen's interment in converting this from abbey to cathedral. The 1541 'Deed of Endowment of a new cathedral' was the subject of a display, appointing John Chambers as the first bishop. Among other things the signing of this deed by Henry VIII:

- Made the Abbey Church a Cathedral
- Created a Bishop of Peterborough
- Made Peterborough a City
- Created a King's School

Indeed the diocese is curious. The city formerly ran its own sub-zone, the Soke of Peterborough, attached to Northamptonshire to the west. But look at the map and you will see its position in Fenland on the cusp of rival territories, a hotbed of vying interests over the centuries. Peterborough is in Cambridgeshire, a county mostly within the diocese of Ely. The see of Peterborough basically comprises Northamptonshire, with Rutland, which itself was abolished as a county in 1974 to be absorbed into Leicestershire. It was thankfully restored as a county in 1997.

The very first sight of Peterborough Cathedral merited photos: it is composed of impressive towers and spires, with the perimeter gatehouse serving in a support role below them. On the way we enjoyed a couple of old buildings, trying to survive among the road works and concrete regeneration, to be generous to official intentions. There were four in the party: Rand (task – drawings), Wakey (observation followed by proof reading) and Mickser (based in the area and with an historical bent, therefore tour guide on a day with no such official provision) and myself. We missed out on Benedicts Café, which was recommended by a warden, but closed. Also, on weekdays we might have joined a mouth-watering tour including the triforium, tower and roof 'in a snakelike format' she said. Benedicts had been promising, affording entry into another former monastic building, unencumbered by the cathedral itself. In this it is unlike many cafés, which are located, with the best of intentions, inside the main event, making them cramped and inefficient.

First we derived full value from the west front, at a distance, then close up. Alec Clifton-Taylor summarized it: 'The dramatically unexpected W front is unique in Europe', with three Early English arches, surmounted by rose windows, featuring the three patron saints. Mickser commented: 'I used to call it "Peter, Paul and Mary."' Conveniently we heard some singing. Eucharist had started, to the strains of 'For all the Saints'. Wakey and I hummed along. We were missing it; also to come to 'Show of Hands – Spires and Beams Tour 2010 with Peterborough Cathedral Choir and the Festival Chorus'. This had been a universal regret, almost by definition: not to be able to return to any cathedral for forthcoming delights. Next stop was to be the Friday lunchtime organ recital at Birmingham. The west front almost concealed the northwest tower, complete with a fine set of bells, unlike Norwich – we had heard them on the way – but the sacrifice didn't matter, nor the lack of a south west tower. To extend that, though it has received bad press, I found the central tower effective, even if squat. Yes, it could have been taller, but as it was the emphasis was on the unremitting mass, particularly of the nave, also north transept and the east end.

We walked round the whole heavy and portentous cathedral, advisedly done as it started raining on the way back. The dramatic curve of the apsidal original was the other feature, apart from the west front, to be more impressive outside than within. By the north side we came across a boulder, heavily empathizing with the backdrop of the north wall. An architectural survey 'had found 30 up in the core of the northwest pier, and a wrought iron stone plinth of the southeast pier of the central tower, rebuilt in 1883–4.' 'I get the feeling it's bulging out,' said Wakey, assessing the northern exterior. 'It's built on silt,' replied Rand, by now cognisant of East Anglian soil types. And it was mostly Barnack stone, generically 'Northamptonshire', the quarry now exhausted and reinvented as 'Barnack Hills and Holes National Nature Reserve,' something we were to run out of time to visit the next day after Clipsham quarry.

Amid a gust of wind, Wakey had caught a birch leaf, gleefully, in groundward trajectory, and Rand once again failed to achieve this. Mickser wasn't bothered, unaccustomed to the annual folly the rest of us went through to earn a year's good luck. Rand wondered if 'bigger is better; anyway it's easier to catch a chestnut leaf as they take more time to fall.' That thinking hadn't helped him up to now. He had caught one in Burnham Overy two days before, but then dropped it. 'It's not like cricket' I said. 'You have to keep it for a whole year.' He was eagerly awaiting the Test matches in Australia at the time. I now reckon we benefited from the perceived need to retrace our steps having meandered all the way round to the southwest corner. There were bins serving to block our way, and an 8' wall behind. What we didn't realize until after the refreshment session, later, was that the toilets were there, like they are in so many cathedrals, accessed by a door from the south transept. My point is that the solid Romanesque building was worth passing again, particularly as we were there on borrowed time. Winter beckoned. The trees were in stunning autumn mode. The surrounds – erstwhile monastic buildings in substantial space – were as seductive as many of Peterborough's peers. No cramped city centre location, but a surprise.

Arriving at the west door, we all admired the porch. A handful of curious detailed features were good to observe after a dose of solid exterior. The Holy Trinity was depicted: the Father with the face of the sun, holding the Son's hand, raised in benediction. A dove represented the Holy Ghost, speaking into the Father's right ear. Then there was a pillar of marble at the bottom of which an upside-down carved man, I read as representing Simon Magus, being tormented by demons. Very good. Moving up to the door where this rested, I asked Mike Hurcombe, welcomer-on-duty, about catering, as Benedicts (the second of this name: I remembered Coventry, which had been open) was closed on Sundays. 'You can get a coffee after the service – in the south transept', said he with a smile. In we went for the latter part of the liturgy, though we had been aiming for evensong as the event of the visit. The sound was tremendous, down to the combined excellence of the choir, the organ and the acoustic. We were right at the back and I turned to examine two wall paintings, both of Robert Scarlett, town sexton, who died in 1594 at the age of 98. One of them 'was uncovered when the oil painting of Scarlett (1747) was taken down for cleaning and subsequently replaced on the S side of the doorway. Underneath the wall painting is this inscription:

> You see old Scarlett's picture stand on high
> But at your feet there doth his body lie
> His gravestone doth his age and death time show

His office by these tokens you may know
Second to none for strength and sturdy limb
A scarebabe mighty voice with visage grim
He had interred two Queens within this place
And this town's householders in his lives space
Twice over: but at length his own turn came
What he for others did for him the same
Was done: no doubt his soul doth live for aye
In Heaven: though here his body clad in clay.

After the service we joined the throng in the south transept for tea and biscuits. Mickser observed one of the hymns to have been set by Ralph (he pronounced the name 'Rrrrayfe' in a seriously guttural manner) Vaughan Williams. He informed us: 'He set to music all of the 500 hymns in the English Hymnal, using English folk tunes and resetting them.' *For all the Saints (Sine Nomine)* was apparently one of his favourites. The task took over two years; quite a labour of love when you consider that he was an agnostic. When it came out in 1906, objection came from the Archbishop of Canterbury (Randall Thomas Davidson) concerning inappropriate references, such as to the virgin birth. However, they have stood the test of time: *Songs of Praise* features them regularly (thank you, Aled Jones). 'One tune is called *Down Ampney* – that was where he was born.' And his remuneration was £5.0.0, or rather, his expenses only. He had been engaged by an eccentric vicar, who wanted RVW to edit the English Hymnal as it then was, to be converted into the *New* English Hymnal. Evidence of the man's eccentricity includes his allowed tramps to sleep on the floor of his sitting room. 'Oh, I accept,' replied Rrrrayfe. It took two years.

It was superbly easy to brush tea cups with the people I would have tried to arrange meetings with more formally, had Mickser not been willing to convey his knowledge and insight. Wakey was the last to join the queue, having been diverted by a notice on the wall. 'Combat Stress with Peterborough Cathedral... Drop In Launch 2 June 2010.' This was a branch of the work of the diocese, echoing what he was involved professionally in the National Health Service. Adjacent, he conveyed, were photos of the cathedral staff. Near the top of the tree were Dean Charles Taylor and Canon Precentor Bruce Ruddock, both of whom I had already found were willing to engage in civilized discourse in mouth-watering sight of the tower, both transepts and the top end of the quire. I looked at that afterwards to confirm names. They would recur when visiting Lichfield a week hence. Of course there was a fraternity not only of deans and canons but everybody, as the Church of England is, in effect, a society unto itself. Further afield was a piece about 'Daily Life of the Diocese of Bungoma, Kenya'.

We were beginning to absorb the essential Norman quality of the building, one of the least altered of its generation. Returning to the west end, it was a marvel to embrace the optical illusion of the richly-painted wooden roof, the longest such in the world. It's true that its diamond shapes build up to an impression of resting on props. It was immensely long, rising in the centre. We were very grateful that, on a dull day, and the clocks having gone back that morning, the triforium was awash with spotlights. We could see it all. Thank you Sunday services! In Norwich the sun had done the job. The prevailing image was of the monolithic nave with its three levels: alternately-styled pillars (really a feeble word for their bulk), the tall and deep triforium (how I'd have loved to mount it and thus do some exercise, sadly missing from the routine on a trip like this) and, at the top, the clerestory, letting in what light there was. I'd be so bold as to describe the Peterborough interior as 'sumptuous.'

Moving up the north aisle, I encountered the verger, at removal work, and a substantial ribbed black Victorian radiator. I took a photo. He, as forthcoming as his colleagues, said the boiler was pretty efficient at keeping the place warm. How many radiators were there, at presumably soundly-determined points on each side? Next was the north transept with its modern windows. I liked them but Rand wasn't so sure. They were certainly intelligently designed, mostly blue, in a staggered, abstract style, so there were blank bits, too. They were certainly much more satisfactory than the ones in the south choir aisle chapel, where the story of a Benedictine saint was told in a leaden manner, the dark-costumed hero dominating every pane.

The Treasury, at the junction of the north transept and choir aisle, was, as it were, a small gem. In fact there were a number of items of worth, to satiate visual need at least. The Ramsey Psalter lay in a glass case. This was from the eponymous abbey, nearby, lost during the Reformation. Destiny could so easily have resulted in a ruined Peterborough Abbey, and Ramsey Cathedral extant. In an inventory Rand found an altar cloth listed for the former Queen's grave. At the Reformation it was becoming realistic to visualize every detail mattering. 'Whipping them away, being used to make patchwork quilts,' commented Rand. There was a collection of goblets in display cabinets, including an odd-shaped one in leather. That was quirkily my favourite – and it looked as if it had the greatest capacity.

The north choir aisle gave us the effigy of Benedict, Abbot from 1177 to 1193, no doubt the inspiration for the name of the catering facility. He should be mentioned as having built the majority of the nave; and the effigy was made of local Alwalton marble and in good condition, complete with the abbey reptile at his feet. You could do a rubbing of it, if such a three-dimensional technique has been invented. Further along was Catherine of Aragon's memorial (the tomb was wrecked during the Civil War in 1643). It is a rather humble slab from 1895. Above it hung flags carrying the pomegranate, her emblem. In this cathedral C of A was so prominent as the major feature that her chosen fruit is chosen for it as the image for the whole. She would have enjoyed a few of them as a daughter of the successful Spanish partnership of Ferdinand and Isabella. I reckon our equivalent to be Willam'n'Mary (III and II), but WIII was the guest to the throne, though through MII, who possessed the entitling blood; and he was a warrior, beating off Catholic James II, and lived longer. Now Mary is remembered through occasional performances of Henry Purcell's anthem and two elegies, composed for her funeral.

The Victorian baldacchino, omitted from any lists I saw, had taken over the presbytery, most effective in its bold, creamy design, in the apsidal east end. At once angular, bulky and tall, I found it blended well at the start of the curved wall. I repeat: I adore baldacchinos. This made three, with Derby and St Paul's. In reaching that point, in any case, the visitor is on the straight and narrow, where beckons the retrochoir. The corner is turned at last and you are driven to raise your head for the rich 15th century fan vaulting. We were informed that it was John Wastell's precursor to that fabulous erection in the public domain (and private enterprise: £5.50 for entry) King's College, Cambridge. How propitious that we were to visit it the very next day, and for a service in the choir. The fans were massive and mature, as a result not completely discrete but segmented, unlike the earlier ones at Gloucester and Oxford, which are my preference. Here we saw them close up, as they were lower down, so to speak. In King's College they assumed an utterly contrasting aura, to wonder at in awe in the carefully contrived lighting. But fan vaulting anywhere is seductive, a master stroke of imaginative building design. Below at the east end lay the Hedda Stone, a refreshingly ancient-looking piece of stone, 'the Monks' Stone' which originated back to the very beginning, depicting Jesus, Mary and ten disciples. Round the corner we found the outstanding marble memorial to 'Mary, relict of Thomas Deacon Esqr, Daughter of John Havey of Spalding Gent', who died in 1730. Which of these elevated chaps did the sculpture feature? It was most singular, of a gentleman in a pose so angular, and effete, that he must have been in agony ever since the 17th century when his image was installed. His elbow reclined upon a skull; the shoes might have been cobbled the day before at Northampton, the cobbling capital up the road, just for this purpose, they are so pristine. And as for the crinkled drapes, and the eternal air of condescension on his face, quite wonderful!

In contrast, moving on, was the Orme Memorial. This was very sad, and most telling about the times of the Civil War. First we came to a large image of what it would have looked like when erected:

Once a very fine and elaborate ornament to Sir Humphrey Orme and his wife Frances – prominent local citizens in the seventeenth century. "Mistake not (Reader) I thee craveThis is an Altar, not a grave,Where fier rack't up in ashes lyesAnd harts are made the sacrificeTill tyme and truth her worth and fameRevive her embers to a flame."

Simon Gunton

Underneath was written:

This was put up by Sir Humphrey when his son's wife died in 1627... Sir Humphrey lived to see the desecration of the memorial by Cromwell's men in 1643, but after the Restoration in 1660, his family decided not to rebuild it. It is said that because the memorial contained the words "Altar" and "Sacrifice", it "did so provoke and kindle the Zealots' indignation" that the Puritans used axes, poleaxes and hammers to destroy and break the memorial.

Next was the reference, for that is all it was, to Mary Queen of Scots, where we learned that 'Stuart' only came to be spelt thus because the French language lacks 'W'. Fancy that! 'The former Queen was buried here in 1587 (following her beheading within Fotheringhay Castle, not far away – it would have been a quick trip down the A1) but her body was removed to Westminster Abbey in 1612', by order of her son James VI and I. That's a shame – it was therefore a comparatively early addition to the clutter there. It should have stayed in Peterborough as a local presence and focus for pilgrims. Further, the fact that her remains just passed through supports the feeling of some, such as Christopher Wood, that there an aura of death pervades at Peterborough. The 'resting place' has really been turned into a display of the life and times of the dead, and absent, queen.

The panels of information served their purpose, and I emerged enlightened after a series about the choral tradition and provision of the cathedral. There were separate choirs of boys and girls, both 20-strong. The hierarchy followed standard lines, down from director of music, through the assistant, the organ scholar/assistant organist and six part-time lay clerks. Taking the whole enterprise, the cost exceeded £250K, constituting a major part of the cathedral's budget. On another tack, we learned that there were 34 buildings to look after, the 23-acre site being enclosed by historically important walls. Constant attention was required, needless to say, I'm sure not helped by the location, abutting a frantic centre of industry and population. This showed an excellently open attitude, rarely displayed to better effect. The bottom line was to promote 'The Company of St Peter – please sign up to make your contribution'. Another piece of interest was the plan of the chapter 'to undertake a programme of parking provisions for approximately 110 additional cars in the east and west end of the Precinct... a ten year rolling programme to carry out these much needed works'.

With Benedicts closed, and Mickser unimpressed by the post-Eucharist liquid offerings, he could contain himself no longer. 'I need to wash the hair off my tongue,' he emoted. Rand and I were immersed in yet more displays. This place had by now established a clear lead in the cathedral education stakes (for all the family, but it wasn't at all patronizing, just lucid). The website had proved to be limpid and helpful, as well. These were in the north aisle of the nave, starting at the shop, under the northwest tower, so a bit near the ring of bells. Mickser was sitting, it transpired not very comfortably, very close to it. 'He wants to go to the Drapers,' whispered Wakey, who quoted him: '"If I don't get a drink soon, my teeth will go soft."' I had thought they were all his own. So, the two of them beat a retreat to the pub, leaving Rand and me to a final quiet time. What obviated total further absorption in the boards, perhaps 20 of them, was brainpower. It had almost reached saturation point. This was a place to which to return, like so many. The subject of note was the technical explanation, general and particular. The latter, which involved the quarries of Barnack and Clipsham, related directly to our first engagement the next morning, at the industry provider, Clipsham Stone Company, within the Diocese of Peterborough, producing the 'Northampton' stone of the vernacular, but actually in Rutland, and convenient for the A1(M) and the whole country.

So we went to join the boys for a cheap pint of fine local ale. The Draper's Arms was in beer festival mode, i.e. an abundance of beer choice, all cheap (£1.99 a pint). We had enough time for a welcome respite in a booth for four. Then would be the service. Bells were ringing. The way was clear back to that west front, still visible, despite the hour and dull day. Evensong was magical, sitting in the perfect position in the rear choir stalls. 'It's not much blighted by Victorian glass,' whispered Rand. Indeed the clear windows had proved a boon: maximum light. The attenders just outnumbered participants. My head count made our lot 32. Afterwards

I had a final exchange with Dean Charles (who told me we'd heard Morten Lauridsen's *O magnum mysterium*, and a Tavener piece, both to be noted). That sent us on our way, past the font I hadn't clocked before. It was a gorgeous curved piece in prime position at the west end of the nave, rings of pale and dark stone had been laid to great effect in the floor below it, repeating the shape. Replete, we found the others for a final pint, then points north.

We had deposited Rand's vehicle in a functionary multi-storey car park near the station in 'Cavell', another reference to the eponymous nurse heroine whose grave we had seen at Norwich. Cavell turned out to be one of several blocks of car park, which baffled us on departure, under pressure to vacate the place by the witching hour of 5.30 pm. We just made it, thwarted by the lack of lifts in Cavell and after confusion about the correct 'level', as rather late on in the proceedings we found that you had to cross between blocks at level 5. The car was on Level 1, chosen for its convenience.

A chicken dinner and glance at Mickser's encyclopaedia were in store, and then an episode of the current television hit *Downton Abbey*. We survived it all. Peterborough had come up trumps, as surprising as Southwell for satisfaction. It would merit a return visit: I could stay with my niece Katie at Whissendine, Rutland and visit its notables: the windmill, and, of course the church, of which I'd heard good things.

Monday 1 October
Rand stayed relaxed in the driving seat (and therefore we had a laidback, but cautious, journey). We enjoyed the country route from the Wash to rural Rutland in increasingly rolling country bedecked with vivid autumn, culminating in the detection of the discreet way in, and the weighbridge, where we were to be picked up in a terrain-beating blue four-by-four, I know not what. The quarry, in the guise of Clipsham Stone Cutting Company, had been run and owned by Sir David Davenport-Handley, who accompanied his daughter, current owner/MD Sue Thomas – since 2004, with her husband Alan, who acted as Sales Director. Rand and I were chaperoned round the stunning site. It evoked the memory of the Valley of the Kings for me, and equally an alien landscape, lunar perhaps, of monochromatic, open terrain, but on a sunny day. Could you incur stone blindness? This connected immediately with some we had seen at Peterborough and, more strikingly, the new tower at St Edmundsbury Cathedral, completed in 2005. In the eastern region the stone could be found at Lincoln (a life sized statue of the Virgin Mary holding the infant Saviour, and at Ely (east end)). They had just completed a new road, to bypass the quarry-built Clipsham village a mile away. This would reduce nuisance – trucks hurtling past before

alarms went off – and distance, getting the drivers closer to the trunk road. Sir David, 91 years old, and involved with the quarry since the Second World War, waxed eloquent about so many aspects. The cathedrals which had received this stone were not only local: Salisbury and Wells were on the list. For that matter, Winston Churchill had been instrumental in its choice for work on the Houses of Parliament.

All the stone was employed, whatever its properties. We witnessed Martin, in partnership with the quarry owners, loading and conveying huge bags of stone for a customer's wall. The north bank of the rock, and residue, was crushed for agricultural lime, road metalling, nothing wasted. That area had now shaken off the protective processes on behalf of peregrine falcons, and crested newts. Everyone was happy. Planning permission, for 15 years from Rutland, had also been secured for further exploration. Who was to discern its quality? Meanwhile the completed areas were undergoing restoration – calcareous grass would prevail. A consultant ecologist and planning consultant were involved. Everything demanded the approval so many layers of bureaucracy: relationships abounded. We could understand more by empirical observation. Sue took us to the ridge where stone was being cut and lifted, a laborious routine, and below where slabs were cleft to size. The star turn was the hardest oolitic limestone, of marine origin and displaying mollusc content on occasion. This stone weathers well.

We were bound for Cambridge, in part to feast upon the delights of quarried and assembled stone. Host Jeremy Purseglove took us on a whistle stop walk round the colleges, culminating in that fan-vaulted extravaganza, King's College Chapel. It represented closure on this trip, to absorb the highest of Perpendicular achievement. It was also good to hear the story of the error with the door at the altar. I enjoyed the example of human pride, the contrast between the purer eastern part of the chapel, courtesy of Henry VI in the 15th century, and the western Tudor part, thankfully not within our sight lines during our sojourn in the choir. Its obvious characteristic was, through coats of arms and personal reference, to proclaim the confident regime. Pilgrimage is writ large in East Anglia, from the ancient shrines of North Norfolk to Tudor urbanity in Cambridge.

38

Birmingham

St Philip

Province: Canterbury
Present building: 1711–25 as parish church
Cathedral status: 1905 – from Worcester diocese

Website: www.birminghamcathedral.com
Tel: 0121 2621840
Email: enquiries@birminghamcathedral.com
Address: Colmore Row, Birmingham B3 2QB

Three to See: Edward Burne-Jones windows;
bull door knocker;
the organ in its showpiece setting, the gallery

Bull

Friday 5 November, 2010
Having passed Chloe Marie on the M5, courtesy of Eddie Stobart, I met Goad outside St Chad's Roman Catholic Cathedral, latterly a pointed landmark adjacent to the inner ring road, known as 'Queensway'. This is what John Betjeman wrote about it:

> *(Augustus Welby Northmore) Pugin (1812–52) idealized the Middle Ages. His drawings were sincere but unfair. The prose accompaniment to them is glowing and witty. In 1842, architects were attaching moral properties to Gothic styles (e.g. Guildford a bit later). Pugin had started this idea. And his successors surpassed him. Since Gothic was the perfect style, what was the perfect style of Gothic? I do not know who it was who started the theory that early Gothic is crude, middle is perfection and late is debased. But certainly from the middle of the 1840s, this theory was held by most of the rising young church architects.*

And so it was.

I knew Goad from college days in the early 1970s, and both of us had lived in the Second City. She still did. Neither of us had ventured inside St Chad's before. Two attractions drew me to this building: the relics of the saint, removed from Lichfield Cathedral, a handful of miles distant, and the relics of Cardinal John Henry Newman, much in the news of late in connection with the Pope's visit. Both proved elusive. We investigated the interior, ornate and deeply adorned with chapels round the outside. A curiosity, or rather a lack of one, occurred to me: no icons in evidence. How bizarre that in every Anglican cathedral there is one, often several, on display, but not in this place with more doctrinal and practical affinity with the eastern church, also rich in colour and adornment in other ways.

There was no admittance to the high altar, but looking up from the communion rail with its notice to that effect, a glory came into view: a baldacchino. It was difficult to unearth a dictionary definition. One I tied down was for 'baldaquin': 'covering or canopy', (*The Phrontistery*). This was the fourth. I have to recall the others to get them fixed in my brain: Derby, St Paul's and Peterborough, all total treats. This was one, too, to be admired from afar and below. I had omitted to retrieve my binoculars from my car boot, so I found myself straining to adjust to a view. It was an Augustus Welby Northmore concoction, to great effect. Soon after this, the Sacristy/storeroom/utility room, started to buzz with chatter. Three people came into view: two women and a man. He was delegating duties to his minions, bizarrely kitted out himself in a bandage wrapped right round his head, like one of Dennis the Menace's victims in *The Beano*. A pair of spectacles, which had seen quite a lot of better days, was perched on the top, resting on a slight bulge where his ears should be, which served to allow him to hear my question. 'Where are St Chad's relics?' 'Up there in the baldacchino.' The word assumed a whole new aura, when uttered in a dulcet Brummie accent. I couldn't bring myself to pursue the matter, and we retraced the half dozen footsteps to the centre to admire the contents of the celebrity item, or rather the discreet casket in which they lay. We were still ignorant as to how and why they were removed here from Lichfield. It's true that the Anglican St Chad's is awash with historical highlights. I didn't begrudge this baldacchino its contents. A baldacchino should always be a matter of policy, divined for a special purpose.

Goad observed the initial M elegantly worked into the ceiling and on the pillars. The M, we decided, must stand for Maria/Mary, the Mother of Jesus. This M was beautifully wrought in reds and golds and etched in the painted ceiling; also on pillars, in fact pretty widespread. The next port of call was the shop, where more sound was emitting than we had heard through the doors during the service. Quasi-religious musical offerings were being relayed from a ghetto blaster, of the tinniest kind. The shop was well-stocked with suggestions for Christmas: calendars making up any space not occupied by enough books for a library, many about John Henry Newman. I retreated from the cacophony down steep stairs, noting a section round a corner dedicated to shirts for the clergy market. There were four shades of grey, one black and one white, and some richly hued ones to lift the spirits. This was a wide range of colour options, within narrow parameters, for clerical torsos.

We emerged from the red building to the incessant traffic, duly overcome. Having reconnoitred St Philip's Cathedral on the way, we had established there to be no satisfactory catering facility, only instant coffee in the northwest corner of the nave. In addition there was a sign: 'From after Christmas, the shop will no longer be providing drinks or biscuits. It will continue to stock a range of products appropriate to our cathedral and heritage.' Ah, a cut!

We proceeded to order a cafetière of Continental Brew in Hudsons, a pleasant enough emporium, and suitable given the time limit. We wanted to be close at hand. It was frustrating that the waitress, having taken her time to produce a menu, then busied herself with many another task and had to be alerted by Goad that we did, in fact, want to place an order. The organ recital was the fixture, at 1.15 pm. There should have been enough time. In fact Goad was to down the contents of a second coffee jar.

The cathedral, the third smallest of all at 720 sq ft, made up for it in style, as a Baroque build in a single space. It is surrounded by a small green sward, which is multi-faceted. It serves as graveyard, a sitting area (in fine weather – very soggy on this occasion), and a walkway, being in a busy area near offices and a rank of bus stops. And of course, more illicit uses, the odd clue to which lay in corners untouched by road sweepers. Goad, helpfully familiar with matters of local interest, pointed out a couple of tombstones. One was very short indeed, from 1819, in memory of the shortest woman, Nanetta Stocker, who reached 33" (for that matter in Bartley Green, southwest Birmingham, is buried the tallest woman, Jane Bunford, 7'9", who died at the age of 26 in 1922; strange that the two were contemporaries). The other celebrated Thomas Lines (1776–1863), the Birmingham painter, whose work had been included in an exhibition on the industrial and social history of the city, at the Gas Hall in 2009. Also, represented on his tombstone, were the names of his sons, who became painters and illustrators in their own right.

There loomed an obvious subject for a photo. Directly outside the west front stood the first Bishop of Birmingham, Charles Gore. Looking up, he cut a fine figure, with the characterful tower above. The entrance door was less impressive. All comers had to use it, whether bearing mitre or coffee or candle money. Inside, beyond the minimal lobby, sat Brian, the box office chap, with grey cash tin on table and tickets in hand. This was a £3/£2 concessions event, while similar occasions had been free ('retiring collection') elsewhere. I asked if gift aid was available. He looked non-plussed, then said: 'You could, but it would have to go through different channels.' I understood, as I had suffered different bits of system and budgets in the past. Having executed the transaction, I tried to obtain a cathedral guide leaflet for our use after the concert. The various officials, in the café, the shopping space next to it and Brian himself, did not knew where the English version was, though there was an impressive array of other languages on a display unit. 'I'll use the French one, then,' (like at Tewkesbury, I thought). Then, looking around, I espied a further unit, partly obscured by Brian at the desk. Lurking there was the English guide, in fact a whole pile. 'Oh, yes, she found some this morning,' said the café assistant, who had joined in the search. I smiled sweetly, not wishing to pursue 'she' or why the assistant hadn't remembered before. Also, the time was nigh for the recital.

I sat down next to Goad, and began to take in the surroundings. Marcus Huxley, Director of Music, had arranged the programme, geared to ¾ hour, and was down to play. That was good – we were to hear the top man. We agreed afterwards that it was an excellent programme: two energetic pieces at beginning (Handel's *La Jouissance)* and end (*Festive March* by Henry Smart), with contemplative choices in between. That Handel piece is also known as *Music for the Royal Fireworks.* Very apposite on this day. I looked up to the ceiling, fresh from the memory of Peterborough's display of colour. Here it was plain, in square shapes, throughout the nave, being treated differently in the Chancel, with a geometric design. It felt completely right. All through I was transfixed by the Edward Burne-Jones 1888 stained glass windows. Just beautiful. Fortunately we were able to get up close in this cathedral, for a proper look, the side ones being obscured by pillars from the nave. It was a grey, damp day, but they were still glorious. Goad commented: 'They look as if they're standing in water.' In fact, the blue stained glass in The Ascension is of an azure similar to water. It gives the impression that Christ and the angels are walking on water above the disciples.

Birmingham's star
The Pre-Raphaelites' works spread afar,
To Victorian eyes, without par.
Now those tableaux please pass
For St Philip's stained glass -
As Burne-Jones is the Birmingham star.

The east window vied with others as dominant on the tour: Gloucester and Coventry, the latter literally east in a building 90 degrees out of kilter, but in the baptistery, not over the altar. The gallery above was also of its time, the eye being led round to the organ on the northeast side, recently rebuilt and cased. It looked good, with enough pipes of the thousands in total to create an impression. We enjoyed the sound it made. Chatting briefly to Marcus Huxley afterwards, it emerged that it dated from 1715 in the west end gallery. Much work had been done in 1970, using casework from a redundant church. Nicholson's, now at Malvern, not far away, were responsible for this achievement.

Bonfire night was upon us, and the Armistice beckoned – a display of poppies at the top of the nave served the purpose normally answered by something flashy from a florist. Their bulging bank of red complemented the rich colours of the east windows. Of course there were icons, in a space reserved for them, following on from the shop area in the north aisle. Goad commented: 'I'm surprised there are icons here.' I put her right. That's what I had thought when I started out. On the other side were door handles representing the four evangelists. The bull (ox) of St Luke just begged you to hold it, which we both did, and so did the lion of St Mark. We failed to unearth the other two. It then occurred to me, in fact both of us, that the emblem of Birmingham should be a bull, strong and purposeful, to denote its ethos. The Bull Ring Shopping Centre statue of such a beast was so evocative of the city, and its cathedral served the cosmopolitan community of the frantic West Midlands.

I joined Goad, lost in an exhibition by Catherine Pinnock, in the well-lit south aisle, called *Light in the Darkness (without light we would not exist)*. Themed in a lavender/purple tone for dark and cream/white for light, there was a table covered in counters carrying aphorisms from all ages. They were so good I committed a few to my notebook:

1   'The light shines in the darkness, but the darkness has not understood' (John 15).
2   'If a donkey brays at you don't bray at him' (George Herbert).
3   'Your word is a lamp to my feet and a light for my path' (Ps 119, 105).
4   Another from George Herbert: 'Storms make the oak grow deeper roots'.
    Definition of Dark: without light, gloomy, difficult to understand, evil.
    Definition of Light: the agency by which objects are made visible; mental or spiritual illumination; a bright appearance. Adj: not dark.

At the end were visitors' books in the same two colours. This was a 'contemplative area where you can write your thoughts in the light'.

Saturated by all the stimuli thus far, I was happy to take up Goad's suggestion of Chez Jules for their lunch special, just making it up the stairs before the offer finished for the afternoon. We endured more erratic service: they charged us for vegetables which never arrived. On enquiry we were told the 'veg of the day' were carrots and broccoli, which wasn't much of an omission, at least for me. We had decided to spend our remaining time at St Martin in the Bull Ring, with which Goad was very familiar. She had availed herself of the Heritage Open Day roof tour in September, the same Saturday that I scaled the heights of St Mary Redcliffe, Bristol and saw many another church there. I should make sure I'm in Brum for a day of building exposure next year, or the year after. Going to St Martin's meant passing the splendid bronze beast, and one by one, posing by it, along with a sequence of other people doing the same. It is the parish church for Birmingham, and a Greater Church. This time I was introduced to Paul Rogoff, who wrote for the church magazine. He was able to give me a phone number to follow up, in due course.

The conditions were not ideal. It was umbrella weather and getting dark. Running late, we had missed tea in the café. We employed a mixture of a sashed woman guide, then Goad herself, along with the information leaflet, to take us round all the substantial points of interest in a church so different from either cathedral. It was like coming home to Gothic architecture, the stock-in-trade of this grand tour. These items were particularly interesting:

1   The font (by Jacqueline Stieger, 2003) was an innovative cascade affair. Striking, it faced you on the approach to the nave, but was not switched on at the time.

2   The Prayer Sculpture, also a new century addition (Antony Robinson, 2000), an inventive display for candles.

3   Not so easy to spot: greengrocery wooden carvings, donated by the market traders after the Second World War. You can see the extensive Bull Ring market from the church.

4   Giving some character to the Staffordshire sandstone in the pulpit, figures of Christ, flanked by Elijah and Moses on one side; St Peter and St Paul on the other. Again, you had to be shown, but it was worth the effort to make them out.

5   Monuments in the chancel and aisles to the church's founders (mid-13th century) of the de Bermingham family. Recognize the name? Peter de B had established the first Bull Ring market in 1166.

6   The east window was subtly tinted in the fading light. The church had suffered bomb damage. The replacement glass illustrated the healing work of Christ.

7   'Reserve Choir': 20 stone angels above the choir stalls – we thought we had identified a few early instruments. Was there a hurdy gurdy?

8   The hammer beam roof, again demure in the gloom. The original wood was used to construct the current choir stalls.

9   It was a treat to see another Burne-Jones window (with William Morris). For me they work in the way his oil paintings fail to. It must owe to the passage of light through them. There is an abundance of those in the Birmingham City museum and Art Gallery: a fine experience there is the highly decorated Edwardian Tea Room, at any time of day.

10   Grotesques dotted around, pulling faces. Also, Goad pointed out that William Shakespeare and Sir Winston Churchill were

reputedly in patriarchal pose aloft outside. You needed both daylight and binoculars to confirm this.

Those are a top 10 of sorts. The whole is greater than the parts, for this was a delightful building, certainly worth the treatment as one of the 31 Greater Churches. I've left the potted history, the time line, until the end. From the leaflet, it is for the City of Birmingham as well as for its parish church, so provides a little of the background for St Philip's Cathedral:

1156 – Henry II grants a charter to Peter de Bermingham.
1255 – The de Bermingham family build a church in red sandstone.
1690 – The church is restored and adapted. Galleries are added to increase its capacity.
1715 – A daughter church is built: St Philip's, which becomes Birmingham Cathedral in 1905.
1872 – St Martin's is demolished and rebuilt by local architect J A Chatwin.
1941 – The church is bombed and extensively damaged – the Burne-Jones window had only just before been removed for safe keeping.
1957 – Restoration completed.
1987 – Hammer beam roof restored and preserved.

The work had involved successful fund-raising campaigns. This has not stopped: the church continued to benefit from dynamic commitment to benefit the church. This is a church in an area without local population. That says a lot, in common with the cathedral. Birmingham is a buoyant, cosmopolitan city, well able to sustain its major churches. We enjoyed all of them.

The next mention has to go to the nearly-sanctified Cardinal Newman. On the way out of Birmingham the following morning, my new companion, Wakey, and I were bound for Stoke-on-Trent and Cheadle (Diocese of Lichfield). A stop at the Cardinal's Oratory was apposite, as it were, to sign off. This enterprise was inspired by St Philip Neri, who founded the Oratory of Rome in the 16th century. Attention to this St Philip caused echoes of the visit to Arundel RC Cathedral, which had been part of the Chichester trip the previous February. An oratory is 'a stable community in which priests and brothers live together in one place, usually in a city, engaged in whatever works their individual talents dictate,' *Catholic Truth Society*.

We were bound for the Cardinal's Shrine. It was in the Sacristy, where a service was nearing its conclusion, a tall, bearded priest informed us. We were resting by the leaflet rack, replete with all manner of booklets, some free, most for a small charge, many of which referred to our intended character. In due course we were able to observe his resting place altar, while a rather small boy, in black cassock, removed the communion paraphernalia bit by bit, genuflecting each time he passed the centrepiece. What was remarkable was how many times he had to cross the line.

That was the past. This is a report to do with the Pope's visit to Birmingham in September 2010: 'BIRMINGHAM celebrates the beatification of Cardinal John Henry Newman with two extraordinary events'.

On 18 September at the Official Beatification Conference 'J.H. Newman by his biographers' at Birmingham ICC (£80, £45 concessions) and 'An extraordinary performance of *The Dream of Gerontius* by Sir Edward Elgar at Birmingham Town Hall (£50 and £75).'

What a contrast was the former Bishop of Birmingham, John Sentamu, who was translated to the Archbishopric of York, after only three years in the Midlands (2002–05). This is one example of his approach:

> **Archbishop keen to move church talks into pub**
> *The Church of England should be open to new ways of conveying its message at Easter, reaching out into the community even in pubs, the Archbishop of York has said. In an interview on GMTV yesterday, Dr John Sentamu, the former Bishop of Birmingham, spoke in favour of debates in pubs as one method of helping to modernise the church.*
>
> *He said: "We've got now in the Church of England… where instead of simply advising people to come into our buildings and our churches, people are doing it in a new way and going to many places. I've actually gone and had endless debates when I was in Birmingham in pubs with a lot of people. I think we've got to find a way of getting our message across."*
> *The Archbishop also spoke of the importance of religious teaching in schools in increasing knowledge about the true meaning of Easter among youngsters.*
>
> Western Daily Press 3/4/10

It was interesting to note the bishop's third name: Mugabe.

Monday 8 November
To gain more insight into the workings of Birmingham, I had arranged an

interview with the Dean, the Very Revd Catherine Ogle, only two months into her post, and, considering the vastness of her task, generous in giving me the time. One dynamic in Catherine's tenure would be the tercentenary celebrations in 2015. She said she had undertaken, to herself, to treat the job as a commitment for at least a decade. The mixed blessing of the cathedral building was that it is compact and easy to manage, but with little scope for development. The west end entrance is the only shortfall – liturgical processions are difficult. This would be a focus.

Regarding the job, there were regional deans' meetings every quarter. Challenges included growing inter-faith work. She was experienced in this from her previous role as parish priest at Huddersfield: 'I had 17 very happy years'. Then she saw the advertisement in *Church Times*. The custom had been like an arranged marriage – invitations were the means of selection. She felt equipped for the new, big, post, having met lots of people in different sections of the community. Being a rare woman dean occurred to her as an advantage – she had peers at Leicester and Salisbury, with St Edmundsbury in the offing. She had always been the first woman, and found a good level of support. A development was afoot: common tenure, meaning more job security. The church was being persuaded to systematize its running. Role descriptions were coming in. A dean was a 'senior priest' and archdeacons, senior deacons. Reaching into a file she listed the order of precedence:

1   Bishop
2   Suffragan; also assistant bishops, when representing the bishop
3   Chancellor (legal responsibilities)
4   Dean
5   Residentiary canon
6   Suffragan and assistant bishops when not representing the bishop
7   Archdeacon (Aston and Solihull in Birmingham)
8   Diocesan registrar
9   Honorary lay canons (clergy honoured for service in the diocese)
10   Lay canons

Where did they live? There was no close at the cathedral. That was the preserve of old foundation cathedrals. The office space where we were chatting was modern, a standard leased office space, with Starbuck's as neighbours. The diocese did own property for canons – family homes in the suburbs. Catherine lived in the desirable Moseley. The budget would always be definite, but tight to control. New income was needed, but there was a limit to charging for events. It had to be balanced with the cathedral's central role. Something in the offing would be the Dean's Dinner, in the cathedral the next year. There were overseas links – Malawi and Tanzania. This was the mother church for the parishes, which in fact ran themselves. Comparison was made with Wakefield with which Catherine was most familiar. They were different: Wakefield diffuse, Birmingham compact, with the emotional appeal of the building. She told the story from Yorkshire of a new church caretaker, who harboured a fear of wasps (spheksophobia: I looked it up). There was a problem with a plague, culminating in his opening the vestry to be confronted with a black cloud of them. She added that that was a year of plague and pestilence.

Commenting on the cessation of coffee in the cathedral, she expressed regret, but brought attention to the conflict between refreshment and prayer. The focus should be on the core calling – people come in to pray. There was only a single space there – no room for a cat – and it was too noisy (as Goad and I had found during the recital). Meanwhile volunteer chaplains were on hand for those in need, as I had found at most major city cathedrals.

I wished her good luck and hoped she would achieve a grander opening to the building. It deserves plenty of pomp, when you enter the building to face those fabulous 1888 windows. While ruminating during the motorway journey, I passed another Eddie Stobart representative: Calamena Amelia, and heard the 'breaking news' that five bishops were to defect to the Roman church, unhappy about the direction of the Anglican Communion. The ordination of women bishops was the headline reason. However, there were practical consequences to consider in resigning, such as loss of stipend, accommodation and pension. Another way of looking at this was that the men concerned were mostly nearing retirement, and were minor bishops. It sounded a bit like the ineffectual wittering of Labour Party members against Gordon Brown not so long before.

39

Blackburn

St Mary

Province: York
Founded: 1820–26 parish church rebuilt
Building extensions: 1938–77 crossing lantern and spire; reconsecrated
Cathedral status: 1926 – created from Manchester diocese

Website: www.blackburncathedral.com
Tel: 01254 503090
Email: lynne.trudgill@blackburncathedral.co.uk
Address: Cathedral Close, Blackburn BB1 5AA

Three to See: Nave ceiling with fairground look;
sculpture on exterior east wall *The Healing of the Nations;*
lantern and its setting

Football

Saturday 20 November, 2010

We endured a tortuous approach to Blackburn, involving nail-biting rail changes at Stockport and Bolton. Each time we seemed to have a woman encumbered with a rucksack as a fellow traveller. Out of the bag protruded a substantial wooden spoon. When we alighted at Bolton (their word; Wakey preferred 'alit') I asked a convenient official which platform we needed (3 minutes to go). It was 'number 4, over that bridge'. Then the first stop was Hall'i'th'Wood, almost as individual as Westward Ho! Devon, I thought, though the latter lacks a station. It was no surprise to come across Spoon Woman later in the cathedral. We had a brief exchange: she was one of two viola players in the concert that evening, and indeed was now clutching her musical instrument. The spoon protruded from her bag on the floor, in begging mode.

Wakey and I had checked in at the Fernhurst Hotel, taking taxis for a mere £4.50 and £4.25 to and from it. I was used to £6 or £7 for similar journeys in the south. We were up against the clock, having booked the only cheap journey from Euston. The time pressure concerned the arrangement I had made to visit Holy Trinity, as a Conservation church. I wanted to know more of this initiative. So, to grab a snack and see the cathedral in daylight we had to get there promptly. The plan worked. Once inside, we witnessed enough of the gradual gathering of musicians and hints at a rehearsal to water our mouths for the 7.30 concert comprising *Monteverdi's 1610 Vespers* (again). That was all that would engage us in the building. The café was staffed, but not for the public, in the afternoon and evening. In fact it became clear by way of several signs and leaflets that it was only open for tea and cakes, and snacks at lunchtime between 10 am and 2.30 pm (or 3 pm, as some were overwritten with a revised closing time), from Tuesday to Friday. We were to remain in ignorance about the worthiness of the facility, as it was scheduled for opening after the service the next morning, after the Eucharist, by which time we had fled the scene for out football game.

The preview was certainly promising. Mickey G, a born and bred local lad, with whom I had upset Geography tutors at college donkey's years before, and whom we met later on this occasion, had said: 'It's a modern cathedral. Elizabeth has sung in it.' That was his daughter, who had defected to Italy (perhaps partly a ploy to avoid yet another season ticket at Blackburn Rovers FC along with father and brother). I emerged, with an armful of leaflets, which we read in the OneRoverSport café, just round the corner in Church Street. This must once have been a main thoroughfare to the church, now cathedral. Now it was a sad little connection between a misguided shopping centre (many old buildings torn out) and the bus station. At least the latter abutted the rail facility. I'm all for synchronized transport services. All credit to the football club; however, to promote a strong presence there, both in a shop full of stock and customers and, an unusual facility, a café at the back, providing exactly what we wanted in the early afternoon. Wakey was expiring with hunger. We had enjoyed a pint of lush Thwaites Wainwright in the hotel bar, while waiting for the room to be prepared, and the taxi to arrive. Now it was a matter of something to eat before the climb up to Holy Trinity. Wakey wolfed down his chilli potato, and chips. My tuna bake (with some greenery) was just right, both accompanied by a pot of tea. I espied the image of a Blackburn Rovers player in mid-kick in the garden outside. That provided:

1   A good photo with backdrop of the cathedral from the northeast.
2   The spark of an idea, which was translated into words by Wakey: 'Why not make a football the icon here. There's a link.'

Blackburn had been incorporated as a borough in 1851; the rival settlement down the Ribble Valley was made 'The City of Preston' in 2002, becoming England's 50th city. One of the 27 contenders had been Blackburn. 'Proud Preston', certainly. Fair enough, as Blackburn has the diocese, founded in 1926. It remains the more populous element of the 'Borough of Blackburn with Darwen'. The following illustrates one instance of life thereabouts:

> The employee of the week is the clerk at a Blackburn job centre, who advised Hayley O'Neil, 23, that her best chance of gaining employment was to put a bag over her head or stand behind a wall during a job interview. Hayley is covered in tattoos and has studs through her cheeks, nose, lips, chin and so on. "Who's going to employ you looking like that?" he asked.
> 'Hayley has complained about being "humiliated" and said, regarding her hideous adornments, "This is who I am." Yep, sweetcheeks, it surely is: i.e. unemployed, and likely to remain so.
> Sunday Times 26/9/10

Concerning the diocese, there is a rhythmic undertow to the saga-like process of diocesan development in Lancashire, which is lifted from the cathedral's website:

The Origins of Blackburn Diocese
The Diocese of Blackburn, in the Province of York, was taken out of the Diocese of Manchester in 1926 when Percy Mark Herbert was appointed Bishop.

The Diocese of Manchester was taken out of the Diocese of Chester in 1847, when James Price was appointed Bishop.

The Diocese of Chester was taken out of the Diocese of Lichfield and York in 1541, when John Bird was appointed Bishop.

The Diocese of Lichfield, which may have been a survivor of an ancient British Diocese, was founded (or re-founded) by the English in 656, when Diuma was appointed Bishop.

The Diocese of York was in existence in the year 314. It was re-founded by the English in 627, when Paulinus was Bishop.

(Finally,) The Diocese of Blackburn consists of the Archdeaconries of Blackburn and Lancaster, which are divided into fourteen Deaneries...

This read like a family tree from the Old Testament, (now, there's an idea for a new stained glass window, inspired by the pervasive presence of Jesse Trees). It was well-expressed for a history lesson on Anglican changes in the region.

It was also the most northerly cathedral on this trek so far, albeit to be eclipsed soon enough by York, Ripon and Carlisle. Blackburn also boasts a church listed as one of the forty featured in *A Brief Visitors Guide to Treasures in Trust,* under the umbrella of The Churches Conservation Trust: Holy Trinity. The entry ran: 'Standing proudly on Mount Pleasant, Edward Sharpe's great hymn to the Middle Pointed Gothic style contains a fascinating social history in the 80 painted heralded panels of its ceiling of c.1840.'

Prompted by this, Wakey and I made our way there for 3 pm, having engaged key holder Chris Ward. His day job, of stocktaker, required constant nationwide movement to such purveyors of goods as B&Q and M&S. I caught him on the phone – first try – the previous Monday, a rare day off at home. Said he: 'You have to take it when you can.' The ascent to the church demanded negotiation of the extensive premises of Thwaites, the independent brewers (still unencumbered – good for them, and us). They occupied a complete block, bounded to the north by Barbara Castle Way. It was reminiscent of the eponymous lady's political style – forthright, direct, no nonsense. As soon as we turned the corner beyond the beer fumes, there stood the towered church above. Having read a paragraph to that effect, I had expected a gruesome array of 1960s blocks behind. One only had survived, and, once we had met, right on time, the hour chiming, Chris led us into the open space of the church. It was satisfyingly bleak in the gloom, necessitating lights to be switched on in the latter stages of our hour-plus presence. The key man did the honours – switches lurked behind panels it seemed – and we were able to admire the fittings themselves, a brass-looking metal circle with three bulbs in each, appealingly antiquated.

John Whittaker had founded the church in 1837 on a green field site, surrounded by hundreds of houses. Paying significant contributions, all manner of people invested in the overhead celebration of their families – of the 80, 56 related to individuals alive at the time. 'Not that that counts,' said Chris. The Victoria Regina centre piece, dominated the crossing, the Queen's Arms 'protected by royal bearing and eight earlier versions of the Royal Arms'. It was 11' square, the surrounding others, 5'6". Some had been restored to good effect. Chris shone a torch of industrial size at a few, recounting the identities of their donors – evidently there was a lot of money about for such generosity, and pride. They were impressive. My memory shot back to the painted ceilings of St Giles, Cheadle (Augustus Welby Northmore Pugin's delightful Staffordshire extravagance. We have to itemize all his names, they're so resonant). The roof also evoked Peterborough Cathedral. So much richness overhead in such a short time! A number of public figures provided presence of different kinds, such as Sir Robert Peel, Prime Minister of the day, in the east window. The Arms of contemporary divines were suitably placed over the chancel with those of the local subscribers: landowners, cotton manufacturers, civic dignitaries in serried and attendant ranks in lesser positions over the nave and transepts.

The stark emptiness of the vast expanse of illuminated ceiling, flat and cruciform, made a telling contrast to what we were to feast our eyes upon in the cathedral. Thank God this building had been saved! To quote the Trust's column on the obverse of the leaflet inside the church *Northern lights... Historic churches in Cheshire, Lancashire, Greater Manchester, Merseyside* (headed up 'A thousand years of English history awaits you'): 'The Churches Conservation Trust is the national charity protecting historic churches at risk.

'We've saved over 340 beautiful buildings (it had been 300 in 1998), which attract more than a million visitors a year. With our help and with your support they are kept open and are in use – living once again at the heart of their communities.' It was established in 1969, as a unique partnership between the State and the Church of England, to care for and conserve historic churches for which there was no longer a parochial need. Then it was called the Redundant Churches Fund. The name was changed in 1994 because the churches were more sensibly regarded as redundant only in the narrowest sense of the word'.

Holy Trinity was not one of their red-starred top 50, but still intriguing. My abiding image is of the massive unoccupied floor. Most of the pews had been sold off.

Broadening the discussion to the diocese, he said that Blackburn Parish Church had been chosen for the new cathedral ahead of rival churches. 'Preston was hemmed in and Lancaster too far north'. I reflected on this: a substantial minority of cathedrals lie near the edge of their dioceses. The effect varied a lot. The key man added that the heiress of Thwaites, Mrs Yarborough, contributed 'pots of money to Blackburn'. Money talks, especially when you want to convert a rundown parish church into a modern cathedral. This duly happened. The cathedral had been a Victorian build, but here are other landmark years:

- 556 – The territory was noted by a medieval writer as occupied by a church.
- 1086 – The Domesday Book recorded St Mary.
- 1451 – A church was endowed by the Earl of Derby, with a song or grammar school attached.

Chris displayed much insight and general knowledge. His special interest was heraldry, but he expounded on various topics, including local history and the central matter of funding. Wakey and I both felt replete with this visit, which left us with insufficient time to try out the Blackburn Museum and Art Gallery, which Mickey G had recommended.

Let us be transported on four hours to the concert, where for a mere tenner we enjoyed a prime north aisle position with an open view. That it was not from the front wasn't critical. It was hugely different from the Lichfield festival performance of the same piece (it was the quarter-centenary) in July, and suited these more modest conditions. To us the sound soared in an entrancing way, organized and conducted to perfection by the outgoing Director of Music, Richard Tanner (1998–2011), who had written in the brochure: 'Members of the Renaissance Singers have been keen to stage a performance of the Vespers for many years, not least because Blackburn has such a perfect acoustic to sing sacred music of the Italian Baroque,' (including 'period instruments such as cornets, sackbuts and theorbos!' Let's hear it for the sackbuts and theorbos, making a splendid presence right in front of us! Spoon Woman was feet away, but her wooden appendage was out of sight. The music was duly executed by superb soloists, with The Renaissance Singers, Blackburn Cathedral Choir and Young People's Choir (kitted out in an alarming vermilion against the black donned by everyone else). Being immersed in the core of the building was as satisfying as at other similar events. The cathedral was a 20th century construct as we experienced it, and succeeded as such. Before, during and afterwards we were able to observe much of it, being a simply designed entity, not the smallest of the parish church cathedrals, but finite and bespoke. One of the surprises was the vastness on the lower, crypt, level, seemingly occupying the entire ground floorplan. An exhibition occupied one corner – we gave it some time, while sipping at the interval red wine (£2.50 paid for in advance, and, inventively using a red slip – what colour was the white?). Wakey had been impressed by the shop, in fact the whole space. It offered a rare 'tot' glass for £6.50, noted for the sake of comparison, as neither of us wanted to collect any more. What caught his eye were the olive wood camels.

This ditty was composed about the experience, suggested by *The Song that Goes Like This*, from *Spamalot* a musical I'd seen twice by then. It was still out on the commercial theatre circuit.

The Vespers Go Like This
Once in this long tour
We find a church like this,
Cathedral with allure,
A modern upgrade, this.
Oh where is the see
With all of this?
Where is it? Blackburn!

A parish church so long,
It casts a magic spell;
The Vespers thrill the throng
We hum along like hell!
This composition you just can't miss
We're all there – there it is!

Now look up at a boss
And Stations of the Cross;
The Vespers are quite enough for me.

The interval's escape
Two glasses from the grape
Which then
He quaffs,
And me.
Now we're near the end
(sob) it's such a subtle blend,
A piece that bucks the trend,

What Monteverdi meant,
It sounds just right in a build like this.

They're sounding mighty fine,
That echo is sublime,
That is this church's way,
To spread the flattest 'A',
Bouncing chords in a build like this.

They all have lots to do,
The singers, players, too,
All working hard among
The punters, motley crew,
Enjoying the Vespers – they still go on.

This will haunt us for days,
We'll have to try out ways
To stop this damned refrain,
The old and new in train,
Cathedral and Vespers fused in bliss.

Afterwards we dropped into the conveniently situated Adelphi for a quick pint of local ale, Thwaites Bomber, the strong one, named after the legendary cricket force, Andrew 'Freddie' Flintoff, now retired from shinpads. A drink was now in the nature of a nightcap. Mickey joined us, on his way to a rather late showing of the newly released Harry Potter film. I expect he had plenty to dream about. We certainly did.

Sunday 21 November
The paradox was that the other thing we had come for was Blackburn Rovers vs. Aston Villa at 1.30 pm. It served to get us up early, as breakfast was to cease at 8.45 am, somewhat early for a Sunday. We were able to reach the cathedral before the end of the Parish Communion, conducted in the north transept. This was after pausing to admire the modern sculpture outside the east end, Mark Jallard's European Regional Development Fund-financed 'colossal 35-foot by 26 foot sculpture', described thus by the council: 'named "The Healing of the Nations" (it) is an abstract steel and copper circular piece and has become a major new attraction in the town. Hydraulics and fibre optics between two copper skins make all seven tons of the awe-inspiring sculpture slowly 'pulse' or breathe' creating patterns of light.' It came across as a blue essence. Wakey reckoned it conveyed

'faith and confidence. It adds something to the cathedral'. This was part of a £400,000 scheme project undertaken in 2000–01, also 'involving the re-building of the east end roofs and parapets'.

Our first target was the display boards illustrating personnel and activity and plans. One thing, which had come to fruition extremely successfully, was the 15 Stations of the Cross, portrait-shaped oil paintings in bold style, placed all around the building. Bold and brilliant, mainly in purples and red, they were effectively displayed with discreet numbered captions nearby, which were unobtrusive but legible: very clever! Headed up as 'the Journey,' they were the subject of a detailed leaflet detailing the inspirations, including horrifying abuses to people around the world, such as the Holocaust, Soweto and Iraq. Canon Chris Chivers had written it. He had recently departed from the diocese, unfortunately, as I had been given him as a contact at Blackburn. I was told he had said, *a propos* of cathedral attendance: 'It's all right as long as you believe in a God of some sort – we do multi-faith stuff.'

The bishop's throne (not 'cathedra' here) was a modern item, under the crossing behind the main altar, replacing the old one (not that old as it dated back to 1953). It was set authoritatively at the back of the north transept under an effective modern stained glass window. One of the good things there was a limited use of stained glass: more light and less distraction. This emphasized the essential contemporaneity of the architecture. Despite this there were eight medieval misericords reputedly originating at Whalley Abbey (now the location for the diocesan conference and retreat centre) in dark wood, four on either side of the former throne. I recalled visits to Whalley with Mickey G in the past. It boasted a lovely setting in the country above Blackburn, and Mitton Hall, a restaurant converted from a 15th century farm house. The misericords were assembled in a single line, which made for more of a statement. But we looked up and beheld! Yes, we saw the lantern, of 1967, not dissimilar from Ely, and thankfully much closer to the viewer than that Fenland stunner. However its condition deteriorated and the roof and spire began to leak, requiring restoration. Admirable were the coloured glass up there and hangings right down to the crown of thorns, a 'Corona', suspended above the altar. Best of all were the bits of organ, a strong image indeed, blue and chrome and lovely, adorning walls the crossing corners at the bottom of the clear-glass clerestory. There was no triforium here, but subtle regular panes throughout the upper level. One benefit was the proximity. You could make out the subjects of the bosses, though Chris Ward's comment: 'They've been repainted so many times that they are obscured,' was probably accurate as well.

There was still time to explore the east end, finding the Jesus Chapel, rather than 'Lady', but that's fine as the cathedral is dedicated to the Virgin. Its centrepiece was an icon. Like the splendid organ before it, this was a modern piece throwing tradition to the winds. The standard cathedral approach was to give pride of place somewhere to something Byzantine in appearance. This one presented Jesus in a white robe with a yellow and orange background, indeed iconic, particularly in a well-lit space. The southeast window had a circular blue glass piece, in a black metal frame, on the sill, 'Looking for Peace', 'commissioned for all asylum seekers and refugees in Blackburn with Darwen' by Kathryn Mark, supported by the Lloyd Trust, Darwen in June 2008. 'The title was inspired by refugees from Somalia.' Both sides of the chapel were of plain glass, with engraved inscriptions. One of these was to St Chad, our friend from Lichfield. This was understandable as this part of the world was for long under its aegis. Here he was referred to as Abbot of Lastingham. The other former diocesan identities also had a place in these panes, and there was reference to a gift from St Andrew and St Michael, Bloemfontein, South Africa. Establishing an important mother church such as a new cathedral had basic ramifications. The diocese had developed relationships which extended far beyond our shores.

Next was St Martin's Chapel, for the East Lancashire Regiment. With the customary banners tatty overhead, the subtly-toned stained glass in its east window seemed a paragon of precise, uplifting art. In the south transept stood the oval font, a contribution by Bishop Claxton (1960–71) and his wife, the egg shape representing new life.

We had done a circuit and, glancing at yet more Stations of the Cross, the post-Crucifixion ones, realized the time to be nigh for the Eucharist service. Dean Christopher Armstrong was president and the procession was more measured and incense-driven than most. The organ playing was strong and affecting throughout. I had learned something rare: the early music instrument the serpent, though absent from the *Vespers*, had been awarded a presence in the organ itself. The stop knobs contained one such in their design. The service was protracted by expansive work by the choir and organist.

There were seven choirs at the cathedral. The Cathedral Choir (Boys and Men) sung at this service. It was Festal Eucharist, 'celebrating the 33rd Anniversary of the Consecration of the Cathedral and the Feast of Christ the King'. That was really the re-Consecration after completion of the internal work on the building. The dean opened by noting the 'success of the concert last night'. The microphone crackled disconcertingly. Then we were able to sing some familiar hymns with good tunes from the New English Hymnal, not entirely those of Vaughan Williams. Most welcome, the Nicene Creed was sung, just like at my old school. The distant view of the high altar was an intriguing, complex one, with a number of features. First was the enclosed choir area, behind which rose the altar itself, 'a unique feature of the Cathedral, designed by Laurence King who was appointed architect in 1961', by the corona, hung by about 16 thick, dark threads, hanging from the lantern. As time passed, these assumed an identity of their own, extending the thorn element aloft. Beyond, was an effective illustration on the east wall, the colours blue, red and green involved, topped by an ogee arch. Looking round, on either side of the nave, through the plain glass windows, trees could be made out, skeletal now, blowing in the wind. It was a cold day. Outside that is. The heating system was effective where we were sitting and no doubt economical.

I examined the ceiling, which suggested a fairground, comprising green and white fan strips leading up from the narrow Perpendicular-style columns, with gold and red in support. Wakey noted a green man in a boss. Every cathedral should have one of those, like icons. Blackburn had passed the test. Moreover, it scored high on confidence, majesty and health, the last because it was so clean. No vermin, no cat required. The style was outgoing, the congregation was embraced. They were also encouraged to join 'Nightsafe's Sleep-Out' appeal. On the night of 3 December Cathedral clergy were to do just that in order to help homeless young people. Sponsorship was requested, by way of forms at the back of the cathedral.

We emerged to meet Mickey in the cathedral's neighbour, the Postal Order pub, a JD Wetherspoon establishment, indeed formerly a post office. It was crowded for 12 noon on a Sunday: it had been open since 10 am, and many imbibers were in advanced preparation for the forthcoming match with a clutter clutching cigarettes on the street outside. 'Blue and white' was the prevailing shirt scheme. From the wide choice we opted strategically: Three B's Brewery (Blackburn)'s Tackler's Tipple. Our companion (who kept to lager, poor sod) looked appropriately washed out, having got to bed at 4 am after hours of *Harry Potter and the Deathly Hallows, Part 1*. Wakey emerged from the bar throng with three pints, just about, after a frustrating debacle with a bar bird who deserted her section, in front of him, just as his turn arrived.

Football and cathedrals can be related: this snippet was lately reported in the Citizen: 'Blackburn Cathedral is to be given a £125,000 grant by an Indian tycoon trying to buy Blackburn Rovers... Ahsad Ali Syed will be handing over £25,000 over the next five years to encourage girls to join the choir... Canon Andrew Hindley said the donation had come "out of the blue... We were approached by representatives of Mr Syed to consider whether we could receive the money. It's a completely personal donation, from his own bank account."' Of course there followed opinions back and forth under the electronic column *Your Say*, mostly from fans concerned about the future of their club, relating to the genuineness of the offer, whether he was Hindu or Muslim etc. At the game we were to endure that afternoon (the home side beat the Villa 2–0), a seated Syed was welcomed at the game, and on television that night, paraded as new owner of BRFC. Both enterprises had been carried off and everyone to do with the club, and cathedral one imagines, was happy… The buyers were officially named as Venky's, an Indian poultry company, for £23m, described as 'the Bernard "Bootiful" Matthews of Asia' and 'the woman who heads up the firm confesses that, until she bought the club… she had never been to a football match.' *Sunday Independent* (19/12/10). It was a baffling series of reportages. I was hoping that the cathedral would get its gift, and Aston Villa better results. Villa were indeed to wreak revenge at home, thrashing Blackburn 4–1 in the reverse fixture.

The football turned out truly to be an appropriate icon for St Mary's in another way. On page 54 in *Rovers Review,* the match programme, the player wearing number 39, Pascal Chimbonda, was sponsored by Blackburn Cathedral, with the caption 'appealing across Lancashire'. These entities, Rovers' Ewood Park for sport and St Mary's for the soul, came across as the two biggest things in Blackburn. Mickey G had recently attended the funeral at the cathedral of Ronnie Clayton, who had died at 76. He had been a star player and the service was attended by 1,000 mourners, including Sir Bobby Charlton, 'current boss Sam Allardyce, along with Chris Samba, Ryan Nelson, Paul Robinson and David Dunn,' all current squad notables, except, of course for poor Sam, who had been unceremoniously dumped by the new regime. I was able to recount my similar sad funeral experience at Exeter Cathedral a few months previously.

All was done. Safely home, the next calendar event after this was St Cecilia's Day. She is the patron saint of music and musicians. The radio evensong was notable for the first reference I'd heard to Christmas lights. They were being turned on in Oxford. The broadcast was from Christ Church Cathedral.

Fig 52

Fig 53

[52] Birmingham: Charles Gore, 1st Bishop, in front of his home patch.
[53] Blackburn: *The Healing of the Nations* greets you at the east end.
[54] York: Roman emperor Constantine in charge of the cafe.

Fig 54

40

York

St Peter

Province: York
Founded: 625–7, then made archbishopric
Present building: 1227 starting with transepts, through to 15th century tower

Website: www.yorkminster.org.uk
Tel: 01904 557216
Email: visitors@yorkminster.org
Address: The Visitors' Department, St William's College, College Street, York YO1 7JF

Three to See: Five Sisters window;
undercroft for the best crypt displays;
in the nave, a crane shaped as a dragon's head, jutting out of the triforium

Heart

We shall open this undertaking with a daytrip to the hinterland of the Diocese of York. Our man for this is Phil Thomas, whom Rand, Wakey and I were to meet two days later in York, where he was resident. I shall introduce him now as our mentor, his title 'Church Buildings Officer & Secretary to the DAC' in this setting on the website: 'Church Buildings Team: These people help care for the churchyards across the Diocese.' It continues, informatively: 'The Diocese of York is led by the Archbishop of York acting with the advice and consent of the Diocesan Synod. "Synod" is a Greek word meaning "coming together and finding a way"'.

Phil had the particular advantage of something meaty in his remit: a disproportionately large number of buildings grouped under the umbrella 'Greater Churches'. This was established in 1991,

> ... *as an informal association of non-cathedral churches, the group aims to provide help and mutual support in dealing with the special problems of running churches of significant age, size, historical, architectural or ecclesiastical importance within the organisational and financial structure of a parish church. We seek to enhance the quality of parish worship in such churches and promote wider recognition of the unique position and needs of churches of this kind.*

There were 31 at this stage. In a phone call with the Hon Sec, she stated that it would stay at that number. They did not wish the group to become unwieldy, recent recruits including the newly-defined minsters of Rotherham and Halifax. Yorkshire boasted seven affiliates over four dioceses. Of these Selby Abbey, Beverley Minster and Holy Trinity, Hull are within the see of York. Phil enjoyed looking after such splendid buildings, and the advantage was two-way: for himself to fulfil the requirements of the job and to the diocese to benefit from his experience and knowledge, Selby was first. The journey there, initially uncertain owing to the residual ice from recent downloadings of snow, and persistent freezing temperatures, did come to fruition. The abbey turned out to be Phil's choice as 'the most complete liturgical arrangement. It works very well'. However the local setting is not so good. Phil called it difficult: problems with local politics. The Dean of Ripon, Keith Jukes, was to echo this, in that Selby, his previous workplace, for 10 years, was 'a challenged area' and the council unsupportive. He recalled this incident: when he was there alone one Good Friday evening (of all days on the church calendar!), a large piece of masonry from the right pinnacle of the central tower fell off into a transept. 'This brought forward the quinquennial report,' and produced a new architect. This in turn produced an urgent stonework programme of £7m. Selby Abbey, the building, was so bad that it appeared on a list of the 100 most endangered sites. The adverse publicity had served to unlock funding. The restoration was split down to eight phases. This was serious stuff, but for our trio of jolly tourists it provided a fine opening to our day out in the hinterland of York.

Selby was also the subject of this headline in *Church Times* (3/12/10):

Police drama by floodlight:
North Yorkshire Police hope that they have struck a blow in their war against church lead thieves after two men were arrested on suspicion of stealing lead from a church roof in Selby.

The men were arrested in Selby after PC Graham Smith, off duty after his shift on Friday 30 October, noticed shadows on floodlit Wistow Parish Church. After PC Smith called for back-up, officers joined him and pulled over a vehicle that contained a large amount of lead roofing.

Dorothea Howland, a member of the parochial church council, said that precautions had been taken by the church after a recent theft. "We had a lot of rain coming in through the roof a couple of weeks ago, and workmen who came in to have a look told us a lot of lead was missing. They said it was probably about £6000's worth – and, because of that, the police advised us to leave the floodlights on all night."

Two men in their early 20s from the York area have been arrested and are now on police bail.

Onto Selby Abbey itself which, between 1069 and 1539, was ruled by 34 or 35 abbots. The Norman west doorway, with fascinating decorative work, was a fine place for Wakey to pause for a minute. He had been scouring the streets for a parking space while Rand and I did a circuit of the building. We took longer. Above, the two towers, raised in 1935, were effective. The glory, as widely advertised, was the east window. Rand wondered about its subject, the Tree of Jesse. As in all the best teaching, repetition works. We were to see many such in the next few days, never boring despite the endless figures depicting the man's descendants. This one was special, particularly the 14th century glass, which made up a significant part of it. It featured Jesse himself, reclining in noble attitude in the middle. An entertaining diversion was available from a table in the form of a rather tatty leaflet with a bad drawing of the mouse with a speech bubble: 'Hi my name's Sam. Can you help me find the Selby Secrets?' This involved finding something in each of 10 zones and drawing its image in the space provided. This would lead you to 'a picture of St Germain telling Benedict the monk to build an Abbey in Selby,' in Zone 3, 'the ugly stone face known as the Selby Devil' in Zone 6, and, in Zone 7, 'a wood carving of Sam, the Selby Abbey mouse'. Aha! This was the work of Mouseman Thompson, Yorkshire-based, whose efforts Wakey and I had enjoyed in Bangor Cathedral.

On we proceeded, and out to the car for the next destination, Beverley, by scenic snowy country roads and Market Weighton. The need for refreshments had somehow abated – a coffee break was originally attached to the Selby stop. No doubt flowing adrenalin and the threat of slippery surfaces wreaked some effect. We were feeling mutual concern about parking. It was late morning and we had decided to spend the rest of the day in this highly regarded destination. In fact the problem was solved at once. Once past the 'Beverley' sign, we followed to outline of the tower of St Mary, accorded four stars by Simon Jenkins, and an appropriate prequel to the main event, the Minster (unsurprisingly given five). Just through the north gate, there was a series of parking spaces at angles with the road – Wakey negotiated the solitary unoccupied one, and struggled out of the driving seat. We were all out in the sludge, espying the metre. A charming man hailed us, donating his parking ticket, which had a remainder of 55 minutes. 'That might be enough,' I said. Our ensemble found itself through the gate and round to the entrance, indicated as being on the south side. We were unable to do our customary circuit as the eastern part was inaccessible. The church was road-locked. We did look up at 'the panelled west front with its polygonal turrets, which might belong to another minster rather than a parish church,' *England's Thousand Best Churches*. It was minster-quality heaven in Yorkshire, clearly. The trouble was that we had missed the morning opening session. A notice on the closed door indicated that it would reopen at 2 pm, time enough for a lunch break. For that we took in the busy surroundings on what was obviously a main road and happened upon The Poppy Seed. With a name like that it had to be what we wanted at this stage: a light snack. And we enjoyed our colcannon (only two left) and fish cakes. Rand had those and the corner I sampled was full of fish, a rare thing in fish cakes. No regrets, though, as the colcannon was excellent, and just the right kind of light dish for now, Wakey and I agreed.

Back to the church, now open, having acquired another period of parking. The rich Perpendicular we encountered was 'the best that late-medieval money could buy, the nave arcades having been rebuilt after the central tower collapsed into the nave in 1520'. So contrasting to Selby, we were to marvel at three entirely different churches that day, an abbey, a church and a minster. I shall mention a handful of items: the cluster of brightly-clad minstrels at the top of a capital at the north end of the nave, in a part of the world where music was a central medieval activity. Looking further up was a star-filled blue roof. A Lewis Carroll connection pervades Yorkshire, we were to discover. There was a wall carving which evoked the familiar image of the White Rabbit, carrying a pilgrim's bag. You had to search for it, being stone on stone. As with green men, the best aspect was the sense of accomplishment at identifying something rather indistinct.

The next phase was less fun, armed with a simplistic map (from Blackburn Tourist Office), Wakey driving round Beverley in search of somewhere to leave the car. This culminated in a parking space – for £5 (horrors!) – in the fairly central Grayburn Lane. It was helpful that this is a market town of modest dimensions, but not when you are battling with black ice, poor road signs, and frustrating repetition. We must have gone down Lord Roberts Lane half a dozen times. Well, it seemed like that. The galling, and enthralling bit, was passing the Minster during this quest. By now we had our bearings fairly confidently. We used a residential back street trail to the grail that is Beverley Minster, an occasional occupant in green wellies shovelling brown and white stuff off their stretch of pavement. In the 12/11/10 issue of *Church Times,* the very first clue (1 across) of the crossword read: 'Yorkshire church could produce stern believer – my! (8, 7)'. I'll give you one guess as to the solution.

We reached the northwest side without absorbing the west front fully: keep it for the end, we decided, as the icing on the cake, or the ice itself, perhaps. Through the Highgate Porch, on the north side, we were welcomed by a retainer in a chair, resident there all day we reckoned. Unfortunately, when I asked about evensong he replied about a future date. But in a few hours there was to be a Christmas event, involving singing. That was to seem strange for, as time passed during this visit the building assumed an increasing aura of closure – unlit and cold, with the few staff huddling as if shortly to retrieve their coats to make an escape. The leaflet provided by the retainer summarized the Ground Plan:

> *The church owes its existence to John of Beverley but is dedicated to St John the Evangelist. This is the fourth building on the site. Building began at the east end, behind the high altar, about 1220 and finished at the west end about 1420. It is in all three phases of the Gothic style.*

We had missed the minster in full landmark mode, while enjoying its joyous frame in our circumnavigation in Dana Banana, Wakey's startlingly yellow car. Now we were to feast on good examples of Early English, Decorated and Perpendicular styles. Rand and I were feeling the effects of the tea and sparkling water in the café, and were directed to the gents, outside the north aisle. Above the bowl (no urinal), we read:

If you miss and make a mess
Help reduce the cleaners' stress.
Please use some toilet rolls,
Then use some more and leave behind
A nice dry floor.

William Shakespeare (honestly)

An immense Christmas tree, lacking lights and rather spooky, took pride of place in the crossing, forming an obstacle to entering the quire, where our attention was directed to the Percy Canopy – Decorated (mid-14th century) and 'believed to be a memorial for a lady of the Percy family. The Percys were the most powerful nobles in the north at that time and had a castle at Leconfield'. It struck me that it had to be true about power, as the family's stronghold was far away in Northumberland. Examining the atlas later, I found Leconfield to be a short distance to the north of Beverley.

Simon Jenkins made this point: 'There are many candidates for 'best' non-cathedral church in England, but Beverley most often takes the palm. Like Selby, Tewkesbury and Christchurch (Dorset), it ranks architecturally with the cathedrals and thus with the best Gothic churches in Europe.' Most parish church cathedrals were chosen primarily for demographically-inspired reasons – an area had burgeoned in population and it became imperative to introduce a new diocese. Rural Yorkshire was busy in the Middle Ages, so it gained a number of fine churches. They couldn't all become cathedrals. Beverley should therefore be enjoyed for what it is, benefitting from a grime-free setting, as against the recently visited Blackburn, which successfully achieves its role in growing from an insignificant parish church into a modern cathedral, fit for purpose for the citizens of Lancashire. It's Yorkshire and Lancashire at odds again – the concepts of Blackburn and Beverley are poles apart.

At Beverley I liked this piece from *English Cathedral and Monastic Carpentry* by Cecil A Hewett (1985): '… on the 20th of September 1188, as more than one medieval chronicler tersely notices, the town of Beverley was burnt "together with the noble church of Blessed John the Archbishop"'. From 1220, there followed a building programme, which 'must have been well advanced when, in 1252, Geoffrey de Langley, Justiciar of Forests, was ordered to supply 40 oaks from Sherwood Forest as a royal gift to the works… ' Then, to an endeavour of a well-known building purveyor:

The Great South Transept: This roof may be part of the work undertaken by Nicholas Hawksmoor in the period 1715–36. It is of oak, some of it re-used, with four common-rafters between tie-beams. The tie-beams are doubled, placed upon one wall-plate and under the other, with four threaded through-bolts. The principal–rafters are double also, with three side-purlins and a ridge-piece. In each truss there is a king-post with two braces, and two queen-posts each with two braces. It is the best roof of the later designs.

Technical, but, I think, worth the mention. Wakey agreed.

Down to ground level, it was light relief to yield to the colourful trompe l'oeil illusion of stepping stones in the choir (18th century). This made me realize that this was quite an earnest place, commanding admiration: austere, despite the musical presence on capitals and, really, wherever you looked. But it was a cold, dreary day. Two positives remained. The north transept was spacious, the room easily accommodating an informative exhibition, a good shop nestling within the eastern part of the double space. Phil was to extol the shop as something the diocese had achieved, and Rand bought a postcard. We were good at mislaying things: Wakey's wallet quite often, Rand's alternate specs (one for driving, another for looking at road signs – no wonder I worry when it's his turn) and now I'd lost my woolly hat. I'd freeze in no time, admiring the west front bare-headed. Retracing steps (all of us, like an army manoeuvre), I may not have been the only one to ask the unwitting man and woman, chatting in the north transept near the shop. No knowledge. On my circuitous route in the gathering gloom of the Minster, I bumped into Rand leaving St Katherine's Chapel. He'd found the article behind a rush chair. Of course! I'd taken it off while attempting a photo of a stained glass window.

Now for the final pleasure, that late 14th century west front, to which we slid on the icy pavement. We admired it through the railings circling the building. Alec Clifton-Taylor considered the effect to surpass the west front of any English cathedral. It was magnificent. In the last light of the afternoon, we found shops, Christmas lights and something you wouldn't expect in a place like this: two portraits attached to the wall over a demure-looking emporium. Most strange. In fact Wakey came out with his customary cod French utterance: 'très strange'. We were looking up for architectural satisfaction: this bit was Georgian. A small amount of shopping ensued (Rand had been combless up to then) and, reaching the

Saturday Market, espied the tower of St Mary's beyond, a block looming above some illuminations. We found the Globe Inn nearby. It was good to sit down quietly with a pint, away from the body of the bar. Towards the end of the supping session – just the one drink for now – the landlord came to our table, having noticed the *Good Beer Guide* on the table. He encouraged us to 'sample' an extremely strong local ale. We did and it was, and tasty as well. But we couldn't stay for more. Next was to be Dana Banana for the return trip. The car was placed precariously by a heap of snow, the only space available when we arrived hours earlier. Wakey and Rand attended to tyre pumping. It was a puncture, slow, to our relief. The return journey seemed easy after a day of delight in the Diocese of York.

Sunday 12 December
    On the Saturday we indulged in a diversion to the diocese of Sheffield, embracing the fine Doncaster Minster, another Greater Church. At last we reached York Minster, but not by way of the City Walls as per Plan A. With desperately slippery streets underfoot, none of us actually yielded to the ice. Not quite. We arrived at Jewbury, where the door to the wall was firmly shackled shut. Well, we missed the overhead view of the Minster, and the rest of the old city, and were unable to take a tower tour. Other things were more important. In 1899, Francis Bond had observed: 'One realises (York Minster's) immensity best from the city walls, where it is seen reflecting every change in the sky, and rising like a mountain above the parochial churches and houses of the city' (*The Cathedrals of England and Wales*). The central tower assumes a low profile, even though it is one of the largest medieval examples in England. In 1407 it twisted and fell, leading to so much Perpendicular architecture in the ensuing programme. It works well to produce a unified effect with its companion towers.
    Theatrical productions have been successfully mounted at York Minster. The Royal Shakespeare Company produced the *Mystery Plays*, directed by Greg Doran, within its confines. Ian Mortimer wrote more generally on the subject in *The Time Traveller's Guide to Medieval England*:

> *Travelling from town to town you are most likely at some point to come across a performance of a play. The most common sorts are the miracle plays and mystery plays which are performed on feast days in the larger towns. The sequences of plays performed at York, Chester and Wakefield are very famous; but you will also find mystery plays put on at ... (list of 14 places, including Beverley). Worcester's five plays or*

pageants are enshrined in the town ordinances. (Definition: mysteries = city guilds).

The day was bright and, once more, very cold. The snaps outside the west front revealed that when we later looked at the ones we posed for in various groupings. We wondered at the west window, noting the 'Heart of Yorkshire' as a main feature, defining the composition. Rand and I came to the mutual conclusion to nominate the heart as York's icon. We entered by an insignificant aperture to the bottom right, actually a substantial doorway, bound straight for the choir stalls. Matins (single 't' here) featured the transcendent performance of a strong choir, the space lit by the rays from the clerestory windows on the south side, and the choristers' candles.

Afterwards, before nourishment in the catering facility, I wanted to establish our ticket status for the two days we were to enjoy the building. Ostensibly the charges were £8, with £7 concessions, and this entitled you to return as much as you liked over 12 months. The cashiers were lined up to prevent illicit entry, and we were behind, already in, following the service. I approached one and explained our situation. She said: 'That's ok, it's free for you.'

Outside the cathedral we found the statue of Roman Emperor Constantine, and behind it the fenced off masons' yard full of tactile yellow stone in varying stages of readiness for use. Then, round the east end, the chance of empirical testing of the catering facility, called the Tea Room. It should have been lovely, but failed. It was wisely omitted from the *Welcome to York Minster* leaflet, which we were to follow (1–16 items, I-X Chapels and A-J Where to find: complicated but worth the effort). There was ghastly music blaring all around us, the coffee lacked flavour, and my fruit cake was dry. Wakey's honey choice contrived to contain too much fat. I think Rand's was coconut. The overall vote was 6 out of 10 for the space and 5 for the fare. It had flattered to deceive, presenting an antique impression on entry. Indeed the building had an attractive courtyard. Still, don't let me put you off: it may have been down to bad management, since then much improved. This has often proved to be the case. There was an ancient codger, well-established near the entrance to the section we entered, his aim no doubt an open view, plying any incomers with his wares, which were seasonal attempts at painting. He did manage a couple of sales while we were there. Following this unsatisfactory break, we re-entered the main venue via the shop, and I couldn't resist a small round pill box (or something) illustrated with a voluptuous green man. The price was knocked down from £4.99 to £1.99: a gift for birthday boy Wakey. The shop was good in shape, with two rooms and a lot of stock. Rand bought a post card. Other items to be noted for timely reference included York Collection Faces from the chapter house, Brontë Calendar £3.99 (I wondered how much they would be in the closer Bradford Cathedral), Favourite prayers (£5.50), a reproduction York Minster carving (£117.50) and a Father Christmas tray (£6.95 – it looked like a chipmunk with goggles).

We decided upon the crypt for a proper session. That is exactly what it became for us, an in-depth investigation, in the 'Undercroft, Treasury and Crypt'. We were soon immersed in an extensive display beneath the building. Part of this showed us its history, witnessed by captioned bits of floor and wall from earlier ages, right back to the Roman. We were told of the 1960/70s discovery of foundation weakness and new construction employing stainless steel and concrete, alongside works from earlier generations. At times the sensation of enclosure, the awareness of that immense weight of stone (and wood, and history) reminded me of my onetime willing incarceration in the great Pyramid at Giza. Yet not claustrophobic. The Treasury was a detour to the left, and bulging with an excellent display, much of which was silver, on empathic purple cloth for the most part; and a lot of stone and brick at every turn to remind you where you were situated. At the rear of this was a font, as it happened closer to the steps to the south transept, therefore just round the corner from where we had started out. It was magnificent, 15th century with an elaborate canopy by Ninian Comper from the 1940s, and very photogenic. I'm sure the cussed old chap had a chuckle over that design. As throughout, there was a 'no photography' sign. We concurred that this would all be an educators' paradise; and suitable for hide and seek.

We had determined to join a standard guided tour the next morning, and now had to decide what to see in the remaining hour before evensong. It was to be the chapter house, which could readily be assimilated from the do-it-yourself cathedral leaflet and other information to hand. So it proved, having gorged ourselves in the north transept, most of all on the grisaille Five Sisters window. It defied description. The chapter house (c.1280) was effective for the lack of central pillar, despite its capacity. It is the largest in England. Southwell is the only other octagonal one. 'Made of wood', observed Rand. The stone work was full of detail, with more grisaille glazing. The entrance passage sported many a green man in repeated circular corbels and bosses. Even with binoculars they were elusive, and I managed no clear photos, even with maximum telephoto facility. It was to be a matter of looking them up in a book, or procure a ladder.

We were doing things in reverse, only at this point attending to the nave. This course of action made a change. The vast west window, stunned us, now, from within, dated from 1338. Below it stands St Peter, the patron saint, with the keys to heaven and hell in his hands. Francis Bond waxed lyrical: '... the great west window in the fine contrast of the pointed arches and the free flow of the great ogee arches and the triple-heart centrepiece, surpasses its only rival, the east window at Carlisle'. And that was to be enjoyed this very month. The window's stone tracery was replaced in the 1990s, was now seen in all its magical combination of glass and stone, quite at odds with the Five Sisters. It was traced out like an inverted ogee in the middle. Rather sad in that setting was the mobile font, on a platform between two pillars. It was insignificant in size, with some strength of recent design, but wan; presumably expedient. It was probably inadvisable to have seen the one in the crypt first. However, something much older offered relief and amusement: the dragon's head jutting out of the triforium, 'a carved pivotal crane' which was probably used to lift a font cover. Had it benefited from an actual font below, there would have been three in the building, and a motley selection, too.

A body of technicians, in the nave throughout this period, were gathering momentum in their endeavours. A Christmas happening was imminent, with huge screens now erected undergoing tests by microphone and headphones. It all abated soon enough, with evensong due in the quire. It was almost 4 pm. Back through that screen, several feet thick, we took up what by now was the customary choice, the back row behind the candled pews of the choristers (preferably facing the organ – not applicable here). The lighting was seductive, the choristers ample for an entrancing sound: 20 girls, 12 men. We'd had Stanford in C in the morning, now Stanford in G for the Psalms, culminating with a Bach voluntary: *Nun komm, der Heiden heiland*. It was the Third Sunday in Advent, preacher Revd Stephen Cope told us, with a reminder of the message that Christmas was coming. A carol service was to follow at 7 pm. The leaflet was succinct on the quire: late 14th century Perpendicular. 'Music has always been an important part of the worship and many of the services in the minster are sung in the quire which is arranged so that the choir is part of the congregation. The wooden choir stalls were restored after the 1829 fire.' The upper parts of the building could be absorbed to good effect in the uplifting atmosphere.

We emerged just about on time for the tryst with Phil. He was waiting patiently in the cold gloom by the front door of the Dean Court Hotel on the southwest side of the Minster. Tea for four and a pink cake (for Wakey, the voracious one) followed, and much conversation about a wealth of relevant matters. The particular diversion was about the imminent outcomes of the diocese commission. Phil rarely went into the cathedral – his job was elsewhere. That evening consisted of a compote of treats. Jeremy Purseglove, who had initiated the contact between Phil and me, joined the party for a drink in the Three Legged Mare, and on we went to a fine pillared restaurant: Ask, in the converted Assembly Rooms. We were talking round the subject. 'Oh yes,' said Jeremy over the bottle of Chilean Merlot, 'they close the Walls as they're dangerous'. With most senses mollified we trudged to the spectacular York Station. The day's exposure could in no way suffice to satiate needs for this city: the Walls, of course and Jorvik Museum at last, but above all more stained glass. Reputedly, York offered fine examples in several churches.

41

Ripon

St Peter & St Wilfrid

Province: York
Founded: 660 as monastery, later pro-cathedral to York
Present building: 12th century
Rebuilds: 1288 and 1458 after collapses; 1502–38 nave and aisles
Restored: 1862–72
Cathedral status: 1836 – from York diocese

Website: www.riponcathedral.org.uk
Tel: 01765 603462
Email: postmaster@riponcathedral.org.uk
Address: Ripon Cathedral Office, Liberty Court House, Minster Road, Ripon, North Yorkshire HG4 1QS

Three to See: The jewel, of course;
Saxon crypt;
Markenfield tombs, noting reversed feet

Jewel

Monday 13 December, 2010

Ripon is the seventh smallest city in the UK. Its population according to the 2001 Census was 15,922. The *England Blue Guide*, which joined the bookshelves in 1920, had it in the 1976 edition that the population of the 'pleasant little cathedral city' was 11,000. At Ripon, the *Inhrypum* of Bede, a monastery dependent on Melrose was founded c.660. About 10 years later St Wilfrid built a church here, and for a short time (681–6) Ripon was a bishop's see (resuscitated in 1836). Ripon thus ranks with York and Beverley as one of the three original Christian centres of Yorkshire. A visitor at the end of the 19th century considered it to be a 'very picturesque object, whether viewed from the country above the river Ure, which adds so much to the beauty of the neighbourhood, or whether approached from Kirkgate, with its fine west front before us'. You have to do both, of course.

The ancient custom is still observed of the blowing of a horn every night at 9 pm at the market cross and in front of the house of the mayor. This was performed by the "Wakeman", i.e. watchman. And so it was in 2010. After the concert upon which we had hung this visit we managed both a pint in the Royal Oak and the sight and sound of the Wakeman. In frozen, slippery conditions, he successfully executed his nightly duty, once before each of the four sides of the cross itself, attired in the customary garb. It looked, through the gloom of an empty market square, to comprise a jacket in beige with black hat and shoes. It was an eerie experience as the only attenders.

We had arrived easily enough from York, checking in at the Old Deanery Hotel, opposite the south side of the cathedral. The new Deanery, Minster House, lay almost as close to the cathedral, round the corner from its west end. The setting for this night's stay was in honour of Wakey's birthday, the previous Saturday. His birthdays tended to go on and on. I think this is connected to the psychological effect of its date, exactly two weeks before Christmas. The hotel afforded a view from the room of the body of the nave with towers surmounting. We tentatively crossed Minster Road, the one. It was very slippery, particularly in the hotel car park. The management should have detailed someone to clear it.

The Revd Malcolm Hanson was the first person I laid my eyes on. He was the friend of a friend, and through a sequence of emails we had arranged for him to take us round the cathedral, followed by an invitation to his house for pre-concert supper. Lovely! Malcolm was a 'freechurchman', which shows a considerable devotion to this building, as its practices did not accord with his own beliefs. As guide/welcomer he was now committed at 2 pm (soon after we arrived) to involvement in a schools group in the cathedral. This had little effect on our full experience in the remaining daylight hours – about two. We were introduced to Andrew Aspland, fairly new as verger, and very enthusiastic and forthcoming. With no ado he complied with my immediate wish to see the 'high parts', as they put it at Wells. We mounted the 75 steps to the bell chamber. Andrew had been an experienced bell ringer in Leeds. He was continuing campanology here: this was his first cathedral job. It was refreshing to receive such positive treatment: no fuss, nor charge. There were 12 bells with a semitone, which made it up to 12.5. The bells dated from 1906, from John Taylor & Co of Loughborough, and were wondrous to behold, and to shake to, as Andrew produced a few ear-splitting notes. Taylors have it as follows: '(2008) Bells 12 + 1 bells 23–0–24 in Eb. The existing frame reordered and extended to accommodate 13 bells on one level and to improve the rope circle. The peal augmented with two matching trebles and a flat 6th. New rope guide installed.' This seemed to me to be the opportunity to include some technical bell information.

Then he showed us the seductive green clock workings, from 1906 as well, courtesy of W Potts of Leeds. They had been converted to electricity in 1964. Meanwhile a set of chimes had been transferred from a redundant church in Ripon's neighbour, Harrogate. There had been a lot of ecclesiastical removal. The formerly Cistercian Fountains Abbey had been the source of medieval bells, and more. Bell practice had changed, as in the fashion for change ringing. Taylors and their rivals, Whitechapel, have dominated the bell founding market for a very long time. This is a point which has been regularly reinforced for me around the cathedrals. There is loyalty in this specialist area and it's wise to invest trust in your supplier. Word would soon get around in this intimate world should a duff bell be installed. Archives could also be interesting, I'm sure. Andrew was eloquent about 78 copper, 22 tin percentages, the 23 cwt tenor bell (no bass) and the 5 cwt treble. I noticed chairs in a recess above and beside the bulk of the bells. 'Yes,' said Andrew, explaining 'storage'. That's the geographical section for now. But we did move across the roof to the southwest tower, refreshingly devoid of contents, though we were told that might change. It was a refreshing space, with architectural decorations. It seemed ready for action.

This was quite a technically aware cathedral. I quote *The Stage*: 'The lighting 'luminaries' were responsible for consultant Jim Morse's (Light and Design Associates) winning the Lighting Design Award for 2010 in the Heritage Projects. The cathedral needed new lighting both internally and externally, which allowed the use of current technology.' I had also noted a prize awarded for floodlighting and internal wiring.

We did as much climbing and masonry gap traversing as was possible. Andrew was giving us the works. Back on the nave floor, in response to my request on descent to ascend the roof, he said: 'Ok, we'll go there now.'

And so we did, onto the triforium space, formerly concealed and now open to the elements. From the nave and quire it looked negligible, but once on the uncertain terrain of the icy roof, there appeared a substantial buttressed area. You could play bowls there, where we spotted a recently deceased pigeon. 'Be careful,' instructed our guide at various points, and we simply used common sense when obstacles and gaps loomed. We were enjoying limitless observation of the building and from the top the wintry patchwork of North Yorkshire all around. Our hotel was confirmed as the natural property of the cathedral, with considerably more space behind it given over to Sainsbury's and its car park. That was a valuable facility for cathedral visitors, as were the public conveniences. This was the only loo-less cathedral encountered, though there was an arrangement with the proprietors of the toilets over the road to remain open during events. I wondered how many of the audience that evening would patronize it.

We made our final descent, at the southeast end of the building. We dropped into the Holy Spirit Chapel, adorned with excellent bright fittings and altar rail, or gate. The leaflet *A Brief Tour* commented: '… controversial decorative metalwork by Leslie Durbin, the maker of a ceremonial sword presented to Stalin by Churchill at Yalta'. Wakey and I both loved the chapel, and Malcolm concurred, on meeting us at that point. He was askance when I told him where we'd been. He'd never done that, and I could advise him honestly to ask Andrew.

We were left to our own devices for a while more. Evensong wasn't many minutes away. So we elected for the choir stalls, where a man was dutifully polishing the eagle lectern. We upended a much-anticipated set of misericords. Dating from 1494, they were the work of local woodcarvers. They were all numbered on a laminated hand board for efficient use. That was just as well as there were 34. There was a sow with bagpipes (a dancing pig denotes lust), Samson carrying off the gates of Gaza, wyverns (two legs) and gryphons (four). And one more: an elephant with a castle on its back, the animal appearing to be more physically accurate than the one at Exeter, which had cloven feet. The cathedra was very similar to the pulpit, but worked as a piece in this setting.

Next we were to experience a first – something rare but clear. There, above the choir stalls on the screen below the organ, was a sinister hand, actually a right one, but whose history had been as a conducting mechanism connected to the organ bench, the only one such in the country. It could still be used, at any rate it moves, 'but these days a person is employed to beat time', said the erudite Malcolm. It transpired that his overall take was one of enquiry, searching to explain what we saw. While on the organ, mention must be made of a clever fund raising leaflet, *Sponsor a Pipe*, the

Ripon Cathedral Organ Appeal. Inside was a colourful graphic spreadsheet showing pipes from 1 to 53, and the amount requested for sponsorship, from £25 to £300 for Octave Tromba or Contra Fagotto.

There were so many items in the building for which there was no convincing explanation, such as the metal ring, and, next to it, the cavity where another should have been, at the base of the narrower pillar at the northeast end of the nave. Fascinating! Wakey suggested a tethering function. The story based itself on the founder St Wilfrid, around 672 AD. 'We have to blame Wilfred Owen for the modern spelling,' Andrew had said. I wonder. The crypt was captivating, a discreet anomalous series of whitewashed spaces under the quire. Malcolm told us the story. There was immense confusion as to dating and function – the historical process. What we all sensed was calm and unity. The leaflet offered paragraphs on the man:

> *St Wilfrid, educated at Lindisfarne, travelled to Rome in 652 and, on his return three years later, became abbot of a Benedictine monastery here. He built a new church, the crypt of which is the oldest existing Saxon crypt in England, forming part of today's Cathedral. At the Synod of Whitby in 664, he was largely responsible for the decision to impose Roman traditions on the Northumbrian Celtic Church.*
>
> *Wilfrid's missionary activity took him to Hexham (with which a number of comparisons were made here, including the 674 crypt there, said Malcolm), Mercia, Sussex, Kent, Frisia and Gaul and he went to Rome three times. Despite this, he is chiefly associated with Ripon, which became a place of pilgrimage on Wilfrid's account for hundreds of years, and remains so today.*

There was a diminutive sculpture on a ledge in the body of the crypt, and a hole through to the passage, through which it was said brides-to-be were wont to pass through to prove their virginity, 'in use in recent memory'. That tiny space would certainly preclude matrons. There was also a connection with St Cuthbert, more readily the saint associated with Durham, but Wilfrid shared the honour of dedication with St Peter. There was a hole which looked suspiciously like a leper squint, but Malcolm told us it was for observation 'to keep out the riffraff,' not dissimilar really.

We moved back upstairs, to the north transept and the Markenfield tombs. We were joined by acknowledged expert Toria Forsyth-Moser, having written books on Ripon Cathedral, to which Malcolm had drawn our attention initially, in the shop, before we were snapped up by Andrew: *The Time Traveller – Treasure Chest* (£7.50) and *The Memorials of Ripon*

Cathedral – Who do they think they were? by a team of heritage volunteers from Ripon Cathedral (£7.95). Other volumes in the shop which I would have considered, had the budget not precluded, included *Lewis Carroll's Ripon* by Maurice H Taylor (£2.50). The last one provokes the 'Alice' question. Having been shown the 'White Rabbit' corbel in St Mary's, Beverley, three days before, we found more such inspirations here: towards the end Malcolm pointed up high in the south transept, but by then in the gloom. We could just about make out the Cheshire Cat and the Queen of Hearts. Returning to the misericords, we also noted 'a gryphon chasing a rabbit whilst another rabbit hides down his hole'. This is held as evidence of Lewis Carroll's inspiration. After all, his father was a canon at Ripon between 1852 and 1868.

The memorials celebrated members of the Markenfield family from different generations, the more crumbly, but finely decorated one was actually later (1497), but suffering from greater erosion, owing to a bad choice of material. The curiosity was the female figure of the two, man and wife, effigies on the older item, dating from 1398. Her feet were upside down, her body in the standard prone stance. Toria, invited to comment as an expert, was convincing in her story that it was a prank by craftsmen in more recent times. The north transept had some Transitional architecture, in contrast with, round the corner into the nave, a striking Art Nouveau Pulpit – 1913 of a bronze which gleamed dark, an effective contrast to the marble columns supporting it.

Andrew had told us about the collapse of the tower in 1450, citing the evidence for it in the upper reaches. Malcolm pointed out the effects down below. The medieval screen had been destroyed. We were shown the replacement, resplendent with figures from 1946. King James I and VI was there, repeated in a donated figure which proudly, but discreetly (the effigy had to be pointed out to us), occupied a slim recess on a nave capital. The king re-founded Ripon as a collegiate church in 1604. It appears that a lot of the building work was funded by indulgences. We admired the Jameses to the strains of *O Come, O Come, Emmanuel*. Children were rehearsing for the 7 pm happening. We were guided to the chapter house, or vestry as was its current purpose. Could a corner not be eked out for a toilet somewhere here? There were fetching porthole-type circular 'splay' windows, throwing light upwards to the roof, to good effect, and unique in these islands.

As With Gladness Men of Old now wafted through. We were taken to the Treasury, located in the Library. The fine silver collection, small but striking and well-polished, featured the long-awaited Ripon Jewel. And a treasure it was, impressively low-key in size and appearance, not as flashy as the bright metals in the cabinet. The bulbs were bright, too (150 watt, I guessed). It is of Saxon origin, but unearthed as recently as 1976. It is a small gold roundel, slightly more than an inch in diameter. The four segments contain amber and the lesser triangular ones have garnet. Though the middle and the inner circle are empty, the whole is a tempting testament to the art of an age long gone. Its existence is down to the perspicacious Wilfrid, who believed that the finest craftsmanship and costliest materials were appropriate for the worship of God. St Cuthbert (of Durham and, partly, here) wore brooches and pendants. The Jewel is the inevitable choice as the emblem of Ripon, augmented by the evocative name, also attached to a fine local beer, Daleside Ale – we were deprived of the chance to sup it as it was absent from the pubs we tried. However, a product I must commit to the page is Ripon Spice Cake. Here is a traditional recipe, for this 'loaf cake,' which involves fruit cake and Wensleydale cheese:

Ripon Spice Cake
Ingredients:
225g/8oz Butter
275g/10oz Granulated Sugar
3 Eggs, beaten
50g/2oz Mixed Peel
50g/2oz Glacé Cherries, chopped
225g/8oz Currants
225g/8oz Raisins
450g/1lb Plain Flour
250ml/¼ pt Milk
50g/2oz Ground Almonds
2 tsp Baking Powder
2 tsp Ground Mixed Spice
Makes 2 loaves.

Method:
Cream together the Butter and Sugar until pale and fluffy.
Add the eggs gradually.
Toss the fruit in a little Flour and stir into the mixture with the Milk and Almonds.
Add the remaining ingredients and fold in.
Divide the mixture between two greased 900g/2lb loaf tins and bake at 150c/300F/Gas 2 for 1 ¾ hours.
When cold, store in an airtight container and serve sliced.
May be served with a piece of Wensleydale Cheese if desired.

On the ceiling were two gargoyles, always welcome, looking out of place inside a building. As waterspouts they should be grimacing at the elements they suffer as their purpose in life. One was in good condition – that was the one we liked. This was an area affected by the collapse of the central spire in 1660, after which the two smaller western ones were removed for fear of a repetition. It's a shame when visual losses occur, but the building looks good spireless, to me, and somehow fit for purpose, particularly in view of the hot news of the recommendations of the Cathedrals Commission. These were of a basic 'bread-and-butter' nature in their possible effect. Simply, Wakefield was named as the cathedral for the revised diocese of West Yorkshire. Ripon and Bradford Cathedrals would comprise a new category of 'area cathedrals', under its aegis. *Hark, the Herald Angels Sing* filled the air. I was mulling over the look of this structure. Perhaps Malcolm was right in thinking the cathedral needed spires, as it 'looks stumpy.' Andrew was administering a censer all around. Evensong was imminent. Upwards was the geometric tracery of the east window. Sir Gilbert Scott had this to say of the east end: 'It stands high among the productions of this admirable style, its east window is a peculiarly fine one of seven lights, and all its details are excellent.' Scott undertook restoration here between 1862 and 1872.

Time was now of the essence, that is, 5 pm had passed. We dipped into the shop in the northwest corner. The books have been noted. I found no shot glasses, but Wakey committed £4.95 to a tea towel, which I coveted when he unwrapped it later on, but not so much the Christmas decoration he bought. The shop was somewhat cramped and had spilled out into the nave. We left with Malcolm to enjoy more cathedral chat with him and his wife Brenda. So much was easily covered in limited time as we were destined to join the queue for unallocated seats. A relaxed chicken supper in their warm house was just right.

We did well for the concert, by finding spots by the south aisle wall with radiator, cushion and a reasonable view. I had been in parsimonious mode in (eventually) securing seats. The ticket process is too shaggy a story to relate, but a lavish hotel price was compensated by £10 seats (maximum £30). Wakey dropped his reading glasses, which he scrabbled to find on the stone floor, as they blended too well. A humorous exchange ensued with the old lady next to him, who laughed: 'You'll have to ask for larger ones for Christmas.' A lavish programme had been provided, gratis (American style), announcing *Christmas Carol Concert by Candlelight with Aysgarth School Choirs in aid of Macmillan Cancer Support*. Abounding with adverts the aim was to surpass the contribution achieved at the same occasion in 2009. Of 52 pages, 49 sported some form of publicity – fair enough in this case. The concert featured valuable contributions from the choirs, solo boys,

Siddiq El Fadil, recognized by Wakey from television, and, at last the Dean, The Very Revd Keith Jukes. A potent orator, he urged: 'dig deep in your pockets' to contribute, perhaps to buy a blooming red poinsettia, of which it seemed hundreds adorned the piano and the ticket desk, 'for a tenner or whatever you can. We have to beat last year's £29,000,' he emphasized. Some found new owners for £50. We had all sung the hymns and the dean commanded a rerun of *Hark the Herald*. He added, wryly: 'We'll take pledges for January,' and, a reference to one of Siddiq's anecdotes: 'Hands up if you're not rearing pigs for Christmas,' to full-bellied guffaws from some. I imagine enough obliged, also acquiescing afterwards in the unctuous provision of mead and mince pies in the south transept. The atmosphere exuded bonhomie, and it finished well in time for us to try out Kirkgate, the Market Square and the curfew.

In the bitter mid-evening, never mind bleak midwinter, we enjoyed a ramble through the deserted streets of this lovely little city, to be compared with Southwell, as a small town with a cathedral, evoking a village ethos. Back in the hotel after a visit to the One-Eyed Rat, we just caught the old glasses lady with her companion. They'd thoroughly enjoyed the evening, polished off with a good meal at the hotel. 'Where do you live?' I asked as they moved towards the front door, car keys in the hands of one of them. 'Staindrop, near Barnard Castle,' she replied. 'It's only an hour away.' And about the meal: 'Very good, but nouvelle cuisine.' 'I hope our breakfast isn't.' We finished with pints of Black Sheep bitter as we wallowed in ample armchairs.

Tuesday 14 December
The breakfast was a hearty 'full Yorkshire' plateful. I paced the few yards to the cathedral office to ask for Judith Bustard, personal assistant to the dean, with whom I had developed a friendly patter as emails advanced. She delicately informed me I was in the wrong place. She took me to Minster House, umbrellaless as the heavens opened, to be greeted by Dean Keith. After the introductions she borrowed en episcopal brolly for her return. 'Yes, please do,' he responded when I asked if I could call him Keith. We settled down to a pot of tea in his living room, with a southern aspect of a garden in better shape than the sogged out grass and a few feeble bushes at the Old Deanery. Perhaps it would have been improved by remaining the dean's residence. The walls were adorned with paintings, some evidently souvenirs of his former jobs, plus a Russian Orthodox CD still on the sideboard.

He had been a clergyman for 33 years, which had included much fund raising experience, coming to Ripon, his first dean job, in 2007, nearly four years before. Keith succeeded John Methuen, who resigned in 2005 'in the wake of complaints about his autocratic style, a number of resignations by cathedral staff, allegations of excessive drinking and inappropriate behaviour towards women,' (went a local report). On the other hand 'in 1999 he was involved in the promotion of Ripon Jewel, a beer that was to be sold at Ripon Cathedral'. We have to applaud that.

The new dean inherited a backlog of projects. Examples were the nave chairs, new lighting inside and out. Next, in 2011, was the Narthex plan we'd heard about from Malcolm, to allow all three west end doors to be used: 'Opening up the building to the community.' That would provide a direct vista of the west front from the town. The initiative was certain to happen according to Keith as funds had been committed by a private donor, not even a member of the congregation. On the fund raising front was the now annual Angel Dinner. This was serious stuff, patrons filling the nave, just like the pillar-pounding concert of the previous evening. This time 550 would be accommodated with a high per capita spend. 'People will come who might not do otherwise,' he surmised. There was now really good fellowship in an open, friendly environment.

Projects, as the dean enumerated them, were:

1   The Narthex, which I found an intriguing, if not lovely, word. I haven't found it used much elsewhere: there was one at Arundel RC Cathedral and another in Santorini, Greece.
2   Toilets – oh yes! And Keith mysteriously conceded that there was a space.
3   The big one: opposite the cathedral, between the Old Deanery and Liberty Court House, there used to be a masons' yard, where his aim was to erect a cathedral hall and cultural centre. £7–9m was the notional target. It could only prove to be worthwhile.

A native of Tunstall, Stoke-on-Trent, Keith had spent 20 years at work in the local diocese, of Lichfield. The tea set was a Dudsons one from Stoke. Keith loved Lichfield, and said: 'Not long ago I would have nominated it as my favourite cathedral, but now I'd have to say Ripon.' He listed reasons: 'It's one of those buildings which could be grand enough when you want it to be (e.g. last night) but can have a sense of real intimacy.' He went on: 'The crypt's connections with Wilfrid and the original journey here makes it a special place.' He cited comments in the visitors' book: 'Coming here and encountering God'. He was incumbent at Selby Abbey for a decade.

Asked about the geographical imbalance of the diocese, concerning

Leeds, which lay within it, he said the bishop now lived there, but visited Ripon regularly: about twice a month, which was more than most bishops, many of whom lived near their cathedrals. And bishops are in truth guests in the cathedral, at the invitation of the dean and chapter. He reckoned that quite a lot of the concert audience would have been from Leeds. 'It's not a difficult journey and the conditions were fine. But a series of St Wilfrid lectures were held, serious stuff on an international scale, six annually, which attracted city dwellers.

This led into the Commission: 'a very interim report. It has quite a lot of good points. The Yorkshire dioceses do need some kind of review', adding I've spent fourteen years in Yorkshire, meeting other deans. It needed a bit of tidying up, but I'm not sure if they've got it right'; an unsurprising response as the Diocese of Ripon and Leeds was set for relegation. 'Wakefield as the hub is ok for the cathedral's location.' He repeated that it was a discussion document. 'The soonest anything could happen is three years from now.' And what about Sheffield? It would survive, and was to receive Barnsley, at present in the Diocese of Wakefield. It would therefore follow the boundaries of South Yorkshire. 'That's part of the point,' said Keith. And there were bits of Durham in his diocese, which would join the rest of that county (Palatine). Overall clarity was needed – this would start emerging.

The door bell rang, providing a natural pause. An ancient dog entered, Keith's 14 year-old pet, Sooty. But there was now no cathedral cat. I felt pleased with this conversation with a most engaging man. He was later pictured in the course of the annual four mile Boxing Day Walk from the cathedral to Fountains Abbey – 'in sub-zero temperatures, too,' reported *Church Times* (14/1/11). 'Five hundred walkers started with a short eucharist in the Cathedral, and then set off, following the River Skell out of the city, and led by the Bishop of Ripon & Leeds, the Rt Revd John Packer, and the Dean, the Very Revd Keith Jukes.'

Dropping into the cathedral for a last look, I bumped into Wakey, who furnished me with my very own tea towel, needless to report featuring Ripon Cathedral and its jewel. He had wanted 'to stay awhile amidst its (Ripon's) ancient charms,' which had served to bring on outmoded vernacular. There were heart-felt signs as we approached the A1(M): 'No motorway services here.' Once on the southbound carriageway, two of Eddie Stobart's lorries were duly overtaken, bearing the names Audra Ann, then Kirsty Luanne. They don't get any better.

42

Carlisle

Holy Trinity

Province: York
Founded: 1102 Augustinian monastery
Present building: 12th century; six bays of nave destroyed 1650
Restored: 1762 badly, better in the 19th century
Cathedral status: 1133

Website: www.carlislecathedral.org.uk
Tel: 01228 548141
Email: office@carlislecathedral.org.uk
Address: Cathedral Office, 7 The Abbey, Carlisle, Cumbria CA3 8TZ

Three to See: The choir stalls and misericords;
medieval paintings in the aisles – uncover them;
baldacchino;
a bonus fourth: look at the well in the south transept, only uncovered in 2010.

Warrior

Monday 27 December, 2010
I liked the description of Carlisle in *Nicholson's guide to Great Britain:*

> *An invigorating hotchpotch full of outspoken chauvinism. Since Roman times Carlisle has been a key defence and trading centre standing near the western end of Hadrian's Wall. Warred over by the Picts, sacked by the Vikings and conquered by the Normans, it then became a perpetual bottleneck for the border wars between England and Scotland. The small sandstone cathedral was begun in 1130. Of interest – the castle founded in 1092; the 15th C tithe Barn; the citadel built by Sir Robert Smirke in 1807; the 18th C town hall.*

There you are. This visit to the cathedral involved a substantial trek up the country at an inhospitable time of year. It was hoped to embrace most of the landmarks of the city, broken up by pubs I wanted to review for the *Football and Real Ale Guide.* Not many people venture to this corner of England.

In fact this foray, which made sense when conjured up and booked (the cheapest Virgin and Cross Country train offers, and a hotel both convenient and reasonable), turned out to be fraught. The elements conspired to threaten the trip right up to the last minute. The timing was geared to a football fixture: Carlisle United vs. Exeter City. Why did the computer come up with this, one of the longest journeys of all, at a notoriously suspect weather period – between Christmas and the New Year? It was duly postponed, the decision being broadcast when it was too late for me to rearrange the voyage, in fact having already embarked upon it. The cathedral visit was carefully worked out for balance and sequence within the grand tour. Despite everything I was glad to have done it.

Wakey had just arrived before me after a nightmare of performances by East Coast and Northern Rail. We spent the evening on an extended reconnaissance of the city, the Hallmark Hotel being most conveniently located next to the station. We shared some joy in espying, then peering at the cathedral in the murky city centre sodium lighting. We did inhale a furtive eyeful of the stunning concept of the east window, its much-vaunted tracery marked out, and were surprised to find little snow on the ground, though it was treacherous underfoot. My best effort was to sink right into a puddle, while trying to make out what was written on an information board near the south entrance. Fortunately I had purchased 'cross-terrainers' for Norwegian mountains, since donned for most days out, especially in the recent conditions. They coped with this: I suffered little waterlogging. It was nothing an evening of exploration in the hostelries of the 'border capital' couldn't sort out. The noticeboard failed to reveal anything helpful.

The next morning was to be spent in cathedral and city centre. The football and real ale guide pubs were more or less the only ones, another example of meagre downtown provision in a place yielding to modern use. There were open spaces, but a plethora of standard shops and accompanying refreshment establishments, such the ubiquitous Costa and Pret a Manger. The Board Room, King's Head and Howard Arms were all tested. They were all that we found which qualified. They were worth a try for anyone visiting the city.

Tuesday 28 December
We walked straight to Carlisle Cathedral, after a hearty breakfast, to find we'd arrived without knowledge of the Eucharist service. It was in progress, directly opposite the south side entrance in St Wilfrid's Chapel. This part of the building is so odd. The two pillars of the nave are solid Romanesque red stone. The very modesty of its extent is overwhelming. I was latching onto gems when they cropped up, and these pillars were worth caressing just for their rarity in this setting.

To the left of the crossing, we found a west-facing chapel below the main west window. This had formerly housed the font. It now served better the tradition of easy access from the entrance, from which it could be seen. The service was advanced and there seemed to be a paucity of attenders – the canon and, maybe, two others. I decided to risk missing the opportunity of a conversation with the celebrant after the service and focus on the Treasury, a treat I was sure. It beckoned, down stairs at the northwestern corner and was good, providing a potted history of the cathedral and the region it occupied, that is, served. Henry I established the Augustinian Priory in 1122, which in 1133 was elevated in status to a cathedral. This made three in the Province of York. Canterbury had 14 at that time. The diocese comprised most of the old county of Cumberland and only part of Westmorland, sadly lost to county maps since 1974. An aspect of the political nature of bishops can be noted from William Shakespeare's *Richard II*, in which the Bishop of Carlisle plays a key role. Siding with the deposed king, he is eventually executed. These are the final few lines of a satisfying rant when all is lost:

> *... My Lord of Hereford here, whom you call king;*
> *and if you crown him, let me prophesy-*
> *the blood of English shall manure the ground,*
> *and future ages groan for this foul act;*

peace shall go sleep with Turks and infidels,
and in this seat of peace tumultuous wars
shall kin with kin and kind with kind confound;
disorder, horror, fear, and mutiny,
shall here inhabit, and this land be call'd
the field of Golgotha and dead men's skulls.
O, if you raise this house against this house,
It will the woefullest division prove
That ever fell upon this cursed earth.
Prevent it, resist it, let it not be so,
Lest child, child's children, cry against you woe.

Richard II Act 4 Scene 1

The Wars of the Roses were to ensue.

In 1856 the diocese was extended to transfer Westmorland and 'Lancashire North of the Sands' (i.e. Barrow-in-Furness, known as 'the longest cul-de-sac'). The new territory chopped off the top off the see of Chester. Carlisle lies at the northern end, with the Scottish border precariously close. While the Norman period saw immense development in administration, as exemplified by the production of the Domesday Book in 1086, Carlisle was to suffer from its remoteness, in addition to its precarious proximity to Scotland and disputed territory. It was poor as well as remote, and without a bishop from 1156 to 1204. Fortunes turned around as time passed. In the 13th century it boasted prominent bishops: Walter Mauclerc (1224–46) was Treasurer of England and Silvester of Everdon (1247–54) was Chancellor to the King.

Carlisle and its cathedral have been a battleground over the centuries, and the image for this building must be the warrior, for the presence of the cathedral is defensive; aggressive, too. Scottish encounters are linked strongly with Edward I, 'Longshanks' or 'The Hammer of the Scots', who used Carlisle Castle as a residence during his campaigns. Parliament was also held there, owing to extended absences from the official seat of power.

It is difficult to imagine what it must have been like. It's best to be positive and recall the uniqueness of this cathedral. There's certainly nothing else to compare. This building can offer a maximum of 600 seats (260 in the main body) at the box office in these days when revenue from events is a key budgeting factor. That it has a short nave owes to the dismantlement of six bays of massive form in 1650. The stone was then applied to strengthening and extending structures, such as the city's wall.

This brings us back to diocesan reform. Up to 1856, Chester's remit had included such solidly Cumbrian communities as Workington and

Cockermouth. The latter featured adversely in the news in November 2009 for an act of God: the horrendous floods, which caused so much disruption, including the destruction of the main bridge over that river, which demonstrated something of the power of unleashed natural forces. Then in 2010 came a different sensation. The Bishop of Carlisle was to be invoked in respect of violence in the community.

> *Police attempting to establish the motive behind Derrick Bird's shooting rampage (in the Whitehaven area) have confirmed he was the subject of an ongoing tax inquiry. The 52-year-old taxi driver shot 12 people dead in Cumbria before shooting himself on Wednesday. Detectives said they were focusing on a number of key issues, including suggestions that he was involved in disputes with fellow drivers. No suicide note or list of targets was found during a search of his home. The Bishop, The Right Revd James Newcome, conveying a message of support, said: "I think in times of disaster, immediately and instinctively people will turn to the Church."*
>
> BBC News 5/6/10

And a further threat could be expected from 2011 – *The Guardian* in its 2010 review noted that 14,200 was the number of workers in Copeland, Cumbria in the public sector – 50.4% of the total workforce, the highest in Britain, at a time of increasing cuts to services. The prospect was bleak.

A short time earlier (28/5/09), this piece had been published:

> *Downing Street announced this morning that "The Queen has approved the nomination of the Right Reverend James William Scobie Newcome MA, FRSA, for election as Bishop of Carlisle in succession to the Right Reverend Geoffrey Graham Dow, MA, BSc, MSc, MPhil, who resigned on 30 April 2009."*

Bishop James accepted the promotion with his eyes wide open, having been Suffragan Bishop of Penrith, with responsibility for the southern part of the see. The question was posed: 'Will the new bishop manage to embarrass Carlisle as much as the old one did?'

Continuing on some of these subjects – floods and Bishop Dow:

> *In July 2007, following widespread storms in parts of England, Dow stated that he believed the resulting flooding (in which several people were killed) was the result of God's "strong*

and definite judgment" on the "moral degradation" of British society. In particular, he blames the economic exploitation of poorer nations and the United Kingdom's introduction of laws aimed at reducing discrimination against gay people. According to an article in The Times, Dow is a specialist in exorcism, explaining in a leaflet entitled 'Explaining Deliverance' that both oral and anal sexual practice is liable to allow entry to spirits".

Getting back to the point, the Treasury was not extensive, in fact somewhat cramped, though it could be entered by way of a wheelchair lift. The shiny chalices, goblets and souvenirs were from another time, and often, place. Peer cathedrals were represented, such as Southwell, Exeter (1280–1980 stated the caption) and Peterborough. They had been donated by a man in memory of his son. Alongside the blinding silver was a more contemporary piece, an enamelled chalice, mainly in blue, by Elizabeth Soederberg (1861–1939). We have to be grateful that some creations like chalices survived the edicts of authority.

Once back in the nave I bumped into Head Verger James Armstrong. 'There's a baptism at 11 o'clock,' he replied to my request for a few minutes of his time. We settled upon 11.40 as a time when he might be free for a few minutes. Breasts were swelling as, a leaflet entitled 'Carlisle Cathedral, a Place of discovery, celebration & beauty' in each of our mitts (I was certainly wearing gloves), we set out to the east, to the showpiece section. First was a viewing of the wooden medieval panels, the three on display telling the stories of the lives of Saints Antony, Cuthbert and the Twelve Apostles. All of them were decayed and difficult to read. We gave up on St Cuthbert, fresh from exposure to him at Ripon. Yet the panels were warming to cast your eyes over. The one depicting and naming the Twelve Apostles was questioned by Wakey as to identity. He was unfamiliar with Thaddeus and Matthias. 'I shall have to go back to the Bible,' he said, adding, 'I think the medieval were a bit illiterate.' I diverted him round to the vast central structure, comprising screen and organ beside the crossing. That was all good, commanding a presence. In the tower hung the ring of 13 bells (the most recent addition in 2005.) All of the multitudinous organ pipes were housed in that impenetrable area. The total delight of the 15th century choir stalls greeted us, with 'tabernacle canopies' above and seats mostly up, so the viewer could admire the fine misericords, 46 of them (from c.1400). I was able on this occasion to rest my modest camera on the surface normally intended for hymnals and the like, so as to steady it for long exposures. The light from the high clerestory was otherwise inadequate. The public was not allowed above ground level, and the triforium, apparently of modest dimensions and without organ pipes, was of a piece between nave and clerestory. I contrived to photograph a few, and they were as evocative as those already encountered at Manchester, as a good example. A Ganymede figure being transported by an eagle and a mermaid with breasts akimbo and the mirror of vanity were two of them. Those were our assessments of subject matter. The eye was led in so many directions:

1   Around the choir stalls, satisfyingly complete, in very fine Decorated style, to the cathedra. All was dark end majestic.

2   Aloft to the blue roof, repainted in 1970, a residual hammer-beam construction at the sides, and whose ends were decorated with colourful angels, shaped like buttresses, and as much use as many, i.e. not!

3   Ahead and up to the east window, especially the upper parts which still contain the Last Judgment portrayed in the glass lights of 1380–84.

4   Down the showpiece through the delectable tracery, upstaging the later stained glass, to my personal favourite, a baldacchino. The verger was to tell me that it was a 20th century addition to guide the congregation's sightline down to the altar, within it. It is a great piece, at once substantial and purposeful, also extremely attractive in rich gold, red and blue. It could contain a four -poster bed, and was the most striking of the five by now encountered. Derby, St Paul's, Peterborough and Birmingham St Chad's had preceded.

5   Round again to the north to the pulpit, of 1559 from Antwerp, but not made for Carlisle. It was purchased in 1963 from the church at Cockayne Hatley, Bedfordshire (Diocese of St Albans). Adjacent was the Salkeld Screen (c.1540), erected by Lancelot Salkeld, the prior who was translated to become the first dean.

Now for a little wander. Having absorbed all these wonders, we passed behind the bulk of the baldacchino below the east window to happen upon the white marble effigy of Samuel Waldegrave, the 57ᵗʰ Bishop (1860–69). We remarked on how short his time had been in the eons of life at the cathedral, but he was noted in the Treasury exhibition as a significant reformer.

In the southeast corner was the Bewcastle Cross. On loan from the city's Tullie House Museum since 2008, a caption read: 'a decision has yet to be made about its display for a longer period'. Doesn't time fly? The cross was outstanding as a curiosity in the corner, so we both applauded its presence. I expect the Tullie could do without it, no doubt full of similar goodies in storage as well as on display. This Anglo Saxon cross dated from 675, in Northumbria. Its meaning is unclear, but some detection has been made, e.g. that it is of St John the Baptist with the Lamb of God.

The south aisle wall was the cathedral's only brass, and that a small one. We couldn't make out the detail, which was supposed to include a depiction of this cathedral, predictably with weapons of war. Then, illuminated in a recess, was The Becket Sword with the tale in prose and a reproduction of illuminated scripts. There was a replica sword and scabbard. A legend was attached that the sword belonged to one of the Canterbury assassins, Sir Hugh de Morville, 'a knight for this county. He is described as Knight of Knaresborough and possessor of the Honour of Westmorland'. Such an appellation simply prompted a raft of questions, so we moved on to the curtain which abutted the choir stalls. It dropped from the capitals to the floor. This concealed the final wooden paintings, of the African St Augustine, of Hippo. We discreetly pulled it back to enjoy a further dose of medieval art. That kind of thing is rare and worth the effort to uncover.

Making our way back to the crossing, Verger James was there and willing to commit some time to a chat. He and I sat in the truncated nave, now the Border Regiment's chapel. It was easy to conjure up the image of its former look, bounded to the north by the two vast dusky extant pillars, steps up to the font under the window, with a canopy rising up to the ceiling. Sir Walter Scott chose this place for his nuptials in 1797.

The space above was now occupied by one of four contemporary candelabra, the subject of a new century initiative. They worked well. James came from Northumberland, born in Hexham with its must-see abbey. He had been in post at Carlisle for 20 years, a period that had seen considerable changes in leadership and the building. The east end had undergone substantial alteration both inside and out, the latter including the removal of four statues, perhaps to be replaced with a different style in due course. There were no shrines here. It was a grass roots place, a down to earth environment. I didn't doubt that, given its violent history, he was emphasizing the contrast with the comfortable south, in this case pertinently. There was an abiding rawness. Wakey, a Yorkshireman whose territory for this purpose was down the map, was uneasy, calling it 'misshapen– it doesn't hang together', that is, deformed, with good bits. I did like the cathedral, as James did overtly, and he said he enjoyed the developments in which he was involved. He cited Worcester as his favourite. I was glad to hear that, as it too had suffered from the efforts of nature and man.

I commented that the 11 am baptism gathering had looked in doubt at 11.10, with him, the man in charge, still standing expectant, a picture of contemplative solemnity for us from the chancel through the screen. There was a South African element, the new recruit being the great niece of a canon. 'They were running on South African time', joked the generously-built James, who came across as a bluff fellow. We returned to the lighting: the four candelabras were now in place as Phase 2. Phase 1 had been to illuminate the main body, 'at last' said the relieved verger, and Phase 3 involved whitewashing aisles and ceiling. The overall theme might be 'Let there be light.' Another thing I had noticed was the hot radiators (a whole bank of them under the east window with a fire extinguisher for company), not performing to much effect on a cold day. 'It's gas central heating,' he said. 'Goes back yonks.' He was wearing a blue garment under the black uniform, which may in part have explained his bulk. 'I don't normally need extra layers,' he said, 'but it's been so cold.'

He told me about the sturdy rectangular medieval building down from the entrance, the Fratry, pronounced with a long 'a'. It doubled as library and café. The Prior's Kitchen was a suitable name. Unfortunately it was closed for Christmas, reopening the next day when we were scheduled for a southbound train. It couldn't count for the catering survey, alas. In fact it used to be the Prior's kitchen/buttery. The cathedral owned all the buildings in the close, all of the same deep red sandstone, forming an appealingly irregular piece of territory. Yes, he lived in one of the houses. Did he enjoy his work? 'Yesterday I was all at sea, today I'm chipper,' he smiled, going on to reveal that the cathedral was staffed with key practitioners: a cleaner 'who's worth her weight in gold,' two handymen and a part-time clerk of works. The last had been full time during the existence of a masonry unit. Review of the fabric was looked after by fee-paid specialists. I was aware of the requirement to have an architect attached, normally through his/her firm. There had been examples of dilapidated masonry leaping off the building. Another recent phenomenon was to be seen outside the south porch: gaps in the medieval carving. The offending patch did look woebegone, comparing badly to the crisply defined counterpart on the other side.

We moved to the subject of management. The Bishop had been fending for himself in covering the whole diocese. He had retained responsibility for Penrith while assuming the overall. They saw Bishop James Newcome from time to time and, betimes, Archbishop Sentamu in his capacity of Chancellor of the University of Cumbria. Sentamu's picture appeared in *The Way, The newspaper of the Church in Cumbria* (Winter 2010/11). He had 'spent two days touring Cumbria during November on an official visit to view some of the work of churches in Carlisle diocese... He visited the sites of the 2009 floods... also visited the BAE shipyard in Barrow... where he (was) pictured with Bishop James in front of the latest Astute submarine, which was due to have its first roll-out in mid-December.' The appropriately dowdy hardhats set off the guys' purple ever so well in front of the busy hangar.

Of the working style, there were more bells and smells now than before – the congregation preferred some incense in the air. A (specialist) Celtic service had been introduced on Mondays, now settling down with an average attendance of 25. On the other days between three and seven was the norm for attendance. He was sure this revealed a general preference, not necessarily endorsed by officials. This diocese had been marked by evangelism, after all. The candle stand, at that moment with five white candles, lit and paid for by visitors, had been introduced after the Lockerbie disaster (21/12/88) this being the closest cathedral to the Scottish town. As you find them everywhere it was surprising to hear it explained in terms of a particular influence. A modern cathedral had to provide broad facilities, in a multi-faith world. One recent, popular, event comprised a double Gamelan performance. It had been linked with the Sage Gateshead.

I asked about icons, and he pointed out one above us. He added that there was one in the south transept, on the wall above the well, which had been discovered by accident a few weeks previously, and was being worked on. The well had become a modest project. It had been dug up to see how much water was there. A 12' ladder was now in place. Curiously the water level had actually dropped since then. We rose to have a look at it, on the way venturing into the choir, to find a shut-eyed Wakey surreptitiously enjoying a respite. We went to peer down the hole in the ground. Something appeared to gleam from below.

It had been a good exchange with this friendly, forthcoming verger. He asked as an afterthought: 'Have you seen the Labours of the Months on the capitals of the piers in the choir?' We hadn't and it would have been extremely remiss, regretful, to omit them. This summed it up:

> ... the most perfect stone calendar in England and will reward careful study. Notice how Janus has three heads – to look back, view the present and look forward to the future. On the piers themselves, especially on the NW side, are numerous interesting examples of medieval graffiti.
>
> Harris's Guide to Cathedrals and Churches

We had examined the masons' marks, and successfully photographed a star on a pillar, and James was to assist us with a month by month guide of occupations. We started with January, just described. Not only a monthly chosen activity was carved, but a lot more besides – foliage, supporting activity such as dancing, even a full-frontal monkey; however the middle months had been covered by the stall canopies, erected since their inception. James said he had managed to photograph all of them, but on this occasion we couldn't really get enough access or space to read them. The ones we saw were magnificent. That was a splendid way to end, with a cursory final glance round the whole area, finishing with the 32' high Willis organ. I wished we could have heard it in action.

James posed for my camera outside the entrance, and showed us the damage to the arch. That was it – it was time for a coffee. The first café we found was Fats, just outside the western gate. It was disappointing (mine, anyway – black, probably instant; Wakey was happy with his cappuccino). The time it took to arrive had hinted at meticulous care and a high strength rating. I'm still moaning about this after all these cathedrals. It was a shame to have to miss the fare of the Prior's Kitchen.

St Cuthbert's Church had been recommended by the Revd John Coldwell in Douglas, IoM. With it he had given us a contact, which came to nothing – a Carlisle United FC supporting cleric. Indeed, the local football club assumed a non-existent profile during this visit. St Cuthbert's lay just round the corner from the cathedral properties, past a series of unprepossessing garages. It sported an impressive cupola and offered a total contrast in style to what we had seen. There was no apparent exhibition of the saint's life and times, as had been advertised. 'No entry' signs were in place, to both altar and gallery in a predominantly light blue and cream Baroque church. This didn't undermine the visit, a cursory wander being sufficient. Though we would have preferred to see the mechanism by which the pulpit could be moved from one position to another (rails on the floor – great engineering!) we thought we could discern it but unfortunately could not get not close enough.

In the entrance hall were piled leaflets for 'Connect at the Lodge'. This building greeted you first on the, main, northwest approach to the cathedral from Citadel and shops. We had hoped it would be open for hospitality as the Fratry was not. The leaflet listed an activity there: 'Tuesday 12–2, Knit and Natter.' After this, Tourist Information was also closed, despite notices giving Bank Holiday opening hours.

We were now in pursuit of touristic fulfillment and decided upon the castle next. It was now afternoon, past 2 o'clock, and everything seemed to close at 4 pm. We scaled the drawbridge, and were offered encouragement to 'Join today and get a refund.' We paid £5 each (no concessions) for a single visit. There followed the Tullie House Museum, rather more impressive, which offered an exhibition titled *Ultima Thule,* an edifying exhibition of large-scale landscape photographs.

We were at the end of 2010. England had annihilated Australia at Melbourne Cricket Ground to retain the Ashes. That was good and so was the Cathedral of the Holy and Undivided Trinity. Carlisle was clearly not a place given to providing information. Perhaps that is a consequence of its remoteness, and lack of visitors. The next example was evening prayer. We had no knowledge of this, but passing by the cathedral again, there was evidence of activity in the form of a dark cassocked figure moving towards a subtly lit cathedral. We followed, to experience the choir stalls in action, with the baptismal canon as president for evening prayer. The choristers were on holiday, of course. It was a quietly joyful experience. We were in the best part of the cathedral, for me at least. Given the building's ill fortune over the centuries, I wondered what the 21st was to bring.

Fig 55

Fig 56

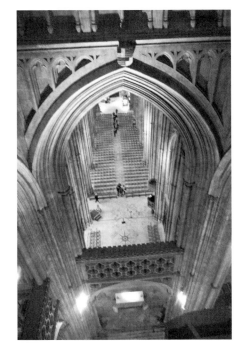

Fig 57

[55] Ripon: 13 bells and a wakeman for the Market Square curfew.
[56] Carlisle: The best baldacchino has a strong presence.
[57] Canterbury: The north aisle from above the Martyrdom.
[58] Canterbury: Laptop gets the top cat award.

Fig 58

43

Canterbury

Christ

Province: Canterbury
Founded: 602, the first of all
Present building: c.1000 as monastic cathedral
Building development: c.1400 nave completed

Website: www.canterbury-cathedral.org
Tel: 01227 762862
Email: enquiries@canterbury-cathedral.org
Address: The Precincts, Canterbury, Kent CT1 2EH

Three to See: Kings screen and tower above if illuminated in the evening;
tomb of the Black Prince;
tread wheel on the climb up Bell Harry

Mitre

Thursday 13 January, 2011

We had settled upon a Churches Conservation Trust day as the prelude to exposure to Canterbury Cathedral. We were bound for Cooling, St James in fact, contriving an extension of the Dickens connections, already established in the first visit to Rochester over a year before. 'The churchyard is believed to be the setting for the first encounter of his hero Pip with the convict Magwitch (in *Great Expectations*), and contains the pathetic tombs of 13 babies, known as Pip's Graves.' In full Dickensian cliffhanger mode, the road suddenly congested with vehicles perched at all angles to reduce the available girth, to the point when, emerging nervously from a bend, Rand was forced to stop. To the side was parked a truck with a purpose, yellow-kitted men proliferating, and ahead a JCB obstructed, in debris-shifting mode. Beyond stood a motley selection of blokes gesticulating to negative effect. Eventually our driver asked: 'Can we get through to Cooling?' 'There's no way through here, mate,' said a youthful yellow-clad worker. He displayed a charming smile I could imagine seducing many a wench on a Friday night in Maidstone (the nearest centre for the persuasive arts). 'There are five more trucks down the road. It's road excavations. You'll have to find another way round.' I looked at Rand's two maps in turn, which at least carried the word 'Cooling', but suggested a considerable detour to south, west and north again. I was quietly upbraiding him that he was too mean to buy an Ordnance Survey map, which would have done the navigating job properly.

Moving on, we did achieve three churches, all from the 'Visit Churches in KENT'. To summarize an eventful tour dogged by problems of direction and feebleness of map provision:

1   St Catherine, Kingsdown. We eventually sought help from one Darren, the first human we had seen for an age. He was building a house and displayed teeth through a gleaming smile, obviously a hallmark for the day. Following his directions, we eventually found the church, nestling in a copse. It bore Puginist hallmarks – Gothic Revival and potentially mad. 'St Catherine's is the only remaining complete Anglican church by Augustus's son Edward Welby Pugin (1834–1875) who was also a Roman Catholic.' All the Trust was really able to do with this as one of a horde of churches sheltering under their umbrella, was to keep it open. The buildings we enjoyed on this occasion had these factors in common: the 'Church open' notice, the stand full of leaflets and a damp book to enter name, address and number in party. The church was satisfying

as a unified whole: mature Decorated style, and all 'Revival.' As ever it was individual features, which made sense of the challenging voyage undertaken to find it.

2   St Mary, Luddenham. A sojourn intervened, a few miles north (correct on the compass, if we'd brought such an aid) at the Black Lion in Lysted, the only inn we'd seen the whole time. We were to be bombasted by a big, loud bloke in the bar, and, to a lesser extent by a man in a suit, taking a long lunch. But the tuna mayonnaise sandwiches were sans pareil, as were the drinks, from Goachers, a local brewery. Big Bloke and Long Lunch were comparing definitions of 'bradawl' and 'awl'. Rand, a technical chap adept at hole-making, whispered the right answer. More than one of my trouser belts, and my waistline, had already survived his bradawl expertise. At last we reached St Mary's, to find an idyllic rustic scene of hay bales, barns, steaming heaps of manure, signs for beef and beer (Shepherd Neame of Faversham, a bit out of place in a remote field) and, yes, the very long church. We happened upon it side on. The Trust: 'This is a hidden gem in a farmyard on the edge of the marshes to the south of the River Swale.' Moving on, there had been an unworkable pedal organ at Kingsdown; the one here emitted an unusual type of sound as we both had a go.

3   St Bartholomew's, Goodnestone. In a flat, even submerged area, the church rested precariously on a slight incline, or 'knoll above Goodnestone Court'. It is a Norman build, restored in the 19th century. The original bits were excellent; including residual stairs up to what had been the rood screen, more recently topped by a gap at the top of the Nave on the north side. The roof is 15th century – 'two tie-beams support vertical crown posts, which in turn support the rest of the roof timbers'. Rand discovered light switches, which proved to be essential. The stark white of the interior set off the striking wooden timbers above to photographic effect. Those regular items could be ticked off to our satisfaction: piscina(e), one formerly being covered up by its own small arched door; unkempt altar and font, this time a diminutive 19th century item 'with concave sides and a traceried stem'. Finally the east window caught our attention, with depictions of the Four Evangelists, St Matthew here being an angel, rather than man, and the lion and ox both bearing wings. A call of nature drew

Rand to an evergreen in the churchyard. For him the yew, for me the view, which extended far afield in the dusk.

We repaired back to base to rescue Wakey from whatever rail company had him in thrall. The evening was nigh, culminating in sweet dreams, no doubt about rescued churches.

Friday 14 January
The real thing! The thrill of arrival was diluted by the exorbitant car parking charge. It turned out that Rand had chosen right, in the Canterbury West station car park, as at 90p per hour it was cheaper than the others we examined during our troll round the streets. Pursuing constitutional exercise in the freezing conditions, we passed the fledgling Marlowe Theatre (a big rebuild project, scheduled for panto opening, but clearly a long way short of the deadline given exposed JCBs and a windowless state), Christ Church Gate and that fine tower, Bell Harry, making for the seriously antique St Martin's. It was later referred to in the cathedral on a number of occasions, so it was an advantage to have visited it first. Chronological order was preferred, and this old church served as a taster. Wakey's navigation from Rand's old coloured tourist office map got us there satisfactorily, in fact in perfect time, as the vicar arrived simultaneously. 'It's not normally open on Fridays,' quoth she, 'but we've got a funeral today.' Excellent!

It dated back to Christian Queen Bertha, the spouse of the pagan Ethelbert, Saxon king. Then Augustine arrived. The rest is history. Living history. It tied in to rub shoulders with funeral attenders in the tiny nave, as a crocodile of them departed for the service up in the churchyard in the far southeast corner. We were left to ourselves. It was a matter of atmosphere rather than content, the best thing within being the elaborately carved font, a cavalier affair of mismatched images: pure entertainment and all the better for that. On uneven surfaces we trudged round the building, solidly white-washed and, naturally enough, washed out. Rand and I were wearing sensible footgear, the same as for fields and copses the previous day. Wakey only had one pair. Thankfully, they didn't leak. The colours of several generations of exterior struck us most – bricks in red, paint, flint, you name it. We recalled the Roman-inspired St Albans tower.

We endured an unsatisfactory coffee experience on the way to the cathedral. It was almost time to meet Clare Edwards, Canon Pastoral. At Christ Church Gate we admired the carving on the front, and Rand pointed out the modern green statue of Christ in the centre recess, showing us a photograph in the book he was carrying. This showed an empty space. It worked, we all concurred. At the ticket station under the arch, I stated our arrangement and we passed to our first full view of the destination from the southwest. Gasps were to be heard. Bell Harry was outstanding in the middle. Jocelyn Prebble, at the desk in the Cathedral Office, was expecting us. I signed a form giving me permission to take and use photographs in the cathedral (not Library or Archive). This was in duplicate, and I added the working title of the book, in hope.

With Day Passes dangling from our necks, we observed comings and goings of guides, delivery people, dog collars. A smiling woman rushed in as I was looking at excavation photos, asking: 'Which one's Mick?' After introductions to and from Clare we established that she could help us most of the rest of the day, and yes, we would be able to climb to the upper levels, even Bell Harry, if the weather relented. It was becoming a routine. Luckily every time I had chosen a bad day, it had ameliorated later on. We would now be shown round, with a lunch break for us all to recover. There was no catering facility, but plenty close by. We agreed the cathedral had been mistaken in this omission: there was an extensive fund-raising unit down the road (a whole shop front), and a sizeable shop, no doubt lucrative and with marketing benefits. We had paused in the shop on the way. Wakey did well with a shot glass – £1.75, and there were sale items such as Canterbury Cathedral Christmas cards reduced from £5.99 to £3 for a pack of ten. The Advent calendar was still £4.99 – for next year, one would conclude. I was interested in *The Canterbury Tales* in case a thread of narrative about pilgrims was to prove worthwhile. There was '*Retelling*' by Peter Ackroyd. But as it was £25 and I was trying to travel light. Along with the Christmas cards it was a case of 'no sale'.

Clare escorted us through the southwest door, amid a bursting of schoolchildren. She held us rapt for a substantial monologue about the work of the cathedral, starting with the end: it was closed every day at 9 pm: 'The doors are closing,' was the customary announcement. Christ Church Gate was fitted with 24 hour cover. 'Between 2 and 3K people pass through daily and it needs to breathe.' Wakey commented: 'It's nice to have that silence.' That was often cited by those who preferred the lower profile cathedrals: the big, popular ones were too busy and noisy. Meanwhile the precincts were full of cathedral residents. In answer to Rand, Clare said that none of the properties was rented out to private individuals (unlike Norwich, I whispered to him). The cathedral did a lot of business, 'but we don't have a betting shop'. The new study centre had been built beyond the Cathedral Office, attracting scholars from overseas as well as British regions. What came across was a fusion between the ecumenical, educational and earning potential. The 'Big Four' – Canterbury, York, St Paul's and Westminster Abbey – were linked by similar practice. This being the last of them to be visited, it would be interesting later to make an assessment. There were other strands of activity, such as archaeological digs and the south transept project. This was entirely under polythene wraps, not, as many guessed, for the stained glass, but the building itself. 15th century piles had expanded with heat. The historic window and panels were on display in the crypt. Methuselah was on show!

The Stonemasonry Department comprised six personnel, headed up by Heather Newton, whom we didn't quite meet – their work was visible in part from on high, as we craned our necks to the east end: we saw lush new stone ready for working. There was no one evident in the yard, hardly surprising on this inclement afternoon. I later picked up a *Sponsor a stone* leaflet. 'From as little as £5 a month,' the options included: 'Single payment... of £60 walling stone' or '£300 decoration stone'.

We heard about the cathedral kestrel, which excited Wakey, bird-lover, but not quite twitterer; also peregrine falcons which, Clare said 'make a hell of a noise'. I wondered if there was a bird/cat correlation. Not really, as Laptop (the cat, of whom more later) was fed by the cleaners, though he sometimes dropped in a dead bird.

Stephen Cox's Water Stoop was a recent, and very effective, addition to the line of vision on entering the cathedral. It was of deep mottled grey marble, and Wakey was sure that the water would make up a few gallons, say five. When I dipped my hand in it, I easily reached the bottom of the curved vessel and reckoned it would hold a pint or two. It was a responsibility of the vergers to keep it fresh and full. That would be performed regularly, given the 1.25m annual visitors, plus 60K free passes (us included) all having a go. Qualifications for passes included local residence (within four miles of the cathedral) and student status. To illustrate the power of the building, Clare told us the story of the non-believing man whose son was doing a cathedral-based project on Thomas Becket, requiring the father to enter it on a regular basis. Eventually he was to say: 'Something's got to me.' What ensued was the multiple baptism of him, with all his family.

Another strand had occurred recently when rock group Jethro Tull were informed: 'It's our tradition to pray at the beginning.' Who knows what effect this had on some present? There were increasing numbers of occasions like this – secular society being engaged in a church. Benedictine origins prevailed. The 'Welcome everybody' theme continued.

We came down to earth with some hard information. In the west end stood the two towers – the northwest housing the clock, the southwest for bell ringing, though this had suffered from the 19th century restoration, the original one being removed. Clare believed in the prevailing approach to leave things as they had become through the passage of time. 'It's who we are,' she maintained. This applied to the decapitations on the west front: 'It's part of our history.' Meanwhile there were 22 chapels round the building. 'All are used, for communion services,' while the nave lacked examples of religious subjects on display, something she had discovered during a session with a group of children, during an attempt to get them to find items on a treasure hunt.

I asked how often Archbishop Rowan visited the cathedral, recalling the stock cathedral answer of 'about once a month'. 'About every fortnight,' was her reply. His responsibility here was somewhat greater than that of the average bishop. The pulpitum faced us at the top of the nave, up a flight of steps, under Bell Harry, which was breath-taking to view from underneath. The Screen of the Six Kings presented itself. We identified, from the list, Edward the Confessor, Ethelbert, Henrys IV, V and VI, and Richard II. They all dated from c.1450, therefore cut off before Edward IV ascended the throne. A shame, I pondered, as he chose the badge of the 'Sun in Splendour', which might have livened things up a bit. In the Trinity Chapel we paused for the memorial to Henry IV, with his queen, Joan of Navarre, then the bronze effigy of the Black Prince (1330–76). He expired the year before he would have expected to ascend the throne, indeed as Edward IV. His dad, EIII, was ageing. The prince's tomb was vivid, his effigy in bronze. His sword was missing – a theft inspired by Cromwell, it was thought. His chantry chapel, in the crypt, was soon to be unlocked for us. There were also various souvenirs from his wardrobe, on display on the aisle wall, but Clare considered his to be 'an unusual approach to battle – rape and pillage'. Regrettable, but maybe not so unusual.

We arrived at the Martyrdom, formerly the northwest transept, renamed for Thomas Becket, who gets everywhere. As for a shrine, there is doubt as to the precise location in this building. It matters not which bit you choose for your devotion, as the effect of disputed identification may mean the dispersal of pilgrims around the building. On the subject of pilgrimage as exemplified by that masterpiece *The Canterbury Tales*, David Dimbleby's *Seven Ages, Episode 2*, identified Geoffrey Chaucer as 'court poet to Richard II'. My favourite is *the Pardoner's Tale*, spinning the yarn of three youths intent upon revelry. They are outwitted by death and expire as victims of their own folly. Just as interesting, is the pardoner himself, a vehicle for Chaucer to send up the hypocrisy of the church. The pardoner sermonizes, sells relics to sinners (with more money than sense, and plenty of guilt). The earnings allowed the practitioner to indulge in those age-old appetites. It was just as well for the pilgrims that St Thomas's Day had been transferred (in 1220) from his deathday of 29 December to 7 July, at a much more forgiving time of year for a hike.

The Martyrdom presented lovely ogee arches, high on a Perpendicular canopy, and in your face as you took the steps down from the body of the cathedral. This was on the tomb of Archbishop William Warham (1503–32). 'Sssshh,' hissed Clare as we stepped down to the crypt, then proceeded to regale us with information in hushed undertones. There was a new sculpture in the offing, *Transport* by Antony Gormley. Next we entered the Black Prince's Chantry, on the south side of this space. It was now the Huguenots' Church: services for the French Protestants were held every Sunday at 3 pm.

It was time for the main attraction, courtesy of the bubbly Clare and her colossal key. We scaled the heights of Bell Harry with gradual intent, as Rand and Wakey were uncertain, but rallied when it came to what we were shown, first a curious cubby hole with an oblique view down many feet (or cubits, no way metres), a disused windowless room with a massive fireplace, and the triforium. That was good, as was the vaulting. We were in a substantial cavity to admire a tread wheel. Everyone should mount this tower and see the wheel in all its faded bulk. At last we reached the summit and Harry's bell. Clare pointed out distant landmarks. Really the greatest interest lay right below in the territory of the cathedral itself, including the dwellings, such as Clare's just to the north, with neighbours such as the dean and the other canons. Each one was occupied by someone attached to the establishment. We saw no birdlife up there, but it was slippery with mess and mulch.

There was a clear view of the King's School. My friend Mervyn had been a pupil there in the mid-1960s. He told some evocative stories about life there, mainly harsh, involving many a trousers-down thrashing, and windows eternally open in the heatless dormitories, even in the depths of winter. He still bore the marks of his suffering: chilblained hands. His invitation to join the ranks followed an encounter with the Red Dean, Hewlett Johnson. Mervyn and his twin brother bumped into the great man in the cloisters, his impressive appearance suggesting to them something special. They reported to the headmaster and their father, who had been discussing their future inclusion in the ranks of the school: 'We've met the Archbishop of Canterbury.' Canon Fred Shirley was the headmaster. The outcome was both places at the school and the provision of necessary funding assistance. The Red Dean gained a reputation for unorthodox views. 'He believed Communism and Christianity could be reconciled, and used to go off to visit China,' to meet, for one, Zhou Enlai, related Mervyn. 'He brought the subject into his sermons.' At the end of one such service, to the strains of Widor's *Toccata*, the procession was moving down the nave. 'The little beadles were scuttling in front. Two old ladies leapt up with umbrellas and attacked him. The beadles didn't know what to do. The dean spread his huge red robes, like Zoroaster, and marched on. The beadles grabbed the ladies. For a moment it looked like a repeat of *Murder in the Cathedral*,' he added. I've seen that play, in a college chapel. How impressive it must be in its thematic setting.

In Mervyn's day the chapter house was used for assembly. Monitors (senior boys) had duties in the cathedral. On Sundays, mattins and evensong were conducted in the crypt. There was considerable exposure to the cathedral, all the school houses being located in the precinct. Pupils would also enjoy the surrounding countryside. This extended to the produce of farmers' orchards. This was, after all, the Garden of England. A complaint was made to the school about such thefts, which were followed by bicycle sprints back to the city. In assembly Headmaster Fred (as he was known), 'asked for people to own up. Eventually about a hundred hands were raised (out of the 600-plus boys at the school). They were all to be given six of the best. After about 60 canings, his arm gave out. The Captain of the School had to do the rest.'

Clare led the downward spiral. We chatted on, having done the 300 steps, as Clare claimed to be the total. I didn't choose to disagree after a breathless count, but she admitted that to achieve the round figure steps up to and down from the bell room might have been included. There was plenty to see in the remaining time. We paced and observed, in, out and about. It was dark and bitingly cold. Evensong was a delightful release, our spirits soaring in sight of the Trinity Chapel and corona. Canon Clare graced the company in her proper station among many choristers and officiators. Afterwards we were treated to what we'd been promised. Requested by our hostess, a verger switched off the main lights as we stood in prime position in front of the Six Kings, above the stark nave and below the tower. Gazing up, it glowed and shimmered in its nocturnal illumination, the fan vaulting displayed to beneficial effect. Outside it was forever a beacon for travellers. As we departed to pick up the car, we all found ourselves looking back, wistfully. 'See the turret lit up,' said Wakey, excitedly. Rand was blinkered with his current spectacles, which had been more effective reading the service sheet. A fumbled change ensued in the gloom. He was glad to make it out at last. It was quite cute, an isolated lancetful of muted light backed up by the solid black silhouette of Bell Harry. Then he drove us to Whitstable for a celebration in seafood and local ales.

Monday 17 January
It was raining again after a sunny Sunday intermission in the Diocese of Rochester. Umbrellas to the fore, after Wakey's departure by train. We

used the opposite platform. The first bonus was exposure to the city walls, complete with intermittent view of Canterbury Cathedral. We had arranged Day Passes as before. We were free for a quiet examination of the cathedral for nearly two hours until the 1 pm appointment at the Library/Archives.

The crypt was favoured first. Rand was immediately disappointed, making for the stunning Romanesque column capitals. 'They're the best anywhere and they're unlit,' he complained, quietly – again – to respect the signage, writ loudly: 'SILENCE.' The meaty capitals sported divers exotic subjects: apemen, provocatively crouched figures and weird beasts. The Treasury lay behind the panels: various fine pieces, including my word of the day: 'Christmatory,' a copper alloy from the 12th century, a container with three compartments for holy oils, found in the roof of St Martin's Church in the 19th century. In this instance it's most likely best kept here, safely, as part of a grand display. One attraction was the gaudy, but effective, silver-plated candelabra, designed by our friend Welby. Augustus Pugin, the Elder, that is. As the morning fled, I observed how on these occasions you end up suspending normal needs, mostly elevenses and lunch. There was no time. Something had to give.

We hadn't yet seen Laptop, the cathedral cat. I had been directed to 'any warm space' by a welcomer on our arrival. 'We know he was fed earlier,' he added. 'He's usually to be found in the cloisters or chapter house,' offered his companion, in a tweed skirt. I was keeping an eye open each time we passed a radiator. These proliferated, with a reassuringly old-fashioned look. They were turned off. We were encouraged on the hour of noon to join in saying the Lord's Prayer 'in your own language'. I could well believe the sentences are of similar length in most languages. That's what we were told, anyway. We surfaced to behold the strainer arches under the crossing, erected as at Wells to support a suspect tower (Bell Harry is big) except in the north transept as the recently erected (15th century) stained glass 'Royal Window' would have been obscured and they cost a lot of money, partly to promote the benefactor. Edward IV made his mark here, at last, depicted in one of the lights.

We returned to the chapter house, built between 1304 and 1320 and heightened at the beginning of the next century. The barrel-vaulted roof was second only to Westminster Hall in size as a medieval structure. Next, the cloisters, indeed all the outside areas to the north, were impressive, and in need of some stone repair. Rand noted the water tower, quietly abutting one wall, while your eye was drawn up to that central tower. All was in mottled stone, which helped to disguise extensive erosion. In the walkway, two brashly orange bowls were resting on the ledge all round the perimeter. On the first circuit they stood, almost devoid of what turned out to be cat breakfast. Then, lo and behold, the animal appeared, ginger and white, bulky (spoiled) with tail erect. He padded to below the dishes and considered the situation. He was, no doubt, weighing up the onlookers – our party of two was augmented by several others, all enjoying the spectacle. Rand had said: 'A pet should be plump, that's what they're for.' Laptop was hefty, but managed to leap up to the dish ledge for nourishment and the ensuing photo session. Patrick Roberts, cat writer, later forwarded me this answer from a verger to his query about the feline, by now a rarity in cathedrals: 'I don't know the official past of Laptop, but as far as I know, he used to belong to one of the King's School houses, and then was adopted by Choir House. I believe it was the choristers who named him Laptop, as he liked jumping onto their laps.'

Our time was nigh for the Library/Archive and the door was just round the corner. Manager Karen Brayshaw took us through to view this facility, having required us to exchange our pens for pencils, resting in a receptacle. It became difficult to make out my writing in intractable lead against the faded parchment tone of my primeval notebook. Instructions were emphatic: 'Do not touch; No photography.' In fact I would have been required to get permission to use my own photos for publication, had I been allowed to take any. We were told about funding for the Library, awarded by the dean and chapter and the University of Kent, fairly secure sources in the current harsh financial climate.

We were shown the post-Reformation versions of the Bible, each one different, and all in English, from the reigns of Henry VIII (1509–47, the volume from 1545) and his successors and the topical prize, James I. Yes, we saw an original 1611 King James Bible. In 2011 many a KJB display was to be presented in cathedrals around the country.

There was more, but space will not allow, except to translate us from Library to Jackie Davidson in the Archive section, whose main room was awash with computer operators, many of whom were surely investigating their family origins. The star attraction had to be the Accord of Winchester, a single piece of vellum from 1072, with crosses for signatures. We were shown this in aside room. William the Conqueror was not alone in being unable to sign his name. Jackie said consort Matilda was literate, but was represented by a demure feminine cross in support of the King. For the Provinces of the Church, Lanfranc; for Canterbury and Thomas, York, were at the centre of this issue. The latter was to leave unhappy, for the Accord served to give Canterbury supremacy. And so it remained.

- We saw the parchment recording the murder of Thomas à Becket in 1170.

- Seals of the priory (of Canterbury): the 3rd from 1386. On the obverse, St Thomas' soul was shown in a state of elevation. The first seal dated from 1152 (under King Stephen), the second from 1175 (Henry II).
- A fine book showing coats of arms – we were subsequently to look for the three 'beckets' (choughs – with red feet) in the west cloister after leaving the Archive, and found it resplendent on a centre boss. No binoculars were needed. Silver was a dominant colour.

Then we saw *Gervasii Cantuariensis Opera Historia*. It didn't mean a lot in a literal sense, but so much for its significance, as we left for a final period of absorption in this supreme edifice. Appearing in the tome was William of Sens, French master mason, who was appointed after the fire of 1174, originating from sparks from a neighbouring house, fanned by a powerful wind, ruined the east end. He appeared in the above document. This is the only documentation about the building of a medieval cathedral. Rand wondered about the whereabouts of the original. He was dismayed at Jackie's revelation that this is lost. We were shown a facsimile.

We left to inhale the atmosphere of the garden, noting old-fashioned herbs like Good King Henry. In we ventured again. We dwelt in the eastern parts, the Trinity Chapel, including second looks at the memorials to Henry IV and the Black Prince. The look benefitted from the diocesan chair at the top of the stairs, square and solid. It complemented the completely different, traditional canopied cathedra at the top of the choir stalls. All around the quire was the famous stained glass, working well, I felt, but not easy to assimilate unlike the massive windows at the extremities of other cathedrals. For me the east end was best, seen from the choir stalls.

Out we went for our tea date with Canon Clare, arranged by mobile phone, in Ferns café where we had lunched on Friday. This time the choice was pots of tea and slices of treacle tart, and cream. This was a gentle, encapsulating finale, with the canon imparting further gems of information. There were 15 guides, who first had to undergo a test of knowledge. They were organized in four zones, plus hundreds of assistants and 350 chaplains. It was a mega-operation. Clare's take on Laptop was that she would come in for duty at 7.30 am to find a cheeky blackbird pinching water from the cat bowl. And he was not the only feline – they proliferated. But he was alone in entering the cathedral. It was his territory.

Rand mentioned stained glass. The outcome was this encore: we were taken to the dedicated department down an alleyway to the southwest of the cathedral. Goodbye Clare; 'Just for a short time, hello,' greeted Leonie

Seliger, a strapping German in charge of the stained glass, but she was generous, showing us the operation at work, and stocks of south transept glass awaiting reinsertion in their tracery. Through the trading arm of the cathedral, 'Enterprises', hard cash was earned from this workshop. We were to agree that we were so lucky to live in an age of preservation and conservation. The medieval colours still rang strong and clear.

That was enough for all of us. Rand and I retreated after yet another day of intense exposure to so many facets of the country's chief cathedral. We tried the Three Tuns for a pint and a half. I explained the nature of a tun. We reflected on how much beer had been brewed by the inmates of this close over the centuries.

Now for a couple of items relating to Robert Runcie, Archbishop of Canterbury from 1980 to 1991. My friend Marilyn Imrie married his son James, and related her memory of visits to her father-in-law in Lambeth and Canterbury. The latter was 'like a little country retreat in the middle of Canterbury – mullioned windows and stone-flagged floor'. Lambeth was poor by comparison. Runcie himself once said: 'In the Middle Ages people were tourists because of their religion, whereas now they are tourists because tourism is their religion.' That was well said from the standpoint of one of the country's biggest draws. And he had two cathedra, chairs of office from which to make pronouncements.

44

Wakefield

All Saints

Province: York
Founded: 15th century as parish church
Building: 18th, 19th, early 20th centuries
Cathedral status: 1888 – from Ripon diocese

Website: www.wakefield-cathedral.org.uk
Tel: 01924 373923
Email: admin@wakefield-cathedral.org.uk
Address: Cathedral Centre, 8–10 Westmorland Street, Wakefield WF1 1PJ

Three to see: St Mark's Chapel at the east end, for serenity and some good artefacts;
organ – you can touch it;
the Chantry Chapel of St Mary, the best bridge chapel in the country and worth the walk

Rhubarb

Thursday 24 February, 2011

This trip provided clear candidates for a double act: Wakefield and Bradford, or 'Wakeford' for brevity. Both are parish church cathedrals, both formerly in the West Riding and now in West Yorkshire; both the subject of the heated debate about the future of the Yorkshire dioceses. Currently, the Diocese of Wakefield enjoyed the prospect of premiership, nominated by the Howe Commission in December 2010 as the centre of three current sees, the third being Ripon and Leeds.

On the way up I was enjoying the relaxation of prebooked, cheapish rail travel, and all the trains were on time. What was going on in other parts of the world was nightmarish. Following the earthquake in Christchurch, New Zealand on 23 February, the 130-year-old Christ Church Cathedral, was to be the subject of 'before and after' photos. I had visited it in May 2009. Now it was a ruin, towerless, reminiscent of so many tales of woe afflicting our own cathedrals, centuries ago: collapses, towers, and even the occasional earthquake. Christchurch had overtaken Wellington as NZ's second most populous city during the stay, and was enjoyed as a safe, scenic place. The best thing was the trolley dinner, doing seven circuits right round the central area, over several hours and much ingestion. I wondered if that service would be restored when given the immense challenge of rebuilding basic infrastructure, such as roads. A bulletin on 3/3/11 estimated that it would take 15 years. One hundred and sixty one people had perished thus far with no survivors under the rubble 'except by a miracle'. There could well be a substantial number of missing persons.

A very different horror story was taking place in Libya, political rather than physical. Hard on the heels of hard-won changes of leader and regime in Tunisia and Egypt, it was their neighbour Libya's turn. Col Gaddafi wasn't capitulating so easily, and was reported as 'deranged'. *The Independent* carried the headline: 'Tripoli: a city in the shadow of death.'

The challenges facing diocesan organization in Yorkshire felt anodyne by comparison, but the matter was eliciting vigorous argument. The first analytical opinion Wakey and I heard against many of the proposals was from Kate Taylor, recently made a lay canon of Wakefield Cathedral. Her contribution would be 'ecumenical', she said, as a dedicated and long-standing local historian. She regretted the recommended ceding of Barnsley by Wakefield to the diocese of Sheffield, as that misunderstood the character of the place. Barnsley was in the administrative county of South Yorkshire, so this was, in part, a further attempt to get ecclesiastical administration to tie in with the rest of bureaucracy (the see of St Albans, founded in 1877, comprised the counties of Beds and Herts). Kate had formidable local knowledge, of the massive erstwhile West Riding of Yorkshire and its age-old structure, broken up in the local government overhaul of 1974.

We had met Kate, by arrangement through the cathedral office, at a rare bridge chapel, the Chantry Chapel of St Mary the Virgin, in the middle of a bridge over the rapid river Calder. She had generously torn herself away from a hot research project to show us round the chapel, which is one of only three surviving in England. One had survived not far away in Rotherham, while the third, in St Ives, Cambridgeshire, might merit a future viewing. Bridge chapels were new to me and were another example of the wildly varied threads of building work in this country over the last millennium.

There were other chapels near bridges – we had missed the one at Rochester when there in January. The legend goes that that iconic monarch (my opinion) Edward IV built the Wakefield chapel after defeat by the Lancastrians at the Battle of Wakefield in 1460. His father, Richard of York, advancing his claim to Henry VI's throne, had fallen in the fray. Edward was to win the throne months later, in 1461. The chapel had actually been erected between 1342, when a new bridge was recorded, and 1356 when it was licensed. No matter, it's a good story, and in any case the 19th century is most in evidence in the building, only the foundations revealing much medieval work. Kate had produced *This Pious Undertaking* in 2003, about the chapel, in the 19th and 20th centuries.

There had passed centuries of very limited records, and care. In 1764 Wakefield had a vicar – the elevation to cathedral status was to come about in 1888. This vicar 'in response to questions from his archbishop... referred to the "chapel upon Wakefield bridge... in which no divine service has been performed time out of mind"'. I wonder if that was the same *Vicar of Wakefield*, eponymously the central character and raconteur of Oliver Goldsmith's 1766 novel, a tame, callow chap, more victim than hero. The novel is both sentimental and satirical, and became a favourite throughout the period of the chapel's restoration, being referred to in novels by Mary Shelley (*Frankenstein*), Charles Dickens (*A Tale of Two Cities*) and Louisa M Alcott (*Little Women*), to name but a few.

Eventually, in 1842, the Yorkshire Architectural Society was founded. 'Its objects were "to promote... the restoration of mutilated remains"... What better than the Chantry?' asked Kate. The outcome was the appointment of George Gilbert Scott (1811–78), who effectively redesigned the chapel. 'The scheme was not to restore or conserve, but to pull it down,' such as the west front, removed in its entirety. It ended up as a folly at the boathouse of Kettlethorpe Hall, not far away and became the subject of published urgings of rescue. They all came to nothing. Instead vandals wrecked it in 1996.

There followed more restorations in the 1880s, 1939–46, 1969–71 and the 1990s, and ongoing, helped by contributions from the Friends. The sequence says a lot about local chemical pollution. It was good to be introduced to the chapel, and having absorbed it, step down to the tiny crypt, betimes under water, visualizing any number of wide-ranging events (RC services, meetings) employing the 40 modern chairs within. 'They ran out of money,' was a recurring phrase from our guide, concerning the amount of plain glass and incomplete stonework. We saw the exterior in the sun, the river many feet below, host to swans and the odd snowdrop. Notables were depicted in corbels on the south side. In the end it was a confident sight, best from the outside, chunky and idiosyncratic, adjacent to a working area of the city, and a busy thoroughfare, Wakefield's south eastern access road. We bid the excellent Kate goodbye: outstanding with a red car, number plate KAT100E. On our walk back towards Kirkgate we had to speed up to avoid a truck with a Sat Nav-challenged driver. That was our conclusion as we contemplated the gentle slope up to the city centre. As we turned the last corner (after a quick pint in the Wetherspoon's Six Chimneys on the way, using discount vouchers), the spire of All Saints Cathedral came into view. It is the tallest in Yorkshire.

I had cheated, or at least got ahead of the game. In waiting for Wakey to join me before the 2 pm appointment with Chantry Kate, I had dropped into the Treacy Centre, an octagonal wooden edifice on the north side of the cathedral. My destination was Cathedral Coffee, I recalled the equivalent St Albans facility, a separate building in a discreet position. Rhubarb and custard it had to be, for this is the centre of that vegetable. Yes, veg it is, and the image of Wakefield, the hub of the Rhubarb Triangle and venue for the Festival of that name, a fixture at the end of each February. That had governed the timing of this visit. We were to see tea towels displaying a Rhubarb Cheesecake recipe for £3.95, near the stall of E Oldroyd. At their farm in the Rhubarb Triangle a couple of years earlier we had been ushered into a low shed to hear the forced rhubarb popping in the dark. Large orders of it were destined for Harrods, to name but one purveyor of superior table-bound provender. This plateful now was duly photographed and devoured, immediately taking Wakefield Cathedral's café to a higher league place than the main event could ever expect. The menu on the cash desk had included: 'breakfast muffin sausage bacon and egg £2.75'. Given that the hotel price didn't include breakfast, it was, perhaps, a pity, given the quality of the rhubarb dish that the facility didn't open early enough for us (9.30 am to 2 pm). Taking advantage of the Gents in the corridor connecting with the ambulatory, we noticed two laminated signs on the door at the end. They were identical, instructing: 'Please close the door.

Cold air in this area puts the organ out of tune.'

I had entered via the west door with time in hand and watch on wrist, having recently read in a piece about the Spring meeting of the Ecclesiastical Architects' and Surveyors' Association (there's no end of publications to pick up at cathedrals), that The Very Revd Jonathan Greener, Dean, wished to see the back of the brightly-coloured kneelers. I found them at least good for a photograph, universally hung on the pew fronts in the dappled light of the nave. In search of sneak previews of the tour proper, I found a second visual delight: the organ pipes in the north choir aisle. Sonorous and honey-gold, they were palpable. And this was the anniversary of the baptism of George Frideric Handel, the tear-off calendar of *Forgotten English* informed.

> *German composer and organ virtuoso, Kazlitt Arvine's Cyclopaedia of Anecdotes of Literature and Fine Arts (1883) related a story involving an envious organist's convoluted opinion of the musical master: "One Sunday, having attended divine worship at a country church, Handel asked the organist to permit him to play the people out, to which... the organist consented. Handel accordingly sat down to the organ and began to play in such a masterly manner as instantly to attract the attention of the whole congregation who, instead of vacating their seats as usual, remained for a considerable space of time fixed in silent admiration. The organist began to be impatient... and at length, addressing the performer, told him that he was convinced that he could not play the people out, and advised him to relinquish the attempt." To prove his point, the miffed, and mediocre, musician proudly resumed playing, emptying the church, according to the same account, 'like the reading of the Riot Act.'*

Wakefield's organ was a parish church cathedral boon: you could reach up and touch bits which were usually aloft and requiring binoculars. Mine were not needed for this. Not having noticed a tour leaflet, I approached a gaggle of women at the shop further down the north aisle. One of them was clearly on duty, smart and jovial in a grey surplice. It was Sister Phyllis. She was from the convent at nearby Horley, on her usual Thursday spot as chaplain. I told her what I was looking for. She marched to a stand, pointing out the glossy guide (£3). I demurred and she handed over a *Look at Wakefield Cathedral* – an attractive 8-page A4 item in bold type, geared to the younger visitor. 'I think they want £1 for this,' she said,

'but take it,' adding: 'There is an audio guide, but it's a "spiritual journey".
It takes 20 minutes.' Not enough time, but ok for later. So rhubarb and
custard it was, after this exchange.

So, the tour! At this stage it was still only me – Wakey was recovering
in horizontal mode from an overdose of work. This was having at last
checked into the hotel (now 3 pm had passed), in itself the best ever value
at £23.50 per room. The Tourist Office had put me onto Travelodge,
apparently a Rhubarb Festival Special. The cathedral offered some special
things, too. The gossips' chain, near the west door, was a rare piece. It used
to have a lockable iron collar. 'Gossips and nagging wives could be chained
up here for a time to think about their "sins"'. It yielded less physical impact
than the hassocks or organ, but was good for a giggle. The nave had grown
ever wider since the enhancement of status, now ample and broad. Add
to that the 20th century eastern extension and the building seems to have
grown like Topsy (I looked this up – the phrase was coined in *Uncle Tom's
Cabin*, 1852, when the church was fit only for the erstwhile borough of
Wakefield, not serving a whole diocese).

I was attempting the audio 'discovery' tour, with headphones,
machine in pocket, camera in other pocket, notebook and pen in hand. This
was enough for the western areas, giving us things permanent: the trapdoor,
'through which the ring of 14 bells was lifted into the belfry,' the video
machine with an illuminating display of interviews, forthcoming events,
and, close to it, a model of the building with an invocation to contribute
any amount, by tossing it through the gap, above nave position. Then came
the pulpit, at which point I remembered my binoculars, untouched in my
shoulder bag. I contrived to extract them on entering the choir, did so in the
stalls, and admired the wooden roof. Verger Emma Brotherton was on hand
to guide. That was helpful as the audio machine had packed up, while she
showed me the misericords, or, more specifically, the one of a green man.
It was lovely, once we found it. Perhaps the long pause after N° 4 was too
much for the machine. I later found I'd lost the binoculars case. However,
I do recommend the choir roof. Following the blue guide I moved through
the various chapels encasing the choir and sanctuary. To the south lay the
Lady Chapel, given over to an extensive display of clay figures all over the
floor. The comical part was the association with an 18th century memorial
beside the wall, of a reclining gentleman. It looked stark and white.

At the far east end beyond the sanctuary lay St Mark's Chapel. It
had an evocative embroidery of the saint. *Look At* commented: 'He was a
teenager when he saw Jesus arrested by the Temple guards in the Garden of
Gethsemane.' In children's literature you sometimes get interesting snippets
like that. Also good for kids was the Robert Thompson mouse. Making

fine furniture from oak, his base was in Kilburn, North Yorkshire. Beyond Ripon. 'Mousey' was responsible for the altar rails and some of the chairs. It was unobtrusively sited at the bottom, rear, of the rails. It was good to discover more of this man's work, pleasantly remembered from Bangor. It was good, too, to be in this space, reserved for quiet prayer, below the east window and, opposite, the sanctuary screen, attractive from both sides. There was one more thing there: something different – an aumbry, within which 'The bread and wine will be taken to people too ill to come to church.'

Emma was looking urgent when I now passed her. It was after 5 pm, when the cathedral was scheduled for closure for an hour until the lead-up to evensong, unusually late at 6.30 pm. I thanked her, while opening my bag to put away the bins. A quick search revealed a lack of case. Lost! This was the result of the self-imposed clutter of my pockets and bag: camera, notebook, pen, glasses to accommodate. A peremptory look round the top of the nave and choir failed. She said she'd look out for it. I said I was returning for the service, so would look then.

I left the nave to follow the guide for 'Outside the Cathedral.' The south porch was the best bit, with 'a small room called a "parvise" as an upper storey (now used as an office – I imagine space is short), and a sundial on the wall above. And below, youths were gathering. There were stones commemorating the stages of the building's extension. Above again, 'at the north-east corner is this (pictured) small tower. It contains a spiral or "newel" stair which gives access to the roof of the cathedral'. It was a pity time had expired to mount it. That would have been welcome, as well as the highest spire in Yorkshire.

Fast forward to Wakey's tour, having extracted him from slumber. He had visited the cathedral before, more than once. We discarded the alternative exhibition, featuring 60 angels, as well-intentioned copies, mostly of familiar images, such as paintings by Fra Angelico. Its time had been extended, as the clay figures had. Overall it made the place seem jumbled. We witnessed a very full and long rehearsal of the men and boys choristers. I suddenly had a thought about the binoculars case: the cathedra. And there it was, on the bishop's cushion. I had received help from more than one person in the congregation, masterminded by a woman who may well be related to the work in hand, asking quite a few for help.

We chose back seats (misericords underneath: mine looked like a fanciful beast) opposite the organ console, and, for that matter, the pipes – two banks of them. It was an appealing service, a female canon singing in monotone, the dean in charge. When it came to the César Franck piece he informed us of the composer's accident in 1890, his cab succumbing under the wheels of a horse-driven bus. I looked it up. It turned out that he died, from pleurisy, later that year, aged 67. We were all invited to the Gala Concert that Saturday: 'entry free and all are welcome'. I was intrigued by the outfits of the men – eight or nine different trims on the red surplices, including sheepskin on a bulky bass. A rarity occurred during the creed: the congregation didn't face the altar. We followed the example of the choir. That's two pieces of unorthodoxy. The various spaces were lit to best advantage, the long nave now dark and cavernous, our choir bright and sculpted with its shiny bosses, the sanctuary topped by simple vaulted stone, and, beyond that most effective screen, St Mark's Chapel soaring and light to culminate the experience. 'Did you see the mouse?' I asked Wakey quietly. No, and after the service we wandered round the back, to the clay exhibits and for him to admire the mouse carving. My companion stated St Mark's as his favourite bit. He wasn't as keen on the cathedral as a whole: 'It's in an appalling location, but makes the most of what it's got. It's the right size for what it does,' he thought.

By then the dean was almost finished with greeting the departing congregation. We engaged in a short conversation. I asked him about the colours. 'Oh, we let everyone wear their university colours. It's a free atmosphere here,' he told us. Then he confirmed what I had read, that he would like to make changes in the nave, not only disposing of the kneelers: 'rather old-fashioned,' he considered, but also the pews, which were restricting. The obstacle was money. Did I hear him say £3.3m? It was good to meet him, having read something of his endeavours in a number of publications: the website, the plethora of leaflets in evidence and displays, one of which covered the Wakefield Mara (Diocesan) Link. Dean Jonathan was chair of the committee, representing 22 years' productive relationship with the Tanzanian diocese, now reorganized into three.

It remained to revisit the Wakefield area to meet the bishop, who had been unavailable on this occasion. The Bishop's Lodge was in Sandal, to the south of the city. On our way to the door I spotted Emma, undertaking duties back in the choir. I rushed to tell her my good news. 'It might not have been found for a while,' said I. 'Oh, the bishop's here most weeks,' she replied. I shouldn't have been surprised. The lesser cathedrals seem to get good value from their diocesan chiefs.

Friday 6 May
To meet Bishop Stephen Platten definitely required a car. It was deeply rewarding to draw up beside the bluebell wood which unfolded before me once into the drive at Bishop's Lodge, clearly a substantial and amenable pile. This was outside Sandal, an opulent suburb of Wakefield. The drawing room was hung with a variety of peer cathedrals, as well as the ruins at

Alnmouth. There were invitations on the mantelpiece. Two caught my roving eye as I waited to be called to the office: from the Fishmongers' Company and for the enthronement of the Bishop of Bradford. Stephen was a personal contact. While in Norwich he had been friends with a connection of mine. They had suggested I meet him. 'He's a great guy,' I was told. In the office I was offered any one of a dozen chairs. I didn't like to try the orange Penguin Books deckchair. It promoted *The Garden Party* by Katherine Mansfield. Stephen commented: 'It's funny: that's always the last one to go.' I said I'd put the Mansfield book on my list for future leisure time. He suggested I add *Flagships of the Spirit: cathedrals in society*. Guess who edited it? He gave me a copy of another work of his, with Christopher Lewis: *Dreaming Spires – Cathedrals in a new age* (2006). It transpired to contain a relevant contribution from James Atwell, Dean of Winchester, who had been arranged as the very last priest I would see on this trail.

Stephen said his was the first case for a long time of a dean of an old cathedral turned bishop of a new one. He had been in post at Wakefield since 2003, after eight years at Norwich. Both jobs and dioceses were in total contrast. He had learned a huge amount as dean in a Romanesque building with all its traditions. He had been instrumental in some of the improvements, which have proved so popular. One drawn out process had been the new building at the cathedral. In the end execution of the plan hung on the widening of a doorway. A war had been waged involving the local authority and English Heritage.

He summarized that people go to cathedrals as pilgrims, tourists and seekers; and that they are marvellous centres locally. There was mention of involvement in re-designing the Norfolk coastline. There had been enormous opportunities in the work of the dean (and chapter). As a bishop his job was more constrained. Bishops were caught up with issues on a national basis. It helped that he was on the Cathedrals Fabric Commission and involved with liturgical discussion. I had seen him quoted in the press. He admitted to liking his public presence. He had graced the House of Lords since 2009.

Of his home in the country, the domain wherein we were seated, Stephen told me the story of its acquisition. Campbell Hone, the Suffragan Bishop of Pontefract (1931–38) had bought it in his own name. When he was promoted to the senior position at Wakefield (in post 1938–45) he sold it to the Ecclesiastical Commissioners, so it ended up in its present role, for him then, and all bishops since. That sounded like a canny move. Cathedrals are seats, but buildings and houses do not belong to the diocese. He was droll about the deanery at Norwich: it was lovely, and local to his workplace.

I wondered about lay canons, having met Kate Taylor. She had only recently been accorded that honour. Deriving from the Cathedrals Measure of 2000, a template for all cathedrals allowed the appointment of 'distinguished Anglicans', individuals of great achievement in their respective fields. Juliet Barker was one such, having written the best book on the Brontës, and Paul Whittaker, in the field of music and the deaf. The Mothers' Union also did key work. This all helped significantly in Wakefield, which lacked financial resources.

Finally Stephen had trouble in naming his favourite cathedral. He nominated a handful, such as Liverpool as a great magisterial statement of the 20th century, but settled on Norwich. I would have been surprised had he chosen anywhere else. He did not anticipate a move, however. He seemed to have wrought a bespoke life rising above the factors constraining a bishop.

45

Bradford

St Peter

Province: York
Founded: 1200 as parish church
Building: 1327, 1430 and 1493
Cathedral status: 1919 – from Ripon diocese

Website: www.bradfordcathedral.org
Tel: 01274 777720
Email: info@bradfordcathedral.org
Address: Cathedral Office, 1 Stott Hill, Bradford BD1 4EH

Three to See: World War I Memorial stained glass window;
west tower, outside and in;
a treasure hunt for the cross keys dotted about the building

Cross keys

Friday 25 February, 2011

Wakey and I spent the day using West Yorkshire Train Dayrover tickets. They cost £5.70, a considerable saving, allowing us to enjoy the Bradford Beer Festival at Saltaire, coupled with a glimpse at its United Reformed Church. This sat, most elegantly, above the river Calder beside Sir Titus Salt's factory, turned museum. Supported by crocuses and snowdrops, any vista there is picturesque, actually built as a mid-19th century model town for the industrialist's alpaca and mohair works, and for the workers to upgrade their living standards, as interpreted by their chief and benefactor. Unfortunately the church does not open during the week.

Casting your eye up and over, in an easterly direction, was Victoria Hall, whither we wended for the lunchtime session. Sir Titus, sitting contentedly in Saltaire church, would not have condoned such a thing. It was, however, a most civilized happening, mainly comprising northern brews. Upstairs (with rows of breweries from A to G) through the windows was more eye-watering architecture; downstairs (H to Z, and perries) a Wurlitzer organ, in pastel colours, periodically rose through its trap door to the stage platform. We found a quiet space in a rear corner to enjoy pies with mushy peas and gravy, washed down by the latter half pints. That was the size of the glass, but a measure was also marked on the vessel for third pints, unorthodox but prudent – this was an increasing trend in the world of discerning ale tasting. We completed the voting forms with the same choice of best beer, of the eight samplings: 'Laguna Seca Blonde' from Burley Street Brewery, Leeds. You can't get much more verbose than that. It was full of character, as they say, and hoppy. Saltaire remains a showpiece, and desirable to live in, in this century for a very different type of resident. It's a world away in all departments. And the beer is surely better nowadays.

We had been warned off Bradford Cathedral, due to the day's event, the funeral of Private Martin Bell, a local paratrooper killed in a bomb blast in Afghanistan. We later saw the news bulletin, involving a packed cathedral and sympathetic words from the Dean, The Very Revd David Ison. The slightly moot point was that Private Bell died while trying to save a colleague, against orders. He was still a hero.

Returning from Saltaire, as it was now after 3 pm, we were able to check in at the recently built Jury's Inn Bradford. Our top floor room afforded views of a car park and faded blocks. This seemed a city in need of renewal.

Saturday 26 February

I had visited the cathedral once before. According to my diary I attended an organ recital as part of a festival in August 1986. I remember more about jazz events in the attractive district of Little Germany nearby. The visit was nigh and our loins were firmly girt on a day which improved from cold and damp to a bit brighter. The first sight of the cathedral was encouraging – the tower had a seductive look – solid, almost squat, chunky Perpendicular. Then we were faced with a long stone wall-gate from the same period, requiring the mounting of a flight of steps under and up. Above were rows of ogee arches superimposed on the stone. Here is a definition of the phenomenon: 'Ogee: a sinuous form of arch, featuring two 'S' curves that appeared in the late 13th century. While it remained until the Reformation, it was a defining feature of the later period of the Decorated style. The adjective is *ogival.*' *Cathedral* by Jon Cannon.

It was a good start, though the east approach to the building needed the flattened tombstones and purple crocuses to give interest. We had hoped that the adjacent Daisies café, built into the former post office below, would be open for breakfast. It was closed, and we were to learn that it was now unconnected with the cathedral. There had been a scandal about financial failure, following a faith exhibition. Cathedrals cannot become bankrupt, but voluntary insolvency ensued. Bradford, while not flush with money, has recovered from the debt, and embarrassment. It sounded like a simple case of poor budgeting, an overestimation of punters. That reminded me of the Worcester sports exhibition. That cathedral is in a higher league, and was able to make up the deficiency with other earnings, not readily available here.

Approaching the main entrance we were uplifted by the sound of young voices emitting: 'Alleluia!' The weather was in keeping with other experiences of tower climbing. We bumped into Head Verger and Lay Reader Jon Howard, in post(s) for six years, so as he was currently available, we left the detailed examination of the compact and easy building until after he had shown us the tower. I asked, he offered. Then Canon Precentor Sam Corley arrived. It was refreshing that neither of them was wearing official garb. Sam was in jeans and an open-necked shirt. I took the opportunity to raise the 'cat' question. Jon's Maisie, a Jack Russell terrier, would have to do. She was a ratter, but mainly scoring in the grounds, not the building. The choral practice continued and we heard about the outreach work into schools through singing. There was an abundance of choristers, who were all voluntary from local schools. No one would sing at all without this initiative from the cathedral. They have even done trips to Canada, Spain etc.

It was quite believable that the tower dated from 1508 – that's how old the stairs seemed. It was after a little persuasion that Jon undertook this task. A Health and Safety Inspector had barred entry to the public after he had come a cropper on the steps. Jon encouraged us further with the information that, not long before, a chorister had broken a leg up there.

'He was larking about.' So we promised to be careful (and well-behaved). The first resting place was the bell chamber, full of atmosphere, and, like the spirals, worn and archaic; complete with sweet wrappers and photos and memorabilia from many a generation. Not much further up Jon contrived to unlock the bell space, the core of the tower. It was hazardous, as we clambered along an unlit space and scaled a moving ladder, hindered by our shoulder bags. Once on the plank straddling the loft, we were within touching distance of some mighty items – massive ancient bells. Jon was completely confident – campanology duties were another part of his extensive remit. Wakey wasn't at all sure – a plummet between the bells would have spelt doom. The piece of wood he had to grasp was in motion, at the top of one of the most forbidding, dull and dusty bells. Actually it was marvellous, as good an informal tower experience as at Ripon, where the bells had also featured strongly.

We were soon on the roof, another bulky key granting access, and presented with a magnetic panorama: the bowl that is Bradford. There were focal points more weird than wonderful. The good bits were the proud Victorian buildings, from town hall to the Alhambra Theatre and, next door, the Odeon, with twin cupolas and abolition in the air. That we surmised, as so much of the city centre had been neglected as mouldy gaps with no prospects, while out of town sites had been developed. Bradford City FC's Valley Parade stadium stood on rising ground on the north side, its cantilevered stands attractively festooned with jutting maroon girders. We were to pay it a visit later on, preceded, of course, by a pub or two on the way. This was where the conflagration had engulfed the old wooden ground in May 1985.

Closer in, the cathedral close was contained behind iron gates. Jon lived there, Sam did too. We were set to meet the latter the next day after the Eucharist service. The original plan had been for him to host us. This had to be retracted. Sam wrote: 'As a family we foster teenagers and a girl who has previously lived with us is coming for that weekend. She is under 16 and Social Services won't allow guests staying overnight.' So we were at Jury's Inn, built less than a year before and next door to the sad Odeon, though there were no rooms overlooking it. I got the feeling that the Odeon's plight would soon yield even more open space in the city. The only positive seemed to the green bit, 'the Urban Garden,' for which we have to thank the bishop.

I now have to introduce the cross keys, the keys of heaven, which feature ubiquitously at Bradford Cathedral. They are chosen as the icon for it, deriving from St Peter, to whom it is dedicated. From the tower was the perfect view of the second vertical section of the building, a shorter tower on the west end with metal cross keys within the spindly spire, or rod, topping it. We proceeded to sight cross keys everywhere:

1   On banners.
2   On the dean's seat in the chapter house.
3   A blue one on a statues mounted on the wall above the high altar (the other statue had red crossed swords).
4   On a powder blue lozenge-shaped mounting on a wall, with the woolsack which told of local industry.
5   Making art of the head of the drainage pipe on the south exterior wall.

Jon subscribed to this notion, by example, with his collection of antiques keys revealing the pleasures of the tower. There was also a poster advertising Artspace, welcoming 'artists, flower arrangers, actors, performers, and dancers from many backgrounds'.

He also made a point of showing us the World War I Memorial Window. The leaflet *Treasures Revealed* stated: 'This window tells part of Bradford's story in an international context, as it commemorates local regiments... and is full of closely observed detail... In the central panel the dying soldier looks to Christ who first said "Greater love has no man than this, that a man lay down his life for his friends."' That text had been delivered by the dean at the military funeral. An excerpt from the publication *The Cathedral Church of St Peter, Bradford* is worth inserting here, as the window is exceptional and demands serious scrutiny:

> *Beginning at the bottom left corner the story unfolds clockwise round the window. We see troops landing in France, followed by the major actions on the Somme, until they arrive at the Rhine in 1919, depicted in the form of Cologne Cathedral. There are many little cameos of life in the trenches in the border design. Hidden amongst the panels there are tiny symbols – poppies, the Yorkshire rose, and pelicans – sign of sacrificial love.*

The centre panel features Christ on the cross, with a fallen soldier below. Jon told us how a school group was shown round. At the end a girl asked: 'Who is that?' pointing at Christ, not the soldier.

Being so compelling and expertly executed, this window got Wakey's and my vote, despite competition from William Morris in the north aisle. Another contender was the purpled hued west window, by Heaton, Butler and Bayne, depicting Women of the Bible, individually and in a centrepiece group of the Resurrection – women at the tomb.

Nearby was the shop, in the south aisle. We bought some greetings cards, economical at £1.30. There were no shot glasses, but stained glass transfers. Wakey pointed out the etched glass Celtic crucifix. Nearby was the font, a Victorian piece. Much better to my mind was its wooden canopy, hanging from on high and dating from 1543. The nave had the chairs Dean Jonathan Greener of Wakefield wished for. The pillars were many and narrow, helping sightlines. You could look up to the ceiling, of dark wood supported by horizontal cross pieces. This had previously been covered by a false ceiling prior to cathedral status, which was conferred in 1920, a generation after that of Wakefield. Much conversion and improvement had been undertaken for the new cathedral.

The chancel and sanctuary were light, with tall plain windows and walls painted white, to see right up to the Lady Chapel. First came the walk round the north side, to the Venerable Bede chapel, whose recognition starts the historical ball rolling. A lot of Bradford's past is honoured in sundry memorials. These plaques stood out:

1   A bronze one for 'a market charter, granted in 1251, which led to the holding of medieval markets on a Sunday, in order to encourage attendance at worship'; it also illustrates the Battle of the Steeple in 1642/3 during the Civil War. Joseph Lister was a young apprentice whose impressions were recorded in vivid detail.

2   To Robert Turner (1923–90) and George Watson (1908–74) 'who pioneered the use of chemotherapy as a treatment for cancer and the people of Bradford to their spirit and vision'.

3   Worldwide contributions totaling £4.25m following the Bradford City FC fire of 1985 are commemorated in a 'Disaster Appeal' plaque. Fifty six perished and more than 300 were injured.

Back in time is the Saxon fragment, built into the north aisle wall – though primarily a Victorian city immersed in the wool trade, Bradford goes back a long way. Our way took us up to the chapels at the east end: The Holy Spirit for quiet prayer and to admire the icon produced for this space, representing the birth of the Christian church: 'at the sides, growing amongst... rocks are... tiny sticks of rhubarb'. This building has its share of interest and diversity. I have just dipped into it. It had been a session of observation, culminating in an exchange in the shop with Kathleen Gray, resident in the area for many years, but hailing from Lincolnshire, actually

Gainsborough. Clearly a woman of wide experience (she was to lead the intercession section of Eucharist the next morning) she was posed with the inevitable question. She replied: 'I adore Lincoln, my local cathedral, how you can see it for miles over the flat countryside; and the rich glow on the west front in the evening. But I would choose Hereford.' That happened so many times in the favourites survey. It is often a head versus heart issue.

Sunday 27 February
Despite a lie-in and a snatched breakfast in the room, comprising one each of scotch eggs, bananas, clementines and pathetic hotel teabags with plastic milk, which tasted like purple top, i.e. devoid of character, we arrived at the cathedral in good enough time to choose our seats and do a bit more wandering.

Kath had warned us about the service that 'there's a baptism too, so it will be rather long'. It lasted for an hour and three quarters. That included the dean taking his time explaining (for the benefit of the baptism party, I wondered) the niceties of what was to follow including a practice of the 'alleluia' sequence, of which the chorister's contribution we seemed to have heard at length the preceding day. The choir was considerable, in membership (occupying all the stalls), as well as volume. These parish church cathedrals are achievers in that department. I was already anticipating the next one, Portsmouth, with relish.

Sam delivered a powerful sermon, hotly trailed by the baptism. This was held on the second birthday of the victim, Isaac, who may have been revealing masochistic tendencies as he gurgled at his total immersion. I think those were plastic knickers encasing his nether regions. Afterwards it was tea and a biscuit at the back for the congregation, then the excellent Sam was free for us to converse on nave chairs. Wakey was having a quiet moment or two, later to opine his favourable feeling of this place: 'It has a bit more space than Wakefield, but is hemmed in, tucked away like an embarrassing relation. It is welcoming and friendly to anyone who comes in. There is a sense of connection.'

Sam was new in this job, through which he was chaplain to the university. It was likely that some of his potential charges had been responsible for the ghastly din we underwent too, on the Friday night, in the normally civilized (said more than one person we met, as 'everyone likes it') Fighting Cock, near the university. The beer was lovely. Speaking of alcohol, Sam had spent his stag event in Portsmouth and Chichester Cathedrals. I interpret 'stags' and 'hens' as being intermeshed with booze. Anyway, he had seen all the English cathedrals but Truro. The customary question was therefore potent. He did prevaricate, but came out with Durham, as he had spent three key years there. He had come to Bradford from Lancaster, and recommended the priory there, a Greater Church, and a fairly near miss for the diocesan choice in 1926, which went to Blackburn. That was even more recent than Bradford. This is the opportunity to bring in outlying parts of the map. The Diocese of Blackburn is notoriously odd, with the city at the bottom southeastern corner, reaching up in a northwesterly direction up as far as Sedbergh, next to Cumbria. New incumbents in senior diocesan positions make a point of visiting their flock, however remote and psychologically and socially removed from Bradford itself. It's not the only bizarrely distributed see. Think of Brecon (with Swansea) or neighbours Blackburn. *Church Times* (17/12/10) had an entertaining story:

> [The Revd Robin Gamble] *never baked so much as a chocolate cake... until he was taken in hand by Edd Kimber, national winner of the recent BBC television series* The Great British Bake Off.
>
> *Mr Kimber and his family have had a long association with Mr Gamble's church, Holy Trinity, in Idle (on the fringes of Bradford), and when Mr Gamble congratulated Mr Kimber and said that if only he could learn to bake a Victoria sandwich or treacle tart, his life would be complete, he was challenged to do just that.*
>
> *The baking lesson was to be a small affair, in the church kitchen, but somehow the event became the Great Bradford Bake Off, in the church itself, in front of "a huge live audience", Mr Gamble says. "They had never seen the Vicar disappear in clouds of flour before."*
>
> *When prepared, the sponge cake, pies, and tart were baked in the church kitchen oven, but he did not taste the results because "they had all been scoffed before I had a chance to get near." His wife said that she was gobsmacked by his efforts.*
>
> *A chocolate-mint-flavoured grasshopper cake, made by Mr Kimber, was raffled to raise £400 for Children in Need. The next thing Mr Gamble hopes to add to his repertoire is "a curry of all curries".*

On the subject of the Howe Commission he reckoned the best approach was to have a single diocese, administered from Leeds, but with three equal ranking cathedrals, that is to leave them all as they are. It sounded promising. He confirmed the central focus of work on interfaith matters in Bradford. Positive relations had been built up. In parallel there were ever stronger links with outside bodies, in the world of education, for example, together with inter-diocesan links and shared resources. Should the cathedral revert to being a mere parish church, it would be unsustainable. The Church Commissioners were called upon to make ends meet – pay for essential things like clergy to keep the enterprise going. Nitty gritty arguments clearly coloured life here: how to fund the conversion of the chapter house had become a project.

Sam was a mere 34 years old; his predecessor had moved on to become the fourth female dean, at St Edmundsbury. I joked about where he would be offered his first diocese, eventually, as bishop. But he was focused on the here and now. There was plenty of that at Bradford, we reflected, jointly and severally as I gathered up Wakey and left Sam to the rest of his Sunday, no doubt busy, from observation. For us lunch in the City Tavern loomed as the final fixture on the Bradford trail, for a Sunday roast, great value at £5.95.

Ogee Bradford

Oh gee! Oh no! How sad, good sense denied:
Those Gothic shapes – Victorian strength turned rot,
A rich arched place, curved Odeon, civic pride:
Neglect's oozed shapeless corrugated grot.
Talk sport: despair's acute up street, and round
A corner: cantilevered Valley
Parade soars angled, sharply yellow sound,
Its City fails. No city block can rally.

The oldest cog's that tower, cubed church shield.
Go: twist up fractured steps, see ogees' style -
Those arches: sharp round curves. St Peter's build
Brings bells, sings songs, support for long square miles.
Its icon's cross keys? Stained glass? Which for prize?
O gee! Those sumptuous ogees: no surprise.

Fig 59

Fig 60

Fig 61

[59] Wakefield: The dean didn't like the bright kneelers.
[60] Bradford: Bradford's pure ogees on the way up the steps.
[61] Bradford: World War I memorial window.
[62] Portsmouth: Organist David Price on his instrument.
[63] Portsmouth: You can see the cathedral tower from the sea and marina.

Fig 62

Fig 63

46

Portsmouth

St Thomas of Canterbury

Province: Canterbury
Founded: 1185 as parish church
Building: from 1935 new nave
Cathedral status: 1927 – created from Winchester diocese

Website: www.portsmouthcathedral.org.uk
Tel: 0239 2823300
Email: enquiries@portsmouthcathedral.org.uk
Address: Cathedral Office, St Thomas's Street, Old Portsmouth, Hampshire PO1 2HA

Three to See: View of cathedral from marina and out on the Solent, if possible;
arcades on either side of choir;
golden barque weather vane from 1710

Anchor

Friday 11 March, 2011

The wider world setting lurked in every headline: the earthquake and tsunami in northeast Japan, so soon after the quake in New Zealand which had occurred at the time of the last cathedral visit, to Yorkshire. The big wave wreaked havoc as far away as Chile and Hawaii. The south coast of England seemed cosy by comparison.

Once at the destination, I checked into my guesthouse, the reasonable Everley in Southsea, and sought guidance from the proprietress as to local bus services. It was approaching 1 pm and I had an appointment with Dr David Price, the cathedral organist, an hour from then. There were challenges in comprehending this strange place, where the various forthcoming events were dispersed all over the promontory which comprises the City of Portsmouth. I battled with various maps to work out the most efficient course of action and its supporting negotiation of routes. This contrived to present difficulties: the various maps were inconsistent. I fought with them and finally made some sense. The trouble was that the cathedral sits west of Southsea, right down at the bottom of Old Portsmouth, delimited by wall and sea and adjacent to the ferry terminal, Gunwharf Quay and the visitor attractions.

The route delivered some insight into the area, jaunting past the promenade with snatches of the foaming Solent, open green spaces and busy streets with promising taverns. I felt a surge in my breast at the first sight of the cathedral on alighting from the 6A bus. As parish church upgrades went, this one looked likely to impress. Clean and bright, it seemed substantial, topped by the tower of 1691, and above that the 1703 cupola. Don't forget the 1693 pulpit and golden baroque weather vane of 1710, all supreme to see. On first impression, the cupola worked to great advantage aesthetically, and no doubt made an evocative landmark from the Solent. That was fair enough as it started life as a naval watch tower.

An anchor appeared on the coat of arms and in purple crocus form under the flagstaff on the north side, in the lawns surrounding the best part of the exterior. It was duly selected as Portsmouth's icon. Two o'clock was nigh, as I approached the Cathedral Music Centre opposite the cathedral, and met David Price, slight in form but very dapper (crisply tied, and what shiny brown shoes: patent leather?) He had joined the staff in 1996 as Organist and Master of the Choristers, has since been awarded an honorary doctorate in music by the University of Portsmouth. He was also an associate of the English Cathedrals Music and Liturgy Committee. Meanwhile, one development has followed another at his workplace. The first subject we covered was the choirs. These have augmented into three: the Cathedral Choir (men and boys), the St Thomas' Parish Choir (anybody) and Cantate (girls, who sing with the men, not the boys), each run by a different member of his team. The others were Marcus Wibberley, Assistant Organist and Andrew Cleary, Director of Music. The benefit of David's developments is the constant availability of a choir, not just at base but throughout the diocese.

Addressing that, it's worth going back in time: in truth not very far, in the context of the history of the Church of England. Portsmouth was awarded city status in 1927. In conjunction it was decided to carve a diocese out of that of Winchester. Earlier excisions had been Southwark in 1905, and Guildford, also in 1927. The latter became a new building project on a hill divorced from the town, while at Portsmouth territory was settled upon southeast Hampshire embracing the Isle of Wight, with one of the city's churches to be developed into a cathedral fit for purpose. There was competition between three of them for the upgrade to cathedral. The obvious one, St Mary's in the city centre, was met with reluctance by its vicar. St Thomas' was the oldest and smallest, located in the seafaring area, awash with pubs and lowlife, described by some as a slum. Even so, it did boast a long history and strong naval associations. It emerged triumphant, its vicar immediately promoted as the first bishop, and the edifice to become the subject of extensions and conversions. While the galleries round the interior east of the organ screen were removed, extra space was added all around, with the east end remaining the earliest part of the church.

David took me up to the organ loft, for a privileged outlook over the eastern parts. The section effected an unanswerable barrier between nave and quire. As there was a substantial gap at ground level, where a tactile modern font resided, sightlines worked from east end to west. He liked it. So did I, despite the immense organ above the screen. What I was already beginning to enjoy was the clean-lined paleness throughout: white walls, simple cylindrical pillars, alongside light wood. The lack of stained glass reinforced this, in window styles evocative of a number of periods. Box pews had been dumped (literally, according to David) like the galleries. The choir stalls were new, like nothing I'd seen before, elegant, tall and easily moved to make space. Ditto the nave chairs, in red: not very many in evidence at this visit. Lots more were housed elsewhere for popular services and events. There were plenty of those. In 2004 occurred 'D Day 60'; in 2005, the bicentenary of the Battle of Trafalgar. The choir was much in demand, overseas as well. Groups tour every 18 months, with visits to France and Germany coming up. 'It's busier than Ely,' said David, who had been Assistant Organist there from 1991 (aged 25) till 1996. Portsmouth had a parish function and sat in an urban environment. Weddings were a regular occurrence here; not so at Ely. David made a number of comparisons between the two, some of which showed his former employer up in a lesser light. However, the cathedral of the eels remained a paramount medieval construction, whose octagon tower and profile in the Fens had won it many a 'favourite' vote: David's was the latest.

The organ states '1718' for all to see, in the typical curved numbering of the time. It is third hand, conveyed from a church in Manchester in 1880, and moved into its present position during the 1990s initiative. The story there is that the process of improving the new cathedral continued up to the outbreak of war in 1939. It was then suspended for 50 years. What we saw was the modified version, completed in 1991; for me successful. The musical side of things had been greatly helped by a windfall in recent memory: a legacy (the Ritchie Music Bequest) plus a promise of money up to half the cost of the plan. The bulk of the bequest was invested. The organ was now insured for £1.5m. The case, empathic with the pervasive wood colour, was purpose built during the more recent stream of improvements. One was the chamber organ we saw by the choir stalls, whose impressive performance I was to witness at evensong, alongside the 18th century showpiece. The new one deserved a caress to confirm the quality of its design, which I duly executed, taking my time over it. The detail included lancet-shaped orifices on the side and shapes of leaves in relief. David explained: 'Our new chamber organ (built by Kenneth Tickell) has been commissioned and built in memory of David Ritchie and was blessed at Evensong on Sunday 13th May 2007; (Stopped Diapason 8', Flute 4', Fifteenth 2", he added).

Wakey and I had heard about 'Sing-up' at Bradford. Here it was again, as an element of the wide-ranging initiatives David had introduced in the area: relationships had been established with schools. This was a people place, which produced such happenings as 'Music in the Round'. The organ had almost 6,000 pipes. Seen from the nave it was a matter of closed doors, symptomatic of Lent, which was upon us. However, while in the loft my host did open them, so I could see how it worked. It was a cramped space, filled with pipes and wood, to the extent that the traditional hole for lifting bells up to their chamber above was covered over. The last time new bells (two of them) were installed, in 2010, installation was necessitated by hoisting it up to a window high above, outside the building.

David treated me to a demonstration on the organ, overlooked by gold-leafed cherubim overhead. He stroked the instrument, producing a pleasing full sound; then he played the cascade effect conveyed by 'cymbalstern', replicated solely at Norwich Cathedral in this country. It was a cascade of eight bells, which could be lengthened. I commented that it might be suitable for Nativity-related events for children, or Christingle. Actually, it was a weirdly hypnotic noise.

At Portsmouth the Lady Chapel lies to the north, the east end being dedicated to St Thomas. We had reached this area. My host pointed out the dark cruciform stain on the floor. This owed to the 200 wax candles placed on a wooden cross after the demise of Diana, Princess of Wales. The intense heat melted the plastic below. The whole area was light and spacious, an impression developing as the character of the whole place.

Time was pacing on, and I had decided to leave a tour of the cathedral, with the 'Welcome' leaflet, until the next morning with Wakey. David offered refreshment back in the office over the road in St Thomas' Street. Tea for two it was and the conversation drifted to processions, which of course demanded maximum organ display. Palm Sunday saw the best piece of staging. The 'performers' (as this was a theatrical piece of work) would congregate at the Royal Garrison church not far away, by the sea wall. A donkey was involved. The proceedings were followed up the High Street and into the nave. Palms proliferated, to find their way to the floor of the cathedral, working as a mat. By the way, the good doctor confirmed this to be a bells and smells place. 'It's the trend,' said he. Attention to liturgical considerations had been central to the work of Provost David Stancliffe (provost 1982–93, before the post was converted to 'dean' in 2000). He was a great reformer. David said he 'finished the nave and re-ordered the entire cathedral in his time'.

Drama and theatre were popular with the congregation, with an ever-increasing need for excitement. The recently retired, then deceased (a leukaemia victim), Bishop Kenneth Stevenson had been David's father-in-law, making for an unusually close relationship within the fraternity. His obituary in *The Guardian* noted: 'Kenneth was a highly public bishop and loved the city's diversity. He was at home at Cowes week or enjoying the hospitality of the Royal Navy, also moving among some of the most deprived communities in Britain.' The bishop's residence was in Fareham, eight miles away, which might suggest a more distant affiliation in prospect, so many bishops' residences being in their cathedrals' closes. There were six houses owned by the cathedral, occupied in the main by the customary senior staff: dean and canons, and some of which, like David's former house, were given over to occupancy by gap year choral scholars. The gap year scholars scheme had been established by him a few years back. It was advertised widely, to recruit and nurture singers, committed to the diocese. This had provided so many benefits, from introducing a textured structure of choral development to the regular touring programme and exchange – there was a twinning arrangement with Stockholm. Those must be quite a presence in the cathedral. Titled 'Heavenly Hunks', calendars were pinned to the office wall illustrating the young men in various entertaining poses, one year in the buff like so many rugby teams, harking back to the original Yorkshire 'calendar girls'. The choral tours were important to the performers and attracted large audiences. There had been a rare exception of a poor attendance, at Tallinn, Estonia, one dark and frozen February evening, but that was at an educational institution. Another point about these forays was the scale. There would be boys, men, parents and superintendents: quite a coachload, in fact a party of 50. David mentioned another contrast with Ely. Whereas here he was in a position of care of child choristers between 3.30 pm and 7 pm, often making a long day, at his previous workplace the boss (remember David was then assistant) would go for a nap in the afternoon. And there, deficits would be absorbed, the institution being comparatively large with substantial assets and reserves. Portsmouth's neighbour Winchester, too, was blessed with 'hordes of administration': pay scales were higher there, and boarding was provided for in the close.

The conversation took a feline turn. At last another cat! However, this one, appearing in *Cathedral Cats* by Richard Surman, was now no longer at large, having died in 2009 at the early age of seven. He had been David's, Ivor by name, 'a genial white and ginger cat with an unusual retroussé nose', and resident 'in a pleasantly ramshackle Georgian house'. His origins were feral, from a farmyard near Sidmouth, Devon. His owner said: 'He took to visitors and used to sit with them. He would be in the cathedral a couple of hours every day.' One guide noticed him dipping in the font on one side, emerging from the other, somewhat bedraggled; and at a particular Christmastide there was bark distributed on the floor around the crib. Ivor was seen to shovel it with his paws, then defecating in the bark, before anyone could stop him. On the other hand his instincts were put to advantage outside the building where he was not shy of killing vermin. Inside, his favourite resting place was the bishop's throne. A photograph in *Cathedral Cats* shows him at the organ keys, with the caption 'Ivor tries out a new voluntary'.

The afternoon was waning and David was overdue for his choristers. I would be able to sit and watch the rehearsals from 5.15 pm. The open air provided sensory benefits: the smell of the water, the rush of the wind, the touch of ancient rough stone, the taste of fine local beer in the Still and West, where patrons were scoffing fish and chips in brown paper. Finally, I got as close as I could to the Royal Garrison church, deconsecrated and currently the subject of an English Heritage-funded restoration. I returned to St Thomas' to the full sound of evensong rehearsal. There were many seating options. I tried the back section of the absorbing strata of the aisles. Apparently only Boxgrove Priory, a few miles away over the West Sussex border in the Diocese of Chichester, had a similar chancel treatment of small arches within a semi-circular design. Like the eastern view from the choir stalls at Wakefield, the sides seen from the choir section showed the effect of clever, theatrical lighting in an area full of varied architectural shapes.

I did indeed enjoy a quiet period in a choir stall, moving to prime position for the service itself. The pillars were created on a human scale and were eminently effective. There were some impressive Norman ones in key positions, but not so as to affect sightlines of conductor, choir and both organists, opposite and above. The service was led by the dean, and was handled efficiently. Psalm 31, or most of it, was well sung by men and boys, on duty that day. The prayers included those 'suffering from the earthquake in Japan, and the tsunami, which followed; also those suffering in Libya'. It was all over in a brief 35 minutes, in stark contrast with the previous event at Bradford (the protracted eucharist/baptism service). Nevertheless I was able to absorb the astute lighting, casting the constituent areas of the north side of the choir into relief. Further up stood a wooden screen, surmounted by an array of ogee arches. This was the first encounter with Lent, scrutinizing the week's service list. Ash Wednesday's big service, at the same hour of 1800, had been 'Sung Eucharist with imposition of Ashes'.

Emerging into the evening gloom, I was reminded it was still March, as an icy wind penetrated over the stretch of water, and the tower was discreetly illuminated. 'You can see it from the sea,' I was told. 'But not at night,' I thought. There remained an evening of reunion with my niece Clemmie, who had taken a train down from her base in Winchester. Aperitifs, for which read thirst-slaking pints, were enjoyed in Monks, a pub opposite the cathedral. On leaving, I thought I discerned a group of men by the further reaches of the bar, recognizing them as David and some lay vicars previously in formal cathedral gear. He confirmed this the next day: 'You should have joined us.' But they looked to be locked in impenetrable discussion and we had an appointment with what proved to be a fine emporium: 'abarbistro', which in a long-lost persona, as the Shipwrights Arms, had housed convicts bound for America. There was something special to come: David had agreed to take Wakey and me up the tower the next morning, a welcome prospect.

Saturday 12 March
And so it was. Wakey had joined me and we took the number 6A to join David and his dad, Basil (as Welsh as his son was pristine English, at least in speech). Basil was a guide, on duty in the subtle shade of orange (more the tone of angostura bitters, really). David, with whom I would have liked to spend more time if only to enjoy further examples of his sartorial expertise, was in an open neck shirt (it was Saturday) and red (paprika?) trousers.

We were bound for the roof. Sensibly he donned a neutral-toned pullover for sea breeze exposure. These all survived the ensuing clamber. Wakey and I were dressed for a football-day-out, and had already checked in at the Royal Beach Hotel, to get such formalities out of the way. This was an internet cheap stay committed by computer.

The nave abounded with Cantate Zimbe Workshop participants. We heard occasional strains of traditional vocals evocative of Africa. Next we were led up to the loft. David was proud of the organ improvements. This time I noticed a deep basket chair, certainly for private recovery. 'It's for one of the gap year boys', said our man. We didn't get to the bottom of this matter, but scrambled up narrow stairs to the bells, having passed through the chamber, as elsewhere awash with the trappings of regular use.

Up at the top of the cupola, we peered through the porthole-like windows. This was a new experience. None like it anywhere else. Some could be opened. Those were the ones for photographs, but I could have waited for the best bit: the perimeter of the tower, supporting the cupola's rounded form. We had to crouch to pass from one corner turret to another, as the wall was low. Poor Wakey underwent a similar brush with a plunge as had threatened him in the bell tower at Bradford. The view was superlative, we all agreed, really as you would expect. This, of all cathedral locations, lies in a prime position for variety. I recalled separate previous occasions, up the Spinnaker Tower with the neighbouring Gunwharf development; beyond lay HMS Warrior and her Dockyard companions. I could still feel the spray protecting the Mary Rose and the greasepaint of *Jack Nasty Face*, a fine puppet show from a lost world. By the sea wall traffic busied itself: naval craft and ferries, such as the Wight vessel, which we watched negotiating its mooring spot in reverse gear. In the distance were the prospects for travel to more counties and dioceses.

On the descent our ears were bombarded with the hour. The chimes were a quarter of an hour fast. David had to agree. Counting 12 bells, (I'd read the number during research, and it was true. David had guessed at nine, rising to eleven), we rejoined Basil, who had rested among bell-ringers' sandwich packets during our final ascent. There were old, pre-1912, clappers on display in the bell room, in an oak frame made from timber for the previous generation. Most notable. John Taylor of Loughborough had always been invested with responsibility for the bells here. In 1957 two were cast and hung to make 10, the 12 being made up in 2010. Satisfied with all we'd seen, down we went, to complete the session with some time in the eastern reaches of the building.

Over the altar were the tester, 'like a bed', said Basil, and pyx, a helpful word for Scrabble. The former occurred to me (cheerily) as the top part of a baldacchino; the latter hung from it and contained the 'reserved sacrament', informed the caption. They were splendidly colourful and made a fine feature in this open space. There was little stained glass, the most attractive bits being quite small, in an east window lancet, beside which were two recesses on either side, in which stood saints Thomas Becket, Columba and Augustine, together with Lancelot Andrewes (1555–1626, a former dean of Winchester). The figures had been sculpted from driftwood.

Basil, priming himself for his stint as guide, drew our attention to an 18th century tomb in the floor. The date read: '174 ½'. He averred that it reflected the national change from the Julian to the Gregorian calendar. Then David told us of the respective Harvest Festival offerings: there had been a cornucopia at Ely including all the local fare, from fish in tanks to saplings to calves. Cattle in the nave! The building would be awash with the quick and the dead. At Portsmouth lobsters would be in evidence. A gentle wander followed, as Basil left to don his orange and David a jacket, smart of course, as we crossed the green, and purple, perimeter to the Dolphin. It claimed to be 'Old Portsmouth's village pub.' It served our purpose well: local Oakleaf brews for Wakey and me, a Merlot for the Master of the Choristers, who was then bound for a rare connubial lunch.

We had time for a final wander round the interior. The nave was satisfyingly idiosyncratic. It had not reached the dimensions intended by architect Sir Charles Nicholson ('The money ran out', said David). The current pale and curved design was a 1935 product, a direct outcome from the new status conferred eight years earlier. Its curves and creaminess reminded me of George Pace's Welch Regiment Memorial Chapel at Llandaff. The spaces in St Thomas' Cathedral are in contrast, rather than at odds, with the chancel up there beyond the font, the screen, the organ. A piece of history should be introduced: the church 'was founded by the wealthy shipowner John de Gisors as a chapel-of-ease and known to be under construction in 1185. This phase is among the best early gothic work in the country; much of the rest of the church was rebuilt after Civil War damage. The church gained a parish of its own in 1320,' *Cathedral* by Jon Cannon (2007).

We had been treated to splendid exposure to this surprising building. Next was the prospect of football interlaced with rumination over what had gone before, rather better than the goalless encounter between Portsmouth and Middlesbrough. The atmospheric old ground, Fratton Park, seemed positively old-fashioned after the unspoiled, anchor-linked cathedral. Boards round the stadium proclaimed 'FA Cup Winners 2008' and 'First Division Champions 1949', and the same for 1950; then 'Play up, Pompey!' and 'Blue Army'. (And *Pompey Chimes* was the name of the free 'parish magazine from Petersfield to the Isle of Wight'). Pompey were relegated in 2010. For six seasons this ground had hosted the elite of the top tier of English football. In societal terms, the football club had adopted an element of philosophy in common with the cathedral, and both with local authority social services, whose job you might think it to be, at the core. A high profile was attached to this area of concern: 'Portsmouth FC working in the community… more than just a football club.' 16,447 were there to see this. 17,170 volunteer hours had been spent 'in the community'.

Long before the invention of football at Fratton (built 1899) and the promotion of St Thomas' Church, 28 years later, Charles Dickens was born in the city: on 7 February 1812. His family emigrated to London, then Chatham, when he was young. Some wishes of the great man hit the news in the 21st century: first his denied request to be buried in Rochester Cathedral (he died in 1870). He was interred in Westminster Abbey. He also wrote in his will that he wanted to be remembered for his work, so did not want any physical memorials: plaques and statues. Rochester had registered a desire in 2010 to honour him with a statue, and in 2011 Portsmouth Cathedral hoped to raise a memorial to his memory. His family supported the idea, while the Dickens Fellowship disagreed, in their view reflecting his wishes. At the time of writing it remained a tantalizing issue at both cathedrals. Would either, or both, achieve their aims? Wakey and I hoped they would. We should honour such a man, and bring his name to the attention of visitors, that is 'spread the word'.

Sunday 13 March

Our experience of a church building at work on a Sunday morning work was not at Portsmouth Cathedral but Romsey Abbey, one of the 31 Greater Churches. This was a modest drive up country after a burst of ozone on Southsea's South Parade Pier, opposite our hotel. Regaled by a sermon from Jonathan Frost, Bishop of Southampton, and afterwards by a bluff choir member/guide, keen on conveying information, we were made excellently welcome. The Romanesque features of the place is a 'must see.' Its foundation dates back to King Alfred, originating as a nunnery. Dedicated to St Mary and St Ethelflaeda, it is a stocky, vigorous building. The nave is the best bit, dominated, like Malvern Priory, by massive pillars. The good thing for us is that the inspired townsfolk had the will and wit to take it over at the Dissolution, unlike so many which were left to ruin and a role as a source of building material. It is monumental in scale in its setting, in a small town, near Southampton for the bustle of life, and Winchester, the local ecclesiastical head quarters.

After the service and short tour of the abbey, we made our way to the church hall, full of elevenses consumers. The bishop engaged us in conversation. We were new faces and fortunate to find him in attendance. What inspired this was the special subject of the day. The leaflet handed out at the service announced: 'Developing our Pastoral Care for the Church Community and wider Parish'. Pastoral Visitors were 'commissioned' as part of the service. But, the lady who lent us her service sheet informed us: 'There is always this number here' (that is, pretty full). Indeed the whole thing conveyed the air of the customary modal church attender in comfortable, rural Hampshire: retired and able to afford the collection each week.

I emerged with a plant for £2 (hellebores are doing well this year) and some Fair Trade stem ginger cookies. This was following an exchange with the bishop, who had waxed enthusiastic with some children at the top of the nave at the service (after their Sunday school absence). His eventual cathedral choice, after ruminating over Durham, was St Albans. It was where his heart lay. The Portsmouth visit had been transformed into a taster for the final fixture, at Winchester two months hence.

47

Newcastle

St Nicholas

Province: York
Founded: 11th century as parish church
Building: 14th, 15th centuries
Cathedral status: 1882 – from Durham diocese

Website: www.stnicholascathedral.co.uk
Tel: 0191 232 1939
Email: office@stnicnewcastle.co.uk
Address: Chapter Office, St Nicholas Churchyard, Newcastle-upon-Tyne
NE1 1PF

Three to See: Crown tower and spire with clock on the side;
early 16th century eagle lectern, endearingly damaged;
the large Thornton brasses in the east end

Bridge

Thursday 14 April, 2011

Venturing upon an extended immersion in the furthest reaches of England, Graham and I made it to Hexham Abbey. We discovered the ancient foundation round a long bend in this rewarding market town. We parked most conveniently and entered. The solid mass of the south transept opened up on the left to a well-worn staircase. Doubling back it led up to a landing in the south transept. At the top through closed doors you would find the former canons' dormitory, adapted these days as the access point for the choir. Other drama was afforded by the memorial stone to a Roman standard bearer (c.80 AD), at the foot of the stairs and, opposite, stood a cross, lending testimony to the age of this pile.

I was able to climb down to the cramped crypt (from c.674, courtesy of St Wilfrid) at the end of this session, hosted by verger Gary Barham. Once upon a time, passages led northwards out to daylight and, in the other direction, to working abbey spaces. On the walls were Roman inscriptions, transferred from the local camp of Corstopitum (Corbridge). The view when leaving the crypt presented a sharp angle up to the font and west window. They looked good. Needless to say, the font is reckoned to be Roman, and is topped by a tall canopy made of 15th century wood: entirely compatible.

Comparatively new features reinforced the antiquity. The 38 misericords, from the mid-15th century, fitted in as well as anything, providing light relief simply evocative of a time far beyond our own experience, and as irreverent as elsewhere. That is good pragmatism, of insertions into the building reflecting the life of the respective generation. In the middle of the chancel stood a stocky stone chair: the Frith stool, allegedly another of Wilfrid's pieces. So Hexham, now a parish church under the dominion of Johnny-come-lately Newcastle, has history as the centre of a see, with this episcopal throne as evidence.

Meanwhile I had picked up a leaflet for a concert on the following Saturday: there had been nothing on the website. We were still to be resident in the area, so it became a mellowing prospect to enjoy the abbey in action for Durufle's *Requiem* and Haydn's *Nelson Mass*. They would be new to the ears of both of us. A surprise treat was therefore in store, and Gary was to advise: 'near the front of the nave would be best. The acoustics are good'. We would have to arrive around 7 pm, when the doors were to open. The neighbouring shop was full of Easter gifts, including fetching empty blue floral egg boxes in some form of cloth, which looked home-made. But no tickets were available. 'We don't sell them here,' said the assistant. 'It's the Hexham Orpheus Choir. You pay at the door.' Perplexing, I was thinking.

Circulating round the building, displays in a recess in the south choir aisle represented a different era: the Anglo-Saxon chalice. *Welcome to*

Hexham Abbey stated: 'This would have been used to take the sacrament of the Eucharist to local communities. The clergy of the Abbey continue this tradition today by taking the Eucharist to the ill and house-bound'; a good point to make. The chalice is a mere 5" high and made of shining copper-gilt. Looking up to the high altar, the north side of the presbytery was replete with a captivating painted wooden screen. We were back in the Middle Ages, to sink most of all into four panels illustrating the macabre Dance of Death.

The whole is a marvellous conglomeration of antiquity. We were anticipating the forthcoming main event, the later build of St Nicholas, Newcastle. It was easy to focus on the aged Hexham. There would be further time to explore and absorb it in the evening, replete with concert-goers. After all there is a modern organ (1974) with a gimmick: electronically controlled doors, so its sound can be aimed at the nave; and in the north aisle of said nave, 'recessed into the more recent 20th century wall are stones found in the abbey at various stages of rebuilding'. There was almost a surfeit of old stuff here.

A Costa coffee later, and latte for Graham, we took advantage of the good directions I had received from a male voice at Newcastle Cathedral, and 22 miles later, I parked right next to the target, again with the essential advantage of Graham's blue badge. It had been helpful at Hexham, as well, in successfully depositing his car right beside the shop and south door. The external aspect is critical for St Nicholas: the tower crowned by an adventurous steeple on flying arches. Building started in the 1340s and was a century in completion (1448). It followed the style of St Mary-le-Bow, London. I had also admired the spire of St Dunstan's-in-the-East, City of London by Sir Christopher Wren, among many such delights around the Square Mile. The idea of this approach spread northwards, reaching its apex at St Giles, Edinburgh, the most familiar of all. I wasn't the only observer to think Newcastle Cathedral's tower looked Scottish.

The clocks on two sides are also fine pieces. Clear and seductive to the eye, the guidebook told us:

> *The first mention of a clock at St Nicholas's occurs in 1565...*
> *a new clock was installed in 1761. Like many clocks of its time*
> *it only had an hour hand; a minute hand was not added until*
> *1826. In December 1829 the clock face was illuminated by*
> *gas, to the great excitement of the crowds gathered to see the*
> *sight, and in 1833 a new, large bell was provided... Its Gothic*
> *style and red gilt give it an unusual continental appearance.*

It served as icing under the cake of the crown spire.

The cathedral itself is almost entirely of the 14th and 15th centuries, therefore profoundly different from where we had just been. We enjoyed the entrances to this building. The west door was the initial novelty. It opened automatically by the press of a disc. While I'm on the subject, on our return to the cathedral for evensong, after noting the statue of the mature Queen Victoria (more of a landmark than source of joy), by Alfred Gilbert, we tried the north door. Once inside, this was adorned elegantly by a structure in pale wood, designed to assist less mobile visitors, such as Graham: stairs on one side, a ramp on the other. 'I'll use the ramp,' said he. It was a good thing they had to space for this piece of practical fun. Newcastle's elevation to city status in 1882 was alongside St Nicholas' promotion to a cathedral for the Northumberland part of the diocese of Durham (at the expense of its rival at Hexham); it was the fourth biggest parish church in England. Others among the quartet may also have joined the joyful band of cathedrals. And, what is the collective noun for cathedrals? What I did read about was the failed attempt to contrive cathedral status in 1553, during the reign of fervent protestant boy king Edward VI. Queen (Bloody) Mary acceded to the throne all too soon and 'reversed the legislation'. St Nicholas had to wait for 329 years to pass before its enhancement in status.

As soon as we arrived in the west end, we were greeted by experienced welcomer, Margaret Hetherington, who was to lend assistance on various fronts. A Durham lass (from Gateshead, she said) she commented about the high profile place just to the south: 'Durham wouldn't have us – what a cheek!' That was about an event to which she had been party. Her favourite cathedral was Canterbury. This was a friendly city building. It was busy with recording arrangements, in progress in various areas during our time there; a group of people busied themselves around the display of misericord photos and captions in the north choir aisle.

While we enjoyed lunch in the cathedral café, Margaret was to occupy a table with her cronies, the café manager moved between that group and another one which, like a moving feast, comprised the girls' choirmaster, the administrator and director of music. The outcome was that the mince and dumplings got a top mark and I bought a guide book, so impressed was I with its content, after Margaret pointed out something of interest therein. Graham alluded to Somerset dialect which called dumplings 'doughboys', at least according to his mother and grandmother. The café building itself was fine, light and, in the roof and upper level, adorned with a painted heraldic (I think) display. Through the agency of our welcomer and Anne, the café assistant who buxomly proffered the steaming platefuls of meaty doughboys, to be washed down by glasses of orange and water, respectively, I managed a productive conversation with both choirmaster and administrator. The subject with the former was about who was to sing at evensong. I had imagined the worst on looking at a notice, which intimated that now, being the Easter holidays, the service would be evening prayer, no choirs being available. But David Stevens, the girls' boss, was able to confirm that it would be the men that day. He showed me the service sheet. Excellent!

Also, the administrator, Julian Haynes, was informative about the history of the library, which had formerly been the function of this building. In this matter we must pay attention to the story of Robert Thomlinson (1668–1748). He was a book collector, facilitated by receiving income from at least four different sources:

1   As afternoon lecturer of St Nicholas' Church.
2   Rector of Whickham, in the diocese.
3   Two appointments in the gift of the Corporation, as master of the hospitals of St Mary the Virgin in 1715 and shortly after St Mary Magdalene.
4   Prebend of St Paul's cathedral.

I picked up a yellow leaflet, yielding the above information and more, on a small display cabinet. This housed two books from his time. In 1736 he outlined plans to leave his library to the people of Newcastle. A small classical structure (Palladian) was designed to house the library, attached to the back of the then church. In 1741 Sir Walter Blackett endowed it with £25 annually to pay for a librarian, as well as increase the book stock. It was noted that Messrs Thomlinson and Blackett were both disciplinarians, applying tight rules. As elsewhere (for example Hereford and Wells) chains were introduced to prevent theft. So far, so good when the benefactor died and his 7,000 books, and bookcases, were moved to the library. The chains seem to have worked after this: there was not a single loss in the book stock when the first librarian, the Revd Nathaniel Clayton, died. After that, general decline set in. Eventually, 'in 1834, a solicitor's clerk was transported for seven years for stealing 174 volumes of books – and there were even rumours that some had been sold for waste paper,' (*The Newcastle Collection*, Newcastle City Council). Moving on a bit, according to the guide book: 'In 1926 a hall, library, vestry and subsidiary rooms were added on the north-east side of the cathedral, designed by the architect W H Wood. They were extended in 1984 by R G Sims.'

This was the progression of a dynamic new cathedral. It was confined in its territory. However, it came across in a very favourable light for what it was: quite big enough, with plenty of space for its function and character.

The special things, for me during a contented post-doughboy examination, were:

1   The lectern: an eagle which idiosyncratically lacked a talon or two. It had also assumed a backward leaning stance. The caption stated: 'This lectern, early 16th century, is the only pre-Reformation lectern in the North of England.' It was a splendid piece.
2   The grand seat, with most demonstrative wings, alone in the front row of the pews.
3   The crucifixes throughout the building, under red wraps, 'for Lent,' the dean was to explain after the service. 'Local people like different seasons to be expressed.' This was the one and only such that I encountered in various churches over the 40 days: very individual!
4   In St Margaret's Chapel, the singular stained glass window of the Madonna feeding the Christ child. This is often called the 'First Supper'.
5   The truncated top parts of medieval arches, above the floor of the south choir aisle.
6   In the south transept, the Maddison Monument, in the guide as 'the most attractive and lively monument... erected in memory of Henry Maddison who died in 1634 and of his wife Elizabeth... beneath them are the figures of their ten sons and six daughters'. It was a 'glorious confection', indeed, 'topped off with effigies representing the ideals of faith, hope and charity'.
7   The immense Thornton Brasses, perhaps the biggest anywhere, facing the east end, they are a Flemish monument cover of the early 15th century (also the date of the font cover).
8   The simple modern stained glass, actually with a minimum of colour, in the north choir aisle. It honours 1,406 Danes who perished on sailing from Newcastle in 1940.
9   The wooden rood screen (1880s), embellished with figures of saints, which leads the eye up to the marvellous contemporary reredos. No matter that it obscures the east window.
10 To finish, the Victorian misericords. We had a look at them all, they were so appealing. I was not surprised that they were 'based on medieval examples in Carlisle and Exeter cathedrals', two of the best elsewhere. They included a sleeping serpent and bird with brood. And, of course, a fulsome green man.

We spent the afternoon interlude on the Gateshead side of the river

Tyne, trying first the Baltic, then the Sage, both highly-rated modern spaces for the arts. Disappointment prevailed, at the limited exhibitions at the former, and the current closure of the latter. We emerged to enjoy recovery back over the swing bridge in Newcastle's proud, Georgian Grey Street, choosing Costa Coffee (latte for him, sparkling water, ice and lemon for me, to wake me up), with a direct view of the currently closed Theatre Royal. On one of its wall a notice screamed out in red signage: 'Brand spanking old: Restoring our historic auditorium in style, modern in comfort'. I'd like to try out the spanking (new) theatre sometime.

After next discovering the opulent Central Arcade, where a busker was regaling us with her pipe, it was time for evensong, back at the cathedral. The service was led by the dean. The six male choristers acquitted themselves well. Prayers included a dedication to Libya and other countries in the Middle East and Africa. There were a number of parts of the world enduring acute distress. We sat with a view of the organ towering above, among a total of nine attenders. The fan vaulting rested above us, to good effect. Graham sat above a lion at feast on a dragon: we lifted the seat to examine the misericord, again. The final foray was to be the westward journey, but only after an essential diversion towards Newcastle Airport. The petrol dial was ominously low. 'It won't get us back to Hexham,' asserted the owner. At £138.9 per litre the airport BP service station was only charging the (horrendous) going rate. We had expected a captive market price enhancement. With the tank full, we could travel to the hinterland in the morning.

Friday 15 April
This was the day off from the cathedrals of the northeast. During our daylong rambles we identified just the one roadside notice at a farm selling its own eggs. Marilyn Framrose was my friend in the area. She was to nominate York as her favourite; her partner Ian Dunsmuir opted for Coventry, and her daughter Sarah 'Liverpool, but I haven't been to any others': they all count. Marilyn had recommended the Hadrian Hotel at Wall, a mere two miles down the road from her establishment. I posit: what other name for a hotel at Wall than the 'Hadrian'? Marilyn's deconsecrated church cottages were full of holidaying walkers, leaving no space for us. Anyway she's running a business.

Ian had produced a leaflet of churches, *Finding the Way in West Northumberland's Eternal Horizons*, marked for advice. We were to manage three of them:

1   St Giles, Chollerton, within sight of Old Church Cottages

(Marilyn's place), and certainly Graham-friendly, that is the passenger door opened right next to the short path up to the open south door. St Giles 'is Grade I listed and dates from c.1100'. We enjoyed the Norman pillars, evocative of Hexham, but on a very local scale in undulating fields with yellow rape in abundance, with the knowledge that the North Tyne lurked beyond trees to the west. A panelled Jacobean reredos created a dark, warm effect, in contrast with the much older, mostly Romanesque, interior. As almost always at churches, a circuit of the outside of the building was rewarding. Spring was in full throttle: lots of yellow and white, the latter a profusion of a particular strain of daffodils in the churchyard.

2   St Aidan, Thockrington, in deepest country, where we truly thought we had reached the end of civilization in an extensive farmyard. We reached it round one more corner. Ian and Marilyn had urged how worthwhile this would be. It was an 11th century product 'situated on an outcrop of the Whinsill and silhouetted against the skyline'. The car had to rest on the uneven grassy verge, by a gate, which opened to suggest the way up to the church through pasture and the churchyard. The exterior included 'the perched bellcote on the west end of the building with its stepped buttress'. Under this lay the tombstone of Welfare State initiator, Lord Beveridge (William Henry, of Tuggal, 1879–1963). The building was a curiosity. The leaflet stated: 'The church has "lost" its village possibly through a sailor bringing back the plague with the consequence that the housing may have been torched.' I liked the language, and the singularity of this place, on ground which, on the east side, dropped immediately onto the farm, immense and motionless, a deserted array of organically erected grey buildings from a previous generation, actually most appealing.

3   St Christopher, Gunnerton; but not before a modest panic as Graham had seen a sign, announcing 'Weak bridge. Road closed.' But, without interruption, we got to it, on the roadside of a village remarkable for impressive detached, mostly modern, houses. The front door of the church bore a notice, to collect a key from a house up the road, eventually achieved. I found myself in a pink interior, with a white ceiling and mid-blue supports. It was the work of John C Hawes (1876–1956). 'Extensive re-modelling began in 2003.' The circular stained glass window was a geometric association of colours, centred

on dark blue. The plethora of the spectrum it cast on the floor reminded me of Paddy's Wigwam. The idea of community struck a chord at this church most of all, in an obvious dormitory village.

It was creditable that this busy place hosted services in its turn, along with Chollerton, the exposed Thockrington and the unseen Birtley in one group. I returned the key and the two of us repaired down straight roads to base. A sign presented itself: 'Weak bridge at Wark'. Ah, Wark, slightly further on, and its bridge, remained untroubled by us.

This was a leisurely day out in scenic Northumberland. In between the churches (more to be seen another time), there were sheep to observe in the fields, ubiquitously outnumbered by playful lambs, with a diversity of markings. We did enjoy fine lamb at table during this stay, also pork chops, the ones Marilyn produced, with colcannon. They were absolutely succulent. This put me in mind of the t-shirt an Australian barman was wearing at a pub-near-farm I had patronized in Somerset. 'Animals – I love 'em. They're delicious.' That was on the front. Turning round, he displayed: 'Kill 'em and grill 'em.'

Casting my mind back just three months, to the hinterland of Canterbury, where the Conservation Trust churches were mainly in need of drying out, these northern ones were all in fine, working condition. Of course, it was now high-spring rather than mid-winter. Soon after this visit, I read about the addition of a further two churches to the complement: 'St Nicholas', Saintbury, a Grade I listed medieval church on the Cotswold Way, and St Leonard's, Linley, a Grade II* listed church in Shropshire... This brings the total number of churches vested in it to 342', (*Church Times*, 1/4/11).

There had been incident in this ostensibly quiet part of the world: in summer 2010, the infamous Raoul Moat had perpetrated heinous crimes in summer 2010, shooting people, and finally despatching himself. Our piece of drama was when we found ourselves facing a long incline, with smoke and flames close as we approached a bend in the road. A black figure stood in silhouette at work, burning his fields.

Monday 18 April
This was the time the Right Revd Martin Wharton, Bishop of Newcastle, had available to see us in his home. 'This is the smallest bishop's house – parts are 17th century' said Bishop Martin, on the junction of the more desirable parts of Newcastle: Gosforth and Jesmond. 'But only two miles away,' he said, 'is a deprived area, with several generations of unemployment.' The

house had been purchased in 1958; the Church Commissioners had sold off Benwell Tower, the previous residence of the bishop. He did think there to be benefits: '

> *... where everyone lived around the cathedral, like Durham and Salisbury. They operate in a particular kind of way. Some have choir schools, for example. This is a commuting cathedral – clergy travel in – which makes it a very different sort of place, a harder place to work. There are challenging questions for the director of music, who has to scout around the state schools and university. There are issues round festivals. What do you do when half the choir clears off during the summer?*

In post at Newcastle since 1997, Martin had been made CBE in the 2011 New Year Honours, for services to the Church of England and the community in the northeast: 'a surprise,' and evidently strongly linked to socially-inclined initiatives. The honour said a lot. Bishop Martin modestly admitted to working quite hard at developing community relations. These were hardly affected by immigration in this region. There had been nothing to come to for overseas job-seekers. The area was quite unlike what he had found in London (Southwark) and over 10 years in Yorkshire (Bradford).

Meanwhile he was also a season ticket holder at Newcastle United; also a supporter of Lancashire CCC: the Barrow-in-Furness area, his place of origin, had been in Lancashire at that time (before its translation to the new Cumbria). Clearly a man of many parts, he was welcoming and informative. He made the point about bishops in the House of Lords, being valuable in their own right – offering wisdom and experience, 'taking a different point of view. There is no whip. It's an independent vote'. These were not reactionary forces but mature and intelligent men. They did tend to agree on certain issues, such as those pertaining to life itself: they were against 'assisted dying'. A telling point was that other faith communities were keen that bishops be retained in the House of Lords. Muslims and Sikhs talked about 'our bishop'. He was their representative. 'A person of belief keeps faith at the centre of public debate.' This would be lost if the (26) bishops were booted out.

On the subject of geography, we covered the burning issue of boundaries and cathedral responsibilities. His stance on the debate about the West Yorkshire dioceses was that the proposals didn't work. No changes, such as the present mooting of Wakefield Cathedral becoming the sole one of the three in West Yorkshire, should be made without including York itself in the argument. Perhaps the answer would be not to make

Ripon and Bradford pro-cathedrals, but to retain them all, and create an administrative centre in Leeds, as the hub.

We turned to local geography. One hundred and forty miles separated Berwick-on-Tweed (top of Newcastle territory) from Stockton-on-Tees (southern outpost in Durham). There were currently difficulties with Berwick, the town itself being in the midst of a move to defect from England to Scotland, with which it felt closer links. Berwick Rangers FC competed in the Scottish Football League! Any thoughts about reorganization would have to consider the Cleveland/Teesside area of North Yorkshire, currently part of the see of York. It really should be added to Durham. There had been inconsistencies when the boundaries were drawn up. Some parishes in Durham were included in Newcastle's remit. Martin had 245 churches to look after, and he was on the road a lot. He attended the cathedral every Friday morning at 7.30 am to pray together at the early service. Otherwise visits were for ordinations and major festivals. 'It's easier for the Bishop of Norwich. He lives bang next to the cathedral.'

The obvious matter of contrast between Newcastle and Durham showed up in stark relief. 'It's a reality of the time. We're chalk and cheese. There's pots of money at Durham'; and its high profile and iconic status continued to make it able to attract funds. Newcastle's recent National Lottery bid for total refurbishment had been turned down. It had no historic resources, and funding was dwindling. The Church Commissioners provided funds, but for revenue purposes, such as to pay staff, not capital. The economic climate was one of struggle. Northumberland had suffered the collapse of heavy industry, and fishing, agriculture and forestry were in decline. The biggest employers were now universities and hospitals. 'The unemployment figure was up more than 11,000 last month. There is an overheating economy in the southeast, and increasing deprivation in the northeast.' Another side to this was the challenge of recruitment. How do you attract the best people to the northeast? This affected the church. 'There are two things going on. A lot of people are overqualified. A small proportion came here to university and stayed.' Recently, an agent for the biggest local landowner had commented that the business was no longer agriculture but property development. Martin said: 'Northumberland is the last feudal county. It still operates like that, down to the power of landed estates. It's an enclosed kingdom.' He pointed to the map on the wall. Indeed, this was a clearly defined area, the sea, two rivers (the Tyne and the Tweed) and high ground defining it, rendering relationships to Newcastle Cathedral difficult. There were 'holy' problems, too, competition coming from Lindisfarne, the old foundation at Hexham Abbey, and Holy Well. Wryly, Martin pointed out that this, the location of the first baptism in the north of England, was hard to find, discouraging visitors. On the other hand this region was, as we had found, rich in interest, with the accent on a long history, including the ecclesiastical. Identity was important: St Cuthbert was so central that his day (he died on 20 March 687) was taken up by the local paper. St Cuthbert (and, of course, the Venerable Bede and St Wilfrid) provided a link elsewhere, for example with Durham, also Ripon to the south.

Poor St Nicholas Cathedral had another cross to bear. It wasn't the automatic choice for the regional capital's civic activities. Of Newcastle's four other Anglican churches in a small city centre, St Thomas', near the Town Hall, was best placed. There was a move underway to create a Geordie Ramblas (following the model of the renowned street in Barcelona), the effect of a corridor of activity, which would embrace the cathedral on its route. 'But where's the money? It's a pipedream,' was his response.

This all sounded bleak. But an extension to the cathedral had been achieved, following a successful purchase of the adjacent building, which nobody else wanted. Certain trusts had helped. This would provide more space for the people in the city. A further appeal was under way for heating and lighting, not to mention a sound system. Bishop Martin swivelled on his chair. Graham cast an eye over the display of books lining the walls. I finished my tea and off we went, after a fine, open discussion.

48

Durham

Christ & St Mary

Province: York
Founded: 999 as monastery, 1081 Benedictine cathedral
Present building: 1093–1135 onwards
Restored: 1874–76 George Gilbert Scott

Website: www.durhamcathedral.co.uk
Tel: 0191 3864266
Email: enquiries@durhamcathedral.co.uk
Address: The College, Durham DH1 3EH

Three to See: 14th century double of cathedra and tomb;
2010 Transfiguration Window;
trick oak table in Galilee Chapel
These assume the obvious, that you can't avoid the nave pillars

Pillar

Saturday 16 April, 2011

The party of three had diminished to me on my own. Rand had rescinded and Graham was forced to remain in the town, in the vicinity of the river Wear. There was no way he could mount the incline up to the cathedral, on a walking stick and with taxis turning us away: 'We could give you a piggy back,' joked one happy cabby. This had arisen, as, despite reassurance from the chapter office that there was disabled parking available 'first come, first served' beside the building, we could not find a way in. We were forced to leave the car in the City car park. The city centre was undergoing roadworks with a vengeance.

Once inside I immediately spent £3.50 (senior) on a tour, and applied the sticker to my lapel, to join a group of three at the back of the nave. Two were from Bridgnorth, diocese of Hereford, 'right at the northern end,' said the woman, who was to negotiate her male wheelchair-bound companion up various inclines, circumnavigating steps. The husband of the third sticker-wearer was involved in educational pursuits in the area over the weekend. She nominated Winchester as her favourite cathedral. 'We haven't got much at home in Northern Ireland,' she explained. Our guide was a Durham girl, Elizabeth Rae.

The tour was fine, an easy perambulation despite large, mostly youthful, groups. We were regaled with fascinating facts. As this is, for many, the very apex of cathedral achievement, I feel it would be presumptuous to make any points about quality. Nikolaus Pevsner compared the size of the nave as similar to its peers, Ely and Gloucester, and wrote: 'The effect is quite different. That has chiefly two reasons: one the design and proportions of the elevations, the other the shape of the chief members used.' My impression, seeing this massive masterpiece in the cold light of a busy Saturday morning, was that the Norman nave is so stunning that it is unanswerable. Chevrons and herringbone are just two of the abstract designs on the columns, which are utterly the image of Durham. Vast and full of rubble. 'Built with lime mortar', said Elizabeth, who told us, then the story of George Gilbert Scott's 19th century restoration. The outcome of this was to replace the full screen between nave and chancel, with the present one featuring a fetching range of stone, especially the Frosterley marble-like limestone, polished black and sleek with fossils contributing decorative interest. She later drew attention to the back of a column, out of sight and rough, without the relentless rubbing of animal skin. However, for me the building would look better with a more substantial division. You can see right through, past the elaborate high altar, to the substantial circular east window. I would rather have the nave standing alone for maximum impact. The quire, and all that surrounds, and follows, is of a different character, to be admired in its own right. We back-tracked to admire the font, the tallest anywhere. That dated from 1663 – 'comparatively modern, in fact', a gift from Bishop John Cosin. At that time in recent memory was the occupation of the building by Scottish soldiers, using it as barracks, causing much destruction. We cast our eyes round to the north door to hear about sanctuary. Those escaping the law would use the north door (no porch here) employing the prominent knocker for up to 37 days in hiding. Then they would face a court. Sackcloth was involved, and a ship from Hartlepool, the local port. To the 37 were added three days for the journey, to make 40, the number of days Jesus was in the wilderness. In the south aisle stood part of the dismantled quire screen which became a miners' memorial with a date of 1946. The coal industry had been strong in County Durham; indeed had contributed to the not inconsiderable coffers of Christ and St Mary. The plaque read: 'He breaketh open a shaft away from where men sojourn they are forgotten of the foot that passeth by.' In answer to my next question, Elizabeth told us the nearest mines were only a couple of miles away.

Between two pillars were severely damaged tombs, of members of the Neville family, celebrating victory at the Battle of Neville's Cross. We had noticed a roundabout of that name on the way in. Into the south transept, we had to admire a clock entirely different from the ornamental one enjoyed on the tower of Newcastle Cathedral. *A Short Guide to Durham Cathedral* said:

> *The cathedral has had a clock since at least 1360. The present one was provided about 1632 when Richard Hunt was Dean. The Victorians disliked it, and, in 1845, removed the case and mounted the face on the wall. In 1938 it was restored, with as much of the original wooden case as could be collected, by the Friends of Durham Cathedral. Originally, it had only an hour hand, hence the 48 quarter-hour divisions on the face.*

I felt I was collecting clocks. I took the opportunity provided by the disabled contingent absenting themselves to find a flat route into the quire, to ask Elizabeth about a cathedral cat. She looked slightly askance at the idea. 'Oh, no, not here!' The misericords to follow were fine. Her simile for them was 'like shooting sticks, for long services. You perched on the end'. She pointed out the 1876 Father Willis organ, restored by Harrison & Harrison Ltd, organ builders, in 1909, and ever since; also a black plastic bucket in place to collect drips of moisture at the bottom in the north quire aisle. Willis organs had been the subject of a recent radio programme. Anyway, we were scheduled, in two days' time, to visit Meadowfield, a few miles to the west, the location of Harrisons'.

Hydraulic pipes had been inserted under the floor, where we were standing. 'Sometimes you can feel movement,' and she was precise about the number of pipes: 5,746. We had arrived at the bishop's throne, prominent above the Hatfield Chantry, referring to Thomas Hatfield (bishop 1345–81) who inspired the whole piece. Apparently it was the highest in the country, erected 2" higher than the pope's in Rome. Perhaps that is a bit of a cheat, as the cathedra itself is not substantial, though pleasantly ornate. The *Guide* told us: 'The Bishop of Durham occupies this seat the first time he comes to the Cathedral, but thereafter sits near the chancel screen.' That was understandable, as at Canterbury. Some cathedrals are sometimes just too big to be entirely practical as designed.

The sanctuary screen confronted us above the altar. It was a gift from the omnipresent Neville family, made by Henry Yvelli (the local spelling) 'the finest mason/architect of the 14th century'. Elizabeth told us of 107 coloured statues, hidden during the Reformation, and never found. The current screen makes impressive sense once you are in the eastern part of the cathedral, your eyes being led up to the rose window in the east end.

There was an altar in every arcade, making for a varying contour round the building. Then there was an aumbry, defined as 'a locker or cupboard of some kind, usually placed in the north chancel wall, for safe keeping of service-books and sacramental vessels'. This was in the south aisle wall, where we also found the window commemorating the millennium of the cathedral, in 1995. Featured were the industries of the northeast, Stevenson's Rocket and the Tyne Bridge; also more recently the Nissan car factory at Sunderland (whose minster was now a 'Greater Church', something else for another time). 'It's doing well,' we were informed of the motor manufactory. 'They make electric cars now.' A woman in purple passed by. 'She's a steward,' said our guide, 'the guides wear red,' she added, in her vermillion garb. I asked about exams for guides. As I was now aware, this was the practice in other cathedrals, to ensure competency. We have an interview and training,' she replied, then apologized for the crowds battering us. 'We have mentors, too,' she added. The recently installed (2010) 7-scene Transfiguration Window appeared above us. It was rare in that it was made in Germany owing to the need for a burnished-gold looking colour, which dominated, and seduced the viewer. I was convinced. This was the caption on the postcard, which I later bought: 'Installed in memory of Michael Ramsey… The artist, Tom Denny, has included St Cuthbert standing outside his cell… and the Cathedral lying above a wooded valley.' The window was given by the Friends of Durham Cathedral, to mark their 75th Anniversary. Michael Ramsey (1904–88) was bishop here, then Archbishop of York, then Canterbury, which represents a kind of grand slam. He was responsible for the establishment of the General Synod, and retirement ages for clergy. It occurs to me that three quarters of a century is a rather insignificant period of time in a building of so long a history to justify such a prominent addition as this window. What was to mark the Friends' centenary? It's a good thing that the piece is so good, as are the Millennium Window, and the Daily Bread Window at the diagonally opposite, northwest corner of the building. All of them fit in with the simple strength of the cathedral. The plaques listing bishops and priors/deans faced us. It showed priors from 1083 to 1540, followed by deans, but there was no space now left at the bottom for future incumbents. What then? There had been a 'to do' in the 16th century, with Robert Horne appearing twice with a few years in between. 'He ordered statues to be destroyed,' said Elizabeth.

We were adjacent to another treat, overlooked by our guide: an ogee arch over a grilled door. Ogees were by now an obsession of mine. Peering through it, the effect was that it was ignored, and had been for a while. There was nothing of note behind it. However, there was something rather good opposite: the 'feretory', which Elizabeth urged us two survivors to ascend, though she would not join us. Apparently the word means 'a shrine for relics during a procession or for a funeral bier'. It abutted the back of the high altar, unique, I think, and it was indeed St Cuthbert's Shrine, elaborately decorated with coloured stone throughout. It also afforded an aerial view of the east end, that is, the Chapel of the Nine Altars (not the standard Lady Chapel here). This was all a bit oppressive, with large parties pervading. We had to make way, as they were bigger than us. I was to enjoy it more later on, when quieter. The proliferation of altars made for consistency and variety at once. After all there were nine divisions to see, but it somehow brought the experience of the cathedral to an abrupt halt. It was a flat finish, albeit elaborated by the odd piece of latter-day art, such a Madonna and Child made of driftwood, and several powerful stained glass windows in the vicinity. Attention was drawn to another product of the fundraising work of the Friends, made by the Cathedral Broderers: the central altar frontal and three back parts, depicting saints Cuthbert, Aidan and Bede. This area is rich in ancient saintly quality. It all made a fine display, lifting the overall look. It featured connections with Cuthbert's life: the 'Cuddy' duck and sea otter; for St Aidan a horse. Bede gave his horse away to the first lame beggar he encountered. He was ever after on foot.

And we heard about the Prince Bishops, introduced soon after the Norman Conquest by William I. This area needed strong control, so far away from the seat of power. These palatinate (derived from 'palace', therefore 'royal') bishops were equivalent to dukes; thus responsible for management of laws and order in their considerable northern territories, even raising troops for the King. Local coinage was in circulation. The PB system continued until 1836.

It was then fast forward to someone whose reputation is more tarnished: the architect James 'Wrecker' Wyatt, at large in the late 18th century, who had successfully truncated the nave at Hereford Cathedral. At Durham his radical recommendations of destruction were not all seen through. He applied the name of truth to a misguided interpretation of medievalism, (he didn't like obstructions, such as screens). The Galilee Chapel is still there, with a replacement roof, saved just in time by the intervention of the dean, but his attempts at restoration did result in the loss of the chapter house, and amendments to the east end. We made our way down the north aisle, where a curious incident occurred. As we were being told that there were 200 purple stewards on the register, an excited man approached our guide, saying: 'It's Elizabeth Rae, isn't it?' 'Yes,' replied she, cautiously. 'I'm David Shaw. We were in the same class at school – in the fifties.' 'Were we?' They confirmed the name of another classmate, and agreed upon a cup of coffee after the tour, now drawing to a close. He went off to admire a window. 'I don't remember him, but it's such a long time ago. Did I say the right thing?' 'It's best to be honest,' I replied. 'He may be trying to pull a fast one.' 'Anyway it'll be nice to have a drink,' she concluded, moving towards another window, depicting the Last Supper seen from above, with Jesus indicated by a purple cross, and Judas facing outwards. The border is streaky purple glass, the seating area has shades of blue and the table is red: very effective. We entered the Galilee (Lady) Chapel at the west end, to whose well-lit delights she introduced us. It was full of photogenic artefacts.

It would have been beneficial to have snapped away for an aide memoire. My average for cathedral visit was about 150 photos. As I write, I have found that, as at St Paul's, I struggle to recall Durham's detail, which quick snaps might have supplied. Also as at St Paul's the favoured picture was to be external: in London the *Resurgam* panel on the south side, here the cloisters in sharp sunlight. My advice is simply to go to the Galilee Chapel, at the end of the visit, as a satisfying finale. My favourite item was the table made of recycled oak. Built into it were the requisites for a meal. It would fold out into an elaborate design for use, very soon on this occasion, as an altar at Easter.

That was it. Tour over, I tried out the 'Undercroft Restaurant at Durham Cathedral', where the filter coffee (£1.30) and banana, cherry and walnut cake (£1.95, no lemon drizzle) were good in value, strength and flavour, respectively. The space was a bit cramped, under a corner of the building at the southwest, near the Treasures of St Cuthbert Exhibition and, outside, functional toilets in a block which looked as if it had been intended as temporary, but had actually been there for a long time. The shop was also nearby. Mugs were £6.95, a wine glass would be rather extravagant purchase at £13.75, and something called a Glitterglobe was £15. A child was being treated to one of these while I queued with my postcards, which included the Transfiguration Window.

Next I decided upon a wander round the delightful close, in full bloom, and with many a car parked in ample space by the grassy bits, so why could a taxi not have brought us up here? I decided to invest further funds. Not the tower (£5), which I had mounted years before, but a ticket giving limited access to the Treasures and Audio-Visual Display. This did not accord with the website, which offered rather more: Monks' Dormitory and Building the Church, as well, which was closed in winter. This was a sunny day in April. You can only take what you are allowed, so I adopted the principle of 'I'm unlikely to return, so "Go for it!"' This was also at variance from my printout indication. In the Treasures, display was somewhat limited. For me the best thing was the original door knocker, which was to be seen from outside the exhibition space to lure in the punters. It did look better close up, I admit. The film was secreted at the far end of the cloister. A genial button presser activated it for me. It proved interesting and good on the history. I was sanguine about these shortfalls, typical of a major icon venue.

I rambled, finally, round the interior, leaving to look back at the replica door knocker. Its widespread fame is explained by this piece in *Church Times*:

> *A would-be thief attempted to prise the knocker from the cathedral's north door between 6 pm on 28 December (2010), when the cathedral was locked up, and 7 am the next day, when staff discovered the damage. The original door-knocker, which is in the form of a lion's head, dates back to 1140. It is extremely valuable, and was placed in the Treasury Museum of the cathedral 30 years ago. A bronze replica was fixed in its place.*

One benefit of the replica is that you may photograph it, being outside the cathedral. Photography was strictly forbidden within the building. There was even a pink leaflet on the subject. 'Photography permits, for specific educational purposes only, may be purchased from the Chapter Office or the Vergers' Vestry, at the weekends. Proof of academic status may be required.' My chosen subject was to be the cloisters, which provided an image of contrasts with sun streaming in.

I emerged onto the cathedral green with a view of all manner of delights, including the castle, which was also closed. The next thing I espied was something of a shock. Disgorging patrons by a clearly marked bus stop was a single decker bus. It provided a shuttle between the railway station and the cathedral. We should have been told! So Graham, consigned to several hours in the shops and cafes below, could have joined me at this top attraction. What a shame! I wandered round corners and down the hill to find the poor chap, who had spent an hour sipping at a smoothie in Café Rouge. 'People watching,' had been his occupation, he conveyed with a wan smile.

I shall invigorate this tale with the recently published culmination of a diocesan story. Paintings by the Spanish artist Zurbaran (Francisco de, 1598–1664, 'the Spanish Caravaggio') had been the subject of a protracted debate. *Church Times* reported (3/12/10):

> *The Church Commissioners have agreed in principle to sell a set of Zurbaran paintings, which hang in Auckland Castle, Durham (the seat of the bishops). The Commissioners have emphasised that the sale could raise more than £15 million for the work of the Church across the nation, especially in areas of need and opportunity. The annual return, when invested – plus the savings in insurance and security costs – is equal to the costs of around ten parish priests. Discussions are taking place with the diocese and local representatives.*

The bishopric wanted to sell them for altruistic benefit to clergy. By January 2011 the matter had attained House of Commons attention. A working party, with the Lord Lieutenant of Durham as chairman, would consider how to keep the paintings at Auckland Castle. The Church Commissioners were intent upon continuing with preparations to auction them in summer 2011. The Second Church Estates Commissioner, Tony Baldry, MP, considered they would fetch c.£500m pa in perpetuity.

There was better news in the spring. The Church Commissioners issued a statement that they would not sell the paintings after all, following a multi-million pound donation from Jonathan Ruffer, an investment manager, to set up a new charitable trust to keep the paintings in the northeast. 'Another £1 million has been committed by the Rothschild Foundation… There are now plans to turn Auckland Castle, which has housed the paintings since 1756, into a "leading public heritage site" for the north-east. This would involve giving "much greater public access" to the castle grounds, although further funding is required for this.' I can echo the need for more access. Not much was open when I tried to pay the place on a previous visit, on that occasion or any other, to judge by the information board.

Palm Sunday, 17 April
Transport continued to prove tricky. Dropping into Hexham railway

station on Saturday's return journey from Durham, I managed to catch the attention of the occupant of one of three uniforms joking together on a deserted platform. The outcome was the information that it would not be viable to get to Durham in time for the Palm Sunday Eucharist. The earliest would mean a seriously late arrival time during the service. And the return journey? Well, it involved two trains, on a Sunday afternoon. That spoke for itself: best not to think about it. That evening, I telephoned Canon James Lancelot, Master of the Choristers and Organist, whom I was due to meet at the cathedral after the service. I obtained his private number after several attempted calls to various published cathedral numbers. It was someone at the school who helped. Thank you, sir! James proved right in unearthing an accurate schedule on his live computer during the phone call, without demur. This showed that I might just join the procession across the green, if I walked apace from the station. The outcome was that I did commit myself to the journey. On a lovely spring day, I emerged from a train from Newcastle in sight of the cathedral, then marched briskly towards it to find the fine aspect of the long line of palm-bearing congregation. They were approaching the sanctuary knocker and the interior it beckoned.

Once inside, I procured a service sheet by way of a charming usher who smartly forced a young couple to share. I chose a row on the south side of the nave, where I could absorb a pillar or two, and admire the reclining memorial to Dr James Britton ('Jacobo Britton'), a 19th century Headmaster of Durham School. After the service, James, who had displayed his skills in full throttle in conducting the choir, met me as arranged under the clock. Sunday lunch ensued in the restaurant. He was the only lay canon among the organists over the country. 'A pleasant surprise' was how he described the offer from the bishop in 2002. On the subject of the building, the acoustic was acceptable. He noted, though, that each of those massive pillars represented the space occupied by about 36 seats. He had been responsible for the introduction of a girls' choir school on equal terms with the boys. The girls' choir were to sing with the men at the 3.30 evensong service, and he urged me to stay for that. (I was marginally concerned about trains. When would I be back? In time for the meal at Marilyn's?) In fact the timing of lunch and his duties afforded a visit to James's house at Nº 6 The College, a lovely red-doored house with a cherry tree in bloom in front of the terrace, and an attractive garden below at the rear. He showed me books in his collection relevant to this project. But now, given the timescale I would have to anticipate for future enjoyment. One such was a 1926 edition of *Cathedrals* by George E Beer, a GWR publication (first edition in 1924). It was a tempting, tactile volume, with a personal note from 'Lambeth Palace, SE' from Randall Davidson, the incumbent Archbishop of Canterbury. He was the 96th in post, from 1903 to 1928, which makes his tenure one of the longest. It was sent to Viscount Churchill, Chairman of the Great Western Railway, that's Victor, not Winston. The archbishop addresses the viscount: 'My dear Churchill', applying the formal address of the time. These days surnames are not even used at the Durham choir schools, something James engineered on introducing girls. This is an excerpt:

> ... *The way in which it presents to the public the beauty and character of the great Cathedrals which stand within your range is beyond praise... You will be rendering a wonderful service to the English people and to visitors from overseas if you will help them to realise better the sacred heritage which is ours...*

I certainly aimed to acquire a copy of the book. James said: 'The nice challenge (I mean nice in its proper sense) that we face in reconciling the fact that Durham Cathedral is not only a world-class building architecturally but also the spiritual home and place of worship of a community of local people (some of them of student age). There's an interesting balance to be struck in our worship between the stately and the intimate – it's a good exercise for us to try to achieve that balance. In many ways I think the music helps in this. And of course it's not only local people – I remember the comment of someone who lived far away and was heard to say "I am a member of the congregation – I visit twice every year!"'

Good point! I now had the leisure to take in the environs of the cathedral, such as committing trespass into my latest source of excitement, the Works yard, complete with an idle concrete mixer. Evensong followed, entirely predictable in the quality of the girls' singing in the setting of such a place. The train journey to Hexham was less satisfactory, but a sociable evening included the prospect of final (for now) visits to Newcastle and Durham to conclude this trip.

This is where I convey Bill Bryson's opinion from *Notes from a Small Island* (1995):

> ... *if you have never been to Durham, go at once. Take my car. It's wonderful... The cathedral, a mountain of reddish-brown stone standing high above a lazy green loop of the River Wear, is, of course, its glory. Everything about it was perfect – not just its setting and execution but also, no less notably, the way it is run today. For a start there was no nagging about money, no 'voluntary' admission fee.*

Things have changed a bit on the financial front, Bill, but it does remain many people's favourite.

Finally, Clue 7 across in the *Crossword* in the 12/4/11 issue of *Church Times* (set by Philip Marlow) was: 'Churl hated drama brewing in big northern church (6, 9)'. You've deduced it: the answer was 'Durham Cathedral', by way of a clever anagram.

Monday 18 April

The AA Routemaster got us to Harrison & Harrison, despite a slight concern at the very end as the industrial estate was rather extensive, and H&H was right at the beginning when we were congratulating ourselves on having reached 'St John's Road' at all. The firm occupies a stylish, award-winning building with a 'pagoda-like silhouette', which opened up into an extremely efficiently laid out workshop. The firm was set up in Rochdale in 1861, moving to Durham in 1872. It's quite well-established then!

Graham and I visited at a time of change of personnel. We met Nancy Radford, three months into the Administrator role, with Chris Batchelor comprising the upper tier of management. Chris had only recently assumed the Managing Director mantle from Chairman Mark Venning, who had preceded him as MD since 1975, having joined the company three years earlier. The staff numbered around 50, in the largest organ building company in Britain. They also worked overseas: for instance the USA has provided several clients, and a major contract was recently completed in Stockholm City Hall.

Most generously in a highly economically-run enterprise, Nancy was to give us more than two hours of detailed information, and informative and attractive paperwork and posters. From all we were given we were able to glean the gamut of H&H's activity. There were men on the books with more than 50 years' service, loyal and deeply proficient, one of whom, Peter Hopps, Head Voicer, was about to retire. 'Organs don't speak until they're voiced', as he put it. Keith Unsworth, 73 years old, had been present as an apprentice when the Royal Festival hall organ was installed – in 1954. Then there was Alan Howarth, who retired from his role as works manager 13 years ago and now worked part-time as a designer, using the computer to create beautiful casework designs.

Organ building demands long hours and careful scheduling. It must be a shock to retire from a workplace so all-consuming and no doubt emotionally committing. The nature of the work has not changed, but there have been technical improvements. The apprenticeship takes four years, but training continues long after that, and organ builders never stop learning. Currently there were as many contracts under way as ever. There were three jobs on the go: Shrewsbury St Chad's, and in London, the Royal Festival Hall and Holy Trinity, Sloane Street. These represented contrasting specifications, requiring repairs, refurbishment and additions. There were no cathedrals at the moment but plenty in the past (Durham, Exeter, Winchester, Lichfield, Salisbury, Hereford, Westminster Abbey, to name a few at random), and more to come. Quotes were being meticulously assembled to achieve a balance of the elements: time, cost, resources. It was all challenging. An organ has an immensely intricate character, like a human being, I was told, and no two organs are alike.

Nancy introduced us to the archives, tidily filed in a room upstairs. We were welcome to peruse the files dedicated to each client. I dipped into St Edmundsbury Cathedral, recalling work done there, and St Mary Redcliffe, Bristol, where I had observed bits of instrument cordoned off all over the floor, and, more recently heard the results of Harrisons' work in a lunchtime recital. There was a stark contrast in the old, frayed, pre-decimal accounts compared with those of mere months ago. This was a matter of few, but big, bills: not a lot of petty cash transactions.

We met and were able to converse closely with men at work, having arrived at the end of a break. Michael Whitfield, the foreman, explained the various processes. Everything had to be right. What we saw included:

- Console, keyboards and stop knobs – Peter Urwin was working on Shrewsbury. Ivory has been replaced by cowbone, but ebony is still freely available. What gorgeous names are used for the stops, such as Nazard and Lieblich Gedeckt.
- Pipes – all manner of them in the metal shop, complete with a bath for washing them, a turning machine and a guillotine. Les Cooper boasted the title 'pipe maker', pure and simple.
- A machine like a small organ, used to test the sound of the pipes during the initial voicing, demonstrated by Peter Hopps.
- A soundboard – a complicated wooden structure on which the pipes stand – being restored. This was for the RFH; completion of the various phases of this big contract is planned for 2014. Wind reservoirs, or bellows, being releathered.

This excellent tour was gruelling for us, focusing on so many parts of an organ, when usually you only see the elegant display pipes in a church (concealing the thousands of pipes which lurk out of sight). It's a kind of open secret; we saw the constituent parts in various stages for three different clients, but a finished piece of work only in photos on the wall. Along with scantily-clad young ladies and Marilyn Monroe, these included the new organ case designed by Harrisons for St Davids Cathedral, featuring a pair of Welsh dragons as a finely chiseled finishing touch.

Mark Venning was to relate this snippet:

> *The cathedral organs of Salisbury and Durham were both built by Willis in 1877 (a remarkable achievement in itself). The Durham organ has been in our care since 1905, and we were intrigued to notice that one of the stops is marked Salisbury. Sure enough, when we restored the Salisbury organ in 1978, we found that the equivalent stop is marked Durham. A pleasingly obscure link between the two cathedrals.*

On the long way home, we spotted two Eddie Stobart lorries, favouring Ann Elizabeth, then Sally Bess. Those brought us down to earth, along with interminable standstill over the barrier on the northbound M6. It was time to go home after first-rate exposure to the northeast.

Fig 64

[64] Newcastle: This dignitary seat
is a feature of the nave.
[65] Durham: You may take
photographs of the cloisters.
[66] Durham: Leslie Cooper,
foreman pipe maker at
Harrison & Harrison.
[67] Winchester: A rare Tournai
font: stories on each side.

Fig 65

Fig 66

Fig 67

49

Winchester

Holy Trinity

Province: Canterbury
Founded: 634
Present building started: 1079; 1350–1410 nave remodelled
Support to foundations: 1906–11 by William Walker, diver

Website: www.winchester-cathedral.org.uk
Tel: 01962 857275
Email: cathedral.office@winchester-cathedral.org.uk
Address: Visitors' Centre, The Close, Winchester, Hampshire SO23 9LS

Three to See: Norman crypt, largely empty owing to flooding frequency;
rare Tournai font;
Izaak Walton stained glass

Diving helmet

Friday 20 May, 2011

It was rewarding to visit the tallest and longest on consecutive days. Our party of four spent a day in Salisbury on the way to this tour's swansong in that endlessly long building. Speaking of songs Winchester Cathedral has proved an inspiration to lyricists. The eponymous song reached the top of the charts in 1966 for the New Vaudeville Band. There were only 17 lines, which doesn't bear comparison with most of the psalms and anthems delivered by the cathedral's renowned choristers. My favourite verse is 'You could have done something/ But you didn't try/ You didn't do nothing/ You let her walk by'. What could be more rooted to the spot than this titan of a building whose suspect foundations required the recruitment of a diver? That may be the point, of course. Then, in 1977 Crosby, Stills and Nash included a song called 'Winchester' on their 1977 record *CSN*. No other cathedral name has assumed muse status like this. Perhaps the name of this building is strangely sonorous, and perhaps evocative. The same thing occurs elsewhere, such as 'Nottingham Forest' among football club names. 'We hate Nottingham Forest!' seems more telling than to use any other team name, even Tottenham Hotspur.

We checked into the Mercure Wessex Hotel, opposite the north side of the building, making sure of rooms with a view (£10 extra per night). Graham's disabled parking disc was again a boon. The hotel made a nightly charge £8 for all vehicles. We were able to find a space in a car park close by with free disabled parking. A full kettle was immediately boiled for refreshment, as we sat for an initial intake of the cathedral through the window, and conducted a quick planning session. Graham needed a rest; Andy, Spencer and I then made our way to St Cross Hospital, a mile down the River Itchen. We would save the cathedral for an in-depth investigation the next morning. The walk took us through intriguing old streets, past Winchester College, church, museum, the Wykeham Arms and other hostelries. It was a fine evening for a stroll.

The church tower came into view. This is 'England's oldest and most perfect almshouse' (and accorded 4 stars by Simon Jenkins in *England's Thousand Best Churches*). The 'Hospital', in the sense of 'hospitality', states 'Welcome to the Hospital of St Cross & Almshouse of Noble Poverty'. We were too late in the day for the practical manifestation of this, initiated by Stephen of Blois when he founded it in 1136. Last seen at Arundel RC Cathedral, AD joined our party the next day having partaken of the Wayfarer's Dole (a small beaker of beer and a morsel of bread). When we arrived at the front entrance, one wooden door was open, with a 'closed' sign nearby. But I had resolved to make sure we saw something, recalling my previous visit a few years earlier. On that occasion Rutz (she who enjoyed St Davids) took us round the premises: her parents were married in St Cross. Once inside the main Tudor quadrangle we were confronted by a glut of visual enticements. It was immediately peaceful. The almshouses were consistent in design with tall chimneys and colourful, well-tended borders as a fringe. The church exterior was chunky, 'a Norman cathedral in miniature', wrote Jenkins. It would have been good to venture inside, but the door was locked when I tried it. At that moment an official emerged from a corner and made it clear that we should not be there. I wondered how the institution was now run, as I had been battling with Anthony Trollope's *The Warden* (1855), which was set in St Cross at a time of poverty and corruption. We identified the alternative route back, which was a treat: alongside the River Itchen, a true babbling brook that day (no doubt prone to flooding), by water meadows, college playing fields and impressive buildings. Towards the end we face Wolvesey Palace, the residence of the bishops of Winchester. Back in the more populous area we got our welcome in the Wykeham Arms to swill some Gale's Ales, still good after the takeover by Fuller's of Chiswick.

Saturday 21 May
The four of us opened operations in the Old Gaol House for breakfast, as the Wessex was charging £15.50, an outrageous amount. Even advance internet booking would not have reduced the price. Most of this J D Wetherspoon hostelry's patrons were enjoying rather early (it was 9 am) pints of a good range of beers. We weren't tempted! Tea was fine to kick start us for a day of concentration and observation, as well as indulgence. There were prints on the wall by the window where Graham had chosen tables (and Kevin contrived to spill three jugs of milk in total, over two incidents). The illustrations served as supporting information for the day's business:

- Cardinal Wolsey (any connection with Wolvesey?): came to live here after his fall from power
- Alfred the Great: Winchester was capital of Wessex.
- King Henry III: supervised the building the castle's great hall

Over the green and into the west end of the cathedral, we underwent two tours, which involved various mentions of St Swithun's special feature, water. There was some deliberation about order of play. The plan had been to join a one hour Cathedral Tour at 10 am, followed by a Crypt Tour (20 minutes) at 12.30 pm, and that was just the morning. A phone call the day before had revealed that all this would be accommodated in a single ticket (£6.50, £5 for oldies) and only the crypt needed booking. Then came a proviso: 'Tomorrow is Healing Day, so not all the spaces will be open all the time.' We settled upon the crypt first, as the most reliable option. As the breakfast process became somewhat protracted, it turned out that we would have been late for the planned tour, anyway, so the crypt it was to be.

Once we were past the cash desk (temperamental computer) we eventually found the entrance round a corner in the north transept. Armed with a key and past a number of hovering people, guide Bill Weeks gave six of us a smart, comprehensive narration. The crypt is apsidal. Only Worcester, Gloucester and Canterbury share this feature. They are all superior, but this is the one to make the **Three to See** list, because of its singularity. It is in three sections, all of which are normally under water for much of the year. This explains the void impression of this Norman construct. We were led down a walkway round each space, with pillars and bits of masonry entire cluttering as relief. It was good and I was glad we'd chosen the right half of the year, when it was open to the public. The pride and joy was *Sound II*, Antony Gormley's 1986 sculpture of a figure, modelled upon the artist. It was intended to stand in water, like those figures off the coast in Lancashire. A seasonal reflection of the Romanesque groin vaulting would make it even more dramatic. A viewing platform was employed to observe the work, which had been offered as a gift, something the cathedral couldn't refuse, but not all our party were in sympathy. What also impressed in the furthest eerie section were the bulky bases of two chantry chapels in the retro choir, for Henry Beaufort and William of Waynflete. Judging by their mass they would prove colossal when we encountered them.

As ever Bill's excellent tour over-ran and we almost gambolled to the west end, for the 11 am cathedral tour. Naomi Davidson was already imparting background information to nine people sitting on the nave chairs. She was out of the fold of Salisbury's Celia Tate as a guide, that is, full of cutting observation and vim. The nave was pointed out for its consistent and continuous style, the west window a mass of re-assembled medieval glass. William of Wykeham, famous for the motto 'Manners maykyth man', was central to the story. While bishop (1366–1404) he remodelled the nave from its Romanesque into the Gothic style. His endeavours were partly as a consequence of the effects of the Black Death: he founded New College, Oxford in 1379 and Winchester College in 1382. The earlier font stood between immense pillars on the north side of the nave: carved from a single block of black marble from Tournai, Belgium, c.1150. It looks like wood, and is one of seven in the country. I had seen one of the others at Lincoln Cathedral. A marvellous thing, it was out of the way for normal baptismal use, but easy to appreciate where it was. Depictions include legends of St Nicholas of Myra, a 4th century subject. On the south face, clear in the light, was the saint giving bags of gold to a nobleman's three daughters. In *Civilisation*

(1969), Kenneth Clark wrote of the font: 'Women were thought of as squat, bad-tempered viragos that we see on the font of Winchester Cathedral: these were the women who accompanied the Norsemen to Iceland'. Opposite, impressively dominant, was the chantry chapel of William Edington.

We moved up a few bays, turning left into the north transept. Naomi wanted to show us the Epiphany Chapel with its Edward Burne-Jones windows, made in William Morris' workshop. It was designated a quiet space for prayer, and was occupied, but we could see some of the rich stained glass, subjects being the Annunciation and the Birth of Christ. I found the north transept entirely magical, much of it the original Norman, as massive and interwoven in design as anywhere. The tower had collapsed in 1107. The central area was redesigned in the 1350s, most effectively, 'working up from the arcade to the gallery to the clerestory,' said Naomi. On the north wall was a 1990s statue of Christ by Peter Eugene Ball of Nottingham. He also worked at Southwell Minster, unsurprisingly.

Let's move to the retrochoir, full of goodies, mostly of a chantry nature. Naomi's first point was damage, in fact vandalism. The statue of Joan of Arc used to hold a sword in her hand. 'It was nicked,' as were bits of Tudor woodwork from the choir stalls. Further, in the course of a service there (Sunday evensong) carving was removed from the Lady Chapel. Members of our audience were aghast. Then, as an untoward sound wafted towards us, our guide posited sharply: 'Is that a mobile phone?' It was time to note the floor, of a hugely varied range of original tiles with an unmistakable slope. We also noted a pillar on the south side, clearly out of kilter. We moved on to the nine icons in a row on the back of the high altar, or rather feretory, as the name was entered on one of the plans. The icons made a convincing display. They were introduced between 1992 and 1996, one subject being St Swithun (c.800–862). Now he has been mentioned it's his turn for exposure. His shrine now lies in front of the icons, in the middle of the retrochoir. It was busy that day, as one of the provisions is healing. Naomi didn't care to get close, I imagine for artistic reasons. She told the story of how the St Swithun myth of precipitation came about. On the day, 15 July 971, when his shrine was at last translated to the retrochoir, it rained, much to the chagrin of all concerned. Precipitation continued for 40 days, so now if it rains on that date, you know what to expect.

This is William Cobbett's take on the saint, whose spelling seems to have changed over the years:

Fareham, Hants.
Here I am in spite of St SWITHIN – The truth is, that the Saint is like most oppressors: rough him! rough him! And he relaxes.

After drying myself, and sitting in the rain, boldly setting the Saint at defiance, and expecting to have not one dry thread by the time I got to Havant, which is nine miles from Fareham, and four from Cosham. To my most agreeable surprise, the rain ceased before I got by SELSEY.

Rural Rides 2/8/1823

That may be because he moved areas. Selsey is in another county, after all.

The old shrine was destroyed by Henry VIII in 1538; the current one was a gift from the Friends in 1962. It is always popular with pilgrims. It had lost its covering, which might have lent more quality to a piece lost between the grand chantries it has as neighbours. The Friends have been productive here. Outside the cathedral on the north side, 'The Fleury Building is the first permanent addition for 500 years, for storage, and a new boiler and heating system and lavatories, mostly funded by the Friends of the Cathedral' *Church Times* (1/4/11). Dom Etienne Ricaud, current abbot of Fleury, opened it, with the Very Revd James Atwell, Dean of Winchester. Fleury Abbey, France, is a partner of the cathedral (as is Florence Cathedral), with links going back to the very start. The Benedictine monastery derived from there. Prayers are said for Fleury in services.

Chantries abound. There are several momentous examples, representing a sequence of bishops, leading up to the Reformation and a change in policy. Dropping intrusive monoliths had got out of hand. We must be grateful that the ones at Winchester survived, being of such high quality. Those bishops celebrated with chapels are as follows:

1346–1366 – William Edington: Chancellor of England; at the time Winchester was the richest see in England

1366–1404 – William of Wykeham: Chancellor, Lord Privy Seal 1363, founder of colleges

1404–1447 – Henry Beaufort: son of John of Gaunt; Chancellor, cardinal 1426

1447–1486 – William of Waynflete: Chancellor, founder of Magdalen College, Oxford 1448

1487–1493 – Peter Courtenay, just to fill in the gap. He had no chantry chapel in Winchester

1493–1501 – Thomas Langton: chaplain to Edward IV, archbishop of Canterbury elect (died too soon)

1501–1528 – Richard Fox: Lord Privy Seal; founded Corpus Christi College, Oxford 1517

Getting more up to date in the east end is the bronze statue of a popular figure: the moustachioed William Walker (1869–1918). This is the synopsis of his work in the *Welcome* leaflet: 'The famous diver who saved the Cathedral with his two bare hands from 1906 to 1911 underpinning the Cathedral's foundations.' His is a heart-warming story.

Moving on to the choir, you have to avoid falling over the plain tomb, probably of William II (Rufus, reigned 1087–1100), who was killed locally in the New Forest, by an arrow through the lung. All around is a profusion of enchanting woodwork, carved between 1308 and 1310, complete with green men, monkeys and mythical beasts. Naomi emitted a shriek and pointed to the top of the north side of stalls, saying: 'Oh, my goodness, that's new!' There was a panel of lurid blue, newly added. A woman in the group tried to console her: 'It'll weather over time.' The organ saved the day. It was magnificent. We could admire the instrument itself, actually built by the well-known specialist, Henry Willis, for the Great Exhibition of 1851. Much of the original workings have survived.

Finally, among so much more which could and should be seen, Naomi moved us to the south transept for some fine stained glass in Prior Silkstede's Chapel, depicting *The Compleat Angler* author, Izaak Walton. He moved with newly-appointed Bishop Morley to Winchester in 1662. The window shows him reading and fishing on the River Itchen, together with a picnic and symbols of fish. The black slab below is his tomb. This is a dramatic portrayal. Other pieces of entertainment here have included *Antiques Roadshow* in 2011, which as well as providing 'a modest amount' of money, according the dean, must have raised the profile of the cathedral given the audience figures of the programme; also, on 26/11/09, Mendelssohn's oratorio *Elijah* featuring bass-baritone Bryn Terfel. My friend JJ Smith worked on the event, as a lighting technician for Imax Lighting, Bristol. There was 'at least 10,000 m of cabling and scaffolding like rugby posts in the massive nave arches. They used floodlights to light the pillars from ground upwards. Architectural lighting'. There was a hundred-strong orchestra and 150 in the choir. 'It was a two-day fit-up. The get-out took 6 hours after the audience had all left. We finished at about six in the morning.' He added: 'There were five van loads of gear.' A company like that gets around. Not just cathedrals but the countryside (for rock festivals) and weddings, though not 'royal' ones, fairly topical as Prince William had recently married Kate Middleton.

We dispersed to relaxation in the Winchester Cathedral Café, a facility which catered for conferences, weddings and the disabled. On a flat and open site, it lay 25 m from the west end, informed the leaflet. It was hard to beat as we were able to augment the various tea and coffee orders by the private table under a gathered parasol with a partial view of the southwest corner of the cathedral. We all chose banana and walnut cake; just as well that it met our demands. Reflection and sharing experiences was a fine luxury at this stage. The whole thing earned a high mark. It would now be a matter of weighing up the list of 30 catering establishments out of the 49 cathedrals. The cathedral shop was part of the café building. It was stocked with contemporary items such as the King James Bible (paperback, £7.99), a LED book light (£4.50), or you could choose a bendable, portable one for £6.99. Despite the catless state of the cathedral, there was 'Love me Love my cat': a Frith sculpture for £29.50, licking its paw. I overheard an exchange between a customer and cashier: 'They did a lovely ploughman's in there'; 'They're always very busy'. A further benefit here must be the convenient location in the city centre. This was the nice part of town. Simon Jenkins, in introducing St Cross, wrote: 'Forget booming Winchester, its college and wrecked city centre'.

It was time for the gallery and library, which our ticket covered. No photography here! First we mounted the 28 steps to the Triforium Gallery in the south transept. It was pleasantly spacious, with open views of the neighbouring parts of the cathedral, and featured the Shaftesbury Bowl 'the only surviving example of late Saxon glass in England' (claimed the website). It served as an introduction to the two rooms below. We ventured into the roost of the Winchester Bible, to be regaled by guide Jennifer Faber about its four volumes produced between 1160 and 1175, even then incomplete. She tried to identify the different dyes used. The best known must be the blue lapis lazuli from Afghanistan. Like similar creations in other cathedral libraries, I, at least, was awe-struck. It had six styles of painting, the artists researched by Walter Oakeshott in 1945. After that it was bound in the current pale leather, with oak boards. That's enough: see it for yourself!

Everyone should undergo this. I am referring to the whole ancient tome display and its setting, on top of that fabulous book.

Finally we crossed to the 17th century Morley Library itself, somewhat cramped and completely lined with books, many of which had white binding. Bishop Morley instructed the purchase of what we admired next: the Castlemayne Globes (1675), 'terrestrial and celestial', located by the rope cordoning off the best part of the dimensions of the room. The celestial globe displayed constellations shown illustratively. *Ursa major* was a large bear.

By now we were sated from hours spent in this rich building with the bible as its climax. We went our separate ways to reunite for evensong. I was engaged to visit the Deanery at 4 pm. I dropped into another St Swithun dedication: on Kingsgate, a small room over the wall. Preoccupation with the cathedral and its environs had precluded following through strong recommendations I had received to visit the Great Hall and Round Table; also, outside the city, St Catherine's Hill, an Iron Age fort with a turf maze. These merely added to the list of reasons for a return visit.

Just before the appointed time, I arrived at the Deanery, a fine building with medieval origins. The front porch was busy with a fund-raising book fair. The Very Revd James Atwell greeted me at the door, offering tea, which was most welcome after further exposure to the cathedral in and out, the latter extending to familiarization with neighbouring streets. I was able to settle down in the upstairs reception room as Dean James took a call while the kettle boiled. 'That was the bishop,' he said. 'We're having a lot of contact as he's leaving soon.' Indeed Rt Revd Michael Scott-Joynt's replacement had not yet been appointed. The new one would be the 97th. I was able to break the ice easily as I had read James' entry 'Les grands projets' in Dreaming Spires, which its co-author (bishop) Stephen Platten had given me at Wakefield. This provided a good subject for discussion: the contrast between parish church and long-established cathedrals. He had moved as dean from one, St Edmundsbury, to the other in 2006. That was a year after the major accomplishment of the completion of the tower at Bury St Edmunds. He considered the award of National Lottery Millennium funding to the project to have been achieved partly because of timing. It was at the end of the three waves for projects. The differences between the two organizations owed mostly to scale, which was completely different. He had moved from 35 staff to 102; from between 200 and 300 to 700; from a budget of £¾m to one of £4m. This all spoke of a fundamental difference regarding control. A smaller enterprise can be run with the chief executive (the dean) able to keep abreast of the whole concern. A large one, like Winchester Cathedral, has to involve delegation, committees, distance. 'Cathedrals get no finance from the diocese; no money from the state,' he said. It was the Diocese of Winchester that was reported as being £1.4m in the red in 2009: no connection with the cathedral itself and its dean and chapter, but moves had become necessary to solve the problem, mainly by staff cuts. One asset at risk was the property, in the close. James had to argue the need to house the fraternity against the commercial possibilities of leasing out, or selling. He said: 'As regards potential for what is called the Close Plan, the possible in-fill areas are the end of Dome Alley and the old masons' yard adjacent to N° 1 The Close (i.e. southeast of the cathedral)'. There was no danger of loss of identity or character.

He mentioned other sources of income, such as the ice rink and Christmas market in the winter, but that was after a rich compote of events through the year. Here are just a few forthcoming samples on the website:

- The Friends 80th anniversary concert (June – £25.75 for a ticket)
- King James Bible lecture series (through to June – £6.75 each)
- Southern Cathedrals Festival (July, in rota with Chichester and Salisbury – from free to £23)
- Calligraphy workshops (October – £10)

The wide range and frequency must be helped by the high profile of the cathedral, its catchment area, and itself serves to spread further word of mouth.

Another aspect of resource management was exemplified in the Board of Education here, shared with the Diocese of Portsmouth. It has been mooted that Winchester should absorb the neighbouring diocese to make a single one for Hampshire. Out of interest Portsmouth has the Isle of Wight and Winchester the Channel Islands in their briefs. The realm of Winchester was immense until 1905 when Southwark was carved out of it. Winchester Palace, or rather its ruins, lies close to the Thames near what is now Southwark Cathedral. In a period of perceived expansion Winchester spawned two more dioceses in 1927: Guildford and Portsmouth. Things seem different now. Rationalization and economy are more of the essence.

For me the conversation with James could have continued, but his watch was consulted with increasing regularity (the clock on the mantelpiece was stuck at 3 o'clock). On the way out there was just time for him to pose for photographs in a smart white jacket in front of his garden portico. The garden looked worthy of a charitable open afternoon. (In fact a forthcoming event applied: 'Deanery open garden' was advertised for 11 June.) He then led me determinedly through various ground floor rooms and corridors. We escaped the Deanery by a rear gate almost abutting the south side of the cathedral. There he found another door. It was so discreet as to suggest mystery. It suddenly made sense that such authors as Charles Dickens and William Golding used ancient cathedrals as settings. They defy comprehension and deny total knowledge. We had now reached some point inside the south transept area. I suddenly registered a physical need and requested the facility. 'Oh, it's in there,' he pointed at a cupboard space. In this monolithic structure such a thing occupied the same floor area as a modern estate house. There were all manner of provisions in the sequence of spaces, from basin to bucket and a man in red stood by the urinal. After a discreet pause for him to recompose his attire, he introduced himself as Canon Michael (St John-Channell), the Precentor. I was to follow the instructions to cross the building, not to the choir stalls as planned but to the quiet Epiphany Chapel with its Burne-Jones windows.

This was to be the launch of the celebration. 'Tour Over' you could call it. The car complement of four was joined by six of my closest relations (aunt, sister, two nieces and their partners) for evensong, drink and food. Substitute prayer for song, and you have it. As 5.30 pm was upon us, it was a matter of brief hugs all round and scrambling together enough prayer books and chairs. That setting was the best. We filled it, together with five others in the congregation, and the precentor (as president) and dean (reader). Around us was some of the best architecture available: a solidly Norman stone presence, with the vivid stained glass at close range.

The problem was that the choir was some miles away at Hambledon that evening at a fund-raising event: beneficial for the cathedral, but not for our gathered party. The service sheet insisted this to be 'Evensong' despite lack of singing.

Afterwards, Dean James met our entourage and encouraged us to return for 'Mayoral Mattins' as he called it. That wasn't the plan, as we hoped to be on a steam train on The Alresford-Alton Watercress Line at the time. It was hard to assimilate conclusion of such a long quest, but an evening of drinks at the William Walker (recently re-named, said my niece Clemmie), the closest pub, followed by a meal at the Loch Fyne restaurant was hard to beat to mark it. The obligatory group photo was taken by a compliant barmaid: the tavern behind, the superbly developed cathedral before us. Suffice it to say that the need for satisfying closure won the day: after a farewell breakfast outside Café Monde on a fresh bright morning, the survivors attended Holy Trinity for a fine processional Choral Mattins service, 'attended by the Right Worshipful Mayor of Winchester and Members of the City Council'. There was a considerable entourage for a city of around 35K population (according to *Historic-UK*). The choristers were in full voice, and that endless nave burst with organ music. The Watercress Line would follow. We took the 11.43 am instead of 11.00 departure. Bemused with steam and cathedrals, it occurred to me that there were to be no more teatimes with deans or assessment of our best diocesan buildings. Steam trains were a growing, going concern. So are cathedrals, and would continue to move us. The workplace of William Walker was apposite as a final venue.

The End

Appendix I – Foundations and Dioceses

Old Foundation/ Monastic	Date of Diocese	Current Building Started (approx)
Canterbury	602	1170
Rochester	604	1178
St Paul's London	604	1675
York	627	1227
Winchester	642	1079
Hereford	676	1079
Worcester	680	1224
Lichfield	700	1195
Wells	909	1186
Exeter	1050	1258
Lincoln	1072	1192
Chichester	1075	1187
Durham	1081	1093
Norwich	1094	1095
Ely	1109	1081
Carlisle	1133	1123
Salisbury	1220	1220
Reformation Upgrades		
Chester	1541	1093
Gloucester	1541	1089
Peterborough	1541	1116
Bristol	1542	1140
Oxford	1542	1158
Modern Era		
Ripon	1836	1220
Manchester	1847	1421
Truro	1876	1880

St Albans	1877	1077
Liverpool	1880	1904
Newcastle	1882	1359
Southwell	1884	1108
Wakefield	1888	1409
Birmingham	1905	1711
Southwark	1905	1220
Chelmsford	1914	c1460
St Edmundsbury	1914	1503
Sheffield	1914	1430
Coventry	1918	1962
Bradford	1919	1458
Blackburn	1926	1820
Derby	1927	1723
Guildford	1927	1936
Leicester	1927	c 1250
Portsmouth	1927	1185
Plus		
Peel	1980	1884
Wales		
Bangor	546	1496
Llandaff	560	1130
St Davids	589	1180
St Asaph	1073	1282
Newport	1921	1080
Brecon	1923	1215

Appendix II – Favourite Cathedrals

Ranking	Public Vote	Author's Vote
1	Wells	Wells
2	Durham	Exeter
3	Lincoln	Lichfield
4	Ely	Winchester
5	Salisbury	Gloucester
6	Gloucester	Southwell
7	Bristol	Peterborough
8	York	Ripon
9	Winchester	Coventry
10	St Paul's	York
11	Exeter	Portsmouth
12	Canterbury	Liverpool
13	St Davids	St Albans
14	Truro	Oxford
15	Coventry	Hereford
16	St Albans	Norwich
17	Chichester	Worcester
18	Norwich	Durham
19	Liverpool	St Asaph
20	Chester and Lichfield	St Edmundsbury

This is completely unscientific. The 'public' vote is the outcome of over 250 responses to the question: 'Which is your favourite Anglican cathedral in England, Wales and the Isle of Man?' The answers included 33 of the 49 names available. There must be a bias in favour of the southwest of England, as the majority of contributors were based there. I would think that Bristol, Wells and Gloucester have benefited from locality. In the end Wells was an easy winner with Durham way ahead of the next three.

What has been interesting is the reason given for choices. First it has to be said that there were two approaches: heart and head. The top two scored highly through both admiration of the respective building and empathy with it. A minority in the survey cited only the quality of the cathedral building in their decision. After all the question itself is biased, as the word 'favourite' invites an emotional rather than intellectual response.

It became obvious that the view from afar counted for many votes for delights like Lincoln, Salisbury and Ely. Also personal association was widely persuasive, often harking back to earlier life. Almost all the respondents explained their choice and frequently listed a number of others contending for the final nomination. Reasons included:

- The one they are most familiar with
- Identifying a preferred style
- Preferring spires to towers
- Broad setting, such as in the city centre or with favourite surroundings
- External impression as a landmark
- The look of the building
- Particular internal features
- Rating the space above its contents, such as not liking clutter
- Occasional preference for quiet, unthreatening atmosphere

Familiarity is a key factor, as I have found in my own reaction to these cathedrals. I have enjoyed every one, and have grown in appreciation of those with which I have developed more of a relationship. That includes parish church cathedrals as well as traditional medieval buildings. In the end a key yardstick was how much I felt the need to pay a return visit to each cathedral: a tricky assessment as there are 49 I want to go back to!

Finally, an observation. We live in an age of care and heritage. Just think what it would have been like to visit many of the current cathedrals in the mid-eighteenth century, in various states of neglect and ruin.

Appendix III – Cats

Name	Colouring	Cathedral	Sighting
Laptop	Ginger and white	Canterbury	Witnessed leaping purposefully to his breakfast bowl in a cloister
Louis	Marmalade	Wells	Spotted beside a radiator, on the Bishop's chantry cushion and in mid-cloister
Doorkins Magnificat	Tabby	Southwark	Observed slumbering over a hot air grille in the south aisle
Wolfie	Black	Salisbury	Unseen but searched for throughout; usual habitat is stonemasons' yard

In every other cathedral the response was some kind of negative, from 'No, he died' or 'He was the previous dean's' to incredulity that such a presence should be countenanced. 'Health and safety' was sometimes mentioned.

Various claims were made for dogs. These included Comet (the black Labrador at Lichfield) and Maisie (the Jack Russell at Bradford). And mention should be made of the robin at Winchester.

Appendix IV – Catering

Ranking	Environment	Provision
1	Chester	Southwark
2	Wells	Newcastle
3	Liverpool	Wakefield
4	Winchester	Winchester
5	Newcastle	St Paul's
6	Southwark	Wells
7	Guildford	Salisbury
8	Southwell	Guildford
9	Worcester	Norwich
10	Hereford	Durham

Of the 49 cathedrals 28 had catering facilities which were visited, six were omitted, in most cases being closed at the time. Unfortunately Manchester's café was due to open two days after the trip there. Fifteen did not have any café or restaurant, a surprisingly high number.

The aim was to try each one out in a similar way, notwithstanding varied times of day. The standard was coffee, or tea, and a cake (preferably the almost universal lemon drizzle). This was the best that could be done and proved to be flawed in that what is on display varied considerably. The coffee cake at Guildford was alarmingly good, as was the rhubarb crumble at Wakefield. It is a highly subjective approach, and should be viewed as a bit of fun.

At cafés it became apparent that the two elements of the situation, setting and aesthetic aspect, the 'environment', was distinct from what you found when you got there, the 'provision'. Whether or not ingestion is enjoyed, Chester has adapted its monks' refectory into a fine café space, Liverpool has a successful north transept conversion into a mezzanine level café, Wells affords fine views on two sides, while Winchester offers nourishment inside, and outside, in a spacious modern building '2.5 metres' from the west front.

Provision is made up of the people part – service and attitude – and what you get in terms of food and drink. The big disappointment has been in the potency of the coffee and cakes. Coffee is frequently too weak. For me, that is. The same has been experienced with cakes. Lemon drizzle has mostly involved no more than a whiff of the fruit flavour. Also, many was the time that the goods failed on a moisture count: dry rather than succulent. It may be preferable to choose savouries and main meals, which have been enjoyed or witnessed at many cathedral cafés.

Happily, on follow-up visits to several a makeover had been done, or management had changed, to result in a significant improvement. The message is to give them all a try as part of the cathedral experience. In general they are increasingly sensitive to the demands of patrons, who are there to enjoy the building, or perhaps just for the café, often as a city centre facility in a pleasing environment.

Appendix V – Map of Cathedrals

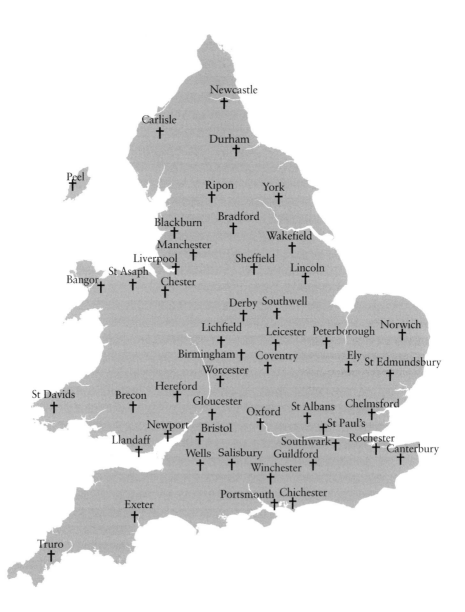

References

AA: *Treasures of Britain* (1968, Drive Publications)

Peter Ackroyd: *London, the Biography* (2000, Vintage and The Random House Group Ltd)

Colin Amery & Richard Reid (ed): *Nicholson's guide to Great Britain* (Robert Nicolson Publications Ltd)

Francis Bond: *The Cathedrals of England and Wales* (1912, B T Batsford)

Prof T G Bonney (ed): *Cathedrals, Abbeys and Churches in England and Wales* (1891, Cassell & Co Ltd)

Bill Bryson: *Notes from a Small Island* (1995, Doubleday)

Jon Cannon: *Cathedral* (2007, Constable & Robinson)

Kenneth Clark: *Civilisation* (1969, BBC/John Murray)

Alec Clifton-Taylor: *The Cathedrals of England* (1967 and 1986, reproduced by kind permission of Thames & Hudson)

William Cobbett: *Rural Rides* (1830)

Tim Cook: *The Works of George Herbert* (1994, Wordsworth Poetry Library)

S Dunkerton: *Robert Bakewell*, Artist Blacksmith

Robert Dunning, Richard Lewis, Melvyn Matthews: *Wells Cathedral* (2005, Scala Publishers Ltd)

Tom Fort: *The Book of Eels* (2002, HarperCollins)

Mike Harding: *A Little Book of the Green Man* (1998, Aurum Press)

Brian L Harris: *Harris's Guide to Cathedrals & Churches: Discovering the Unique and Unusual in over 500 Churches and Cathedrals* (2006, Ebury Press, reprinted by permission of The Random House Group Ltd)

Simon Jenkins: *England's Thousand Best Churches* (2000, Penguin Group)

Samuel Johnson: *Dictionary of the English Language* (1755)

Jeffrey Kacirk: *Forgotten English* (2009) and calendars for 2010 and 2011

Ian Mortimer: *The Time Traveller's Guide to Medieval England* (2009, Vintage and The Random House Group)

The Observer's Books: *Volume 43 – Cathedrals* (1972, Frederick Warne)

John Oliver: Dickens' Rochester (1978, John Hallewell)

Nikolaus Pevsner: *The Buildings of England – Cambridgeshire, Herefordshire* and *Warwickshire* (Penguin Group)

Jeremy Purseglove: *Taming the Flood* (1988, OUP/Channel 4)

Richard Surman: *Cathedral Cats* (2006, Collins)

Also:

Churches Conservation Trust: *An Inspiration of Churches* (1998) and website information (2011)

Pitkin Pictorial guides to various cathedrals

Patrick Roberts: *Featuring Felines/Purr-n-Fur*: www.purr-n-fur.org.uk

The Football and Real Ale Guide (Stedders Guides)

www.footballandrealaleguide.co.uk

Church Times, Stage, The Times, The Independent and other publications